SOCIAL AND PERSONALITY DEVELOPMENT

DEVELOPMENT

AN ADVANCED TEXTBOOK

SOCIAL AND PERSONALITY DEVELOPMENT

AN ADVANCED TEXTBOOK

Edited by

Michael E. Lamb
University of Cambridge
Eunice Kennedy Shriver National Institute of
Child Health and Human Development

and

Marc H. Bornstein
Editor, Parenting: Science and Practice

Psychology Press
Taylor & Francis Group
NEW YORK AND HOVE

Published in 2011
by Psychology Press
711 Third Avenue
New York, NY 10017
www.psypress.com

Published in Great Britain
by Psychology Press
27 Church Road
Hove, East Sussex BN3 2FA

Psychology Press is an imprint of the Taylor & Francis Group, an Informa business

Copyright © 2011 by Psychology Press

Typeset in Times by RefineCatch Limited, Bungay, Suffolk
Printed in the USA by Sheridan Books, Inc. on acid-free paper
Cover design by Andrew Ward

10 9 8 7 6 5 4 3 2 1

Library of Congress Cataloging-in-Publication Data
Social and personality development : an advanced textbook / edited by Michael E. Lamb and
Marc H. Bornstein.
     p. cm.
  Includes bibliographical references and index.
  ISBN 978–1–84872–926–1
  1. Developmental psychology.   2. Personality development.   I. Lamb, Michael E.,
1953– II. Bornstein, Marc H.   III. Title.
  BF713.S652 2011
  155.2′—dc22

                                                                    2011006532

ISBN: 978–1–84872–926–1

Visit the Taylor & Francis Web site at http://www.taylorandfrancis.com and the Psychology Press Web site at
http://www.psypress.com

CONTENTS

PREFACE

Developmental science constitutes a unique, comprehensive, and significant domain of intellectual endeavour for three main reasons. First, developmental scientists offer an essential perspective on psychological theory and research. When, for example, psychologists study personality, emotional, or social development, they usually concentrate on social, emotional, or personality development in individuals of a particular age—infants, children, adolescents, adults, or the elderly. In so doing, they gain important knowledge about social experience, emotional development, or personality. To study psychological phenomena at only one point in the life cycle, however, is to limit our knowledge of them by failing to consider such factors as their stability and continuity through time that are the province of developmental study. Indeed, it could be argued that, when we undertake a comprehensive analysis of any psychological phenomenon, we necessarily incorporate a developmental perspective. The question is, how well is that perspective addressed? The chapters in this textbook on substantive areas of psychology—emotion, social interaction, emergent personality, and the application of empirical research—all demonstrate that the developmental perspective transcends and enriches any narrow focus on particular points in the life span. One purpose of this textbook, then, is to furnish inclusive developmental perspectives and the substantive chapters included in this volume underscore the dynamic and exciting status of contemporary developmental science.

Second, developmental science is a major sub-discipline in its own right. It has its own history and systems, its own perspectives, and its own methodologies and approaches to measurement and analysis, as each of the contributions to this textbook illustrates. If studying psychology comprehensively involves attending to development, then there are special traditions, perspectives, and methodologies to which students of psychology must also attend. These traditions, perspectives, and methods are masterfully introduced and reviewed in the chapters that follow.

Third, many aspects of developmental science have obvious and immediate relevance to real-world issues and problems. Each of the chapters in this textbook exemplifies the everyday relevance of developmental science through reviews of the history, theory, and substance of the sub-discipline. Furthermore, the last chapter focuses directly and explicitly on the application of developmental research to policy and practice.

In summary, developmental science provides a perspective that illuminates substantive phenomena in psychology, applies across the life span, has intrinsic value, and manifest relevance to daily life. It is for these reasons that we undertook the study of social, emotional, personality and applied development and subsequently prepared this advanced introduction to the field.

This volume can be used at the advanced undergraduate and introductory graduate levels. It is hardly possible today for any single individual to convey, with proper sensitivity and depth, the breadth of contemporary developmental science on these aspects of development. For that reason, we invited experts to prepare comprehensive, and topical treatments developmental science with respect to these aspects of development. We then organized and edited their contributions, with the cooperation and good will of our contributors, into a single coherent volume. All chapters represent faithfully the current status of scholarly efforts with respect to these key aspects of social, emotional, personality, and applied developmental psychology. The volume is also supported by resources developed by Trey Buchanan of Wheaton College, which can be found on the password protected website at http://www.psypress.com/textbook-resources/; the website features material for students as well as material that is accessible only to instructors. Students will find chapter outlines, topics to think about before reading the chapters, a glossary, and suggested readings with active reference links. Instructors will have access to this material as well as electronic access to all of the text figures and tables, suggestions for classroom assignments and/or discussion, and a test bank with multiple-choice, short-answer, and essay questions for each chapter. *Social and Personality Development* provides a comprehensive and up-to-date introduction to the field for advanced students.

Social and Personality Development has many purposes. We hope that readers of this textbook will obtain a new perspective on social and emotional development, a greater appreciation of the varied phenomena that constitute these aspects of developmental psychology, and a fundamental grounding in developmental science itself.

In addition to our outstanding contributors, we also wish to thank many reviewers for thoughtful ideas about this book, including Trey Buchanan (Wheaton College), Annie M. Cardell (Mountain State University), Lisa K. Hill (Hampton University), and Rebecca Wood (Central Connecticut State University). In addition, we are grateful to Mandy Collison, Andrea Zekus, and Debra Riegert at Psychology Press for their excellent editorial and production support.

Michael E. Lamb, University of Cambridge
Marc H. Bornstein, NICHD

SOCIAL AND PERSONALITY DEVELOPMENT: AN INTRODUCTION AND OVERVIEW

Michael E. Lamb
Cambridge University
Eunice Kennedy Shriver National Institute of Child Health and Human Development
Marc H. Bornstein
Editor, Parenting: Science and Practice

INTRODUCTION

When lay people think of psychology, they tend to focus on the nature and origins of intelligence or personality. These concerns have characterized the reflections of men and women on their own nature since Aristotle first pondered the nature of mankind and individual diversity. Despite its long history, however, studies of intelligence and personality development are still marked in large measure by dissension rather than consensus, by assertion rather than documentation. This state of affairs may reflect both the inadequacies of scientific psychology and the complexity of the issues that developmentalists confront. Fortunately, recent advances in our understanding of development are transforming these areas of scholarship, as authors in this book make clear.

Developmental science addresses the full spectrum of human thinking, feeling, and behavior and how they vary from one culture to another (Bornstein, 2009), and it is concerned with children's futures as well as the future of society. In undertaking this privileged burden, developmental science has four related goals: (a) *Description*—what people are like at different ages and how they change or stay the same over time; (b) *Explanation*—the origins of individual differences and the causes of development; (c) *Prediction*—what an individual will be like at a later point in development based on what is known about the individual's past and present characteristics; and (d) *Intervention*—how best to use developmental knowledge to improve well-being.

Development is usually identified with growth and change. In the realm of language development, for example, growth and change are especially salient. As the toddler emerges out of the infant and the child out of the toddler, one of the most readily observable developmental characteristics is growth and change in the child's language. Although development implies growth and change over time, development is not just any kind of growth and change. When a child gains weight, his or her body grows bigger, but weight gain is not development. Developmental growth and change are special in three ways; consider language development again. (a) Developmental growth and change constitute better adaptation to the environment. When a child can say how she feels and what she wants, she has developed from being a baby who can only cry to communicate. Developing language enables a child to actively participate

1

in her own development as well. (b) Developmental growth and change proceed from simple and global to complex and specific. In acquiring language, children move from single words that express simple and general thoughts to putting words together to express ever more sophisticated thoughts. (c) Developmental growth and change are relatively enduring. Whereas simple change is transitory, once a child acquires language it is permanent. Developmental growth and change therefore reflect relatively lasting transformations that make an individual better adapted to his or her environment by enhancing the individual's abilities to understand and express more complex behavior, thinking, and emotions.

But the coin in this (as in other realms of) development has two sides. The complement of growth and change in development is continuity and stability. Although development is commonly identified with growth and change, some features of development are theorized to remain (more or less) consistent over time. In biology, a goal of the organism is to maintain internal stability and equilibrium or homeostasis.

SOME CENTRAL ISSUES IN DEVELOPMENTAL SCIENCE

Norms and Individual Differences

In studying almost every characteristic (construct, structure, function, or process) of development, developmental scientists consider both norms and individual differences. Norms represent average outcomes on some characteristic; normative development is the pattern over time that is typical or average. For example, very few adults are either 4 or 7 feet tall; many more stand between 5 and 6 feet. This distribution during the childhood and adolescent years tells us how height varies in the population and provides guidance for pediatricians to determine whether a child or adolescent is developing normally.

However, typical development, based on what occurs on average, is only part of the story because children who are the same age vary within every domain of development. It is commonly understood that variation among individuals in diverse characteristics appears in normal distributions in the population. So, to continue our example, at virtually every age, children vary in terms of individual differences in their language. On average, children begin to talk and walk at about 1 year of age. But the range of individual differences in both achievements is considerable. Some children say their first word at 9 months, others not until 29 months; some children first walk at 10 months, others at 18 months. It is also the case that development can follow many different paths to the same or to different ends. Children may develop at different rates, but eventually reach the same height. Others may develop at the same rate, but stop growing at different heights. And different children may develop at different rates and reach different heights. All these paths illustrate individual differences. Understanding development requires an understanding of individual differences—the variation among individuals on a characteristic—as well as norms or what is typical.

The Constant Interplay of Biology and Experience

All children come into the world with the set of genes they inherit from their parents, but only a few traits (such as eye color) are genetically determined. All children have experiences in the world, but only a few experiences are formative by themselves. Rather, the characteristics an individual develops are the result of interaction between genetic and experiential influences over time (Gottlieb, Wahlstein, & Lickliter, 2006). A child may inherit a genetic tendency to be inhibited, for instance, but whether this leads to painful shyness or quiet confidence depends on the child's experiences. Likewise, language development is the product of genes and experience (Waxman & Lidz, 2006). Adopted children are like both their biological and adoptive parents with respect to their language abilities. Differences in the timing and rate of puberty among adolescents growing up in the same general environment result chiefly, but not exclusively, from genetic factors (Dick, Rose, Pulkkinen, & Kaprio, 2001; Mustanski, Viken, Kaprio, Pulkkinen, & Rose, 2004), but puberty occurs earlier among adolescents who are better nourished throughout their prenatal, infant, and childhood years.

Development is Dynamic and Reciprocal

Development is not the result of an environment operating on a passive organism; in many respects people help to create their own development through their thoughts and actions. People shape their own development by selecting experiences (children choose their friends); by appraising their experiences (children who believe that their parents love them have fewer mental health problems); and by affecting their experiences (children engender parents or peers to behave toward them in certain ways).

Development is Cumulative

To understand an individual at a given point in the life span, it is helpful to look at earlier periods (Lamb, Freund, & Lerner, 2010; Overton & Lerner, 2010). The quality of the infant's relationships at home lays the groundwork for the relationships the child forms with school friends, which in turn shape relationships the adolescent develops with intimate friends and lovers, and so on. The pathway that connects the past with the present and the future is a "developmental trajectory" (Nagin & Tremblay, 2005). A child who has poor early relationships is not destined to have bad relationships throughout life, but the child who is launched on a healthy trajectory clearly has an advantage.

Development Occurs Throughout the Lifespan

Development is a lifelong process, and individuals have the potential for continuing growth and change. This view contrasts with the notion that individual trajectories are determined by early experiences. Early experiences are, of course, important because they lay the foundation for later development, but their impact can be overridden by later experiences. No one period of development prevails over all others. Development continues from birth to death, and change is almost always possible, in infancy, childhood, adolescence, adulthood, and old age (Baltes, Lindenberger, & Staudinger, 2006; Elder & Shanahan, 2006).

Systems in Development

Dynamic systems theory looks at the many facets of development as part of a single, dynamic, constantly changing system. Thus, development in one area of life influences others. Children's motor achievements affect other, sometimes surprising, aspects of their psychological growth (Howe & Lewis, 2005; Thelen & Smith, 2006; van Geert & Steenbeek, 2005). For example, infants perceive depth (the ability to correctly judge distances) at 2 months, but they do not show fear of heights until they are able to crawl on their own, regardless of the age at which they begin to crawl. Crawling (motor development) allows the infant to estimate distances more accurately than before (cognitive development), which later translates into fear (emotional development). Exercise affects brain development and learning; being more physically fit is related to higher scores on standardized math and reading tests (Castelli, 2005; Castelli, Hillman, Buck, & Erwin, 2007). Obesity presents a social and emotional hazard. Boys and girls who are overweight are subject to teasing and are more likely to be excluded from friendship groups; tend to have less confidence in their athletic competency, social skills, and appearance; and have lower opinions of their overall self-worth (Bradley et al., 2008; O'Brien et al., 2007). They score lower than normal-weight children on measures of quality of life (Schwimmer, Burwinkle, & Varni, 2003).

Consider another example of the interface between physical and psychological development. Hearing problems affect about half of those aged 75 and older (Pleis & Lethbridge-Çejku, 2006). Hearing problems are a deficit in themselves, but they can make it difficult for older adults to follow conversations, interfere with social interactions, frustrate others, or lead them to view the older person as confused or incompetent, reactions that can undermine the older person's confidence or feelings of self-worth (Kampfe & Smith, 1998) and so cause some older adults to become hesitant when interacting with others or to avoid interaction altogether (Desai, Pratt, Lentzner, & Robinson, 2001).

PRINCIPAL THEORIES OF DEVELOPMENT

Scientific theories are ideas or principles based on empirical findings that explain sets of related phenomena. Members of the scientific community accept a theory because it stands up under empirical testing and fits the known facts. Theories help scientists to organize their thinking, decide which phenomena are significant, and generate new questions and hypotheses. Developmental science covers a vast array of topics. Without theories, developmental scientists would be lost. But theories are not permanent; the history of science consists of widely accepted theories being replaced by new approaches. Theories are refined in response to new scientific discoveries.

Through most of the twentieth century, the study of development was guided by "classical theories" or overarching visions that sought to explain every aspect of development from birth to adulthood. Although less influential now than before, classical theories laid the foundation for today's science of development. Perhaps the most prominent and enduring theoretical orientation to development is the belief that development results from the predominance or the interplay of **nature and nurture**. The contemporary view of the nature–nurture debate emphasizes interaction and transaction, and their mutual influence through time.

Nature–Nurture

One perennial issue in discussions of intelligence or personality development can be summarized in three words: "heredity or experience?". Although it is common to attribute the earliest salvos to the European empiricists and nativists of the seventeenth and eighteenth centuries, the dispute over the relative importance of innate biological influences ("heredity") versus the role of the environment ("experience") in individual development was initiated by Aristotle and his contemporaries much earlier (Brett, 1912–1921).

The heredity–experience dichotomy crudely labels the two principal points of view on the origins of the individuality and uniqueness of each person. Extreme hereditarians proposed that individual differences could be attributed to constitutional and genetic factors. Just as biology determines the characteristics that make all humans similar, they argued, so biological factors account for the features that make each member of the species recognizably unique. In contrast, the extreme empiricists argued that the experiences inherent in living determined both the course of development and the uniqueness of the individual. Men and women develop particular attitudes and behavioral styles because they have been trained to behave, think, or feel in such fashions. In the language of the scientific empiricists, differential reinforcement—both positive and negative—accounted for the strengthening of some behavior patterns and the elimination of others. Individuality consequently resulted from a unique history of experiences, just as species-specific similarities may result from uniformities in patterns of reinforcement.

In the nineteenth century, Charles Darwin (1859) initiated movements that were destined to engender the scientific study of psychology. The psychologists succeeding Darwin emphasized the biological aspects of development at the expense of the experiential. When Sigmund Freud subsequently formulated his **psychoanalytical** explanation of personality development, for example, he did so largely within this biological framework. Although critical formative experiences (such as the Oedipus complex) in the life of each person were described, Freud made clear that these events need not be concretely experienced; rather, many of the conflicts and "experiences" were believed to be inevitably (that is, biologically) predetermined (Freud, 1916/1917).

Scientists and philosophers stressing the importance of innate or biological determinants of intelligence and personality became known as **nativists**, and their dominance was rudely shattered in 1924 with John B. Watson's publication of a Behaviorist Manifesto. Watson's **behaviorism** was greeted enthusiastically by psychologists, and behaviorists' subsequent relentless emphasis on the observable and the tangible, and their rejection of any explanatory concept that rested on unobservable biological bases, transformed psychology. Watson's behaviorist theory was no less speculative than the theories against which he railed; the reinforcement histories, the experiences, and the training he identified were postulated, not observed. The strength of the behaviorist doctrine lay in its apparent precision and the extent to which it seemed open to refutation or confirmation.

For the next half-century the behaviorists dominated developmental science. Studies of intelligence and personality development drew on behaviorist notions, and official publications aimed at lay persons and parents paraphrased behaviorist pronouncements. However, psychoanalytic theory remained the predominant point of view among those working with disturbed children in clinical settings and continued to provide many of the concepts and to identify many of the phenomena with which other theories dealt. Psychoanalytic theory focuses on the inner self and how emotions determine the way we interpret our experiences and therefore how we act. Learning theory stresses the role of external influences on behavior. In 1950, Dollard and Miller attempted to translate psychoanalytic theory into behaviorist terms with the aim of making it both precise and scientific. Throughout this book the reader will encounter references to critical or formative experiences.

Unfortunately, the brash promise of the behaviorists was never fulfilled. Although Watson and his students published some experimental studies substantiating behaviorist notions that behavioral patterns could be established by reward and extinguished by punishment, their successors were less empirical. In their zeal to explain intellectual or personality development with a "scientific" theory, they were rather less careful about the manner in which they conducted research. Instead of observing the function of stimulus–response contingencies in the development of specific children, for example, they attempted to answer questions posed more generally (for example, do "smarter" parents have "smarter" children? or do "hostile" parents have "aggressive" children?) and they relied almost exclusively on retrospective accounts of the behavior of both children and adults. Alas, a half-century of dogmatic pronouncements yielded a peculiarly inconclusive set of findings: Few clear associations between styles of parenting and styles among children emerged.

During the decades that the behaviorists dominated American psychology, they were vehemently criticized by the **maturationist** Arnold Gesell (1925), who deserves recognition as the most ardent and vociferous proponent of the nativist position. Gesell and his colleagues spent years carefully documenting the emergence of cognitive, motor, and social skills in infants and young children. Ironically, while Watson and his behaviorist colleagues were railing against the psychoanalysts for postulating unobservable and therefore unverifiable processes, it was the maturationists who actually observed children, although their conclusions were no more acceptable to Watson and other behaviorists than were those of Freud. According to Gesell, children become increasingly skillful for the same reason that they grow taller and heavier—because they mature. Two-year-olds behave as they do because they are in the "two-year-old" phase. Unfortunately, the vigor with which Gesell expounded "maturationism" led others in the field to discount his theory and his behavioral observations as well as his insistence that genetic and constitutional factors must be given more than token attention.

Interaction and Transaction

In 1958 Ann Anastasi published a seminal paper in which she denounced the excesses of both the extreme nativists and the radical behaviorists. Clearly, she argued, the biological and genetic heritage of young children influences intelligence and personality, just as children's experiences influence the manner in which they develop. However, it is essential to recognize that both experience and heredity are important determinants of development and that these determinants interact in children. Different experiences may yield similar or different outcomes when they interact with different genetic propensities.

Anastasi's interactionist position was widely perceived as superior to either of the extreme positions she criticized, and after 1958 most authors and almost all popular textbooks declared their commitment to an interactionist perspective, usually appending admonitions that further discussion of the nature–nurture controversy is pointless. Nevertheless, with the exception of a few studies it was only in the 1970s that developmental scientists undertook investigations that seriously considered constitutional and experiential factors together. More importantly, it was only with the revolutionary transformation of molecular genetics in the past two decades that researchers began documenting **interactionism**, rather than proclaiming it. For example, a longitudinal study in New Zealand showed that children were differentially affected by exposure to maltreatment, with some showing profound consequences in later life but others apparently unaffected by maltreatment (Caspi et al., 2003). Importantly, a specific genetic allele appeared to distinguish between those children who were and those who were not adversely affected.

Interaction is sometimes more than and different from the combination of nature and nurture. A teaspoon of vinegar and a teaspoon of baking soda are, by themselves, inert, but mixed together they fizz and bubble. Thus, the result of their interaction is something qualitatively different from the initial ingredients. So it is with development. Measuring genetic and experiential influences fails to account for development; the key to development is how genes and experiences interact through time.

Take physical development. What factors contribute to growth? Heredity is certainly a vital ingredient. Studies that have contrasted growth in identical twins (monozygotes who share 100% of their genes) and fraternal twins (dizygotes who share, on average, 50% of their genes) find that about two-thirds of the variation in height and weight can be attributed to genetic inheritance (Plomin, 2007). But heredity is only part of the story. Changes in nutrition can increase height and weight, as they have done in the past 100 years in most parts of the world (Hoppa & Garlie, 1998; Magkos, Manios, Christakis, & Kafatos, 2005; Zhen-Wang & Cheng-Ye, 2005).

In modern times, classical broad-brush theories have given way to more specialized perspectives. Cognitive-developmental theory is concerned with development of thinking; ecological theory asserts that context is key to understanding development; the sociocultural perspective stresses that development constitutes adaptation to specific cultural demands; behavioral genetics studies inherited bases of behavior; and the evolutionary perspective looks at development in light of the evolution of the human species.

Multiple Sources of Influence

Children are profoundly affected by their interpersonal relationships, the social institutions that touch their lives, their culture, and the historical period in which they are developing (Bronfenbrenner & Morris, 2006). The prevailing way developmental scientists think about how experiences influence child development is in terms of an ecological perspective. Developmental characteristics in children are influenced by some forces that are close at hand (parents, extended family, peers); other forces that are somewhat removed (their neighborhood, their parents' workplaces); and still other forces that are quite removed, although still influential (social class, culture). Closer influences are called "proximal," and more remote influences are called "distal." Generally speaking, distal forces influence child development through proximal forces. For example, low socioeconomic status (a distal influence) is linked to poor intellectual development in children through, say, parenting (a proximal influence) (Bornstein, 2002; McLoyd, Aikens, & Burton, 2006).

Most developmental characteristics have multiple distal and proximal determinants. That is, the development of intelligence and personality alike is influenced in many different ways. It is necessary to consider all the likely sources of influence before it is possible to explain how and why an individual thinks or feels in specific ways. Caspi and colleagues (2003) focused on a specific gene that affects susceptibility to adverse influences on development, but researchers have identified a number of specific genes that appear to make children more vulnerable so it is likely both that children can be vulnerable for different reasons and that some children may be especially vulnerable, because they have more than one source of **vulnerability**. No single process is sufficient to explain any aspect of development fully.

Moreover, no single process appears to be necessary to explain any given characteristic of development. Most important aspects of intelligence and personality are over-determined, which means that there are many ways of assuring the same outcome. This implies that the failure or absence of any single experience need not have a profound impact on the child. Consider the child's adoption of a gender role, for example. Various studies implicate hormonal and biological status, maternal behavior, paternal behavior, imitation of parents, imitation of siblings, societal expectations, the media, and peer pressure as influences on gender-role adoption (Hines, 2010). None of these sources of influence necessarily plays a role in every individual case, and none on its own is sufficient to ensure that the child develops a secure and appropriate gender role. This determination holds not only for gender-role development but also for every other aspect of development.

Although the concept of over-determination complicates explanation and understanding, it makes good sense from an evolutionary perspective. The survival of a species as characteristically social as ours would be seriously jeopardized if the appropriate acculturation and **socialization** of each member of the species depended on the occurrence of a large number of complex, narrowly defined experiences. Survival would be facilitated if, as we find is indeed the case, there were many experiential and genetic determinants of intelligence and personality development. That there is considerable plasticity ensures the potential for further adaption to changing environments; that there are **multiple determination** and over-determination delimits the likelihood of radical changes in behavior that might be inimical to a species' adaption to the environment. One unfortunate consequence, however, is that the task of those seeking to understand and explain intelligence and personality development is rendered vastly more challenging.

Stability and Instability; Continuity and Discontinuity

In developmental science time is a fundamental consideration, and so the field is centrally concerned with the consistency or inconsistency of thoughts, feelings, and behaviors through time. Consistency can be measured at the level of the individual or the group. Stability describes consistency in the relative standing of individuals on some characteristic through time. Stability in language development, for example, characterizes development when some children display a relatively high level of language at one point in time *vis-à-vis* their peers and continue to display a high level at a later point in time, where other children display consistently lower levels at both times. Instability in language occurs when individuals do not maintain their relative rank order through time. The other side of development is group average performance through time, the so-called developmental function. **Continuity** describes group mean level consistency; change in the developmental trajectory of a characteristic in its mean level signals discontinuity.

The study of developmental stability and continuity is important for several reasons. One reason is that findings of consistency tell us about the overall developmental course of a given characteristic. Whether individuals maintain rank order on some characteristic through time not only informs about individual variation, but contributes to understanding the possible nature, future, and origins of the characteristic as well. Past performance is often the best predictor of future performance. So, in language, it is believed that the major predictor of developmental status at a given age is language at an earlier age. Two additional reasons knowledge about developmental stability and continuity is essential are that child characteristics—especially consistent ones—signal developmental status to others and affect the child's environment. For example, children's vocalizations and words used during social interactions have been employed to quantify how children socialize with others. Furthermore, interactants often adjust to match consistent characteristics in an individual. For example, adults modify their language to harmonize with the language of children. Thus, mothers fine-tune the contents of their utterances in concert with their children's level of understanding.

In a nutshell, developmentalists are broadly interested in how characteristics manifest themselves and in their individual and group developmental course—their stability and continuity through time. From this perspective the developmental trajectory of a psychological characteristic may consist of any of the four possible combinations of individual stability/instability and group **continuity/discontinuity**. If all children increase in their vocabulary as they grow (as they do), then vocabulary will be discontinuous. If, within the group, children who have more vocabulary when they are young tend also to have more vocabulary when they are older, then vocabulary will be stable. As a whole, vocabulary will be stable and discontinuous. Stability in individuals and continuity in the group are independent of one another. A considerable amount of developmental scholarship focuses on identifying factors that promote stability or continuity over time as well as factors that result in possible instability or discontinuity, both when they are desirable (e.g., potential for effective intervention) and undesirable (e.g., impact of traumatic life events).

CONTEMPORARY DEVELOPMENTAL SCIENCE

The fields that are embraced by broad labels such as "cognitive and intellectual development" or "social and personality development" have been energized by a variety of theoretical perspectives; researchers have adopted various techniques with which to explore the underlying processes. Theoretical frameworks and methodologies, such as are detailed in Chapters 2 and 4 of this volume by Lerner and colleagues and Hartmann and colleagues, must be considered together, because they are closely intertwined and because theoretical frameworks can confirm or disprove hypotheses only to the extent permitted by the research method adopted. Progress in our understanding of development consequently depends on sophistication of methodology as much as on precision in theory. This is an important point to bear in mind when moving from the foundations chapters in the first part this book to the substantive areas of developmental science in the second part.

The usefulness of developmental research has been enhanced by the increased sophistication of many researchers and the parallel awareness that, because the processes involved in intelligence and personality development are extraordinarily complex, traditional simplistic hypotheses are inadequate. With appreciation that both environmental and constitutional factors influence the course and outcomes of these processes through time, there is promise that current and future research will advance our understanding of development more than investigations of the past.

Processes of development exert their influences on the human organism from the time of conception until long past the stage when the individual begins to play a role in the socialization of others. In fact, if we talk not of socialization—a term that implies a conscious effort to influence the behavior of another through the exercise of power or control—but of formative social interaction, even fetuses can be said to exert influence, albeit unwittingly, on their parents. From the time of birth, infants enter into reciprocal interaction with significant others in their social world. This interaction, as this book makes clear, is the source of socializing input to young children, but it is also the medium by which children— genetically unique individuals with specific behavioral predispositions—contribute to the development of their parents, siblings, and others around them. The facts that these patterns of influence are reciprocal, the sources of influence multiple, and the products diverse combine to make the study of intelligence and personality development complex, challenging—and resistant to simplistic interpretations and explanations of either process or outcome.

There are, or course, a number of ways in which a person's genetic heritage contributes to the development of his or her intelligence and personality. Genetic factors may mediate predispositions characteristic of the species that interact with environmental factors in affecting individual development. For example, ethologically oriented theorists argue that infants are born with behavioral propensities shaped by evolution; these propensities are realized only through association with specific adult behaviors. If the appropriate adult behaviors do not occur, developmental deviations (and hence differences in intelligence and personality) are to be expected.

For the most part, however, discussions of genetic determinants refer to the effects of the individual's inherited tendencies on their behavioral development. There are multiple ways in which these effects can be mediated. Not the least important are the relatively rare cases in which a severe pathological condition is directly attributable to gene effects or chromosomal damage (e.g., Down's syndrome).

There are also cases in which genetically mediated abnormalities establish predispositions that will be followed unless a particularly benign environment is encountered. For example, most scientists now recognize that schizophrenia, the most commonly diagnosed psychotic condition, occurs among only a portion of the individuals who are genetically predisposed toward it. Individuals whose environments are unusually supportive (including those in which the individual is never subject to severe stress) retain the genetic predisposition and may pass it along to their children, but they themselves avoid psychotic breakdowns. Similarly, Caspi et al.'s research showed that children with the "susceptibility" gene develop normally provided they are not exposed to maltreatment, but will be especially harshly affected (relative to peers without that gene) when exposed to such experiences.

Another illustration of genetic predisposition interacting with the environment occurs in the case of a syndrome called phenylketonuria (PKU), which causes profound mental retardation. Geneticists have determined that the individual's inability to metabolize the amino acid phenylalanine is to blame. Toxins such as phenylpyruvic acid build up and cause functional brain damage. If the disorder is diagnosed at birth, however, and the child is placed on a special diet that excludes phenylalanine, injury to the nervous system is avoided and the child develops with a normal intellect. Furthermore, the diet can be terminated in middle childhood, after the period of rapid brain development during which the nervous system is maximally sensitive to injury.

The predisposition to PKU is determined by a single recessive gene, so it is fairly simple to determine the cause of the syndrome. Unfortunately, most aspects of intelligence and personality that are subject to genetic influence are mediated not by single genes but by many genes acting concurrently. This has two important implications. First, it means that there are many different types and degrees of predisposition toward a particular intellectual or personality trait. Each will require association with a different type of environment for the trait to be expressed. Second, it means that most traits will not be bimodal, with a person being *either* X *or* non-X. Instead there will be a range of possible outcomes. For example, environmental conditions will not simply determine whether or not a person who is predisposed to be introverted will actually become introverted; they will also determine how much or how little introverted he or she will become.

Intelligence and personality are neither innate nor fixed in early life. Certainly genes contribute to general intellectual or personality development, but experience in the world is a major contributing factor to all psychological functions, including intelligence and personality, and to be inherited does not mean to be immutable or nonchangeable. Longitudinal studies show that individuals definitely change over time. Even heritable traits depend on learning for their expression, and they are subject to environmental effects (Lerner, Fisher, & Gianinno, 2006). So, in the social context perspective development is assisted and guided by others.

Genetic differences affect the way people are influenced by their experiences, and inborn tendencies shape the way people behave and partially determine what types of treatment they elicit from others. Thus, children's experiences modify their behavior, which leads to changes in the parents' behavior. The final outcome is the result of a long and complex transaction between experiential conditions and genetically determined tendencies.

A specific example may be helpful. Babies differ from birth in the extent to which they enjoy close physical contact or cuddling. Consider what effects a baby's lack of enthusiasm for cuddling may have on new parents, most of whom are eager to hold their baby. Many will interpret the baby's apparent rejection of their attempts as a personal rebuff, to which they respond with hostility or withdrawal of affection. These attitudes may influence their behavior and thus the baby's development. Innate differences in irritability, distractibility, and adaptability may have similar long-term effects. In the case of these characteristics, the baby's temperament may elicit parental practices that interact with the baby's enduring propensities. For example, infants with different degrees of adaptability will respond differently to attempts by parents to discipline or guide them, and they will elicit different types of parental behaviors and differential sensitivity in children to socializing pressures.

To say only that biological factors are important is to gloss over the complexity of genetic influences. Hereditary factors do not merely "cause" variation in intelligence and personality. They do not simply set up predispositions that will be translated into undesirable or desirable traits depending on the environment. They are of greatest interest to students of intelligence and personality development because they establish predispositions that affect the types of treatment individuals will experience and modulate the impact of socializing stimuli.

Environmental influences are also complex, as developmentalists have elucidated a number of significant processes that mediate the impact of the environment. The simplest of these are the processes elaborated by learning psychologists—classical and operant conditioning. The popularity of strict learning models is probably attributable to their evident simplicity, to the fact that parents and other socializing agents do attempt to alter the behavior of children by giving rewards and administering punishment, and to the fact that parents' efforts often have the desired effects. **Learning theorists** have shown that partial reinforcement is usually most effective in securing long-term effects, that prompt punishment and reward are ideal, and that the demands made and the reinforcements applied should be consistent. Theorists have also stressed observational learning. Children imitate behavior of models even when they are not rewarded for doing so. Furthermore, the immediate activity may be only an unobservable process called acquisition, with performance of the newly acquired behavior deferred until a more auspicious occasion.

Real or anticipated rewards greatly affect the performance of behaviors that have been acquired through observational learning, however, showing that these two modes of learning are best viewed as complementary rather than mutually exclusive. Furthermore, under the influence of cognitively oriented theorists, **social learning theorists** have increasingly emphasized the role of individual cognitive and motivational factors influencing the impact of observational learning. For example, children not only come to know their gender and realize that this characteristic affects others' expectations; thereafter, children pay attention to same-gender models (see **sex-role models** in the glossary) and try to imitate their behavior while ignoring or trying not to imitate opposite-gender models. Similarly, children who feel especially fond of a parent may be motivated to emulate that parent's behavior and values in ways that children in strained relationships do not. Such motivational and cognitive factors are very important because there are of course myriad models that children could emulate, and it is increasingly obvious that they play crucial roles in choosing models. In sum, then, we see that the different processes by which the environment influences the development of the young organism cannot be viewed as mutually exclusive. All processes are probably implicated in all but the most elementary types of socialization.

OUTLINE OF THIS BOOK

This book is divided into two parts. The next three chapters in Part I introduce the intellectual history of developmental science, review the cultural orientation to thinking about human development, and introduce the manner in which empirical research on development is conducted. Unlike chapters in the second part of the book, these three chapters do not focus much on substantive areas in development, such as intelligence and personality, but on issues that are of central importance to all areas of developmental science. The chapters that follow them, in Part II, move to cover development of temperament, emotions, and self, mother–child and peer relationships, social institutions such as neighborhoods and schools, and social policy. It is well to remember in considering these separate substantive topics—as well as the separation of cognitive and socioemotional development—that we do this as a way of organizing information. In the real world, all domains of development are closely linked.

In Chapter 2, Lerner, Lewin-Bizan, and Alberts Warren describe the philosophical origins and history of systems in developmental science, with special emphasis on the contextual systems view of contemporary developmental study that Lerner and his colleagues have long embraced and advocated. As these authors explain, there have been shifts over time in the definitions of development proposed by competing theorists and in the manner in which central issues in development (e.g., nature versus nurture, stability versus instability, continuity versus discontinuity) are portrayed. Lerner and his colleagues end their chapter with a discussion of the interface between "pure theory" and application in the real world—thereby foreshadowing issues later addressed in more detail by Malloy, Lamb, and Katz (Chapter 9). Developmental theories embody principles based on empirical findings that explain developmentally related phenomena. Without theories, developmental scientists would be lost. However, the history of developmental science is one of widely accepted theories being replaced by new approaches.

In Chapter 3, Cole and Packer provide a sweeping account of the deeper understanding gained when scholars adopt a cultural perspective on development. These authors discuss the implications of alternative definitions of culture before describing several specific examples of interrelations between culture and development. As Cole and Packer show convincingly, culture infuses virtually every facet of human growth, and all developmental scientists must thus be sensitive to its pervasive and diverse influences. For example, infant sleep states are affected by culture. Among the Kipsigis people in East Africa, infants sleep with their mothers and are permitted to nurse on demand. During the day they are strapped to their mothers' backs, accompanying them on their daily rounds of farming, household chores, and social activities. They often nap while their mothers go about their work, and so they do not begin to sleep through the night until many months later than US children who follow a much different course of developmental experiences. No one ever died of wrinkles, gray hair, or baldness, but in some societies they signal the passing of a generation to the next; in other parts of the world, however, these outward signs of aging are associated with maturity, wisdom, and nurturance.

Like all good science, developmental science relies on good methods, design, and analysis. These factors set limits on understanding. For example, developmentalists agree that Piaget seriously underestimated infants' perceptual and cognitive capacities, in some measure because of limitations on his methods. In the last of the foundational chapters in Part I (Chapter 4), Hartmann, Pelzel, and Abbott discuss the diverse ways in which scientists gather, analyze, and interpret developmental evidence. Developmental scientists are methodologically eclectic and rely on experiments, observations, and interviews and questionnaires to obtain their data. They then marshal an array of descriptive and inferential statistical techniques to analyze those data and reach conclusions. The authors discuss these quantitative issues and also offer a unique review of qualitative approaches to data gathering and analysis. Because most studies conducted by developmentalists involve children, a special set of ethical issues attends developmental research, and these too are discussed in this chapter.

The chapters in Part II of this book examine personality and social development in the context of various relationships and situations in which developing individuals function and by which they are shaped. Thompson, Winer, and Goodvin show, in Chapter 5, how temperament, emotions, and self-concepts converge in shaping the emergence of personality in individual children. To explain these complex processes, Thompson and his colleagues explain what each of these key dimensions involves, how each develops, and the ways in which each contributes to the psychological make-up of the individual. The self unfolds in close relation to temperament, emotions, and personality in the course of early psychological development.

However, the self emerges in social contexts. One primary social context for developing individuals is represented by the family. In Chapter 6, Lamb and Lewis recount the development of social relationships within the family during the first years of life. They describe normative developmental progressions in the emergence of these relationships as well as factors that account for individual differences in relationships, creating some that foster healthy adjustment and development and others that subvert developmental processes and lead to the emergence of behavioral pathology.

In Chapter 7, Rubin, Coplan, Chen, Bowker, and McDonald shift the focus to relationships children have with other children outside the family, notably with peers. As Rubin and his coauthors point out, relationships with peers play a central and formative role in children's development. These authors document how, with increasing age, peers in various kinds of groups account for a growing proportion of children's social experiences, creating an increasingly important context within which children manifest their distinctive personality and social styles and by which these styles are modified and honed. Initially, peers punish the breach of societal mores, which they regard as moral imperatives, whereas their parents may regard them as broad and flexible guidelines. Subsequently, peers gain importance by defining new standards for the regulation of the group's activities. In adolescence and adulthood, peers provide models to imitate and perhaps models whose behaviors one must attempt to complement. How peer influences are measured, why individual children are influenced by peers, how children essentially negotiate their relationships with friends, and the consequences of good and poor peer relationships in children's lives are topics of keen interest in contemporary developmental science.

As most children grow, self and social relationships are increasingly organized within institutional contexts such as school and community. These social institutions serve as environments in which children are expected to perform and by which their tendencies, preferences, and abilities are shaped. School and community are therefore, as Eccles and Roeser show in Chapter 8, pervasive and powerful developmental ecologies for children. Although developmentalists have often viewed the family as the primary context within which children are reared, and peers as close runners-up, Eccles and Roeser make clear that children are profoundly influenced by relationships and experiences outside the family, although earlier theorists and researchers failed to consider fully the potential impact of teachers on children's development. Seminal research has dramatically alerted social scientists to the fact that teachers' expectations can have substantial impacts on the subsequent performances of their pupils. It is important to note that the influence of teachers supplements, complements, and interacts with the influences of other socializing agents. Teaching styles have different impacts on children with different personalities, gender, and backgrounds, ensuring that the socialization process is complex, enduring, and broad.

As explained by Lerner and his colleagues in Chapter 2 and as noted in many of the proceeding chapters, developmental science is not only a subdiscipline in which scientists seek basic knowledge of developmental processes. The individuals at the centre of developmental research face real problems and challenges, and the results of developmental research often have implications for the design of intervention programs and for the initiation of social policy. An increasing portion of attention in developmental science today is paid to applied as well as basic research issues. In the concluding chapter (Chapter 9), Malloy, Lamb, and Katz illustrate the ways in which developmental thinking and research affect and are affected by practice and social policy. Their chapter is a guide to students who would like see their work affect and benefit the society at large.

CONCLUSIONS

Contemporary developmental science is positioned to have a powerful impact on how people mature and how society functions. It can do so through its associations with and impacts on all of those involved in human development. Developmental science provides parents with information on what behavior is typical or atypical at a given age and what effects different approaches to parenting have on children. Knowledge about development allows teachers to develop age-appropriate curricula. Knowing what is developmentally typical and atypical helps healthcare professionals diagnose problems and design more effective treatments.

Government officials write and enforce laws regarding children and decide which programs should be supported. All of these people have a stake in the success of developmental science.

REFERENCES AND SUGGESTED READINGS (📖)

📖 Anastasi, A. (1958). Heredity, environment, and the question 'how?' *Psychological Review*, *65*, 197–208.

📖 Baltes, P. B., Lindenberger, U., & Staudinger, U. M. (2006). Life-span theory in developmental psychology. In W. Damon & R. M. Lerner (Eds.), *Handbook of child psychology: Vol. 1. Theoretical models of human development* (pp. 569–664). New York: Wiley.

📖 Bornstein, M. H. (Ed.). (2002). *Handbook of parenting* (2nd ed.), *Volume 1: Children and Parenting. Volume 2: Biology and Ecology of Parenting. Volume 3: Status and Social Conditions of Parenting. Volume 4: Applied Parenting. Volume 5: Practical Parenting*. Mahwah, NJ: Lawrence Erlbaum Associates.

📖 Bornstein, M. H. (Ed.). (2009). *The handbook of cultural developmental science. Part 1. Domains of development across cultures. Part 2. Development in different places on earth*. New York: Psychology Press.

Bradley, R. H., Nader, P., O'Brien, M., Houts, R., Belsky, J., Crosnoe, R., et al. (2008). Adiposity and internalizing problems: Infancy to middle childhood. In H. D. Davies & H. E. Fitzgerald (Set Eds.) and H. E. Fitzgerald & V. Mousouli (Vol. Eds.), *Obesity in childhood and adolescence: Vol. 2. Understanding development and prevention* (pp. 73–91). Westport, CT: Praeger.

Brett, G. S. (1912–1921). *A history of psychology* (3 volumes). London: Allen.

Bronfenbrenner, U., & Morris, P. (2006). The bioecological model of human development. In W. Damon & R. Lerner (Series Eds.) and R. Lerner (Vol. Ed.), *Handbook of child psychology: Vol. 1. Theoretical models of human development* (6th ed., pp. 793–828). New York: Wiley.

Caspi, A., Sugden, K., Moffitt, T. E., Taylor, A., Craig, I. W., Harrington, H., et al. (2003). Influence of life stress on depression: Moderation by a polymorphism in the 5-HTT gene. *Science*, *301*, 386–389.

Castelli, D. (2005). Academic achievement and physical fitness in third-, fourth-, and fifth-grade students. *Research Quarterly for Exercise and Sport*, *76*(1), A-15.

Castelli, D. M., Hillman, C. H., Buck, S., & Erwin, H. E. (2007). Physical fitness and academic achievement in 3rd and 5th grade students. *Journal of Sport and Exercise Psychology*, *29*, 239–252.

Darwin, C. (1859). *The origin of species*. New York: Signet Classics.

Desai, M., Pratt, L. A., Lentzner, H., & Robinson, K. N. (2001). Trends in vision and hearing among older Americans. National Center for Health Statistics. *Aging Trends*, *2*, 1–8.

Dick, D. M., Rose, R. J., Pulkkinen, L., & Kaprio, J. (2001). Measuring puberty and understanding its impact: A longitudinal study of adolescent twins. *Journal of Youth and Adolescence*, *30*, 385–400.

Dollard, J., & Miller, N. E. (1950). *Personality and psychotherapy*. New York: McGraw-Hill.

Elder, G., Jr., & Shanahan, M. (2006). The life course and human development. In W. Damon & R. Lerner (Series Eds.) and R. Lerner (Vol. Ed.), *Handbook of child psychology: Vol. 1. Theoretical models of human development* (6th ed., pp. 665–716). New York: Wiley.

Freud, S. (1916/1917). *Introductory lectures on psychoanalysis*. London: Hogarth Press.

Gesell, A. (1925). *The mental growth of the preschool child*. New York: Macmillan.

Gottlieb, G., Wahlsten, D., & Lickliter, R. (2006). The significance of biology for human development: A developmental psychobiological systems view. In W. Damon & R. Lerner (Series Eds.) and R. Lerner (Vol. Ed.), *Handbook of child psychology: Vol. 1. Theoretical models of human development* (6th ed., pp. 210–257). New York: Wiley.

Hines, M. (2010). Gendered behavior across the lifespan. In M. E. Lamb, A. Freund, & R. M. Lerner (Eds.), *The handbook of lifespan development (Vol. 2): Social and emotional development* (pp. 341–378). Hoboken, NJ: Wiley.

Hoppa, R. D., & Garlie, T. N. (1998). Secular changes in the growth of Toronto children during the last century. *Annals of Human Biology*, *25*, 553–561.

Howe, M. L., & Lewis, M. D. (2005). The importance of dynamic systems approaches for understanding development. *Developmental Review*, *25*, 247–251.

Kampfe, C. M., & Smith, S. M. (1998). Intrapersonal aspects of hearing loss in persons who are older. *The Journal of Rehabilitation*, *64*(2), 24–28.

📖 Lamb, M. E., Freund, A., & Lerner, R. M. (Eds.) (2010). *The handbook of lifespan development (Vol. 2): Social and emotional development*. Hoboken, NJ: Wiley.

Lerner, R. M., Fisher, C. B., & Gianinno, L. (2006). Editorial: Constancy and change in the development of applied developmental science. *Applied Developmental Science*, *10*, 172–173.

Magkos, F., Manios, Y., Christakis, G., & Kafatos, A. G. (2005). Secular trends in cardiovascular risk factors among school-aged boys from Crete, Greece, 1982–2002. *European Journal of Clinical Nutrition*, *59*, 1–7.

McLoyd, V. C., Aikens, N. L., & Burton, L. M. (2006). Childhood poverty, policy, and practice. In K. A. Renninger &

I. E. Sigel (Eds.) and W. Damon (Series Ed.), *Handbook of child psychology: Vol. 4. Child psychology in practice* (6th ed., pp. 700–775). Hoboken, NJ: Wiley.

Mustanski, B. S., Viken, R. J., Kaprio, J., Pulkkinen, L., & Rose, R. J. (2004). Genetic and environmental influences on pubertal development: Longitudinal data from Finnish twins at ages 11 and 14. *Developmental Psychology*, *40*, 1188–1198.

Nagin, D. S., & Tremblay, R. E. (2005). Developmental trajectory groups: Fact or useful statistical fiction? *Criminology*, *43*, 873–904.

O'Brien, M., Nader, P. R., Houts, R. M., Bradley, R., Friedman, S. L., Belsky, J., et al. (2007). The ecology of childhood overweight: A 12-year longitudinal analysis. *International Journal of Obesity*, *31*(9), 1469–1478.

Overton, W., & Lerner, R. M. (Eds.) (2010). *The handbook of lifespan development (Vol. 1): Cognition, biology, and methods.* Hoboken, NJ: Wiley.

Pleis, J. R., & Lethbridge-Çejku, M. (2006). Summary health statistics for U.S. adults: National Health Interview Survey, 2005. *Vital Health Statistics*, Series 10, *232*, 1–153.

Plomin, R. (2007). Genetics and developmental psychology. In G. W. Ladd (Ed.), *Appraising the human developmental sciences: Essays in honor of Merrill-Palmer Quarterly* (pp. 250–261). Detroit, MI: Wayne State University Press.

Schwimmer, J. B., Burwinkle, T. M., & Varni, J. W. (2003). Health-related quality of life of severely obese children and adolescents. *Journal of the American Medical Association*, *289*, 1813–1819.

Thelen, E., & Smith, L. B. (2006). Dynamic systems theories. In W. Damon & R. Lerner (Series Eds.) and R. Lerner (Vol. Ed.), *Handbook of child psychology: Vol. 1. Theoretical models of human development* (6th ed., pp. 258–312). Hoboken, NJ: Wiley.

Van Geert, P., & Steenbeek, H. (2005). Explaining after by before: Basic aspects of a dynamic systems approach to the study of development. *Developmental Review*, *25*, 408–442.

Watson, J. B. (1924). *Behaviorism.* New York: People's Institute Publishing Company.

Waxman, S. R., & Lidz, J. L. (2006). Early word learning. In W. Damon & R. M. Lerner (Series Eds.) and D. Kuhn & R. S. Siegler (Vol. Eds.), *Handbook of child psychology: Vol. 2. Cognition, perception, and language* (6th ed., pp. 299–335). Hoboken, NJ: Wiley.

Zhen-Wang, B., & Cheng-Ye, J. (2005). Secular growth changes in body height and weight in children and adolescents in Shandong, China between 1939 and 2000. *Annals of Human Biology*, *32*, 650–665

FOUNDATIONS OF DEVELOPMENTAL SCIENCE

❖ 2 ❖

CONCEPTS AND THEORIES OF HUMAN DEVELOPMENT

Richard M. Lerner
Tufts University
Selva Lewin-Bizan
Tufts University
Amy Eva Alberts Warren
Institute for Applied Research in Youth Development

INTRODUCTION

The meaning of the term "development" continues to engage scholars in philosophical and theoretical debate (e.g., Collins, 1982; Featherman, 1985; Ford & Lerner, 1992; Harris, 1957; Kaplan, 1983; Lerner, 2002, 2006; Overton, 1998, 2003, 2006; Reese & Overton, 1970). The existence of the debate is itself indicative of a key feature of the meaning of the term: Development is not an empirical concept. If it were, inspection of a set of data would indicate to any observer whether development was present. However, different scientists can look at the same data set and disagree about whether development has occurred.

In this chapter, we discuss the concept of development as it has been and currently is used within human developmental science. We review both the philosophical foundations and the historical roots of the concept and explain how its use within contemporary, cutting-edge theoretical models of human development finds its basis in this philosophical and historical record.

Past concepts of development were predicated on Cartesian philosophical ideas about the character of reality that separated, or "split," what was regarded as real from what was relegated to the "unreal" or epiphenomenal (Overton, 1998, 2003, 2006). In human development, major instances of such splitting involved classic debates about nature versus nurture as "the" source of development, continuity versus discontinuity as an appropriate depiction of the character of the human developmental trajectory, and stability versus instability as an adequate means to describe developmental change. Today, most major developmental theories eschew such splits, and use concepts drawn from **developmental systems theories** (e.g., Lerner, 2006; Overton, 1998, 2003, 2006) to depict the basic developmental process as involving relations—or "fusions" (Thelen & Smith, 2006; Tobach & Greenberg, 1984)—among variables from the multiple levels of organization that comprise the ecology of human development (e.g., see Bronfenbrenner, 2001, 2005). In contemporary developmental science, the basic process of development involves mutually influential (i.e., bidirectional) relations between levels of organization ranging from biology through individual and social functioning to societal, cultural, physical, ecological, and, ultimately, historical levels of organization (e.g., Baltes, Lindenberger, & Staudinger, 1998, 2006; Elder & Shanahan, 2006; Ford & Lerner, 1992).

As a consequence, contemporary developmental theory transcends another split that has characterized the field of human developmental science—a split between basic science and application (Fisher & Lerner, 1994; Lerner, 2006). The relational character of development means that some degree of change is always possible within the developmental system, as the temporality of history imbues each of the other levels of organization within the developmental system with the potential for change. Temporality means that at least relative **plasticity** (the potential for systematic change) exists within the integrated (fused) developmental system. Temporality creates changes in the mutually influential relations between individuals and their contexts. These mutually influential relations may be represented as individual ↔ context relations.

Theoretically predicated attempts to change the course of development—the trajectory of individual ↔ context relations—constitute both tests of the basic, relational process of human development *and* (given ethical mandates to act only to enhance human development) attempts to improve the course of life. These interventions into the life course may be aimed at individuals, families, communities, or the institutions of society, and may involve such actions as instituting community based programs or enacting broad rules (i.e., social policies) governing the structure or function of such programs (Lerner, 2002, 2006). Thus, from the viewpoint of the developmental systems theories that define the cutting edge of contemporary developmental science, there is no necessary distinction between research on the basic, relational process (relational development) linking individuals to their multi-tiered ecological systems and applications aimed at promoting positive individual ↔ context relations.

How did developmental science traverse a conceptual course from split conceptions of the bases and course of development to integrative concepts and models that emphasize the relational character of human development and the synthesis of basic and applied foci? To answer this key question, which in essence tells the story of past and contemporary defining features of human developmental science, we need to consider first what developmental scientists may or may not assume about the nature of their subject matter.

THE ASSUMPTIONS OF HUMAN DEVELOPMENTAL SCIENTISTS

Scientists begin their study of development with some implicit or explicit concept of what development is. Then, when they inspect a given set of data, they can determine whether the features of the data fit with their concepts. Thus, debates among scientists about the meaning of development arise because different scientists have different conceptual templates. These conceptual differences exist because different scientists are committed to distinct philosophical and theoretical beliefs about the nature of the world and of human life.

Nevertheless, despite the philosophical and theoretical differences that exist among scientists in their conceptions of development, there is some agreement about the minimal features of any concept of development. In its most general sense, development refers to change. But "change" and "development" are not equivalent terms. Whenever development occurs there is change, but not all changes are developmental ones. Changes must have a systematic, organized character for them to be labeled as developmental. But systematicity, or organization, does not suffice to define development. For organized, or systematic, changes to be developmental ones, they have to have a *successive* character. The idea of successive changes indicates that the changes seen at a later time are at least in part influenced by the changes that occurred at an earlier time, if only to the extent that the range of changes probable at the later time is limited by earlier occurrences.

Despite a relatively high degree of consensus about the point that development is a theoretical concept that, at least, connotes systematic and successive change in an organization, there is a good deal of disagreement among developmental scientists about what particular ideas need to be added to define the term adequately. These differences in definitions are associated with theoretical differences that, ultimately, are based on their commitments to different philosophical positions (Kuhn, 1962; Lerner, 2002; Overton, 2003, 2006; Pepper, 1942). These philosophical positions involve implicit and explicit assumptions that scientists make regarding their theories, hypotheses, and the methods they use to design their research or to make observations.

The philosophical models of the world used by scientists have a pervasive effect on the scientific positions they adopt. In developmental science, they specify the basic characteristics of humans, and of reality itself, and thus function either to include or to exclude particular features of humans and/or of the world's events in the realm of scientific discourse. Hence, science is relative rather than absolute. Facts are not viewed as naturally occurring events awaiting discovery. According to Kuhn (1962), science "seems an attempt to force nature into [a] preformed and relatively inflexible box . . . No part of the aim of normal science is to call forth new sorts of . . . phenomena; indeed those that will not fit the box are often not seen at all. Nor do scientists normally aim to invent new theories, and they are often intolerant of those invented by others" (p. 24).

As we explain below, a range of models exist within developmental science. As such, full understanding of human development cannot be obtained from any one theory or methodology, nor can it be obtained from a cataloging of empirical "facts." The integration of philosophy, theory, method, and research results is required to attain a complete understanding of any instance of scientific scholarship. Within such an integration, theory and research are given meaning. They are developed and interpreted within the context of a given philosophical perspective. Thus, it is necessary to understand the different philosophical assumptions on which the study of development can be based and to examine the models, or world views, that are used today in the study of human development.

CONCEPTUAL SPLITS IN THE HISTORY OF DEVELOPMENTAL SCIENCE

Have people always believed that humans develop? Have people always said that infants are different from children and that both are different from adolescents and adults? Have "special" portions of the life span, such as adolescence or the aged years, always been held to exist? Have people always believed that there is such a phenomenon as human development, and if not, when and why did such a belief arise?

Focusing on the Western world, many of the central questions and controversies about human development are quite old, with roots in ancient Greece and the traditions of Western philosophy. In both the 2,000 years of this philosophy and about 150 years of pertinent science, the ideas advanced to explain development have revolved around the same few issues. These issues represent the core concepts in any discussion of development, and differences among philosophers and scientists can be understood by looking at the stances they take in regard to such basic conceptual issues. These pertain most directly to one issue: the **nature–nurture** controversy.

In its most extreme form, the nature–nurture controversy pertains to whether behavior and development derive from nature (or in modern terms, heredity, maturation, or genes) or, at the other extreme, whether behavior and development derive from nurture (or in more modern terms, environment, experience, or learning). However, whatever terms are used, the issue raises questions about how nature characteristics (for example, genes) may contribute to development and/or how nurture characteristics (for example, stimulus–response connections, education, or socialization) may play a role in development.

Once the analysis of development is framed in such a split fashion, it is generally further assumed that some set of empirical investigations will ultimately record a definitive answer to the either/or question. The simple empirical observation that generations of empirical investigations have failed to resolve any of these issues demonstrates the inadequacy of the assumption that research done will resolve controversies about splits. As a consequence, the fundamental conceptual prejudice of seeing the world in **conceptual splits** continues to hold the controversies in place as controversies (Overton, 1998). For instance, despite decades of evidence from biology and comparative psychology that genes function as fused entities within an integrated organism ↔ context relational system (e.g., see Gottlieb, 1992, 1997, 2004; Gottlieb, Wahlsten, & Lickliter, 2006), there exist repeated appeals to partition variance associated with genes from variance associated with the context (e.g., Plomin, 2000; Rowe, 1994; Rushton, 2000).

In fact, one can regard the history of developmental science as involving the swinging of a pendulum. This pendulum moved from conceptions of human development stressing nature to conceptions stressing nurture. At this writing, there is a focus on conceptions stressing that neither extreme is appropriate. Notions such as interactions, relationism, fusion, integration, or dynamic systems are used today to understand how the bases of human development combine to foster systematic change across the life span (Lerner, 2002, 2006).

Nature versus Nurture

Anastasi (1958) explained why split conceptions fail. She noted that the first way that scholars inquired into the nature–nurture problem was to ask, "Which one? Does nature *or* nurture provide the determining source of behavior?" Those who posed the issue in this way were assuming that the independent, isolated action of one *or* the other domain provided the source of a behavior.

However, this split way of posing the problem should be rejected because it is illogical. There would be no one in an environment without heredity, and there would be no place to see the effects of heredity without environment. Genes do not exist in a vacuum. They exert their influence on behavior in an environment. At the same time, if there were no genes or heredity, the environment would not have an organism in it to influence. Accordingly, nature and nurture are inextricably tied together and they never exist independent of the other. As such, Anastasi (1958) argued that *any* theory of development, to be logical and to reflect life situations accurately (to have *ecological validity*), must stress that nature and nurture are always involved in all behavior; both are completely necessary for any organism's existence or for the existence of any behavior.

Some psychologists (e.g., Hebb, 1949; Lehrman, 1953; Schneirla, 1956, 1957) had recognized the inappropriateness of the "which one?" question even before Anastasi (1958). Others had asked another question that Anastasi maintained also was inappropriate because it too led to a conceptual dead end. The question was: "Granted that nature and nurture are always involved in any behavior, *how much* of each is needed for a given behavior?" This question is also fruitless because it too is based on the same split and hence inappropriate underlying assumption. In the case of the "how much?" question, the instantiation of the split assumption may be termed the independent, additive-action assumption. It suggests that the way in which nature and nurture are related to each other is that the contribution of one source is added to the contribution of the other to provide a basis of behavior. However, the "how much?" question leads to separating out (splitting) the independent, isolated effects of nature and nurture, as in the "which one?" question. That is, the "which one?" question is just a special case of the "how much?" question, implying a split between nature and nurture of 100 percent/0 percent (or vice versa).

Thus, a conceptualization of the independent action of either source (in either an isolated or an additive manner) leads to a conceptually vacuous dead end. Two assertions follow directly from the above argument. First, nature and nurture are always completely involved in all behavior. Any method of inquiry into the source of behavioral development that does not take cognizance of this statement and seeks to make artificial distinctions between nature and nurture can lead only to conceptual confusion and an empirical blind alley. Second, because independent-action conceptualizations of the contributions of nature and nurture similarly lead to conceptual dead ends, an alternative conceptualization of their contributions, that of *dynamically interactive* or *fused* action, seems more appropriate.

This alternative indicates that nature and nurture interact dynamically (as components or dimensions of a fused, developmental system) to provide a source of behavioral development. Because both sources are necessarily completely present, and because it is inappropriate to speak of their contributions as adding to each other, then the appropriate questions seem to be: "*How* do nature and nurture dynamically interact to produce behavioral development? *How* do the effects of each multiply (or reciprocally interrelate within a fused developmental system) to provide a source of development?"

This third question, Anastasi argued, is the appropriate way to formulate the issue, because it takes cognizance of the logical necessity of the material existence of both domains for a living organism (or living system; Ford & Lerner, 1992). This question denies a split between nature and nurture or the contention that one domain is real and the other is pseudo-phenomenal (e.g., as in Rowe, 1994). Instead, there exists a relation in which the full presence of each source is completely intertwined with the other. As such, nature never affects behavior directly; it always acts in the context of internal and external environments. Environment never directly influences behavior either; it will show variation in its effects depending on the heredity-related characteristics of the organism on which it acts.

The fused approach to nature and nurture presented by Anastasi (1958) helps frame other key issues involved in understanding the characteristics of human development. One of these is the **continuity–discontinuity issue**.

Continuity–Discontinuity

If behavior seen at one point in the life span can be represented or depicted in the same way as behavior at another point, then descriptive continuity exists. If behavior seen at one point in the life span cannot be represented or depicted in the same way as behavior at another point, then descriptive discontinuity exists. Consider, for instance, recreational behavior studied in adolescence and young adulthood. If the same activity (for instance, bike riding) was the major form of recreational behavior at both points in the life span, then descriptive continuity would exist. If, when as adolescent, the person rode a bike for recreation but, in adulthood, went hiking, then there would be descriptive discontinuity across these portions of ontogeny.

Changes in the description of behavior across a person's life can occur for many reasons. In fact, even the same change, whether continuous or discontinuous, can be explained by many reasons. If the same explanations are used to account for behavior across a person's life, then this means that behavior is interpreted as involving unchanging laws or rules. In this case there is explanatory continuity. If, however, different explanations are used to account for behavior across a person's life, then there is explanatory discontinuity.

Descriptions or explanations of development can involve quantitative or qualitative changes. Descriptively, quantitative changes involve differences in how much (or how many) of something exists. For example, in adolescence quantitative changes occur in such areas as height and weight because there is an adolescent growth spurt and these changes may be interpreted as resulting from quantitative increases in the production of growth stimulating hormone. Descriptive qualitative changes involve differences in what exists, in what sort of phenomenon is present. The emergence in adolescence of a drive-state never before present in life (a reproductively mature sexual drive; Freud, 1969) and the emergence in adolescence of new and abstract thought capabilities not present in younger people (formal operations; Piaget, 1950, 1970) are instances of changes interpreted as arising from qualitative alterations in the person. It is believed that the person is not just "more of the same;" rather the person is seen as having a *new* quality or characteristic.

Explanations of development can also vary in regard to whether one *accounts* for change by positing quantitative changes (for example, increases in the amounts of growth stimulating hormone present in the bloodstream) or by positing a new reason for behaviors (e.g., an infant's interactions in his or her social world are predicated on the need to establish a sense of basic trust in the world, whereas an adolescent's social interactions involve the need to establish a sense of identity, or a self definition). In other words, it is possible to offer an explanatory discontinuous interpretation of development involving *either* quantitative or qualitative change. Figure 2.1 illustrates the various combinations of quantitative and qualitative, descriptive and explanatory, continuity and discontinuity that can occur intra-individually across ontogeny.

Virtually any statement about the character of intraindividual development involves, explicitly or implicitly, taking a position in regard to three dimensions of change: (1) descriptive continuity–discontinuity; (2) explanatory continuity–discontinuity; and (3) the quantitative versus the qualitative character of descriptions and explanations—that is, the quantitative–qualitative dimension pertains to both description and explanation.

The particular couplings that one posits as involved in human life will depend on the substantive domain of development one is studying (e.g., intelligence, motivation, personality, or peer group relations) and primarily on one's theory of development. Any particular description or explanation of intraindividual change is the result of a particular theoretical view of development. Accordingly, commitment to a theory that focuses only on certain variables or processes will restrict one's view of the variety of changes that may characterize

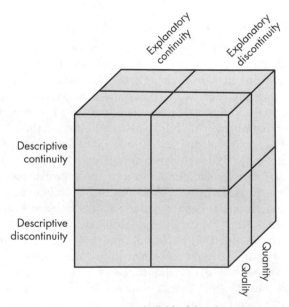

FIGURE 2.1 The intraindividual change box. Intraindividual involves change along three dimensions: descriptive continuity–discontinuity; explanatory continuity–discontinuity; and a quantitative–qualitative dimension (adapted from Lerner, 2002, p. 109).

development. Focusing only on "stages of development" (e.g., Freud, 1954; Piaget, 1950) may lead to an emphasis only on qualitative discontinuity in both descriptions and explanations. Focusing only on stimulus–response connections (e.g., Bijou & Baer, 1961) may result in an emphasis on explanatory continuity and descriptive discontinuity (in regard to the number of connections present in a person's behavioral repertoire). Thus, especially in the case of theories that are based on nature–nurture splits, the range of possible intraindividual changes included in a person's development are split into sets associated with a specific theoretical model. In short, theory, not data, is the major lens through which one "observes" continuity or discontinuity in development.

Stability–Instability

The **stability–instability issue** describes differences that arise between people within groups as a consequence of within-person change. Thus, two types of alterations involving people are occurring simultaneously. People may be changing over time, and because not all people change in the same way or at the same rate, people's locations relative to others may alter as well. Accordingly, to understand all dimensions of a person's alteration over time, both aspects of change (continuity–discontinuity *and* stability–instability) should be considered simultaneously. Only through such a joint, simultaneous focus can development across the life span best be portrayed.

If a person's position relative to his or her reference group changes with development, this is *instability*. If a person's position relative to his or her reference group remains the same with development, this is *stability*. These terms describe a person's ranking relative to some reference group. However, whether stability or instability occurs says nothing whatsoever about whether or not any within-person change took place. A person can change, and this change may still be labeled stability. This could occur if others in the reference group also changed and if the target person remained in the same relative position. By contrast, a person could remain the same from Time 1 to Time 2 and yet his or her position relative to the reference group could be termed unstable. This would occur if others in the group changed while the target person did not. Hence, the terms stability and instability describe relative, not absolute, changes.

Any developmental change may be characterized as being either continuous or discontinuous *and* either stable or instable, and different theories of development proscribe and prescribe the character of the changes that may be involved in human development. Theories that vary in their commitment to nature, to nurture, or to nature–nurture interactional or synthetic ideas may be contrasted in regard to their inclusion of ideas pertinent to qualitative and quantitative, descriptive and explanatory continuity and discontinuity.

Towards the Healing of Conceptual Splits

We have seen that some scholars took split positions in regard to human development, whereas others favored what Overton (1998, 2006) labeled relational conceptions, a set, or "family," of theories labeled developmental systems perspectives. Relational positions aim to "heal" the nature–nurture split (1) by offering categories that describe the biological and the social–cultural as alternative ways of viewing the same whole (e.g., Gottlieb, 1992; Overton, 1973, 2003, 2006; Tobach, 1981) and (2) by suggesting that action constitutes a broad-based mechanism of development that itself differentiates into biological and social–cultural manifestations (e.g., Brandtstädter, 1998, 2006; Overton, 2006).

Prior to Overton's (1998, 2006) discussion of split-versus-relational ideas in philosophy, Overton and Reese (1973, 1981; Reese & Overton, 1970) focused their attention on the import for theory and method in human development of two world views—the mechanistic and the

Willis F. Overton.

organismic—which, historically, have been central in influencing theories of development. Although many theories of development associated with mechanism and organicism were similar in adopting split views of nature and nurture, Reese and Overton advanced the understanding of human development significantly by describing the different "families" of theories and methodological traditions associated with mechanistic- and organismic-related theories.

The work of Reese and Overton was seminal in promoting among other developmental scientists an interest in exploring the potential role of other world hypotheses in shaping theories of development. Reese and Overton (Overton, 1984; Overton & Reese, 1981; Reese, 1982) and Lerner (e.g., 1984; Lerner & Kauffman, 1985) discussed the ways in which a "contextual" world hypothesis (Pepper, 1942) could be used to devise a theory of development. In turn, Riegel (1975, 1977) discussed the potential use of a "dialectical" model of development.

Although Pepper (1942) claimed that it was not philosophically permissible to "mix metaphors" and combine mechanistic, organismic, and contextual world views, often scholars believed it was possible to do just this. Arguing on the basis of criteria of usefulness (e.g., in regard to developing statements that, in comparison to those of other positions, account for more variance in developmental data sets, lead to more novel discoveries than do ideas associated with other positions, or integrate a broader range of phenomena pertinent to development than is the case with other positions), Overton (1984) and Lerner and Kauffman (1985) advanced the notion of combining organicism and contextualism to frame a new approach to developmental theory.

The conceptual attractiveness of an integration between contextualism and organicism has resulted within contemporary developmental science in an interest in and elaboration of various instantiations of developmental systems theories.

DEVELOPMENTAL SYSTEMS PERSPECTIVES

The power of a developmental systems perspective is constituted by four interrelated and in fact "fused" (Tobach & Greenberg, 1984) components of such theories: (1) change and relative plasticity; (2) relationism and the integration of levels of organization; (3) historical embeddedness and temporality; and (4) the limits of generalizability, diversity, and individual differences. Although these four conceptual components frame the contemporary set of developmental systems theories within the field of human development (Lerner, 1998), each has a long and rich tradition in the history of the field (Cairns, 1998).

Change and Relative Plasticity

Developmental systems theories stress that the focus of developmental understanding must be on (systematic) change. This focus is required because of the belief that the potential for change exists across (1) the life span and (2) the multiple levels of organization comprising the ecology of human development. Although it is also assumed that systematic change is not limitless (e.g., it is constrained by both past developments and contemporary ecological, or contextual, conditions), developmental systems theories stress that *relative plasticity* exists across life (Lerner, 1984).

There are important implications of relative plasticity for understanding the range of intraindividual variation that can exist over ontogeny (Fisher, Jackson, & Villarruel, 1998) and for the application of development science. For instance, the presence of relative plasticity legitimates a proactive search across the life span for characteristics of people and of their contexts that, together, can influence the design of policies and programs promoting positive development (e.g., Birkel, Lerner, & Smyer, 1989; Kurtines et al., 2008; Lerner & Overton, 2008): for example, the plasticity of intellectual development that is a feature of a systems view of mental functioning, and provides legitimization for educational policies and school- and community-based programs aimed at enhancing cognitive and social cognitive development (Dryfoos, Quinn & Barkin, 2005; Lerner, 2004a, 2007). Such implications for the design of policies and programs stand in marked contrast to those associated with mechanistic, genetic reductionistic theories that suggest that genetic inheritance constrains intellectual development (e.g., Herrnstein & Murray, 1994; Rushton, 2000).

Relationism and the Integration of Levels of Organization

Developmental systems theories stress that the bases for change, and for both plasticity and constraints in development, lie in relations that exist among the multiple levels of organization that comprise the substance of human life (Schneirla, 1957; Tobach, 1981). These levels range from the inner biological, through the individual/psychological and the proximal social relational (e.g., involving dyads, peer groups, and nuclear families), to the sociocultural level (including key macro-institutions such as educational, public policy, governmental, and economic systems) and the natural and designed physical ecologies of human development (Bronfenbrenner, 1979, 2001, 2005; Bronfenbrenner & Morris, 2006; Riegel, 1975). These tiers are structurally and functionally integrated, thus underscoring the utility of a developmental systems view of the levels involved in human life.

A developmental systems perspective promotes a *relational* unit of analysis as requisite for developmental analysis: Variables associated with any level of organization exist (are structured) in relation to variables from other levels; the qualitative and quantitative dimensions of the function of any variable are shaped as well by relations of the variable with ones from other levels. Unilevel units of analysis (or the components of, or elements in, a relation) are not an adequate target of developmental analysis; rather, the relation itself—the interlevel linkage—should be the focus of such analysis (Lerner, Dowling, & Chaudhuri, 2005a; Overton, 2006; Riegel, 1975).

Relationism and integration have a clear implication for unilevel theories of development. At best, such theories are severely limited, and inevitably provide a non-veridical depiction of development, due to their focus on what are essentially main effects embedded in higher-order interactions (e.g., see Walsten, 1990). At worst, such theories are neither valid nor useful. Thus, neither nature nor nurture theories provide adequate conceptual frames for understanding human development (see Hirsch, 1970, 2004; Lewontin, 1992). Moreover, many nature–nurture interaction theories also fall short in this regard because theories of this type still treat nature- and nurture-variables as separable entities, and view their connection in manners analogous to the interaction term in an analysis of variance (e.g., Bijou, 1976; Erikson, 1959; Hartmann, Pelzel, & Abbott, Chapter 4, this volume; Plomin, 2000; cf. Gollin, 1981; Hebb, 1970; Walsten, 1990). Developmental systems theories move beyond the simplistic division of sources of development into nature-related and nurture-related variables or processes; they see the multiple levels of organization that exist within the ecology of human development as part of an inextricably fused developmental system.

Historical Embeddedness and Temporality

The relational units of analysis of concern in developmental systems theories are understood as change units. The change component of these units derives from the ideas that all the levels of organization involved in human development are embedded in the broadest level of the person–context system: history. That is, all other levels of organization within the developmental system are integrated with historical change. History—change over time—is incessant and continuous, and is a level of organization that is fused with all other levels. This linkage means that change is a necessary, an inevitable, feature of variables from all levels of organization. In addition, this linkage means that the structure, as well as the function, of variables changes over time.

Because historical change is continuous and temporality is infused in all levels of organization (Elder, Modell, & Parke, 1993; Elder & Shanahan, 2006), change-sensitive measures of structure and function *and* change-sensitive (i.e., longitudinal) designs are necessitated in contemporary theories of human development (Baltes, Reese, & Nesselroade, 1977; Brim & Kagan, 1980). The key question *vis-à-vis* temporality in such research is not whether change occurs but whether the changes that do occur make a difference for a given developmental outcome (Lerner, Schwartz, & Phelps, 2009; Lerner, Skinner, & Sorell, 1980).

Given that the study of these historical changes will involve appraisal of both quantitative and qualitative features of change, which may occur at multiple levels of organization, there is a need to use both quantitative and qualitative data collection and analysis methods, ones associated with the range of disciplines having specialized expertise at the multiple levels of organization at which either quantitative or qualitative change can occur (Shweder et al., 2006). In essence, the concepts of historical embeddedness and temporality indicate that a program of developmental research adequate to address the relational, integrated, embedded, and temporal changes involved in human life must involve multiple occasions, methods, levels, variables, and cohorts (Baltes, 1987; Baltes, Lindenberger, & Staudinger, 2006; Schaie & Strother, 1968).

A developmental systems perspective, and the implications it suggests for research through concepts such as temporality, may seem descriptively cumbersome; inelegant (if not untestable) in regard to explanations of individual and group behavior and development; and, as a consequence, of little use in formulating interventions aimed at enhancing individual and social life. However, in the face of the several profound historical changes in the lives of children and their families that have occurred across the past century (e.g., see Elder et al., 1993; Elder & Shanahan, 2006; Hernandez, 1993), it would seem, at best, implausible to maintain that the nature of the human life course has been unaffected by this history. Accordingly, it would seem necessary to adopt some sort of developmental systems perspective to incorporate the impact of such historical changes, and of the contemporary diversity they have created, into the matrix of covariation considered in developmental explanations and the interventions that should, at least ideally, be derived from them (Lerner & Miller, 1993).

Yet, it would be traditional in developmental science to assert that the historical variation and contemporary diversity of human (individual and group) development was irrelevant to understanding *basic* processes. Indeed, within developmental science, the conventional view of basic process, whether involving cognition, emotion, personality, or social behavior, is that a developmental process is a function generalizable across time and place. However, data such as those presented by Elder et al. (1993) and Hernandez (1993)—which document the profound impact of historical change on individual and family life over the course of just the past two centuries—constitute a serious challenge to the ontological presuppositions that have grounded this view of basic process and, as such, of developmental psychology's theory and research about people's ontogenies.

The traditional view of basic process found in developmental science (i.e., the prototypic view for much of the past 50 to 60 years) cannot be defended in the face of the historical and contextual variation characterizing American individuals and families across the past century. Indeed, without adequate tests of, and evidence for, its presuppositions about the irrelevance of temporality, context, and diversity for its view of basic process, the field of developmental science fails in even an attempt to represent veridically the course of human life (Cairns, 1998).

By weaving historical change and contextual specificities into the matrix of causal covariation that shapes human developmental trajectories, a developmental systems perspective reconstitutes the core process of human development from a reductionistic and individualistic one to a synthetic, or multilevel integrated, one. Through the seemingly simple step of integrating historical change, contextual variation, and individual developmental change, a developmental systems perspective provides a paradigmatic departure from the psychogenic, biogenic, or reductionistic environmentalist models of causality that have undergirded most theories of human development (Gottlieb, 1992; Lerner, 1991).

The Limits of Generalizability, Diversity, and Individual Differences

The temporality of the changing relations among levels of organization means that changes that are seen within one historical period (or time of measurement), and/or with one set of instances of variables from the multiple levels of the ecology of human development, may not be seen at other points in time (Baltes et al., 1977; Bronfenbrenner, 1979; Bronfenbrenner & Morris, 2006). What is seen in one data set may be only an instance of what does or what could exist. Accordingly, contemporary theories focus on diversity—of people, of relations, of settings, and of times of measurement (Lerner, 2006). Diversity is the exemplary illustration of the presence of relative plasticity in human development (Fisher et al., 1998; Lerner, 1984). Diversity is also the best evidence that exists of the potential for change in the states and conditions of human life (Brim & Kagan, 1980).

In essence, ethnic, cultural, and developmental diversity must be understood systemically to appreciate the nature and variation that exists within and across time in human behavior and development. In other words, individual differences arise inevitably from the action of the development system; in turn, they move the system in manners that elaborate diversity further.

EXAMPLES OF DEVELOPMENTAL SYSTEMS THEORIES

The above four components constitute a developmental systems perspective. This perspective leads us to recognize that, if we are to have an adequate and sufficient science of human development, we must integratively study individual and contextual levels of organization in a relational and temporal manner (Bronfenbrenner, 1974; Zigler, 1998). **Developmental contextualism** is an instance of developmental systems theory. Consistent with the emphases on integrative, or fused, relations between individuals and contexts found in other instances of such systems perspectives, the central idea in developmental contextualism is that changing, reciprocal relations (or dynamic interactions) between individuals and the multiple contexts within which they live comprise the essential process of human development (Lerner & Kauffman, 1985). We consider below this instance of developmental systems theories.

In addition, we briefly review other major examples of such approaches to the understanding of human development.

Richard M. Lerner's Developmental Contextualism

Developmental contextualism is a theoretical approach to the science of, and service to, human development. Building on the integrative ideas found in Schneirla's (1956, 1957; Tobach, 1981) thinking, developmental contextualism represents a model of human life that transcends the dichotomies, or splits (Overton, 2006), found so often in the study of human development.

Developmental contextualism stresses that bidirectional relations exist among the multiple levels of organization involved in human life (e.g., biology, psychology, social groups, and culture) (Bronfenbrenner, 1979; Bronfenbrenner & Morris, 2006; Lerner, 2006). These dynamic relations provide a framework for the structure of human behavior (Ford & Lerner, 1992). In addition, this system is itself dynamically interactive with historical changes. This temporality provides a change component to human life (Dixon, Lerner, & Hultsch, 1991). In other words, within developmental contextualism a changing configuration of relationships constitutes the basis of human life (Ford & Lerner, 1992).

Developmental contextualism reflects the ideas of dynamic interaction, levels of integration, and self-organization associated with other instances of open, living, developmental systems theories of human development. As such, scholarship framed by the model eschews reductionism, unilevel assessments of the individual, and time-insensitive and atemporal analyses of human development. Instead, integrative/holistic, relational, and change-oriented research focused on the individual-in-context is promoted (e.g., Magnusson, 1999a, 1999b; Magnusson & Stattin, 2006). Such research, necessarily embedded in the actual ecology of human development (Bronfenbrenner & Morris, 2006), has another significant feature—its import for actions (e.g., intervention programs and policies) that may enhance human development.

From a developmental contextual perspective, research must be conducted with an appreciation of the individual differences in human development, differences that arise as a consequence of diverse people's development in distinct families, communities, and sociocultural settings. In turn, policies and programs must be similarly attuned to the diversity of people and context to maximize the chances of meeting the specific needs of particular groups of people. Such programs and policies must be derived appropriately from research predicated on an integrative multidisciplinary view of human development. As noted earlier, the evaluation of such applications should provide both societally important information about the success of endeavors aimed at the enhancement of individuals *and* theoretically invaluable data about the validity of the synthetic, multilevel processes posited in developmental contextualism to characterize human development.

Meeting the challenge represented by the need to merge research with policy, and with intervention design, delivery, and evaluation, will bring the study of people and their contexts to the threshold of a new intellectual era. The linkage between research, policy, and intervention will demonstrate to scientists that the basic processes of human behavior are ones involving the development of dynamic, reciprocal relations between individually distinct people and the specific social institutions they encounter in their particular ecological settings. Such demonstrations may then enable developmental scientists to collaborate with communities to use scholarship to promote positive human development and to enhance civil society (Lerner, 2004a; Lerner, Fisher, & Weinberg, 2000). The developmental contextual approach represents an important example of the family of developmental systems theories, but other theories are also quite influential.

We discuss below several other family members that stand out as particularly influential in the creation of the family of developmental systems theories. A brief presentation of these theories will further illustrate the commonality of ideas shared across diverse members of this theoretical family and, at the same time, underscore the unique and important contributions to theory made by each model. Because of its central generative role in the past and present development of developmental systems models in general, and in the other instances of this family of perspectives, the life-span view of human development will be considered first. For more than three decades the work of Baltes and his colleagues has provided the core conceptual and empirical foundation for this theory of human development.

Paul Baltes' Life-Span Developmental Theory

Life-span developmental theory (Baltes, 1987, 1997; Baltes, Reese, & Lipsitt, 1980; Baltes et al., 2006) deals with the study of individual development (ontogenesis) from conception into old age. A core assumption of life-span developmental science is that development is not completed at adulthood (maturity). Rather, the basic premise of life-span developmental science is that ontogenesis extends across the entire life course and that lifelong adaptive processes are involved. In the context of these assumptions, Baltes et al. (2006) note that life-span developmental theory has several scientific goals, ones that span and integrate the basic-to-applied continuum of interest in other members of the developmental systems theory family.

Levels of analysis in life-span developmental scholarship. To pursue the goal of life-span developmental theory, Baltes and his colleagues conduct scholarship at five levels of analysis. Baltes et al. (2006, p. 574) explain that the first level of analysis is the:

> most distal and general one, [and] makes explicit the cornerstones and "norms of reaction" or "potentialities" . . . of life-span ontogenesis. With this approach, which is also consistent with the levels of integration notion of Schneirla or more recently S.-C. Li . . . we obtain information on what we can expect about the general scope and shape of life-span development based on evolutionary, historical, and interdisciplinary views dealing with the interplay between biology and culture during ontogenesis.

They go on to note that:

> Levels 2 and 3 move toward psychological theories of individual development. On these levels of analysis, while keeping the initial overall framework in mind, we shall describe, using an increasingly more fine-grained level of analysis, specific conceptions of life span developmental psychology. On Level 4, we advance one concrete illustration of an overall life span developmental

Margaret M. Baltes and Paul B. Baltes.

theory, a theory that is based on the specification and coordinated orchestration of three processes: Selection, optimization, and compensation. Subsequently, and corresponding to a putative
Level 5, we move to more molecular phenomena and functions. Specifically, we characterize life
span theory and research in areas of psychological functioning such as cognition, intelligence,
personality, and the self (Baltes et al., 2006, p. 574).

In presenting the theoretical ideas associated with life-span developmental theory, Baltes
and his colleagues stressed both (1) the commonality of theoretical ideas between life-span
developmental theory and other instances of developmental systems theories (e.g., in regard
to plasticity and to the embeddedness of development in a dynamic system composed of
levels of organization ranging from biology through culture and history) and (2) ideas about
human development that are specifically brought to the fore by a life-span perspective (e.g.,
development as a life-long process, the dynamic between gains and losses, the integration of
ontogenetic and historical contextualism, and the functional dynamic between processes of
selection, optimization, and compensation that is involved in successful/adaptive development). To illustrate how Baltes and his colleagues conceptualized the five levels of analysis
used in the study of development across the life span, consider the interest within Level of
Analysis 2 in understanding the structure of gain and loss integrations across ontogeny. To
appreciate the character of the developmental process involved across the life span in these
integrations, Baltes et al. (1998, p. 1041) saw it as necessary to investigate four dimensions of
changing person–context relations: (1) an age-related general reduction in the amount and
quality of biology-based resources as individuals move toward old age; (2) the age-correlated
increase in the amount and quality of culture needed to generate higher and higher levels of
growth; (3) the age-associated biology-based loss in the efficiency with which cultural
resources are used; and (4) the relative lack of cultural, "old age-friendly" support structures.
This example of the way in which Baltes and his colleagues used the propositions associated
with life-span developmental theory to conceptualize and study developmental phenomena
associated with the five levels of theoretical analysis they envision illustrates the use by
Baltes et al. (1998, 2006) of ideas both common to members of the developmental systems
theoretical family (e.g., in regard to life-span changes in plasticity) and specific to life-span
theory (e.g., the thorough integration of sociocultural influences across the breadth of the
life span).

Given the unique and important role played in life-span developmental theory of propositions specific to this instance of developmental systems theory, it is useful to discuss
these features of the conceptual repertoire of this perspective in more detail. In particular,
it is useful to review the ideas of Baltes and his colleagues regarding ontogenetic and
historical contextualism as paradigm and the concepts of selection, optimization, and
compensation. The former instance of the propositions of life-span developmental theory
serves as an important conceptual bridge to life-course models of human development,
whereas the latter instance is associated closely with action theoretical accounts of human
development.

Ontogenetic and historical contextualism as paradigm.   To illustrate the specific
theoretical contributions of the life-span developmental perspective, it is useful to discuss
how Baltes and his colleagues integrated individual ontogeny and the historical context of
human development. Baltes et al. (2006, p. 586) note that:

> individuals exist in contexts that create both special opportunities for, and limitations to, individual
> developmental pathways. Delineation of these contexts in terms of macrostructural features, like
> social class, ethnicity, roles, age-based passages and historical periods, is a major goal for the
> sociological analysis of the life course.

Baltes and his colleagues offered a tripartite model for integrating ontogenetic development with features of historical change, and thus for synthesizing sociological approaches (e.g., Elder & Shanahan, 2006) and individual-psychological ones (Hetherington & Baltes, 1988) to understand the bases of development. The three components of this model involve: (1) normative, age-graded influences; (2) normative, history-graded influences, and (3) nonnormative, life-event influences (Baltes et al., 1980).

Normative, age-graded influences consist of biological and environmental determinants that are correlated with chronological age. They are normative to the extent that their timing, duration, and clustering are similar for many individuals. Examples include maturational events (changes in height, endocrine system function, and central nervous system function) and socialization events (marriage, childbirth, and retirement).

Normative, history-graded influences consist of biological and environmental determinants that are correlated with historical time. They are normative to the extent that they are experienced by most members of a *birth cohort* (that is, a group of people who share a common year of birth or, somewhat more broadly, a group born during a specific historical period). In this sense normative, history-graded events tend to define the developmental context of a given birth cohort. Examples include historic events (wars, epidemics, and periods of economic depression or prosperity) and sociocultural evolution (changes in sex-role expectations, the educational system, and childrearing practices).

Both age-graded and history-graded influences *covary* (change together) with time. Nonnormative, life-event influences are not directly indexed by time because they do not occur for all people, or even for most people. Rather, they are idiosyncratic in development (Baltes et al., 1998, 2006). Thus, when non-normative influences do occur, they are likely to differ significantly in terms of their clustering, timing, and duration. Examples of nonnormative events include illness, divorce, promotion, and death of a spouse.

In short, variables from several sources, or dimensions, influence development. As such, life-span developmental theory stresses that human development is *multidimensional* in character. Variables from many dimensions (ones ranging from biology-related, age-graded events through the normative and the non-normative events constituting history) are involved in developmental change. As we have emphasized, in life-span developmental theory the relationships among the sources of contextual influence—normative, age-graded; normative, history-graded; and non-normative, life-event—are seen as *dynamic*, that is, *reciprocal*. They may continually change, and each influence has an effect on the others and is affected by them.

Baltes et al. (1980) suggested that these three sources of influence exhibit different profiles over the life cycle. Normative, age-graded influences are postulated to be particularly significant in childhood and again in old age, and normative, history-graded influences are thought to be more important in adolescence and the years immediately following it; this is thought to reflect the importance of the sociocultural context as the individual begins adult life. Finally, nonnormative, life-event influences are postulated to be particularly significant during middle adulthood and old age, promoting increasing divergence as individuals experience unique life events. The three sources of time-related influences on development suggested by Baltes reflect a concept of multidirectional development across the life span. The role of the "dynamic collaborations" (Fischer & Bidell, 1998, p. 476) suggested by Baltes et al. (1998, 2006) as a key part of individual development is consistent with dynamic, developmental systems theoretical approaches to development (e.g., Fischer & Bidell, 1998, 2006; Rogoff, 1998).

Conclusions. Life-span developmental theory constitutes a conceptually rich and empirically productive instance of developmental systems theory. The breadth and depth of the sets of ideas of Baltes and his colleagues offer a means to understand the dynamic links between individuals and contexts. These relations underscore the changing character of plasticity across the life span and enable individuals to play an active role throughout their lives in promoting their own positive development.

The conceptual integrations involved in life-span developmental theory span levels of organization ranging from biology through culture and history and, as such, provide a means to achieve another sort of integration, one related to the five levels of analytic work pursued by life-span developmentalists. That is, life-span developmental theory provides a means to synthesize into discussions of the course of human life other instances of developmental systems theories, ones spanning a range of interests from more micro, individual-level psychological interests to more macro, social institutional and historical interests.

For instance, we have seen that the theoretical propositions of life-span developmental theory provide an integration of models associated with historical contextualism and the individual actions taken by people seeking to pursue their immediate and long-term goals within the context of the actual ecologies of their lives. In other words, life-span developmental theory provides a means to see the integrative relevance of individual action, of the institutional/sociological setting of the life course, and of the broad ecology of human development. Accordingly, we turn now to discuss theories associated with these other domains of developmental systems theory.

Jochen Brandtstädter's Action Theories of Human Development

Scholarship pertinent to the nature of human plasticity within developmental systems theories suggests that **developmental regulation**—that is, the processes of dynamic person–context relations—should be a key focus of inquiry in the study of human development. **Action theory** (Brandtstädter, 2006; Brandtstädter & Lerner, 1999) is an exemplar of an approach that is focused on these relational processes (the Baltes and Baltes [1990; Freund, Li, & Baltes, 1999; Gestsdóttir & Lerner, 2008] selection, optimization, and compensation [SOC] model is another). The focus on such self-regulative actions reflects an interest in the ways that the "individual is both the active producer and the product of his or her ontogeny. The central tenet of an action-theoretical perspective thus holds that human ontogeny, including adulthood and later life, cannot be understood adequately without paying heed to the self-reflective and self-regulative loops that link developmental changes to the ways in which individuals, in action and mentation, construe their personal development" (Brandtstädter, 2006, p. 516). Thus, the central feature of action theories is isomorphic with a key idea in the developmental contextual version of developmental systems theory, that of individuals acting as producers of their own development (Gestsdóttir, Lewin-Bizan, von Eye, Lerner, & Lerner, 2009; Lerner, 1982; Lerner & Busch-Rossnagel, 1981; Lerner, Theokas, & Jelicic, 2005b; Lerner & Walls, 1999).

Regulation and plasticity in human development. Across their ontogeny humans actualize a rich potential for cognitive and behavioral plasticity (Lerner, 1984). However, the evolutionary gains in complexity (anagenesis) that underlie human plasticity have come "at a price" that is the ontogenetically protracted development of humans' eventually high-level cognitive and behavioral capacities (Gould, 1977). As discussed by Heckhausen (1999, p. 8),

> the relative dearth of biologically based predetermination of behavior gives rise to a high regulatory requirement on the part of the human individual and the social system. The social and cultural system and the individual have to regulate behavior so that resources are invested in an organized and focused way, and that failure experiences lead to an improvement rather than to a deterioration of behavioral means.

For humans, then, the complexity of their nervous systems and the multiple levels of their contexts mean that there is no one necessarily adaptive relation between context and behavior; what behaviors are requisite for adaptation are uncertain. As a consequence, although plasticity affords vast variation in behavior, the evolutionary status of humans means that the selection of adaptive options from within the array of behaviors available to them constitutes the key challenge in human development. Thus, according to Heckhausen (1999, p. 7):

> Selectivity and proneness to failure as basic challenges both result from the extensive variability and flexibility of human behavior. Other nonprimate species are far more programmed in terms of their repertoire of activities and behavioral responses to the environment, with more instinct-driven behavior and substantially more constrained behavioral options. Humans, in contrast, have evolved with the ability to adapt flexibly to a great range of environmental conditions, and in particular with the ability to generate new systems of behavior.

Similarly, Brandtstädter (1999, p. 46) indicated that:

> a basic evolutionary feature that makes possible—and at the same time enforces—cultural and personal control of ontogeny is the great plasticity and openness of development . . . These features of human ontogeny imply adaptive potentials as well as vulnerabilities, and they have concomitantly evolved with mechanisms to cope with the latter. The capacities to create, maintain, and enact culture, and to plot the "trajectory of . . . life on the societal map" (Berger, Berger, & Kellner, 1967, p. 67), are rooted in this coevolutionary process. Generally, developmental plasticity is already implicated in the notion of culture, as far as this notion connotes the cultivation of some process that is open to modification and optimization.

In essence, the regulation by individuals of their relations with their complex and changing physical, social, cultural, and historical context is the key problem for successful development across life (Baltes et al., 2006). Arguably, the understanding of the system involved in linking individuals and contexts becomes the essential intellectual challenge for developmental science. Indeed, as noted in our earlier discussion in this chapter of the Level 2 analyses that Baltes and his colleagues pursued to understand the cultural embeddedness of gain–loss processes, as the biological underpinnings of human behavior recede in ontogenetic significance as people traverse their post-reproductive years, the need for humans to intentionally draw on either individual-psychological or collective (e.g., cultural) resources (means) to promote their successful development becomes both increasingly salient and the necessary target of life-span developmental analysis (Baltes & Carstensen, 1998; Baltes & Baltes, 1990; Freund & Baltes, 2002).

Accordingly, to understand development as conceived within a dynamic, developmental systems perspective and to appreciate the role of a person's own contributions to this development, focus should be placed on the role of an individual's actions in regulating the course of engagement with the context and in fostering constancy and change (in actualizing plasticity) across life. In the theoretical and empirical scholarship associated with this action theory perspective, the work of Brandtstädter has been the most important in framing and advancing the key conceptual issues in the instance of developmental systems theory. Accordingly, it is useful to continue our discussion of action theory by considering his scholarship.

The contributions of Jochen Brandtstädter.   Brandtstädter conceptualized actions as a means through which individuals affect their contexts and, through the feedback resulting from such actions, organize their ideas about their contexts and themselves. As a consequence of this understanding, individuals then develop a set of "guides"—that is, motivations (e.g., intentions, goals), or regulators—for or of future actions. The outcome of this reciprocal, "action–feedback–self-organization–further action" process is, to Brandtstädter (2006), human development. Thus, action constitutes the "engine" of development and, as such, of person–context relations. Indeed, it is the self—the person who reflects on his or her own intentions, goals, and interests and who understands therefore who he or she is at the moment and who he or she would like to be at some future time—that acts to regulate relations with the context.

Thus, akin to other members of the developmental systems theoretical family, action theory as conceptualized by Brandtstädter (1998, 2006) emphasizes the fused, dynamic relations between individuals and their contexts as constituting the core process of human development. However, as is the case with other members of this theoretical family, Brandtstädter's action theory also has attributes specific to it. One key distinctive feature is the central role given to the intentionality of the individual in moderating exchanges occurring between person and context. A second feature is a focus on the changes in development deriving from these intention-based exchanges. That is, as Brandtstädter (2006, p. 535) explained, other instances of developmental systems theory have placed primary emphasis on:

> development as the result of person–environment transactions, rather than as a target area of intentional action; in other words, the relation between action and development has been conceptualized primarily as a functional rather than an intentional one.

Although Brandtstädter (1998, 2006) noted that the functional emphasis is appropriate for the early portions of the life span (e.g., the initial infancy period), by the end of this initial phase of life and certainly thereafter across the life span, intentionality must play a central role in moderating the individual's interactions with his or her physical and social world.

Given this central role of the individual's intentions within the person–context fusions involved in the developmental system, Brandtstädter (2006, pp. 523–524) defined actions as:

> behaviors that (a) can be predicted and explained with reference to intentional states (goals, values, beliefs, volitions); (b) are at least partly under personal control, and have been selected from alternative behavioral options; (c) are constituted and constrained by social rules and conventions or by the subject's representation of these contextual constraints; and (d) aim to transform situations in accordance with personal representations of desired future states.

Contextual and developmental constraints on action. Accordingly, to Brandtstädter, actions link the person dynamically to his or his social context. The plasticity of the individual enables him or her to regulate what he or she does to and in the context and to circumscribe to some extent the influence of the context on him or her.

The developmental capacities of the individual also constrain, or moderate, his or her interactions with the context and, especially in regard to Brandtstädter's emphasis on the centrality of intentions in developmental regulation, the person's changing cognitive capacities are particularly important in respect to possessing the ability to form intentions.

Conclusions. Brandtstädter's action theory placed central emphasis on an individual's intentions in his or her regulatory actions. These actions both reflect and propel development. As such, actions constitute the means through which the active individual, fused with his or her active context, actualizes his or her potential for plasticity in ways that develop, support, and elaborate the self. At the same time, Brandtstädter (1998, 2006) explained that the intentions of the self are limited in the developmental goals that can be actualized due to both individual and contextual constraints on plasticity.

Accordingly, Brandtstädter (1998, 2006) envisioned three dimensions of scholarship that should be pursued to understand the dynamic relations between plasticity and constraints, a relation brought to the fore of conceptual attention by an action theoretical perspective. That is, he recommended that:

> in analyzing the ontogeny of intentional self-development, three basic lines of development should be considered: (1) the development of intentional action in general, and of cognitive and representational processes related to intentionality; (2) the formation of beliefs and competencies related to personal control over development; and (3) the development of the self (or self-concept) as a more or less coherent structure of self-referential values, beliefs, and standards that guides and directs self-regulatory processes. (2006, p. 545)

Other action theorists have pursued theoretical and empirical agendas that correspond to the scholarly vision of Brandtstädter. In particular, Heckhausen (1999) has taken on the challenge of developing a program of work that addresses directly the issue of plasticity and constraints that is of concern in action theory.

Action theory provides a means to understand dynamic relations between individuals and their contexts that exist across the life span. From the point in ontogeny when cognitive development is sufficiently advanced to form intentions and/or to devise strategies for primary control (controlling a goal by acting on it) or secondary control (controlling a goal by thinking differently about it), and then for the rest of the life span, individuals may influence their social world that is influencing them.

Accordingly, to understand the integrations among the levels of the developmental system that comprise the action context for human development we must include a discussion of the social system within which people develop and of the historical/contextual focus used to specify the role of the social world within the developmental system. This social system approach to human development has been termed **life-course theory** and the scholarship of Glen H. Elder, Jr. has been central in understanding the importance of the life course in influencing the character of human development—the transitions in social situations or institutions involved in people's lives and the shaping of the trajectory of human life by its embeddedness in the institutions of society.

Glen H. Elder, Jr.'s Life-Course Theory

As envisioned by Elder (1998, p. 969), this theory is predicated on the following proposition:

> Human lives are socially embedded in specific historical times and places that shape their content, pattern, and direction. As experiments of nature or design, types of historical change are experienced differentially by people of different ages and roles . . . The change itself affects the developmental trajectory of individuals by altering their life course.

Glen H. Elder, Jr.

The life-course theory of human development has emerged over the past 30 years, based on theoretical and empirical contributions derived from three general areas of scholarship. These areas are the study of: (1) social relations, for example, involving scholarship about the study of self (as, for instance, in action theory), social roles, role transitions (for instance, from student to worker), and the linkages among generations (for instance, involving children, parents, and grandparents); (2) **life-span developmental theory**, for instance, as we have discussed earlier in this chapter in regard to the work of Baltes and his colleagues; and (3) age and temporality, for example, involving birth cohort, age, and the role of normative and non-normative historical variation.

Elder (1998; Elder & Shanahan, 2006), in recounting these roots of life-course theory, explained that this perspective emerged, often in collaboration with life-span developmental theory, to meet three interrelated sets of conceptual and empirical challenges to devising an integrated and dynamic view of the entire course of human life. A first challenge was to extend the theoretical frame used to study people from a child-focused one emphasizing only development or growth to one useful across the life span, and thus one encompassing development and aging, growth and decline, or gain and loss. A second challenge was to employ such a frame to develop a set of concepts for depicting the organization of and the changes in humans' lives across their ontogenies and, as well, across different historical events and eras. The third challenge was to use these concepts about ontogeny and history to integrate human lives with the changing social contexts within which each individual and all birth cohorts live across their life spans.

Elder (1998; Elder & Shanahan, 2006) saw life-course theory as enabling scholars to move beyond an additive or simple interactional view of the social system within which development unfolds. Rather, life-course theory synthesizes the social systems into the actual constitution of the structures and functions constituting human development. The means through which this integration is seen to occur in life-course theory is one emphasized as well in life-span developmental theory (Baltes et al., 1998, 2006) and in action theory (Brandtstädter, 1998, 2006); that is, through the selective and intentional regulative actions of individuals, functioning as producers of their own development.

Because of its evolution in intellectual proximity to the also evolving theory of life-span development, the two perspectives have come to rely on very similar ideas about the dynamics of individuals and contexts in the development of the structures and functions constituting the course of human life. Moreover, through this collaboration Elder drew on action theoretical concepts (which of course life-span developmental theory does as well) and emphasized the role of the active individual in the construction of life-course changes. Indeed, as a consequence of these linkages, Elder (1998; Elder & Shanahan, 2006) adopted a theoretical view of developmental process that is completely consistent with life-span developmental theory, with action theory, and with the other instance of developmental systems theory. Elder & Shanahan (2006, p. 679) stated that:

> human development in life course theory represents a process of organism–environment transactions over time, in which the organism plays an active role in shaping its own development. The developing individual is viewed as a dynamic whole, not as separate strands, facets or domains, such as emotion, cognition, and motivation.

Thus, as did Baltes et al. (1998, 2006), Elder saw human development as an interpersonally relational—a dynamically collaborative (Fischer & Bidell, 1998; Rogoff, 1998) social—process. The distinctive features of life-course theory are associated with the link that Elder (1998; Elder & Shanahan, 2006) drew between individual development and the social relationships within which the person's ontogeny is dynamically collaborative.

Constructing the life course.   We have noted that Elder (1998; Elder & Shanahan, 2006) specified that the substantive roots of life-course theory lie in the integration of scholarship pertinent to life-span developmental theory, human agency, timing, linked lives, and historical time and place. Elder and Shanahan (2006) presented five principles framing life-course theory. The principles were:

1. the principle of life-span development, which means that human development and aging are life-long processes
2. the principle of human agency, which indicates that individuals construct their own life course through the choices and actions they take within the opportunities and constraints of history and social circumstance
3. the principle of timing, which refers to the fact that the developmental antecedents and consequences of life transitions, events, and behavior patterns vary according to their timing in a person's life
4. the principle of linked lives, which involves the idea that lives are lived interdependently and social–historical influences are expressed through this network of shared relationships
5. the principle of historical time and place, which means that the life course of individuals is embedded in and shaped by the historical times and places they experience over their lifetime.

Accordingly, Elder indicated that the life course is constructed through the *simultaneous* contribution of actions made by individuals dynamically interacting with other individuals while embedded in a context changing along three temporal dimensions: "Life" or "onto-genetic" time (one's age from birth to death), "family" time (one's location within the flow of prior and succeeding generations), and "historical" time (the social and cultural system that exists in the world when one is born and the changing circumstances regarding this system that occur during one's life). That is, Elder (1998, pp. 951–952) pointed out that:

> The life course is age-graded through institutions and social structures, and it is embedded in relationships that constrain and support behavior. In addition, people are located in historical settings through birth cohorts and they are also linked across the generations by kinship and friendship . . . Both the individual life course and a person's developmental trajectory are inter-connected with the lives and development of others.

The postulation of a dynamic integration between an individual's regulatory actions and a social system constituted by the people, social institutions, and historical events that vary across these three temporal dimensions provided, for Elder (1998), a means to represent the life course of an individual. As such, Elder's (1998) vision resulted in a theoretical system of singular creativity and enormous value to developmental systems theories of human development. His theory merges within a given person the micro (ontogenetic biological, behavioral, and psychological) and macro (social system) levels of organization that are held to be fused within developmental systems theory.

In short, then, Elder's model constitutes a means to integrate an individual's life into the social system from the moment of his or her birth. Birth provides for his or her immediate membership into (1) a familial flow of generations; and (2) a society that exists at a given point in history with its extant but evolving set of institutions, roles, and socially defined life pathways.

Conclusions.   Life-course theory adds a new dimension to the set of concepts associated with developmental systems theories. Building on the ideas associated with other members of this theoretical family—most prominently, life-span developmental theory and, to a somewhat lesser but nevertheless significant extent, action theory—Elder's (1998; Elder & Shanahan, 2006) view of the life course provides a dynamic means to integratively bring the social system into the ontogeny of individuals.

There is always the danger that when scholars whose training or interests are in a discipline more macro than the disciplines having focal units of analysis involving individuals, or even units more molecular than individuals (e.g., genes), the course of an individual life may be interpreted in "sociogenic" terms, that is by exclusive reference to the institutions of society, the rules of culture, or the events of history. Just as we would wish to avoid the alternative conceptual "danger" of a psychogenic or a biogenic interpretation of the life span of a person, such a sociogenic view of human development would not be theoretically desirable (in regard, at least, to the perspective of human development advanced by developmental systems theory) or empirically supportable. Just as Overton (1998, 2006) has cautioned scholars of human development to "avoid all splits," we can offer a similar warning: Avoid all interpretations of human development that are based on the hegemony of one discipline over all others.

The significance of Elder's formulation of life-course theory, then, is that he is able to weave the importance of macro, social system influences into the development of individuals in a manner that is neither disciplinarily "isolationist" (or hegemonist) nor simply additive. Elder's scholarship is an example of the relationism, the multilevel fusions, that define a developmental systems perspective. He brings the social system to human development, not as a context for development but—in the essence of what is sought for in developmental systems theory—as part of the very constitutive fabric of human ontogeny.

There is at least one scholar whom Elder and we would agree integrates person and context seamlessly. Urie Bronfenbrenner has, for a half century, provided a vision for—and a theoretical and empirical literature supportive of—the integration of all levels of organization within the ecology of human development (e.g., see Bronfenbrenner, 2005).

Urie Bronfenbrenner's Bioecological Theory of Developmental Processes

In his 1979 book, *The Ecology of Human Development*, Bronfenbrenner explained the importance for human ontogeny of the interrelated ecological levels, conceived of as nested systems, involved in human development. Bronfenbrenner described the *microsystem* as the setting within which the individual was behaving at a given moment in his or her life and the *mesosystem* as the set of microsystems constituting the individual's developmental niche within a given period of development. In addition, the *exosystem* was composed of contexts that, if not directly involving the developing person (e.g., the work place of a child's parent), had an influence on the person's behavior and development (e.g., as may occur when the parent has had a stressful day at work and as a result has a reduced capacity to provide quality caregiving to the child). Moreover, the *macrosystem* is the superordinate level of the ecology of human development; it is the level involving culture, macro-institutions (such as the federal government), and public policy. The macrosystem influences the nature of interaction within all other levels of the ecology of human development. Finally, time—the *chronosystem*—cuts through all other components of the ecology of human development. As a consequence, change becomes an integral feature of all systems.

Bioecological theory. His 1979 book made an enormous contribution to such a conception of human development, through giving scholars conceptual tools to understand and to study the differentiated but integrated levels of the context of human development. Bronfenbrenner also recognized that his theory would be incomplete until he included in

Urie Bronfenbrenner.

it the levels of individual structure and function (biology, psychology, and behavior) fused dynamically with the ecological systems he described. Accordingly, Bronfenbrenner and his colleagues (e.g., Bronfenbrenner, 2005; Bronfenbrenner & Ceci, 1993; Bronfenbrenner & Morris, 2006) worked to integrate the other levels of the developmental system into the model of human development he was formulating. The span of the levels he seeks to synthesize in his model—biology through the broadest level of the ecology of human development—accounts for the label *bioecological* he attaches to the model.

As Bronfenbrenner described it, the defining properties of the model that has emerged from this scholarship involve four interrelated components: (1) The developmental *process*, involving the fused and dynamic relation of the individual and the context; (2) the *person*, with his or her individual repertoire of biological, cognitive, emotional, and behavioral characteristics; (3) the *context* of human development, conceptualized as the nested levels, or systems, of the ecology of human development he has depicted (Bronfenbrenner, 1979); and (4) *time*, conceptualized as involving the multiple dimensions of temporality that we have noted that Elder and Shanahan (2006) explain are part of life-course theory. Together, these four components of Bronfenbrenner's formulation of **bioecological theory** constituted a process–person–context–time (PPCT) model for conceptualizing the integrated developmental system and for designing research to study the course of human development. Bronfenbrenner believed that just as each of the four components of the PPCT model must be included in any adequate conceptual specification of the dynamic human development system, so too must research appraise all four components of the model to provide data that are adequate for understanding the course of human development.

In turn, in regard to the three remaining defining properties of the model—person (the developing individual), context (the micro-, meso-, exo-, and macro-systems), and time (the chronosystem)—Bronfenbrenner and Morris (2006, p. 795) noted that they give priority in their scholarship to defining the biopsychosocial characteristics of the "Person," because, as noted by Bronfenbrenner in 1989, his earlier formulations of the model (e.g., Bronfenbrenner, 1979) left a gap in regard to this key feature of the theory.

Indeed, Bronfenbrenner redefined the character of the microsystem to link it centrally to what he regarded as the "center of gravity" (Bronfenbrenner & Morris, 2006, p. 814)—the biopsychosocial person—within his theory as it has now been elaborated. That is, although, as in 1979, he saw the ecology of human development as "the ecological environment . . . conceived as a set of nested structures, each inside the other like a set of Russian dolls" (p. 3), he magnified his conception of the innermost, microsystem structure within this ecology by incorporating the activities, relationships, and roles of the developing person into this system. That is, he noted that:

> A microsystem is a pattern of activities, social roles, and interpersonal relations experienced by the developing person in a given face-to-face setting with particular physical, social, and symbolic features that invite, permit, or inhibit, engagement in sustained, progressively more complex interaction with, and activity in, the immediate environment. (Bronfenbrenner, 1994, p. 1645)

What may be particularly significant to Bronfenbrenner in this expanded definition of the microsystem is that he included not only the person's interactions with other people in this level of the ecology but, as well, the interactions the person has with the world of symbols and language (with the semiotic system)—a component of ecological relationships that action theorists also believe is especially important in understanding the formulation of intentions, goals, and actions (cf. Brandtstädter, 1998, 2006). That is, Bronfenbrenner noted that:

> The bioecological model also introduces an even more consequential domain into the structure of the microsystem that emphasizes the distinctive contribution to development of proximal processes involving interaction not with people but with objects and symbols. Even more broadly, concepts and criteria are introduced that differentiate between those features of the environment that foster versus interfere with the development of proximal processes. Particularly significant in the latter sphere is the growing hecticness, instability, and chaos in the principal settings in which human competence and character are shaped—in the family, child-care arrangements, schools, peer groups, and neighborhoods. (Bronfenbrenner & Morris, 2006, p. 796)

Finally, Bronfenbrenner noted that the emphasis on a redefined and expanded concept of the microsystem leads to the last defining property of the current formulation of his theory of human development, i.e., time (the chronosystem). Bronfenbrenner and Morris (2006, p. 796) indicated that:

> the fourth and final defining property of the bioecological model and the one that moves it farthest beyond its predecessor [is] the dimension of Time. The 1979 volume scarcely mentions the term, whereas in the current formulation, it has a prominent place at three successive levels: (1) micro-, (2) meso-, and (3) macro-. *Microtime* refers to continuity versus discontinuity in ongoing episodes of proximal process. *Mesotime* is the periodicity of these episodes across broader time intervals, such as days and weeks. Finally, *Macrotime* focuses on the changing expectations and events in the larger society, both within and across generations, as they affect and are affected by, processes and outcomes of human development over the life course.

Conclusions.   Bronfenbrenner's bioecological model is in at least two senses a living system (Ford & Lerner, 1992). First, the theory itself depicts the dynamic, developmental relations between an active individual and his or her complex, integrated and changing ecology. In addition, the theory is itself developing, as Bronfenbrenner (2005) sought to make the features of the theory more precise and, as such, create a more operational guide for PPCT-relevant research about the dynamic character of the human developmental process.

At this writing, then, the bioecological model has developed to include two propositions. Both these sets of ideas promote a dynamic, person–context relational view of the process of human development. As explained by Bronfenbrenner and Morris (2006, p. 797), Proposition 1 of the bioecological model states that:

> Especially in its early phases, but also throughout the life course, human development takes place through processes of progressively more complex reciprocal interaction between an active, evolving biopsychosocial human organism and the persons, objects, and symbols in its immediate external environment. To be effective, the interaction must occur on a fairly regular basis over extended periods of time. Such enduring forms of interaction in the immediate environment are referred to as proximal processes. Examples of enduring patterns of proximal process are found in feeding or comforting a baby, playing with a young child, child–child activities, group or solitary play, reading, learning new skills, athletic activities, problem solving, caring for others in distress, making plans, performing complex tasks, and acquiring new knowledge, and know-how.

Thus, in the first proposition in his theory, Bronfenbrenner emphasized a theme found in the other instances of developmental systems theory—the role of the active individual as an agent in his or her own development. In fact, the idea of the contribution of the individual to the developmental process is present as well in the second proposition of bioecological theory.

> The form, power, content, and direction of the proximal processes effecting development vary systematically as a joint function of the characteristics of the developing person; of the environment —both immediate and more remote—in which the processes are taking place; the nature of the developmental outcomes under consideration; and the social continuities and changes occurring over time through the life course and the historical period during which the person has lived (Bronfenbrenner & Morris, 2006, p. 798).

As is evident from the two propositions, Bronfenbrenner regards proximal processes as the primary sources of development, an assertion that is compatible with the several versions of action theory discussion in this chapter (Baltes & Baltes, 1990; Brandtstädter, 2006; Heckhausen, 1999). That is, in all of the proximal processes described by Bronfenbrenner in the first proposition of the bioecological model, goal selections, intentions, developing means to engage goals, the primacy of primary control, and the importance of compensatory behaviors and/or of secondary control may be involved. In turn, the propositions also point to the fusions across the developmental system described by Bronfenbrenner as providing the dynamism that enables the proximal processes to drive the developmental system.

In addition, the role of the individual, as an active agent in his or her own development, is central in the bioecological model. Indeed, Bronfenbrenner and Morris (2006, p. 798) asked their readers to consider:

> Characteristics of the person actually appear twice in the bioecological model—first as one of the four elements influencing the "*form, power, content, and direction of the proximal process,*" and then again as "*developmental outcomes*"—qualities of the developing person that emerge at a later point in time as the result of the joint, interactive, mutually reinforcing effects of the four principal antecedent components of the model. In sum, in the bioecological model, the characteristics of the person function both as an indirect producer and as a product of development. (emphasis in original)

In sum, then, as has been the case in all of the instances of developmental systems theory we have discussed in this chapter, and as emphasized over a half century ago by Schneirla (1957), the active, developing individual was seen by Bronfenbrenner as a central force of his or her own development. This contribution to the process of development is made by a synthesis, an integration, between the active person and his or her active context. We see stress on such individual ↔ context relations in both of the two final instantiations of developmental system theories we discuss.

Esther Thelen and Linda Smith's Dynamic Systems Theory

Thelen and Smith (1998, 2006) noted that their version of developmental systems theory—which they term **dynamic systems theory**—derives from both systems thinking in biology and psychology and the study of complex and nonlinear systems in physics and mathematics. They explained that in its simplest sense the idea of dynamic systems refers to changes over time among elements that are interrelated systemically. Although this idea can be extended more technically or formally, through specific mathematical equations, Thelen and Smith (2006) noted that there are two key features of any physical or biological system: (1) Development can only be understood as the multiple, mutual, and continuous interaction of all levels of the developing system, from the molecular to the cultural. (2) Development can only be understood as nested processes that unfold over many time scales, from milliseconds to years (p. 258). To Thelen and Smith (1998, 2006), dynamic systems theory can be applied to different species, age levels, or domains of development, e.g., from "molecular" patterns of motor functioning involved in walking or reaching to "molar" changes in cognition that may be gained through the integration of humans' actions on their context and the context's actions on them.

The development of novel forms across life.   Thelen and Smith (1994, 1998, 2006) believed that dynamic systems theory affords understanding of what they regard as the defining feature of development: the creation of new forms. That is, Thelen and Smith contended that the essence of those changes termed "developmental"—the property of change that enables one period of life to be designated as involving a distinct point in development—is qualitative discontinuity, emergence, epigenesis, or simply novelty. Once such novelty has been described, however, a central explanatory issue becomes evident: "Where does this novelty come from? How can developing systems create something out of nothing?" (Thelen & Smith, 2006, p. 259).

Answers to these questions have been associated with nature, nurture, and interactionist perspectives. Not surprisingly, Thelen and Smith rejected both nature and nurture explanations and, implicitly, those interactionist positions representative of weak or moderate views of interaction. Instead, consistent with the ideas of developmental systems theorist Gottlieb (1997, 2004; Gottlieb et al., 1998), they noted that:

> The tradition we follow, that of *systems theories of biological organization*, explains the formation of new forms by processes of *self-organization*. By self-organization we mean that *pattern and order emerge from the interactions of the components of a complex system without explicit instructions*, either in the organism itself or from the environment. Self-organization—processes that by their own activities change themselves—is a fundamental property of living things. (Thelen & Smith, 2006, p. 259; emphasis in original)

Other developmental systems theorists agree. For instance, Gottlieb (e.g., 1997), in his view of the coactions that are involved in epigenesis, and Schneirla (1957), in his notion of circular functions and self-stimulation in ontogeny, provided examples of these self-organizational processes.

In turn, Thelen and Smith (1998, 2006) drew on evidence from embryology and morphology that indicates how highly complicated structural patterns arise within dynamic systems *not* from information specifically coded in genes but, instead, from simple initial conditions. For instance, they explained that neither the spots of leopards nor the striped tails of raccoons are derived from genes for these bodily features. Rather, these features are constructed during development when specific chemical and metabolic attributes of these animals—each one mutually facilitating and constraining the others—spontaneously organize themselves into patterns (Thelen & Smith, 2006).

Similarly, behavioral characteristics and patterns can emerge in development without the requirement of specific genetic coding for them, as is held in theories that rely on split concepts of nature and nurture, such as models within the field of behavior genetics (e.g., Plomin, 2000; Rowe, 1994) or as forwarded in concepts such as instinct (e.g., Lorenz, 1937, 1965). The processes that produce such developmental change are again those associated with the probabilistic epigenetic view of organism ↔ context relations associated with the work of Schneirla, Gottlieb, Tobach, Lehrman, and others. Probabilistic epigenetics refers to the view that the changes that occur across the life span are *not* ones performed in the genes and are *not* invariant in regard to norms. Instead, changes *emerge* because of organism ↔ context relations that occur across life and, because the timing of these relations will inevitably vary from one organism to another, the characteristics that emerge are probable, but not certain, in regard to fitting with any norms of development. Simply, because of variation in the timing of organism ↔ context relations, there is diversity in development.

In short, then, Thelen and Smith (1998, 2006) drew on the evidence provided by the scholarship of embryologists, and by comparative psychologists taking a probabilistic epigenetic perspective, to assert that the basis for novelty in development arises from the integrated relation of intra- and extra-organism levels of organization—and not from either genetic or environmental "instructions" for such change.

The dynamics of the developmental system. The probabilistic epigenetic character of the developmental process meant, to Thelen and Smith (1998, 2006), that the duality, or split (Overton, 2006), between individual and context, or between structure and function, should be eliminated from scientific discourse. In their view, then, contextual levels of organizations (e.g., culture) did not just support the course of development, they "are the very stuff of development itself" (Thelen & Smith, 2006, p. 266). They explained that the essential difference between the developmental systems perspective they favor:

> and more individual-centered approaches is that the levels are conceptualized as *more* than just interacting; instead they are seen as integrally fused together. Behavior and its development are melded as ever-changing sets of *relationships* and the history of those relationships over time. (Thelen & Smith, 2006, p. 267; emphasis in original)

Thelen and Smith (1998, 2006) believed that, because of this fusion, we must reject linear systems of causality wherein there is a direct, unidirectional line from an antecedent, "causal" event or structure (e.g., the possession of a gene) to a consequent behavior (e.g., a particular motor behavior, personality attribute, or cognitive capacity, that is where "X" → "Y"). In the place of such linear notions of causality, developmental systems theories suggest a configural view of causality (Ford & Lerner, 1992), wherein bidirectional relations within and across fused levels of organization change interdependently across time.

The causal system presented in this theory coincides with the view of causality conceived of by Thelen and Smith (1998, 2006), wherein the key features of developing individuals—

self-organization, nonlinearity, openness, stability, complexity, wholeness, the emergence of novelty, and change—are produced by the fused, multilevel influences that constitute the developmental system. The outcomes of development—"form"—are products of this process of bidirectional relations (Thelen & Smith, 1998, p. 586).

Thelen and Smith (1998, 2006) indicated that the key feature of dynamic systems is that the many heterogeneous parts of the system (e.g., the different cells, tissues, and organs within the individual and the various individuals, institutions, and physical features of the context of any person) are free to combine in a virtually infinite number of ways. Theoretically at least, there is no limit to the actual number of combinations that might occur. However, in actuality, the patterns of relations that are seen are far less. In regard to the notion of "relative plasticity" discussed earlier in this chapter, the relation among the multiple parts of the system are sources of constraints as well as of variability. Thus, because of this relative plasticity, an order (a pattern) emerges from the complexity of the system as, through the relations within the system, the system organizes itself.

Thelen and Smith (1998, 2006) explained that order emerges from disparate parts because human development is an *open system*; that is, a system wherein energy is taken into the system and is used to increase order within it. Such a system stands in contrast to a *closed system*, wherein there is no infusion of energy into the system. In that an open, human development system increases its organization over time, it exists in "violation" of the second law of thermodynamics (Brent, 1978; Prigogine, 1978). According to this law, a system changes in the direction of greater disorganization, termed *entropy*. However, some systems—open ones—can show *negentropy*; that is, changes in the direction of greater organization.

The Nobel laureate chemist, Prigogine (1978), has shown that negentropic change can occur because an open system draws energy from its context to increase its internal order. Prigogine demonstrated that such use of energy within an open system does result in an overall dissipation in order outside of it; that is, in the universe as a whole; thus, in the broader system there is an increase in entropy, and the second law is actually not violated.

Thelen and Smith (1998, 2006) noted that when the parts involved in an open system interrelate in a nonlinear manner, integration (i.e., a pattern, an organization, structural relations) emerges. Such integration enables the system to be described via reference to fewer dimensions, or parameters, than was the case at the beginning of the development of the system. Heinz Werner's (1948, 1957) concept of orthogenesis is an example of a general principle of systematic change in developing organisms wherein the globality of the individual's organization is reduced through the emergence of hierarchic integration. In turn, Thelen and Smith (1998, 2006) noted that the integrative variables that emerge within an open system to reduce its dispersion and increase its organization, or pattern, may be termed either *collective variables* or *order parameters*.

The emergence of such collective variables not only reduces the theoretically infinite number of combinations within a dynamic (open) system to some much smaller actual subset but, in so doing, the integration reflected by the collective variables provides continuity and stability within the system. As Thelen and Smith (2006, p. 272) explained:

> The system "settles into" or "prefers" only a few modes of behavior. In dynamic terminology, this behavioral mode is an *attractor* state, because the system—under certain conditions—has an affinity for that state. Again in dynamic terms, the system prefers a certain location in its *state*, or *phase space*, and when displaced from that place, it tends to return there . . . All the initial conditions leading to a particular fixed point attractor are called *basins of attraction*. (emphasis in original)

Thelen and Smith (1998, 2006) described one type of attractor, the *chaotic* attractor, that seems to be involved in many biological systems (e.g., involving changes in heart rate, the sense of smell, and motor movements during the fetal period). Within dynamic systems, chaos describes a situation wherein the relation among the parts of a system seems random (i.e., lacking any pattern or order). However, when the time period used for viewing a state space is extended over a significantly long time period, non-randomness—order—is evident. In fact, chaotic change is represented by highly elaborate geometric patterns (Gleick, 1987).

Stability and change in dynamic systems. Thelen and Smith (1998, 2006) noted that in the study of human development the most important characteristic of an attractor is its relative stability; that is, the likelihood that the system will exist in a given state (or show a specific behavioral pattern) as compared to other ones. The presence of relative stability means that there is a higher statistical probability of one specific behavioral pattern than another and that if the system is dislodged from its preferred state it will return to it. Moreover, the system will "work" to maintain the preferred state. Thus, in regard to the idea that continuity of behavior can be underlain by dynamic interactions between the individual and the context (Cairns & Hood, 1983), the relative stability of a developmental system does not gainsay the fact that dynamic exchanges are occurring within it.

The relative stability of a system is related to the relative plasticity of the course of development. Although organisms—through their dynamic interactions with their context—maintain the capacity for systematic change across the life span (Baltes et al., 1998; Lerner, 1984), these same organism ↔ context relations constrain the variability in functional change that can be seen; as a consequence, plasticity—although ubiquitous—is relative, not absolute. Similarly, Thelen and Smith (1998, p. 626) observed that "adaptive systems live in quasi-stability; reliable enough to make predictions about what is appropriate in a context, but flexible enough to recruit different solutions if the situation changes."

The ontogenetic changes that exist in plasticity mean that, at advanced developmental levels, when the reserve capacity for plasticity has narrowed (Baltes, 1997; Baltes et al., 1998), change is still possible but a larger than previously necessary level of intervention would be required to produce it (Lerner, 1984; MacDonald, 1985). Similarly, Thelen and Smith (2006) noted that, "Very stable attractors take very large pushes to move them from their preferred positions, but they are dynamic and changeable nonetheless" (p. 274). In other words, the system is not fixed, with hard-wired, immutable connections; rather it is *softly assembled*.

Such soft assembly is the essence of plasticity in human development and, to Thelen and Smith (1998, 2006), the defining feature of a dynamic view of development. The presence of soft assembly means that the concept that human development involves the functioning of permanent, immutable structures is not valid. Rather, developmentalists must view the development of the person as involving a dynamic linkage between (1) the stability of the system, conceived of as the resistance to change existing among the collective states and (2) the fluctuations around the stable states, changes that provide the functional source of novelty within the system.

Transitions in systems. Fluctuations within the system, as well as changes from the context that impinge on the system, can alter the patterns of the system. In either case, the system will change in a manner that increases order, that enhances coherence. The parts of the system will interact, or "cooperate," in the terms of Thelen and Smith (2006, p. 271), in the occurrence of a "phase shift" or, in other terms, a "nonlinear phase shift." To illustrate, Thelen and Smith (2006, p. 275) indicated that:

> For example, we can walk up hills of various inclines, but when the steepness of the hill reaches some critical value, we must shift our locomotion to some type of quadrupedal gait—climbing on

all fours . . . In dynamic terminology, the slope change acted as a *control parameter* on our gait style. The control parameter does not really "control" the system in traditional terms. Rather, it is a parameter to which the collective behavior of the system is sensitive and that thus moves the system through collective states. (emphasis in original)

For instance, Thelen and Smith (1998) noted that the "disappearance" of the newborn stepping response (i.e., stepping movements made by the newborn when he or she is held upright), which occurs after a few months of life, occurs in relation to the gain in weight, and especially in body fat, during this period. As the infants' legs get heavier across these months there is no corresponding increase in muscle mass. As a consequence, infants have difficulty lifting their legs—not because of a neuronal change within the brain that "suppressed" the reflex, but because they do not have the muscles to do this when in the biomechanically difficult upright position (Thelen & Smith, 1998). Thus, underscoring the coherence of the changing dynamic system, one wherein patterns emerge through self-organization among components, Thelen and Smith (2006, p. 275) noted that, "Body fat deposition is a growth change that is not specific to leg movements, yet it affected the system such that a qualitative shift in behavior resulted."

Times scales within dynamic systems.   The time frame for the phase shift involved in the infant stepping response involves several months within the early life of humans. One important temporal parameter of dynamic systems illustrated by this example is that the state of the system in regard to stepping when upright at a later time in ontogeny (e.g., when a lot of body fat had been gained) was related to the system state at the prior time (when the ratio of body fat to muscles afforded stepping while upright). This temporal linkage is an example of the point that the condition of the system at any one point in time provides the basis for the condition of the system at the next immediate point in time.

Thus, as discussed in regard to the notion of successive change as being a core component of the definition of development, Thelen and Smith (1998, 2006) noted that there is always a successive character to change within a dynamic system; that is, the state of the system at Time 1 shapes the state of the system at Time 2, and the state of the system at Time 2 determines the state at Time 3, etc. Thelen and Smith (1998, 2006) noted, then, that dynamic systems are *reiterative*; that is, each state within the system is shaped by the prior state of the system.

Moreover, the time scale dividing the successive influences may vary considerably. Times 1, 2, and 3 may be divided (e.g., along the *x*-axis of a graph) by seconds, days, weeks, months, years, etc. Nevertheless, the same sort of successive interdependency of states, and therefore the same linkages across time, will be evident whether the state-to-state observational interval is months (as in the example of the infant stepping response) or years (as may be seen in regard to changes in IQ scores; Bloom, 1964). Thelen and Smith (1998, 2006) explained that there is, then, a self-similarity of the system across many different levels of temporal observation.

However, because different components of the system have their own developmental course and, as a consequence, because the relations among components change continuously, the time scale used within developmental studies to observe the system, and make judgments about its stability or fluctuation, is critical. For example, in attempting to understand connections between the state of the system in early infancy in regard to the presence and disappearance of the stepping response, appraisal of fat-to-muscle ratios across a monthly time parameter may be useful; however, if the interest is the emergence within the system of the ability to run efficiently, then neither such ratios nor a month-by-month perspective would be useful (Thelen & Smith, 1998, 2006). Instead, different system components (involving, for instance, the development of muscle coordination and lung vital capacity) and different time divisions (e.g., years) may be required to see the reiterative character of the system and the bidirectional influences across levels within it.

Conclusions. Thelen and Smith (1998, 2006) offered a nuanced conception of the dynamic character of the human developmental system. Their theory underscored the important role of dynamic interactions, fusions, in human development, and the centrality of plasticity— of softly assembled systems—in providing within-person variability across life and between-person differences in such life-span changes. Their theory, and the data they marshal in support of it (Thelen & Smith, 1994, 1998, 2006), thus highlighted the active role of the individual as a central agent in his/her own development and fosters an integrative, holistic understanding of the individual and his/her context. They saw important and singular promise for their dynamic systems theory:

> Only a dynamic account captures the richness and complexity of real-life human behavior. The issue is not just how people learn to think in formal, logical, and abstract terms, but how they can do that *and* all the other things people do in this society: use tools, operate sophisticated machinery, find their way around, play sports and games, create art and music, and engage in complex social interactions. These activities require active perception, precisely timed movements, shifting attention, insightful planning, useful remembering, and the ability to smoothly and rapidly *shift* from one activity to another as the occasion demands. They happen in time and they recruit all the elements in the system. The challenge for developmentalists is to understand the developmental origins of this complexity and flexibility. Only dynamics, we believe, is up to the task. (Thelen & Smith, 1998, p. 626; emphasis in original)

We agree with the appraisal of Thelen and Smith about the challenge that may be met by, and the potential benefits of meeting it through, the dynamic, developmental systems theory they forward. Other developmentalists agree as well and, in addition, have advanced theories consonant with Thelen and Smith (1998, 2006). One instance of such a theory has been formulated by Magnusson who, over the course of more than a quarter century, has contributed to scholarship about developmental systems.

Magnusson's Holistic Person–Context Interaction Theory

Magnusson's theoretical formulations and research programs, including his **holistic person– context interaction theory**, have emphasized the fundamental role of context in human behavior and development (e.g., Magnusson, 1995, 1999a, 1999b; Magnusson & Stattin, 1998, 2006). His intellectual vision includes a compelling conceptual rationale and substantive basis for internationally contextualized, comparative scholarship (e.g., Magnusson, 1995, 1999a, 1999b) and is built on four conceptual pillars: interactionism, holism, interdisciplinarity, and the longitudinal study of the person.

These themes emerge in Magnusson's theory, which stresses the synthesis, or fusion, of the person–environment system. Magnusson sought to understand the structures and processes involved in the operation of this system and the way in which the individual behaves and develops within it. Given this integrative emphasis on person and context, Magnusson (1995) termed his theory a *holistic approach*. He stated that:

> The individual is an active, purposeful part of an integrated, complex, and dynamic person– environment (PE) system . . . Consequently, it is not possible to understand how social systems function without knowledge of individual functioning, just as individual functioning and development cannot be understood without knowledge of the environment. (Magnusson & Stattin, 2006, p. 401)

David Magnusson.

Causality in holistic interactionism.   To Magnusson, then, as is seen also in respect
to the theories of Schneirla (1957), Kuo (1976), Gottlieb (1997) and Thelen and Smith
(1998, 2006), the cause of development—the emergence of novel forms across life—was
an outcome of the coactions of the components of the dynamic person–context system.
This self-organizational source of developmental change stands in contrast to either the
unidirectional, single source (nature or nurture) or the weak or moderate interactional ideas
regarding the causes of development.

In what Magnusson termed the modern interactionist perspective, or the holistic interactionist viewpoint, the basis of development lies in two types of interaction: inner interactions,
involving bidirectional relationships among biological, psychological, and behavioral characteristics; and outer, person–context interactions, involving continual exchanges between the
person and his or her environment. Magnusson explained that holistic interaction builds
and extends the ideas of interactionism found in what he terms "classical interactionism"
(Magnusson & Stattin, 2006, p. 406).

Holistic interactionism expands on this classic conception of interaction by, first, placing greater emphasis on the dynamic, integrated character of the individual within the
overall person–environment system and, second, stressing both biological and behavioral
action components of the system. Thus, and drawing on many of the same literature
sources relied on by Gottlieb (for example, in regard to neuropsychology and developmental
biology, Damasio & Damasio, 1996; Rose, 1995) and by Thelen and Smith (for example,
in regard to chaos and general systems theory, e.g., Gleick, 1987; von Bertalanffy, 1968),
and buttressed by what Magnusson (1995, 1999a, 1999b) saw as the growing importance
of holistically oriented longitudinal studies of human development (e.g., Cairns & Cairns,
1994). Magnusson and Stattin (2006, p. 407) specified the five basic propositions of holistic
interaction:

1. The individual is an active, intentional part of a complex, dynamic PE system.
2. The individual functions and develops as a total, integrated organism.
3. Individual functioning in existing psychobiological structures, as well as development
    change, can best be described [as] an integrated, complex, and dynamic process.
4. Such processes are characterized by continuously ongoing interactions (including
    interdependence) among mental, behavioral, and biological components of the indi-
    vidual and social, cultural, and physical components of the environment.
5. The environment functions and changes as a continuously ongoing process of inter-
    actions and interdependence among social, cultural, and physical factors.

Features of the person–environment system.   The holistic interactionist theory has profound implications for the conduct of developmental science. Indeed, the far-reaching character of these implications extends to even the role of the concept of "variable" in developmental research.

Magnusson and Stattin (1998, 2006) noted that in most approaches to developmental science the concept of "variable" is embedded within a theoretically reductionistic model of humans. Within this perspective, the "variable" becomes the unit of analysis in developmental research. However, within the context of what they term *the holistic principle*, Magnusson and Stattin (1998, 2006) forwarded a person-centered view of development and, as such, forward the individual, the whole person, as the core unit of developmental analysis. That is, the holistic principle

> emphasizes an approach to the individual and the person–environment system as organized wholes, functioning as totalities . . . The totality derives its characteristic features and properties from the functional, dynamic interaction of the elements involved, not from each isolated part's effect on the totality. (Magnusson & Stattin, 2006, p. 404)

Accordingly, if the totality, the whole person or, better, the person–environment relation characterizes the essence of developmental change, then developmental analysis that assesses single aspects of the system (single variables, for instance) is necessarily incomplete. Only a distorted view of development can be derived from appraising variables divorced from the context of other, simultaneously acting variables (Magnusson & Stattin, 1998, 2006). It is this integration of variables from across the person–environment system that constitutes the core process of human development and, as such, the necessary focus of developmental science.

Indeed, within holistic interactionist theory, the developmental *process* involves a continual flow of integrated, reciprocally related events. Time becomes a fundamental feature of individual development given that, within the probabilistic epigenetic view taken by Magnusson (1995, 1999a, 1999b) of the interrelation of the constituent events constituting the process of development, the same event occurring at different times in ontogeny will have varying influences on behavior and development. As a consequence, "A change in one aspect affects related parts of the subsystem and, sometimes, the whole organism . . . At a more general level, the restructuring of structures and processes at the individual level is embedded in and is part of the restructuring of the total person–environment system" (Magnusson & Stattin, 2006, p. 433).

Thus, to Magnusson (1995, 1999a, 1999b; Magnusson & Stattin, 1998, 2006), individual development is marked by a continual restructuring of existing patterns and—through the facilitation and constraint of the biological through sociocultural levels of the total person–environment system—the emergence of new structures and processes. In other words, as also specified within the Thelen and Smith (1998, 2006) dynamic systems theory, *novelty* in structures and processes, in forms and patterns, arises through principles of system self-organization. Indeed, *self-organization* is a guiding principle within the developmental systems theory proposed by Magnusson. Thus, development, novelty, arises in the living world because the parts of the organism produce each other and, as such, through their association create the whole (Magnusson & Stattin, 1998, 2006).

Also consistent with the theories of Gottlieb (1997, 2004), Thelen and Smith (1998, 2006), and others (Lerner, 1991, 2002; Schneirla, 1957; Tobach & Greenberg, 1984), was Magnusson's view (1995, 1999a, 1999b; Magnusson & Endler, 1977) of the character of the relation among the components of this system: That is, holistic interaction is synonymous with *dynamic interaction*. Indeed, Magnusson and Stattin (2006, p. 434) noted that, "Functional interaction is a characteristic of the developmental processes of an individual in the life-span perspective; from the interaction that takes place between single cells in the early development of the fetus . . . to the individual's interplay with his or her environment across the lifespan."

Magnusson (1995, 1999a, 1999b; Magnusson & Stattin, 1998, 2006) noted that two key concepts are involved in understanding the character of dynamic interaction: *reciprocity* and *nonlinearity*. Magnusson and Stattin (1998, 2006) pointed to data on the mutual influences of parents and children (e.g., Lerner, Castellino, Terry, Villarruel, & McKinney, 1995) as the best illustration of reciprocity in the person–environment system. Similar to Schneirla's (1957) idea of circular functions, Magnusson and Stattin noted that reciprocity occurs in parent– child interactions. The behaviors of each person in the relationship act as an influence on the behavior of the other person. At the same time, change occurs as a consequence of the influence of the other person's behavior.

As do Thelen and Smith (1998, 2006), Magnusson (1995, 1999a, 1999b; Magnusson & Stattin, 1998, 2006) noted that nonlinearity is the prototypic characteristic of the relationship among constituents of the person–environment system. Non-systems perspectives typically approach scholarship with the perspective that the relation among variables is linear and, as well, that linear relations among variables that are identified by appraising differences between people may be generalized to the relations that exist among variables within a person (Magnusson & Stattin, 1998, 2006). However, increases (or decreases) in one variable are not always accompanied by proportional increases (or decreases) in another variable, either across people or within individuals. That is, rather than finding such linear changes to be ubiquitous, changes in one variable may be accompanied by disproportionate changes in another variable. Such relationships are curvilinear in character and, for instance, may take the form of U- or ∩-shaped functions. For example, low levels of stress may not provide enough impetus to elicit high levels of performance on a given task or skill; high levels of stress may overwhelm the person and produce performance "paralysis" rather than high-level performance; but moderate levels of stress may be associated with the greatest likelihood of high-level performance (Magnusson & Stattin, 1998, 2006; Strauss, 1982).

Together, the notions of reciprocity and nonlinearity associated with dynamic interaction underscore the bidirectional causality involved in the developmental system envisioned by Magnusson (1995, 1999a, 1999b), and return us to the point that his model challenges the key concepts of non-systems approaches to human development, even insofar as fundamental notions, such as the definition of the concept of "variable," are concerned:

> concepts of independent and dependent variables and of predictors and criteria lose the absolute meaning they have in traditional research assuming unidirectional causality. What may function as a criterion or dependent variable in statistical analyses at a certain stage of a process, may at the next stage serve as a predictor or independent variable. (Magnusson & Stattin, 2006, p. 436)

Moreover, Magnusson's theory changed the emphasis in developmental science from one of a search for information that will allow generalizations to be made about how variables function across individuals to one of attempting to understand how variables function within the person. That is, because of the nonlinear relation among variables within the individual, and because the individual's "internal" distinctiveness is both a product and a producer of his or her distinct pattern of exchanges with the other levels of organization within the total person–environment system, individual differences are a fundamental feature of human development. Indeed, to understand the development of the individual, one must identify the particular factors that are pertinent to his or her life and the specific ways these factors are organized and operate within him or her (Magnusson & Stattin, 1998, 2006). In short, "developmental changes do not take place in single aspects isolated from the totality. The total individual changes in a lawful way over time; individuals, not variables, develop" (Magnusson & Stattin, 1998, p. 727).

The complexity of this person-centered analysis is underscored when, as Magnusson (1995, 1999a, 1999b; Magnusson & Stattin, 1998, 2006) explained, one understands that the contextual component of the person–environment system is as multifaceted and individualistic as are the levels of organization having their primary loci within the individual (e.g., biology, cognition, personality, behavior). That is:

> The total, integrated, and organized person–environment system, of which the individual forms a part, consists of a hierarchical system of elements, from the cellular level of the individual to the macro level of environments ... In actual operation, the role and functioning of each element depends on its context of other, simultaneously working components, horizontally and vertically. (Magnusson & Stattin, 2006, p. 421)

Magnusson and Stattin (1998, 2006) depicted the complexity of these contextual components of the person–environment system by noting that the environment may be differentiated on the basis of its physical and social dimensions, and that a person may be influenced by the actual and/or the perceived features of these two dimensions. Either dimension may serve as a source of stimulation for behavior and/or a resource for information. In addition, environments may differ in the extent to which they provide an optimal context for healthy development, and in regard to the extent to which they serve over time as a basis for developmental change (i.e., as a *formative* environment; Magnusson & Stattin, 1998, 2006) or as a source for a specific behavior at a particular point in time (i.e., as a *triggering* environment; Magnusson & Stattin, 1998, 2006).

In addition, environments may be differentiated on the basis of their proximal or distal relation to the person. For instance, the family or the peer group may constitute proximal contexts for the person, whereas social policies pertinent to family resources (e.g., policies regarding welfare benefits for poor families) may be part of the distal context of human development (Bronfenbrenner & Morris, 1998, 2006).

Conclusions. When the complexity of the environment is coupled with the multiple dimensions of the person (e.g., his or her biology; mental system; subconscious processes; values, norms, motives, and goals; self-structures and self-perceptions; and behavioral characteristics; Magnusson & Stattin, 1998, 2006), the need for a holistic, integrated theory of the developmental system is apparent. This system must be engaged to understand the course of human development and, as well, to enhance or optimize it. Consistent with our earlier discussions of the implications of plasticity for intervention to enhance the course of human life, Magnusson saw the need to involve all levels of the person and the system to not only design a comprehensive scientific research agenda but, as well, to devise strategies to apply developmental science in ways that will integratively promote positive human change:

> The holistic interactionistic view on individual functioning and development, as advocated here, implies that in the development of societal programs for intervention and treatment, the total person–environment system must be considered, not single problems of individual functioning and single risk factors in the social context ... Multiple agencies, programs, and initiatives must be integrated if the breadth of the person-context system is to be adequately engaged. (Magnusson & Stattin, 1998, p. 740)

Magnusson's ideas about holistic interaction underscore the integral connection between science and application involved in a developmental systems perspective. His views of the scientific and societal utility of such theories, which are consistent with, and buttressed by, the ideas of other developmental systems theorists (e.g., Baltes et al., 1998, 2006), underscore the importance of transcending the basic science–applied science split and of discussing the integral role that application plays in contemporary theory in human developmental science.

Moreover, Magnusson's ideas emphasize that to conduct science that has applicability to policies and programs that can positively impact human development, developmental researchers must enact their science in manners that are sensitive to the diverse developmental trajectories and the participants in their studies, and to the complex and changing ecologies of human development. Only research that is sensitive to such diverse changes of individuals and their settings can hope to be useful for applications that can increase the probability of the positive direction of such time-ordered variation.

Accordingly, as illustrated by the ideas of Magnusson, the theoretical concepts we have discussed have important implications for the methods of developmental science, as well as for the application of such scholarship. As such, we will first discuss briefly the implications of developmental science theory for the methods of developmental science, and then return to the issue of how theory and methods coalesce in developmental science to promote positive human development.

METHODOLOGICAL AND APPLIED IMPLICATIONS OF DEVELOPMENTAL SYSTEMS THEORIES

The integrated levels of organization comprising the developmental system require collaborative analyses by scholars from multiple disciplines. Multidisciplinary knowledge and, ideally, interdisciplinary knowledge is sought. The temporal embeddedness and resulting plasticity of the developmental system requires that research designs, methods of observation and measurement, and procedures for data analysis be change-sensitive and able to integrate trajectories of change at multiple levels of analysis.

Representative Instances of Change-Sensitive Methodologies: Framing the Research Agenda of Human Development

What becomes, then, the key empirical question for developmental scientists interested in describing, explaining, and promoting positive human development? The key question is actually five interrelated "what" questions:

1. What attributes?; of
2. What individuals?; in relation to
3. What contextual/ecological conditions?; at
4. What points in ontogenetic, family or generational, and cohort or historical, time?; may be integrated to promote
5. What instances of positive human development?

Answering these questions requires a non-reductionist approach to methodology. Neither biogenic, psychogenic, nor sociogenic approaches are adequate. Developmental science needs integrative and relational models, measures, and designs (Lerner et al., 2005a). Examples of the use of such methodology within developmental systems-oriented research conducted about adolescent development include the scholarship of Eccles and her colleagues on stage ↔ environment fit (e.g., Eccles, Wigfield, & Byrnes, 2003); of Damon and his colleagues on the community-based youth charter (Damon, 1997, 2004; Damon & Gregory, 2003); of Theokas (2005; Theokas & Lerner, 2006; Urban, Lewin-Bizan, & Lerner, 2009) on the role of actual developmental assets associated with families, schools, and neighborhoods on positive youth development; and of Leventhal and Brooks-Gunn (2004), and Sampson, Raudenbush, and Earls (1997) on the role of neighborhood characteristics on adolescent development.

The methodology employed in individual ↔ context integrative research must also include a triangulation among multiple and, ideally, both qualitative and quantitative approaches to understanding and synthesizing variables from the levels of organization within the developmental system. Such triangulation usefully involves the "classic" approach offered by Campbell and Fiske (1959) regarding convergent and discriminant validation through multitrait–multimethod matrix methodology.

Of course, diversity-sensitive measures are needed within such approaches. That is, indices need to be designed to measure change and, at the same time, to possess equivalence across temporal levels of the system (age, generation, history), across differential groups (sex, religion), and across different contexts (family, community, urban–rural setting, or culture). Moreover, to reflect the basic, integrative nature of the developmental system, researchers should seek to use scores derived from relational measures (e.g., person–environment fit scores) as their core units of analysis. Accordingly, trait measures developed with the goal of excluding variance associated with time and context are clearly not optimal choices in such research. In other words, to reflect the richness and strengths of our diverse humanity our repertoire of measures must be sensitive to the diversity of person variables, such as ethnicity, religion, sexual preferences, physical ability status, and developmental status, and to the diversity of contextual variables such as family type, neighborhood, community, culture, physical ecology, and historical moment.

Diversity- and change-sensitive measures must of course be used within the context of change-sensitive designs. Options here include longitudinal or panel designs (Cairns & Cairns, 2006; Lerner et al., 2005a; Magnusson & Stattin, 2006) and the various sequential designs proposed by Schaie (1965; Schaie & Baltes, 1975). Moreover, it is particularly important that our change-sensitive designs and measures be sensitive as well to the different meanings of time. Divisions of the x-axis in our designs—and in the analyses of our data—should be predicated on theoretical understanding or estimation of the nature of the changes prototypic of a given developmental process (Lerner et al., 2009).

For example, are the changes continuous or abrupt? For instance, are there periods of "punctuated equilibria" (e.g., Gould, 1976, 1977) that are preceded or followed by rapid change in the slope of growth? Are changes linear or curvilinear? Moreover, because understanding the developmental process is of paramount importance in such analyses, developmental scientists should consider inverting the x- and the y-axis, and make age the dependent variable in analyses of developmental process (Wohlwill, 1973). That is, if we believe that a process is linked systematically to age, we should be able to specify points along the x-axis that reflect different points in the process and these points should then be associated with distinct ages.

Not unrelated here, of course, is the selection of participants in developmental research. Theory should decide what types of youth are studied at what points in ontogenetic time. In addition, researchers should decide whether it is important theoretically to use age as the selection criterion for participants or whether different statuses along a developmental process should be used as the basis for the selection of youth and for the partitioning of participant variance.

Insightful formulations about the different meanings of time within the dynamic developmental system have been provided by Elder (1998; Elder & Shanahan, 2006), Baltes (Baltes et al., 2006), and Bronfenbrenner (2005; Bronfenbrenner & Morris, 2006). Our methods must appraise age, family, and historical time and must be sensitive to the role of both normative and non-normative historical events in influencing developmental trajectories.

Choices of data analytic procedures should also be predicated on optimizing the ability to understand the form and course of changes involving multiple variables from two or more levels of organization. Accordingly, multivariate analyses of change, involving such procedures as structural equation modeling, hierarchical linear modeling, or growth curve analysis, should be undertaken. It is important to note here that, over the course of the past decade or so, there have been enormous advances in quantitative statistical approaches, arguably especially in regard to the longitudinal methods required to appraise changing relations within the developmental system between the individual and the context (e.g., see Duncan, Magnuson, & Ludwig, 2004; Hartmann, Pelzel, & Abbott, Chapter 4, this volume; Laub & Sampson, 2004; Little, Card, Preacher, & McConnell, 2009; McArdle & Nesselroade, 2003; Molenaar, 2004; Nesselroade & Molenaar, in press; Nesselroade & Ram, 2004; Phelps, Furstenberg, & Colby, 2002; Raudenbush & Bryk, 2002; Singer & Willett, 2003; Skrondal & Rabe-Hesketh, 2004; von Eye, 1990; von Eye & Bergman, 2003; von Eye & Gutiérrez Peña, 2004; Willett, 2004; Young, Savola, & Phelps, 1991). Moreover, there has been an increased appreciation of the importance of qualitative methods, both as valuable tools for the analysis of the life course and as a means to triangulate quantitative appraisals of human development; as such, there has been a growth in the use of traditional qualitative methods, along with the invention of new qualitative techniques (e.g., Burton, Garrett-Peters, & Eaton, 2009; Giele & Elder, 1998; Mishler, 2004).

From Method and Theory to Application

To enhance the ecological validity of developmental scholarship and, as well, to increase the likelihood that the knowledge gained from research will be used in communities and families to improve the lives of young people, our research methods should be informed not only by colleagues from the multiple disciplines with expertise in the scholarly study of human development, but also by the individuals and communities we study (Burton et al., 2009; Lerner, 2002, 2004b; Villarruel, Perkins, Borden, & Keith, 2003). They too are experts about development, a point our colleagues in cultural anthropology, sociology, and community youth development research and practice recognize.

Most certainly, participants in community-based research and applications are experts in regard to the character of development within their families and neighborhoods. Accordingly, research that fails to capitalize on the wisdom of its participants runs the real danger of lacking authenticity, and of erecting unnecessary obstacles to the translation of the scholarship of knowledge generation into the scholarship of knowledge application (Jensen, Hoagwood, & Trickett, 1999).

In short, the possibility of adaptive developmental relations between individuals and their contexts and the potential plasticity of human development that is a defining feature of ontogenetic change within the dynamic, developmental system (Baltes et al., 2006; Gottlieb et al., 2006; Thelen & Smith, 2006) stands as a distinctive feature of the developmental systems approach to human development and, as well, provides a rationale for making a set of methodological choices that differ in design, measurement, sampling, and data analytic techniques from selections made by researchers using split or reductionist approaches to developmental science. Moreover, the emphasis on how the individual acts on the context to contribute to plastic relations with the context that regulate adaptive development (Brandtstädter, 2006) fosters an interest in person-centered (as compared to variable-centered) approaches to the study of human development (Magnusson & Stattin, 2006; Overton, 2006; Rathunde & Csikszentmihalyi, 2006).

Furthermore, given that the array of individual and contextual variables involved in these relations constitute a virtually open set (e.g., there may be as many as 70 trillion potential human genotypes and each of them may be coupled across life with an even larger number of life course trajectories of social experiences; Hirsch, 2004), the diversity of development becomes a prime, substantive focus for developmental science (Lerner, 2004a; Spencer, 2006). The diverse person, conceptualized from a strength-based perspective (in that the potential plasticity of ontogenetic change constitutes a fundamental strength of all humans; Spencer, 2006), and approached with the expectation that positive changes can be promoted across all instances of this diversity as a consequence of health-supportive alignments between people and settings (Benson, Scales, Hamilton, & Semsa, 2006), becomes the necessary subject of developmental science inquiry.

The conduct of such scholarship illuminates the character of the basic relational process of human development and, as well, provides information about how to promote positive human development in real-world settings, in the ecology of everyday life (Bronfenbrenner, 2005). Depending on the levels of analysis involved in the contexts being studied in relation to the developing individuals involved in a given research project, the work of providing information about the promotion of positive development may be termed "intervention research;" such research may be targeted at the level of either community programs or social policies (Lerner, 2004a). Yet, such "applied" work is at the same time the very work that is required to understand the character of (adaptive) developmental regulations. As such, within a developmental systems approach to developmental science, there is no split between theoretically predicated research about basic processes and practically important research elucidating how knowledge may be applied to foster programs or policies better able to promote positive development (Lerner, 1995, 2002, 2004a, 2005).

For instance, Jensen, et al. (1999) described an instance of such research in the arena of community-based programs aimed at enhancing mental health. Termed an "outreach scholarship" model, Jensen et al. (1999) explained how researchers and their universities collaborate with community members to go beyond demonstrating what programs could work in the abstract to identifying what mutually beneficial relations between universities and their community can produce programs that are effective in fostering mental health and, as well, are palatable, feasible, durable, affordable, and hence ultimately sustainable in communities.

The outcome of such synthetic basic ↔ applied scholarship is twofold: positive human development and social justice! At the individual level, we learn how to identify and align the developmental assets of contexts to promote positive human development among diverse individuals. For instance, in regard to youth development we can answer an optimization question such as "What contextual resources, for what youth, at what points in their adolescence, result in what features of positive youth development (PYD)?" In answering this question, we learn at the contextual level the sectors and features of the context that are needed to maximize positive development among diverse youth. For instance, Theokas and Lerner (2006) found that greater access in schools to high-quality teachers (e.g., as operationalized through lower teacher–student ratios) is linked to PYD; however, the opportunity for a youth to be in such a relation with a teacher obviously varies in relation to socioeconomic issues pertaining to a given school or school district (e.g., involving teacher salaries).

Accordingly, given that developmental science is aimed at optimization of developmental changes, as well as at description and explanation of such change (Baltes et al., 1977), theoretically predicated changes in the developmental system need to be evaluated in regard to whether positive human development can be equally promoted among individuals whose socioeconomic circumstances lower the probability of positive development. Identifying means to change the individual ↔ context relation to enhance the probability that all people, no matter their individual characteristics or contextual circumstances, move toward an equivalent chance to experience positive development is scholarship aimed at promoting social justice; that is, the opportunity within a society for all individuals to have the opportunity to maximize their chances to develop in healthy and positive ways.

In short, then, enhancing the presence of social justice in society is a necessary goal of a developmental science that is based on developmental systems theory and relational metatheory; that is concerned, therefore, with learning how to foster adaptive developmental regulations between all individuals and all contexts; and, as such, that is committed to the tripartite scientific mission of description, explanation, and optimization. Consistent with the integration of basic and applied science inherent in the developmental systems perspective, the developmental scientist, through her or his research, needs to be as much an agent of social change in the direction of social justice as a scholar seeking to understand the nomothetic and idiographic laws of human development. Indeed, without theory-predicated tests of how to foster social justice for all youth, our research will be inevitably limited in its potential generalizability and ecological validity. Without the promotion of social justice as a key scholarly goal, developmental science is critically incomplete.

CONCLUSIONS

Contemporary developmental science—predicated on a relational metatheory and focused on the use of developmental systems theories to frame research on dynamic relations between diverse individuals and contexts—constitutes a complex and exciting approach to understanding and promoting positive human development. It offers a means to do good science, informed by philosophically, conceptually, and methodologically useful information from the multiple disciplines with knowledge bases pertinent to the integrated individual ↔ context relations that compose human development. Such science is also more difficult to enact than the ill-framed and methodologically flawed research that followed split and reductionist paths taken during the prior historical era (Cairns & Cairns, 2006; Overton, 2006; Valsiner, 2006). Of course, because developmental science framed by developmental systems theory is so complex, it is also more difficult to explain to the "person in the street" (Horowitz, 2000).

The richness of the science and the applications that derive from developmental systems perspectives, as well as the internal and ecological validity of the work, are reasons for the continuing and arguably still growing attractiveness of this approach. Moreover, this approach underscores the diverse ways in which humans, in dynamic exchanges with their natural and designed ecologies, can create for themselves and others opportunities for health and positive development. As Bronfenbrenner (2005) eloquently put it, it is these relations that make human beings human.

Accordingly, the relational, dynamic, and diversity-sensitive scholarship that now defines excellence in developmental science may both document and extend the power inherent in each person to be an active agent in his or her own successful and positive development (Brandtstädter, 2006; Lerner, 1982; Lerner & Busch-Rossnagel, 1981; Lerner et al., 2005b; Magnusson & Stattin, 1998, 2006; Rathunde & Csikszentmihalyi, 2006). A developmental systems perspective leads us to recognize that, if we are to have an adequate and sufficient science of human development, we must integratively study individual and contextual levels of organization in a relational and temporal manner (Bronfenbrenner, 1974; Zigler, 1998). Anything less will not constitute adequate science. And if we are to serve individuals, families, and communities in the United States and the world through our science, if we are to help develop successful policies and programs through our scholarly efforts, then we must accept nothing less than the integrative temporal and relational model of diverse and active individuals embodied in the developmental systems perspective.

Through such research, developmental science has an opportunity to combine the assets of our scholarly and research traditions with the strengths of our people. We can improve on the often-cited idea of Lewin (1943) that there is nothing as practical as a good theory. We can, through the application of our science to serve our world's citizens, actualize the idea that nothing is of greater value to society than a science that devotes its scholarship to improving the life chances of all people. By understanding and celebrating the strengths of all individuals, and the assets that exist in their families, communities, and cultures to promote those strengths, we can have a developmental science that may, in these challenging times, help us, as a scientific body and as citizens of democratic nations, to finally ensure that there is truly liberty and justice for all.

ACKNOWLEDGMENTS

The preparation of this chapter was supported in part by grants from the National 4-H Council, the John Templeton Foundation, and the Thrive Foundation for Youth.

REFERENCES AND SUGGESTED READINGS (📖)

Anastasi, A. (1958). Heredity, environment, and the question "how"? *Psychological Review, 65,* 197–208.

Baltes, M. M., & Carstensen, L. L. (1998). Social-psychological theories and their applications to aging: From individual to collective. In V. L. Bengtson & K. W. Schaie (Eds.), *Handbook of theories of aging* (pp. 209–226). New York: Springer.

Baltes, P. B. (1987) Theoretical propositions of life-span developmental psychology: On the dynamics between growth and decline. *Developmental Psychology, 23,* 611–626.

Baltes, P. B. (1997). On the incomplete architecture of human ontogeny: Selection, optimization, and compensation as foundations of developmental theory. *American Psychologist, 52,* 366–380.

Baltes, P. B., & Baltes, M. M. (1990). Psychological perspectives on successful aging: The model of selective optimization with compensation. In P. B. Baltes & M. M. Baltes (Eds.), *Successful aging: Perspectives from the behavioral sciences* (pp. 1–34). New York: Cambridge University Press.

📖 Baltes, P. B., Lindenberger, U., & Staudinger, U. M. (1998). Life-span theory in developmental psychology. In W. Damon (Series Ed.) & R. M. Lerner (Volume Ed.), *Handbook of child psychology: Vol. 1. Theoretical models of human development* (5th ed., pp. 1029–1144). New York: Wiley.

Baltes, P. B., Lindenberger, U., & Staudinger, U. M. (2006). Life span theory in developmental psychology. In R. M. Lerner (Ed.), *Handbook of child psychology: Vol. 1. Theoretical models of human development* (6th ed., pp. 569–664). Hoboken, NJ: Wiley.

Baltes, P. B., Reese, H. W., & Lipsitt, L. P. (1980). Life-span developmental psychology. *Annual Review of Psychology, 31,* 65–110.

Baltes, P. B., Reese, H. W., & Nesselroade, J. R. (1977). *Life-span developmental psychology: Introduction to research methods.* Monterey, CA: Brooks/Cole.

Benson, P. L., Scales, P. C., Hamilton, S. F., & Semsa, A., Jr. (2006). Positive youth development: Theory, research, and applications. In R. M. Lerner (Ed.). *Handbook of child psychology: Vol. 1. Theoretical models of human development* (6th ed., pp. 894–941). Hoboken, NJ: Wiley.

Berger, P. L., Berger, B., & Kellner, H. (1967). *The homeless mind: Modernization and consciousness.* New York: Random House.

Bijou, S. W. (1976). *Child development: The basic stage of early childhood.* Englewood Cliffs, NJ: Prentice Hall.

Bijou, S. W., & Baer, D. M. (1961). *Child development: A systematic and empirical theory* (Vol. 1). New York: Appleton-Century-Crofts.

Birkel, R., Lerner, R. M., & Smyer, M. A. (1989). Applied developmental psychology as an implementation of a life-span view of human development. *Journal of Applied Developmental Psychology, 10,* 425–445.

Bloom, B. S. (1964). *Stability and change in human characteristics.* New York: Wiley.

Brandtstädter, J. (1998). Action perspectives on human development. In W. Damon (Series Ed.), & R. M. Lerner (Vol. Ed.), *Handbook of child psychology: Vol. 1. Theoretical models of human development* (5th ed., pp. 807–863). New York: Wiley.

Brandtstädter, J. (1999). The self in action and development: Cultural, biosocial, and ontogenetic bases of intentional self-development. In J. Brandtstädter & R. M. Lerner (Eds.), *Action and self-development: Theory and research through the life-span* (pp. 37–65). Thousand Oaks, CA: Sage.

Brandtstädter, J. (2006). Action perspectives on human development. In R. M. Lerner & W. Damon (Eds.), *Handbook of child psychology: Vol. 1. Theoretical models of human development* (6th ed., pp. 516–568). Hoboken, NJ: Wiley.

Brandtstädter, J., & Lerner, R. M. (Eds.). (1999). *Action and self-development: Theory and research through the life-span.* Thousand Oaks, CA: Sage.

Brent, S. B. (1978). Individual specialization, collective adaptation and rate of environment change. *Human Development, 21,* 21–33.

Brim, O. G., Jr., & Kagan, J. (1980). Constancy and change: A view of the issues. In O. G. Brim, Jr. & J. Kagan (Eds.), *Constancy and change in human development* (pp. 1–25). Cambridge, MA: Harvard University Press.

Bronfenbrenner, U. (1974). Developmental research, public policy, and the ecology of childhood. *Child Development, 45,* 1–5.

Bronfenbrenner, U. (1979). *The ecology of human development.* Cambridge, MA: Harvard University Press.

Bronfenbrenner, U. (1989). Ecological systems theory. In R. Vasta (Ed.), *Six theories of child development: Revised formulations and current issues* (pp. 185–246). Greenwich, CT: JAI Press.

Bronfenbrenner, U. (1994). Ecological models of human development. In T. Husen & T. N. Postletwaite (Eds.), *International encyclopedia of the social and behavioral science.* Oxford, UK: Elsevier.

Bronfenbrenner, U. (2001). The bioecological theory of human development. In N. J. Smelser & P. B. Baltes (Eds.), *International encyclopedia of the social and behavioral sciences* (pp. 6963–6970). Oxford, UK: Elsevier.

Bronfenbrenner, U. (2005). *Making human beings human.* Thousand Oaks, CA: Sage.

Bronfenbrenner, U., & Ceci, S. J. (1993). Heredity, environment, and the question "How?" A new theoretical perspective for the 1990s. In R. Plomin & G. E. McClearn (Eds.), *Nature, nurture, and psychology* (pp. 313–324). Washington, DC: American Psychological Association.

Bronfenbrenner, U., & Morris, P. A. (1998). The ecology of developmental process. In W. Damon (Series Ed.) & R. M. Lerner (Vol. Ed.), *Handbook of child psychology: Vol. 1. Theoretical models of human development* (5th ed., pp. 993–1028). New York: Wiley.

Bronfenbrenner, U., & Morris, P. A. (2006). The bioecological model of human development. In R. M. Lerner & W. Damon (Eds.), *Handbook of child psychology: Vol. 1. Theoretical models of human development* (6th ed., pp. 793–828). Hoboken, NJ: Wiley.

Burton, L. M., Garrett-Peters, R., & Eaton, S. C. (2009). "More than good quotations": How ethnography informs knowledge on adolescent development and contest. In R. M. Lerner & L. Steinberg (Eds.), *Handbook of adolescent psychology: Vol. 1. Individual bases of adolescent development* (3rd ed., pp. 55–91). Hoboken, NJ: Wiley.

Cairns, R. B. (1998). The making of developmental psychology. In W. Damon (Series Ed.) & R. M. Lerner (Vol. Ed.), *Handbook of child psychology: Vol. 1. Theoretical models of human development* (5th ed., pp. 419–448). New York: Wiley.

Cairns, R. B. & Cairns, B. D. (1994). *Lifelines and risks: Pathways of youth in out time.* New York: Cambridge University Press.

Cairns, R. B., & Cairns, B. D. (2006). The making of developmental psychology. In R. M. Lerner (Ed.), *Handbook of child psychology: Vol. 1. Theoretical models of human development* (6th ed., pp. 89–165). Hoboken, NJ: Wiley.

Cairns, R. B., & Hood, K. E. (1983). Continuity in social development: A comparative perspective on individual difference prediction. In P. B. Baltes & O. G. Brim, Jr. (Eds.), *Life-span development and behavior* (Vol. 5, pp. 301–358). New York: Academic Press.

Campbell, D. T., & Fiske, D. W. (1959). Convergent and discriminant validation by the multitrait–multimethod matrix. *Psychological Bulletin, 56*(2), 81–105.

Collins, W. A. (1982). *The concept of development: The Minnesota symposia on child psychology* (Vol. 15). Hillsdale, NJ: Lawrence Erlbaum Associates.

Damasio, A. R. & Damasio, H. (1996). Making images and creating subjectivity. In R. R. Llinas & P. S. Churchland (Eds.), *The mind–brain continuum: Sensory processes* (pp. 19–27). Cambridge, MA: MIT Press.

Damon, W. (1997). *The youth charter: How communities can work together to raise standards for all our children.* New York: The Free Press.

Damon, W. (2004). What is positive youth development? *Annals of the American Academy of Political and Social Science, 591,* 13–24.

Damon, W., & Gregory, A. (2003). Bringing in a new era in the field of youth development. In R. M. Lerner, F. Jacobs, & D. Wertlieb (Eds.), *Applying developmental science for youth and families—Historical and theoretical foundations: Vol. 1. Handbook of applied developmental science—Promoting positive child, adolescent, and family development through research, policies, and programs* (pp. 407–420). Thousand Oaks, CA: Sage.

Dixon, R. A., Lerner, R. M., & Hultsch, D. F. (1991). The concept of development in the study of individual and social change. In P. van Geert & L. P. Mos (Eds.), *Annals of theoretical psychology* (Vol. 7, pp. 279–323). New York: Plenum Press.

Dryfoos, J. G., Quinn, J., & Barkin, C. (Eds.). (2005). *Community schools in action: Lessons from a decade of practice.* New York: Oxford University Press.

Duncan, G. J., Magnuson, K. A., & Ludwig, J. (2004). The endogeneity problem in developmental studies. *Research in Human Development, 1*(1/2), 59–80.

Eccles, J., Wigfield, A., & Byrnes, J. (2003). Cognitive development in adolescence. In I. B. Weiner (Editor-in-Chief) & R. M. Lerner, M. A. Easterbrooks, & J. Mistry (Eds.), *Handbook of psychology: Vol. 6. Developmental psychology* (pp. 325–350). New York: Wiley.

Elder, G. H., Jr. (1998). The life course and human development. In W. Damon (Series Ed.) & R. M. Lerner (Vol. Ed.), *Handbook of child psychology: Vol. 1. Theoretical models of human development* (5th ed., pp. 939–991). New York: Wiley.

Elder, G. H., Modell, J., & Parke, R. D. (1993). Studying children in a changing world. In G. H. Elder, J. Modell, & R. D. Parke (Eds.), *Children in time and place: Developmental and historical insights* (pp. 3–21). New York: Cambridge University Press.

Elder, G. H., Jr., & Shanahan, M. J. (2006). The life course and human development. In R. M. Lerner & W. Damon (Eds.), *Handbook of child psychology: Vol. 1. Theoretical models of human development* (6th ed., pp. 665–715). Hoboken, NJ: Wiley.

Erikson, E. H. (1959). Identity and the life-cycle. *Psychological Issues, 1*, 18–164.

Featherman, D. L. (1985). Individual development and aging as a population process. In J. R. Nesselroade & A. von Eye (Eds.), *Individual development and social change: Explanatory analysis* (pp. 213–241). New York: Academic Press.

Fischer, K. W., & Bidell, T. (1998). Dynamic development of psychological structures in action and thought. In W. Damon (Series Ed.) & R. M. Lerner (Vol. Ed.), *Handbook of child psychology: Vol. 1. Theoretical models of human development* (5th ed., pp. 467–561). New York: Wiley.

Fischer, K. W., & Bidell, T. R. (2006). Dynamic development of action and thought. In W. Damon & R. M. Lerner (Eds.), *Handbook of child psychology: Vol. 1. Theoretical models of human development* (6th ed., pp. 313–399). New York: Wiley.

Fisher, C. B., Jackson, J. F., & Villarruel, F. A. (1998). The study of African American and Latin American children and youth. In W. Damon (Series Ed.) & R. M. Lerner (Vol. Ed.), *Handbook of child psychology: Vol. 1. Theoretical models of human development* (5th ed., pp. 1145–1207). New York: Wiley.

Fisher, C. B., & Lerner, R. M. (1994). Foundations of applied developmental psychology. In C. B. Fisher & R. M. Lerner (Eds.), *Applied developmental psychology* (pp. 3–20). New York: McGraw-Hill.

Ford, D. L., & Lerner, R. M. (1992). *Developmental systems theory: An integrative approach.* Newbury Park, CA: Sage.

Freud, A. (1969). Adolescence as a developmental disturbance. In G. Caplan & S. Lebovic (Eds.), *Adolescence* (pp. 5–10). New York: Basic Books.

Freud, S. (1954). *Collected works, standard edition.* London: Hogarth Press.

Freund, A. M., & Baltes, P. B. (2002). Life-management strategies of selection, optimization and compensation: Measurement by self-report and construct validity. *Journal of Personality and Social Psychology, 82*, 642–662.

Freund, A. M., Li, K. Z., & Baltes, P. B. (1999). The role of selection, optimization, and compensation in successful aging. In J. Brandtstädter & R. M. Lerner (Eds.), *Action and self-development: Theory and research through the life-span* (pp. 401–434). Thousand Oaks, CA: Sage.

Gestsdóttir, G., & Lerner, R. M. (2008). Positive development in adolescence: The development and role of intentional self regulation. *Human Development, 51*, 202–224.

Gestsdóttir, S., Lewin-Bizan, S., von Eye, A., Lerner, R. M., & Lerner, J. V. (2009). The structure and function of selection, optimization, and compensation in middle adolescence: Theoretical and applied implications. *Journal of Applied Developmental Psychology, 30*, 585–600.

Giele, J. Z., & Elder, G. H., Jr. (1998). *Methods of life course research: Qualitative and quantitative approaches.* Thousand Oaks, CA: Sage.

Gleick, J. (1987). *Chaos: Making a new science.* New York: Viking.

Gollin, E. S. (1981). Development and plasticity. In E. S. Gollin (Ed.), *Developmental plasticity: Behavioral and biological aspects of variations in development* (pp. 231–151). New York: Academic Press.

Gottlieb, G. (1992). *Individual development and evolution: The genesis of novel behavior.* New York: Oxford University Press.

Gottlieb, G. (1997). *Synthesizing nature–nurture: Prenatal roots of instinctive behavior.* Mahwah, NJ: Lawrence Erlbaum Associates.

Gottlieb, G. (2004). Normally occurring environmental and behavioral influences on gene activity: From central dogma to probabilistic epigenesis. In C. Garcia Coll, E. Bearer, & R. M. Lerner (Eds.), *Nature and nurture: The complex interplay of genetic and environmental influences on human behavior and development* (pp. 85–106). Mahwah, NJ: Lawrence Erlbaum Associates.

Gottlieb, G., Wahlsten, D., & Lickliter, R. (1998). The significance of biology for human development: A developmental psychobiological systems view. In W. Damon (Series Ed.) & R. M. Lerner (Vol. Ed.), *Handbook of child psychology: Vol. 1. Theoretical models of human development* (5th ed., pp. 233–273). New York: Wiley.

Gottlieb, G., Wahlsten, D., & Lickliter, R. (2006). The significance of biology for human development: A developmental psychobiological systems view. In R. M. Lerner & W. Damon (Eds.), *Handbook of child psychology: Vol. 1. Theoretical models of human development* (6th ed., pp. 210–257). Hoboken, NJ: Wiley.

Gould, S. J. (1976). Grades and clades revisited. In R. B. Masterton, W. Hodos, & H. Jerison (Eds.), *Evolution, brain, and behavior: Persistent problems* (pp. 115–122). New York: Lawrence Erlbaum Associates.

Gould, S. J. (1977). *Ontogeny and phylogeny*. Cambridge, MA: Belknap Press of Harvard.

Harris, D. B. (Ed.). (1957). *The concept of development*. Minneapolis, MN: University of Minnesota Press.

Hebb, D. O. (1949). *The organization of behavior*. New York: Wiley.

Hebb, D. O. (1970). A return to Jensen and his social critics. *American Psychologist, 25*, 568.

Heckhausen, J. (1999). *Developmental regulation in adulthood: Age-normative and sociocultural constraints as adaptive challenges*. New York: Cambridge University Press.

Hernandez, D. J. (1993). *America's children: Resources for family, government, and the economy*. New York: Russell Sage Foundation.

Herrnstein, R., & Murray, C. (1994). *The bell curve: Intelligence and class structure in American life*. New York: Free Press.

Hetherington, E. M., & Baltes, P. B. (1988). Child psychology and life-span development. In E. M. Hetherington, R. M. Lerner, & M. Perlmutter (Eds.), *Child development in a life-span perspective* (pp. 1–19). Hillsdale, NJ: Lawrence Erlbaum Associates.

Hirsch, J. (1970). Behavior–genetic analysis and its biosocial consequences. *Seminars in Psychiatry, 2*, 89–105.

Hirsch, J. (2004). Uniqueness, diversity, similarity, repeatability, and heritability. In C. Garcia Coll, E. Bearer, & R. M. Lerner (Eds.), *Nature and nurture: The complex interplay of genetic and environmental influences on human behavior and development* (pp. 127–138). Mahwah, NJ: Lawrence Erlbaum Associates.

Horowitz, F. D. (2000). Child development and the PITS: Simple questions, complex answers, and developmental theory. *Child Development, 71*, 1–10.

Jensen, P., Hoagwood, K., & Trickett, E. (1999). Ivory towers or earthen trenches?: Community collaborations to foster "real world" research. *Applied Developmental Science, 3*(4), 206–212.

Kagan, J. (1980). Perspectives on continuity. In O. G. Brim, Jr. & J. Kagan (Eds.), *Constancy and change in human development* (pp. 26–42). Cambridge, MA: Harvard University Press.

Kaplan, B. (1983). A trio of trials. In R. M. Lerner (Ed.), *Developmental psychology: Historical and philosophical perspectives* (pp. 185–228). Hillsdale, NJ: Lawrence Erlbaum Associates.

Kuhn, T. S. (1962). *The structure of scientific revolutions*. Chicago: University of Chicago Press.

Kuo, Z.Y. (1976). *The dynamics of behavior development: An epigenetic view*. New York: Plenum Press.

Kurtines, W. M., Ferrer-Wreder, L., Berman, S. L., Lorente, C. C., Briones, E., Montgomery, M. J., et al. (2008). Promoting positive youth development: The Miami Youth Development Project (YDP). *Journal of Adolescent Research, 23*(3), 256–267.

Laub, J. H., & Sampson, R. J. (2004). Strategies for bridging the quantitative and qualitative divide: Studying crime over the life course. *Research in Human Development, 1*(1/2), 81–99.

Lehrman, D. S. (1953). A critique of Konrad Lorenz's theory of instinctive behavior. *Quarterly Review of Biology, 28*, 337–363.

Lerner, R. M. (1982). Children and adolescents as producers of their own development. *Developmental Review, 2*, 342–370.

Lerner, R. M. (1984). *On the nature of human plasticity*. New York: Cambridge University Press.

Lerner, R. M. (1991). Changing organism–context relations as the basic process of development: A developmental–contextual perspective. *Developmental Psychology, 27*, 27–32.

Lerner, R. M. (1995). *America's youth in crisis: Challenges and options for programs and policies*. Thousand Oaks, CA: Sage.

Lerner, R. M. (1998). Theories of human development: Contemporary perspectives. In W. Damon (Series Ed.) & R. M. Lerner (Vol. Ed.), *Handbook of child psychology: Vol. 1. Theoretical models of human development* (pp. 1–24). New York: Wiley.

Lerner, R. M. (2002). *Concepts and theories of human development*. Mahwah, NJ: Lawrence Erlbaum Associates.

Lerner, R. M. (2004a). *Liberty: Thriving and civic engagement among America's youth*. Thousand Oaks, CA: Sage.

Lerner, R. M. (2004b). Innovative methods for studying lives in context: A view of the issues. *Research in Human Development, 1*(1), 5–7.

Lerner, R. M. (2005, September). *Promoting positive youth development: Theoretical and empirical bases*. White paper prepared for the Workshop on the Science of Adolescent Health and Development, National Research Council/Institute of Medicine. Washington, DC: National Academies of Science.

Lerner, R. M. (2006). Developmental science, developmental systems, and contemporary theories of human development. In R. M. Lerner (Ed.). *Theoretical models of human development: Vol. 1. Handbook of child psychology* (6th ed.) (pp. 1–17). Hoboken, NJ: Wiley.

Lerner, R. M. (2007). *The good teen: Rescuing adolescents from the myths of the storm and stress years*. New York: Crown.

Lerner, R. M., & Busch-Rossnagel, N. A. (1981). *Individuals as producers of their development: A life-span perspective.* New York: Academic Press.

Lerner, R. M., Castellino, D. R., Terry, P. A., Villarruel, F. A., & McKinney, M. H. (1995). A developmental contextual perspective on parenting. In M. H. Bornstein (Ed.), *Handbook of parenting: Biology and ecology of parenting* (Vol. 2, pp. 285–309). Hillsdale, NJ: Lawrence Erlbaum Associates.

Lerner, R. M., Dowling, E., & Chaudhuri, J. (2005a). Methods of contextual assessment and assessing contextual methods: A developmental contextual perspective. In D. M. Teti (Ed.), *Handbook of research methods in developmental science* (pp. 183–209). Cambridge, MA: Blackwell.

Lerner, R. M., Fisher, C. B., & Weinberg, R. A. (2000). Toward a science for and of the people: Promoting civil society through the application of developmental science. *Child Development, 71*, 11–20.

Lerner, R. M., & Kauffman, M. B. (1985). The concept of development in contextualism. *Developmental Review, 5*, 309–333.

Lerner, R. M., & Miller, J. R. (1993). Integrating human development research and intervention for America's children: The Michigan State University Model. *Journal of Applied Developmental Psychology, 14*, 347–364.

Lerner, R. M., & Overton, W. F. (2008). Exemplifying the integrations of the relational developmental system: Synthesizing theory, research, and application to promote positive development and social justice. *Journal of Adolescent Research, 23*(3), 245–255.

Lerner, R. M., Schwartz, S. J., & Phelps, E. (2009). Problematics of time and timing in the longitudinal study of human development: Theoretical and methodological issues. *Human Development, 52*(1), 44–68.

Lerner, R. M., Skinner, E. A., & Sorell, G. T. (1980). Methodological implications of contextual/dialectic theories of development. *Human Development, 23*, 225–235.

Lerner, R. M., Theokas, C., & Jelicic, H. (2005b). Youth as active agents in their own positive development: A developmental systems perspective. In W. Greve, K. Rothermund, & D. Wentura (Eds.). *The adaptive self: Personal continuity and intentional self-development* (pp. 31–47). Göttingen, Germany: Hogrefe & Huber.

Lerner, R. M., & Walls, T. (1999) Revisiting individuals as producers of their development: From dynamic interactions to developmental systems. In J. Brandtstädter & R. M. Lerner (Eds.), *Action and self-development: Theory and research through the life-span* (pp. 3–36). Thousand Oaks, CA: Sage.

Leventhal, T., & Brooks-Gunn, J. (2004). Diversity in developmental trajectories across adolescence: Neighborhood influences. In R. M. Lerner & L. Steinberg (Eds.), *Handbook of adolescent psychology* (pp. 451–486). New York: Wiley.

Lewin, K. (1943). Psychology and the process of group living. *Journal of Social Psychology, 17*, 113–131.

Lewontin, R. C. (1992). Foreword. In R. M. Lerner (Ed.), *Final solutions: Biology, prejudice, and genocide* (pp. vii–viii). University Park, PA: Penn State Press.

Little, T. D., Card, N. A., Preacher, K. J., & McConnell, E. (2009). Modeling longitudinal data from research on adolescence. In R. M. Lerner & L. Steinberg (Eds.), *Handbook of adolescent psychology: Vol. 1. Individual bases of adolescent development* (3rd ed., pp. 15–54). Hoboken, NJ: Wiley.

Lorenz, K. (1937). Ober den begriff der instinkthandlung. *Folia Biotheoretica, 2*, 17–50.

Lorenz, K. (1965). *Evolution and modification of behavior.* Chicago: University of Chicago Press.

MacDonald, K. (1985). Early experience, relative plasticity, and social development. *Developmental Review, 5*, 99–121.

Magnusson, D. (1995). Individual development: A holistic integrated model. In P. Moen, G. H. Elder, & K. Lusher (Eds.), *Linking lives and contexts: Perspectives on the ecology of human development* (pp. 19–60). Washington, DC: APA Books.

Magnusson, D. (1999a). Holistic interactionism: A perspective for research on personality development. In L. A. Pervin & O. P. John (Eds.), *Handbook of personality: Theory and research* (2nd ed., pp. 219–247). New York: Guilford Press.

Magnusson, D. (1999b). On the individual: A person-oriented approach to developmental research. *European Psychologist, 4*, 205–218.

Magnusson, D. & Endler, N. S. (1977). Interactional psychology: Present status and future prospects. In D. Magnusson & N. S. Endler (Eds.), *Personality at the crossroads: Current issues in interactional psychology* (pp. 3–31). Hillsdale, NJ: Lawrence Erlbaum Associates.

Magnusson, D., & Stattin, H. (1998). Person–context interaction theories. In W. Damon (Series Ed.) & R. M. Lerner (Vol. Ed.), *Handbook of child psychology: Vol. 1. Theoretical models of human development* (5th ed., pp. 685–759). New York: Wiley.

Magnusson, D., & Stattin, H. (2006). The person in context: A holistic–interactionistic approach. In R. M. Lerner & W. Damon (Eds.), *Handbook of child psychology: Vol. 1. Theoretical models of human devleopment* (6th ed., pp. 400–464). Hoboken, NJ: Wiley.

McArdle, J. J., & Nesselroade, J. R. (2003). Growth curve analysis in contemporary psychological research. In I. B. Weiner (Editor-in-Chief) & J. A. Schinka & W. F. Velicer (Vol. Eds.), *Handbook of psychology: Vol. 2. Research methods in psychology* (pp. 447–477). Hoboken, NJ: Wiley.

Mishler, E. G. (2004). Historians of the self: Restorying lives, revising identities. *Research in Human Development, 1*(1/2), 101–121.

Molenaar, P. C. M. (2004). A manifesto on psychology as a idiographic science: Bringing the person back into scientific psychology, this time forever. *Measurement, 2*, 201–218.

Nesselroade, J. R. & Molenaar, P. C. M. (in press). Methods—person-centered (intraindividual) & variable-centered (intervariable) approaches. In W. Overton (Vol. Ed.) & R. M. Lerner (Editor-in-Chief), *The handbook of lifespan development: Vol. 1. Cognition, Neuroscience, Methods.* Hoboken, NJ: Wiley.

Nesselroade, J. R., & Ram, N. (2004). Studying intraindividual variability: What we have learned that will help us understand lives in context. *Research in Human Development, 1*(1/2), 9–29.

Overton, W. F. (1973). On the assumptive base of the nature–nurture controversy: Additive versus interactive conceptions. *Human Development, 16*, 74–89.

Overton, W. F. (1984). World views and their influence on psychological theory and research: Kuhn-Kakatos-Lauden. In H. W. Reese (Ed.), *Advances in child development and behavior* (Vol. 18, pp. 191–225). New York: Academic.

Overton, W. F. (1998). Developmental psychology: Philosophy, concepts, and methodology. In W. Damon (Series Ed.) & R. M. Lerner (Vol. Ed.), *Handbook of child psychology: Vol. 1. Theoretical models of human development* (5th ed., pp. 107–187). New York: Wiley.

Overton, W. F. (2003). Development across the life span: Philosophy, concepts, theory. In B. Weiner (Series Ed.) and R. M. Lerner, M. A. Easterbrooks, & J. Mistry (Vol. Eds.), *Handbook of psychology: Vol. 6. Developmental psychology* (pp. 13–42). New York: Wiley.

Overton, W. F. (2006). Developmental psychology: Philosophy, concepts, and methodology. In W. Damon & R. M. Lerner (Eds.), *Handbook of child psychology, Vol. 1. Theoretical models of human development* (6th ed., pp. 18–88). New York: Wiley.

Overton, W. F., & Reese, H. W. (1973). Models of development: Methodological implications. In J. R. Nesselroade & H. W. Reese (Eds.), *Life-span developmental psychology: Methodological issues* (pp. 65–86). New York: Academic.

Overton, W. F., & Reese, H. W. (1981). Conceptual prerequisites for an understanding of stability change and continuity–discontinuity. *International Journal of Behavioral Development, 4*, 99–123.

Pepper, S. C. (1942). *World hypotheses.* Berkeley, CA: University of California.

Phelps, E., Furstenberg, F. F., & Colby, A. (2002). *Looking at lives: American longitudinal studies of the twentieth century.* New York: Russell Sage Foundation.

Piaget, J. (1950). *The psychology of intelligence.* New York: Harcourt Brace.

Piaget, J. (1970). Piaget's theory. In P. H. Mussen (Ed.), *Carmichael's manual of child psychology* (3rd ed., Vol. 1, pp. 703–723). New York: Wiley.

Plomin, R. (2000). Behavioral genetics in the 21st century. *International Journal of Behavioral Development, 24*, 30–34.

Prigogine, I. I. (1978). Time, structure, and fluctuation. *Science, 201*, 777–785.

Rathunde, K., & Csikszentmihalyi, M. (2006). The developing person: An experiential perspective. In R. M. Lerner & W. Damon (Eds.), *Handbook of child psychology: Vol. 1. Theoretical models of human development* (6th ed., pp. 465–515). Hoboken, NJ: Wiley.

Raudenbush, S. W., & Bryk, A. S. (2002). *Hierarchical linear models: Applications and data analysis methods* (2nd ed.). Thousand Oaks, CA: Sage.

Reese, H. W. (1982). Behavior analysis and developmental psychology: Discussant comments. *Human Development, 35*, 352–357.

Reese, H. W., & Overton, W. F. (1970). Models of development and theories of development. In L. R. Goulet & P. B. Baltes (Eds.), *Life-span developmental psychology: Research and theory* (pp. 115–145). New York: Academic.

Riegel, K. F. (1975). Toward a dialectical theory of development. *Human Development, 18*, 50–64.

Riegel, K. F. (1977). The dialectics of time. In N. Datan & H. W. Reese (Eds.), *Life-span developmental psychology: Dialectical perspectives on experimental research* (pp. 4–45). New York: Academic Press.

Rogoff, B. (1998). Cognition as a collaborative process. In W. Damon (Series Ed.) & R. M. Lerner (Vol. Ed.), *Handbook of child psychology: Vol. 1. Theoretical models of human development* (5th ed., pp. 679–744). New York: Wiley.

Rose, S. (1995). The rise of neurogenetic determinism. *Nature, 373*, 380–382.

Rowe, D. C. (1994). *The limits of family influence: Genes, experience, and behavior.* New York: Guilford Press.

Rushton, J. P. (2000). *Race, evolution, and behavior* (2nd special abridged edition). New Brunswick, NJ: Transaction.

Sampson, R., Raudenbush, S. W., & Earls, F. (1997). Neighborhoods and violent crime. A multilevel study of collective efficacy. *Science, 277*, 918–924.

Schaie, K. W. (1965). A general model for the study of developmental problems. *Psychological Bulletin, 64*, 92–107.

Schaie, K. W., & Baltes, P. B. (1975). On sequential strategies in developmental research: Description or explanation? *Human Development, 18*, 384–390.

Schaie, K. W., & Strother, C. R. (1968). A cross-sequential study of age changes in cognitive behavior. *Psychological Bulletin, 70*, 671–680.

Schneirla, T. C. (1956). Interrelationships of the innate and the acquired in instinctive behavior. In P. P. Grasse (Ed.), *L'instinct dans le comportement des animaux et de l'homme* (pp. 387–452). Paris: Masson et Cie.

Schneirla, T. C. (1957). The concept of development in comparative psychology. In D. B. Harris (Ed.), *The concept of development* (pp. 78–108). Minneapolis, MN: University of Minnesota.

Shweder, R. A., Goodnow, J. J., Hatano, G., LeVine, R. A., Markus, H. R., & Miller, P. J. (2006). The cultural psychology of development: One mind, many mentalities. In R. M. Lerner (Ed.), *Handbook of child psychology: Vol. 1. Theoretical models of human development* (6th ed., pp. 716–792). Hoboken, NJ: Wiley.

Singer, D., & Willett, J. B. (2003). *Applied longitudinal data analysis: Modeling change and event occurrence.* New York: Oxford University Press.

Skrondal, A., & Rabe-Hesketh, S. (2004). *Generalized latent variable modeling: Multilevel, longitudinal, and structural equation models.* Boca Raton, FL: Chapman & Hall.

Spencer, M. B. (2006). Phenomenology and ecological systems theory: Development of diverse groups. In R. M. Lerner & W. Damon (Eds.), *Handbook of child psychology, Vol. 1. Theoretical models of human development* (6th ed., 829–893). Hoboken, NJ: Wiley.

Strauss, S. (1982). *U-shaped behavioral growth.* New York: Academic Press.

Thelen, E., & Smith, L. B. (1994). *A dynamic systems approach to the development of cognition and action.* Cambridge, MA: MIT Press.

Thelen, E., & Smith, L. B. (1998). Dynamic systems theories. In W. Damon (Series Editor) & R. M. Lerner (Vol. Ed.), *Handbook of child psychology: Vol. 1. Theoretical models of human development* (5th ed., pp. 563–633). New York: Wiley.

Thelen, E., & Smith, L. B. (2006). Dynamic systems theories. In R. M. Lerner (Ed.). *Theoretical models of human development. Vol. 1. Handbook of child psychology* (6th ed., pp. 258–312). Hoboken, NJ: Wiley.

Theokas, C. (2005). *Promoting positive development in adolescence: Measuring and modeling observed ecological assets.* Unpublished dissertation. Medford, MA: Tufts University.

Theokas, C., & Lerner, R. M. (2006). Observed ecological assets in families, schools, and neighborhoods: Conceptualization, measurement, and relations with positive and negative developmental outcomes. *Applied Developmental Science, 10*(2), 61–74.

Tobach, E. (1981). Evolutionary aspects of the activity of the organism and its development. In R. M. Lerner & N. A. Busch-Rossnagel (Eds.), *Individuals as producers of their development: A life-span perspective* (pp. 37–68). New York: Academic Press.

Tobach, E., & Greenberg, G. (1984). The significance of T. C. Schneirla's contribution to the concept of levels of integration. In G. Greenberg & E. Tobach (Eds.), *Behavioral evolution and integrative levels* (pp. 1–7). Hillsdale, NJ: Lawrence Erlbaum Associates.

Urban, J., Lewin-Bizan, S., & Lerner, R. M. (2009). The role of neighborhood ecological assets and activity involvement in youth developmental outcomes: Differential impacts of asset poor and asset rich neighborhoods. *Journal of Applied Developmental Psychology, 30*(5), 601–614.

Valsiner, J. (2006) The development of the concept of development: Historical and epistemological perspectives. In R. M. Lerner (Ed.). *Handbook of child psychology: Vol. 1. Theoretical models of human development* (6th ed., pp. 166–209). Hoboken, NJ: Wiley.

Villarruel, F. A., Perkins, D. F., Borden, L. M., & Keith, J. G. (Eds.). (2003). *Community youth development: Programs, policies, and practices.* Thousand Oaks, CA: Sage.

von Bertalanffy, L. (1968). *General systems theory.* New York: Braziller.

von Eye, A. (1990). *Statistical methods in longitudinal research: Principles and structuring change.* New York: Academic Press.

von Eye, A., & Bergman, L.R. (2003). Research strategies in developmental psychopathology: Dimensional identity and the person-oriented approach. *Development and Psychopathology, 15*, 553–580.

von Eye, A., & Gutiérrez Peña, E. (2004). Configural frequency analysis—The search for extreme cells. *Journal of Applied Statistics, 31*, 981–997.

Walsten, D. (1990). Insensitivity of the analysis of variance to heredity–environment interaction. *Behavioral and Brain Sciences, 13*, 109–120.

Wapner, S. (1995). Toward integration: Environmental psychology in relation to other subfields of psychology. *Environment and Behavior, 27*, 9–32.

Werner, H. (1948). *Comparative psychology of mental development.* New York: International Universities Press.

Werner, H. (1957). The concept of development from a comparative and organismic point of view. In D. B. Harris (Ed.), *The concept of development* (pp. 125–148). Minneapolis, MN: University of Minnesota.

Willett, J. B. (2004). Investigating individual change and development: The multilevel model for change and the method of latent growth modeling. *Research in Human Development, 1*(1&2), 31–57.

Wohlwill, J. F. (1973). *The study of behavioral development.* New York: Academic Press.

Young, C. H., Savola, K. L., & Phelps, E. (1991). *Inventory of longitudinal studies in the social sciences.* Newbury Park, CA: Sage.

Zigler, E. E. (1998). A place of value for applied and policy studies. *Child Development, 69*, 532–542.

CULTURE IN DEVELOPMENT

Michael Cole
University of California, San Diego
Martin Packer
Duquesne University and *University of the Andes, Bogotá*

INTRODUCTION

Although it is generally agreed that the need and ability to inhabit a culturally organized environment are among the defining characteristics of human beings, it is a curious fact that until recently the role of **culture** in constituting human nature received relatively little attention in basic textbooks and leading journals, either of general or developmental psychology. This situation seems to be changing at an increasingly rapid pace. Since the early editions of this textbook, specialized handbooks and journals devoted to the topic of culture and psychology, much of it developmentally oriented, have appeared (Bornstein, 2009; Kitayama & Cohen, 2007; Valsiner & Rosa, 2007). Culturally inclusive psychological research has spawned new journals such as *Culture and Cognition* and *Culture and Psychology*, in addition to attracting more attention in major journals, some devoted specifically to development (e.g., *Human Development*) and some not (e.g., *Psychological Review* and *Psychological Bulletin*). Coverage of research featuring cultural themes has now become common in a number of introductory developmental psychology texts.

Culture: Independent Variable or Medium?

Implicit in a good deal of the extant treatment of culture in the psychological literature is the notion that culture is synonymous with cultural *difference*. This assumption is made explicit by Hinde (1987), who argued that culture is "better regarded as a convenient label for many of the diverse ways in which human practices and beliefs differ between groups" (pp. 3–4). This notion has underpinned decades of research exploring the causes and consequences of these differences in the approach known as **cross-cultural psychology**, in which culture is treated as an antecedent or independent variable that acts on psychological processes. In the past decade this emphasis on cross-cultural psychology has been complemented by what is referred to as *cultural psychology*, an approach in which culture is treated as the species-specific medium of human life within which people acquire and share symbolic meanings and practices, so that cultural contributions to psychological processes can be can be fruitfully studied among people within a given cultural group. There is currently a broad discussion about the relation between cultural psychology and cross-cultural psychology (see, e.g., Atran, Medin, & Ross,

TABLE 3.1
Cross-cultural Psychology and Cultural Psychology

Cross-cultural Psychology	Cultural Psychology
Culture as an independent variable	Culture as a medium of human life
Generally compares different cultural groups	Studies people within and between cultural groups
Uses tests and other measures in experimental or quasi-experimental settings	Uses ethnographic methods. If tests are used they are derived from local practices

2005, or Valsiner & Rosa, 2007). Some (e.g., Berry, 2000) identify **cultural psychology** as a sub-field of cross-cultural psychology which, along with indigenous psychologies and the use of the comparative method, defines the "generic field." Others are more likely to see cross-cultural research as a specific method within the toolkit of cultural psychology (Greenfield, 2000; Shweder et al., 2006; see Table 3.1).

The two approaches share a common interest in "the systematic study of relationships between the cultural context of human development and the behaviors that become established in the repertoire of individuals growing up in a particular culture" (Berry, Poortinga, & Pandey, 1997, p. x). However, differences between the two approaches influence how their practitioners go about conducting their research. Greenfield (1997, p. 306) identified the crux of the matter when she wrote that "the ideal in cultural psychology is for problems and procedures to flow from the nature of culture, both in general and specific terms." By contrast, cross-cultural psychology relies more "on the methodological armoire of psychology, rather than on the nature and practice of culture." This difference corresponds to treating culture as a medium, rather than as an independent variable (Cole & Hatano, 2007; Valsiner, 2000). There is growing discussion of the need to view culture in new ways (e.g., Atran et al., 2005).

To cover the diversity of views on this topic we organize this chapter as follows. The next section begins with a summary of alternative conceptions of culture used by psychologists concerned with culture and development. The alternatives generate different approaches to, and conclusions about, the role of culture in development. We then offer a conception of culture in relation to development that appears to be emerging as a kind of consensual meeting ground among various researchers who, however, remain diverse in their particular substantive concerns and preferred domains of research. The third section presents prominent examples of research on how culture enters into the process of development at different periods of the lifespan. This survey draws on both intra-cultural and cross-cultural studies to emphasize several points: (1) that cultural mediation of development is a universal process expressed in historically specific circumstances at different levels of social aggregation; (2) that culture and biology are intertwined in human development; and (3) that there are methodological opportunities and problems associated with the study of cultural constituents of development, both intra-culturally and cross-culturally.[1] This survey is organized in a chronological fashion, with different key issues that apply to all of development highlighted in different periods of life. We end by returning to discuss the general theoretical and methodological challenges that need to be confronted to improve our understanding of the roles of culture in development.

---

[1] For excellent, and still up-to-date, discussions focused on the methodological problems of conducting cross-cultural research on development, see Atran et al. (2005), Bornstein (1980), Greenfield (2009), and Kitayama and Cohen (2007).

CLASSICAL THEORIES OF DEVELOPMENT AND A GENERALIZED CULTURAL ALTERNATIVE

For most of the twentieth century, theories of human development could usefully be summarized by three approaches. The first held that endogenous (phylogenetic) factors dominate development, which passes through a series of invariant stages. Each stage is characterized by a qualitatively distinctive structure of the organism and a qualitatively distinct pattern of interaction between organism and environment. Gesell (1940, p. 13) wrote, for example:

> Environment . . . determines the occasion, the intensity, and the correlation of many aspects of behavior, but it does not engender the basic progressions of behavior development. These are determined by inherent, maturational mechanisms.

The causal relations of development to culture are neatly summarized in Gesell's metaphorical declaration that "Culture accumulates; it does not grow. The glove goes on the hand; the hand determines the glove" (1945, p. 358).

Gesell's ideas went out of fashion in the 1950s, but recent years have witnessed a significant revival of interest in innate biological constraints on development (Grotuss, Bjorklund, & Csinady, 2007; Pinker, 2002). Some of these approaches adopt the view that the role of the environment is restricted to "triggering" the realization of endogenous structures, whereas others emphasize ways in which culture is necessary to complete the process of development and accumulating evidence that the causal relations between culture and development travel in both directions (Li, 2007).

The view that the environment, both cultural and natural, provides the major influence on developmental change provides the traditional opposite to the endogenous view. An extreme version of this exogenous view was put forward by Skinner (1953, p. 91) in the following striking statement:

> Operant conditioning shapes behavior as a sculptor shapes a lump of clay. Although at some point the sculptor seems to have produced an entirely novel object, we can always follow the process back to the original undifferentiated lump, and we can make the successive stages by which we return to this condition as small as we wish. At no point does anything emerge which is very different from what preceded it. The final product seems to have a special unity or integrity of design, but we cannot find a point at which this suddenly appears. In the same sense, an operant is not something which appears full grown in the behavior of the organism. It is the result of a continuous shaping process.

In this view, the environment, the "sculptor," is the active agent in development, not the past coded in the genes; moreover, new forms emerge from this process in a continuous fashion. Contemporary psychologists sympathetic to an environmentalist perspective may consider Skinner's position somewhat exaggerated. The analogy between the organism and a lump of clay is especially unfortunate, because it implies a totally passive organism (contrary to Skinner's own principles!), but his emphasis on the dominant role of the environment in shaping development continues to have many adherents (e.g., Bandura, 2002; Kitayama, Duffy, & Uchida, 2007). Insofar as the "sculptor" is a metaphorical embodiment of society, all of development is engendered by processes of socialization.

Piaget, perhaps the most influential developmental theorist of the twentieth century, argued forcefully for the equal weight of endogenous and exogenous factors in development (Smith, 2002). On one hand, he asserted that "Mental growth is inseparable from physical growth; maturation of the nervous and endocrine systems, in particular, continue until the age of sixteen" (Piaget & Inhelder, 1969, p. viii). At the same time, like those who adopt an environmental shaping perspective, Piaget argued that the role of environmental input goes well beyond determining the occasioning, intensity, and correlation of behavioral aspects:

> The human being is immersed right from birth in a social environment which affects him just as much as his physical environment. Society, even more, in a sense, than the physical environment, changes the very structure of the individual . . . Every relation between individuals (from two onwards) literally modifies them. (Piaget, 1973, p. 156)

Piaget's view is often contrasted with the maturational and environmental shaping views in his emphasis on the crucial role of active organisms, which construct their own development through attempts to adapt to the environment. But culture plays a very limited role in Piaget's theory, restricted in the main to providing differing amounts of raw material for the processes of assimilation and accommodation to "feed upon" in given social circumstances.

Although they differ in the weights that they assign to phylogenetic constraints and ontogenetic experiences as well as to the importance of children's active modifications of their environments, the adherents of all three positions conceive of development as an interaction between *two* juxtaposed forces (nature/nurture, individual/environment, and phylogeny/ontogeny). Gesell, Skinner, Piaget, and their modern followers all implicitly or explicitly suggest that the environmental side of the equation can be partitioned into cultural or social factors versus the physical environment, but these distinctions are not well developed in their writings. Moreover, when culture is identified as a factor in development, it is often conceived of as separate from the organism, merely an influence acting on it (Lucariello, 1995).

A fourth view, which we adopt here, explicitly includes culture as an inseparable constituent of development. According to this cultural-mediational view, the two interacting factors in the previously described approaches do not interact directly. Rather, their interactions occur in the medium of culture—that is, biology and social experience are mediated through a third factor, culture, the accumulation of knowledge, experience, and learning of prior generations that forms the medium for development (Cole & Hatano, 2007; Li, 2007). From this perspective human development is conceived of as an emergent process of **bio-social-cultural change**, in which none of the constituents is reducible to the others.

To develop this fourth perspective, which we will use to guide the exposition of empirical issues in this chapter, it is now necessary to consider the concept of culture as it is used in current academic discourse about development.

CONCEPTIONS OF CULTURE

In its most general sense, the term "culture" refers to patterns of behavior that are passed from one generation to the next through extra-somatic means. It is the socially inherited body of past human behavioral patterns and accomplishments that serves as the resources for the current life of a social group ordinarily thought of as the inhabitants of a country or region (D'Andrade, 1996).[2] When applied to human beings, the notion of culture ordinarily assumes that its creators/bearers/users are capable of symbolic behavior. So, for example, Tylor (1874, p. 1), the titular father of anthropology, defined culture as "that complex whole which includes knowledge, belief, art, morals, law, custom, and any other capabilities and habits

---

[2] Note that when defined in this abstract fashion, many creatures besides human beings exhibit cultural modes of behavior (McGrew, 2002).

acquired by man as a member of society." Tylor's conception is echoed by Herskovitz's (1948, p. 17) widely used definition of culture as "the man made part of the environment."

In trying to specify more carefully the notion of culture as social inheritance, anthropologists have historically tended to emphasize culture either as "something out there," as the term "man made part of the environment" implies, or as "something inside the head," as the terms "knowledge" and "beliefs" imply. As D'Andrade has noted, during the first half of the twentieth century the notion of culture as something "superorganic" and material dominated anthropological thinking. However, as part of the "cognitive revolution" in the social sciences, the pendulum shifted, so that for several decades the "culture-as-knowledge" view has reigned. This view is most closely associated with the work of Goodenough, for whom culture consists of "what one needs to know to participate acceptably as a member in a society's affairs" (Goodenough, 1994, p. 265). This knowledge is acquired through learning and, consequently, is a mental phenomenon. As Goodenough (1976, p. 5) put it:

> in anthropological practice the culture of any society is made of the concepts, beliefs, and principles of action and organization that an ethnographer has found could be attributed successfully to the members of that society in the context of dealing with them.

From this perspective culture is profoundly subjective. It is in people's minds, the mental/symbolic products of the social heritage.

Other anthropologists, as well as psychologists, are seeking to transcend this "ideal versus material culture" dichotomy. In an oft-quoted passage, Geertz (1973, p. 45) wrote that his view of culture begins with the assumption that:

> human thought is basically both social and public—that its natural habitat is the house yard, the market place, and the town square. Thinking consists not of "happenings in the head" (though happenings there and elsewhere are necessary for it to occur) but of trafficking in . . . significant symbols—words for the most part but also gestures, drawings, musical sounds, mechanical devices like clocks.

In recent years it has become common to see efforts to combine the "culture is out there/material" and the "culture is in here/mental" views in definitions of culture. For example, Shweder and his colleagues (2006) define human culture as *both* a symbolic *and* a behavioral inheritance:

> The *symbolic inheritance* of a cultural community consists of its received ideas and understandings . . . about persons, society, nature, and the metaphysical realm of the divine . . . [whereas] the behavioral inheritance of a cultural community consists of its routine or institutionalized family life, social, economic, and political practices. (pp. 719–720; emphasis in original)

Weisner and his colleagues developed a similar perspective. For example, Weisner (1996) argued that the locus for cultural influences on development is to be found in the activities and practices of daily routines that are central to family life. The relation between individuals and activities is not unidirectional, however, because participants take an active role in constructing the activities in which they participate. Consequently, "the subjective and objective are intertwined" in culturally organized activities and practices (Gallimore, Goldenberg, & Weisner, 1993, p. 541).

Our own way of transcending the ideal–material dichotomy with respect to culture is inspired by the work of the Russian "cultural–historical school of psychology" (Vygotsky, 1987). It is to think of the cultural medium as both material and mental. It is a species-specific medium in which human beings live as an environment transformed by the **artifacts** of prior generations, extending back to the beginning of the species (Cole & Hatano, 2007). The basic function of these artifacts is to coordinate human beings with the physical world and each other; in the aggregate, culture is then seen as the species-specific *medium* of human development: as, so to speak, "history in the present." Because artifact mediation was present hundreds of thousands of years prior to the emergence of *Homo sapiens*, it is not appropriate to juxtapose human biology and human culture. The human brain and body co-evolved over a long period of time within our species' increasingly complex cultural environment (Li, 2007; Plotkin, 2002; Quartz & Sejnowski, 2002).

As Geertz (1973, p. 68) pointed out, as a result of their tangled relations in the course of human phylogeny culture and biology are equally tangled in the course of human ontogeny, disallowing a superficial view of the role of culture in human nature:

> Rather than culture acting only to supplement, develop, and extend organically based capacities logically and genetically prior to it, it would seem to be ingredient to those capacities themselves. A cultureless human being would probably turn out to be not an intrinsically talented though unfulfilled ape, but a wholly mindless and consequently unworkable monstrosity.

It is important to keep in mind this long-term, phylogenetic perspective when considering the ontogeny of children, for it reminds us that causal influences do not run unidirectionally from biology to culture. Rather, human beings are hybrids of phylogenetic, cultural–historical, and ontogenetic sources (Cole & Hatano, 2007; Li, 2007; Wertsch, 1985).

For this perspective to be useful it is essential to understand how the artifacts that constitute culture-as-medium are combinations of the conceptual/ideal and the material, because it is this combination that makes necessary the linking of phylogeny and cultural history in ontogeny. On one hand, artifacts have a mental/ideal/conceptual aspect in that they embody goal-directed interactions of which they were previously a part and which they mediate in the present (e.g., the structure of a pencil carries within it the history of representing spoken language in a different medium, manufacturing processes, communicative practices, and so forth). On the other hand they are embodied in material form, whether in the morphology of a spoken or written or signed word, or in a solid object such as a pencil. D'Andrade (1986, p. 22) made this point when he said that "Material culture—tables and chairs, buildings and cities—is the reification of human ideas in a solid medium." As a consequence of the dual conceptual–material nature of the systems of artifacts that are the cultural medium of their existence, human beings live in a double world, simultaneously natural and artificial. Hence, the environment into which children are born is more than a material world; both the mental and the material aspects of that world envelop the developing child.

This conception of the relation between culture and the special properties of human nature was expressed in particularly powerful language by the American anthropologist White (1942, p. 372):

> Man differs from the apes, and indeed all other living creatures so far as we know, in that he is capable of symbolic behavior. With words man creates a new world, a world of ideas and philosophies. In this world man lives just as truly as in the physical world of his senses . . . This world comes to have a continuity and a permanence that the external world of the senses can never have . . . Temporally, it is not a succession of disconnected episodes, but a continuum extending to infinity in both directions, from eternity to eternity.[3]

---

[3] It would be an error, in view of decades of work on proto-cultural features among primates, to overstate the discontinuities between *Homo sapiens* and other species (Premack & Hauser, 2006). Hinde (1987) argued that these phenomena do not imply culture in the way in which human beings have culture. We concur, even though we disagree with his identification of culture only with difference.

Among other properties White attributes to culture in this passage, his emphasis on the way it creates an (artificial) continuity between past and future merits special attention, as we show later. It is also significant that both White and Soviet cultural–historical psychologists (e.g., Luria, 1928; Vygotsky, 1987) emphasize that, as mediators of human action, all artifacts can be considered tools. As White (1959, p. 236) expressed the relation:

> An axe has a subjective component; it would be meaningless without a concept and an attitude. On the other hand, a concept or attitude would be meaningless without overt expression, in behavior or speech (which is a form of behavior). Every cultural element, every cultural trait, therefore, has a subjective and an objective aspect.

There are a great many suggestions about the forms taken by the artifacts in terms of which culture operates as a constituent of human activity. One well-known formulation offered by Geertz is that culture should be conceived of by analogy with recipes or computer programs: what he referred to as "control mechanisms." A complementary notion of artifacts constitutive of the medium of culture is offered by D'Andrade, who suggested the term "cultural schemes" to refer to units that mediate entire sets of conceptual–material artifacts. In D'Andrade's (1984, p. 93) terms:

> Typically such schemes portray simplified worlds, making the appropriateness of the terms that are based on them dependent on the degree to which these schemes fit the actual worlds of the objects being categorized. Such schemes portray not only the world of physical objects and events, but also more abstract worlds of social interaction, discourse, and even word meaning.

Finally, psychologists such as Bruner (1990) and Nelson (1981, 2007) identified "event schemas" embodied in narratives as basic organizers of both culture and cognition. Referred to as "scripts" by Nelson, these generalized event schemas specify the people who participate in an event, the social roles that they play, the objects that are used during the event, the sequences of actions required, the goals to be attained, and so on. Nelson's account of scripted activity is similar in many ways to Geertz's and D'Andrade's suggestions for basic units of cultural structure. Her emphasis on the fact that children grow up inside of other people's scripts, which serve as guides to action before the children are ready to understand and execute culturally appropriate actions on their own, leads naturally to her conclusion that "the acquisition of scripts is central to the acquisition of culture" (Nelson, 1981, p. 110).

A Developmentally Relevant Conception of Culture

The properties of culture-as-medium discussed so far—its foundation in artifact-mediated human activities, its co-evolution with the human brain and body, the dual material–conceptual nature of artifacts, the close relation (perhaps identity) of artifact and tool, and (as noted by White in the quotation above) the unique time extension provided by the medium—are all important to understanding the relation between culture and development. Not only the past and present, but the child's future, are present at the child's birth.

In thinking about culture as it relates to development, we have found it useful to begin with the intuitive notion underlying this word, as it has evolved since entering English from Latin many centuries ago (Cole, 1996). As Williams (1973, p. 87) noted, the core features that coalesce in modern conceptions of culture originate in terms that refer to the process of helping things to grow: "Culture, in all of its early uses was a noun of process: the tending of something, basically crops or animals." From earliest times the notion of culture included a general theory of how to promote development: Create an artificial environment in which young organisms could be provided optimal conditions for growth. Such tending required tools, both material (hoes) and knowledge (don't plant until winter is over), perfected over generations and designed for the special tasks to which they were put.

Although it would be foolish to over-interpret the metaphorical parallels between the theory and practice of growing next generations of crops and next generations of children, the exercise has considerable heuristic value. To begin with, the properties that one associates with gardens bear some obvious affinities to classical definitions of culture offered by anthropologists. A garden conceived of as an artificial environment-for-growing-living-things is, as classical definitions of culture emphasize, a "complex whole," and gardening requires both knowledge and beliefs, as well as material tools.

The **garden metaphor of culture** is also useful because it reminds us that gardeners must attend not only to a specialized form of environment created inside the garden but also to the ecological circumstances surrounding the garden. These two classes of concern often seem to be addressable independently of each other, but in reality they are interdependent, as a long tradition of research in ecological psychology has emphasized (Barker, 1968; Heft, 2003; Tudge, 2008; Turvey, 2009). Ecological psychologists' uses of the term "ecological" orient us to the interdependence of each component within a system as well as between the sub-system of interest and its context. Although it is possible to raise any plant anywhere in the world, given the opportunity first to arrange the appropriate set of conditions, it is not always possible to create the right conditions, even for a short while. So, if one is interested in the creation of conditions that not only enhance the needed properties of the artificial (cultural) environment but do so in a sustainable way, then it is essential to attend to how the system in which the garden is embedded shapes the properties of the garden itself.

Inside the garden one must consider the quality of the soil, the best way to till the soil, the right kinds of nutrients to use, the proper amount of moisture, as well as the best time to plant and nurture the seeds, and the need to protect growing plants against predators, disease, and so forth. Each of these tasks has its own material needs, associated tools, beliefs, and knowledge. Consequently, the theory and practice of development require us to focus on finding exactly the right combination of factors to promote development within the garden walls.

With respect to gardens, we can note that, in addition to having a wall separating them from their surroundings, they also have internal organization; different plants are not scattered at random within the garden walls. And so it is with culture. As Super (1987, p. 5) commented:

> Rarely in the developmental sciences . . . does theory acknowledge that environments have their own structure and internal rules of operation, and thus, that what the environment contributes to development is not only isolated, unidimensional pushes and pulls but also structure.

Humanizing the Garden Metaphor

Although the garden metaphor is useful for thinking about culture and development because it emphasizes the fact that human beings live in an artificial environment, and that cultures exist within, are shaped by, and in turn shape their ecological settings, it fails to consider the fact that human beings are not plants; nor does it capture several aspects of modern conceptions of culture that need to be elaborated in the study of development. Fortunately, modern theorizing about culture and development suggests parallels between the metaphor of garden-as-culture and the cultural organization of human development.

For example, Super and Harkness (1997) used the term **developmental niche** to refer to the child's location within the complex set of socio-cultural–ecological relations that form the proximal environment of development. Developmental niches are analyzed in terms of three components: (1) the physical and social settings in which the child lives, (2) the culturally regulated childrearing and socialization practices of the child's society, and (3) the psychological characteristics of the child's parents, especially parental theories about the process of child development and their affective orientation to the tasks of childrearing. Super and Harkness emphasized that these three components of the developmental niche operate in (imperfect) coordination with each other, providing the proximal structured medium through which children experience the world (see Gauvain, 2005, for a similar argument).

As the work of cultural psychologists clearly indicates, a "developmental niche" is roughly synonymous with a "life world." It incorporates many "micro niches" which include not only the circumstances where children are in close proximity to their parents, who might be thought to "mold" their behavior, but also the range of activities that their parents choose for them to experience (Whiting, 1980). Simple examples of such indirect parental influences over enculturation include the differential work roles assigned to boys and girls in agricultural and industrialized societies and decisions about whether and which children attend school, and if so for how long (Tudge, 2008).

Before proceeding to the issue of how culture-as-medium enters into the process of ontogenetic development, we need to address two important issues: First, the question of cultural variability, and especially the issue of **cultural evolution**; and second, the question of the "level" of the social unit to which the term "culture" is applied.

Tylor (1874), whose notion of culture was discussed earlier, believed that cultures could be classified according to their level of development, and characterized by the sophistication of their technology, the complexity of their social organization, and similar criteria, a view referred to in the literature as *cultural evolution*. He assumed in addition that all people are born with the same potential to use culture (an assumption dubbed the *doctrine of psychic unity* in anthropology) but that certain societies developed more fully than others, with industrialized societies at the top of the heap. Combining these two assumptions with the assumption that the cultural traits observed in various cultures were arrived at through a process of independent invention, Tylor believed that he could reconstruct the stages of development of humankind through a comparative analysis of societies at different levels of cultural development.[4]

This line of thinking (discussed at greater length in Cole, 1996; Jahoda, 1993; Laboratory of Comparative Human Cognition, 1983) fit with and gave respectability to the idea that the members of societies judged to be at an earlier stage of cultural evolution were also at an earlier stage of mental development. Captured in the colorful phrase that "primitives think like children," this belief in the mental superiority of people living in industrially advanced countries was held by a vast majority of nineteenth- and early twentieth-century psychologists, anthropologists, and sociologists, and remains a serious issue in the study of culture and development (Hallpike, 1979; Jahoda, 1993).

Despite its modern-sounding claim that there is an intimate relation between culture and thought, this unilinear theory of cultural–mental evolution has long had its critics, starting with Herder (1784/1803), who argued that the history of a culture can only be understood with respect to the specific development of single peoples and communities; general comparisons are deceiving. This idea of the historical specificity of cultures came into modern anthropology largely through the work of Boas (1911), one of the first major figures in

---

[4] Tylor (1874) acknowledged, but did not build on, the fact that "if not only knowledge and art, but at the same time moral and political excellence be taken into consideration, it becomes more difficult to scale societies from lower to higher stages of culture" (p. 29).

anthropology to do fieldwork in societies outside of Europe (see Stocking, 1968, for an interpretive account of Boas' contribution to modern thinking about culture).

Boas conducted research among the peoples of the American and Canadian Northwest with the objective of obtaining first-hand evidence about their technology, language use, art, custom, and myth to determine the empirical validity of evolutionary theorizing. His findings shattered his initial expectations. On the basis of comparative ethnographic data, Boas concluded that borrowing from other groups was a major source of cultural traits among the peoples he studied, undermining the basis for historical reconstruction. Moreover, the within-society heterogeneity of cultural traits contradicted either a simple diffusionist or independent-invention account of cultural change: Tribes with similar languages were found to have quite different customs and beliefs, and tribes with quite different languages were found to have very similar customs and beliefs. Assignment of societies to particular cultural levels was undermined by the great heterogeneity of levels of complexity in different domains of life in a single society. Among the Kwakiutl, for example, the graphic arts revealed a quite abstract way of representing natural forms whereas the technology was relatively unsophisticated.

From these and other observations, Boas concluded that each culture represents a combination of locally developed and borrowed features, the configurations of which are adaptations to the special historical circumstances of the group. Because all societies are characterized by heterogeneous constituent elements with respect to any single criterion of development, and because all societies can be considered equally valid responses to their own historically and ecologically posed problems of survival, there can be no basis for comparisons across societies with respect to *general* levels of development. Such comparisons illegitimately tear aspects of a culture out of context as if these aspects played an equivalent role in the life of the people being compared, when they do not.

Adopting Boas' position has direct implications for how one studies culture and development. It means that if we want to understand a behavior being manifested in any particular cultural context, we need to know the way that this context fits into the pattern of life experiences of the individuals being studied, as well as into the past history of interactions between and within cultures that have shaped the contexts where we make our observations. To fail to consider a behavior in its cultural–historical context is to risk misinterpreting its meaning, and hence its overall psychological significance for the people involved. (See Rogoff, 2003, for an elaboration of this point.)

From this rather truncated discussion of conceptions of culture, we can abstract the following essential points.

1. Culture is the residue in the present of past human activity in which human beings have transformed nature to suit their own ends and passed the cumulated artifacts down to succeeding generations in the form of tools, rituals, beliefs, and ways of conceiving of the world in general. The subjective/ideal and objective/material aspects of culture are inextricably interconnected.

2. Culture is not a random assortment of artifacts; it comes packaged in the form of conceptual systems, social institutions, and a multitude of values—acceptable ways of feeling and behaving in a wide variety of activities. The proximal environment of cultural influences on development consists of activities and practices that can be thought of as a "developmental niche."

3. Culture is a medium. When culture is treated as an independent variable, severe methodological difficulties can arise that compromise the ability of analysts to make clear inferences about causation. Despite these difficulties, varieties of cultural configurations, associated with different historical experiences (where "history" is assumed to

extend back to the first creatures dubbed *Homo sapiens* although we have written records dating back only a few thousand years), make it tempting to treat cultures as independent variables and to privilege observations based on standardized methods instead of making comparisons secondary to locally derived procedures. When cultural variations are studied conceiving of culture as an antecedent, independent variable, the fact that cultures are organized patterns of artifacts means that it will prove difficult or impossible to unpackage them to determine precisely which aspects of culture contribute to the development of particular behavioral outcomes (Whiting, 1976, referred to culture used in this way as a "packaged variable"). In the sections that follow we illustrate these and other psychologically important aspects of culture in development and some of the analytic dilemmas they pose.

The Socially Distributed Nature of Culture

When Mead went to study the people of Samoa and New Guinea in the 1920s and 1930s, it was generally assumed that a culture was widely shared by the adult population. In fact, it was thought to be sufficiently homogeneous that one could talk to a small number of people and generalize to all the people sharing that cultural system. In terms of the garden metaphor, this would be as if all the plants in a garden were the same and all grew at a uniform rate and developed into identical "cultural" clones of each other. Today, it is widely recognized among anthropologists that cultural knowledge is only partially shared, even among members of small face-to-face societies who have lived together over many generations (Romney & Moore, 2001). Within a garden, each plant has its own interaction with its own, intensely local, "micro-climate." Thus, heterogeneity within culturally defined populations ought to be taken into account in any cross-cultural investigation. Only rarely has this been done in developmental research (Medin, Unsworth, & Hirschfeld, 2007).

Level of culture is important, and as a final preliminary consideration concerning the notion of culture in relation to human development, it has long been realized that it is essential to consider what are termed "levels of the environment," ranging from the proximal and local to the distant and global (Bronfenbrenner, 1979; Laboratory of Comparative Human Cognition, 1983). With respect to understanding the role of culture in cognitive development we find it helpful to consider the processes involved in terms of three levels of social groupings: human beings as a mammalian species, societies (thought of as the population of a particular geographical and political region that exhibits common cultural features), and **cultural practices** (thought of as recurrent ways of accomplishing valued social activities in concert with some group of one's proximally circumscribed social unit). These levels are not independent of each other. It is helpful to think of each "smaller" unit of cultural analysis as embedded within the more inclusive levels both spatially (in terms of the number of people involved) and temporally (in terms of time span over which the given cultural feature or formation has existed). Just as geopolitically defined populations can be thought of as branches of a tree of human life extending back to *Australiopithecus*, all of which involve the mediation of experience by culture, so the different cultural practices within a society represent variations in the ways that people organize their everyday lives within the set of possibilities to be found in highly similar ecological circumstances. As a consequence, specifying the linkages among specific cultural practices within more inclusive sociocultural formations, and the linkages of those sociocultural formations within historically formed modes of life, is a major ongoing challenge to the study of culture and development. We will attempt to illustrate how this challenge is currently addressed in the examples of research presented in later sections.

Figure 3.1 (see over) represents the relations in cultural psychology.

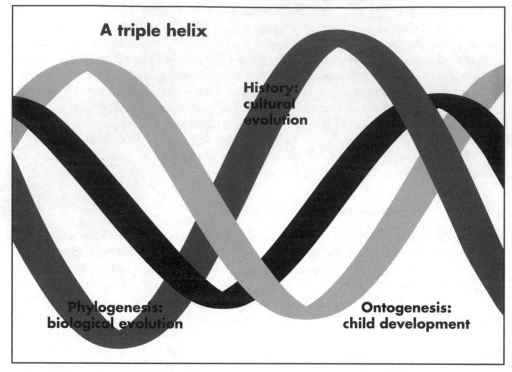

A triple helix

History: cultural evolution

Phylogenesis: biological evolution

Ontogenesis: child development

FIGURE 3.1   Cultural psychology studies the interrelations among history (cultural evolution), phylogenesis (biological evolution), and ontogenesis (child development).

TRACKING A DYNAMICAL SYSTEM OVER TIME

One enormous challenge facing students of development in general, and human development in particular, is that they seek to explain the lawful changes in the properties of a complex, interacting system in which different aspects of the system are themselves developing at different rates. As a means of orienting ourselves in attempting to describe this process of growth, we employ a framework proposed by Emde, Gaensbauer and Harmon (1976), who in turn were influenced by what Spitz (1958) called *genetic field theory*. Emde et al.'s basic proposal was to study developmental change as the emergent synthesis of several major factors interacting over time. In the course of their interactions, the dynamic relations among these factors appear to give rise to qualitative rearrangements in the organization of behavior that Emde and his colleagues referred to as *bio-behavioral shifts*. Cole and Cole (1989) expanded on this notion by referring to **bio-social-behavioral shifts** because, as the work of Emde and colleagues shows quite clearly, every bio-behavioral shift involves changes in relations between children and their social world as an integral part of the changing relations between their biological makeup and their behavior. Cole and Cole also emphasized that the interactions out of which development emerges always occur in cultural contexts, thereby implicating all of the basic contributors to development that a cultural approach demands.

In this section, we present a series of examples illustrating how culture is central to the process of development, focusing on major developmental periods and bio-social-behavioral shifts between periods. To keep this chapter within the scope of normal developmental study, we choose examples from broad age periods that, if perhaps not universal stages of development, are very widely recognized in a variety of cultures (Whiting & Edwards, 1988). The examples have been chosen for a variety of reasons. In some cases, our goal is to illustrate one or another universal process through which culture enters into the constitution of developmental stages and the process of change. In other cases, examples are chosen to highlight the impact of particular configurations of cultural mediation. Yet other examples highlight the special difficulties scientists must cope with when they focus on culture in development.

We adopt this strategy because, owing to restrictions on length, we cannot hope to treat all of the relevant issues at every age level. Instead, we have opted to emphasize particular aspects of culture–development relations at different points in the temporal trajectory from conception to adulthood. What is really called for is a life-span perspective in which the manifestations of all of the basic ideas are present, in varied configurations, at all ages.

Prenatal Development: The Cultural Organization of Development

It might seem capricious to begin an examination of cultural influences on development with the prenatal period. After all, the child does not appear to be in contact with the environment until birth. This view is implicit in Leiderman, Tulkin, and Rosenfeld's (1977) introduction to *Culture and Infancy*, which begins with the assertion that "the human environment is inescapably social. From the moment of birth, human infants are dependent on others for biological survival" (p. 1). A little reflection will reveal that the same can be said of prenatal development, with the proviso that the child's experience is, for the most part, mediated by the biological system of the mother. We need the proviso "for the most part" because there is increasing evidence that prenatal humans are sensitive to, and are modified by, culturally organized events occurring in the environment of the mother. The best documented way in which the cultural organization of the mother's experience influences the development of her child is through the selection of food and other substances that she ingests. Current public attention to the devastating effects of alcohol, cigarette smoke, and drug ingestion provides an obvious and painful reminder of cultural effects on prenatal development with long-term consequences (for a summary, see Cole, Cole, & Lightfoot, 2005, pp. 85ff.). At a more mundane level, research in both industrialized and non-industrialized societies demonstrates that beliefs about appropriate foods for expectant mothers are quite variable in ways that are likely to influence such important indicators of development as birth weight and head size. In one of the few intra-cultural studies on this topic, Jeans, Smith, and Stearns (1955) compared the health of babies born to mothers whose diets were judged as either "fair to good" or "poor to very poor." The women were all from a single rural area and did not differ in any indices of social class; it was their choice of foods that differed. The mothers judged as having fair to good diets had markedly healthier babies. When social class does differ, and with it the associated nutritional status of mothers and their offspring, the consequences can be devastating, including death of the infant (Pollitt, Saco-Pollitt, Jahari, Husaini, & Huang, 2000).

There is also reasonably good evidence that pregnant women who inhabit stressful environments have more irritable babies (Chisholm, Burbank, Coall, & Gemmiti, 2005; Leigh & Milgrom, 2008). For example, Chisholm and his colleagues have shown that Navajo women who live within Navajo communities rather than Anglo areas have less irritable babies. Chisholm provided suggestive data implicating high blood pressure resulting from the stress of living in fast-paced and generally unsupportive urban centers dominated by Anglos as the cause of increased infant irritability.

With the advent of modern medical technologies there is an obvious new source of cultural influence on prenatal development through genetic screening techniques, especially the ability to learn the gender of the expected child. In a number of countries selective abortion of females is being reported, where previously female infanticide practices were delayed until the child made its appearance (Sharma, 2003).

More benignly, there is also ample evidence that prenatal humans are sensitive to, and are modified by, the language spoken in the environment of the mother (Kisilevsky et al., 2009; Lecanuet, Graniere-Deferre, Jacquet, & DeCasper, 2000; Mastropieri & Turkewitz, 1999; Mehler, Dupoux, Nazzi, & Dehaene-Lambertz, 1996).

Birth: Evidence for a Universal Mechanism of Cultural Mediation

The realignment of biological, social, and behavioral factors at birth makes it perhaps the most dramatic bio-social-behavioral shift in all development. There is ample evidence of great cultural variation in the organization of the birthing process (Newburn, 2003), but it is also the case that this fundamental transition provides some of the clearest evidence of universal mechanisms relating culture to development (Richardson & Guttmacher, 1967).

When babies emerge from the birth canal and the umbilical cord is cut, their automatic supply of oxygen and nutrients comes to an abrupt halt. Neonates are no longer bound to their environments through a *direct* biological connection. Following birth, even essential biological processes occur *indirectly*—they are mediated by culture and other human beings. The baby's food no longer arrives predigested through the mother's bloodstream, but neither, generally speaking, is it raw. Rather, it is transformed by a preparative process that is neither purely biological nor purely natural, a process that has been shaped as an integral part of the cultural history of the group.

To survive in an environment mediated by culture, the baby must act on the nurturing environment in a qualitatively different way than was true before birth. This is not to say that the baby is ever inactive. With the beginning heartbeat early in embryogenesis, the organism becomes and remains active until it dies. Without such activity during the prenatal period, more complicated neural circuits needed for coordinated movement and thought could not develop adequately. However, the effects of fetal activity on the environment inside and outside its mother's womb are minimal.

Following birth, changes in babies' impact on their environments are no less marked than changes in the way the environment acts on them. They make urgent, vocal demands on their caregivers. They become social actors who reorder the social relationships among the people around them. At birth, *development becomes a co-constructive process* in which *both* the social environment *and* the child are active agents (Valsiner, 2000).

From existing ethnographic evidence, we know that both the mother's and child's experiences at birth vary considerably across societies of the world according to cultural traditions that prescribe the procedures to be followed in preparation for, during, and after the birth. In a few societies, birthing is treated as a natural process that requires no special preparation or care. Shostak (1981) recorded the autobiography of a !Kung-san woman living in the Kalahari desert in the middle of the last century who reported that she observed her mother simply walk a short way out of the village, sit down against a tree, and give birth to her brother. In most societies, however, birthing is treated as dangerous (and in some places as an illness), requiring specialized help (see Cole, Cole, & Lightfoot, 2005, p. 95, for additional examples and references).

Rather than concentrate on the potential consequences of these cultural variations in birthing practices, we focus on the way that birth provides evidence of a universal mechanism of cultural mediation of development—the process through which the ideal side of culture is transformed into material–cultural organization of the child's environment. This example (taken from the work of pediatrician MacFarlane, 1977) also demonstrates in a particularly clear fashion White's point that culture provides a specifically human form of temporal continuity.

Figure 3.2 presents in schematic form five different time scales simultaneously operating at

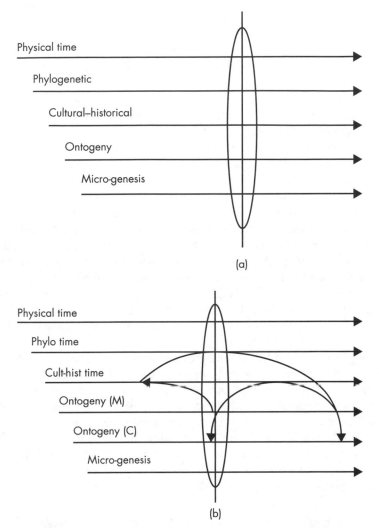

FIGURE 3.2   (a) The kinds of time in effect at the moment a child is born (marked by the vertical line). (b) How culture is converted from an ideational or conceptual property of the mother into a material or interactional organization of the baby's environment. Note that two ontogenies are included, the mother's and the baby's. The curved lines depict the sequence of influences: The mother thinks about what she knows about girls from her (past) cultural experience; she projects that knowledge into the child's future (indicated by remarks such as "It will never be a rugby player"); this ideal or conceptual future is then embodied materially in the way the mother interacts with the child.

the moment at which parents see their newborn for the first time. The vertical ellipse represents the events immediately surrounding birth, which occurs at the point marked by the vertical line. At the top of the figure is what might be called physical time, or the history of the universe that long precedes the appearance of life on earth.

The bottom four time lines correspond to the developmental domains that, according to the cultural psychological framework espoused here, simultaneously serve as major constraints for human development (Cole, 2006). The second line represents phylogenetic time, the history of life on earth, a part of which constitutes the biological history of the newborn individual. The third line represents cultural–historical time, the residue of which is the child's cultural heritage. The fourth line represents ontogeny, the history of a single human being, which is the usual object of psychologists' interest. The fifth line represents the moment-to-moment time of lived human experience, the event called "being born" (from the perspective of the child) or "having a baby" (from the perspective of the parents) in this case. Four kinds of genesis are involved: **phylogenesis**, cultural–historical genesis, **ontogenesis**, and microgenesis, with each lower level embedded in the level above it.

MacFarlane's example reminds us to keep in mind that not one but two ontogenies must be represented in place of the single ontogeny in Figure 3.2a. That is, at a minimum one needs a mother and a child interacting in a social context for the process of birth to occur and for development to proceed. These two ontogenies are coordinated in time by the simultaneous organization provided by phylogeny and culture (Figure 3.2b).

Now consider the behaviors of the adults when they first catch sight of their newborn child and discover if the child is male or female. Typical comments include "I shall be worried to death when she's eighteen," or "She can't play rugby." In each of these examples, the adults interpret the biological characteristics of the child in terms of their own past (cultural) experience. In the experience of English men and women living in the mid-20th century, it could be considered common knowledge that girls do not play rugby and that when they enter adolescence they will be the object of boys' sexual attention, putting them at various kinds of risk. Using this information derived from their cultural past and assuming that the world will be very much for their daughters what it has been for them, parents project probable futures for their children. This process is depicted in Figure 3.2b by following the arrows from the mother to the cultural past of the mother to the cultural future of the baby to the present adult treatment of the baby.

Of crucial importance to understanding the contribution of culture in constituting development is the fact that the parents' (purely ideal) projection of their children's future, derived from their memory of their cultural past, becomes a fundamentally important material constraint organizing the child's life experiences in the present. This rather abstract, nonlinear process is what gives rise to the well-known phenomenon that even adults totally ignorant of the real gender of a newborn will treat the baby quite differently depending on its symbolic or cultural gender. Adults literally create different material forms of interaction based on conceptions of the world provided by their cultural experience when, for example, they bounce boy infants (those wearing blue clothing) and attribute manly virtues to them, while

Social change can invalidate projected ontogenetic trajectories, as illustrated by the rise of women's rugby. Photo source: Selective Focus Photography, www.flickr.com/photos/scottnh/3394339933

they treat girl infants (those wearing pink clothing) in a gentle manner and attribute beauty and sweet temperaments to them (Rubin, Provezano, & Luria, 1974). Similar results are obtained even if the child is viewed *in utero* through ultrasound (Sweeney & Bradbard, 1988). Parental expectations of aspects of infant temperament have been found to anticipate these in time, and so presumably influence them (Pauli-Pott, Mertesacker, Bade, Haverkock, & Beckmann, 2003).

MacFarlane's example also demonstrates that the social and the cultural aspects of the child's environment cannot be reduced to a single "source of development" although the social and the cultural are generally conflated in two-factor theories of development, such as those presented schematically in Figure 3.1. "Culture" in this case refers to remembered forms of activity deemed appropriate to one's gender as an adolescent, whereas "social" refers to the people whose behavior is conforming to the given cultural pattern. This example also motivates the special emphasis placed on the social origins of higher psychological functions by developmental scientists who adopt the notion of culture presented here. As MacFarlane's transcripts clearly demonstrate, human nature is social in a different sense from the sociability of other species. Only a culture-using human being can reach into the cultural past, project it into the (ideal or conceptual) future, and then carry that ideal or conceptual future back into the present to create the (material/ideal) sociocultural environment of the newcomer.

In addition, this example helps us to understand the ways in which culture contributes to both continuity and discontinuity in individual development. In thinking about their babies' futures these parents are assuming that the "way things have always been is the way things will always be," calling to mind White's telling image (see above) that, temporally, the culturally constituted mind "is not a succession of disconnected episodes, but a continuum extending to infinity in both directions, from eternity to eternity." In this manner, culture is the medium that allows people to project the past into the future, providing an essential basis of psychological continuity.

This assumption, of course, is sometimes wrong. The invention of new ways to exploit energy or new media of representation, or simple changes in custom, may sufficiently disrupt the existing cultural order to be a source of significant developmental discontinuity. As an example, in the 1950s American parents who assumed that their daughters would not be soccer players at the age of 16 would have been correct. But by 1990 a great many American girls were playing soccer.

We know of no recordings equivalent to MacFarlane's from very different cultures, but an interesting account of birthing among the Zinacanteco of south-central Mexico appears to show similar processes at work. In their summary of developmental research among the Zinacanteco, Greenfield, Brazelton, and Childs (1989, p. 177) reported a man's account of his son's birth at which the son "was given three chilies to hold so that it would . . . know to buy chili when it grew up. It was given a billhood, a digging stick, an axe, and a [strip of] palm so that it would learn to weave palm." Girls are given weaving sticks, in anticipation of one of their central cultural roles as adults. The future orientation of differential treatment of the babies is not only present in ritual; it is coded in the Zinacantecan saying, "For in the newborn baby is the future of our world."

Infancy: Biology and Culture Working Together

It has long been recognized that there is an intimate link between the relative immaturity of the human newborn, which will require years of nurturing before approaching something akin to self-sufficiency, and the fact that human beings inhabit a culturally mediated environment. Both are distinctive characteristics of our species. Infancy (from a Latin word meaning one who does not speak) is widely, if not universally, considered a distinctive period of development that extends from birth until approximately the age of 2½.

The newborn infant is physically separate from the mother but still completely dependent on others for the basic necessities of life. Parents must wait until social smiling appears at around 2 months for the infant's first acknowledgement of their existence (a change to which they respond with more and more complex speech to the infant, at least in Western middle-class families: Henning, Striano & Lieven, 2005). But the infant is thoroughly embedded in a social situation from the outset, and has an innate "general relational capacity" (Selby & Bradley, 2003). Later we will consider children's acquisition of language, but it is important to recognize that communication between infant and adults occurs from birth in an "intersubjectivity" that at first does not require deliberate or specialized communicative acts on the part of the former (Trevarthen, 2005). Children's later verbal communication will grow out of this preverbal interaction, in which child and adult are best described as a single system rather than as two individuals transmitting coded information.

The system has been characterized as one of "**co-regulation**," "a form of coordinated action between participants that involves a continuous mutual adjustment of actions and intentions" (Fogel & Garvey, 2007). What Bruner (1982) referred to as "formats" and Nelson (1981, 1986) as "scripts" are event-level cultural artifacts, embodied in the vocabulary and habitual actions of adults, which act as structured media within which children can experience the covariation of language and action while remaining coordinated in a general way with culturally organized forms of behavior. In the process of negotiating such events with enculturated caregivers, children discover the vast range of meanings encoded in their culture at the same time as they find new ways to carry out their own intentions.

The cultural orchestration of this communication varies considerably. Cross-cultural research supplements intra-cultural studies by disclosing the incredible diversity of ways in which infants are involved in adult-led activities (de Villiers & de Villiers, 1978). Cross-cultural studies have shown that adults in all societies adopt something akin to a baby-talk mode when speaking to their children, before and while the children are acquiring language, using higher pitch and intonation, simplified vocabulary, grammatically less complex sentences, and utterances designed to highlight important aspects of the situation (Bryant & Barrett, 2007). Cross-cultural data have shown that, although adults everywhere speak to young children differently than they speak to older children and other adults, the particular form of infant-directed speech of middle-class American parents is not universal. Middle-class US parents treat the infant as a social being and as an "addressee" (Schieffelin & Ochs, 1986). Kaluli mothers consider their infants to be "soft" and without understanding, and carry them facing outwards. They talk with other people *about* the child, but rarely *to* the child. In Samoa, talk is directed *at* the infant but not *to* them.

Getting on a schedule.   The neonate's dependence requires that the child participates in a social and cultural system. The earliest, essential condition for continued development following birth is that the child and those who care for him or her must coordinate their conduct in this system. Adults must accumulate enough resources to accommodate the newcomer. They must come to know their child. The newborn must learn how to meet needs through the actions of others, because the child's own behavior is so limited. In this process one sees an intricate interplay between the initial characteristics of children and the cultural environment into which they are born, what Super and Harkness (1986, 2002) refer to as the developmental niche.

A clear illustration of the cultural character of the process of achieving coordination is the contrasting patterns of sleep in the months following birth in American urban dwelling and rural Kenyan (Kipsigis) children (Super & Harkness, 1997). Newborns in the United States show a marked shift toward the adult day/night cycle a few weeks after birth; by the end of the second week, they are averaging about 8½ hours of sleep between the hours of 7 p.m. and 7 a.m. Between 4 and 8 months the longest sleep episode increases from about 4 to 8 hours a night. The pressures toward sleeping through the night are not difficult to identify. American urban dwellers live by the clock. When both parents have jobs the child must be ready when they leave home in the morning. Parents are likely to push as hard as possible for the child to sleep when it is convenient for them.

Among Kipsigis infants, the course of getting on a schedule is very different. At night they sleep with their mothers and are permitted to nurse on demand. During the day they are strapped to their mothers' backs, accompanying them on their daily rounds of farming, household chores, and social activities. They do a lot of napping while their mothers go about their work. At 1 month, the longest period of sleep reported for babies in a Kipsigis sample was 3 hours, and their longest sleep episode increased little during the first 8 months of postnatal life.

This seemingly simple case contains some important lessons. First, the coordination that produces different patterns of sleeping is more than a temporary convenience. Assuming there is little change in Kipsigis life circumstances, the children socialized into a flexible sleep schedule will become more flexible adults than their American counterparts. Second, cultural variations in sleeping arrangements reflect the tacit moral ideals of the community (Shweder, Jensen & Goldstein, 1995), so the pattern the infant comes to participate in is as much ethical as it is practical.

From sucking to nursing.   In the 1940s Mead and Macgregor (1951) set out to test Gesell's ideas about the relation between growth (maturation) and learning through cross-cultural research. All biologically normal children are born with a sucking reflex that can be triggered by many different stimuli. But Mead and Macgregor argued that basic principles of the way that cultures interweave learning and maturation can be seen in the way the change from reflex sucking to nursing is organized, and in the long-term behavioral implications of this organization. Some cultures, they noted, take advantage of the sucking reflex by putting the baby to the mother's breast immediately to stimulate the flow of milk, although the baby remains hungry; others provide a wet nurse; others will give the baby a bottle; and so on. In an immediate sense, all of these routes to mature nursing are equally adequate. However, they have different implications in the short, and even the long, run. Mead and Macgregor pointed to one potential short-run effect: Babies who are bottle fed until their mother's milk comes in may elaborate nursing behaviors that interfere with breast-feeding, changing both short-run nutritional and social–interactional experiences. More recent research has shown that mothers who breast feed their children also engage in more touching and gazing at their child than mothers of bottle fed babies, indicating that the choice of feeding method influences interpersonal mother–infant interactions (Lavelli & Poli, 1998).

The future in the present: A cross-cultural example.   In Cole (2005) an example from work by Bornstein and his colleagues was used to illustrate processes of cultural mediation in infancy similar to those displayed in the conversations of parents greeting their newborns recorded by MacFarlane. That study of the interactions between American and Japanese mothers and their 5-month-old offspring (living in New York and Tokyo, respectively) showed different responses to the infants' orientations to events in the environment or to the mothers themselves (Bornstein, Tal, & Tamis-LeMonda, 1991; Bornstein, Toda, Azuma, Tamis-LeMonda, & Ogino, 1990; Bornstein et al., 1992). Infants in the two cultures behaved in a similar manner, in particular displaying equal levels of orientation to their mothers and to physical objects in the environment, but there was a distinctive difference in the way their mothers responded to them. American mothers were more responsive when their children oriented to physical objects in the environment; Japanese mothers were more responsive when their infants oriented to them. Moreover, American mothers diverted children's attention from themselves to objects, whereas Japanese mothers showed the opposite pattern. Bornstein et al. proposed that the influence was bidirectional and could lead to "dramatically divergent ontogenetic paths" (1992, p. 818).

Bornstein's more recent work illustrates another aspect of how development is channeled by cultural value systems embodied in distinctive cultural practices. Bornstein, Haynes, Pascual, Painter, & Galperín (1999) compared mothers' play with their 20-month-old infants in the US (Washington) and Argentina (Buenos Aires). Not surprisingly, at this age of infants, *both* mothers and infants differed across cultures. Argentine children and their mothers engaged more in representational play and less in (the presumably less advanced) exploratory play than US children and their mothers. Bornstein et al. attributed this to an emphasis in Argentine parenting on control and interdependency, and an emphasis in US parenting on independence and exploration. When Cote and Bornstein (2009) compared the play with their 20-month-old infants of South American immigrant mothers to the US (from Argentina, Colombia, and Peru) and US-born mothers, they found no such differences. Apparently the immigrant parents quickly adjusted to the value systems of their new socio-cultural milieux. In at least some circumstances, "dramatically divergent ontogenetic paths" exhibit a good deal of plasticity.

A shift in socioemotional and cognitive development at 6 to 9 months. The period from 6 to 9 months of age is strategically useful for illustrating several points about culture and development. First, there is a good deal of evidence pointing to a universal and distinct-ive reorganization of the overall way in which children interact with their environments at this time, illustrating the stage-transformation process that we referred to earlier as a bio-social-behavioral shift (Cole, Cole, & Lightfoot, 2005). Second, there are many cross-cultural data that allow us to address both general and culture-specific ways in which this change occurs. The cross-cultural data are as interesting for the general methodological problems of cross-cultural research that they raise as for their substantive contributions to understanding the role of culture in development.

The universal changes occurring at 6 to 9 months of age are apparent in all aspects of the bio-social-behavioral shift. With respect to the biological strand, we find that new patterns of electrical activity, associated with increased levels of myelinization, arise in several parts of the brain (Pujol et al., 2006; Richmond & Nelson, 2007). The affected areas include the frontal lobes (which play a crucial role in deliberate action and planning), the cerebellum (which is important in controlling movement and balance), and the hippocampus (important in memory). In addition, the muscles have become stronger and the bones harder than they were at birth, providing support for increasingly vigorous movement.

Increased motor skills associated with these changes allow children to move around objects, pick them up, taste them, and attempt to use them for various purposes (Adolph & Berger, 2010). This increased exploratory capacity has been shown to have important psycho-logical consequences because it enables the infant to discover the invariant properties of objects. Campos and his colleagues (2000), for example, showed that children given extensive experience moving around in baby walkers before they could locomote on their own displayed improved social, cognitive, and emotional development, referential gestural communication, wariness of heights, the perception of self-motion, distance perception, spatial search, and spatial coding strategies.

For these new forms of experience to have a cumulative impact, infants must be able to remember them. Evidence from a number of sources (Mandler, 2004; Schacter & Moskovitch,

1984) indicates that between 6 and 9 months of age children show a markedly enhanced ability to recall prior events without being reminded of them. Closely related is a shift in the propensity to categorize artificially constructed arrays of objects in terms of conceptual properties (Cohen & Cashon, 2006; Mandler, 1997). Taken together, these enhanced memory and categorizing abilities increase the degree to which children can structure information from past experience, enabling them to deal more effectively with current circumstances. The combination of increased mobility and increased remembering also brings increased awareness of the dangers and discomforts the world has in store. These changes, in turn, are associated with changes in children's social relationships with caregivers, about whom children have begun to build stable expectations.

Once children begin to crawl and walk, caregivers can no longer directly prevent mishaps, no matter how carefully they arrange the environment. Newly mobile babies keep a watchful eye on their caregivers for feedback about how they are doing—called *social referencing* (Tamis-LeMonda & Adolph, 2005). At the same time, children become wary of strangers and become upset when their primary caregivers leave them. This complex of apparently related social behaviors has led a number of psychologists to hypothesize that a new quality of emotional relationship between caregiver and child emerges, called "**attachment**."

Attachment.   Although various aspects of the complex of changes that occur between 6 and 9 months of age have been investigated cross-culturally (e.g., Kagan, 1977, reported data supporting the hypothesis of cross-cultural universals with respect to various aspects of remembering and object permanence), by far the greatest number of data have been collected on cultural contributions to attachment, so it is on this issue that we focus.

After the complete social dependence of the neonate and the diffuse sociality after the first 2 months, infants form their first specific social relationships in the period of 6 to 9 months. The attachment relationship clearly demonstrates biology and culture working together.

Despite the fact that there are competing theories to account for how and why children form special emotional bonds with their caregivers (see Cassidy & Shaver, 2008, for a representative sample of views), current research still takes as its starting point Bowlby's (1969, 1982) attempts to explain why extended periods of separation from parents are upsetting to small children, even though they are maintained in adequate circumstances from a purely physical point of view. His explanation, briefly stated, was that one has to interpret contemporary forms of behavior in terms of the environment in which our species evolved, the "environment of evolutionary adaptedness." In this view, behaviors that might seem irrational today were once crucial to survival, becoming a part of the human biological repertoire through natural selection.

The development of attachment would seem to be a necessary, universal biological requirement to be found in all cultures under normal circumstances because it is a species-specific consequence of our phylogenetic heritage. However, even if the attachment system is a biologically based universal, this in no way contradicts the principle of cultural mediation. Indeed, in the phenomenon of attachment we see clearly the interweaving of biology and culture. Our description of the newborn illustrated that it is overstating the case to say that "cultural learning begins with the attachment relationship" (Grossmann & Grossmann, 2005, p. 208), but certainly "It seems as if nature wanted to make sure that infants begin their lifelong education by first learning about the values of their own people" (p. 207). The biological system of attachment is interwoven with cultural practices because it ensures that the infant relates primarily with kin at the age when he or she is developing important social and cognitive abilities, especially language.

During the past three decades there has been a heated dispute on the implications of cultural variations in the outcomes of this interweaving. The dispute is worth examining in some detail because it is typical of difficulties facing the use of cross-cultural approaches to culture and development. Appropriately, the studies that began the modern debate on culture and attachment arose from comparison of the behaviors of mother–child pairs observed in their homes in the United States and Uganda by Ainsworth (1967; Ainsworth, Blehar, Waters, & Wall, 1978). Ainsworth was struck by the fact that children in both cultural groups exhibited similar patterns of attachment-related behavior (distress during brief, everyday, separation from their mothers, fear of strangers, and use of the mother as a secure base from which to explore). However, the Ugandan children seemed to express these behavior patterns more readily and intensely than did the American children Ainsworth studied. In laboratory studies using the "strange situation," Ainsworth identified three differing patterns of infant response to separation from and reunion with the parent: Type A (anxious–avoidant), Type B (securely attached), and Type C (anxious–resistant). Subsequent work has identified an additional pattern, Type D (disorganized) (Main & Solomon, 1990; Hesse & Main, 2006). Mothers of B babies have been found to typically be sensitively responsive to their infants, mothers of A infants are found rejecting, and mothers of C infants are found inconsistently responsive. Since the 1970s there has been a great deal of research on the behavior produced in the strange situation, its antecedents, and its sequelae (see the articles in Cassidy & Shaver, 2008, for reviews, leading areas of contention, and references to additional primary sources of information).

For at least two decades there has been sharp disagreement among developmentalists concerning how the attachment system is expressed in different cultures. Research initially suggested significant cultural variation in the proportion of infants showing each pattern. For example, several decades ago, children living in some Israeli kibbutzim (collective farms) were reared communally from an early age. Although they saw their parents daily, the adults who looked after them were usually not family members. When at the age of 11 to 14 months such communally reared children were placed in the strange situation with either a parent or a caregiver, many became very upset; half were classified as anxious/resistant, and only 37% appeared to be securely attached (Sagi et al., 1985). Sagi and his colleagues suspected that the high rate of insecure attachment among these children reflected the fact that the communal caregivers could not respond promptly to the individual children in their care, and staffing rotations did not allow the adults to provide individualized attention. To test this hypothesis these researchers compared the attachment behaviors of children reared in traditional kibbutzim, where children slept in a communal dormitory at night, with those of children from kibbutzim where children returned to sleep in their parents' home at night (Sagi, van IJzendoorn, Aviezer, Donnell, & Mayseless, 1994). Once again they found a low level of secure attachments among the children who slept in communal dormitories. But those who slept at home displayed a significantly higher level of secure attachments, supporting the idea that cultural differences in the opportunities for sensitive caregiving accounted for differences in attachment quality.

Some have argued that these different proportions of attachment patterns are important cultural variations in attachment and that the very notion of human relatedness which is a part of the concept of attachment is culturally specific (Rothbaum, Weisz, Pott, Miyake, & Morelli, 2000). Others have argued that cultural variations are the result of insufficiently rigorous adherence to the procedures for administering the test, and still others have argued that children display a universal tendency toward secure attachment but insecure attachment is manifest in various ways (van IJzendoorn & Sagi, 1999).

A low percentage of securely attached babies has also been observed among northern (but not southern) German children. Researchers in one study found that 49% of the 1-year-olds tested were anxious–avoidant and only 33% were securely attached (Grossmann, Grossmann, Spangler, Suess, & Unzner, 1985). Having made extensive observations of northern German home life, Grossmann et al. were able to reject the possibility that a large proportion of northern German parents were insensitive or indifferent to their children. Rather, they contended, these parents were adhering to a cultural value that calls for the maintenance of a relatively large interpersonal distance and to a cultural belief that babies should be weaned from parental bodily contact as soon as they become mobile. The researchers suggested that among northern German mothers, "the ideal is an independent, non-clinging infant who does not make demands on the parents but rather unquestioningly obeys their commands" (p. 253).

In Japan, Miyake and his colleagues found a large proportion of anxious–resistant infants among traditional Japanese families, and no anxious–avoidant infants at all (Miyake, Chen, & Campos, 1985; Nakagawa, Lamb, & Miyake, 1992). Miyake and his colleagues explained this pattern by pointing out that traditional Japanese mothers rarely leave their children in the care of anyone else, and they behave toward them in ways that foster a strong sense of dependence. Consequently, the experience of being left alone with a stranger is unusual and upsetting to these children. This interpretation is supported by a study of nontraditional Japanese families in which the mothers were pursuing careers requiring them to leave their children in the care of others (Durrett, Otaki, & Richards, 1984). Among the children of these mothers the distribution of the basic patterns of attachment was similar to that seen in the United States.

The evidence of cultural variation has been brought into question and balanced by evidence that there is a general tendency in all societies for children to become attached to their caregivers. An influential review of research on attachment spanning many cultures conducted by van IJzendoorn and Sagi reported that, although the proportion of children displaying one or another pattern of attachment behaviors may vary in a small number of cases, the overall pattern of results is remarkably consistent with Ainsworth's initial findings and Bowlby's theory (van IJzendoorn & Sagi, 1999, p. 731). The global distribution was found to be 21% type A, 65% type B, and 14% type C, with greater variation within countries than between them.

When Behrens, Hesse, and Main (2007) tried to replicate Miyake's findings with older Japanese children, using the 6th-year parent–child reunion procedure (Main & Cassidy, 1988) and the Adult Attachment Interview (Main, Goldwyn, & Hesse, 2002), they found a distribution of A, B, C categories similar to worldwide norms, but 47% of the children were in category D or unclassifiable. Maternal attachment using their categorization scheme was strongly related to children's attachment in infancy, with securely attached mothers having securely attached children.

One consequence of the view that "sensitive" parenting (especially mothering) is the same for all cultures and all times, however, is that much of human history must then be seen as marked by "epochal derailments" of the attachment system (Grossmann, Grossmann, & Keppler, 2006). According to this view, the history of parental treatment of children is a grim one of "widespread neglect, indifference, maltreatment, sexual abuse and abandonment of infants and children over the ages, particularly during the 18th and early 19th centuries" (Grossmann, 2000, p. 86). It is difficult to reconcile such an account with the notion that attachment has had universal survival value. The possibility should not be ruled out that what seems in hindsight maltreatment of children had functional value in the society of the time. Furthermore, neither the universality of attachment in human relations nor a universal distribution of patterns of attachment behavior excludes the likelihood that attachment develops in specific ways that depend on the cultural niche in which the child has to survive (van IJzendoorn & Sagi, 2001). For example, when attachment researchers offered the "competence hypothesis" that "secure attachment is related to higher competence in dealing with developmental, social, and cultural challenges," they have added that competence has to be defined "in accordance to each specific cultural group" (Grossmann, Grossmann, & Kepler, 2006, p. 83). In the US, for example, maternal sensitivity is associated with children's exploratory response to challenging situations; in Japan it is related to cooperativeness. The proposal is that securely attached children "will grow up to value their parents' values" (p. 83).

Associating maternal sensitivity with infant attachment also tends to construe a dyadic interaction as a one-way influence. Evans and Porter (2009) found that patterns of co-regulated interaction (Fogel & Garvey, 2007) were predictive of attachment outcomes, suggesting that both partners play a role.

Attachment researchers grant that "phenotypic attachment behaviors are bound to have specific characteristics," that is, "Attachment behaviors (e.g., actively seeking proximity or only passively crying when left alone, exuberant or subdued greeting behaviors on reunion, more or less expressed separation anxiety) will differ in distinct cultures and in different epochs depending on differences in customs of child care, family or social structure, devastating or benign living conditions and similar environmental circumstances" (Grossmann & Grossmann, 2005, p. 220). But the different categories of attachment—A, B, C, and D—would themselves seem to be phenotypic forms of the common genotypic attachment system, leaving unanswered the question of whether secure attachment can appropriately be considered optimal for all places and times.

Language development.   At around the same time that children form specific attachments, they speak their first words. Although acquisition of language has been one of the major battlefields on which the nature–nurture controversy has been fought (see Bruner, 1983; Elman et al., 1996; Pinker, 1995, for discussions of the contending viewpoints), consensus is emerging that here too we see the intersection of biology and culture. It is evident that the capacity to acquire language is common to all humans and has a biological basis. This places a lower bound on the evolutionary phase at which hominids acquired this ability, because the last common ancestor in the diverse radiation of human beings across the planet was around 100,000 years ago. The upper bound would be the point at which human evolution split from primate evolution, around 160,000 years ago, because language ability is unique to humans: Attempts to teach apes forms of language that compensate for the anatomical limitations of their vocal apparatus (chiefly sign language) have had only limited success (though the case of Kanzi, an "enculturated" bonobo, is a possible exception; Segerdahl, Fields, & Savage-Rumbaugh, 2006).

Obviously, children acquire the language of the social group and culture in which they live. Children need interaction with competent adult speakers to acquire a language. What is less obvious is the details of how biology and culture work together in the development of the ability for symbolic communication. The earliest psycholinguistic studies focused on syntax (Brown, 1973), but it is now recognized that the pragmatics of language—how utterances are used in context—is equally or more important.

Furthermore, although learning language has often been considered a specific domain of children's development, a compelling argument can be made that language acquisition and socialization should not be considered two separate processes. Ochs and Schieffelin (1984) pointed out, on the basis of research in several societies, that "the primary concern of caregivers is to ensure that their children are able to display and understand behaviors appropriate to social situations. A major means by which this is accomplished is through language" (p. 276). Learning a language and becoming a member of a community are mutually implicative. It is no accident that the infant's first words can generally be understood only by those who share their current situation and have had a history with them: the members of their family. These competent speakers surround the child with the adult form of language, and the acquisition of oral language is woven in this web of social relations and interactions. Parents provide a "dynamically adjusted frame in which infants' communicative capacities may unfold" (Papousek, 2007, p. 259). Language is a product of adult biology as much as infant biology.

Children's first words are prototypical speech acts (proto-imperatives and proto-declaratives; Bates, 1976) that accomplish social actions. Semantically, the first words are "holophrasic," containing a wealth of meaning packed into a single lexical unit, and adults interpret them with attention to setting, gesture, and facial expression. Although children speak only in one-word phrases, adults talk to them in syntactically complex sentences with a large vocabulary, adjusted to the child's comprehension.

As children move from these holistic utterances to differentiated grammatical sequences, phenomena such as over- and under-extension of reference, simplifying phonological strategies, and overgeneralization of grammatical rules show that they actively construct the language they speak, rather than simply copying adult forms or rules.

Adult talk provides conversational resources—metalinguistic directions—sufficient for children to learn new word meanings, and vocabulary acquisition may be better explained by pragmatic factors than by innate constraints on the mapping of words to meaning (Clark, 2007). In many societies, adults deliberately teach vocabulary, along with styles of address and other linguistic features. There are subcultures within the United States (e.g., working-class people in Baltimore; Miller, 1982) in which it is firmly believed that children must be explicitly taught vocabulary, using quite rigid frames of the sort "How do you call this?" (see Schieffelin & Ochs, 1986, for a wide range of examples). However, although the adults involved in such practices may believe that such special tailoring is helpful to their children's language acquisition, the data indicate that significant benefits associated with deliberate teaching of language are found rather rarely and in restricted domains (Snow, 1995).

As speech becomes more complex, the meaning—the semantic content—of children's words develops. The words of the family language, and the ways in which these words are used in everyday contexts, provide children with ready-made templates for the meanings and distinctions that are important in their community. As Brown (1965) phrased it, words are "invitations to form concepts." The meaning of the word "doggie" is not the same at 12 months as at 3 years, and this suggests an important interaction between language and thought. Words inevitably generalize—even the infant applies the word "doggie" to more than one referent—and generalization serves important cognitive functions. If language were a structurally distinct module there would be no particular relation between language and thought. Insofar as culturally organized experience is essential to the acquisition of language, then language, thought, and development are likely to be intimately connected. This is a topic that requires more extensive treatment than we can give it here.

Studies of deaf children reared with both deaf and hearing parents show a normal pattern of early language acquisition, whether the children are (1) monolingual in sign language, (2) bilingual in oral and sign language, or (3) bilingual in two different sign languages. Hearing children reared to sign by deaf parents show the same pattern (Petitto, 2005). An interesting contrast is children born deaf to hearing parents who do not believe that it is useful for their children to sign, insisting instead that they learn to interact through oral language (Goldin-Meadow, 2007; Goldin-Meadow, Butcher, Mylander, & Dodge, 1994). These children are reared in an environment that is rich in culturally mediated social interactions; they lack only the linguistic behavior that fills the gaps between movements and provides accounts of the rationale and prior history of those actions. Under these circumstances children spontaneously begin to employ *home sign*, a kind of communication through gesture which exhibits a number of properties also found in the early stages of natural language acquisition. Children who start signing in the absence of adult signers begin to make two, three, and longer sign sequences around their second birthdays, at about the same time that hearing children create multiword sentences. Moreover, Goldin-Meadow and Mylander (1996) showed that home sign takes very similar forms in very different cultural/linguistic environments: Chinese and American deaf children showed the same patterns of early gesture sentences. These researchers concluded that the development of these gesture systems is "buffered against large variations in environmental conditions and in this sense can be considered 'innate' " (p. 281).

However, the language development of deaf children born to hearing parents who do not sign comes to a halt at this point. Unless such children are provided access to some form of language as a part of the culturally organized environments they participate in, they will not develop the more subtle features of language on which sustainable cultural formations depend. An illustration of this is the way children joining a new school for the deaf in Nicaragua pooled their different home signs to create their own language, which new arrivals made richer and more complex. In only a few years it became as grammatically structured as any natural language (Senghas, Kita, & Ozyürek, 2004).

Such studies demonstrate that the biological predisposition for language operates at a very general level, and in no way depends on the brain mechanisms of hearing or vocalization. One component appears to be a sensitivity to rhythmical and distributed patterning, whether it be verbal or auditory (Petitto, 2005). They also show that the social environment is crucial. Bruner (1982, p. 15) captured the essence of the view that culture plays an essential role in language development when he wrote that the latter cannot be reduced to:

> either the virtuoso cracking of a linguistic code, or the spinoff of ordinary cognitive development, or the gradual takeover of adults' speech by the child through some impossible inductive tour de force. It is rather, a subtle process by which adults artificially arrange the world so that the child can succeed culturally by doing what comes naturally, and with others similarly inclined.

A similar attempt to overcome the long-standing opposition between nature and nurture in explanations of language acquisition is found in "emergentism," the view that language acquisition is a dynamic process, located not in an individual but in a system, a matter of "simple learning mechanisms, operating in and across the human systems for perception, motor-action, and cognition as they are exposed to language data as part of a communicatively-rich human social environment by an organism eager to exploit the functionality of language" (Ellis, 1998, p. 657; Ke & Holland, 2006; MacWhinney, 2006).

The most secure overall generalization about language acquisition is that culturally organized joint activity which incorporates the child into the scene as a novice participant is one necessary ingredient. Conversely, language plays a central role in the process of children's participation in culturally organized activities (Nelson, 2003; Rogoff, 2003). Language bridges gaps in understanding between people, and allows them to coordinate in shared activities. Language acquisition is a bidirectional process in which biology and culture are equally important. But more than this, in acquiring the capacity to speak effectively (knowing not just what to say, but how and when to say it) children are transformed as cultural participants. The sociocultural niche into which a child is born provides the necessary conditions for language to emerge, but as children struggle to understand objects and social relations to gain control over their environments and themselves, they recreate the culture into which they are born, even as they reinvent the language of their forebears. The consequences of this interplay of language and cultural participation for children's psychological functions have only begun to be explored.

Early Childhood: The Role of Culture in Conceptual Development

In contrast to infancy, which is a good candidate for a universally acknowledged stage of development, there is some uncertainty about how one should specify later parts of the lifespan. Whiting and Edwards (1988), following Mead (1935), divide the period between

2½ and 6 years of age, often designated as early childhood, into two parts: 2- to 3-year-olds are referred to as "knee children," who are kept close at hand but not continuously on the mother's lap or in a crib; 4- to 5-year-olds are referred to as "yard children," because they can leave their mothers' sides but are not allowed to wander far. In many modern, industrialized countries, children between 3 and 5 to 6 years of age spend part of every day in an environment designed to prepare them for school, which has led many to call this time of life the preschool period.

The future in the present in early childhood.   With children this age we can find more illustrations of how adults bring the future into the present, shaping children's experiences and future development. Tobin, Hsueh, and Karasawa (2009) conducted a follow-up to their 1985 study of preschool socialization in Hawaii, Japan, and China. They showed recordings of classroom interactions made 20 years ago and today to teachers and other audiences in all three countries, to evoke their interpretations, identify the "informal cultural logic" of preschool education, and consider historical changes in this important institution. In 1985, teachers in Japan, China, and the US had markedly different views about matters such as the appropriate size of a preschool class, the relative importance of character and ability versus effort, when and how a teacher should intervene in conflicts, as well as the degree of acceptable bodily contact among the children and between teacher and child. For instance, where US teachers would intervene in conflicts among children, Japanese teachers considered this inappropriate, for they believed the conflicts provided a valuable opportunity to develop social skills. Twenty years later, the Chinese preschool had changed dramatically. A concern in 1985 with spoiling the child had been replaced by emphasis on promoting independence and creativity, "characteristics needed to succeed in entrepreneurial capitalism" (p. 226). At the same time, concern was growing to ensure that young Chinese do not lack social and moral values. In Japan, after more than a decade of economic difficulties, Tobin and his colleagues found the view that preschools should conserve traditional values, perspectives, and skills. People spoke derisively of modernization. In the US, they found a growing emphasis on academic readiness, accountability, and scientifically based practice. Play-oriented curricula are now out of favor, and there is pressure to credential both teachers and programs. But Tobin, Hsueh, and Karasawa suggest that in each country the implicit cultural logic has not changed, largely because it goes unnoticed. Class size in Japanese preschools remains larger than in the United States, in part because of the implicit cultural value that children need to be socialized to relate to others and their group. In China, the implicit emphasis on mastery and performance is unaltered. In the United States, freedom of choice and individual self-expression are still taken for granted. We can see here again how culture creates an effect conditioned not so much by present necessity as by deep beliefs about "how things work" in adulthood, an effect that may have relatively minor consequences in the present life of the child, but major consequences in the long-term organization of his or her behavior.

The role of biology and culture in children's conceptual development.   In early childhood, children's rapidly increasing facility with language gives researchers new and different opportunities to study their knowledge and reasoning. Piaget proposed, in his early writings, that reasoning at this age is "animistic," failing to make a distinction between biological and nonbiological entities (Piaget, 1937). In his later writings he described this form of reasoning as "preoperational" and "precausal," lacking the ability to reason logically and in particular to provide causal explanations (Piaget, 1969). Contemporary work suggests that young children recognize core ontological distinctions, reason about specific causes in distinct knowledge domains, and have interconnected frameworks of knowledge. Frequently, the domain-specificity of young children's conceptual knowledge and reasoning is taken to imply that such knowledge is innate, but logically these are separate matters (Wellman & Gelman, 1992). Whether "core domains" of knowledge are necessarily based on biological "mental modules," innately specified and developing on a species-wide maturational timetable, as some have suggested, is a matter of widespread scholarly dispute.

Chomsky's proposal that there exists a unique and specialized language-learning faculty (the "language acquisition device" or LAD) remains influential in current thinking about early conceptual development as well as in the domain of language. He considered syntax to be of such complexity, and the environmental input so impoverished, that a child must be born with an innate capacity to learn language (Chomsky, 1986). Fodor (1983) coined the term "mental module" to refer to any "specialized, encapsulated mental organ that has evolved to handle specific information types of particular relevance to the species" (Elman et al., 1996, p. 36). Often mental modules are associated with particular regions of the brain: Broca's area, for example, is taken to be the brain locus of the mental module for language.

If domain-specific knowledge were the outcome of maturation of a mental module, the role of culture would presumably be restricted to speeding up or slowing down the fixed course of development (Carey & Spelke, 1994). But just as Chomsky's linguistic nativism has been countered by those who argue that social relations and adult "input" provide sufficient cues for the child to learn language (as we described in the last section), the explanation of domain-specific conceptual knowledge in terms of mental modules has been countered by those who argue that biological constraints provide only "**skeletal principles**" for conceptual development. These principles serve to bias developing children's attention to relevant features of the domain, but they do not determine knowledge completely; on the contrary, concepts *require* the infusion of cultural input to develop past a rudimentary starting point (Chen & Siegler, 2000; Gelman, 2009; Hatano, 1997). This kind of argument has also been made by those neuroscientists focused on the brain bases of development who refer to themselves as "cultural biologists" (e.g., Quartz & Sejnowksi, 2002). They emphasize that, whatever the phylogenetic constraints on development, specific brain areas are neither entirely dedicated to a single function nor unaffected by environment, so, for example, when there is damage to a specific area of the brain early in life the functions ordinarily located in that area often shift to an entirely different area (Battro, 2000; Stiles et al., 2003).

Reviewing the literature on the development of core, or **privileged domains**, Hatano and Inagaki (2002) argued that if innately specified knowledge is only *skeletal* it is essential to study the ways in which cultural groups organize children's experience to enhance and perhaps, in some cases, to modify the knowledge endowed by evolution. Because children everywhere need to understand physical objects, plants and animals, and other people, researchers have focused a great deal of research on children's naive physics, naive biology, and naive psychology. We will review evidence concerning the development of knowledge in the last two of these areas, to provide examples of how biology and culture "co-construct" adult knowledge.

Naive psychology.   The knowledge-specific domain of naive psychology is often referred to as "folk psychology." In this case, during early childhood, children are said to form a "**theory of mind**"—a capacity "to construe people in terms of their mental states and traits" (Lillard & Skibbe, 2004). An important strategy for testing this idea comes from "false-belief" tasks, where a child is asked about a situation in which a person has beliefs that contradict the facts (Liu, Wellman, Tardif, & Sabbagh, 2008). By the end of the first year of life infants show they can distinguish intentional from non-intentional behavior (Gergely, Egyed & Király, 2007). By the time they are 3, children can engage in deception in collaboration with an adult; that is, they can enter into creation of a false belief (Sullivan & Winner, 1993). Three-year-olds can reason about others' desires, but have difficulty reasoning about others' beliefs (Wellman, 2002). Children subsequently master the ability to reason about false belief and mental representations, and their understanding grows to encompass secondary emotions such as surprise and pride. (See Cole, Cole, & Lightfoot, 2005, for more detailed account of these developments.)

Bloom and German (2000) questioned the validity of the false-belief task as a measure of naive psychology, arguing that other tasks show theory of mind is acquired much earlier, and that children show similar difficulties with tasks that don't require theory of mind. But Wellman, Cross, and Watson (2001) concluded from a meta-analysis that the phenomenon is robust.

Primates seem to have some understanding of the intentional character of others' behavior, and some understanding of mental states. The situation is well described by the title of a recent article in these debates, "Chimpanzees have a theory of mind, the question is, which parts" (Tomasello, Call, & Hare, 2003). For example, socially subordinate chimpanzees attend not just to the presence of a dominant but to what they infer the dominant can see (Hauser, 2005; Tomasello & Carpenter, 2007). But there is no doubt that young children's understanding of other people rapidly outpaces primates. The question that interests us is the role of culture in this process.

Cross-cultural research has explored whether or not theory of mind is a universal developmental phenomenon, impervious to cultural variation in timing. Such a result would be somewhat surprising, because cultures around the world show an enormous variety in the extent and ways that mental states and actions are spoken about and presumably how they are conceived (Lillard, 1998; Vinden, 1998). In terms of sheer number, English is at one extreme of the continuum, possessing more than 5000 emotion words alone. By contrast, the Chewong people of Malaysia are reported to have only five terms to cover the entire range of mental processes, translated as *want, want very much, know, forget, miss or remember* (Howell, 1984). Anthropologists have also reported that in many societies there is a positive avoidance of talking about other people's minds (Paul, 1995).

At present, opinion about cultural variation using locally adapted versions of theory of mind tasks is divided (Lillard & Skibbe, 2004; Liu et al., 2008). In an early study, Avis and Harris (1991) reported that children in rural Cameroon developed the ability to make inference on the basis of other's false beliefs, but in other studies, where people were less likely to talk in terms of psychological states in the head, performance on the theory of mind task was absent or partial (Vinden, 1999, 2002). It is unclear whether performance was poor because people lacked the vocabulary or inclination, or because they could not articulate their intuitive understanding in words.

To avoid the confound of a cultural group's mental vocabulary and performance on false belief tasks, Callaghan et al. (2005) conducted a study that used a minimally verbal procedure where it was unnecessary to use difficult-to-translate words such as belief and emotion. They hid a toy under one of three bowls with two experimenters present. Then one experimenter left and the other induced the child to put the toy under a different bowl before asking the child to point to the bowl the first experimenter would pick up when she returned. Notice that the procedure uses language only at the level of behavior (asking the child to point) with no reference to mental terms, so the prediction that the absent experimenter would look where the toy had been when she left would indicate the ability to think about others' beliefs independent of vocabulary.

Under these conditions a large number of children 2½ to 6 years of age were tested in Canada, India, Samoa, Thailand, and Peru. Performance improved over age, with 4½ to 5 years of age being the point where 50% of the children performed correctly, and 5½ to 6 years of age the point at which all the children responded correctly. Here is a case of careful standardization of a precise procedure conducted in such a way that performance did not depend on the ability to communicate using mental language among people who do not use such terms. A common pattern was found (in line with the modularity view). But note that children were asked to demonstrate only the most skeletal core of their understanding of others, devoid of enrichment by the local vocabulary and without needing to reason about beliefs. In contrast, Vinden (1999) found that, whereas children from a variety of small-scale, low-technology groups in Cameroon and New Guinea were able to understand how belief affects behavior, they had difficulty predicting an emotion based on a false belief.

Using a different task, in which children were asked to explain the bad behavior of a story character, Lillard, Skibbe, Zeljo, and Harlan (2001) found culture, regional, and class differences in whether children attributed the behavior to an internal, psychological trait or to external circumstances. Children in all groups gave both kinds of responses, internal and situational, but the frequency and patterns of use differed. Lillard and her colleagues (2001) make the important point that "cultural differences are usually a matter of degrees, of different patterns and frequencies of behaviors in different cultural contexts" (a view put forward early by Cole, Gay, Glick, & Sharp, 1971). They attribute the results to language socialization practices in the different communities, noting, for example, that low-socioeconomic status (SES) children or rural children are more likely to have parents who make situational attributions of behavior and model this form of interpretation for their children, whereas high-SES/urban parents are more likely to use an internal model of interpretation which they embody in their interactions with their children.

So, it seems that when carefully stripped down versions of false-belief tasks are presented to people of widely different cultural backgrounds, they perform the same, but cultural variations appear when language and explanation are made part of the assessment. This pattern of results supports the idea of Hatano and Inagaki (2002) that development is a combination of "skeletal biological constraints" plus "participation in cultural practice." Both phylogeny and cultural history are necessary contributors to the development of an adult mode of thinking about the thoughts and situations of oneself and others.

There is indeed consistent evidence that young children's understanding of false beliefs is related to their language development (Slade & Ruffman, 2005). Deaf children reared by hearing parents show a language delay (as mentioned above) and also a late understanding of false beliefs. This suggests that coming to understand behavior in terms of beliefs and desires—or whatever the local concepts are—depends on participation in a language community (Perner & Ruffman, 2005). Astington and Baird (2005) suggested that this is because language supports the distinction between what is real and what is hypothetical or counterfactual. But the proposal that language makes possible the capacity for representation of propositional attitudes (de Villiers & de Villiers, 2000) has not been supported by comparison of English- and German-speaking children (Perner, Sprung, Zauner, & Haider, 2003). Understanding of desire preceded understanding belief in both cases, even though the grammatical encoding of these processes was the same in German but different in English.

The notion that theory of mind is based on an innate mental module still has its supporters (e.g., Leslie, 2005). But the evidence for specific brain localization is not compelling (Leekam, Perner, Healey, & Sewell, 2008). Moreover, Ruffman and his colleagues have demonstrated the importance of the family context for theory of mind. Children perform better on theory of mind tasks if they have more siblings (Perner, Ruffman, & Leekam, 1994), older siblings (Ruffman, Perner, Naito, Parkin, & Clements, 1998), and mothers who encourage them to reflect on feelings (Ruffman, Perner, & Parkin, 1999) and who talk about mental states (Ruffman, Slade, & Crowe, 2002) and emotions (Taumoepeau & Ruffman, 2008). In contrast, general parenting style (warmth/sensitivity) is not associated with children's performance on theory of mind tasks, although it is associated with children's cooperative conduct (Ruffman, Slade, Devitt, & Crowe, 2006). It has been proposed that mothers' talk helps to make explicit the child's implicit understanding of other minds (Taumoepeau & Ruffman, 2006, p. 478; 2008, p. 297).

But are psychologists explaining children's naive psychology in the correct terms? "Theory of mind" research assumes (1) that mind is a distinct realm and (2) that young children form theories. On the first point, many philosophers have argued that mind–body dualism is inconsistent and should be avoided. If children are dualists, that is an important and interesting fact (Bloom, 2004; Wellman & Johnson, 2008), but if psychologists are dualists theoretical problems ensue, as we noted in the introduction (cf. Costall & Leudar, 2007; Vygotsky also identified the pressing need to overcome dualism in psychology, 2004). Yet theory-of-mind researchers assume the representational character of the mind: that beliefs, and other mental states, refer to a world outside the mind (Gopnik, 2009). Is this more than a metaphor we in the West live by (Lakoff & Johnson, 1980)?

The idea that young children and even infants understand the world around them in terms of abstract entities ("theory theory," see Gopnik & Wellman, 1994) is challenged by those who see infancy and the start of childhood as a period of situated, embodied understanding and tacit comprehension. According to this view, as we proposed in earlier sections, and as Ruffman's work is suggesting, understanding other people emerges in a history of co-regulated interactions with them (e.g., Fogel & Garvey, 2007). Theory-of-mind research effaces the distinction among different developmental forms of knowledge in ontogenesis (Perner, 2008). It also treats understanding other people as a matter of indifferent cognition, whereas evidence shows that deep-seated emotional systems are involved (Trevarthen, 2005). Our own view is that young children understand other people's actions implicitly, emotionally, and pragmatically before they reason explicitly, using the terms of their local language, about mental states.

Naive biology. A second area of research concerning young children's knowledge and reasoning has focused on the domain of plants and animals. Some have argued that children show "rapid conceptual change" in this domain, others that there is merely "knowledge enrichment"—that is to say, the debate is again over qualitative reorganization versus gradual change. Carey (1985) argued for the former idea, proposing that children do not distinguish the biological from the psychological until as late as age 10. This conclusion would suggest that young children should distinguish plants from animals but not animals from humans. They would have no specifically biological kind of explanation, or distinguish psychological from biological phenomena. Data now exist to disprove all three suggestions.

For example, Inagaki and Hatano (1993) showed that 4- and 5-year-olds distinguish psychological and biological causes, and understand vitalism—that living things have a vital energy—as one among several kinds of biological causation. Their understanding is animistic and personifying this is the result not of confusion between the psychological and biological, but of the children applying their greater knowledge of people to reason by analogy—to make "educated guesses"—about plants and animals. Hatano argued that children's biological knowledge contains an innate "skeletal" component but this skeleton is supplemented by a sociocultural component that varies both between and within cultures. Because children in postindustrial societies have little direct experience of plants and animals, they can only reason by analogy to people. But even a city-dwelling child who has direct experience—for example, taking care of a goldfish—will draw analogies to the familiar animal rather than to humans (Inagaki, 1990). Of course, children in different cultures will gain different kinds of direct experience of animals, a point we will return to below (Waxman & Medin, 2007).

Claims to the contrary notwithstanding, young children's reasoning about biology is not like that of a scientist. Researchers have increasingly come to recognize that scientific biology employs various distinct interpretive frameworks, and that scientific reasoning is not the necessary endpoint of conceptual development. For some time it seemed that, in every human society studied, adults tend to think about plants and animals in terms of taxonomic hierarchies, organized around generic species (e.g., oak and robin, rather than tree and bird) which have a common essence, and reason about the features of these species in teleological terms (Atran, Medin, & Ross, 2004). This way of thinking differs significantly from scientific biology, which considers humans to be animals and deals with interrelated genera, rather than species with distinct essences.

But researchers have now discovered significant variation in the forms of adult reasoning about biological kinds in different cultures. Even if there is a universal way of organizing knowledge about biology (a presumption that now has to be doubted), people from different cultures certainly reason from this organization in systematically different ways. Two distinct ways are now distinguished in the literature. Adults in industrialized societies tend to treat the taxonomic hierarchy as a basis for inference about groups and their shared properties. In contrast, the Yukatek Maya, for example, are primarily concerned with "ecological and morpho-behavioral relationships" and they reason in a "systemic" way (a distinction that has relevance for our discussion of **schooling** below) (Atran et al., 2004). In "ecological thinking," two biological kinds would be included in the same category not because of similar biological characteristics but because of their interrelation in the ecology in which they both live.

Researchers increasingly point out that adults in industrial societies lack both scientific knowledge and detailed folk biological knowledge, so their children's reasoning is likely to be limited as a consequence. One result is growing interest in both children and adults in other cultures. For example, research by Atran and colleagues (2001) showed that, in cultures that value ecological reasoning, young children become able to reason in this way. These researchers suggest that the anthropocentric bias of American children results from lack of familiarity with non-human biological kinds. They compared young Yukatek Maya children (aged 4 to 5) with Maya adults. The task (based on Carey's work) was to infer to what degree a property possessed by a base item would be characteristic of a set of target items. For example, they were shown a picture of a wolf and told "Now there is this stuff called *andro* that is found inside some kinds of things. One kind of thing that has *andro* inside is a wolf. Now I will show you other things and you tell me if you think they have *andro* inside like wolves do." This questioning frame was used with a number of inferential "bases" (human, wolf, bee, goldenrod, water) and a larger number of "target objects" from each of the taxonomic categories represented by the bases (for example, raccoon, eagle, rock) to see if the child or adult would reason that "andro" would also be found in the target object. The Maya adults decreased their inductions from humans to other living kinds and then to non-living kinds, following the pattern predicted by standard biological taxonomies. But when "bee" was the base they often inferred that properties would be shared not only with other invertebrates, but also with trees and humans. Atran et al. interpreted this pattern of inference as based on ecological reasoning: Bees build their nests in trees, and bees are sought after by humans for their honey. The participants often explicitly used such ecological justifications in their responses. Most importantly, the young Maya children's responses were very similar to those of the adults. Whatever the base concept, inductive inferences decreased as the target moved from mammals to trees. And, like the adults, the children showed no indication of anthropomorphism: Inferences from humans did not differ from inferences from animals or trees, and the Mayan children did not appear to favor humans as a basis of inference. They did not interpret the biological world anthropocentrically. This evidence highlights the importance of culturally organized experience in the development of inferences in the domain of biology, supporting the conclusion that the anthropocentric bias observed with urban American children reflects their lack of intimate contact with plants and animals.

Citing these and a variety of other studies using historical as well as experimental data, Medin, Ross, and Cox (2006) arrived at the conclusion that over the past 200 years there has been decreased knowledge of, and decreased ability to reason about, the natural world among the increasingly urbanized, schooled populations of the world. In short, with respect to understanding the environment, it is the culturally "less developed" people who are cognitively more sophisticated. Further work by Atran, Ross, Medin, and their colleagues, designed, in their terms, to tease apart the contributions of culture and experience, will be described below when we turn to middle childhood.

In short, neither Piaget's acultural account of reasoning in early childhood nor its explanation in terms of innate mental modules is fully adequate. Young children seem more capable in their reasoning about biological kinds than Piaget recognized. In fact, the research that has been conducted with young children whose culture brings them into close, everyday, practical contact with plants and animals shows that they are capable of sophisticated ecological reasoning. The findings of less advanced reasoning with children in urban, technologically dependent settings seem to reflect their lack of experience, the "devolution" of knowledge (Atran, Medin, & Ross, 2004; Wolff & Medin, 2001), rather than innate or universal abilities (but cf. Ergazaki & Andriotou, 2010). What is innate, if anything, is still unclear.

The studies we have reviewed are informative, but they raise important methodological questions. Frequently, language is used as though it were a transparent medium of communication. For example, Coley (1995) asked young children to name drawings of animals. When the name was "correct" they were told so; when not he provided the "correct label." Then he asked questions ("Can Xs think?") that required only a yes/no answer. Such a procedure offers children little opportunity to articulate their understanding of an animal name, and actually discards useful information about their concepts that is contained in their "incorrect" names.

Consequently, when Medin and Atran (2004, p. 966) suggest that "many different people, observing many different exemplars of dog under varying conditions of exposure to those exemplars, may nonetheless generate more or less the same concept of *dog*" (we have doubts: A child who is familiar with a dog as the family pet is unlikely to form the same concept as one for whom a dog is trained to herd or hunt, or guard the house, or fight).

A further limitation of many studies is that they consider the child largely in isolation, rather than as a participant in cultural practices. Atran, Medin, and colleagues do consider the degree of exposure to animals children have in different societies, but they do not consider the qualitative differences in contact. Children in the United States are likely to have household pets that are spoken to and treated as having personalities, beliefs, and desires. Their other main contact with animals is likely to be in the form of cuts of beef and chicken, purchased at the store. Maya children are likely to be surrounded by domestic animals whose rearing they will participate in, and wild animals which the family may hunt, or venerate. Categorization of animals is a social practice—or system of practices—before it is an individual cognitive scheme.

Middle Childhood: Apprenticeship in Adult Skills

One of the most pervasive changes in the cultural organization of children's lives is the new social arrangements that adults make for their children when they reach 5 to 7 years of age (Rogoff, 2003; Sameroff & Haith, 1996). Across all societies children are expected to stop playing childish games, start learning skills that will be essential to them when they grow up, and to be held accountable if they fail to live up to adult expectations. For example (Read, 1960), among the Ngoni of Malawi in Central Africa (when Read lived there several decades ago), the boys must leave the protection of their home and move into dormitories where they must submit to male authority and begin to engage in at least rudimentary forms of adult work. Read described the effects of this abrupt change by writing that "From having been impudent, well fed, self-confident, and spoiled youngsters among the women many of them quickly became skinny, scruffy, subdued, and had a hunted expression" (1960, p. 49). The Ifaluk of Micronesia identify this age as the time when children acquire "social intelligence," which includes the acquisition of important cultural knowledge and skills, as well as the ability to work, to adhere to social norms, and to demonstrate compassion for others—all valued adult behaviors (Lutz, 1987). In Western Europe and the United States, this same transition has long been considered the advent of the "age of reason" (White, 1996).

This ubiquitous change in parental expectations of, and arrangements for, their children has a corresponding set of changes in biological, behavioral, and social characteristics of children that illustrate clearly the idea of a major bio-social-behavioral shift, specifics of which depend on cultural circumstances. Especially notable in the biological realm are changes in the organization of brain functioning, dexterity and coordination, and physical strength (Bogin, 2009; Janowsky & Carper, 1995; Luria, 1973).

In virtually every country in the modern world, the most striking change in the organization of children's activities is that they begin to attend formal schools. Although schooling has a long history, and its forms have changed over many centuries, the dominant form of schooling adopted currently around the world is based on a European model that evolved in the nineteenth century and followed conquering European armies into other parts of the world. Serpell and Hatano (1997) have dubbed this form of education "institutionalized public basic schooling" (IPBS) (see LeVine, LeVine, & Schnell, 2001; Serpell & Hatano, 1997, for a more extensive treatment of the evolution of formal schooling).

At present, IPBS is an ideal if not a reality all over the world (the Islamic world providing one alternative in favor of adherence to religious/social laws, as written in the Qur'an—a word that means "recitation" in Arabic). This "Western-style" approach operates in the service of the secular state, economic development, the bureaucratic structures through which rationalization of this process is attempted, and exists as a pervasive fact of contemporary life. According to a survey published by UNESCO (2009), there are large disparities among regions in the level of education achieved, varying from almost 100% high school graduation in some industrialized countries to countries in which many children complete few, if any, years of schooling. Nonetheless, experience of IPBS has become a pervasive fact of life the world over.

When we contrast the experiences of children who spend several hours a day, 5 days a week, attending formal schools where literacy and numeracy form the core of the curriculum with comparable children who remain at home helping their mothers with cooking, child care, or gardening, or who accompany their fathers into the fields or forests to assist in farming, hunting, or making mortar bricks with which to build houses, certain prominent characteristics of the classroom experience stand out quite clearly (Cole, 2006; Gaskins, 2000; Serpell & Hatano, 1997).

1. The settings in which schooling occurs are distinctive in that they are removed from contexts of practical activity. Students are trained in the use of mediational means such as writing and provided with dense exposure to the conceptual content of various cultural domains, which are supposed to provide the means to later productive activity.
2. There is a peculiar social structure to formal schooling, in which a single adult interacts with many (often as many as 40 or 50, sometimes as many as 400) children at a

time. Unlike most other settings for socialization, this adult is unlikely to have any familial ties to the learner, rendering the social relationships relatively impersonal. This structure defines abstract positions of "teacher" and "student" to which children must adapt (Packer, 2001a, 2001b).

3. There is a distinctive value system associated with schooling that sets educated people above their peers and that, in secular education, values change and discontinuity over tradition and community. One ubiquitous feature of schooling is the "sorting" of children in terms of this system (Packer, in press; Varenne & McDermott, 1999).

4. There is a special mediational skill, writing, that is essential to the activity of schooling. Writing is used to represent both language and non-verbal systems (e.g., mathematics).

5. On-the-spot assistance is considered inappropriate, in sharp contrast with learning/ teaching interactions in many other contexts, and emphasis is placed on learning as an individual achievement (Serpell & Hatano, 1997).

6. All these factors taken together result in a situation in which language is used in distinctive ways. Perhaps the best documented example of this is the pattern of interaction in which teachers ask children to answer questions, the answers to which the teachers already know (Mehan, 1978).

This characterization of the distinctive nature of the activity settings associated with formal schooling does not do justice to all the differences between formal schooling and other socialization settings that might be considered educational in the broad sense. (For more extended discussions see Greenfield & Lave, 1982; Schliemann, Carraher, & Ceci, 1997.) However, it is sufficient to see that cultural discontinuities occurring during middle childhood present an especially attractive proving ground for testing theories about culture and cognitive development (for reviews see Berry, Poortinga, Segall, & Dasen, 2002; Gardiner & Kosmitzki, 2007).

From the many specific developmental phenomena that might be chosen for illustration, we discuss four here: the development of logical operations, memory, the ability to analyze language, and induction based on classification. Each of these psychological processes is the object of a great deal of traditional pedagogical research, and it seems plausible to believe that the many thousands of hours of instruction children experience during middle childhood should be a powerful cultural influence on their development.

Schooling and the development of logical operations.   For purposes of discussion, the logical operations in question are those that form the basis for Piagetian theory, within which it is assumed that concrete operations consist of organized systems (classifications, serial ordering, correspondences) that allow children to think through the consequences of an action (such as pouring water from one pitcher into another) and mentally to reverse that action. However, such operations remain limited in the sense that they proceed from one partial link to the next in a step-by-step fashion, without relating each partial link to all the others, and they must be carried out on actual objects. Formal operations, which Piaget hypothesized to arise in adolescence, differ in that all the possible combinations are considered, they can be carried out without reference to actual objects, and each partial link is grouped in relation to a "structured whole" (Inhelder & Piaget, 1958).

Early in his career, Piaget believed that there would be large cultural differences in cognitive development associated with the difference between primitive and technologically advanced societies (Piaget 1928/1995). However, when he began to address the issue of cultural variations and cognitive development in the 1960s he assumed that the sequence of cognitive changes that he had observed in Geneva was universal, and he restricted his attention to various factors that might modify the rate at which children progressed (Piaget, 1973). The key factor was the amount of operational exercise, the constant interplay of assimilation and accommodation that drives the system to higher, more inclusive, levels of equilibration. Some societies, he speculated, might provide greater opportunities for operational exercise by helping children to confront and think about their environment with greater frequency. However, he was dubious about the extent to which schooling actually accomplished this task because the authority structure of the classroom resulted in accommodation markedly exceeding assimilation, thus hindering equilibration.

Although it would seem that cross-cultural comparisons involving children who had and had not been to school should be well suited to testing Piaget's hypotheses, the history of this line of research has proved as much a cautionary tale about the difficulties of cross-cultural research. The difficulties confronting researchers are well illustrated by studies initiated by Greenfield and Bruner (Greenfield, 1966; Greenfield & Bruner, 1969). Working in rural Senegal, Greenfield and Bruner observed the steady development of conservation among schooled children and its absence among about half of the non-educated adults, leading them to speculate that schooling might actually be necessary for the development of concrete operations. This kind of result was picked up by Hallpike (1979), who claimed that adults in nonliterate societies, as a rule, fail to develop beyond preoperational thought (a conclusion hotly denied by, among others, Jahoda, 1993).

The crucial ambiguity in this research is similar to that which we have already encountered in the work on attachment: When a social context representing a test situation with particular meanings in one cultural system is imported into another, how do we know that the participants have understood the task in the way the experimenter intended so that the results are comparable? For at least some of the research on schooling and the development of concrete operations in which unschooled children fail, results point clearly to the conclusion that the individuals who failed to conserve also failed to enter into the framework of the problem as intended by the experimenter, although they complied in a surface way with instructions. Thus, for example, in the study by Greenfield (1966) among the Wolof of Senegal, it appeared that, unless children attended school, many failed to achieve conservation of volume. However, in a follow-up study, Irvine (1978) asked children to play the role of an informant whose task it was to clarify for the experimenter the meaning of the Wolof terms for equivalence and resemblance. In their role as "participant," these individuals gave non-conserving responses when liquid was poured from one beaker into another. However, in their role as "linguistic informants," they indicated that, although the water in one beaker had increased as a result of pouring, the amounts were the same (using different vocabulary to make the appropriate distinctions). Greenfield's own research also pointed to interpretational factors that interfere with conservation judgments; when she permitted Wolof children to pour water themselves, conservation comprehension improved markedly. Greenfield (2004) currently argues for differential interpretation of the tasks associated with different discourse modes and familiarity with task contents as the explanation of differential performance.

Two additional lines of evidence support the conclusion that problems in interpreting the Piagetian interview situation, not a failure to develop concrete operations, account for cases in which cultures appear to differ. First, Siegal (1991) demonstrated that even 4- to 5-year-old children display an understanding of conservation principles but misunderstand what is being asked of them by the experimenter. Second, in a number of instances no differences between the conservation performance of schooled and unschooled children from developing countries have been observed when the experimenter was a member of the cultural group in question (Kamara & Easley, 1977; Nyiti, 1978). Although some ambiguities remain in this research, it appears most sensible to conclude that concrete operational thinking is not influenced by schooling; what is influenced by schooling is people's ability to understand the language of testing and the presuppositions of the testing situation itself.[5]

Schooling and memory. The basic expectation underlying research on culture and memory is quite different from that of work on logical operations. At least since the time of Plato, there have been speculations that acquisition of literacy (which, in most circumstances, occurs in school) could actually decrease powers of memory because people could always return to their store of written materials to recall information relevant to the issues at hand (see Cole & Scribner, 1977, for a review of theoretical approaches). Early empirical work was conducted on adults and did not involve schooling as a variable. Nadel (1937), for example, compared recall of a story constructed to be familiar in form and general content to members of two Nigerian groups, the Yoruba and the Nupe. On the basis of prior ethnographic analysis, Nadel predicted that the Yoruba would emphasize the logical structure of the story, whereas the Nupe would emphasize circumstantial facts and details because these two emphases fit their dominant sociocultural tendencies and associated schemes. His results confirmed his expectations, as did a follow-up study many years later by Deregowski (1970).

Research that has contrasted schooled and unschooled people of different ages has found marked effects on performance of the materials to be remembered and specifics of the task used for assessment on memory performance. Clearly, schooling confronts children with specialized information-processing tasks such as committing large amounts of esoteric information to memory in a short time and producing lengthy written discourses on the basis of memorized information. These, and similar tasks that are a routine part of schooling, have few analogies in the lives of people from societies in which there is no formal schooling. Hence, it is only to be expected that, when confronted with such tasks, which carry within them highly specialized histories and associated practices, there would be marked differences in performance—and there are. In line with these expectations, a number of studies show that schooling promotes the ability to remember unrelated materials (Rogoff, 1981; Wagner, 1982). For example, when a list of common items that fall into culturally recognized categories is presented repeatedly to children who are asked to recall as many of them as possible in any order, those children who have completed 6 or more years of schooling remember more and cluster items in recall more than nonschooled comparison groups (Cole et al., 1971; Scribner & Cole, 1981). By contrast, **schooling effects** are generally absent in tests of recall of well-structured stories or when the materials are embedded in a locally meaningful task (Dash & Mishra, 1989; Mandler, Scribner, Cole, & de Forest, 1980; Rogoff & Waddell, 1982).

Thinking about language. As we pointed out above, schooling involves special ways of using language, both in the forms of oral discourse and in its constant mediation through written language. Several studies that speak to the issue of the consequences of schooling provide evidence that literacy in the context of schooling creates lasting effects on the development of knowledge about spoken language and even of differences in the brain morphology of people who have or have not been to school (Ardila, Roselli, & Rosas, 1989; Bornstein, Arterberry, & Mash, 2010; Castro-Caldes, 2004; Ostrosky-Solís, Ramirez, &

---

[5] The cross-cultural evidence is unclear with respect to the universality of formal operations, which are not expected until adolescence. Generally speaking, when Piagetian tasks have been used to measure formal operations, developing peoples who have not attended school fail, and even those who have attended several years of formal schooling rarely display formal operations (see Berry, Poortinga, Segall, & Dasen, 1992, for a review and additional sources). However, the same result has been claimed for US college students, although the matter is under dispute, and the question of the necessary and sufficient conditions for displaying formal logic remains open (see Cole, Cole, & Lightfoot, 2005, for a review of the issues and relevant data).

Ardila, 2004). Collectively, these studies have involved a variety of populations ranging from cases of cultural practices in a Portuguese study where older girls were kept at home while second-borns went to school and were tested decades later, to cross-sectional studies of adults who had experienced various of levels of education and come from different parts of the same country. Results of these studies have lead Castro-Caldes to conclude that it is possible to identify brain structures that correspond to the functions of reading and writing, both from functional and anatomical points of view. Note that every one of these effects is specific to analysis of oral language. No evidence of generalized brain changes for problem solving in general or even of different forms of language use associated with schooling have been reported.[6]

Inductions based on classification. In a well-known series of studies conducted in Central Asia in the early 1930s, Alexander Luria reported an increased likelihood of people (many as young adults) who had attended school categorizing objects taxonomically (given the items hoe, axe, and wood, hoe and axe go together as tools) rather than functionally (axe and wood go together because you cut the wood with an axe). This finding was replicated by Cole and his colleagues, who confirmed that unschooled adults did not lack vocabulary corresponding to the relevant taxonomic categories and that their use of such taxonomic categories was manifested in a variety of experimental conditions, appearing to make Luria's results task-specific (Cole et al., 1971).

That schooling alone could account for differences in experimental categorization tasks has been cast into doubt by Li, Zhang, and Nisbett (2004), who report that college students at Beijing University were most likely to carry out such categorization functionally, like Luria's peasants. Something more, or something else, is involved in the performance changes that Luria attributed to cultural-historical progress and schooling, but it remains unclear what those "somethings" might be.

Other recent cross-cultural research raises further questions about categorization. In a series of studies Ross and his colleagues compared the development of inductive reasoning about biological kinds among rural Menominee Native Americans, Anglo-American children living in a town in the same rural area, and Anglo counterparts living in a large city (Ross, Medin, Coley, & Atran, 2003). They report that, whereas all but the youngest city-dwelling Anglo children showed an appreciation of biological categories and the similarities among them, the rural children, including the Menominee rural children, showed a form of the ecological thinking we described earlier. This ecological thinking was present among the rural Anglo children, although in weaker form, but did not appear even among the oldest urban children.

In summary, school-aged children from indigenous communities, like the younger children we described in the last section, are capable of ecological reasoning. Where Luria considered this a less advanced kind of reasoning that schooling would, and should, replace with taxo-nomic reasoning, we propose that these are two distinct reasoning styles, each relevant in the appropriate situation. Ecological reasoning, however, is likely to clash with treatments of biology in the classroom, for these tend to start with model species and build gradually to a systems perspective, and often introduce ecosystems without reference to humans (Bang, Medin, & Atran, 2007).

Cross-generational studies of schooling effects. The most convincing evidence for a generalized impact of schooling on development comes not from cross-sectional experimental

---

[6] It is also relevant that Scribner and Cole (1981) provided evidence of increased ability to analyze language among Vai adults who had become literate without attending school. Their results reinforce the view that cultural influences on the development of particular psychological functions are specific to the practices involved.

studies of cognition, but from studies of the intergenerational effect of schooling on parenting practices of mothers and the effect of these practices on subsequent generations. LeVine and his colleagues have provided convincing evidence of the cognitive and social consequences of schooling. These researchers focused on the ways in which formal schooling changes the behavior of mothers toward their offspring and their interactions with people in modern, bureaucratic institutions, as well as the subsequent impacts on their children (LeVine & LeVine, 2001; LeVine et al., 2001). These researchers propose a set of plausible habits, preferences, and skills that children acquire in school which they retain into adulthood and apply in the course of rearing their own children. These changes in parenting behavior include, in addition to use of rudimentary literacy and numeracy skills:

1. discourse skills that involved using written texts for purposes of understanding and using oral communication that is directly relevant to the negotiation of interactions in health and educational settings involving their children
2. models of teaching and learning based on the scripted activities and authority structures of schooling, such that when in subordinate positions schooled women adopt and employ behaviors appropriate to the student role and, when in superordinate positions adopt behaviors appropriate to the teacher role
3. an ability and willingness to acquire and accept information from the mass media, such as following health prescriptions more obediently.

As a consequence of these changes in the maternal behavior of young women who have attended at least through elementary school, LeVine and his colleagues find that the children of such women experience a lower level of infant mortality, better health during childhood, and greater academic achievement. Hence, if schooling may or may not produce measurable, generalized, cognitive affects at the time, such experience does produce context-specific changes in behavior that have quite general consequences with respect to the task of childrearing, which in turn produces general consequences in the next generation.

Converging evidence of a different kind comes from the work of Correa-Chávez and Rogoff (2009) on changes in children's tendency to learn from closely observing the behavior of their parents carrying out tasks they will be expected to deal with in the future. The tendency to learn effectively by close observation decreased as the level of mother's education increased.

Casting this broader research net indicates that new forms of activity involved in schooling engender not only new, restricted cognitive "tricks of the literate trade" but a more general elaboration of various verbal skills and a "modernist" ideology associated with schooling and modern work that structures the enculturation environment of subsequent generations. It also indicates that some effective ways of learning decrease as an effect of maternal education. In effect, research on the cognitive consequences of education teaches us something about our own cultural practices that should make us more cautious in our claims about the cognitive benefits of schooling, independent of the value we place on the specific abilities that children acquire there and the modes of life made possible and more sensitive to indirect effects associated with generational change.

From Childhood to Adulthood: A Site for Examining the Idea of Developmental Stages

In common parlance, adolescence is so routinely treated as a clearly marked period of development that it is rarely remembered that when Hall (1904) launched the modern study of adolescence over a century ago, he referred to an age period in the life cycle that spanned the ages from 14 to 25 years. At the present time, although it is common to encounter claims of a new period of life that spans all or part of the years that Hall identified as adolescence, there is widespread disagreement on whether those years mark a distinct period of development or a more or less protracted transition to adulthood, which has itself been subjected to extensive changes in definition and periodization in terms of chronological age (Johnson-Hanks, 2002).

For many decades, scholarly interest in the time period identified by Hall as adolescence (a term that came into English from French and Latin, referring to "a youth between childhood and manhood" [sic] Oxford English Dictionary, Second Electronic Edition, 1989) has focused only on the earlier years in Hall's proposed age period, roughly from 13 to 18, so that "teenager" and "adolescent" became virtually synonymous terms. In 1970, Keniston claimed that new socioeconomic circumstances, at least for the educated elite in advanced industrialized countries, justified the addition of a "new" stage of development, "youth" (ages 18 to 25), between adolescence as it was then understood and adulthood. A decade later the period now accepted as adolescence was further subdivided into early and late "sub-stages" with the inauguration of The Journal of Early Adolescence, which focused on the age roughly from 12 to 14 on the grounds that its developmental processes were distinct from those of later adolescence. Later still, the period that Keniston identified as youth was renamed "emerging adulthood," defined by Arnett (1998, p. 312) as "a period of development bridging adolescence and young adulthood, during which young people are no longer adolescents but have not yet attained full adult status." This specification is quite similar to the way that adolescence had been treated as a period bridging childhood and adulthood in earlier eras. Arnett attributed the emergence of this stage to political, economic, and social changes occurring primarily in societies that have undergone a change from industrial to informationbased economies, and characterized it as "the age of instability, the self-focused age, the age of feeling in between, the age of possibilities" (Arnett, 2007, p. 208).

During this same period, adulthood, which had traditionally been treated as qualitatively different from both old age and childhood, itself began to be redefined. Social commentators began to talk about a "Third Age" of adulthood, the years from 50 to 74 years:

> Old age is what you make of it. Science has underscored this message by, for example, announcing that grey cells also reproduce themselves in old age, but only if the brain is kept fit. The threat of senility can be countered. Important muscles can, within one or two years, be trained to reach the capacity of those of middle-aged people. In sum, a high quality of life during one's "third age" is not only a gift. It is also one's duty—a duty that consists of exercise, healthy foods, education, and enriching social networks. Those who have neither money nor the motivation to work on themselves, fail. (Greenberg & Muehlebach, 2006, p. 195)

These changing conceptions of "the transition to adulthood" highlight in particularly clear form the interplay of biological and cultural–historical factors in the constitution and interpretation of "stages" of ontogenetic development, because all the proposed stages display cultural and historical variation in the way they are manifested and organized in different societies at different times.

Stages or transitions? Single or multiple?   The stage-versus-transition discussion is important not only because cultural factors are clearly involved in its specification but also because it speaks to the basic question of the existence of, and sources of, discontinuity in development. As ordinarily used by psychologists, the terms "transition" and "stage" are not synonymous. A *stage* is a more or less stable, patterned, and enduring system of interactions between the organism and the environment; a *transition* is a period of flux, when the "ensemble of the whole" that makes up one stage has disintegrated and a new stage is not firmly in place. According to this set of ideas, can adolescence, youth, emerging adulthood,

adulthood and so on be considered stages, even in societies that give them a name and treat them as distinct? Or are they best considered, despite popular understanding, heterogeneous, contingent transitions, whose "stage-like-ness" is itself a cultural construction?

The cultural contingency of adolescence as part of the life cycle. Adolescence is an advantageous point at which to investigate such questions because what is indisputable is that some time near or following the end of a decade of life (the exact onset time depends greatly on nutritional and other factors), a cascade of biochemical events begins that will alter the size, the shape, and the functioning of the human body. The most visible manifestations of these changes are a marked growth spurt and development of the potential for individuals to engage in biological reproduction (Bogin, 2009; Gordon & Laufer, 2005). These biological changes have profound social implications for the simple reason that reproduction cannot be accomplished by a single human being (replaying, in inverted form, the social dependency of infancy). As their reproductive organs reach maturity, boys and girls begin to engage in new forms of social behavior because they begin to find such activity attractive. According to many psychologists, some combination of these biological changes in brain and changes in sociocultural circumstances also gives rise to new cognitive capacities (Nasir, 2005; Tamnes et al., 2010).

The evidence from phylogeny and cultural history. Arguments for the universality of adolescence are sometimes made on the basis of studies of the fossil record in the hominid line, and sometimes on the basis of similarities to non-human primates, often chimpanzees (Bogin, 2009; Leigh, 2004). On the basis of an examination of the fossil record available in the prior edition of this book, Bogin concluded that the emergence of a distinctive stage of life between childhood and adulthood occurred with the evolution of *Homo sapiens* from *Homo erectus*, approximately 125,000 years ago. Bogin argued (1999, p. 216) that "adolescence became a part of human life history because it conferred significant reproductive advantages to our species, in part by allowing the adolescent to learn and practice adult economic, social, and sexual behavior before reproducing." Bogin (2009) now argues that there is no event corresponding to the adolescent growth spurt among chimpanzees, so that adolescence is a peculiarly human part of the life cycle. Others argue that changes associated with sexual maturation and altered social behavior (decreased association of males with their mothers and increased association with older males, decreased play of both sexes with juveniles, and increased aggressive behaviors) point toward the presence of adolescence among chimpanzees (King, Weiss, & Sisco, 2008; Ross, Bloomsmith, Bettinger & Wagner, 2009), so the issue is probably best considered uncertain.

Schlegel and Barry (1991), focusing on variation across human societies, side with those who believe in the presence of adolescence among non-human primates as a starting point for their claim of adolescence as a universal stage of development among humans. They go on to provide data from a sample of 186 societies included in the Human Area Files to substantiate claims that a socially marked period of adolescence is a human universal. Consistent with this line of reasoning, Bloch and Niederhoffer (1958) suggested that one of the universal features shared by the notion of a "transition to adulthood" and "adolescence" is a struggle for adult status. In all societies, the old eventually give way to the young. It is not easy for those in power to give it up, so it is natural to expect that, to some degree, the granting of adult status, and with it adult power, will involve a struggle. A good candidate for a second universal feature of the transition from childhood to adulthood is that it arouses tension because children, who have long identified strongly with members of their own gender while avoiding contact with the opposite gender, must now become attached to a member of the opposite gender (or a member of the same gender, which causes a different set of tensions). But if such evidence is sufficient to indicate a period of transition in which individuals from different generations must readjust their relations with each other, it does not indicate the presence of a distinct stage, as this term is generally used.

Sometimes the argument for the universality of adolescence as a stage of development is based on historical evidence, such as Aristotle's characterization of the young as prone to sexuality, lack of self-restraint, and insolence (cited in Kiell, 1964, pp. 18–19). Combining such historical evidence with similar accounts from various non-industrialized societies around the world today, Schlegel (2008) asserted that the experience of adolescence is universal. However, the data supporting the universality of adolescence as a unified stage are by no means unequivocal.

First, reverting to the primate literature, it is striking that marked shifts in social behavior are reported more frequently for males than for females. The same appears true when we turn to Aristotle's description of adolescents and similar descriptions from other ancient societies (Kiell, 1964): The people being talked about were most often males. Moreover, they were urban males of the moneyed classes who had to undergo a period of extended training, often including formal schooling, which created a delay between puberty and full adult status. Generally speaking, women and most members of the lower classes did not undergo such specialized training, and there is a corresponding lack of evidence that they were included in the category of adolescents. Among the upper classes in Athens, for example, girls were often married and sent to live in their mother-in-law's house before they had gone through puberty, and did not undergo institutionalized formal training to be considered adults.

Moreover, although some of the evidence from other cultures may support the idea that adult status universally brings with it new responsibilities, anxieties, and uncertainty, there is equally strong evidence that adolescence, as the term is used in modern industrialized societies, exists only under particular cultural circumstances, that when it exists it is more a transition accomplished by a variety of means at a variety of ages than a stage, and that it is not necessarily accompanied by the kind of conflict and anxiety said to exist in modern, industrialized societies (Johnson-Hanks, 2002; Whiting, Burbank, & Ratner, 1986). When we consider the actual organization of life in ancient Greece, Europe in the middle ages, and contemporary non-industrialized societies, in terms of the role of culture in development, we are reminded that the process of biological reproduction by itself is insufficient for the continuation of our species. As indicated by Schlegel and others who argue for the universality of adolescence among humans, any biological factors must be complemented by the process of cultural reproduction (education, broadly conceived), which ensures that the designs for living evolved by the group will be inherited by the next generation. Accordingly, in our view, adolescence will exist as a distinctive period of life only under specific cultural or historical circumstances. For example, among the Inuit of the Canadian Arctic in the early twentieth century, special terms were used to refer to boys and girls when they entered puberty, but these terms did not coincide with Western notions of adolescence (Condon, 1987). Young women were considered fully grown (adult) at menarche, a change in status marked by the fact that they were likely to be married and ready to start bearing children within a few years. Young men were not considered fully grown until they were able to build a snow house and hunt large game unassisted. This feat might occur shortly after the onset of puberty, but it was more likely for boys to achieve adult status somewhat later because they had to prove first that they could support themselves and their families. In view of the different life circumstances of these people, it is not surprising that they developed no special concept corresponding to adolescence that applied to boys and girls alike; such a concept did not correspond to their reality.

Closer to the present is the example of the Aka of the rainforests of the Central African Republic and the Northern Congo. The Aka live in bands of 25–35 and engage in hunting which is carried out by entire families. As reported by Bentz (2001), teenagers spend most of their days in the presence of their parents. They are extremely close to their siblings and peers, living in what Bentz refers to as an intense intimacy, closeness, and bonds of tenderness and affection. Aka girls build their own houses when they are 9 to 10 years old, often at the first signs of puberty but well before they are likely to bear children, whereas the boys move into what Bentz refers to as a "bachelor's pad." Girls may begin to engage in sexual activity at this time, but when and who they marry is a matter for them to decide, sometimes earlier, sometimes later. They may or may not take their parents' advice on a suitable husband, as they choose. The result of these arrangements, in which male and female cooperate in both hunting and child care, is, according to Bentz, a pattern that combines characteristics that appear antithetical when viewed from a North American perspective. There is clearly a period of transition between childhood and adulthood, but it results not in conflict between autonomy and closeness to one's parents, nor in alienation between generations, but in additional autonomy within the family unit combined with closeness to peers and minimal levels of conflict. In this society it appears that adolescence is more a process of transition than a stage marked off from those that proceed and follow it.

Societies in which technology and an extended period of formal education are absent may still produce conditions in which adolescence exists as a stage, either for males or for females. Such an example is provided by the Ache, a forest-dwelling, hunter-gatherer group in Paraguay (Hill & Hurtado, 1996). Until they came in contact with modern cultural institutions, the Ache lived in small groups and moved so frequently that they did not set up permanent settlements in the forest. At the age of 9 or 10, before reaching menarche, roughly 85% of Ache females had experienced sexual intercourse with at least one adult male, and many married before puberty. Nevertheless, Hill and Hurtado report that even at such a young age "their behavior would be aggressively flirtatious but sexually coy to the point of causing frustration anxiety among most of their suitors . . . The major activity of girls at this time is walking around in small groups laughing and giggling and carrying on in any manner that will attract attention" (p. 225). Boys, who went through puberty later than girls, exhibited behaviors reminiscent of Western teenage boys: "In particular, males of this age appear extremely insecure and often engage in obnoxious or high-risk behavior in order to gain attention" (Hill & Hurtado, p. 226).

Our conclusion is that although the biological changes associated with the ability to reproduce are universal, there is enormous variability in the extent to which the transition to adulthood can be considered a stage in the accepted sense of that term. Among human beings, the capacities for biological and cultural reproduction are intertwined in ways that continue to defy simple generalizations.

Adolescents/youth in periods of rapid social change. A related issue of particular contemporary concern is the impact of rapid social change on the specification of developmental periods, particularly under conditions of extensive inter-cultural contact marked by economic and political inequality. Chandler and his colleagues (Chandler, Lalonde, Sokol, & Hallett, 2003; Chandler & Proulx, 2006) documented the cause for such concerns in their study of suicide among 15- to 24-year-old First Nations young people in British Columbia, Canada. For the period from 1987 to 1992 the suicide rate among First Nations adolescents/ youth was five times greater than that for all other ethnic groups combined. Chandler and his colleagues argued that First Nations young people are especially at risk for suicide due to a number of repressive policies pursued by the government, which have deprived them of their land, their fishing rights, their language, their right to self-governance, and control over their own cultural institutions. Combined with poor educational facilities and job discrimination, these conditions could, indeed, produce a sense of hopelessness at a time of life when, according to the normative characterization of adolescence and emerging adulthood in most textbooks, it should be a period of adult identity formation. Chandler and his colleagues hypothesized that the exceedingly high suicide rates among this population were the result, in part, of a failure to solve the problem of self-continuity (the understanding of oneself as the same person through time despite obvious changes in size, appearance, and knowledge). They used comic book renditions of classical stories in which people went through marked changes during their lifetime, such as Scrooge in Dickens' *A Christmas Carol*, and asked their participants to talk about their own sense of self-continuity. They found that European-origin adolescents were likely to explain self-continuity over time as the result of some essential feature such as their fingerprint or DNA. By contrast, First Nations adolescents provided narratives of how various events in their life produced a sequence of changes in them without negating the fact that they were the same person. These First Nations youths' narratives of self-continuity, Chandler and his colleagues argued, are particularly vulnerable to conditions of cultural destruction because the narrative tradition on which such self-construals were based was itself destroyed, leaving adolescents without the resources to form a sense of self-continuity. This study is not alone in providing evidence that cultural discontinuities in a period of rapid social change endanger successful passage from childhood to adulthood, implicating cultural modes of thought in the process of adolescent/youth development (see also Cole & Durham, 2008).

CONCLUSIONS

At the outset of this chapter, we noted the growing attention that psychologists are paying to the role of culture in human development. Our (necessarily abbreviated) review has illustrated, we hope, both the importance of culture in the process of human development and the complexities of studying it. We have argued for an approach that considers culture as a medium rather than a variable while acknowledging the usefulness of cross-cultural research when it is conducted with sufficient care and modesty about the claims made (see Table 3.2).

Culture serves as the specifically human medium in which biological, cognitive, social, and emotional factors are co-occurring throughout development. This change can often be considered "progressive" insofar as the developing individual achieves greater freedom of action in a broader range of relevant activities. But such "progress" must always be evaluated with respect to some, preferably well-specified, set of cultural values and often what appears to be progress in one domain involves losses in others.

We have noted that during certain time periods, different contributing developmental factors converge and become coordinated in particular cultural circumstances such that they mutually amplify each other, giving rise to qualitatively new forms of living, in what

TABLE 3.2
Implications of Considering Culture as a Medium

- The "progress" of development should be evaluated with respect to a set of cultural values; often what appears to be progress in one domain involves losses in others.
- The existence of a specific stage of development may be the consequence of particular cultural–historical circumstances.
- The transition between stages is a phase change in which different developmental factors converge, become coordinated in particular cultural circumstances, mutually amplify each other, and give rise to a qualitatively new form of living.
- This new form of living then becomes embodied in cultural practices and identified as a new stage of development.

amounts to a phase transition that becomes embodied in cultural practices and identified as a "new stage of development." We saw this clearly at 6 to 9 months, where bone and muscle and brain growth make possible locomotion (although the precise timing of onset of motility depends on adult arrangements); locomotion changes the child's practical understanding of space, which transforms the conditions of social interaction with still-essential caregiver attention and the spatial characteristics of joint attention, making new distal forms of communication necessary, and simultaneously introducing a new emotionality into the caregiver–child relation which now becomes specific where before it was diffuse.

Considering culture first and foremost as a medium also has methodological consequences for the study of culture in development. Experimental research in cross-cultural studies is fraught with problems. Although the goal is to provide a neutral set of conditions where "all other things are held equal," experimentation removes participants from their social setting and introduces a new cultural situation with new demands that are rarely neutral with respect to the comparisons being made. When culture is then treated as an independent variable, it can produce the semblance of rigor while masking the fact that the fundamental requirement of true experimentation—the random assignment of participants to treatments—is violated. The very reason for conducting cross-cultural research is to study people who have *not* been assigned to cultures at random!

There is an instructive parallel between the difficulties of conducting convincing cross-cultural research in the late twentieth century and the dispute between Boas and evolutionary anthropologists such as Tylor in the nineteenth century. Recall that Tylor believed he could rank cultures with respect to level of development using a standardized criterion such as "extent of scientific knowledge" or "complexity of social organization." Boas demurred, insisting that the very meaning of these terms shifted with its cultural context and that heterogeneity of functioning depending on the domain studied had to be taken into account. Like Tylor, cross-cultural psychologists who use standardized instruments that they carry from place to place can rank people with respect to developmental level. However, as Boas would have predicted, their conclusions are suspect because the meaning of their criterial instruments changes with its cultural context. Eventually cross-cultural psychologists must engage in local ethnographic work to establish the relation of their testing procedures to the local culture and the kinds of experiences that people undergo over their life spans. It is a giant undertaking, for which there are only a few extended examples on which to draw.

Despite their shortcomings, cross-cultural methods can help us to identify variations in want of deeper analysis and can sometimes help us to understand the contributions of particular kinds of experience to the development of particular kinds of characteristics (as in the cases of the effects of forced change of prolonged sleep episodes in early infancy and modes of explaining self-continuity in adolescence). Cross-cultural research alerts us to the possibility that the very existence of certain stages of development may be the consequence of particular cultural–historical circumstances and not universal, as in the case of adolescence. It also serves the important function of getting us to question the sources of age-related differences observed in our own culture, as indicated by research on the effects of schooling in middle childhood. The fact that we are left wondering about the generality of the resulting changes in many cases (schooling effects being a major case in point) is disappointing, of course, but the good news is that it puts us on our guard against the ever-present danger of overgeneralizing the results of work conducted in our own societies.

When we take seriously the garden metaphor of culture-as-medium (what Valsiner, 1989, referred to as an *organizing variable*), entirely new avenues of research are opened up, and at the same time new challenges. When we take the step from cross-cultural to cultural psychology we stand the usual relation between everyday experience and experimentation on its head. From this viewpoint, experiments themselves need to be considered as social situations. Studies of the child or infant in isolation can tell us little about what they can do in interaction with others—something that we have argued is crucial. Laboratory experiments with children remove them from the particular social networks in which they live and grow. They "limit the subject's freedom to initiate communication inventively" (Trevarthen, 2005) in ways that often destroy the phenomena they seek to investigate, especially with infants. The child's interaction with the researcher, through talk and nonverbal communication, is often not considered an important factor, though it may "prime" the child's responses in ways the researcher does not intend and remains unaware of (Oyserman & Lee, 2008). We need experiments that study children *in their relations* (Selby & Bradley, 2003).

Naturalistic studies become a necessary part of our toolkit. Instead of starting with presumably culture-free measures of psychological process, we begin with observation of everyday activities as part of a culturally organized sequence with its own internal logic and goals. Experiments then become ways to conveniently model existing cultural practices to externalize their inner workings (Scribner, 1975). When we begin in this way, we come across such new (theoretically speaking) phenomena as the revelation of the projection of ideal or mental models of past gender relations onto ideal or mental models of a child's future and the transformation of this ideal model into concrete reality. Or we are led into an analysis of the organization of everyday conversations between mothers and children to understand how their structure is related to the society's world view (Bornstein, 1989; Goodnow, 1984), or school activities to determine how to make instruction developmentally beneficial (Newman, Griffin, & Cole, 1989).

Such analyses are often, from the perspective of experimental psychology, messy and difficult. However, a growing literature on this topic, only a small part of which we have been able to touch on in this chapter (Packer, 2011), suggests that it holds great promise for the future development of the science of human development.

ACKNOWLEDGMENTS

Preparation of this chapter was supported in part by a Grant from the Spencer Foundation. It could not have been completed without the support of colleagues and staff at the Laboratory of Comparative Human Cognition, whose humor and good will are a constant source of inspiration.

REFERENCES AND SUGGESTED READINGS (📖)

Adolph, K. E., & Berger S. E. (2010). Physical and motor development. In M. H. Bornstein & M. E. Lamb (Eds.), *Developmental science: An advanced textbook* (6th ed., pp. 241–302). Hove, UK: Psychology Press.

Ainsworth, M. D. (1967). *Infancy in Uganda: Infant care and the growth of love*. Baltimore, MD: Johns Hopkins Press.

Ainsworth, M. D., Blehar, M. C., Waters, E., & Wall, S. (1978). *Patterns of attachment*. Hillsdale, NJ: Lawrence Erlbaum Associates.

Ardilla, A. M., Roselli, P., & Rosas, P. (1989). Neuro-psychological assessment in illiterates: Visuospatial and memory abilities. *Brain and Cognition, 11*, 147–166.

Arnett, J. J. (1998). Learning to stand alone: The contemporary American transition to adulthood in cultural and historical context. *Human Development, 41, 5–6*, 295–315.

Arnett, J. J. (2007). Socialization in emerging adulthood: From the family to the wider world, from socialization to self-socialization. In J. E. Grusec & P. D. Hastings (Eds.), *Handbook of socialization: Theory and research.* (pp. 208–231). New York: Guilford Press.

Astington, J. W., & Baird, J. A. (2005). Representational development and false-belief understanding. In J. W. Astington & J. A. Baird (Eds.), *Why language matters for theory of mind* (pp. 163–185). New York: Oxford University Press.

Atran, S., Medin, D., Lynch, E., Vapnarsky, V., Ek, E. U., & Soursa, P. (2001). Folkbiology does not come from

Folkpschology: Evidence from Yukatek Maya in cross-cultural perspective. *Journal of Cognition and Culture*, *1*(1), 3–41.

Atran, S., Medin, D., & Ross, N. O. (2004). Evolution and devolution of knowledge: A tale of two biologies. *Journal of the Royal Anthropological Institute*, *10*(2), 395–421.

Atran, S., Medin, D., & Ross, N. O. (2005). The cultural mind: Environmental decision making and cultural modeling within and across populations. *Psychological Review*, *112*(4), 744–776.

Avis, J., & Harris, P. L. (1991). Belief–desire reasoning among Baka children: Evidence for a universal conception of mind. *Child Development*, *62*, 460–467.

Bandura, A. (2002). Social cognitive theory in cultural context. *Applied Psychology*, *51*(2), 269–290.

Bang, M., Medin, D. L., & Atran, S. (2007). Cultural mosaics and mental models of nature. *Proceedings of the National Academy of Sciences of the United States of America*, *104*(35), 13868–13874.

Barker, R. (1968). *Ecological psychology*. Stanford, CA: Stanford University Press.

Bates, E. (1976). *Language and context: The acquisition of pragmatics*. New York: Academic Press.

Battro, A. (2000). *Half a brain is enough: The story of Nico*. New York: Cambridge University Press.

Behrens, K. Y., Hesse, E., & Main, M. (2007). Mothers' attachment status as determined by the adult attachment interview predicts their 6-year-olds' reunion responses: A study conducted in Japan. *Developmental Psychology*, *43*(6), 1553–1567.

Bentz, B. (2001). Adolescent culture: An exploration of the socio-emotional development of the Aka adolescents of the Central African Republic. *Oriental Anthropologist*, 1(*2*), 25–32.

Berry, J. W. (2000). Cross-cultural psychology: A symbiosis of cultural and comparative approaches. *Asian Journal of Social Psychology*, *3*(3), 197–205.

Berry, J. W., Poortinga, Y. H., & Pandey, J. (1997). *Handbook of cross-cultural psychology, Vol. 1: Theory and method* (2nd ed.). Boston: Allyn & Bacon.

Berry, J. W., Poortinga, Y. H., Segall, M. H., & Dasen, P. R. (1992). *Cross-cultural psychology: Research and applications*. New York: Cambridge University Press.

Berry, J. W., Poortinga, Y. H., Segall, M. H. & Dasen, P. R. (2002). *Cross-cultural psychology: Research and applications* (2nd ed.). New York: Cambridge University Press.

Bloch, H. A., & Niederhoffer, A. (1958). *The gang: A study in adolescent behavior*. New York: Philosophical Library.

Bloom, P. (2004). *Descartes' baby: How the science of child development explains what makes us human*. New York: Basic Books.

Bloom, P., & German, T. P. (2000). Two reasons to abandon the false belief task as a test of theory of mind. *Cognition*, *77*(1), B25–B31.

Boas, F. (1911). *The mind of primitive man*. New York: Macmillan.

Bogin, B. (1999). *Patterns of human growth* (2nd ed.). New York: Cambridge University Press.

Bogin, B. (2009). Childhood, adolescence, and longevity: A multilevel model of the evolution of reserve capacity in human life history. *American Journal of Human Biology*, *21*, 567–577.

Bornstein, M. (1980). Cross-cultural developmental psychology. In M. H. Bornstein (Ed.), *Comparative methods in psychology* (pp. 231–281). Hillsdale, NJ: Lawrence Erlbaum Associates.

Bornstein, M. H. (1989). Cross-cultural comparisons: The case of Japanese American infant and mother activities and interactions. What we know, what we need to know, and why we need to know. *Developmental Review*, *9*, 171–204.

Bornstein, M. H. (Ed.). (2009). *The handbook of cultural developmental science. Part 1. Domains of development across cultures. Part 2. Development in different places on earth*. New York: Taylor & Francis.

Bornstein, M. H., Arterberry, M. E., & Mash, C. (2010). Perceptual development. In M. H. Bornstein & M. E. Lamb (Eds.), *Developmental science: An advanced textbook* (6th ed., pp. 303–352). Hove, UK: Psychology Press.

Bornstein, M. H., Haynes, O. M., Pascual, L., Painter, K. M., & Galperín, C. (1999). Play in two societies: Pervasiveness of process, specificity of structure. *Child Development*, *70*(2), 317–331.

Bornstein, M. H., Tal, J., & Tamis-LeMonda, C. S. (1991). Parenting in cross-cultural perspective: The United States, France, and Japan. In M. H. Bornstein (Ed.), *Cultural approaches to parenting* (pp. 69–90). Hillsdale, NJ: Lawrence Erlbaum Associates.

Bornstein, M. H., Tamis-LeMonda, C. S., Tal, J., Ludemann, P., Toda, S., Rahn, C. W., et al. (1992). Maternal responsiveness to infants in three societies: The United States, France, and Japan. *Child Development*, *63*(4), 808–821.

Bornstein, M. H., Toda, S., Azuma, H., Tamis-LeMonda, C. S., & Ogino, M. (1990). Mother and infant activity and interaction in Japan and in the United States: II. A comparative microanalysis of naturalistic exchanges focused on the organization of infant attention. *International Journal of Behavioral Development*, *13*, 289–308.

Bowlby, J. (1969). *Attachment and loss: Vol. 1. Attachment*. New York: Basic Books.

Bowlby, J. (1982). *Attachment and loss: Vol. 1. Attachment* (2nd ed.). New York: Basic Books.

Bretherton, I., & Waters, E. (Eds.). (1985). Growing points in attachment theory. *Monographs of the Society for Research in Child Development*, *50*(12), Serial No. 209.

Bronfenbrenner, U. (1979). *The ecology of human development*. Cambridge, MA: Harvard University Press.

Brown, R. (1965). *Social psychology*. New York: Free Press.

Brown, R. (1973). *A first language: The early stages*. Cambridge, MA: Harvard University Press.

Bruner, J. S. (1982). The formats of language acquisition. *American Journal of Semiotics, 1*, 1–16.

Bruner, J. S. (1983). *Child's talk*. New York: Norton.

Bruner, J. S. (1990). *Acts of meaning*. Cambridge, MA: Harvard University Press.

Bryant, G. A. & Barrett, H. C. (2007). Recognizing intentions in infant-directed speech: Evidence for universals. *Psychological Science, 18*(8), 746–751.

Callaghan, T., Rochat, P., Lillard, A., Claux, M. L., Odden, H., Itakura, S., et al. (2005). Synchrony in the onset of mental-state reasoning: Evidence from five cultures. *Psychological Science, 16*(5), 378–384.

Campos, J. J., Anderson, D. I., Barbu-Roth, M. A., Hubbard, E. M., Hertenstein, M. J., & Witherington, D. (2000). Travel broadens the mind. *Infancy, 1*(2), 149–219.

Carey, S. (1985). *Conceptual change in childhood*. Cambridge, MA: MIT Press.

Carey, S., & Spelke, E. (1994). Domain-specific knowledge and conceptual change. In L. A. Hirschfeld & S. A. Gelman (Eds.), *Mapping the mind: Domain specificity in cognition and culture* (pp. 169–200). New York: Cambridge University Press.

Cassidy, J., & Shaver, P. R. (2008). *Handbook of attachment: Theory, research, and clinical applications* (2nd ed.). New York: Guilford Press.

Castro-Caldes, A. (2004). Targeting regions of interest for the study of the illiterate brain. *International Journal of Psychology, 39*(1), 5–17.

Chandler, M. J., Lalonde, C. E., Sokol, B. W., & Hallett, D. (2003). Personal persistence, identity development, and suicide. *Monographs of the Society for Research in Child Development, 68*(2), Serial No. 278.

Chandler, M., & Proulx, T. (2006). Changing selves in changing worlds: Youth suicide on the fault-lines of colliding cultures. *Archives of Suicide Research, 10*(2), 125–140.

Chen, Z., & Siegler, R. S. (2000). Intellectual development in childhood. In R. Sternberg (Ed.), *Handbook of intelligence* (pp. 92–116). New York: Cambridge University Press.

Chisholm, J. S., Burbank, V. K., Coall, D. A., & Gemmiti, F. (2005). Early stress: Perspectives from developmental evolutionary ecology. In B. J. Ellis & D. Bjorklund (Eds.). *Origins of the social mind: Evolutionary psychology and child development* (pp. 76–107). New York: Guilford Press.

Chomsky, N. (1986). *Knowledge of language: Its nature, origin, and use*. London: Praeger.

Clark, A. (2007). A sense of presence. *Pragmatics & Cognition, 15*(3), 413–433.

Cohen, L., & Cashon, C. H. (2006). Infant cognition. In D. Kuhn, R. S. Siegler, W. Damon, & R. M. Lerner (Eds.), *Handbook of child psychology: Vol. 2. Cognition, perception, and language* (6th ed., pp. 214–251). Hoboken, NJ: Wiley.

Cole, J., & Durham, D. (Eds.). (2008), *Figuring the future: Children, youth, and globalization*. Santa Fe, NM: SAR Press.

Cole, M. (1996). *Cultural psychology: A once and future discipline*. Cambridge, MA: Belknap Harvard.

Cole, M. (2005). Culture in development. In M. H. Bornstein & M. E. Lamb (Eds.), *Developmental science: An advanced textbook* (5th ed., pp. 45–102). New York: Psychology Press.

Cole, M. (2006). Culture and cognitive development in phylogenetic, historical, and ontogenetic perspective. In D. Kuhn & R. S. Siegler (Eds.), *Handbook of child psychology, Vol. 2: Cognition, perception, and language* (6th ed., pp. 636–686). New York: Wiley.

Cole, M., & Cole, S. (1989). *The development of children*. San Francisco: Scientific American.

Cole, M., Cole, S., & Lightfoot, C. (2002). *The development of children* (5th ed.). New York: W. H. Freeman.

Cole, M., Cole, S., & Lightfoot, C. (2005). *The development of children* (5th ed.). New York: Worth.

Cole, M., Gay, J., Glick, J. A., & Sharp, D. W. (1971). *The cultural context of learning and thinking*. New York: Basic Books.

Cole, M., & Hatano, G. (2007). Cultural–historical activity theory: Integrating phylogeny, cultural history, and ontogenesis in cultural psychology. In S. Kitayama & D. Cohen (Eds.), *Handbook of cultural psychology* (pp. 109–135). New York: Guilford Press.

Cole, M., & Scribner, S. (1977). Cross-cultural studies of memory and cognition. In R. V. Kail & J. W. Hagen (Eds.), *Perspectives on the development of memory and cognition* (pp. 239–271). Hillsdale, NJ: Lawrence Erlbaum Associates.

Coley, J. D. (1995). Emerging differentiation of folkbiology and folkpsychology: Attributions of biological and psychological properties to living things. *Child Development*, 1856–1874.

Condon, R. G. (1987). *Inuit youth*. New Brunswick, NJ: Rutgers University Press.

Correa-Chávez, M., & Rogoff, B. (2009). Children's attention to interactions directed to others: Guatemalan Mayan and European-American patterns. *Developmental Psychology, 45*(3), 630–641.

Costall, A., & Leudar, I. (2007). Getting over "The problem of other minds": Communication in context. *Infant Behavior & Development, 30*(2), 289–295.

Cote, L. R., & Bornstein, M. H. (2009). Child and mother play in three U.S. cultural groups: Comparisons and associations. *Journal of Family Psychology, 23*(3), 355–363.

D'Andrade, R. (1984). Cultural meaning systems. In R. A. Shweder & R. A. LeVine (Eds.), *Culture theory: Essays on mind, self, and emotion* (pp. 88–119). New York: Cambridge University Press.

D'Andrade, R. (1986). Three scientific world views and the covering law model. In D. Fiske & R. Shweder (Eds.), *Meta-theory in the social sciences: Pluralisms and subjectivities* (pp. 19–41). Chicago: University of Chicago Press.

D'Andrade, R. (1996). Culture. *Social science encyclopedia* (pp. 161–163). London: Routledge.

Dash, U. N., & Mishra, H. C. (1989). Testing for the effects of schooling on memory in an ecocultural setting. *Psychology and Developing Societies*, *1*(2), 153–163.

Deregowski, J. (1970). Effect of cultural value of time upon recall. *British Journal of Social and Clinical Psychology*, *9*, 37–41.

de Villiers, J. G., & de Villiers, P. A. (1978). *Language acquisition*. Cambridge, MA: Harvard University Press.

de Villiers, J. G., & de Villiers, P. A. (2000). Linguistic determinism and the understanding of false beliefs. In P. Mitchell & K. J. Riggs (Eds.), *Children's reasoning and the mind* (pp. 191–228). Hove, UK: Psychology Press.

Durrett, M. E., Otaki, M., & Richards, P. (1984), Attachment and the mother's perception of support from the father. *International Journal of Behavioral Development*, *7*(2), 167–176.

Ellis, N. C. (1998). Emergentism, connectionism and language learning. *Language Learning*, *48*(4), 631–664.

Elman, J., Bates, E., Johnson, M. H., Karmiloff-Smith, A., Parisi, D., & Plunkett, K. (1996). *Rethinking innateness: A connectionist perspective on development*. Cambridge, MA: MIT Press.

Emde, R. N., Gaensbauer, T. J., & Harmon, R. J. (1976). *Emotional expression in infancy: A behavioral study*. Psychological Issues Monograph Series, *10*(1), Serial No. 37. New York: International Universities Press.

Ergazaki, M., & Andriotou, E. (2010). From "forest fires" and "hunting" to disturbing "habitats" and "food chains": Do young children come up with any ecological interpretations of human interventions within a forest? *Research in Science Education*, *40*, 187–201.

Evans, C. A., & Porter, C. L. (2009). The emergence of mother–infant co-regulation during the first year: Links to infants' developmental status and attachment. *Infant Behavior and Development*, *32*(2), 147–158.

Fodor, J. (1983). *Modularity of mind: An essay on faculty psychology*. Cambridge, MA: MIT Press.

Fogel, A., & Garvey, A. (2007). Alive communication. *Infant Behavior & Development*, *30*(2), 251–257.

Gallimore, R., Goldenberg, C. N., & Weisner, T. S. (1993). The social construction and subjective reality of activity settings: Implications for community psychology. *American Journal of Community Psychology*, *21*(4), 537–559.

Gardiner, H. W., & Kosmitzki, C. (2007). *Lives across cultures: Cross-cultural human development* (4th ed.). Boston: Allyn & Bacon.

Gaskins, S. (2000). Children's daily activities in a Mayan village: A culturally grounded description. *Cross-Cultural Research*, *34*(4), 375–389.

Gauvain, M. (2005). Sociocultural contexts of learning. In A. Maynard & M. I. Martini (Eds.), *Learning in cultural context: Family, peers, and school* (pp. 11–40). New York: Kluwer Academic/Plenum Publishers.

Geertz, C. (1973). *The interpretation of cultures*. New York: Basic Books.

Gelman, R. (2009). Innate learning and beyond. In M. Piattelli-Palmarini, J. Uriagereka, & P. Salaburu (Eds.), *Of minds and language: A dialogue with Noam Chomsky in the Basque country* (pp. 223–238). New York: Oxford University Press.

Gergely, G., Egyed, K., & Király, I. (2007). On pedagogy. *Developmental Science*, *10*(1), 139–46.

Gesell, A. (1940). *The first five years of life* (9th ed.). New York: Harper & Row.

Gesell, A. (1945). *The embryology of behavior*. New York: Harper & Row.

Goldin-Meadow, S. (1985). Language development under atypical learning conditions. In K. E. Nelson (Ed.), *Children's language* (Vol. 5, pp. 197–245). Hillsdale, NJ: Lawrence Erlbaum Associates.

Goldin-Meadow, S. (2007). Pointing sets the stage for learning language—and creating language. *Child Development*, *78*(3), 741–745.

Goldin-Meadow, S., Butcher, C., Mylander, C., & Dodge, M. (1994). Nouns and verbs in a self-styled gesture system: What's in a name? *Cognitive Psychology*, *27*, 259–319.

Goldin-Meadow, S., & Mylander, C. (1996). Spontaneous sign systems created by deaf children in two cultures. *Nature*, *391*, 279–281.

Goodenough, W. H. (1976). Multiculturalism as the normal human experience. *Anthropology & Education Quarterly*, *7*(4), 4–7.

Goodenough, W. H. (1994). Toward a working theory of culture. In R. Borofsky (Ed.), *Assessing cultural anthropology* (pp. 262–273). New York: McGraw-Hill.

Goodnow, J. (1984). Parents' ideas about parenting and development. In A. L. Brown & B. Rogoff (Eds.), *Advances in developmental psychology* (Vol. 3, pp. 193–242). Hillsdale, NJ: Lawrence Erlbaum Associates.

Gopnik, A. (2009). *The philosophical baby: What children's minds tell us about truth, love, and the meaning of life*. New York: Farrar, Straus & Giroux.

Gopnik, A., & Wellman, H. M. (1994). The theory theory. In L. A. Hirschfeld & S. A. Gelman (Eds.) *Mapping the mind: Domain specificity in cognition and culture* (pp. 257–293). New York: Cambridge University Press.

Gordon, C. M., & Laufer, M. R. (2005). Physiology of puberty. In S. J. H. Emans, D. P. Goldstein, & M. R. Laufer (Eds.). *Pediatric and adolescent gynecology* (5th ed.). Philadelphia: Lippincott, Williams & Wilkins.

Greenberg, J., & Muehlebach, A. (2007). The old world and its new economy. In J. Cole & D. L. Durham (Eds.), *Generations and globalization: Youth, age, and family in the new world economy* (pp. 190–214). Bloomington, IN: Indiana University Press.

Greenfield, P. M. (1966). On culture and conservation. In J. S. Bruner, R. P. Olver, & P. M. Greenfield (Eds.), *Studies in cognitive growth* (pp. 225–256). New York: Wiley.

Greenfield, P. M. (1997). Culture as process: Empirical methods for cultural psychology. In J. W. Berry, Y. H. Poortinga, & J. Pandey (Eds.), *Handbook of cross-cultural psychology: Theory and method* (pp. 301–346). Boston: Allyn and Bacon.

Greenfield, P. M. (2000). Three approaches to the psychology of culture: Where do they come from? Where can they go? *Asian Journal of Social Psychology*, *3*(3), 223–240.

Greenfield, P. M. (2004). *Weaving generations together: Evolving creativity in the Maya of Chiapas*. Santa Fe, NM: SAR Press.

Greenfield, P. M. (2009). Linking social change and developmental change: Shifting pathways of human development. *Developmental Psychology*, *45*(2), 401–418.

Greenfield, P. M., Brazelton, T. B., & Childs, C. P. (1989). From birth to maturity in Zinacantan: Ontogenesis in cultural context. In V. Bricker & G. Gossen (Eds.), *Ethnographic encounters in southern Mesoamerica: Celebratory essays in honor of Evon Z. Vogt* (pp. 177–216). Albany, NY: Institute of Mesoamerican Studies, State University of New York.

Greenfield, P. M., & Bruner, J. S. (1969). Culture and cognitive growth. In D. A. Goslin (Ed.), *Handbook of socialization theory and research* (pp. 633–660). New York: Rand McNally.

Greenfield, P. M., & Lave, J. (1982). Cognitive aspects of informal education. In D. A. Wagner & H. E. Stevenson (Eds.), *Cultural perspectives on child development* (pp. 181–207). New York: Freeman.

Grossmann, K. E. (2000). The evolution and history of attachment research and theory. In S. Goldberg, R. Muir, & J. Kerr (Eds.), *Attachment theory: Social developmental, and clinical perspectives* (pp. 85–121). New York: Analytic Press.

Grossmann, K. E., & Grossmann, K. (2005). Universality of human social attachment as an adaptive process. In C. S. Carter, L. Ahnert, K. E. Grossmann, S. B. Hardy, M. E. Lamb, S. W. Porges, et al. (Eds.), *Attachment and bonding: A new synthesis. Dahlem workshop report*. Cambridge, MA: MIT Press.

Grossmann, K. E., Grossmann, K., & Keppler, A. (2006). Universal and culture-specific aspects of human behavior: The case of attachment. In W. Friedlmeier, P. Chakkarath, & B. Schwarz (Eds.), *Culture and human development: The importance of cross-cultural research to the social sciences* (pp. 75–97). New York: Psychology Press.

Grossmann, K., Grossmann, K. E., Spangler, S., Suess, G., & Unzner, L. (1985). Maternal sensitivity and newborn orientation responses as related to quality of attachment in northern Germany. In I. Bretherton & E. Waters (Eds.), Growing points of attachment theory. *Monographs of the Society for Research in Child Development*, *50*(1–2), Serial No. 209.

Grotuss, J., Bjorklund, D. F., & Csinady, A. (2007). Evolutionary developmental psychology: Developing human nature. *Acta Psychologica Sinica*, *39*(3), 439–453.

Hall, G. S. (1904). *Adolescence*. New York: Appleton.

Hallpike, C. R. (1979). *The foundations of primitive thought*. Oxford, UK: Clarendon Press.

Hatano, G. (1997). Commentary: Core domains of thought, innate constraints, and sociocultural contexts. In H. M. Wellman & K. Inagaki (Eds.), *The emergence of core domains of thought: Children's reasoning about physical, psychological, and biological phenomena* (pp. 71–78). San Francisco: Jossey-Bass.

Hatano, G. & Inagaki, K. (2002). In W. W. Hartup & R. K. Silbereisen (Eds.), *Growing points in developmental science: An introduction* (pp. 123–142). Philadelphia: Psychology Press.

Hauser, M. (2005). Our chimpanzee mind. *Nature*, *437*(7055), 60–63.

Heft, H. (2003). Affordances, dynamic experience, and the challenge of reification. *Ecological Psychology*, *15*(2), 149–180.

Henning, A., Striano, T., & Lieven, E. V. M. (2005). Maternal speech to infants at 1 and 3 months of age. *Infant Behavior and Development*, *28*(4), 519–536.

Herder, J. G. V. (1784/1803). *Outlines of a philosophy of the history of man*. London: Luke Hansard.

Herskovitz, M. J. (1948). *Man and his works: The science of cultural anthropology*. New York: Knopf.

Hesse, E., & Main, M. (2006). Frightened, threatening, and dissociative parental behavior in low-risk samples: Description, discussion, and interpretations. *Development and Psychopathology*, *18*, 309–343.

Hill, K., & Hurtado, A. M. (1996). *Ache life history: The ecology and demography of a foraging people*. New York: Aldine de Gruyter.

Hinde, R. A. (1987). *Individuals, relationships and culture: Links between ethology and the social sciences*. New York: Cambridge University Press.

Howell, S. (1984). *Society and cosmos*. Oxford, UK: Oxford University Press.

His, B. L., & Adinolfi, M. (1997). Prenatal sexing of human fetuses and selective abortion [editorial comment]. *Prenatal Diagnosis*, *17*(1), 13.

Inagaki, K. (1990). The effects of raising animals on children's biological knowledge. *British Journal of Developmental Psychology, 8*(2), 119–129.

Inagaki, K., & Hatano, G. (1993). Young children's understanding of the mind–body distinction. *Child Development, 64*, 1534–1549.

Ingold, T. (2000). *The perception of the environment: Essays on livelihood, dwelling, and skill.* London: Routledge.

Inhelder, B., & Piaget, J. (1958). *The growth of logical thinking from childhood to adolescence.* New York: Basic Books.

Irvine, J. (1978). Wolof "magical thinking": Culture and conservation revisited. *Journal of Cross-Cultural Psychology, 9*, 38–47.

📖 Jahoda, G. (1993). *Crossroads between culture and mind: Continuities and change in theories of human nature.* Cambridge, MA: Harvard University Press.

Janowsky, J. S., & Carper, R. (1995). A neural basis for cognitive transitions in school-aged children. In M. Haith & A. Sameroff (Eds.), *Reason and responsibility: The passage through childhood.* Chicago: University of Chicago Press.

Jeans, P. C., Smith, M. B., & Stearns, G. (1955). Incidence of prematurity in relation to maternal nutrition. *Journal of the American Dietary Association, 31*, 576–581.

Johnson-Hanks, J. (2002). On the limits of life stages in ethnography: Toward a theory of vital conjunctures. *American Anthropologist, 104*(3), 865–880.

Kagan, J. (1977). The uses of cross-cultural research in early development. In P. H. Liedaman, S. Tulkin, & A. Rosenfeld (Eds.), *Culture and infancy: Variations in the human experience* (pp. 271–286). New York: Academic Press.

Kamara, A. I., & Easley, J. A. (1977). Is the rate of cognitive development uniform across cultures? A methodological critique with new evidence from Themne children. In P. R. Dasen (Ed.), *Piagetian psychology: Cross-cultural contributions* (pp. 26–63). New York: Gardner.

Ke, J., & Holland, J. H. (2006). Language origin from an emergentist perspective. *Applied Linguistics, 27*(4), 691–716.

Keniston, K. (1970). Youth: A "new" stage of life. *American Scholar, 39*, 631–654.

Kiell, N. (1964). *The universal experience of adolescence.* New York: International Universities Press.

King, J. E, Weiss, A., & Sisco, M. M. (2008). Aping humans: Age and sex effects in chimpanzee (*Pan troglodytes*) and human (*Homo sapiens*) personality, *Journal of Comparative Psychology, 122*(4), 418–427.

Kisilevsky, B. S., Hains, S. M., Brown, C. A., Lee, C. T., Cowperthwaite, B., Stutzman, S. S., et al. (2009). Fetal sensitivity to properties of maternal speech and language. *Infant Behavior & Development, 32*(1), 59–71.

📖 Kitayama, S., & Cohen, D. (2007). *Handbook of cultural psychology.* New York: Guilford Press.

Kitayama, S., Duffy, S., & Uchida, Y. (2007). Self as cultural mode of being. *Handbook of cultural psychology* (pp. 136–174). New York: Guilford Press.

Laboratory of Comparative Human Cognition (LCHC). (1983). Culture and development. In P. H. Mussen (Series Ed.) & W. Kessen (Vol. Ed.), *Handbook of child psychology: Vol. 1. History, theory, and methods* (pp. 295–356). New York: Wiley.

Lakoff, G., & Johnson, M. (1980). *Metaphors we live by.* Chicago: University of Chicago Press.

Lavelli, M. & Poli, M. (1998). Early mother–infant interaction during breast- and bottle-feeding. *Infant Behavior & Development, 21*(4), 667–683.

Lecanuet, J. P., Graniere-Deferre, C., Jacquet, A. Y., & DeCasper, A. J. (2000). Fetal discrimination of low-pitched musical notes. *Developmental Psychobiology, 36*(1), 29–39.

Leekam, S., Perner, J., Healey, L., & Sewell, C. (2008). False signs and the non-specificity of theory of mind: Evidence that preschoolers have general difficulties in understanding representations. *British Journal of Developmental Psychology, 26*(4), 485–497.

Leiderman, P. H., Tulkin, S. T., & Rosenfeld, A. (Eds.). (1977). *Culture and infancy: Variations in the human experience.* New York: Academic Press.

Leigh, B., & Milgrom, J. (2008). Risk factors for antenatal depression, postnatal depression and parenting stress. *BMC Psychiatry, 8*, 24.

Leigh, S. R. (2004). Brain growth, life history, and cognition in primate and human evolution. *American Journal of Primatology, 62*, 139–164.

Leslie, A. M. (2005). Developmental parallels in understanding minds and bodies. *Trends in Cognitive Sciences, 9*(10), 459–462.

LeVine, R. A., & LeVine, S. (2001). The schooling of women. *Ethos, 29*(3), 259–270.

LeVine, R. A., LeVine, S. E., & Schnell, B. (2001). "Improve the women": Mass schooling, female literacy, and worldwide social change. *Harvard Educational Review, 71*(1), 1–50.

Li, J., Zhang, Z., & Nisbett, R. (2004). Is it culture or is it language? Examination of language effects in cross-cultural research on categorization. *Journal of Personality and Social Psychology, 87*(1), 57–65.

Li, S.-C. (2007). Biocultural co-construction of developmental plasticity across the lifespan. In S. Kitayama & D. Cohen (Eds.), *Handbook of cultural psychology* (pp. 528–544). New York: Guilford Press.

Lillard, A. (1998). Ethnopsychologies: Cultural variations in theories of mind. *Psychological Bulletin, 123*(1), 3–32.

Lillard, A. & Skibbe, L. (2004). Theory of mind: Conscious attribution and spontaneous trait inference. In R. Hassin, J. S. Uleman, & J. A. Bargh (Eds.), *The new unconscious* (pp. 277–308). Oxford, UK: Oxford University Press.

Lillard, A. S., Skibbe, L., Zeljo, A., & Harlan, D. (2001). *Developing explanations for behavior in different communities and cultures.* Unpublished manuscript, University of Virginia, Charlottesville.

Lindzey, G., & Aronson, E. (Eds.) (1986) *Handbook of social psychology* (Vol. 2, 3rd ed.). New York: Random House.

Liu, D., Wellman, H. M., Tardif, T. & Sabbagh, M. A. (2008). Theory of mind development in Chinese children: A meta-analysis of false-belief understanding across cultures and languages. *Developmental Psychology, 44*(2), 523–531.

Lucariello, J. (1995). Mind, culture, person: Elements in a cultural psychology. *Human Development, 38*(1), 2–18.

Luria, A. R. (1928). The problem of the cultural development of the child. *Journal of Genetic Psychology, 35*, 493–506.

Luria, A. R. (1973). *The working brain.* New York: Basic Books.

Lutz, C. (1987). Goals, events and understanding in Ifaluk emotion theory. In D. Holland & N. Quinn (Eds.), *Cultural models in language and thought* (pp. 290–312). New York: Cambridge University Press.

MacFarlane, A. (1977). *The psychology of childbirth.* Cambridge, MA: Harvard University Press.

MacWhinney, B. (2006). Emergentism: Use often and with care. *Applied Linguistics, 27*(4), 729–740.

Main, M., & Cassidy, J. (1988). Categories of response to reunion with the parent at age 6: Predictable from infant attachment classifications and stable over a 1-month period. *Developmental Psychology, 24*, 415–426.

Main, M., Goldwyn, R., & Hesse, E. (2002). *Adult attachment scoring and classification system.* Unpublished manuscript, University of California, Berkeley.

Main, M., & Solomon, J. (1990). Procedures for identifying infants as disorganized/disoriented during the Ainsworth strange situation. In M. T. Greenberg, D. Cicchetti, & E. M. Cummings (Eds.), *Attachment in the preschool years* (pp. 121–160). Chicago: University of Chicago Press.

Mandler, J. M. (1997). Development of categorisation: Perceptual and conceptual categories. In G. Bremner, A. Slater, & G. Butterworth (Eds.). *Infant development: Recent advances* (pp. 163–189). Hove, UK: Taylor & Francis.

Mandler, J. M. (2004). *The foundations of mind.* Oxford, UK: Oxford University Press.

Mandler, J., Scribner, S., Cole, M., & de Forest, M. (1980). Cross-cultural invariance in story recall. *Child Development, 51*, 19–26.

Mastropieri, D., & Turkewitz, G. (1999). Prenatal experience and neonatal responsiveness to vocal expressions of emotion. *Developmental Psychobiology, 35*(3), 204–214.

McGrew, W. C. (2002). The nature of culture: Prospects and pitfalls of cultural primatology. In de Waal, F. B. M. (Ed.), *Tree of origin: What primate behavior can tell us about humans* (pp. 229–254). Cambridge, MA: Harvard University Press.

Mead, M. (1935). *Sex and temperament in three primitive societies.* New York: William Morrow.

Mead, M., & Macgregor, F. C. (1951). *Growth and culture.* New York: Putnam.

Medin, D. L., & Atran, S. (2004). The native mind: Biological categorization, reasoning, and decision making in development and across cultures. *Psychological Review, 111*(4), 960–983.

Medin, D. L., & Atran, S. (Eds.). (1999). *Folkbiology.* Cambridge, MA: MIT Press.

Medin, D., Ross, N., & Cox, D. (2006). *Culture and resource conflict: Why meanings matter.* New York: Russell Sage.

Medin, D., Unsworth, S. J., & Hirschfeld, L. (2007). Culture, categorization, and reasoning. In S. Kitayama & D. Cohen (Eds.), *Handbook of cultural psychology* (pp. 615–644). New York: Guilford Press.

Mehan, H. (1978). *Learning lessons.* Cambridge, MA: Harvard University Press.

Mehler, J., Dupoux, E., Nazzi, T., & Dehaene-Lambertz, G. (1996). Coping with linguistic diversity: The infant's viewpoint. In J. L. Morgan, & K. Demuth (Eds.), *Signal to syntax: Bootstrapping from speech to grammar in early acquisition* (pp. 106–116). Mahwah, NJ: Lawrence Erlbaum Associates.

Miller, P. (1982). *Amy, Wendy and Beth: Learning language in south Baltimore.* Austin, TX: University of Texas Press.

Miyake, K., Chen, S., & Campos, J. J. (1985). Infant temperament, mother's mode of interaction, and attachment in Japan: An interim report. *Monographs of the Society for Research in Child Development, 50*(1–2), 276–297.

Nadel, S. F. (1937). Experiments on culture psychology. *Africa, 10*, 421–435.

Nakagawa, M., Lamb, M. E., & Miyake, K. (1992). Antecedents and correlates of the strange situation behavior of Japanese infants. *Journal of Cross-Cultural Psychology, 23*, 300–310.

Nasir, N. (2005). Individual cognitive structuring and the sociocultural context: Strategy shifts in the game of dominoes. *Journal of the Learning Sciences, 14*(1), 5–34.

Nelson, K. (1981). Social cognition in a script framework. In J. H. Flavell & L. Ross (Eds.), *Social cognitive development.* Cambridge, UK: Cambridge University Press.

Nelson, K. (1986). *Event knowledge: Structure and function in development.* Hillsdale, NJ: Lawrence Erlbaum Associates.

Nelson, K. (2003). Making sense in a world of symbols. In A. Toomela (Ed.), *Cultural guidance in the development of the human mind* (pp. 139–158). Westport, CT: Ablex.

Nelson, K. (2007). *Young minds in social worlds: Experience, meaning, and memory.* Cambridge, MA: Harvard University Press.

Newburn, M. (2003). Culture, control and the birth environment. *Practical Midwife*, 6(8), 20–25.

Newman, D., Griffin, P., & Cole, M. (1989). *The construction zone: Working for cognitive change in the school.* New York: Cambridge University Press.

Nyiti, R. (1978). The development of conservation in the Meru children of Tanzania. *Child Development*, 47(6), 1122–1129.

⊞ Ochs, E., & Schieffelin, B. B. (1984). Language acquisition and socialization: Three developmental stories and their implications. In R. Shweder & R. Levine (Eds.), *Culture theory: Essays on mind, self, and emotion* (pp. 276–320). Cambridge, UK: Cambridge University Press.

Ostrosky-Solis, F., Ramirez, M., & Ardila, A. (2004). Effects of culture and education on neuropsychological testing: A preliminary study with indigenous and nonindigenous population. *Applied Neuropsychology*, 11(4), 186–193.

Oyserman, D., & Lee, S. W.-S. (2007). Priming "culture": Culture as situated cognition. In S. Kitayama & D. Cohen (Eds.), *Handbook of cultural psychology* (pp. 255–282). New York: Guilford Press.

Oyserman, D., & Lee, S. W.-S. (2008). Does culture influence what and how we think? Effects of priming individualism and collectivism. *Psychological Bulletin*, 134(2), 311–342.

Packer, M. (2001a). The problem of transfer, and the sociocultural critique of schooling. *Journal of the Learning Sciences*, 10, 493–514.

Packer, M. J. (2001b). *Changing classes: School reform and the new economy.* New York: Cambridge University Press.

Packer, M. (2011). *The science of qualitative research.* New York: Cambridge University Press.

Packer, M. (in press). Schooling: Domestication or ontological construction? In T. Koschmann (Ed.), *Theories of learning and research into instructional practice.* New York: Springer.

Papousek, M. (2007). Communication in early infancy: An arena of intersubjective learning. *Infant Behavior & Development*, 30(2), 258–266.

Paul, R. A. (1995). Act and intention in Sherpa culture and society. In L. Rosen (Ed.), *Other intentions: Cultural contexts and the attribution of inner states* (pp. 15–45). Santa Fe, NM: School of American Research Press.

Pauli-Pott, U., Mertesacker, B., Bade, U., Haverkock, A., & Beckmann, D. (2003). Parental perceptions and infant temperament development. *Infant Behavior and Development*, 26(1), 27–48.

Perner, J. (2008). Who took the cog out of cognitive science? Mentalism in an era of anti-cognitivism. In P. A. Frensch et al. (Eds.), *International Congress of Psychology 2008 Proceedings*. Hove, UK: Psychology Press.

Perner, J., & Ruffman, T. (2005). Psychology. Infants' insight into the mind: How deep? *Science*, 308(5719), 214–216.

Perner, J., Ruffman, T., & Leekam, S. R. (1994). Theory of mind is contagious: You catch it from your sibs. *Child Development*, 65, 1228–1238.

Perner, J., Sprung, M., Zauner, P., & Haider, H. (2003). *Want that* is understood well before *say that, think that*, and false belief: A test of de Villiers's linguistic determinism on German-speaking children. *Child Development*, 74(1), 179–188.

Petitto, L. A. (2005). How the brain begets language. In J. McGilvray (Ed.), *The Cambridge companion to Chomsky* (pp. 84–101). Cambridge, UK: Cambridge University Press.

Piaget, J. (1937). *The construction of reality in the child.* London: Routledge & Kegan Paul.

Piaget, J. (1969). *Judgment and reasoning in the child.* London: Routledge & Kegan Paul.

Piaget, J. (1973). *The psychology of intelligence.* Totowa, NJ: Littlefield & Adams.

Piaget, J. (1995). Genetic logic and sociology. In J. Piaget (Ed.), *Sociological studies* (pp. 184–214). London: Routledge. (Original work published 1928).

⊞ Piaget, J., & Inhelder, B. (1969). *The psychology of the child.* New York: Basic Books.

Pinker, S. (1995). *The language instinct.* New York: Norton.

Pinker, S. (2002). *The blank slate: The modern denial of human nature.* New York: Viking.

Plotkin, H. C. (2002). *The imagined world made real: Towards a natural science of culture.* London: Allen Lane.

Pollitt, E., Saco-Pollitt, C., Jahari, A., Husaini, M. A., & Huang, J. (2000). Effects of an energy and micronutrient supplement on mental development and behavior under natural conditions in undernourished children in Indonesia. *European Journal of Clinical Nutrition*, 54, 80–90.

Premack, D., & Hauser, M. (2006). Why animals do not have culture. In S. C. Levinson & J. Pierre (Eds.), *Evolution and culture: A Fyssen Foundation symposium* (pp. 275–278). Cambridge, MA: MIT Press.

Premack, D., & Premack, A. J. (1983). *The mind of an ape.* New York: Norton.

Pujol, J., Soriano-Mas, C., Ortiz, H., Sebastian-Galles, N., Losilla, J. M., & Deus, J. (2006). Myelination of language-related areas in the developing brain. *Neurology*, 66(3), 339–343.

Pusey, A. E. (1990). Behavioural changes at adolescence in chimpanzees. *Behaviour*, 115, 203–246.

Quartz, S. R. & Sejnowski, T. J. (2002). *Liars, lovers, and heroes: What the new brain science reveals about how we become who we are.* New York: Morrow.

Read, M. (1960). *Children of their fathers: Growing up among the Ngoni of Malawi.* New York: Holt, Rinehart & Winston.

Richardson, S. A., & Guttmacher, A. F. (1967). *Childbearing: Its social and psychological aspects.* Baltimore, MD: Williams & Wilkins.

Richman, A. L., Miller, P. M., & LeVine, R. A. (1992). Cultural and educational variations in maternal responsiveness. *Developmental Psychology*, *28*(4), 614–621.

Richmond, J., & Nelson, C. A. (2007). Accounting for change in declarative memory: A cognitive neuroscience perspective. *Developmental Review*, *27*(3), 349–373.

Rodriguez, C. (2007). Object use, communication, and signs: The triadic basis of early cognitive development. In J. Valsiner & A. Rosa (Eds.), *The Cambridge handbook of sociocultural psychology* (pp. 257–276). Cambridge, UK: Cambridge University Press.

Rogoff, B. (1981). Schooling and the development of cognitive skills. In H. C. Triandis & A. Heron (Eds.), *Handbook of cross-cultural psychology* (Vol. 4, pp. 233–294). Boston: Allyn & Bacon.

Rogoff, B. (2003). *The cultural nature of human development*. New York: Oxford University Press.

Rogoff, B., Gauvain, M., & Ellis, S. (1984). Development viewed in its cultural context. In M. H. Bornstein & M. E. Lamb (Eds.), *Developmental psychology: An advanced textbook* (pp. 139–151). Hillsdale, NJ: Lawrence Erlbaum Associates.

Rogoff, B., Sellers, M. J., Pirrotta, S., Fox, N., & White, S. H. (1975). Age of assignment of roles and responsibilities to children: A cross-cultural survey. *Human Development*, *18*, 353–369.

Rogoff, B., & Waddell, K. J. (1982). Memory for information organized in a scene by children from two cultures. *Child Development*, *53*(5), 1224–1228.

Romney, A., K., & Moore, C. C. (2001). Systemic culture patterns as basic units of cultural transmission and evolution. *Cross-Cultural Research*, *35*(2), 154–178.

Ross, S. R., Bloomsmith, M. A., Bettinger, T. L., & Wagner, K. E. (2009). The influence of captive adolescent male chimpanzees on wounding: Management and welfare implications. *Zoo Biology*, *28*, 1–12.

Ross, N., Medin, D., Coley, J. D., & Atran, S. (2003). Cultural and experimental differences in the development of folkbiological induction. *Cognitive Development*, *18*(1), 25–47.

Rothbaum, F., Weisz, J., Pott, M., Miyake, K., & Morelli, G. (2000). Attachment and culture: Security in the United States and Japan. *American Psychologist*, *55*(10), 1093–1104.

Rowe, M. K., Thapa, B. K., LeVine, R., LeVine, S., & Tuladhar, S. K. (2005). How does schooling influence maternal health practices? Evidence from Nepal. *Comparative Education Review*, *49*(4), 512–533.

Rubin, J. Z., Provezano, F. J., & Luria, Z. (1974). The eye of the beholder: Parents' view on sex of newborns. *American Journal of Orthopsychiatry*, *44*, 512–519.

Ruffman, T., Perner, J., & Parkin, L. (1999). How parenting style affects false belief understanding. *Social Development*, *8*(3), 395–411.

Ruffman, T., Perner, J., Naito, M., Parkin, L., & Clements, W. A. (1998). Older (but not younger) siblings facilitate false belief understanding. *Developmental Psychology*, *34*(1), 161–174.

Ruffman, T., Slade, L., & Crowe, E. (2002). The relation between children's and mothers' mental state language and theory-of-mind understanding. *Child Development*, *73*(3), 734–751.

Ruffman, T., Slade, L., Devitt, K., & Crowe, E. (2006). What mothers say and what they do: The relation between parenting, theory of mind, language and conflict/cooperation. *British Journal of Developmental Psychology*, *24*(1), 105–124.

Sagi, A., Lamb, M. E., Lewkowicz, K. S., Shoham, K. R., Dvir, R., & Estes, D. (1985). Security of infant–mother,–father,–metapelet, attachments among kibbutz-raised Israeli children. In I. Bretherton & K. Watas (Eds.), Growing points of attachment theory. *Monographs of the Society for Research in Child Development*, *50* (1–2, Serial No. 209), 257–275.

Sagi, A., van IJzendoorn, M. H., Aviezer, O., Donnell, F., & Mayseless, O. (1994). Sleeping out of home in a kibbutz communal arrangement: It makes a difference for infant–mother attachment. *Child Development*, *65*, 992–1004.

Sameroff, A. J. & Haith, M. M. (Eds.) (1996). *The five to seven year shift: The age of reason and responsibility*. Chicago: University of Chicago Press.

Schacter, D. L., & Moscovitch, M. (1984). Infants, amnesics, and dissociable memory systems. In M. Moscovitch (Ed.), *Infant memory* (pp. 173–216). New York: Plenum.

Schieffelin, B., & Ochs, E. (1986). *Language socialization across cultures*. New York: Cambridge University Press.

Schlegel, A. (2008). A cross-cultural approach to adolescence. In D. L. Browning (Ed.). *Adolescent identities: A collection of readings*. (pp. 31–44). New York: Analytic Press/Taylor & Francis.

Schlegel, A., & Barry, H. (1991). *Adolescence: An anthropological inquiry*. New York: Free Press.

Schliemann, A. D., Carraher, D. W., & Ceci, S. J. (1997). Everyday cognition. In J. W. Berry, P. R. Dasen, & T. S. Saraswathi (Eds.), *Handbook of cross-cultural psychology, Vol. 2: Basic processes and human development* (2nd ed., pp. 177–216). Needham Heights, MA: Allyn & Bacon.

Scribner, S. (1975). Situating the experiment in cross-cultural research. In K. F. Riegel & J. A. Meacham (Eds.), *The developing individual in a changing world: Historical and cultural issues*. The Hague, The Netherlands: Mouton.

Scribner, S., & Cole, M. (1973). Cognitive consequences of formal and informal education. *Science*, *182*, 553–559.

Scribner, S., & Cole, M. (1981). *The psychology of literacy*. Cambridge, MA: Harvard University Press.

Segerdahl, P., Fields, W., & Savage-Rumbaugh, S. (2006). *Kanzi's primal language: The cultural initiation of primates into language*. Basingstoke, UK: Palgrave Macmillan.

Selby, J. M., & Bradley, B. S. (2003). Infants in groups: A paradigm for the study of early social experience. *Human Development*, *46*(4), 197–221.

Senghas, A., Kita, S., & Ozyürek, A. (2004). Children creating core properties of language: Evidence from an emerging sign language in Nicaragua. *Science*, *305*(5691), 1779–1782.

Serpell, R., & Hatano, G. (1997). Education, schooling, and literacy. In J. W. Berry, P. R. Dasen, & T. S. Saraswathi (Eds.), *Handbook of cross-cultural psychology, Vol. 2: Basic processes and human development* (2nd ed., pp. 339–376). Needham Heights, MA: Allyn & Bacon.

Sharma, D. C. (2003). Widespread concern over India's missing girls. Selective abortion and female infanticide cause girl-to-boy ratios to plummet. *Lancet*, *363*(9395), 1553.

Shostak, M. (1981). *Nissa: The life and words of a !Kung woman*. Cambridge, MA: Harvard University Press.

Shweder, R. A., Jensen, L. A., & Goldstein, W. M. (1995). Who sleeps by whom revisited: A method for extracting the moral goods implicit in practice. *New Directions for Child Development*, *67*, 21–39.

Shweder, R. A., Goodnow, J. J., Hatano, G., LeVine, R. A., Markus, H. R., & Miller, P. J. (2006). The cultural psychology of development: One mind, many mentalities. In R. M. Lerner & W. Damon, London (Eds.). *Handbook of child psychology (6th ed.): Vol. 1, Theoretical models of human development* (pp. 716–792). Hoboken, NJ: Wiley.

Siegal, M. (1991). A clash of conversational worlds: Interpreting cognitive development through communication. In J. M. Levine & L. B. Resnick (Eds.), *Socially shared cognition*. Washington, DC: American Psychological Association.

Skinner, B. F. (1953). *Science and human behavior*. New York: Appleton, Century, Crofts.

Slade, L., & Ruffman, T. (2005). How language does (and does not) relate to theory of mind: A longitudinal study of syntax, semantics, working memory and false belief. *British Journal of Developmental Psychology*, *23*(1), 117–142.

Smith, L. (2002). Piaget's model. In U. Goswami (Ed.), *Blackwell handbook of cognitive development* (pp. 515–537). Malden, MA: Blackwood.

Snow, C. (1995). Issues in the study of input: Finetuning, universality, individual and developmental differences, and necessary causes. In P. Fletcher & B. MacWhinney (Eds.), *The handbook of child language* (pp. 180–193). Oxford, UK: Blackwell.

Snow, C. E., & Ferguson, C. A. (Eds.). (1977). *Talking to children*. Cambridge, UK: Cambridge University Press.

Spitz, R. (1958). *A genetic field theory of ego development*. New York: International Universities Press.

Stiles, J., Moses, P., Roe, K., Akshoomoff, N., Trauner, D., Hesselink, J., et al. (2003). Alternative brain organization after prenatal cerebral injury: Convergent fMRI and cognitive data. *Journal of the International Neuropsychological Society*, *9*(4), 604–622.

Stocking, G. (1968). *Race, culture, and evolution*. New York: Free Press.

Sullivan, K., & Winner, E. (1993). Three-year-olds' understanding of mental states: The influence of trickery. *Journal of Experimental Child Psychology*, *56*(2), 135–148.

Super, C. (1987). The role of culture in developmental disorder. In C. Super (Ed.), *The role of culture in developmental disorder* (pp. 1–8). New York: Academic Press.

Super, C. M., & Harkness, S. (1982). The infant's niche in rural Kenya and metropolitan America. In L. Adler (Ed.), *Issues in cross-cultural research* (pp. 47–56). New York: Academic Press.

Super, C. M., & Harkness, S. (1986). The developmental niche: A conceptualization at the interface of child and culture. *International Journal of Behavioral Development*, *9*, 545–569.

Super, C. M., & Harkness, S. (1997) The cultural structuring of child development. In J. W. Berry, P. S. Dasen, & T. S. Saraswathi (Eds.), *Handbook of cross-cultural psychology, Vol. 2: Basic processes and human development* (2nd ed., pp. 1–40). Needham Heights, MA: Allyn & Bacon.

Super, C. M., & Harkness, S. (2002). Culture structures the environment for development. *Human Development*, *45*(4), 270–274.

Sweeney, J., & Bradbard, M. R. (1988). Mothers' and fathers' changing perception of their male and female infants over the course of pregnancy. *Journal of Genetic Psychology*, *149*(3), 393–404.

Tamis-LeMonda, C. S., & Adolph, K. (2005). Social referencing in infant motor action. In B. D. Homer & C. S. Tamis-LeMonda (Eds.), *The development of social cognition and communication* (pp. 145–164). Mahwah, NJ: Lawrence Erlbaum Associates.

Tamnes, C. K., Østby, Y., Fjell, A. M., Westlye, L. T., Due-Tønnessen, P., & Walhovd, K. B. (2010). Brain maturation in adolescence and young adulthood: Regional age-related changes in cortical thickness and white matter volume and microstructure. *Cerebral Cortex*, *20*, 534–548.

Taumoepeau, M., & Ruffman, T. (2006). Mother and infant talk about mental states relates to desire language and emotion understanding. *Child Development*, *77*, 465–481.

Taumoepeau, M., & Ruffman, T. (2008). Stepping stones to others' minds: Maternal talk relates to child mental state language and emotion understanding at 15, 24, and 33 months. *Child Development*, *79*(2), 284–302.

Tobin, J., Hsueh, Y., & Karasawa, M. (2009). *Preschool in three cultures revisited: China, Japan, and the United States*. Chicago: University of Chicago Press.

Tomasello, M., Call, J., & Hare, B. (2003). Chimpanzees understand psychological states—The question is which ones and to what extent? *Trends in Cognitive Sciences, 7*(4), 153–156.

Tomasello, M., & Carpenter, M. (2007). Shared intentionality. *Developmental Science, 10*, 121–125.

Trevarthen, C. (2005). Stepping away from the mirror: Pride and shame in adventures of companionship. Reflections on the nature and emotional needs of infant intersubjectivity. In C. S. Carter et al. (Eds.). *Attachment and bonding: A new synthesis. Dahlem Workshop Report 92* (pp. 55–84). Cambridge, MA: MIT Press.

Tudge, J. (2008). *The everyday lives of young children: Culture, class, and child rearing in diverse societies*. New York: Cambridge University Press.

Turvey, M. (2009). On the notion and implications of organism–environment interaction. *Ecological Psychology, 21*(2), 97–111.

Tylor, E. B. (1874). *Primitive culture: Researches into the development of mythology, philosophy, religion, language, art, and custom*. London: J. Murray.

UNESCO Institute for Statistics (2009). Global education digest 2009: Comparing education statistics across the world. New York: UNESCO.

Valsiner, J. (1989). From group comparisons to knowledge: Lessons from cross-cultural psychology. In J. P. Forgas & J. M. Innes (Eds.), *Recent advances in social psychology: An international perspective* (pp. 69–106). Boston: Allyn & Bacon.

Valsiner, J. (2000). *Culture and human development*. Thousand Oaks, CA: Sage.

Valsiner, J. & Rosa, A. (2007). *The Cambridge handbook of sociocultural psychology*. New York: Cambridge University Press.

van IJzendoorn, M. H., & Sagi, A. (1999). Cross-cultural patterns of attachment: Universal and contextual dimensions. In J. Cassidy & P. R. Shaver (Eds.), *Handbook of attachment: Theory, research, and clinical applications* (pp. 713–734). New York: Guilford Press.

van IJzendoorn, M. H., & Sagi, A., (2001). Cultural blindness or selective inattention? *American Psychologist, 56*(10), 824–825.

Varenne, H., & McDermott, R. (1999). *Successful failure: The school America builds*. Boulder, CO: Westview Press.

Vinden, P. G. (1998). Imagination and true belief: A cross-cultural perspective. In J. de Rivera & T. R. Sarbin (Eds.), *Believed-in imaginings: The narrative construction of reality* (pp. 73–85). Washington, DC: American Psychological Association.

Vinden, P. G. (1999). Children's understanding of mind and emotion: A multi-culture study. *Cognition & Emotion, 13*(1), 19–48.

Vinden, P. G. (2002). Understanding minds and evidence for belief: A study of Mofu children in Cameroon. *International Journal of Behavioral Development, 26*(5), 445–452.

Vygotsky, L. S. (1987). Thinking and speech. In N. Minick (Ed. & Trans.), *The collected works of L. S. Vygotsky: Vol. 1. Problems of general psychology* (pp. 39–285). New York: Plenum.

Vygotsky, L. S. (2004). The historical meaning of the crisis in psychology: A methodological investigation. In R. W. Rieber & D. K. Robinson (Eds.), *The essential Vygotsky* (pp. 227–357). New York: Kluwer Academic/Plenum Publishers.

Wagner, D. A. (1982). Ontogeny in the study of culture and cognition. In D. A. Wagner & H. W. Stevenson (Eds.), *Cultural perspectives on child development* (pp. 105–123). San Francisco: Freeman.

Wagner, D. A., (1993). *Literacy, culture, and development: Becoming literate in Morocco*. New York: Cambridge University Press.

Waxman, S. R., & Medin, D. (2007). Experience and cultural models matter: Placing firm limits on childhood anthropocentrism. *Human Development, 50*, 23–30.

Weisner, T. S. (1996). The 5 to 7 transition as an ecocultural project. In A. Sameroff & M. M. Haith (Eds.), *The five to seven year shift: The age of reason and responsibility* (pp. 295–326). Chicago: University of Chicago Press.

Weisner, T. (2002). Ecocultural understanding of children's developmental pathways. *Human Development, 45*(4), 275–281.

Wellman, H. C. (2002). Understanding the psychological world: Developing a theory of mind. In U. Goswami (Ed.), *Blackwell handbook of childhood cognitive development* (pp. 167–187). Malden, MA: Blackwell.

Wellman, H. M., Cross, D., & Watson, J. (2001). Meta-analysis of theory-of-mind development: The truth about false belief. *Child Development, 72*(3), 655–684.

Wellman, H. M., & Gelman, S. A. (1992). Cognitive development: Foundational theories of core domains. *Annual Review of Psychology, 43*, 337–375.

Wellman, H. M., & Johnson, C. N. (2008). Developing dualism: From intuitive understanding to transcendental ideas. In A. Antonietti, A. Corradini, & E. J. Lowe (Eds.), *Psycho-physical dualism today: An interdisciplinary approach* (pp. 3–36). Plymouth, UK: Lexington Books.

Wertsch, J. (1985). *Vygotsky and the social formation of mind*. Cambridge, MA: Harvard University Press.

White, L. (1942). On the use of tools by primates. *Journal of Comparative Psychology, 34*, 369–374.

White, L. (1959). The concept of culture. *American Anthropologist, 61*, 227–251.

White, S. H. (1996). The child's entry into the "age of reason". In A. J. Sameroff & M. M. Haith (Eds.), *The five to seven year shift: The age of reason and responsibility* (pp. 17–30). Chicago: University of Chicago Press.

Whiting, B. B. (1976). The problem of the packaged variable. In K. F. Riegel & J. A. Meacham (Eds.), *The developing individual in a changing world* (Vol. 1). Chicago: Aldine.

Whiting, B. B. (1980). Culture and social behavior: A model for development of social behaviors. *Ethos, 8*, 95–116.

Whiting, B. B., & Edwards, C. P. (1988). *Children of different worlds: The formation of social behavior*. Cambridge, MA: Harvard University Press.

Whiting, J. W. M., Burbank, V. K., & Ratner, M. S. (1986). The duration of maidenhood. In J. W. M. Whiting, V. K. Burbank, & M. S. Ratner (Eds.), *School-age pregnancy: Biosocial dimensions* (pp. 273–302). New York: Aldine de Gruyer.

Williams, R. (1973). *Keywords*. New York: Oxford University Press.

Wolff, P., & Medin, D. L. (2001). Measuring the evolution and devolution of folkbiological knowledge. In L. Maffi (Ed.), *On biocultural diversity: Linking language knowledge and the environment* (pp. 212–27). Washington, DC: Smithsonian Institution.

DESIGN, MEASUREMENT, AND ANALYSIS IN DEVELOPMENTAL RESEARCH

Donald P. Hartmann
University of Utah
Kelly E. Pelzel
University of Iowa
Craig B. Abbott
National Institute of Child Health and Human Development

INTRODUCTION

This chapter is concerned with technical aspects of traditional developmental research, including the following topics: the **design** of studies, the **measurement** of variables, the analysis of data, and ethical considerations. To the neophyte who has attempted to read the method and results sections of developmental papers, these largely "methodological" aspects of research appear to be bewildering, and infinitely varied in type, form, and perhaps function.

However complex the technical aspects of research may be, it is important to emphasize from the start the dependence of research technology on the *theoretically based* questions motivating empirical investigations. The question to be answered should determine the most effective design, the most appropriate measures, and the most informative forms of analysis applied to the resulting scores. When the technical tail wags the substantive dog, research questions tend to be unsystematic, atheoretical, and of dubious use in advancing the science of development. The dependence of research technology on the substance of experimental questions places an additional burden on investigators: They must find or develop *the* design, *the* measurement operations, and *the* methods of analysis that are uniquely suited to their research questions.

The aspects of design, measurement, and analysis presented in this chapter are not intended to qualify individuals to select their own design, measurement, and analysis procedures. Instead, this chapter shows how design, measurement, and analysis function by specifying commonly used methods, indicating major issues, noting more serious pitfalls, and suggesting where additional information might be obtained.

The section on *design* focuses on four classes of threats to validity and on how non-experimental, quasi-experimental, and true experimental designs meet, or fail to meet, the challenges represented by these threats. Special attention is paid to design difficulties that plague developmental investigators, and to the traditional as well as newer designs developed in response to these difficulties.

The section on *measurement* addresses the purposes of measurement, the types of scores generated by developmental investigators, and the criteria used for judging the worth of these scores. **Standardization**, **reliability**, and validity criteria emerge as uniquely important for assessing the quality of scores. Many aspects of measurement—including the nature of the underlying constructs, accessible characteristics of target responses, relevant comparison standards for deciphering the meaning of scores, and available sources of information—determine how scores are operationalized as well as judged.

The section on *analysis* begins with a presentation of the distinctions between **categorical** and **quantitative** approaches to data. We focus on quantitative procedures, beginning with preliminary data analysis: methods of appropriately laundering data and developing an intimate familiarity with them. Formal statistical analysis is viewed as serving two interrelated functions: describing data by means of various indices of typical performance, variability, and relation; and testing whether the value of these indices is consistent with theoretical expectations or differs from null values—that is, whether the data are statistically significant.[1] A substantial number of techniques for serving these functions are described, with brief mention made of pitfalls and problems in their use and of the sources for learning more about them. These techniques of analysis accommodate the two major purposes of developmental research: assessing average performance across time (e.g., the developmental function; Wohlwill, 1973) as well as variation about the average, or individual, differences (e.g., Baltes & Nesselroade, 1979). Univariate and multivariate analytic techniques for categorical and quantitative data are described, and three increasingly popular techniques (hierarchical linear modeling, structural modeling, and meta-analysis) are singled out for special attention. The analysis section ends with a brief discussion of statistical significance, **effect size**, importance, and their interrelations.

The chapter's penultimate section is a brief discussion of *qualitative methods*, which are assuming an increasingly important role in the methodological armamentarium of developmentalists.

The chapter ends with a short discussion of *ethical issues* in developmental research. The discussion is aimed primarily at those issues that directly affect child research participants, including justifiable risk, invasion of privacy, and informed consent.

DESIGN

Traditional science has three main purposes: the prediction of important criteria, the control of relevant outcomes, and the search for causal relations between independent variables (IVs) and dependent variables (DVs). The substantive area of investigation determines the most important of these goals and the variables investigated. Once an investigator chooses the research question—and thereby defines the purposes of the research—a design must be constructed so that that question can be answered in as unambiguous a manner as is

---

[1] The long history of controversy over null hypothesis testing (e.g., Nickerson, 2000) has entered a new level of intensity (e.g., Harlow, Mulaik, & Steiger, 1997). Even the often staid American Psychological Association established a study group to determine whether null hypothesis testing should be discouraged from its journals (see Wilkinson & the Task Force on Statistical Inference, 1999). Abelson (1997a, p. 13) typified the dilemma confronting investigators this way: "Whatever else is done about null-hypothesis tests, let us stop viewing statistical analysis as a sanctification process. We are awash in a sea of uncertainty, caused by a flood tide of sampling and measurement errors, and there are no objective procedures that avoid human judgment and guarantee correct interpretations of results." A variety of approaches has been recommended as adjuncts to, or even substitutes for, null hypothesis testing. These procedures include, foremost, a model-comparison approach to data analysis that emphasizes the use of goodness of fit indices; critical thinking and sound judgment; confidence intervals and effect-size estimates; Bayesian statistics, and appropriate consideration of power (see, e.g., Harlow, 1997; Judd, McClelland, & Culhane, 1995; Wilkinson & the Task Force on Statistical Inference, 1999). These issues are examined in more detail in the analysis section.

reasonable given the ethical, technological, and practical constraints under which we function. Design involves the structure of investigations, the extent and means by which investigators exercise control over their independent, as well as other, variables that might be operating in the investigative context, so that appropriate conclusions can be drawn from the research.

Experimental design is intended to guard against alternative or competing plausible interpretations of the phenomena under study. These competing interpretations have been construed as *threats* to the validity of the investigation. This section describes the most common of these validity threats, with attention directed to problems common to the research experiences of developmentalists. The solutions to these problems afforded by a variety of design variations, including true experimental, quasi-experimental, and **nonexperimental designs**, are described. Special attention is paid to the designs defined by the developmental variables of age, cohort, and time of assessment, both in their traditional combination and in their more complex combination in sequential designs. The section ends with a listing of suggested readings for readers who may want additional information on these issues.

Validity Threats

Campbell and his associates (Campbell & Stanley, 1963; Cook & Campbell, 1979; Shadish, Cook, & Campbell, 2002) distinguished four classes of threats to the validity of investigations that developmental, as well as other researchers, must confront. These four classes, their definitions, and specific examples are given in Tables 4.1–4.4 (also see Huck & Sandler, 1979, for illustrations of many of the frequently discussed validity threats).

Statistical conclusion validity. Threats to **statistical conclusion validity**—or to the validity of the inferences we make from statistical tests—are easier to understand with at least some acquaintance with traditional statistical decision theory. Table 4.1 illustrates a simple decision matrix that describes the decisions that might be made as a result of **null hypothesis testing**. Two decisions and two states of nature are shown: The decisions are to accept or to reject the null hypothesis; the states of nature are that the null hypothesis is either true or false. The resulting decision matrix shows two types of correct and two types of incorrect decisions. The incorrect decisions are referred to as *Type I* and *Type II errors*.

Type I errors occur when a true null hypothesis is rejected mistakenly. True null hypotheses are incorrectly rejected with a probability equal to α, where α is the critical value required for rejection of the null hypothesis, traditionally set at either $p = .05$ or $p = .01$.

TABLE 4.1
A Matrix Illustrating Statistical Decision Theory

State of Nature: H_0

		True	False
	Reject H_0	Type Error (α)	Correct Rejection (Power)
Investigator's Decision			
	Accept H_0	Correct Acceptance	Type II Error (β)

Note. H_0 refers to the null hypothesis.

Type II errors occur when a false null hypothesis is accepted wrongly. Rejection of a false null hypothesis occurs when we fail to detect a real effect that exists in nature. The probability of a real effect not being detected is equal to β, where $[1 - \beta] = $ **power**.

Threats to statistical conclusion validity represented by Type I errors occur as a result of conducting one of the many kinds of fishing expeditions that investigators are known to perform on their data. One of the more egregious forms of fishing occurs when a data analyst performs numerous statistical tests on the same set of data, such as comparing each of $k = 6$ means to every other mean, resulting in $k(k-1)/2 = 15$ comparisons. Unless the analyst makes adjustments for the number of statistical tests conducted (e.g., the Bonferroni correction, where α is set for the entire collection of tests), Type I error mushrooms for the entire *set* of tests, and clearly exceeds α. Additional threats represented by distortions of Type I error occur when certain kinds of statistical assumptions are violated (e.g., Judd et al., 1995; Kenny & Judd, 1986; Kirk, 1995). Failure to meet the assumptions of statistical tests can be particularly lethal when the assumptions of independence are violated and when testing causal models (see the discussion of nesting and structural equation modeling).

Threats represented by Type II errors also can occur when statistical assumptions are violated; however, they primarily occur when *power*—the probability of rejecting a false null hypothesis—is low. The notion of power is so critical in research that we digress here to amplify its implications. To the extent that our theory directs us to important phenomena that produce real, nontrivial effects, the likelihood that we will detect (in a statistical sense) these effects is given by the power of our investigation. Power depends on the size of the effect we are attempting to detect—a factor that ordinarily may not be under our control—plus a variety of factors that are controllable (see Table 4.2 and Shadish et al., 2002, pp. 46–47). These factors deserve our careful attention because our success as investigators hinges critically on the power of our investigations. This occurs in part because the value of manuscripts reporting "failure to find significant effects" is severely limited. Thus, we strongly recommend

TABLE 4.2
Statistical Conclusion Validity Threats: Definition and Examples[a]

Are the results of the statistical tests—acceptance or rejection of each of the null hypotheses—valid? OR Is statistical conclusion validity threatened by design or analytic weaknesses or errors?

Fishing Expeditions: Have Type I errors been inflated—sometimes referred to as probability pyramiding (Neher, 1967)—as a result of excessive, overlapping analysis of the data?

Violation of the Assumptions of the Statistical Tests: Has an incorrect conclusion been drawn—either an incorrect rejection (Type I error) or an incorrect acceptance of the null hypothesis (Type II error)—because an important assumption of the statistical test has been violated?

Low Power or Power Incorrectly Estimated: Is failure to reject a null hypothesis ascribable to the fact that the null hypothesis was true and there was no effect to be detected or to low power (a Type II error)? Low power might occur as a result of

(1) inadequate sample size
(2) measures that are lacking in construct validity or reliability (the latter perhaps due to too few waves or panels in a longitudinal study or too few or too short data collection sessions in an observational investigation)
(3) weak or inconsistent manipulation of the independent variable
(4) poor experimental control (random irrelevancies present in the investigative setting)
(5) excessive respondent heterogeneity
(6) weak statistics
(7) excessively small alpha levels.

---

[a] Strictly speaking, no null hypothesis may be precisely true. Trivial differences may even be found for the null hypothesis such as that involving the equivalence in IQ of people living east of the Mississippi in comparison to those living west of the Mississippi (see Morrison & Henkel, 1970). The relevant difference to be detected is not *any* difference, but any difference large enough to be interesting to the investigator.

conducting power analyses (Cohen, 1988; Maxwell, Kelley, & Rausch, 2008) prior to implementing any investigation.

Internal validity.   Threats to **internal validity** (Table 4.3) represent mistaken inferences about the causal connectedness between independent variable and dependent variable in a particular investigation. These threats, called confounds, are, with few exceptions, easily understood. One of the more knotty confounds is regression to the mean. Regression occurs when participants (poor readers, highly aggressive children, or insensitive mothers) are selected on the basis of the extremity of their scores. If the measures used to select these extremely performing individuals are less than perfectly reliable—which is almost always true in our study of the empirical world—the individuals can be expected to score less deviantly when they are reassessed. Thus, as a group, poor readers appear to be less deviant in their reading performance on a second reading assessment—even one that occurs immediately following the first assessment! Why? Because the poor readers were deviant in part because chance factors contributed to the extremity of their scores, and these chance components are unlikely to reoccur.

A second seemingly opaque class of confounds involves ambiguity about the direction of causal influence. However, this threat to internal validity is recognizable as the old adage that "correlation does not imply causation." Even if all potential third variable causes can be excluded (the troublesome variable Z, when variables X and Y are investigated), it is still possible, particularly in nonexperimental investigations, that X (the putative IV) is caused by Y (the ostensible DV), rather than the other way around.

TABLE 4.3
Internal Validity Threats: Definition and Examples

Can the observed findings be attributed to the independent variable? OR Is internal validity threatened by some methodological confound?

History: Did some event intervene, say, between the pretest and the posttest that produced an effect that might be confused with an effect produced by the independent variable (IV)?

Maturation: Are the observed findings ascribable to the growth or other internal changes in the participant rather than to the IV?

Testing: Did the participant's familiarity with the assessment device produce the observed changes in the dependent variable (DV)?

Instrumentation: Did the measurement instrument itself change over the course of the study so that differences are a result of changes in the calibration of the instrument and not to changes produced by the IV?

Regression: Are observed changes due to the selection of deviant respondents based on their performance on an unreliable assessment device, and their scores moving toward the mean on repeated testing as a function of the combination of selection and unreliability, rather than as a result of changes produced by the IV?

Selection: Are observed differences attributable to preexisting differences in the individuals assigned to the groups compared, rather than to effects produced by differences in exposure to the IV?

Mortality: Are observed differences due to differential dropouts or attrition in the groups compared?

Interactions with Selection: Are the observed findings ascribable to the interaction of selection with, say, maturation (because of selection factors, groups of participants are maturing at different rates) rather than to the effects of the IV?

Ambiguity about the Direction of Causal Influence: Is the causal connection from the presumed DV to the IV rather than the other way around?

Diffusion of Treatments, Compensatory Equalization of Treatments, or Compensatory Rivalry: Is the *lack of* observed differences a result of the fact that the non-treated participants were inadvertently exposed to the treatment, provided with compensatory treatments, or "worked harder" because they did not receive the favored treatment?

Resentful Demoralization: Was the effect observed attributable to the demoralized responding of participants who thought that they received a less desirable treatment?

Most threats to internal validity can be avoided by random assignment of participants to conditions, a critical method of control in psychological research and a characteristic of **true experiments**. However, even randomization may not rule out some threats to internal validity, such as those represented in the last two paragraphs of Table 4.3 (e.g., diffusion of treatments and resentful demoralization).

Construct validity.   In general, threats to **construct validity** occur when the variables, as operationalized, either underrepresent the intended constructs or include surplus components. For example, the construct "anxiety" that did not include physiological, ideational, and behavioral components might be faulted for construct underrepresentation. However, a paper-and-pencil measure of anxiety that correlated highly with verbal IQ might be criticized for including surplus irrelevancies.

Construct validity threats can be sustained by either the IV or the DV. Consider, for example, the use of a single male and a single female model (an example of mono-operation bias—see Table 4.4) in a study of the effects of model gender on the imitation of aggression. In this example, mono-operationalization of the IV might result in a unique characteristic of one of the models, such as attractiveness, producing an effect that is confused with a gender effect. A construct validity threat to DVs might occur when all of the outcome variables are assessed using a single method, such as self-report. In such cases of monomethod bias, relations found between the outcome variables might be produced by the self-report method that they share (Campbell & Fiske, 1959), rather than by actual interdependence of the constructs.

Campbell and Fiske's (1959) notion that a score is a joint function of the construct, trait, or

TABLE 4.4
Construct Validity Threats: Definition and Examples

Do the critical variables in the study (the independent and dependent variables) measure the intended constructs? OR Is construct validity threatened by one or more methodological artifacts?

Inadequate Preoperational Explication of Constructs: Does the meaning of the construct as used in the investigation match (include neither more nor less than) the ordinary meaning of the construct as used in this area of study?

Mono-operational Bias: Have the critical variables in the study been operationalized in only one way, so that the results are a function of the particular operationalization employed?

Mono-method Bias: Have the operationalizations of a construct or constructs all used the same method, so that the results might be ascribable to overlapping method variance rather than overlapping construct variance?

Hypothesis Guessing: Are the results attributable to participants acting consistently with their hypotheses about the study, or how they believe the experimenter wants them to behave (the Hawthorne effect)?

Evaluation Apprehension: Is some "subject effect" (Webber & Cook, 1972) such as fear of evaluation responsible for the observed changes in performance, rather than the IV?

Experimenter Expectancies: Are the results a function of the expectancies of the experimenter—a treatment-correlated irrelevancy—which are somehow transmitted to the participant?

Confounding Constructs and Levels of Constructs: Is it the particular level of the IV that produced (or failed to produce) the observed effect, rather than the entire range of levels of the IV?

Interaction of Different Treatments: Is the effect observed a result of the particular combination or sequence of IVs employed, rather than to the pivotal treatment variable?

Interaction of Testing and Treatment: Does the putative effect of treatment require the use of pretesting— where participants may be primed to respond in a particular manner?

Restricted Generalizability across Constructs: Does the IV affect a range of outcome constructs, or instead, just the more or less narrow range of outcome constructs employed in the investigation?

Treatment-Sensitive Factorial and Reactive Self-Report Changes: Do the treatments or the selection process (e.g., being assigned to the control versus the treatment condition) interact with the assessment method so that the resulting scores have different meaning for the groups compared (see Shadish et al., 2002, p. 77)?

characteristic it is intended to assess *and* the method used to produce it has profound implications. The wise investigator uses multiple measures (or indicators, as they are sometimes called) when assessing constructs to minimize the irrelevant components of each measure and produce more construct-valid assessments (e.g., Pedhazur & Schmelkin, 1991).

Construct validity threats include not only measurement artifacts, but other artifacts as well that distort the meaning of either the IV or DV. Among these are:

1. "subject effects" (e.g., evaluation apprehension and the distrusting participant) that produce atypical responding
2. experimenter effects such as expectancies that influence participants in irrelevant ways
3. pretest assessments that sensitize the participants to the treatments
4. a particular sequence or combination of treatments that modifies the effect of the target treatment.

External validity.   Issues of **external validity** are sometimes labeled as issues of ecological validity, generalizability, or representativeness. Whatever label is attached, the primary concern is the extent to which the results of studies are applicable to individuals, settings, treatments, and times different from those existing during the conduct of the study (see Table 4.5). Generalizability is one of psychology's seminal issues and requires continued vigilance. Are the results of research performed on rural European American adolescents applicable to African American adolescents living in urban settings? Are the findings of research conducted in the 1930s on the effects of nursery school applicable to nursery school experiences in the twenty-first century, when the nature of nursery schools and the parents who enroll their children in them differ? Shadish et al. (2002) presented a grounded theory of generalized causal inference based on the practices that scientists have used to generalize in a variety of investigative areas. Their analysis broadened the issue of generalizabilty from the context of participant sampling,[2] where it largely had resided for many years, to encompass other important facets of generalizability, including settings, treatments, and measurements. The principles developed by Shadish et al. (2002) for assessing the likelihood of generalizing an experimental finding include:

TABLE 4.5
External Validity Threats: Definition and Examples

Can the results of the investigation be generalized broadly? OR Is external validity threatened by contrived settings, unusual participants, or other factors that limit the generality of the results of the study?
Interaction of Selection and Treatment: Are the results limited to the particular sample investigated, or can they be generalized to a broader range of participants?
Interaction of Setting and Treatment: Are the effects produced applicable to other settings than the specific settings employed in the present investigation?
Interaction of History and Treatment: Can the results be generalized to other time periods, or are they limited to the particular historical circumstances in which the study was conducted?
Context-Dependent Mediation: Is the mediator or process operating to produce the effect limited to the particular investigative context?

---

[2] Even the more tractable issue of generalization across participants has been treated in a rather cavalier manner by many investigators—as if any sampling method would do, whether it be convenience or accidental sampling, or involves snowballing (one subject recommends a second, and so on), coercion, or bribery. Unless it is implausible that participant variables could modify important conclusions drawn from the research, such an attitude seems scientifically perilous.

1. *surface similarity*—judging the apparent similarities between the relevant characteristics of the present investigation and the target of generalization
2. *ruling out irrelevancies*—identifying those attributes that seem irrelevant because they do not change a generalization (e.g., parental eye color and the effectiveness of induction procedures)
3. *making discriminations*—making discriminations that limit generalization, such as the effect of ethnicity on parental punishment
4. *interpolation and extrapolation*—for example, parent training demonstrated to be effective in laboratory and home settings would probably also be effective when applied in a clinician's office
5. *causal explanation*—generalization based on developing and testing theories about explanatory mechanisms, for example, that the beneficial effects on children in interaction with both parents and teachers are mediated by warmth and reasonable expectations (e.g., Baumrind, 1991).

No investigator can thwart all of these common validity threats, as some requirements conflict with others. For example, the uniform application of treatments may increase statistical conclusion validity, but at the cost of external validity. No study has been, nor will any ever be, perfect. Basic researchers, those studying basic processes of development, may tend to emphasize internal, construct, and statistical conclusion validity to the detriment of external validity, whereas applied researchers studying social policy issues may emphasize internal, external, and statistical conclusion validity at the cost of construct validity. Investigators must consider the risks of the various validity threats with the potential uses of the research outcomes.

Seminal Design Issues for Developmental Investigators

All investigators, whatever their focus or interest, must confront these four classes of validity threats. In addition to these generic threats to the validity of research findings, there are other design concerns that are more or less the province of developmental investigators. These special issues, not surprisingly, concern the modifiability of the variables studied by developmentalists; the changing form of the phenomena they study; their participants' limited abilities to perceive or describe their experiences; the complexity out of which the behavior they study develops; the dangerous causal biases held by them, as well as by many students of development; and attrition—the loss of data because a participant fails to answer one or more questions in a questionnaire or interview or because the participant is unavailable on one or more occasions of measurement.

Intractable variables. Many of the important variables investigated by developmental researchers are relatively intractable. For example, a pivotal question to the field is the means by which heredity and environment conspire to produce behavior. But heredity cannot be manipulated, except in studies of non-human species, and environments are likewise generally not modifiable over broad sweeps or for extensive periods of an individual's life. Even that most popular of all developmental variables, age, has clear limitations as a causal variable. Age cannot be modified or manipulated, although individuals of various ages can be chosen for investigation. And although it is unquestionably useful to find that a phenomenon covaries with age, neither age nor the related variable time is a causal variable; changes occur *in time*, but not as a result of time. Instead, time or age is part of a context in which causal processes operate. At best, age may serve as a *proxy* for variables that are causally potent for development. Thus, in an important sense, the most studied developmental variable (see Miller, 2007) is causally impotent (Wohlwill, 1970).

Change.   The study of development is foremost the study of change. Historically, the study of change has associated with it a variety of thorny technical problems (Gottman, 1995; Rogosa, 1988) including the reliability of change scores and the negative correlation of change scores with initial scores. However, some of the "seminal" problems associated with the assessment of change literally disappeared as a result largely of a simple improvement in methodology: employing multiwave, instead of the traditional two-wave (e.g., pre- and post-test), **longitudinal designs**. Collecting multiwave data dramatically increases the precision and reliability of the growth measurement—an extra wave of data may double or triple the reliability of the growth rate. Additionally, multiwave data tell us about the shape of change—does change occur immediately after the first assessment or is it steady or delayed?—and may permit a more sophisticated individual model of growth to be adopted (Singer & Willett, 2003; Willet, 1989, 1994). However, not all of the problems associated with change participated in this disappearing act. A construct may itself change in topography or other important characteristics with development, for example, such that a measure of emotional control appropriate for an early developmental level may be inappropriate for assessing emotional control during a later phase of development. When measures do not assess the same construct across occasions (or groups), interpretation of score comparisons is at best muddied, and may result in inferences that are "potentially artifactual and . . . substantively misleading" (Widaman & Reise, 1997, p. 282). This vexing and technically complex issue of "measurement equivalence" is variously discussed by Hartmann (2005) and by Knight and Hill (1998).

Change may be incremental (i.e., gradual and linear) or transformational (e.g., sudden, nonlinear reorganization of system-wide processes). The parameters of change may also vary: For some individuals, change may occur briefly and comparatively late; for others, change may occur early and over more protracted periods of time. A lack of sensitivity to these temporal parameters of change may mean that the time period when a process is most open to inspection will be missed, and that measurements may occur either with insufficient frequency to "resolve" the underlying process or over shorter duration than is necessary to capture the entire process.

Limited availability of self-reports.   Unlike the sophisticated college student often studied by cognitive and social psychologists, the participants in many developmental investigations are unable to aid the investigator by describing their experiences—because either they are unaware of the relevant behaviors or processes or they do not have a communicative system that can be accessed readily. Other complex methods must be used to address even limited aspects of the young child's mental and emotional experiences: Sophisticated technology, participant observers, such as parents and teachers, or independent raters must be relied on to gain access to even the more obvious manifestations of these experiences (Bornstein, Arterberry, & Mash, 2010).

Complexity of causal networks.   Most developmental phenomena are embedded intricately in a complex, interacting network of environmental and genetic–constitutional forces that defies simple analysis or study. And in many cases, the factors of presumed importance—such as severe environmental deprivation—cannot be reproduced with humans because of obvious ethical concerns. As a result, investigators are forced to the laboratory where analogs of naturally occurring phenomena are created, and where complex, naturalistic conditions are greatly simplified. The consequences of these actions are that external and construct validity may be substantially strained.

Directional causal biases.   Developmentalists traditionally have attributed causal agency to adults rather than children, to families rather than cultural factors, and to environmental rather than complexly interacting biological and environmental determinants. The reasons for these biases are undoubtedly complex and are not widely discussed—although the research by Bell (1968) on the direction of effects in the socialization literature is cited widely and appears to have an important impact on developmental research. Nonetheless, we must be cautious in imputing direction of causation, particularly for findings that are produced by passive observational (*ex post facto*) studies, because requirements for inferring causality are difficult to meet (Shonkoff & Phillips, 2000, Chapter 4). Not only does correlation not imply causation in these designs, but a lack of correlation does not disprove causation (Bollen, 1989, p. 52). Furthermore, we must exercise constraint in not overemphasizing the causal importance of proximal variables (such as parents), while underplaying the role of more distal variables, such as unemployment or inequitable distribution of wealth. And we must be wary of overstating the causal importance of currently "politically correct" causes to the detriment of equally important but unpopular causes. We may, for example, be prone to attribute children's aggressive behavior to violence in TV programming rather than to competitive learning environments in our educational institutions, when both factors are equally plausible and potent determinants of aggression. Finally, we must be wary of making simple dichotomous causal judgments (e.g., heredity *or* environment is the cause of a behavior) when the answer is almost certainly setting-specific, and causal processes involve complex interacting systems (e.g., Anastasi, 1958; Fischer & Bidell, 1998; also see Hoffman, 1991).

Attrition.   Attrition and its consequence, unplanned missing scores,[3] are problems that developmental researchers will surely grapple with, especially those doing longitudinal research. "Scientists engaged in longitudinal research deal with unplanned missing data constantly; in fact, it is difficult to imagine a longitudinal study without at least some unplanned missing data" (Collins, 2006, p. 521). Attrition threatens statistical conclusion validity by decreasing statistical power and internal validity when dropouts in different study conditions differ in ways related to the outcome (Shadish & Cook, 2009). Dealing with attrition starts in the planning stages of the study, should be monitored during the course of the study, and must be considered when analyzing and interpreting the data. To minimize attrition, developmental researchers plan for and carefully implement strategies that help prevent it, such as recording complete demographic information of the participants and their family, friends, and coworkers; training research staff to build rapport with the participants; and offering appropriate financial or other incentives for continued participation. Excellent and thorough summaries for retaining and tracking participants are found in Cauce, Ryan, and Grove (1998) and in Ribisl et al. (1996); see also Hartmann (2005) and Shadish et al. (2002). Despite our best preventive efforts, however, attrition will occur, and researchers need to know how to deal with missing scores. Procedures that are based on statistical theory, such as multiple imputation and maximum likelihood, are recommended over *ad hoc* procedures such as casewise deletion and mean substitution (Collins, 2006; Graham, 2009; see also footnote 7 in "preliminary analysis" section).

Design Variations

Developmental investigators have employed a variety of design variations in response to the validity threats and problems already discussed. Many of the common variations are

---

[3] "Unplanned missing data" refers to data loss that is out of the control of the investigator. Some designs however include "planned missing data" for reasons of economy and reduction in the response burden on participants. Known as efficiency designs, their value depends on the investigator's ability to use analysis procedures for handling missing data (Graham, Taylor, Olchowski, & Cumsille, 2006).

summarized in Table 4.6. As the footnote to that table suggests, a design chosen to control one type of validity threat may promote another. For example, contrived settings have allowed investigators to exercise experimental control over unwanted sources of variation—but at the expense of external validity. The study of natural treatments promotes external validity, but the complexity and "noise" associated with these treatments often blurs their meaning or construct validity. The intensive study of a few individuals may allow investigators to capture the complexity of their target phenomena, but may raise questions of generalizability.

TABLE 4.6

The Advantages of Design Variations Intended to Solve Validity Threats and Other Design Concerns

Versus	
Experimental Control: Nuisance variables are precluded from occurring by isolation or selection. Improves internal validity by avoiding error variance.	*Statistical Control:* Nuisance factors are removed by statistical means (e.g., using partial correlation techniques). Promotes internal validity by reducing error variance. Preserves external validity by not tampering with the setting.
Contrived Setting: Modifies settings so that target behaviors occur and extraneous variables are controlled (e.g., laboratories). Promotes internal validity by exercising tight control over nuisance variables. Saves investigative time by decreasing dross rate.	*Field Setting:* Employs untampered settings for investigations. Facilitates external validity by providing a natural context. Provides estimates of naturally occurring rates of behaviors.
Artificial Treatments: Introduces ideal or prototypical forms of treatments. Improves construct validity of causes by control over the nature of the DV.	*Natural Treatments:* Examines naturally occurring treatments. Promotes external validity by studying natural variation in treatment implementation.
Crossed Designs: Designs in which each level of every factor is paired with each level of every other factor (e.g., in an Age × Gender design, girls and boys are represented for each age group). Allows for the assessments of interactions.	*Nested Designs:* Designs in which each level of every factor is *not* paired with each level of every other factor. Improves efficiency by omitting treatment conditions of little interest. Facilitates construct validity by precluding certain forms of multiple-treatment interference.
Within-Subjects Designs: Uses each respondent as own control. Promotes statistical conclusion validity by controlling error variance.	*Between-Subjects Designs:* Control provided by random assignment of participants to condition. May foster construct validity by avoiding multiple treatment interference. Uses investigative time efficiently by allowing simultaneous study of many treatments.
Intensive (Idiographic) Designs: Designs in which one or a few participants are intensively assessed, usually across time as in a longitudinal or time-series study. Furthers the study of performance across time (e.g., the study of trends). Accommodates the complexity of performance changes across time. Provides access to where the laws of behavior reside—in the individual.	*Extensive (Nomothetic) Designs:* Many participants are assessed, but typically only once. Makes efficient use of investigative time.

Note. The advantages of one alternative typically, though not always, are the limitations of the parallel alternative.

Perhaps the most important differences between families of designs are those based on the nature of the causal statement allowed by the designs. Campbell and his associates (Campbell & Stanley, 1963; Cook & Campbell, 1979; Shadish et al., 2002) distinguished three levels of investigation based on the design's allowable causal implications: true experiments, **quasi-experiments**, and nonexperiments.

True experiments.   True experiments include manipulation of the independent variable by the investigator and control of extraneous variables by random assignment of participants to conditions. Random assignment of participants has a number of truly astounding consequences (Shadish et al., 2002, p. 248).

1. It ensures that alternative causes are not confounded with treatment conditions.
2. It reduces the plausibility of a variety of validity threats by distributing them randomly over conditions.
3. It equates groups on the expected value of all variables at pretest—whether or not they are measured.
4. It allows the investigator to know and model the selection process correctly.
5. It allows computation of a valid estimate of error variance that is independent or orthogonal to treatment.

Not surprising, true experimental designs, if conducted properly, allow investigators to make strong inferences regarding the causal effect exerted by the IV over the DV. Table 4.7 illustrates two true experimental designs: the simplest of all true experimental designs—and from which all other true experimental designs are derived—the experimental–control group design with posttests only; and the more complex, Solomon four-group design (Solomon & Lessac, 1968). The Solomon four-group and other true experimental designs are discussed in most design texts, including those by Campbell and his associates (e.g., Campbell & Stanley, 1963).

Quasi-experiments.   Quasi-experiments are investigations in which control procedures are instigated, but assignment to conditions is not random. In such cases, the thread connecting cause and effect is less susceptible to clear delineation, although some causal inferences often are possible.[4] Panel A of Table 4.8 illustrates two quasi-experimental designs frequently used by applied behavior analysts, the ABA and multiple baseline designs (e.g., Gelfand & Hartmann, 1984). With the ABA or interrupted time-series design, a single case (e.g., an individual, family, or classroom) is observed repeatedly under a control series (the repeated Os at the beginning of the series); then a treatment is imposed and observation continues during that treatment phase (the repeated X_1O linkages). The initial observation phase is reinstituted (the second set of Os), and in many cases, a second phase of treatment–observations (X_1Os) is also reinstated. (The reintroduction of the second treatment phase formally makes this an ABAB design.)

With the multiple baseline design, treatment is introduced successively into each of two or more units (behaviors, participants, or contexts) following a series of control observations. These and other quasi-experimental designs can, with the addition of special features (e.g.,

---

[4] An underutilized but promising quasi-experimental design for estimating causal effects is the regression discontinuity design (RDD). The design assigns participants to conditions based on a cutoff score on an ordered assignment variable. A regression is fit to predict outcome from the assignment variable and dummy-coded treatment variable. Treatment effects are estimated from the discontinuity (change in slope or intercept) at the cutoff between treatment and control (Cook & Wong, 2008; Shadish & Cook, 2009).

TABLE 4.7
Illustrations of True Experimental Designs

Experimental-Control Group Design Employing Posttest-Only Assessments:
Group

Experimental	R:	X	O
Control	R:		O

Solomon Four-Group Design:
Group

Experimental	R:	O	X	O
	R:		X	O
Control	R:	O		O
	R:			O

Note. By convention, R indicates random assignment of participants to groups, O indicates an assessment, and X indicates a treatment.

TABLE 4.8
Illustrations of Quasi-Experimental and Nonexperimental Design

Panel A: Quasi-experimental Designs

Interrupted Time-Series (ABA) Design:

Group (or Participant)

Unit 1:   O. .O. .O. .X_1O. .X_1O. .X_1O. .O. .O. .O

Interrupted Time-Series (Multiple Baseline) Design

Group (or Participant)

Unit 1[a]	O. .O. .O. .X_1O. .X_1O. .X_1O. .
Unit 2	O. .O. .O. .O. .X_1O. .X_1O. .X_1O
Unit 3	O. .O. .O. .O. .O. .X_1O. .X_1O. .X_1O

Panel B: Nonexperimental Designs
One-Group, Pretest and Posttest Design

Group
Experimental: O   X   O

Note. The separation of events by . . indicates that the event may be repeated one or more times.
[a] Units can represent individuals or treatment settings or behaviors for an individual. Individuals may be either a single individual or an aggregate of individuals such as a classroom of students (e.g., Gelfand & Hartmann, 1984).

the random assignment of treatment order to units in the multiple baseline design), exclude many or even all plausible alternative interpretations, and allow strong causal inferences.

Nonexperimental designs. Nonexperimental designs employ neither randomization nor adequate control conditions. Designs in this class provide a product that does not allow investigators to reach conclusions about causality. Included in this group are case studies, one-group pretest and posttest designs (see Panel B of Table 4.8), and similar designs that are used primarily for hypothesis generation. *Ex post facto* or passive observational designs also are members of the nonexperimental design family. (In the past, these designs were sometimes referred to as *correlational designs*. However, that is an unfortunate term, as correlations are statistical measures of association, not designs, and can be applied to the data from any of the three types of designs just described.)

The lack of clarity regarding causal connections between the variables investigated in nonexperimental designs is generally well known. Nonetheless, they serve the important role of *probing* (in contrast to *testing*) potential causal models. Certainly a causal model relating X and Y is probed if X and Y are found to be uncorrelated. But even then, one could argue that the relation was too complex to be revealed by the design, or that the investigator made a poor decision in choosing the time delay between putative cause and effect (e.g., hunger is undoubtedly causally related to food intake, but self-reported hunger and observed food ingestion might only be correlated if eating was assessed for the meal immediately following the assessment of hunger). Unfortunately, many traditional developmental designs are closer to nonexperimental designs than to true experimental designs in the level of causal inference allowed.

Developmental Design

Developmentalists have been concerned traditionally with two issues: the normative changes that occur in developing individuals and individual differences in these developmental changes. The pursuit of these goals involves generally the variable of age, and age typically has been investigated using either cross-sectional or longitudinal designs.

Before discussing these and other developmental designs, it is useful to examine three variables that distinguish the various developmental designs: cohort, age, and time of assessment (Schaie & Caskie, 2005). *Cohorts* are groups of participants who are born—or experience some other common event—in the same time period. Thus, we speak of the 1979 cohort and of the cohort of baby boomers. Age has its usual meaning, as does time of assessment.

The design-defining variables of cohort, age, and time of assessment are not independent. This lack of independence can be seen by specifying a cohort and a time of assessment in the matrix shown in Table 4.9. Once the values for these two variables are specified, age—the variable indicated in the body of the matrix—is not free to vary, but instead is fixed or determined. Herein lies one of the major problems with the designs derived from this matrix: The variables of cohort, age, and time of assessment in these designs are inherently confounded. Consider the cross-sectional design (shown in Panel A of Table 4.10).

Cross-sectional designs are those in which at least two cohorts are assessed at the same time of assessment. As a result, the cohorts differ in age. If DV performance in a cross-sectional study differed across the age groups, one would be tempted to attribute the performance difference to age or development. However, note that the same variation in performance on the DV also can be attributed to cohort differences! Cohort differences might be produced by genetic variation resulting from changes in migration patterns or exposure to radiation, or they might stem from environmental variation (such as educational reform associated with living during a somewhat different historical epoch). Each of the simple developmental designs diagrammed in Tables 4.9 and 4.10 shares an analogous confound. These elementary developmental designs

TABLE 4.9
Cohort × Time of Assessment Matrix Illustrating Simple
Developmental Designs

Cohort	Time of Assessment		
	1975	*1980*	*1985*
1960	15[bc]	20[ab]	25[b]
1965	10	15[ac]	20
1970	5	10[a]	15[c]

Note. Age is given in the body of the table
[a] Cross-sectional design; [b] Longitudinal design; [c] Time-lagged design.

TABLE 4.10
Simple Developmental Designs

Panel A

Cross-Sectional Design:	*Cohort*	
	1965	*1970*
Time of Assessment: 1980	15	10

Panel B

Longitudinal Design:	*Age*	
	15	*20*
Cohort: 1960	1975	1980

Panel C

Time-lagged Design:	*Time of Assessment*	
	1980	*1985*
Age: 15	1965	1970

Note. Age is given in the body of the table in Panel A; Time of Assessment is given in the body of the table in Panel B; Cohort Is given in the body of the table in Panel C.

also share two other interpretive difficulties. First, the variables of cohort and time of assessment are *not* causally active—a status that has already been noted for age. At best, the variables of cohort, age, and time of assessment are *proxy* variables for the real causal processes that operate in time or are associated with cohort or time of assessment. Second, the variables of cohort, age, and time of assessment are not manipulated in these designs, nor are participants assigned randomly to cohorts or ages, although they can be assigned randomly to times of assessment—but not after age and cohort are assigned. Thus, the aspects of these developmental designs involving cohort, age, and time of assessment are not truly experimental. Indeed, the designs are nonexperimental (*ex post facto*), and the resulting data do not lend themselves to strong causal inferences regarding the effects of age, cohort, or time of assessment.

A prototypic longitudinal design is illustrated in Panel B of Table 4.10. Longitudinal designs have been described as "the lifeblood of developmental psychology" (McCall, 1977, p. 341). Nonetheless, they confound age and time of assessment and are nonexperimental with respect to these two variables. In addition, age and time of assessment are only proxies for active causal variables. We have already considered some of the causally active variables for which age could serve as a proxy; in the case of time of assessment, the causal variables may be events such as a turndown in the economy, the death of a prominent official, or a natural disaster.

A time-lagged design, the last of the simple designs (but not a true developmental design), is illustrated in Panel C of Table 4.10. Time-lagged designs confound the variables of cohort and time of assessment and are nonexperimental with respect to these two variables as well. Although these simple designs suffer from a variety of interpretive problems, they provide valuable information to developmentalists as to whether standing on important DVs varies as a function of age, cohort, or time of assessment. Once such a discovery has been made, the search for the explanation—the underlying process responsible for the finding—can begin.

In an attempt to remedy some of the problems associated with these simple developmental designs, more complex developmental designs—called *sequential designs*—have been developed (Schaie, 1965; Schaie & Caskie, 2005). These designs are illustrated in Tables 4.11 and 4.12. Table 4.11 displays a *Cohort × Time of Assessment* matrix similar to the one shown in Panel A of Table 4.10. In this case, however, the designs that are derived from the matrix are more complex than those derived from the matrix in Table 4.9. Each of the sequential designs

TABLE 4.11
Cohort × Time of Assessment Matrix Illustrating Complex (Sequential)
Developmental Designs

| | Time of Assessment | | |
| | 1975 | 1980 | 1985 |
Cohort			
1960	15[b]	20[bc]	25
1965	10	15[abc]	20[abc]
1970	5	10[a]	15[ac]

Note. Age is given in the body of the table.
[a] Cohort × Time of Assessment (cross-sequential) design; [b] Age × Cohort (cohort-sequential) design; [c] Time of Assessment × Age (time-sequential) design.

TABLE 4.12
Sequential Developmental Designs

Panel A
Cohort × Time of Assessment Design

| | Cohort | |
	1965	1970
Time of Assessment: 1980	15	10
1985	20	15

Panel B
Age × Cohort Design

| | Age | |
	15	20
Cohort: 1960	1975	1980
1965	1980	1985

Panel C
Time of Assessment × Age Design

| | Time of Assessment | |
	1980	1985
Age: 15	1965	1970
20	1960	1965

Note. Age is given in the body of the table in Panel A; Time of Assessment is given in the body of the table in Panel B; and Cohort is given in the body of the table in Panel C.

(Panels A–C in Table 4.12) represents the crossing (see Table 4.6 for the definition of crossing) of two of the three definitional variables of cohort, age, and time of assessment.

Consider the cross-sequential design (Panel A of Table 4.12) and note how the design is generated and how its findings might be interpreted. The cross-sequential design—renamed the *Cohort × Time of Assessment* design—represents the crossing of the two variables, cohort and time of assessment. That is, each level of the cohort variable is combined with each level of the time of assessment variable to generate the conditions included in the design. (In many design books, the × symbol represents the operation of crossing.) The *Cohort × Time of Assessment* design depicted in Panel A of Table 4.12 can be compared to the cross-sectional design illustrated in Panel A of Table 4.10, which compared 10- and 15-year-olds when they were assessed in 1980. The presence of a second group of l5-year-olds (from the 1970 cohort assessed in 1985) assists in determining whether the performance of the l5-year-olds from the 1980 cohort is ascribable to age or to cohort differences. Furthermore, if the two cohorts of 15-year-olds respond similarly (*converge*), the data might be treated analogously to the data obtained from a longitudinal design with age ranging from 10 through 20 years—but instead of requiring 10 years to conduct, the study would take only 5 years (Anderson, 1995)!

One must be wary in interpreting the data from even these more complex sequential designs, however. Figure 4.1 displays data from a *Cohort × Time of Assessment* design such as the one shown in Panel B of Table 4.10. Exactly the same data are graphed as a function of age (Panel A of Figure 4.1) and as a function of time of assessment (Panel B of Figure 4.1). Are the results a linear function of age (Panel A) or joint main effects of cohort and of time of assessment (Panel B)?

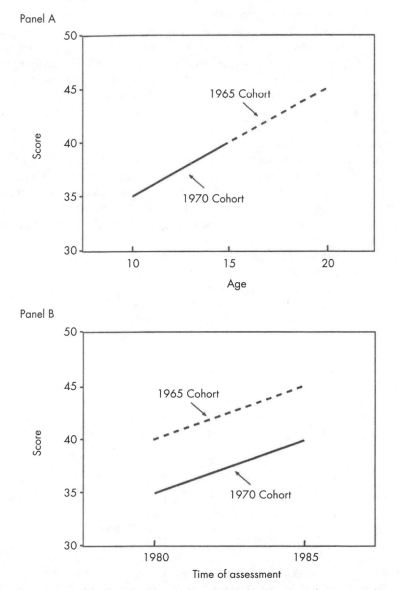

FIGURE 4.1 The same set of data graphed by age (Panel A) and by the time of assessment (Panel B).

The two remaining sequential designs, renamed the *Age × Cohort* design and the *Time of Assessment × Age* design (as the two designs represent the crossing of the two variables included in their names) are shown in Panels B and C of Table 4.12. The interpretation of the data from these designs is analogous to that made for the *Cohort × Time of Assessment* design.

Sample Size for Power and Accuracy

A key aspect of research design is sample size planning. It is important both for the individual researcher who wants a reasonable probability of finding statistically significant results and for a research domain striving to build a cumulative knowledge base. With respect to the latter goal, one of the consequences of low-powered studies is an abundance of apparent contradictions in the published literature (Kelley & Maxwell, 2008). A sample size that is too small or too large for the objectives of the study can have negative economic consequences and—because it misleads and needlessly exposes participants to risk—may be unethical (Lenth, 2001).

Before sample size planning can occur, investigators must clearly identify their goals for the study. A first step is to assess what is known about the subject of inquiry and where the study fits along the continuum of scientific understanding. Formal sample size analyses may not be necessary for exploratory or pilot studies, but well-reasoned sample size analyses are required for studies designed to reach confirmatory or confident conclusions (O'Brien & Castelloe, 2007). Study goals can be conceptualized in a 2 × 2 table (see Table 4.13) with the level of effect, an omnibus or targeted effect, along one dimension, and either power or accuracy along the second dimension (Kelley & Maxwell, 2008). For example, for multiple **regression analysis**, the investigator may be interested in the overall fit of the model, R^2 (omnibus effect), or in the regression coefficients of specific predictor variables, β (focused effect), or both. With respect to the second dimension, the goal may be to reject the null hypothesis and establish the direction of an effect (power), or to estimate the magnitude of the effect accurately (accuracy), or both. Accuracy in estimating the parameter effect (AIPE; Maxwell et al., 2008) involves estimating the **confidence interval** of an effect, where a narrower confidence interval implies greater accuracy or certainty that the observed parameter closely approximates its population parameter. Other things being equal, an appropriate sample size will vary depending on the desired objective. Often larger sample sizes are required for accurately estimating parameters than for detecting even small effects.

A second, and often the most troublesome (Lipsey, 1990), step in sample size planning is specifying an expected effect size. A commonly used approach is to use Cohen's (1988) suggested guidelines for "small," "medium," or "large" standardized effect sizes (see chapter section "interpreting the results of statistical tests"), but this approach has been criticized by Lenth (2001). Other options include basing effect sizes on those obtained in published studies, meta-analyses, and pilot studies (Kelley & Maxwell, 2008). If these options are not available, Lenth describes questions that can be asked about what differences are expected or would be of scientific or clinical interest (see also Bloom, 2008). In some instances, an unknown effect

TABLE 4.13
Conceptualization for Sample Size Planning for Multiple Regression
Parameters Given the Investigator's Study Goals and Desired Effect

| | | Effect | |
		Omnibus	Targeted
Goal	Power	Power of R^2	Power of β
	Accuracy	Accuracy of R^2	Accuracy of β

size is not a major problem for sample size planning for accuracy because the formulas for computing narrow confidence intervals are not dependent on the value of the effect size (Maxwell et al., 2008).

Additional Concerns and References

Experimental design issues do not end with our brief discussion of generic and special developmental validity threats and problems, and design variations that have been developed to address these concerns. Additional topics, such as philosophy of science considerations underlying the choice of design, participant selection, and single-subject design strategies, also are major aspects of design that are given short shrift in this chapter. Interested readers are referred to the following references.

1. *General design issues:* Alasuutari, Bickman, & Brannen (2008), Appelbaum and McCall (1983), Baltes, Reese, & Nesselroade (1988), Cairns, Bergman, & Kagan (1998), Meehl (1978), Miller (2007), Pedhazur and Schmelkin (1991), Rosenthal and Rosnow (1969), and Teti (2005).
2. *Implications of the philosophy of science for design:* Braybrooke (1987), Cook and Campbell (1979, Chapter 1), Kuhn (1970), the volume edited by Lerner (1998)—but particularly the chapter by Overton (1998)—and Popper (1959).
3. *Selecting, assigning, recruiting, and maintaining participants:* Cauce et al. (1998), Hartmann (2005), Pedhazur and Schmelkin (1991, Chapter 15), Ribisl et al. (1996); Shadish et al. (2002, pp. 323–340), and Suen and Ary (1989, Chapter 3).
4. *General and special issues when doing internet-based research:* Kraut et al. (2004) and Skitka & Sargis (2006).
5. *Change and growth:* Among many others, see Cohen and Reese (1994), Collins and Horn (1991), Gottman (1995), and Willett (1988).
6. *Power and its analysis:* Cohen (1988, 1990) and sources for power analysis software: Lenth (2001) and Thomas and Krebs (1997).
7. *Single-subject designs:* Franklin, Allison, and Gorman (1997), Iwata et al. (1989), Kratochwill and Levin (1992), and—for a somewhat different look—Valsiner (1986).

MEASUREMENT

Measurement includes the operations that are used to obtain scores. In developmental research, the scores provided by measurement operations assess DV performance, evaluate participants' IV status, and also determine their standing on other dimensions used to describe the research sample or to control for differences among individuals or groups. These research-related decision-making functions of measurement, or *scaling* as it is sometimes called, require that the resulting scores be both relevant and of high quality.

Issues of measurement quality are particularly acute in developmental investigations because of the vicissitudes of assessing participants occupying the ends of the developmental spectrum. Youngsters in particular present problems "of establishing rapport and motivation; of ensuring that instructions are well understood; of maintaining attention; and, of coping with boredom, distraction, and fatigue" (Messick, 1983, p. 479). In addition, because of children's rapid changes in many cognitively based activities, it may be difficult to capture their transient performance levels. Furthermore, the meaning of test scores may change in concert with changes in the children's development, as we previously noted (see also Patterson's, 1993, discussion of this issue—which he terms a "chimera" in the context of antisocial behavior).

As a result of these problems in measuring children's performance, developmental investigators have an added responsibility to demonstrate that their measures are of high quality.

The assessment of measurement quality, not surprisingly, depends on the nature of the research and the specific questions put forward for investigation. Nevertheless, certain criteria are generally relevant to judgments of quality: They include whether or not the measurement device is applied in a standard fashion; and whether or not the resulting scores are replicable (reliable) and measure what they are supposed to measure—a notion that bears very close resemblance to the notion of construct validity. Still other criteria, such as the presence of a meaningful zero point for the measurement scale, may be required by the nature of the statistical methods that are to be applied to the resulting scores.

Precisely how these criteria or standards are applied, and which are relevant, may also depend on various technical or theoretical considerations—sometimes referred to as measurement *facets* and *sources* (Messick, 1983; see also Baltes, Lindenberger, & Staudinger, 1998). The facets include the nature of the characteristics assessed—whether they are stable traits or changing states, structures or functions, and competence or typical performance. Other facets involve whether the scores are used for interindividual (normative) or intraindividual (ipsative) comparisons, and depend for their interpretation on norms (norm-referenced) or on objective performance standards (criterion-referenced).

The sources of measurement include whether the assessment responses are based on self-reports, constitute test responses, or are reports of performance in naturalistic settings by participant or independent observers. We briefly discuss scores—which are the products of measurement—and then the criteria for evaluating scores, measurement facets, and sources of data. The section on measurement ends with a listing of recommended sources for additional study.

Types of Scores

Scores come in a bewildering assortment of types. Most scores obtained from participants in developmental research will be straightforward and understandable either from reading the description of the study's procedures or from examining the study's tables or figures. Examples include scores that are expressed in basic units of measurement such as extension, frequency, and duration (see Johnston & Pennypacker, 1993) as well as aggregate scores resulting from the addition of item scores obtained on questionnaires and tests. These scores need not concern us further.

Other scores pose slight interpretive problems because they are constructions of the original scores—percentiles and "alphabet scores" (T and z scores)—which come with additional interpretive baggage. These scores are often designed to meet the assumptions of statistical tests or to remedy some perturbation, such as skewness, in the original distribution of scores. Such scores are described in Table 4.14, as are the defects they are intended to remedy and the interpretive warnings with which they are associated.

Still other scores represent more complicated transformations of the original data— difference or change scores, scores obtained from Q-sorts, and age- or grade-equivalent scores; they must be treated with some caution.

Difference scores. Perhaps the most troublesome of these prudence-demanding scores are simple difference scores, X_2 (posttreatment or Time 2) − X_1 (pretreatment or Time 1), popularly used in the past to index change over some period of development or as a result of treatment. Difference scores were often employed to assess change or growth, but are widely regarded as multiply flawed—for example, Cronbach and Furby (1970), Harris (1963); but compare with Rogosa (1988) and Willett (1988). Difference scores suffer from problems of

TABLE 4.14
Transformed Scores, Their Purposes and Qualifications to Their Interpretation

Transformation	Purpose	Interpretive Qualifications
$[X + 1]^{\frac{1}{2}}$, log X, arc sin X	Regularize (e.g., normalize) distributions for data analytic purposes	Interpretation must be applied to transformed scores
Proportion of X_1, X_2, etc.	Control for variation in respondent productivity	All participants have the same total score (across all variables)[a]
Standard score: $z = (X - M)/SD$	Control for disparate Ms and SDs for variables	All variables have Ms = 0 and SDs = 1.0[b]
Percentile rank of X	Reduce the disparity of extreme scores	All variables are given identical ranges (i.e., 1 to 99)

Note. X is the symbol for the original raw scores, M for the mean, and SD for the standard deviation.
[a] See discussion of ipsative scores.
[b] Distributions of standardized scores can be generated with any convenient mean and standard deviation. For example, if the transformed score distribution has a mean of 50 and a standard deviation of 10, the scores are referred to as T scores. T scores are generated by the following equation: $T = 50 + z(10)$.

unreliability—although the scores that are differenced may themselves be reliable! This is so because (1) the non-error variance in the two measures that are differenced is largely used up by the correlation between the two measures, so the precision of the difference scores is low, or (2) the variation in the difference scores is low, thus precluding high reliability because of restriction in range. Difference scores are not base free as is sometimes believed, but are frequently negatively correlated with initial or prescores because individuals who score low on the initial assessment are likely to have larger change scores than individuals who score higher. Additional problems occur when the characteristic that is assessed changes across the period of assessment. Many, although not all, of these problems are substantially reduced or eliminated when multiwave data are employed to assess *growth*, rather than two-wave data to assess *change—as* pointed out previously.

Q-sorts. A Q-sort is a forced-choice method of assessment. The method requires participants to order or sort a set of items (e.g., trait descriptors or behaviors) from least characteristic to most characteristic of some target person. The sort may be restricted to a specific number of categories or follow a prescribed distribution (e.g., a normal distribution); scores are assigned to items based on the category into which they are sorted: Often the resulting scores are used in ipsative, rather than normative comparisons; that is, an item score is compared only to other item scores for the target individual. However, a common use of the Q-sort compares an individual's sort to some criterion or prototypic sort, such as a consensual sort by experts (Strayer, Verissimo, Vaughn, & Howes, 1995). Such a comparison might be summarized by a correlation coefficient, the correlation reflecting the degree to which the individual's sort corresponds to or matches the criterion. Like all correlations, these Q-sort-based scores range from +1.0 (perfect correspondence) through 0.0 (no relation) to −1.0 (perfect inverse correspondence) with the criterion sort. And because correlations are not isomorphic with our ordinary number system, an $r = .40$ is not twice as similar to the criterion as an $r = .20$.

Age-(grade-)adjusted scores. Other problematic scores are age- or grade-equivalent (e.g., "mental age" or MA) and age-adjusted scores (e.g., IQ). Age-equivalent scores are, of course, only as good as the normative groups on which they are based. In addition, they may vary in meaning at different locations on the measurement scale. For example, during periods when skills and abilities are improving dramatically, the performance differences between adjacent age or grade groups may be appreciable; yet during periods of sluggish growth, performance differences between adjacent groups may be minimal. Consider the differences in mental ability between 2- and 5- year-old children and between 22- and 25-year-old adults. In the former case the differences are substantial; in the latter case they are trivial. Thus, developmental researchers need to exercise caution in interpreting differences expressed in age equivalents.

Age-adjusted scores such as IQ scores are not only encumbered by the surplus meanings attributed to them (e.g., that IQ scores are fixed in the way eye color is fixed—see Hunt, 1961; Neisser et al., 1996), but also by the special measurement properties shared by all such age-adjusted scores. Equal scores for children of different ages do not indicate equal skill or ability, but instead indicate equivalent statuses for the children in their respective age groups. Thus, groups of 8-year-olds and 10-year-olds with equal mean IQs of 115 do not have equivalent cognitive skills. Indeed, the 10-year-olds clearly are the more skillful. What the two groups of children do have in common is that they are both one standard deviation above their age-group means with respect to IQ. Age-adjusted scores, similar to age-equivalent scores, must be interpreted with care.

Criteria for Evaluating Scores

The quality of scores usually is judged by their conformity to standard psychometric criteria. These criteria include the standardization of administration and scoring procedures and the demonstration of acceptable levels of reliability and validity (American Educational Research Association, 1999). Some of these criteria require modification as a result of the nature of the variable under investigation. For example, because many performance variables, such as children's social skills, are assumed to be consistent over at least a few weeks, scores that assess these variables must demonstrate temporal reliability or stability over that time period. However, a measure of some transient characteristic, such as mood, would be suspect if it produced scores displaying temporal stability over a 2-week period.

Standardization. Standardization is intended to ensure that procedurally comparable scores are obtained for all participants assessed. Thus, standardization requires the use of equivalent administrative procedures, materials (such as items for tests or questionnaires and the timing and setting for observations), and methods of recording responses and of arriving at scores. In addition, it may be necessary to provide directions on how to develop and maintain rapport, whether to modify instructions for disabled participants (e.g., allow more time), when to present assessment materials and social commentary, and how to ensure that participants understand necessary instructions (Miller, 2007). Even slight variation from standardized procedures can introduce substantial noise into data and ambiguity into the interpretation of individual studies or even groups of studies as has occurred, for example, in the literature on the assessment of children's fears using behavioral avoidance tests (Barrios & Hartmann, 1988).

Reliability. Reliability concerns the dependability, consistency, or generalizability of scores (e.g., Cronbach, Gleser, Nanda, & Rajaratnam, 1972). Theoretical treatises on reliability decompose obtained scores (X) into at least two generic components: true or universe scores (X_t) and error scores (e_x).

$$X = X_t + e_x$$

The true score portion of one's obtained score ordinarily is the part that remains constant across time. This component is sometimes defined as the mean of an infinite number of measurements, or across all parallel forms of an instrument, or across all relevant measurement conditions (also sometimes referred to as *facets*), such as occasions, scorers, and the like. The error component is the portion of one's score that changes across time and results in inconsistent performance. Inconsistent performance might be produced by any number of factors, including chance events such as breaking a pencil during a timed test of mathematical problem solving, temporary states of the assessment setting (e.g., a crowded, noisy room) or of the participant (e.g., being ill, elated, or angry), or idiosyncratic aspects of the measurement instrument such as inconsistent observer behavior or scorer error. Unfortunately, the factors that produce consistent and inconsistent responding on measurement instruments vary depending on how reliability is assessed. For example, an illness might affect a child's playground aggression consistently across an observation session broken into temporal parts; aggression would thus be consistent or reliable across these parts. However, aggression would be inconsistent across observation sessions separated by longer intervals during which the child's health status changed.

As this discussion suggests, reliability may be assessed in a number of ways that differently divide obtained scores into true and error scores, including the following.

1. *Internal consistency* measures assess the consistency of performance across a measure's internal or constituent parts. Internal consistency reliability is one of the only forms of reliability that does not require repeated administration or scoring of an instrument. The Spearman-Brown prophesy formula (e.g., Nunnally & Bernstein, 1994) allows estimation of the internal consistency of an instrument from information about its items. Consider a test containing $k = 20$ items that have average intercorrelations ($\bar{r}_{ij}$) equal to .20. Absolutely speaking, these are low intercorrelations, but they would not be considered particularly low for test items. The internal consistency reliability, (r_{kk}) of the test $= k\bar{r}_{ij}/[1 + (k - 1)\bar{r}_{ij}] = .83$, a very respectable value.

2. *Interobserver* (or *interscorer*) *reliability* assesses the extent to which observers or scorers obtain equivalent scores when assessing the same individual. Interobserver reliability is assessed or measured with agreement statistics (e.g., percent agreement or kappa) or with traditional reliability statistics (e.g., correlation coefficients).

3. *Parallel-form reliability* determines the degree to which alternate (parallel) forms of an instrument provide equivalent scores. Parallel form reliability is to tests as interobserver reliability is to direct observations.

4. *Situational consistency* (generalizability) indexes the extent to which scores from an instrument are consistent across settings. For example, is the punctuality of children in the completion of their mathematics assignments consistent with their punctuality in the completion of their writing assignments? This form of reliability is analogous to the concept of the external validity of investigations.

5. *Temporal reliability* (stability) measures the degree to which an instrument provides equivalent scores across time. Test–retest correlations frequently are used to assess stability.

Two types of reliability, internal consistency and interobserver agreement, are required for most uses of assessment instruments. The scores obtained from an instrument composed of internally consistent parts assess a single characteristic or a set of highly interrelated characteristics. In contrast, assessment procedures containing internally inconsistent items, time periods, or analogous constituent parts measure a hodgepodge; as a result, scores obtained from them will not be comparable. For example, two children who obtain identical total scores on an internally inconsistent measure may perform quite differently from one another on the instrument's parts.

Interobserver reliability likewise is requisite for the minimal interpretability of scores. Without adequate agreement between observers, the very nature of the phenomenon under study is unclear (e.g., Hartmann & Wood, 1990). Interobserver reliability is sometimes surprisingly low even when the phenomenon of interest is clearly defined and easily observed. When this occurs, it may be that differences between observers are confounded with setting differences. For example, parents and teachers may disagree about an easily observed behavior because the teacher observes the child in school and the parents observe their child at home. In addition, if the same teacher rates all children but each child is rated by a different parent, disagreements may occur because parents use the rating scale in an idiosyncratic manner.

The remaining forms of reliability, situational consistency and temporal stability, are required when an investigator wishes to generalize, respectively, across settings and time. Such would be the case if, for example, infants' attachment to their mothers assessed in the laboratory at age 10 months were used to infer their attachment in the home at age 10 months (situational consistency or setting generalizability) or their attachment in the laboratory at age 24 months (temporal stability). Temporal stability is found to be negatively correlated consistently with the length of time between assessments. Indeed, the decreasing stability with increasing interassessment time (sometimes described as *simplex* in structure) has been observed so commonly in investigations of stability that it has assumed the character of a basic law of behavior. Over a standard time interval, temporal consistency increases typically with age during childhood. Brief temporal consistency often exceeds situational consistency (Mischel & Peake, 1983), although this finding is open to some dispute (Epstein & Brady, 1985).

It is important to note that test–retest statistics are sometimes used mistakenly. One frequent error is to describe stability without providing the interval over which it is assessed. A second common error occurs when developmental researchers interpret low stability as evidence against measurement equivalence. The latter interpretation can be dangerous as test–retest correlations "confound issues of construct validity, instrument equitability over time, and interindividual differences in growth" (Willett, 1988, p. 362).

Despite the quite different meanings of the various forms of reliability, they are often assessed in much the same manner—by correlating pairs of participants' scores. The scores may be paired across items, observers, time, or settings, depending on the type of reliability assessed. The statistics commonly used to summarize reliability data are noted in Table 4.15. The advantages and disadvantages of various statistics for summarizing reliability analyses are described by Hartmann (1982a) and Suen and Ary (1989).

Reliability gains general importance because it places a very specific limit on an instrument's empirical validity. If validity is indexed by an instrument's correlation with a criterion (r_{xy}), and the instrument's reliability is expressed as r_{xx}, the upper limit of r_{xy} is $r_{xx}^{1/2}$. That is, $|r_{xy}| \leq r_{xx}^{1/2}$—which is a form of the well-known correction for attenuation formula (e.g., Nunnally & Bernstein, 1994). Thus, a measuring instrument with $r_{xx} = .50$ could not expect to correlate $> .707$ with any criteria.

Measurement validity.   Although all of the abovementioned psychometric criteria involve the interpretation or meaning of scores, validity is the psychometric criterion most directly relevant to their meaning. Instruments, and the scores that they produce, may have various forms of validity.

1. *Face validity* refers to whether the instrument *appears* to be a valid measure of some construct, as would a measure of altruism that asked children about the amount of money they donated to charity. Except for its public relations value, face validity is the least important form of **measurement validity**.

TABLE 4.15
Commonly Used Statistical Techniques for Summarizing Reliability Data

Statistical Technique	Primary Use
Coefficient Alpha (α)[a]	Describes internal consistency reliability. Ranges from .0 to +1.0.
Intraclass Correlation (*ICC*)	General method of summarizing reliability data. *ICC* indicates the ratio of subject variance to total variance. Typically ranges from .0 to +1.0
Kappa (κ)	Summarizes the reliability of categorical data. Recommended because it corrects for chance agreement. κ ranges from <.0 to +1.0.
Kuder-Richardson-20 and -21	Assesses the internal consistency reliability of a device composed of dichotomous items, such as true–false achievement test items.
Product Moment Correlation (r_{xx})	General method of summarizing reliability data. r_{xx} indicates the ratio of true score to total variance; $1-r_{xx}$ indicates the proportion of error variance. Typically ranges from .0 to +1.0.
Raw (Percent) Agreement	Method of summarizing interobserver reliability data; criticized for its failure to correct for chance agreement.
Spearman-Brown Prophesy Formula	Used for estimating the internal consistency reliability of lengthened or shortened assessment devices.

Note. For more extended lists of statistics used for summarizing reliability data, see Berk (1979), Fleiss (1975), and House, House, and Campbell (1981).
[a] Not to be confused with α, the level of significance chosen for testing a null hypothesis.

2. *Content validity* assesses the degree to which the content of the instrument constitutes a representative sample of some substantive domain (e.g., do the items on an exam represent the material taught in the course adequately?). This form of validity is particularly important for achievement tests and observational coding systems.

3. *Factorial validity* indexes the extent to which an instrument taps some substantive construct or factor, and is most often determined for instruments developed using factor analysis. Factorial validity is closely related to the notion of internal consistency.

4. *Predictive validity* indicates the degree to which the scores from an assessment device are useful for predicting certain future criteria, such as academic success. This form of validity is similar to concurrent validity. Indeed, predictive and concurrent validity are sometimes referred to as various forms of "criterion-related validity." Criterion-related validity is typically assessed with a correlation coefficient. A correlation of $r = .50$ between predictor and criterion measures indicates that the percentage of variance that overlaps between the two is 25%. Percent overlap equals $100 \times r^2$ (McNemar, 1969, pp. 152–153; also see Ozer, 1985, and Steiger & Ward, 1987).

5. *Concurrent validity* indicates an instrument's correspondence with an important, currently assessed criterion. A test with substantial concurrent validity may be preferred over the device against which it is validated, if it is more efficient or less expensive than the criterion measure.

6. *Construct validity* indicates the extent to which an instrument assesses some theoretical construct, such as concrete operational reasoning, anxiety, or self-efficacy. Construct validity is perhaps the most basic, and at the same time most inclusive form of validity. Indeed, some have argued that validity is basically unitary, and the various types of validity are merely subclasses of construct validity (e.g., Messick, 1994).

Silva (1993, p. 69) nicely summarized current notions of validity as well as highlighting the inadequacies of earlier formulations, as follows:

- Validity is associated with each inference made from assessment information.
- It is not the instrument that is validated but rather the interpretation of scores obtained from the instrument.
- Validity is an integrative judgment, reached after considering all of the information—both empirical evidence and theoretical rationales. It is not reducible to a coefficient or set of coefficients.
- Types and classes of validity are misnomers for types and classes of *arguments*. The concept of validity is essentially unitary.
- There is no limit to the range of data used to estimate validity. Any information may be relevant in the validation process—which is simply the process of hypothesis construction and testing.

Traditionally, construct validity depends on the congruence between the pattern of results an instrument provides and the theoretical superstructure for the construct it presumably measures. The demonstration of congruence usually involves numerous sources of information. For example, the scores obtained from a construct-valid measure of children's interpersonal self-efficacy expectations (Bandura, 1997) presumably would distinguish socially successful from less successful children; show reasonable temporal stability except when following treatments intended to improve children's self-efficacy expectations; and correlate modestly with traditional measures of intelligence and moderately with peer-based measures of popularity and self-perceived competence. The more extensive and collaborative the interconnections between theory and measure, the stronger is the evidence of the validity of the measure for assessing the construct.

Wise investigators provide evidence for the construct validity of their measures: evidence that is independent of the results of the study that uses the measures to answer substantive questions. Failure to do so may result in a serious interpretive dilemma, particularly if the investigation does not work out as predicted. Critics may ask: Did the assessment instrument assess the construct inadequately? Was the theory supporting the construct faulty? Or did the study itself contain fatal validity threats? Without independent support for the construct validity of the measures, it may not be possible to decide among these three vastly different alternative interpretations.

Other criteria.   With some interpretations of scores, the standard psychometric criteria must be supplemented with additional quantitative requirements. These requirements may include that (1) the scores have a meaningful zero point, (2) the differences between scores have direction, and (3) the differences between scores are scaled (Nunnally & Bernstein, 1994). For example, if the differences between popularity scores are scaled, interpretations such as "Suzy is as different from Chen in popularity as Sigerdur is from Abdul" are possible. If, in addition, the popularity scale has a meaningful zero point, interpretations such as "Ling is twice as popular as Danielle" also are possible. Whichever of these criteria is met establishes the *level* of measurement obtained by the instrument's scores. The level of measurement relates not only to the interpretations that can be applied to the scores, but also to the statistics that are most commonly used with them. The typically distinguished levels of measurement, along with illustrations, interpretations, and statistics typically applied to them, are summarized in Table 4.16.

Data Facets

Measurement specialists and personality theoreticians have described an array of conceptualizations or facets of measurement that concern developmental investigators. The

TABLE 4.16
Typically Distinguished Levels of Measurement

Level	Example	Interpretation	Typical Statistics
Nominal	Gender	= or ≠	Counts; chi-square
Ordinal	Friendship rankings	< or >	Centiles and rank-order correlations
Interval	Grade equivalent	differences are =, <, or >	Ms, SDs, rs, and ANOVAs; t and F
Ratio	Height	ratios	Geometric and harmonic means; coefficient of variation

Note. The interpretations and typical statistics appropriate for more primitive levels of measurement also are applicable to higher levels of measurement.

more important of these facets concern the organization, stability, and content of the constructs assessed, the characteristic or property of the response that is targeted for assessment, and the standards against which scores are compared. These facets are generally noteworthy because they influence the planning, execution, analysis, and interpretation of developmental investigations. More specifically, they determine which of the psychometric standards are relevant to judging the adequacy of scores.

Nature of the measurements. The variables that developmentalists assess in their empirical investigations invariably represent classes or categories. These categories may be narrow and seemingly simple, such as smiles or sitting at desk; or they may be broad and encompassing, such as dominance, achievement orientation, or aggression. These response categories may be conceptualized as *traits* (relatively enduring, internally organized patterns of responding), *as response classes* (sets of responses that are elicited and/or maintained by similar environmental contingencies), or as *states* (relatively transient conditions of the organism).

Whichever of these conceptualizations is adopted has implications for the internal consistency and the temporal stability of the scores used in an investigation. For example, behaviors composing a trait should display substantial internal consistency, temporal stability, and perhaps situational consistency as well, but only internal consistency would be expected of behaviors constituting a response class or state.

The responses assessed can also be considered as *samples* of behavior of interest or as *signs* of some substrate not directly accessible. Children's eye contact, for example, might be a sample of an important aspect of social skill, or a sign of the trait of introversion. In the former case, the investigator must be concerned about the representativeness of the sample of eye contact obtained, and in the latter case about the extent to which eye contact correlates with other measures of introversion.

The substrate assessed need not be some relatively enduring, organized *structure*, such as a trait, but could instead be a *process* or function, such as social problem solving. And either children's *competence* (i.e., their capability or capacity) or their current level of *performance* on these structures or processes could be targeted for assessment. According to Messick (1983, p. 484), "Competence embraces the structure of knowledge and abilities, whereas performance subsumes as well the processes of accessing and utilizing those structures and a host of affective, motivational, attentional, and stylistic factors that influence the ultimate responses." The distinction between competence and performance is particularly important for developmental researchers, as it is tempting to imply that children are incompetent based on their inadequate performance. However, it may be erroneous to imply, for example, that young children do not have the concept of conservation because they fail to solve Piaget's water-glass problem, or that they do not have a particular linguistic structure because they do not use the structure in their spontaneous verbalizations. Instead, the failure may belong to the investigator, who did not elicit competent responses because of faulty selection of test stimuli or setting, or because of the use of inadequately motivating instructions.

Responses can also be conceptualized in terms of whether they assess behavior, attitudes and images, or physiological responding. This triple response *mode* distinction has been particularly useful for the assessment of the constructs of fear and anxiety, for example, which are construed as being represented in varying degrees by different individuals through the three modes (Barrios & Hartmann, 1988).

Response characteristics. There are many properties of responses that could form the basis for scoring systems. Some of these properties, such as number, duration, and amplitude, are simple and easy to measure. Other characteristics of responses are more complex, and must be inferred or judged by some standard that exists beyond the response, such as the correctness or the goodness of the response. In assessing correctness, scoring of responses usually occurs by comparing the responses to a list of acceptable alternatives, and a total score is obtained by accumulating all correct or partially correct responses. This is the procedure that is followed typically in scoring achievement and ability tests. Response goodness may be substantially more difficult to judge and to summarize. To illustrate this difficulty, consider the situation in which children's block play is scored for the uniqueness of their constructions. The children may use quite different building strategies, with some of them generating a few, highly elaborated constructions, others generating many simple ones, and still others some mixture of these two strategies. Thus, a summary response score may need to be based on some weighting of response number, complexity, and uniqueness, although the last of these is of primary interest.

This example illustrates a ubiquitous characteristic of performance—that responses differ not only in substance, but also in style. The stylistic aspects of responding initially captured the attention of measurement specialists because they were a nuisance; differences in style were targets of control as they colored judgments of substance. Later, when the ugly duckling had turned into the Prince Charming, so to speak (McGuire, 1969, p. 20), and style became the focus of investigation, measurement specialists were faced with the opposite task—of assessing style untainted by substance! This latter focus on the manner or style of responding led to the creation of a number of major style constructs, including social desirability, cognitive tempo, and field dependence.

Comparison standards. Because most scores are not meaningful in themselves, they must be compared to some standard in order to achieve meaning. Traditionally, scores have acquired meaning by comparison with the average performance of some relevant comparison group, called a *norm group*. Such scores, not surprisingly, are called *normative* scores. Typical standard scores and percentile ranks are normative scores. *Ipsative* scores, in contrast, are obtained by comparing the scores to other scores obtained by the same individual (Cattell, 1944).[5] Proportion scores obtained from observational measures of children's social behavior are ipsative scores; they indicate, for example, how the individual's total behaviors were

---

[5] A somewhat related distinction is made between whether the methods and procedures of investigation are designed to discover general laws (the *nomothetic* approach) or to discover laws that may be unique to the individual (the *idiographic* approach); see, for example, Allport (1937) and West (1983). This distinction is one of those that separate behavioral assessment from more traditional branches of assessment (Hartmann, Roper, & Bradford, 1979).

apportioned to the observational categories. Ipsative scores can be perplexing and sometimes troublesome, first, because they have unusual statistical properties. For example, the mean of a set of k ipsative subscales is $1/k$, their average intercorrelation is $-1/(k-1)$, and their average correlation with a criterion is exactly zero. Second, ipsative scores pose knotty problems of interpretation when investigators use both normative and ipsative comparisons. For example, one could be in the difficult position of having to explain how a child who scores consistently below par (normatively) on an IQ test could score higher (ipsatively) on the vocabulary subscale than another child scoring consistently above average (normatively) on the very same test.

Another possible method of inducing meaning in scores is to compare them with a criterion or a behavioral referent. Using this *criterion-referenced* approach, a child might be said to have mastered the ability to add two-digit numbers or to have mastered 80% of the tasks necessary to replace the rear wheel of a bicycle. Instruments that are constructed with the intent of using criterion-referenced scoring have substantially different statistical properties than have instruments developed with the intent of employing normative scoring. The primary statistical differences between these two approaches to test construction are summarized in Table 4.17.

Sources of Data

Assessment data in developmental studies come from a number of sources: from self-/ other-reports, from objective tests, and from observations in more or less natural settings. These three sources can be further subdivided. For example, self-/other-reports can be open-ended or provided in response to standard questions, their content can be narrowly focused or far-ranging, and they can be intuitively judged or formally scored.

Each of the sources of assessment information is associated with a relatively unique set of distortions. The presence of these method-specific distortions (called method variance) prompted Campbell and Fiske (1959) to propose that the construct assessed and the method of measurement contribute to the resulting scores. As a consequence, total score variation is sometimes decomposed into two variance components: construct variance and method variance. To avoid research results that are limited in generality by method variance, investigators assess their major constructs with multiple measures that differ in method-specific variation (see threats to construct validity in the design section).

The primary distortions (contributors to method variance) associated with the three sources of assessment information are summarized in Table 4.18. It is important to note in interpreting this table that the distortions lose their unique associations with the sources if, for

TABLE 4.17
Distinguishing Features of Criterion-referenced and Norm-referenced Assessment Instruments

Method	Purpose	Statistical Characteristics
Criterion-referenced	Determining what a child can do, or what a child knows	Truncated, sometimes dichotomous score distributions. Items have variable intercorrelations; many easy or difficult items.
Norm-referenced	Determining how a child compares to other children	Highly variable, often normal score distributions. Items are moderately intercorrelated. No very easy or very difficult items.

TABLE 4.18

Sources of Method Variance for Self-report, Objective-test, and Observational Sources of
Assessment Data

Sources of Data	Distortions
Self- or Other-Report	Misinterpretations; atypical use of descriptors (differing "anchor points")
	Degree of relevant knowledge; observational skills; memory; verbal skills
	Reactive effects such as deception, defensiveness, and impression management
Objective-Test	Cognitive styles such as impulsivity and field dependence
	Response styles such as acquiescence or position preferences (e.g., prefer first alternative)
	Instrumentation effects such as differential familiarity with various item formats and content selection biases
Observations	Observer biases and expectancies
	Observer distortions including memory loss and leveling (Campbell, 1958)
	Instrumentation effects such as halo error, leniency error, and central tendency errors (Guilford, 1954)
	Reactivity effects, such as avoidance of the observational setting

example, the participant is aware of the purpose of an objective-test assessment, or is even aware that an observational assessment is under way. In these two cases, the distortions produced by deception, defensiveness, and impression management are shared by all three sources.

It is not uncommon in assessment research to confound mode (behavior, images or thoughts, and physiological responses) with source in examining the consistency of responding in the three modes. For example, fearful behavior measured observationally might be compared with fearful images and physiological responses assessed by means of self-report. It would not be surprising in these comparisons to find greater correspondence between self-reports of fearful images and physiological responses than between either of these two and observed fearful behavior. This pattern of responding may not reflect greater agreement or synchrony between imaginal and physiological response systems. Instead, it may be attributable to the self-report method variance shared by the imaginal and physiological response measures.

Additional References

More specific information on the development of observational procedures may be found in Bakeman and Gottman (1987), Hartmann (1982b), and Haynes and O'Brien (2000). General information on measurement and scaling is available in Anastasi (1988), Cohen, Montague, Nathanson, and Swerdlik (1988), Crocker and Algina (1986), and especially Nunnally and Bernstein (1994); on measurement considerations in developmental research, in Baltes et al. (1998); on multimethod measurement Eid and Diener (2006); and on reliability statistics in behavioral observations, in Hartmann and Wood (1990) and Suen and Ary (1989). Information on measurement using the internet and web-based methods may be found in Birnbaum (2004) and Reips (2006).

ANALYSIS

Analysis refers to those procedures, largely although not exclusively statistical in nature, that are applied to the products of measurement (scores) to describe them and assess their meaning. Methods of analysis, because they are equated with sometimes difficult and obscure aspects of mathematics, are sometimes more distressing than any other aspect of scientific inquiry. This section discusses some of the technical aspects of statistical analysis as well as more friendly graphic methods.

Once scores have been obtained, preliminary operations are performed so that the scores will be suitable for formal analysis. These operations include adjusting the data for missing scores and outliers (extreme scores that indicate either errors in handling data or atypical participant responding). These preliminary operations also include any additional measurement manipulations that need to be completed such as the construction of composite scores—difference scores, ratio scores, or total scores—and transformations of the scores in cases where they fail to meet the assumptions of the statistical tests that will be performed on them. With intractable or otherwise troublesome data sets, these adjustments—sometimes referred to as "cleaning" or "laundering" the data—may occur repeatedly and at various points during the data analysis process.

Another important goal of preliminary analysis is to become familiar with the data through hands-on experience. This familiarization process often occurs as part of, preceding, or following adjustments of the data. It may involve careful study of frequency distributions and scrutiny of descriptive statistics calculated on the scores, such as measures of central tendency, variability, and correlation.

Once the data's general meaning is understood, the investigator conducts formal inferential tests. These tests function as decision aids that supplement the "binocular" tests conducted during the familiarization stage. The statistical tests determine which of the effects—hypothesized or not—are unlikely to be a function of chance variation in the data; that is, are statistically significant or reliable.

The statistical analysis, whether intended to describe the data or to test hypotheses relevant to them, differs depending primarily on the research question, and secondarily on the nature of the data. Most research questions can be conceived as belonging to one or two analytic classes. In one class are research questions that involve either the correlates of individual differences or the consistency of individual differences across time, settings, or behaviors. The data from these studies require some form of correlational, that is **Pearsonian, analysis**. Correlation analysis includes simple, part, partial, and multiple regression analysis, factor analysis, and structural equation modeling. In the other class are questions about longitudinal changes or cross-sectional differences in average performance. The data from these studies often are subjected to some form of **Fisherian analysis**, such as the **analysis of variance (ANOVA)**. Both Pearsonian and Fisherian approaches to data analysis are based on the general linear model (e.g., Kirk, 1995). However, the distinction between these approaches has been associated with design, subject matter, and other aspects of research strategy (Cronbach, 1957).

As has already been indicated, scores differ in a variety of ways. Two of these dimensions have particular relevance for the selection of statistical tests. The first dimension is whether the scores are categorical or quantitative in nature. Categorical scores include binary (e.g., yes–no) and other few-categorized discrete scores, such as "like–neutral–dislike" scales. Quantitative scores are continuous and multipointed, and include ratio, interval, and near-interval scores such as ratings on 5-point Likert scales. Categorical scores often require some form of contingency table analysis, not unlike common chi-square analyses, whereas quantitative scores usually are analyzed using some form of the analysis of variance or traditional regression analysis.

The second dimension concerns the number and type of scores contributed by each sampling unit (sampling units usually are composed of individual participants, but sometimes are composed of dyads or larger groups such as a family or a classroom). If each sampling unit contributes one score, then a **univariate analysis** is performed; if one score is repeatedly assessed over time or setting, then a repeated-measures univariate analysis may be conducted; or for multiple scores, ordinarily obtained during the same time period, a multivariate analysis is conducted.

These analyses require a wide variety of specific statistical tests, each of which has its assumptions, advantages, and pitfalls. Whatever the form of analysis, the ubiquitous $p < .05$ or $p < .01$ resulting from the analysis has a specific technical meaning that is critical to an understanding of hypothesis testing as it is currently practiced. Unfortunately, that meaning is widely misunderstood. These, and related issues, are addressed in the following section.

Preliminary Analyses

Adjusting scores. Scores, like toddlers, require constant vigilance and repeated intervention if they are to stay out of trouble. Some participants have missing scores, and we must decide whether estimated scores should be derived for them, or whether those individuals should be omitted from some or all of the analyses.[6] Other scores may be transcribed incorrectly on data sheets or entered mistakenly into the computer. Most of these errors can be avoided if investigators emphasize accuracy in their scientific work, provide instructions in how to attain error-free data, institute frequent accuracy checks, and provide incentives for accurate results (Hartmann & Wood, 1990).

Still other data inaccuracies may reflect respondents' misunderstandings of instructions, their incorrect use of answer sheets, or even faking or cheating on their part. If these and other errors cannot be avoided by suitable instructions or by performance monitoring, they might be detected—and either corrected or eliminated—if the erroneous data are sufficiently atypical. Unusual scores are detectable if they are substantially different in value from those of neighboring scores. For example, a child who scored 2 *SD* either above or below his or her nearest scoring classmate on an observational assessment of aggression would certainly be a candidate for further investigation, and for possible removal from the data set. Incorrect scores also may be detectable because they represent an improbable *pattern* of responding. Examples include responding to the same question differently when it is asked twice; missing three very easy problems but answering correctly four more difficult problems; and admitting to taking birth control pills by someone who indicates being a 10-year-old boy. Sieves for the detection of errors of this sort require close scrutiny of the data by members of the research team, perhaps supplemented by computer programs developed to detect unusual responses or patterns of responses (see Tabachnick & Fidell, 2007, Chapter 4).

Still other adjustments may have to be made to the data before they are suitable for analyses. For example, it is not uncommon for scores to be combined or aggregated prior to major data analysis. The item, or other subpart, scores may be combined based on purely theoretical considerations—all items measure the same construct, and so the item scores are simply summed to generate a composite total score. Instead, the item scores may be combined

---

[6] The advent of modern computers facilitated a revolution in statistical procedures for handling missing data. Referred to as methods of data imputation, these procedures have had a major impact on longitudinal studies. According to Shadish et al. (2002), imputation methods enable investigators "to make use of all the data that are present and to eliminate much of the bias associated with nonrandom attrition" (p. 482). These procedures are reviewed and described in, for example, Graham (2009), Little and Rubin (1987), Schafer and Graham (2002), and Shadish et al. (2002).

on empirical bases, including the item intercorrelations, their reliability, or their correlations with a criterion (see Nunnally, 1978, for a not entirely dispassionate discussion of these alternative empirical strategies for combining assessment information).[7] Finally, and most often, scores are combined with an eye to theoretical and empirical considerations. Simultaneously serving more than one criterion need not be troublesome, unless of course the criteria suggest opposite courses of action, as may happen when theoretically appropriate items are inconsistently correlated with one other. In that case, after suitable digging into the data in an effort to make sense of the inconsistencies, investigators must rely on their good judgment and perhaps the good judgment of colleagues.

Another common preliminary manipulation of the data involves equating scores for differences in overall rates of behavior. For example, children may be evaluated on the number and kinds of errors they make in solving mathematics problems, but may differ in the number of problems attempted. In such cases, investigators adjust scores by prorating, by shifting to proportion or percentage scores, or by employing other ratios such as rate per unit of time. Still other transformations of scores, such as square root, log, and arc sin transformations (see Table 4.14) may be required because the original scores violate the assumptions of statistical tests that will be performed on them. These transformations and their effects were outlined earlier in the section on measurement. Following, as part of, or sometimes interspersed between such laundering operations, investigators are wise to construct graphs of their data and calculate descriptive statistics on them.

Becoming familiar with data. Informal or **exploratory data analysis**—consisting of constructing graphs, charts, and plots, and calculating simple descriptive statistics—is critically important to understanding the meaning of data. Indeed, some investigators argue that these procedures, particularly the scrutiny of graphic displays, should constitute the primary method of judging the outcomes of experiments (Baer, 1977; also see Shadish, 1986).

Whether these methods are primary, or merely contributory for judging the outcomes of experiments, there is little doubt of their importance. Unfortunately, it seems that novice investigators omit all, or the greater portion of, the preliminary stages of data analysis: The excitement of having completed data collection is quickly followed by the need to know if the data contain anything "statistically significant." And so the data are prematurely formally analyzed, perhaps using only standard or "canned" computer programs, with results that unnecessarily support the adage "garbage in, garbage out." This misplaced enthusiasm deprives investigators of the opportunity to experience a sense of intimacy with their data— the kinds of hands-on experiences from which serendipitous findings and otherwise new perspectives are discovered. Unfortunately, there is not a large literature on the procedures useful for gaining familiarity with data, and so the procedures tend to be idiosyncratic and somewhat artistic in nature. Generally, however, they involve constructing graphic displays and calculating standard as well as "quick and dirty" descriptive statistics (Tukey, 1977).

Graphing data. Useful graphic displays range from freehand sketches of univariate and bivariate frequency distributions to computer-crafted, publication-ready, three-dimensional drawings of multiple time series (see Parsonson & Baer, 1978). The concern during preliminary data analysis is not with beauty, however, but with utility. For example, when groups

---

[7] One of the alternative strategies discussed by Nunnally (1978) is item response theory (IRT) or item characteristic curve (ICC) theory. IRT is a well-established alternative to classical measurement theory for the model of measurement error. It is popular in educational testing, but it has not achieved widespread use in developmental science, although it is potentially very relevant. Explanations and applications to developmental science of IRT are available in Boivard and Embretson (2008), Bornstein, Hahn, Haynes, Manian, & Tamis-LeMonda (2005), and Embretson & Reise (2000).

are being compared, simple bar graphs (Figures 4.2–4.4) of each group's performance can readily be drawn.

Each display might be checked for atypical performances (Figure 4.2) if this has not already been done in some other way, and a decision might be made concerning the treatment of unusual respondents—sometimes termed outliers (see Tabachnick & Fidell, 2007, for a discussion of outliers and their detection, including tests of significance). Other aspects of the data also might be noted, such as the modality or peakedness *(kurtosis)* of the distribution of scores (see the bimodal distribution in Figure 4.2), their symmetry (see the positively skewed distribution in Figure 4.3), and whether floor and ceiling effects (also see Figure 4.2) are present. Bimodal distributions are found when a sample is composed of scores for two different types of respondents, such as a distribution of birth weights for a sample composed of term and preterm infants. *Skewness*, or lack of symmetry in the scores, might occur for a variety of reasons, including the presence of floor or ceiling effects. These latter forms of asymmetry are observed when a substantial proportion of participants receives the lowest scores (floor effect) or the highest scores (ceiling effect) on the assessment instrument. In ability testing, the presence of a floor effect suggests that the test was too difficult, and a ceiling effect suggests that the test was too easy. The statistical significance of skewness and kurtosis can also be analyzed more formally (e.g., Fidell & Tabachnick, 2003).

If the data are approximately normal in their distribution, both the mean and standard deviation can be readily estimated from graphic displays. The mean will lie approximately in the center of the distribution, and the ratio of the group's range to its standard deviation varies from approximately 3 ($N \approx 10$), to 4 ($N \approx 30$), to 5 ($N \approx 100$), and to 6 ($N \approx 450$); see Guilford (1965, p. 81) and the data shown in Figure 4.4.

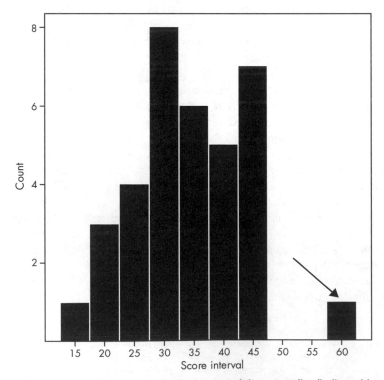

FIGURE 4.2 Univariate bimodal frequency distribution containing an outlier (indicated by arrow). With the outlier, $M = 34.3$, $SD = 9.56$, and $N = 35$; without the outlier, $M = 33.5$, $SD = 8.57$ and $N = 34$.

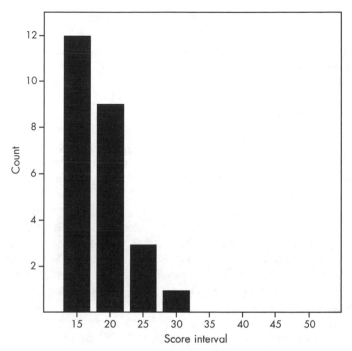

FIGURE 4.3 Illustration of a positively skewed frequency distribution with a distinct floor effect. For this distribution, $M = 18.6$, $SD = 4.21$, skewness $= 1.049$, and $N = 25$.

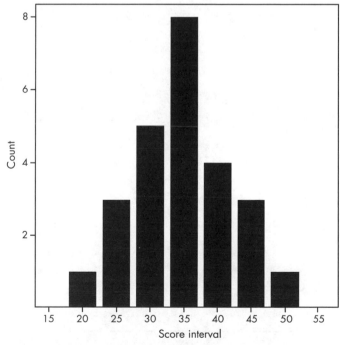

FIGURE 4.4 Illustration of an approximately normal frequency distribution for which rules of thumb provide close approximations to the M and SD of the distribution. $M = 34.8$ (estimated $M = 35$). $SD = 7.29$ (estimated $SD =$ range/3.8 $= 35/3.8 = 7.89$); $N = 23$.

When investigations employ more than one DV, it often proves useful to cross-tabulate the scores or to sketch their bivariate frequency distribution (Figure 4.5). The resulting displays—sometimes referred to as *scatter diagrams*—can be examined for a number of disturbances, including the presence of outliers. When outliers are present, they can change dramatically the magnitude of the correlation between the variables. (Compare the value of r for the data in Figure 4.5 when the outlier is included and when the outlier is excluded.)

Scatter diagrams also can be checked for the extent to which the regression between the variables is linear. Nonlinear regression is illustrated in Figure 4.6. Because the product moment correlation (r) assesses the linear part of the relation between variables, r will under-estimate the relations between variables that are nonlinearly related. Compare, for example, the value of r and of η (eta, the curvilinear correlation coefficient) for the data shown in Figure 4.6.

In addition to disclosing the presence of outliers and nonlinear regressions, scatter dia-grams can indicate *heteroscedasticity* (unequal dispersion of scores about the regression line). Heteroscedasticity indicates that errors of predictions vary depending on the value of the predictor score. With the data displayed in Figure 4.7, Y scores are less accurately predicted for individuals with high X scores than for individuals with low X scores. Scatter diagrams and other graphic plots serve both as important detection devices and as judgmental aids in the hands of experienced investigators.

More on descriptive statistics.   Means, standard deviations, and correlation coefficients are the most commonly used descriptive statistics. In addition, a number of other statistics are sufficiently common to deserve brief mention. First we consider a number of the many

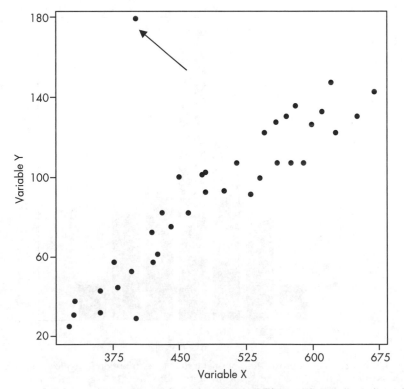

FIGURE 4.5   Illustration of a positive linear relation between variables X and Y. Outlier indicated by arrow. With the outlier included, $r = +.81$; with the outlier omitted, $r = +.95$. The dispersion of scores with each X-array is approximately normal (homoscedasticity). $N = 37$ with outlier included.

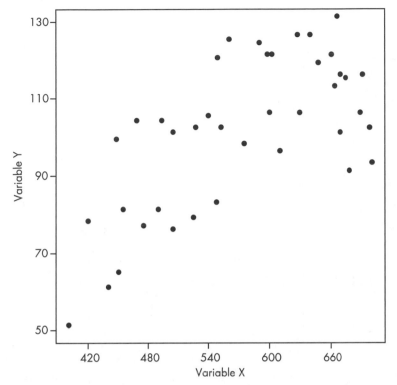

FIGURE 4.6   Illustration of curvilinear relation between X and Y. The value of the linear correlation is +.66, whereas the value of eta, the curvilinear correlation, for predicting Y from X is .99 and for predicting X from Y is +.94. The dispersion of scores within X-arrays is approximately equal (homoscedasticity). $N = 40$.

descriptive statistics related to r, the correlation coefficient: part and partial correlation, kappa (see Table 4.15), and conditional probability.

Part and *partial correlations* are ordinary product-moment correlations that deserve special names because of the nature of the scores to which they are applied. Using the three variables of age, height, and weight, the distinctions between simple correlations and part and partial correlations are illustrated by the Venn diagrams shown in Figure 4.8. Either one (part) or both (partial) of the scores correlated are corrected for uncontrolled variation in a third variable. For example, in a three-variable regression problem involving height, weight, and age, the correlation between height and weight, with age corrected, is called the partial correlation and is symbolized $r_{hw.a}$ (see Figure 4.8, Panel B). The partial correlation between height and weight is equal to the correlation between these two variables when calculated for participants who all are at the mean age of the group. Partial correlation is used when the effects of a third variable, such as age in the abovementioned example, cannot be experimentally controlled. If age were partialed out of weight, but not out of height, the resulting correlation would be the part correlation between height and weight (see Figure 4.8, Panel A). This part correlation is symbolized $r_{h(w.a)}$. Part correlations play an important role in multiple regression, as they indicate the overlap of the criterion with the unique portion of each of the predictors.

Kappa is an agreement statistic that is used to summarize interjudge reliability data, particularly for observational data. Assume that two observers each classified independently the same 200 10-s observation intervals into whether a target child interacted with her peers, interacted with her teacher, or failed to interact. The resulting data might resemble those given in Figure 4.9. A typical, older, and flawed method of summarizing these data is simply

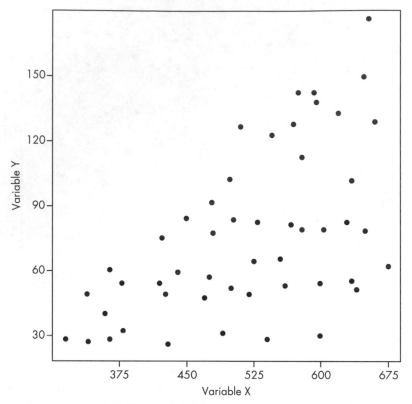

FIGURE 4.7   Illustration of heteroscedasticity (unequal dispersion of scores within each X-array). $r = +.56$ and $N = 50$.

to tabulate the proportion of intervals for which the two observers agreed. For the data in Figure 4.9, the observers agreed on 95 intervals scored as "interacted with peers," 25 intervals rated as "interacted with teacher," and 40 intervals classified as "alone." These 160 intervals, when divided by 200 (the total number of intervals during which observations were taken), gives a proportion of agreement of .80. When kappa is calculated on these same data, a somewhat lower estimate of agreement is obtained, as kappa corrects for agreements that might have occurred by chance. Kappa is equal to

$$(p_o - p_c)/(1 - p_c)$$

where p_o is the proportion of observed agreements and p_c is the proportion of chance agreements.

For the data in Figure 4.9, p_o is .80, as we have already determined in the calculation of the simple agreement statistic, and p_c is equal to the sum of the expected values for each of the agreement cells in Figure 4.9 divided by the total number of observation intervals ($p_c = .4275$).[8] Kappa is then equal to

$$(.80 - .4275)/(1 - .4275) = .65.$$

---

[8] The expected values are determined in exactly the same manner as they typically are for chi-square tables, that is by summing the products of corresponding marginal values and dividing by N. For the data given in Figure 4.9, the expected value for the agreement cell for "interacts with peers" is $(120 \times 110)/200 = 66$; for the agreement cell "interacts with teacher" the expected value is $(30 \times 30)/200 = 4.5$; and for the agreement cell "alone," the expected value is $(50 \times 60)/200 = 15$. Summing these values and dividing by N yields $p_c = (66 + 4.5 + 15)/200 = .4275$.

Figure A

Figure B

Figure C

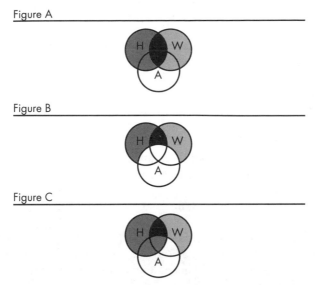

FIGURE 4.8 Venn diagrams illustrating the distinctions between simple correlations, and partial- and part-correlations. In general, the lightly shaded areas indicate the independent portions of the two variables correlated, and the darkly shaded portion indicates the overlapping or nonindependent portions of the variables. For the simple correlation between height and weight (r_{hw})—shown in Panel A—the darkly shaded area that overlaps portions of the entirety of H and W indicates the degree of correlation. For the partial correlation ($r_{hw.a}$)—shown in Panel B—the darkly shaded area overlapping the *remaining* portions of H and W indicates the degree of correlation. Finally, for the part correlation, $r_{h(w.a)}$—shown in Panel C—the darkly shaded area that overlaps portions of the entirety of H and portions of the *remaining* of W indicates the degree of correlation.

	Observer 1 Child interacts with			
Observer 2	Peer	Teacher	No one	Totals
Peer	95	05	10	110
Teacher	05	25	00	30
No one	20	00	40	60
Totals	120	30	50	200 = N

(Child interacts with)

FIGURE 4.9 Joint, but independent, observations of a child's interactions by Observer 1 and Observer 2 used to illustrate the calculation of interobserver reliability using Cohen's kappa. *N* = the number of observation intervals, not the number of participants. The values in the principal diagonal cells—the cells for which like categories intersect for the two observers and extending from upper left to lower right—represent observation intervals for which the observers agreed. The values in the off-diagonal cells represent disagreements between the two observers (e.g., the 10 entries in the cell defined by the first row and third column are those for which Observer 2 indicated that the child was interacting with her peers, but Observer 1 stated that she was alone).

Conditional probabilities play an important role in analysis of fine-grained interactional data, sometimes called micro-analytic analysis (Bakeman & Gottman, 1997; Kerig & Lindahl, 2001). These probabilities perhaps can best be understood by examining 2 × 2 table data, such as those shown in Figure 4.10. The data in Figure 4.10 describe the temporal patterning of talking by a mother and her child. These data can be summarized in various ways: by a correlation statistic such as the phi coefficient or by means of a conditional probability. The conditional probability of the child talking given that her mother talked in the prior interval is equal to the joint probability that the child talked and the mother talked in the previous interval divided by the probability that the mother talked in the previous interval. For the example given in Figure 4.10, the conditional probability of the child talking at time $t + 1$ given that her mother talked in the previous interval is equal to

$$(B/N)/[(A + B)/N] = B/(A + B) = 40/(10 + 40) = .80$$

The conditional probability is often compared with its unconditional probability. The unconditional probability of the child talking is $(B + D)/(N) = (40 + 20)/(100) = .60$. Thus, the mother's talking in the previous interval increases the likelihood that the child will talk in the following interval from .60 to .80.

The final descriptive statistic, one similar to an ordinary variance, is the characteristic root or the eigen value of a matrix. *Eigen values* are to matrices what the variance is to a distribution of numbers. Not surprisingly, then, eigen values (symbolized as γ) are frequently encountered in **multivariate analysis**, where one deals with matrices of scores. For example, in principal component analysis, a factoring technique, the eigen value for each principal component may be thought of as the amount of variance in the original standardized variables associated with that principal component. In multivariate ANOVAs, the eigen value can be thought of as the variance between the group centroids. (A centroid is to multiple dependent variables what a mean is to a single dependent variable.)

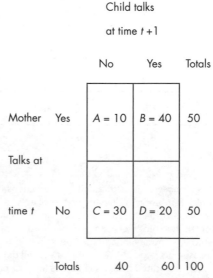

FIGURE 4.10 Temporal sequence of mother and child talking (mother talking at time *t* and child talking at time *t* + 1) used to illustrate the calculation of conditional probabilities. *N* = the number of observation intervals, not the number of participants.

Null Hypothesis Testing

Following the calculation of descriptive statistics, several methods are available to judge the significance of the statistics. Significance in this context refers to whether or not the effects of interest, which are presumably reflected in the data and in the summary descriptive statistics applied to the data, could have arisen by chance. The primary method that developmentalists use to judge the statistical significance of their results is null hypothesis testing. Preference for this method of assessing statistical significance exists despite the very substantial criticism directed at null hypothesis testing procedures (see Harlow et al., 1997; Meehl, 1978; Morrison & Henkel, 1970, Nickerson, 2000).

Null hypothesis testing, as currently employed, is a multistep process (see Table 4.19) that begins with the development of two models or hypotheses about the data. One model, sometimes called the *experimental model*, contains the putative effect of interest to the investigator, such as treatment, age, or gender. The other model, often called the *null* or *restricted model*, does not contain this effect or states that the effect of interest equals zero. Null models or hypotheses often are stated in one of two forms. In one form of the null hypothesis, some effect or parameter is assumed to equal zero in the population under investigation. The parameter, for example, may be a simple correlation coefficient or a beta weight in a multiple regression analysis (e.g., $\beta = 0$). In another form of the null hypothesis, the values of the parameter of interest for two or more populations are assumed to be equal. The parameters to be compared most often include population means or variances (e.g., $\sigma_w^2 = \sigma_b^2$).

In the second step of null hypothesis testing, the investigator decides how unlikely the obtained results must be before concluding that the null hypothesis is probably false. The logic implied here is that if the sample data are unlikely to have occurred under the null model, then that model must not be true. This step is sometimes referred to as "selecting an α level." α levels (or probabilities) of .05 or .01 are the conventional ones used in deciding whether to reject null models or hypotheses. However, it is important to add that the selection of α should be based

TABLE 4.19
Illustration of Null Hypothesis Testing

Step 1. An investigator explores the relation between the number of observed positive social requests and sociometric status in a group of 6-year-old children. The null hypothesis states the following about the population correlation, ρ (rho):

$\rho = .00$. This null hypothesis is contrasted with an alternative hypothesis that states that (ρ) $\neq .00$

Step 2. α, the probability associated with rejection of the null hypothesis, is set at $p = .05$. Therefore, the obtained finding must have a probability of occurrence $\leq .05$ before the null hypothesis will be rejected and the alternative hypothesis accepted.

Step 3. The obtained correlation is tested with the z test for the significance of r using Fisher's r to z_r transformation.

$z = (z_r - 0)/\sigma_{z_r}$, and $\sigma_{z_r} = 1/(N - 3)^{\frac{1}{2}}$

With $r = .50$, and $N = 19$, $z_r = .549$ and $\sigma_{z_r} = 1/(19 - 3)^{\frac{1}{2}} = .25$, so

$z = (.549 - 0)/.25 = 2.20$

Step 4. The two-sided probability value associated with $z = 2.20$, according to the normal curve table, is approximately $p = .028$.

Step 5. Because $p = .028$ meets the criterion established in Step 2 where α was set at $p = .05$, the null hypothesis is rejected. Therefore, it is concluded that positive social requests and sociometric status are significantly correlated in 6-year-old children.

Note. This traditional approach described in Step 5 has been replaced with simply providing the obtained p-value associated with the value of the inferential statistic.

on the consequences of rejecting a true null hypothesis (a Type I error) versus the consequences of accepting a false null hypothesis (a Type II error), and not by convention. If the consequences of rejecting a true null hypothesis are substantial—say, millions of dollars may be spent in changing an existing social policy—and the consequences of accepting a false null hypothesis are minor, a very, very small α level, such as .0001, might be employed.

In the third step, the investigator uses the sample data to compute the value of a test or inferential statistic. This test statistic measures the extent of the deviation of the sample data from those expected on the basis of the null hypothesis. Traditional univariate test statistics are the z (normal curve) test, the t test, the F test, and the chi-square (χ^2) test.

In the fourth step, the investigator determines the probability associated with the test statistic, often by reference to statistical tables or computer output. In order for these sources to provide appropriate probability values, the sample data must be consistent with a set of assumptions required by the statistical test. Although each statistical test has its own set of assumptions, some assumptions are common to many inferential tests. Typical among these shared assumptions are that scores (usually error or residual scores) must be distributed normally, homogeneously, and independently. Violation of these assumptions—particularly that of independence and to a lesser degree that of homogeneity—can result in highly erroneous probability values (Judd et al., 1995; Kirk, 1995). To help insure the correctness of probability values that result from the major statistical analyses, the tenability of critical assumptions should be tested formally (e.g., Kirk, 1995; Tabachnick & Fidell, 2007).

In the final step of null hypothesis testing, it was traditional to compare the probability value associated with the statistical test with the value of α selected by the investigator. As a result of this comparison, the null hypothesis and the model on which it is based were either rejected or not rejected. However, standards recommended by the American Psychological Association (Wilkinson & the Task Force on Statistical Inference, 1999, p. 599) state that "It is hard to imagine a situation in which a dichotomous accept–reject decision is better than reporting an actual p value . . . [and] never use the unfortunate expression 'accept the null hypothesis.' "

It is also important to understand just what a reported p value means, as they are often misinterpreted. Consider a study reporting that $p = .05$. What is the appropriate interpretation of this probability value? It is clearly incorrect to conclude that the result is important, that the probability of this result being replicated is .05, that the probability is .95 ($1 - .05$) of the obtained result having occurred, or that the probability is .05 that the obtained result is 0. If you chose any of these interpretations you were incorrect, but you are also in good company, as even statisticians frequently err in interpreting the probability values from experiments (Tversky & Kahneman, 1971). Instead, the p value provides the likelihood of the obtained or more extreme result given that the null hypothesis model is correct (see Gigerenzer, Krauss, & Vitouch, 2004; Hartmann & George, 1999).

The statistical testing procedures just outlined differ in detail depending on a variety of considerations. These considerations include the descriptive statistic that answers the investigator's question. For example, questions answered by examining means may require different testing procedures than do questions concerned with variability or correlation. Another consideration involves whether each independent experimental unit[9] receives a

---

[9] The number of independent experimental units (called *units of analysis*) usually, although not always, is equal to the number of participants. Exceptions occur when the sampling units are themselves aggregates, such as dyads, families, or classrooms. In these exceptional cases, the responses of individual respondents may be linked (dependent), and the independent experimental units are given by the number of dyads, families, or classrooms, respectively. When the number of units of analysis exceeds the number of sampling units, one is often in imminent danger of lethally threatening statistical conclusion validity. See, for example, the discussion of dependency by Kenny and Judd (1986) and of "nested" subjects by Anderson and Anger (1978) and by Cairns (1983).

score on a single dependent variable (univariate analysis), more than one score on a single dependent variable (**repeated-measures analysis**), or one or more scores on more than one dependent variable (multivariate analysis). Still another consideration is whether categorical or quantitative data are tested for significance. The following sections address significance testing in these various circumstances—which, as we shall find out a bit later, are all examples of the **generalized linear model**. Because of the large number of combinations of circumstances involved, however, only those commonly occurring are discussed.

Analysis of Categorical Data

Categorical data are those that are typically obtained from nominal scales (see Table 4.16). Sometimes, however, quantitative scores are split artificially, say, at the median, and treated as if they were categorical. Such a strategy is almost always foolhardy, as degrading scores in this way is equivalent to throwing away information, and results in lowered power.

Chi-square analysis.   The analysis of categorical data typically has involved some form of chi-square or closely related analysis. Less frequently used are other nonparametric tests, such as Fisher's Exact Test and parametric tests that are more appropriate for quantitative data. Chi-square tests have a variety of uses in the statistical testing of categorical data. For example, they are used to determine whether proportions or frequencies differ from one another, whether categorical variables are correlated, and whether distributional assumptions, such as normality, hold. These uses of chi-square and of other traditional nonparametric testing procedures have been ably described in a large number of books, including those by Conover (1999), Fleiss, Levin, and Paik (2003), and Hollander (1999), and are not cataloged here. Instead, some common errors made in these analyses are noted, and then a number of relatively new methods for analyzing complex categorical data are described.

Perhaps not surprising in view of their general utility, chi-square tests have long been a favorite for abuse. The sources of this abuse are clearly spelled out in a sequence of critical papers, including Lewis and Burke (1949, 1950) and Delucchi (1983). Perhaps the most serious of the many errors made in the use of chi-square is violation of the independence assumption. This error occurs when investigators shift experimental units from participants to the events in which they engage. Consider a set of fictitious data gathered to assess a prediction derived from a theory of moral development: that 4-year-olds would cheat more frequently in turn-taking than would 6-year-olds. The data gathered to test this hypothesis might take the form of the number of violations of turn-taking observed during 10-min samples of free play for 15 4-year-old and 15 6-year-old children. If the number of cheating incidents totaled 40, and individual scores ranged from 0 to 3, some investigators might be tempted to conduct the chi-square analysis summarized in Panel A of Figure 4.11 (also see the data display in Panel A). It is apparent from inspection of this figure that the investigator has shifted experimental units from children ($N = 30$) to some combination of children and cheating incidents ($N = 40$). The 19 entries in cell A represent the number of incidents of cheating engaged in by nine 4-year-old children. It is difficult to argue that these cheating incidents were independent, as individual children contributed as many as three entries to this cell.

The correct display of the data is shown in Panel B of Figure 4.11, maintaining children as the unit of analysis. The proper analysis of these data is given in the Panel B description. As can be seen from this latter analysis, the two age groups do not differ significantly in the proportion of children who are observed cheating; that is, age and cheating are not

PANEL A

AGE OF CHILD

CHEATING	4	6	
Occurrences	A = 19	B = 6	25
Nonoccurrences	C = 6	D = 9	15
Totals	25	15	40

PANEL B

AGE OF CHILD

CHEATER	4	6	
Yes	A = 9	B = 6	15
No	C = 6	D = 9	15
Totals	15	15	30

Panel A. Chi square (χ^2) calculations based on $A = 19$ (see Panel A).

$$\chi^2 = \Sigma\Sigma[(o_{ij} - e_{ij})^2/e_{ij}],$$

where o_{ij} is the observed frequency in the ith row and jth column, e_{ij} is the expected frequency in the ith row and jth column and is equal to the product of the ith row frequency and the jth column frequency divided by N.

$$\chi^2 = [(19 - (25 \times 25/40))^2/(25 \times 2540)] + 2 \times [(6 - (25 \times 15/40))^2/(25 \times 15/40)]$$
$$+ [(9 - (15 \times 15/40))^2/(15 \times 15/40)] = 5.184.$$

which, with 1 degree of freedom is associated with $p < .05$.

Panel B. Chi square calculations based on $A = 19$ (see Panel B).

$$\chi^2 = 2 \times [(9 - (15 \times 15/30))^2/15 \times 15/30)] + 2 \times [(6 - (15 \times 15/30))^2/(15 \times 15/30)] = 1.20,$$

which, with 1 degree of freedom is associated with $p > .20$.

FIGURE 4.11   Incorrect (Panel A) and correct (Panel B) data displays for cheating during turn-taking in 15 4-year-old and 15 6-year-old children, and incorrect (Part A) and correct (Part B) applications of chi-square analyses to these data. Note that even though some of the cells in the correct (Part B) analysis included small expected values, no correction for continuity was included. Simulation research indicates that the correction usually is unnecessary as long as N exceeds 20; indeed, use of the correction produces overly conservative probabilities (Delucchi, 1983).

significantly correlated in these data.[10] Comparing the results of the appropriate and inappropriate analyses illustrates that violating the independence assumption can produce serious distortions in chi-square probabilities. Similar distortions of chi-square probabilities have been noted by Gardner, Hartmann, and Mitchell (1982) in the analysis of dyadic time series data when an interacting dyad provides all of the data entries (see Figure 4.10 for an example of data of this type).

Log-linear analysis.   The newer methods of analyzing categorical data are variously called *log-linear analysis* and (multidimensional) *contingency table analysis*. These approaches allow investigators to analyze complicated cross-classified categorical data, such as the data presented in Figures 4.10 and 4.11 made more complex with the inclusion of additional variables. The analytic approach is similar to that used in an ANOVA. As in ANOVA, a linear model is developed that expresses a table entry (a frequency) as a function of main and interaction effects. Multidimensional contingency table analysis differs from ANOVA in that in the former case the *logarithms* of the putative effects are summed. Because the equation is linear in its log form, the approach is referred to as log-linear. In addition, testing procedures

---

[10] The analysis given in Figure 4.11 is a test of the difference between independent proportions. That is, is the proportion of 4-year-olds who engage in cheating different from the proportion of 6-year-olds who engage in cheating? As such, the analysis is one of the differences between independent means (as the two group proportions in this problem are really group means). The analyses can also be viewed as one of the correlation between group status (age) and cheating. Thus, in an important sense, differences between means and correlations are but two alternative ways of viewing data analysis.

resemble those used with data from unbalanced ANOVA designs. That is, a hierarchical model testing procedure is followed in which each lower-level model might be tested until a model that adequately fits the data is encountered. A set of hierarchical models for the data shown in Figure 4.10 would look like this:

(1) $m_{ij} = \mu$

(2) $m_{ij} = \mu + \lambda^M$

(3) $m_{ij} = \mu + \lambda^M + \lambda^I$

(4) $m_{ij} = \mu + \lambda^M + \lambda^I + \lambda^{MI}$ (the saturated model, including all effects)

where m_{ij} = the log expected frequency in the ith row and jth column; μ = the log of N/rc, or the average cell frequency; and λ^M, λ^I, and λ^{MI} = the log expected row (mother), column (infant), and interaction (Mother × Infant) effects, respectively.

A large value of the test statistic for a model (say, model 2) indicates that additional parameters must be included in the model—as in models 3 and 4—whereas a small value of the test statistic indicates that the model adequately fits the data. This *model comparison* approach to statistical testing is popular (see structural equation modeling; Judd et al., 1995).

The test statistic used for multidimensional contingency table analysis is either the ordinary chi-square statistic or the likelihood ratio statistic, G^2. G^2 involves the logarithm of the ratio of observed and expected frequencies, rather than the squared discrepancy between observed and expected frequencies that the ordinary chi-square test involves.

These techniques for analyzing multidimensional table data have the advantages of the ANOVA: They provide omnibus (overall) tests of main and interaction effects in factorial investigations, allow for subsequent contrast tests, and control for Type I error rates. These advantages come with some cost, however. According to Appelbaum and McCall (1983), multidimensional contingency analysis requires large numbers of participants, particularly when repeated-measures versions of this approach are used.

When these as well as other methods of statistical analysis are used for the first time, the computer program as well as the user should be tested by replicating a textbook example. After an example from any of the standard texts—such as Fleiss et al. (2003), Kennedy (1992), or Wickens (1989)—is analyzed successfully, the new data are ready for analysis. Additional useful material on multidimensional table analysis can be found in Knoke and Burke (1980) and Landis and Koch (1979).

Loglinear analysis is used to test the association between multiple categorical factors that are all regarded as response variables. However, when one of the factors is regarded as a response variable and the other factors are regarded as explanatory variables, *logistic regression analysis* is appropriate (Agresti, 1996).

Logistic regression. Logistic regression can be applied when the response variable is binary (binomial logistic regression) or polytomous (multinomial logistic regression). The explanatory variables are used to model the probability, $\hat{p}$, of the response. Whereas log-linear analysis models the natural log of the expected cell counts of a contingency table, logistic regression models the natural log of the odds of the response variable (Christensen, 1997). The natural log of the odds, $\ln\left(\frac{\hat{p}}{1-\hat{p}}\right)$, is called the logit or logistic unit, hence the name logistic regression. The logit form of the logistic regression equation is

$$\ln\left(\frac{\hat{p}}{1-\hat{p}}\right) = \beta_0 + \beta_1 X_1 + \beta_2 X_2 + \ldots + \beta_k X_k$$

The regression coefficient, β_k, indicates the amount of linear change in the logit for a one-unit change in the predictor. Because logits are difficult to interpret, regression coefficients are typically transformed into odds ratios or probabilities for interpretation. For example, using the contingency table in Figure 4.11, Panel B, the logistic regression equation for predicting cheating from age is logit(Cheating) = .41 − .811(Age). Transforming −.811 by taking the inverse of the natural log, $e^{-.811}$, gives .44, which is an odds ratio. It indicates that cheating by 6-year-old children is .44 times less likely than cheating by 4-year-old children. Logistic regression is a very flexible analytic technique. It accommodates multiple explanatory variables that can be a mix of all types (continuous, discrete, and dichotomous), and that can represent interactions between predictors and polynomials. Detailed presentations and worked examples of logistic regression are found in Agresti (2007), Cohen, Cohen, West, & Aiken (2003), Pampel (2000), and Tabachnick and Fidell (2007).[11]

Quantitative Analysis[12]

Often data are multipoint and ordered, such as Likert scale data,[13] and can be analyzed with one or other of the general methods of quantitative analysis. The more common of these are the ANOVAs and regression/correlation analysis. Both methods are based on the general linear model, in which a score is conceived of as a linear combination of main and interaction effects, plus error. Although in many respects ANOVA and regression analysis can be thought of as alternative approaches to the analysis of quantitative data, certain problems are more closely tied to one approach than to the other. Consequently, the following material discusses the two approaches separately. However, it is important to recognize that the problems discussed under one or the other approach do not disappear when one shifts from regression analysis to the ANOVA, or vice versa. The problems, such as lack of independence of the predictor variables (referred to as *nonorthogonality* in the analysis of variance), inflating Type I error by conducting many tests of significance on the same set of data, and the like must be dealt with whatever the form of analysis.

Regression analysis.   Regression analysis is the most general approach for the analysis of quantitative data. It accommodates data aimed at answering the two general types of question asked by developmentalists: questions regarding group trends and those involving individual differences. Most readers will be familiar with the latter use of regression analysis, for example, to explore the correlates of popularity in a group of 8-year-old children. That regression analysis also can evaluate group trends may be less familiar—but review the discussion of the data on cheating in 4- and 6-year-olds.

---

[11] Two other methods for analyzing categorical data that are growing in use are survival or time-event occurrence analysis (Bornstein et al., 2005; Singer & Willett, 2003; Willett & Singer, 2004) and latent class analysis (LCA; Collins, 2006; Magidson & Vermunt, 2004). Rindskopf (2004, p. 106) described LCA as the "categorical variable analog of factor analysis."

[12] For clarity of exposition, we have omitted an intermediate category: ranked data. Statistical procedures appropriate for ranked data typically are found in books on order, ranking, or nonparametric statistical procedures (e.g., Maritz, 1995; Reiss, 1989).

[13] Likert, or summated rating, scales typically ask the participant to respond to items using a 5-point scale with anchors ranging from *strongly agree* (perhaps scored 4) to *strongly disagree* (then scored 0). Total scores are obtained by summing scores on the individual items composing the scale.

A special use that regression analysis serves is as a test of mediation effects (MacKinnon, Fairchild, & Fritz, 2007). A mediator variable is one through which another variable operates to produce its effect on some outcome. For example, the effect of parental SES on children's social skills might be mediated by child IQ (also see Figure 4.15). Baron and Kenny (1986) distinguish mediator variables from moderator variables—the latter change the direction or strength of the relation between IV and DV. Gender, for example, may moderate the relation between popularity and intimacy. It clearly does not mediate the relation between these two variables.

In all its applications, regression analysis is plagued with difficulties for the unwary. Many of these difficulties are primarily interpretive in nature, rather than involving problems in statistical testing. Nevertheless, they seem worthy of note, and the conditions responsible for these difficulties are summarized in Table 4.20. Additional information on the foibles associated with the interpretation of regression/correlation analysis can be found in Darlington (1990, Chapters 8 and 9), McNemar (1969, Chapter 10) and Cohen et al. (2003).

The effects tested in regression/correlation analysis involve either correlation coefficients (bivariate rs or multiple Rs) or statistics such as path coefficients and beta weights that are a function of correlation coefficients. Tests of these statistics most often employ the F distribution (after Fisher), but in certain simple or unusual cases the t test or the normal curve (or z) test may be used (see the analysis conducted in Table 4.19).

As in many uses of statistical testing, problems occur when investigators are insufficiently sensitive to violations of independence assumptions when conducting statistical tests in conjunction with regression/correlation analysis. Nonindependence (dependence) affects statistical tests in regression analysis in at least two ways. First, tests may be conducted on nonindependent statistics from a regression analysis, but the testing procedure may only be appropriate for independent statistics. This may occur whenever investigators attempt to answer the generic question, "Is X more highly correlated with Y than S is correlated with Z?" and both r_{xy} and r_{sz} are obtained from the same individuals. Because they are obtained from the same respondents, such correlation coefficients are likely to be correlated, and their testing requires adjustments to accommodate the dependency between the coefficients (Meng, Rosenthal, & Rubin, 1992).

The second dependency problem occurs when the pairs of scores on which the correlation coefficient is calculated are not independent. (A similar problem was discussed with

TABLE 4.20
Disturbance Factors in Regression and Correlation Analysis

Disturbance factors	Consequences
Unreliable measurement	Correlation is underestimated.
Restricted score range	Correlation typically underestimated.
Non-normal distributions	Maximum value $|r| < 1.0$ unless the variables correlated are identically non-normal.
Small N to IV ratio	R overestimated; R regresses toward zero when cross-validated.
Correlated IVs	$r^2_{(xy)}$ does not give the proportion of variance in Y (the DV) uniquely associated with X_i; $\Sigma r^2_{(xy)}$ does not equal R^2.
Highly correlated IVs[a] (multicollinearity)	Beta weights (βs) unstable.

[a] Correlated IVs (called nonorthogonal IVs) also produce complicated issues of statistical testing when data are analyzed via ANOVA. The problem of correlated independent variables in the analysis of variance is discussed by Kahneman (1965) and by Cohen (1968). Appelbaum and his associates (Appelbaum & Cramer, 1974; Appelbaum & McCall, 1983) have presented methods of analyzing these data.

respect to the cheating data shown in Figure 4.11.) This dependency problem occurs, for example, when more than one member of a family contributes pairs of scores to the correlation analysis, or when the same individual contributes all of the scores entering into the analysis.

A final problem in testing correlational statistics occurs when a large number of variables are intercorrelated, and the correlation between each pair of variables is tested for significance in the usual manner. When this is done, the probability of making one or more Type I errors (see Table 4.1) may approach 1.0. To avoid the problem of inflating Type I errors with a large matrix of intercorrelations, the entire matrix is first tested to ensure that some significant covariation exists in the matrix as a whole.[14] If that test proves to be significant, then statistical tests are conducted on the individual correlations with α adjusted so as to hold the probability of a Type I error for the entire collection of tests to some specified level (Larzelere & Mulaik, 1977). This procedure has the effect of using a much more conservative alpha for tests of the significance conducted on the individual correlations.

ANOVA.   ANOVA is the approach most often used to assess differences in means for the variables investigated in developmental research, such as age and time of measurement. ANOVA, like regression, is a general approach to data analysis that can accommodate the data from a wide variety of experimental designs. ANOVA can be used when all design facets involve between-subject effects (i.e., completely randomized designs), within-subject effects (randomized block or repeated-measures designs), or within- and between-subject effects (mixed or split-plot designs). ANOVA procedures also can be applied when additional measured variables are included to statistically control unwanted sources of variation (analysis of covariance, ANCOVA), and when the design employs multiple dependent variables (multivariate analysis of variance, MANOVA and multivariate analysis of covariance, MANCOVA).

An ANOVA is illustrated with a 4 (age) × 2 (gender) × 3 (time of measurement) split-plot factorial design in Part A of Table 4.21. The ANOVA of the data from that design might be used to test whether the means for the groups defined by age, gender, and time of testing, alone and in combinations, vary significantly. The latter tests of combinations of variables are referred to as tests of interactions. The tests performed require that the scores used in the analysis meet certain assumptions, including those of normality, homogeneity (equivalence) of variance, and "homogeneity" of covariance or correlation between the repeated measures. ANOVA is relatively robust (insensitive) to violations of the former assumptions as long as each group contains approximately the same number of participants and sample sizes are not very small (Glass, Peckham, & Sanders, 1972; but see Judd et al., 1995). It is not robust, however, to violations of the requirement concerning the correlation between the repeated measures (Kirk, 1995). This requirement is often violated whenever more than two times of testing are employed. This is because the essence of the assumption is that all of the repeated measures are equally correlated. However, scores almost always correlate more highly with measures that are adjacent in time, and less highly with temporally more remote measures. Hence, with even three repeated measures, the correlations between Time 1 and Time 2 scores,

---

[14] The simultaneous test for a sample correlation matrix, **R**, is accomplished by testing the multivariate hypothesis that the population correlation matrix is an identity matrix, H_0: **P** = **I**, which means that all correlations between variables are simultaneously equal to zero, against the alternative H_1: **P** ≠ **I**. The test statistic is, $\chi^2 = -[(N-1) - (2p+5)/6]\ln|\mathbf{R}|$, where N is the sample size, p is the number of variables in **R**, and $\ln|\mathbf{R}|$ is the natural logarithm of the determinant of the sample correlation matrix. H_0 is rejected if χ^2 exceeds the critical value at the $100(1-\alpha)$ percentile point of the chi-square distribution with $p(p-1)/2$ degrees if freedom (Larzelere & Mulaik, 1977, p. 560; Morrison, 2000, pp. 116–118).

TABLE 4.21
Schematic Design and ANOVA Summary Table for an Age by Sex by Time of Testing Factorial Design

Part A. Design Schematic		Testing Period		
Age	Gender	1	2	3
4	Girl ($n = 5$) Boy ($n = 5$)			
6	Girl ($n = 5$) Boy ($n = 5$)			
8	Girl ($n = 5$) Boy ($n = 5$)			
10	Girl ($n = 5$) Boy ($n = 5$)			

Part B. ANOVA Summary Table

Source	Degrees of Freedom (df)	MS	F	p
Between Subjects				
Age (A)	$(a - 1) = 4 - 1 = 3$	25.0	5.00	<.01
Gender (B)	$(b - 1) = 2 - 1 = 1$	5.5	1.10	>.25
A × B	$(a - 1)(b - 1) = 3$	10.0	2.00	<.25
Error (S/A × D)	$ab(n - 1) = 32$	5.0		
Within Subjects				
Assessments (D)	$(d - 1) = 3 - 1 = 2$	8.4	3.36	<.05 (<.10[a])
D × A	$(d - 1)(a - 1) = 6$	10.0	4.00	<.01 (<.05[b])
D × B	$(d - 1)(b - 1) = 2$	2.8	1.12	>.25 (>.25[a])
D × A × B	$(d - 1)(a - 1)(b - 1) = 6$	3.1	1.24	>.25 (>.25[b])
Error (D × S/A × B)	$ab(n - 1)(d - 1) = 64$	2.5		

Note. MS indicates "mean square." The lower case letters in the summary table equal the number of levels for the source indicated in the corresponding upper case letter. For example, there are 4 ages, so the source age (A) has four levels ($a = 4$). In generating F-tests, age, gender, and time of testing are considered fixed so that all between-subjects and within-subjects effects are tested with their respective subject—S/A × B or D × S/A × B—error terms (Kirk, 1995).
[a] Tested with 1 and 32 degrees of freedom (Geisser-Greenhouse correction).
[b] Tested with 3 and 32 degrees of freedom (Geisser-Greenhouse correction).

and between Time 2 and Time 3 scores, are likely to exceed the correlation between Time 1 and Time 3 scores. When the assumption of "homogeneity" of covariance is violated, the probability values obtained from ordinary statistical testing are too small (i.e., the effects appear to be "more significant" than they are). A number of procedures have been developed to remedy the biasing of probability values when this assumption may be violated, the most popular of which is the procedure developed by Geisser and Greenhouse (1958). The Geisser-Greenhouse adjustment was applied to all of the within-subject tests conducted in Part B of Table 4.21. That is, the degrees of freedom used in determining the probability values for the tests were reduced by dividing the usual degrees of freedom by the degrees of freedom associated with the repeated measure $(d - 1)$. The resulting statistical tests indicate that the main effect of age and the interaction between age and time of assessment significantly "determine" performance. The interaction between age and time of assessment is shown in Figure 4.12. From an inspection of this figure, it can be discerned that the interaction, revealed by a lack of parallelism of the four data lines, is due largely to the performance of the

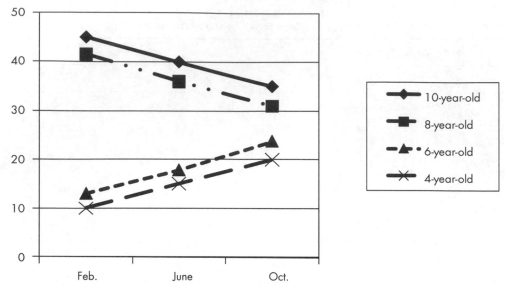

FIGURE 4.12   Illustration of the interaction between age and time of assessment for the design shown in
Table 4.20.

two older age groups of children in comparison with that of the two younger age groups of
children. That is, the 8- and 10-year-olds slightly deteriorate in performance across time,
whereas the 4- and 6-year-olds improve somewhat with each repetition of the assessment
procedures. Note that the presence of a significant interaction requires qualification of the
lower-level effects of which the interaction is composed; that is, interactions take precedence
interpretively over their component effects. In our example, we would interpret the significant
D × A (assessments *by* age) interaction rather than the two component main effects (assessments *and* age)—even if these component main effects were significant. The significant D × A
interaction requires us to recognize that the effect of age varies depending on which time of
assessment one focuses on, or alternatively that the differences between assessment times vary
depending on which age group one focuses on.

The standard tests conducted by ANOVA can be supplemented (and sometimes replaced)
by other statistical tests under at least two sets of circumstances. First, additional tests usually
are conducted to determine exactly what level(s) of a factor differ from which other level(s)
following a significant ANOVA test involving more than one degree of freedom. (More than
one degree of freedom means that more than one contrast—e.g., two groups—are being
compared.) The procedures used for these follow-up tests involve some form of trend test, test
of simple main effects, or other comparisons between combinations of means. Generically,
these tests are referred to as *multiple comparison tests*. Their intent is to determine which
specific levels of the IVs included in the omnibus test are significantly different, while maintaining some control of Type I error rate produced by conducting multiple tests of significance on a set of data. (See the related discussion in the regression analysis section.)
Of course, neither these nor any other form of significance testing are appropriate for "test
hopping"—that is, hopping from one inferential testing procedure to another until "significant" results are found.[15]

_____

[15] A subtle and common, but nonetheless illegitimate, variant of test hopping involves switching the form of the data
as well as the method of analysis. For example, an investigator interested in differences in prosocial behavior between
children of different ages may initially analyze rate of donation with a *t* test, and finding the test nonsignificant, switch
to a chi-square analysis conducted on the transformed data of whether or not each child donated.

Many multiple comparison tests are available. Table 4.22 summarizes the characteristics of 30 multiple comparison tests, most of which are available in major statistical software packages such as SAS and SPSS. The selection among tests is based on a number of considerations, including the experimental model, what statistical assumptions are met (e.g., homogeneity of variance), whether confidence intervals are required, the level of control of the Type I error rate, whether the comparisons were planned prior to data analysis (*a priori* comparisons) or are selected after examining the data (*a posteriori* comparisons or fishing expeditions), and the types of comparisons to be conducted (e.g., all pairwise or more complex comparisons among means, or all condition means contrasted with a control group mean). In addition to the procedures listed in Table 4.22, simulation methods are available for complex designs such as repeated measures ANOVA, or ANCOVA (see Westfall, Tobias, Rom, Wolfinger, & Hochberg, 1999). Recent developments have extended the application of multiple comparison procedures to a broad class of parametric and semi-parametric statistical models, including generalized linear models, mixed models, models for censored data (survival analysis) and more (Hothorn, Bretz, & Westfall, 2008). Detailed explanations of multiple comparison tests and recommendations for their use are available in Hochberg and Tamhane (1987), Hsu (1996), Kirk (1995), Tamhane (2009), Toothaker (1991), and Westfall et al. (1999).

The second basis for not relying solely on omnibus tests from ANOVA relates to a central tenet of statistical application: The analysis should suit the question, and the standard tests performed by ANOVA may not adequately evaluate the comparisons that are involved in an *a priori* hypothesis. Consider the interaction illustrated in Figure 4.13 among the four levels from a 2×2 completely randomized factorial design. (In a completely randomized design, all effects involve between-subjects comparisons.) Using standard ANOVA tests, the variation associated with this interaction would be split between the main effects of age and of gender, and the Age $\times$ Gender interaction. All of the tests of these effects may be nonsignificant, yet a contrast written specifically for this expected pattern of interaction[16] might be highly significant. And of course, this is exactly the approach that should be taken with a typical *a priori* hypothesis: The contrast for the expected effect should be constructed and then tested. These *a priori* contrast tests may be conducted prior to, or even instead of, the traditional omnibus ANOVA tests (see Rosenthal & Rosnow, 1985).

In addition to these general issues associated with the use of ANOVAs, specific concerns accrue with the use of special, commonly used ANOVA designs. Two of these designs are hierarchical analysis of variance and the analysis of covariance.

Hierarchical designs.   Formally, hierarchical designs are those in which the levels of one factor are nested within the levels of another factor. The design would be hierarchical, for example, if both second- and fourth-grade girls and boys were taught spelling using mnemonic devices, but different procedures were used for the second graders and for the fourth graders. Such obvious examples of nesting (think of the grades as nests, and the mnemonic devices as eggs within the nests) are unlikely to be analyzed mistakenly. Mistakes do occur, however, when a nuisance variable such as classroom, play group, or family is nested within an experimental factor. Consider the case in which child aggression comprised the DV, the design factor concerned whether aggression was disregarded or interpreted, and children were assessed and treated within play groups. In this example, a particularly aggressive group member might instigate counteraggression from other group members. As a result, the scores for all or most members of this play group would be elevated, scores for members within the

---

[16] In this case, we might write the numerator of contrast as the mean for 10-year-old girls minus the average of the three remaining means: $\mu_{\female 10} - .33(\mu_{\male 16} + \mu_{\female 16} + \mu_{\male 10})$.

TABLE 4.22

Characteristics of Multiple Comparison Tests

	Pairwise Only	Pairwise or Non-pairwise	Equal ns Only	Equal ns or Unequal ns	Homogeneous Variances	Heterogeneous Variances	Confidence Intervals[a]	Error Rate
A Priori Orthogonal Comparisons								
Student t[bc]		X		X	X		X	PC
Student t with Welch df		X		X		X	X	PC
k[d] − 1 a Priori Nonorthogonal Comparisons Involving a Control Group Mean								
Dunnett[bc]	X			X[e]	X	X[e]	X	FW
C[f] a Priori Nonorthogonal Comparisons								
Dunn (Bonferroni)[bc]		X		X	X		X	FW
Dunn with Welch df		X		X		X	X	FW
Dunn-Sidak[bc]		X		X	X		X	FW
Dunn-Sidak with Welch df		X		X		X	X	FW
Holm[c]		X		X	X			FW
Holm with Welch df		X		X		X		FW
All Pairwise Comparisons (a Posteriori)								
Fisher LSD[bc]	X			X	X		X	PC
Fisher-Hayter	X			X	X		X	FW
Tukey HSD[bc]	X		X		X		X	FW
Tukey-Kraemer[bc]	X			X	X		X	FW
Hockberg GT2[bc]	X			X	X		X	FW
Gabriel[bc]	X			X	X		X	FW
Games-Howel[b]	X			X		X	X	FW
Dunnett T3[b]	X			X		X	X	FW
Dunnett C[b]	X			X		X	X	FW
Tamhane T2[b]	X			X		X	X	FW
REGW Q[bc]	X		X		X			FW
REGW F[b]	X			X	X			FW
Shaffer-Ryan	X		X		X			FW
Peritz Q	X		X		X			FW
Peritz F	X			X	X			FW
Peritz Shaffer-Ryan	X		X		X			FW

			All Comparisons Including Non-pairwise Comparisons (a Posteriori)		Table Note
Newman-Keuls[bc]	X	X	X		FW[g]
Duncan[bc]	X	X	X		PC[g]
Waller-Duncan[bc]	X		X		
Scheffe[bc]	X	X	X	X	FW
Brown-Forsythe	X	X	X	X	FW

Note. **FW** (familywise error rate)—Type I error rate (rejecting a true null hypothesis) is controlled at α for the family of comparisons. A set of contextually related comparisons is a family (e.g., the six pairwise comparisons for comparing the means of a treatment with four levels). **PC** (per comparison error rate)—Type I error rate is controlled at α for each comparison. Procedures that control α at the PC rate will generally exceed α at the FW rate and are generally not recommended; however, contemporary practice favors adopting the PC error rate for a priori orthogonal comparisons. The Waller-Duncan test minimizes risk based on a Bayesian approach instead of controlling for Type I error. [a] Single-step multiple comparison procedures (procedures that use the same critical value for all tests compared; e.g., Dunn, Tukey) yield $100(1 − α)$% confidence intervals and are generally preferred because they provide the greatest level of inference. Confidence intervals can be computed for Students *t* and Fisher's *LSD* but are not simultaneous confidence intervals since they are not adjusted for multiplicity. Multiple-step procedures (procedures that adjust the critical value at each step of the hypothesis; e.g., Holm, REGW Q) do not yield confidence intervals but are generally more powerful and are recommended when confidence intervals are not needed. [b]Supported by SAS. [c]C is the number of comparisons. [d]Supported by SPSS. [e]With modification. [f]C is the number of comparisons. [g]Although supported in major statistical packages, the Newman-Keuls and Duncan procedures are not recommended because they fail to control FW error rates when the number of groups is $k > 2$ for the Duncan and $k > 3$ for the Newman Keuls; the REGW, Shafer-Ryan, and Peritz methods are recommended instead.

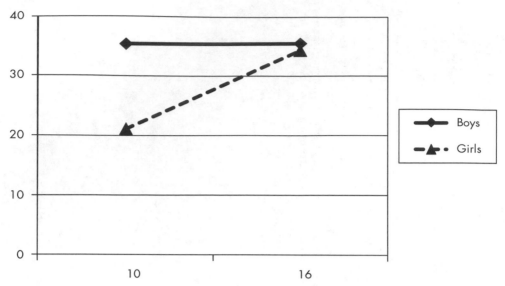

FIGURE 4.13 Illustration of a predicted interaction between gender and age not adequately assessed using standard omnibus ANOVA tests.

group likely would be *interdependent*, and play group membership may be a substantial source of nuisance variation. Thus, the dependency between scores for members of a group and the effect of the group itself must be accommodated in the data analysis—or else serious inferential errors may be made (Kenny & Judd, 1986). Various methods for integrating nested variables into the statistical analysis are discussed by Anderson and Anger (1978), Kraemer and Jacklin (1979), Raudenbush and Bryk (2002), and Kirk (1995).

ANCOVA. ANCOVA is involved when one or more measured variables are used to control unwanted sources of variance through statistical means in any of the standard ANOVA designs. (This is not unlike the method of statistical control served by partial correlations.) For example, in an experiment on methods of teaching reading, children's IQ scores might be used as a covariate to reduce naturally occurring differences in "reading potential" for the children participating in the experiment. Because unwanted sources of variability can be reduced statistically when they cannot be controlled experimentally, ANCOVA is a popular means of increasing statistical power or sensitivity. However, its use requires strict attention to a rigorous set of requirements. These include the usual assumptions of ANOVA of having errors due to treatment that are normally and independently distributed and equal variance across experimental conditions (homogeneity of variance). Additional requirements include homogeneity of the within-group regression slopes, independence between treatment scores and the covariate, covariate values measured without error, a linear relationship between outcome and the covariate, and errors due to the covariate (regression) that are normally and independently distributed with equal variance across the levels of the covariate (Huitema, 1980; Kirk, 1995; Tabachnick & Fidell, 2007).

Two particularly serious problems can occur as a result of using ANCOVA incorrectly: One problem results from violating the ANCOVA assumptions; the other occurs when ANCOVA is asked to perform roles for which it is ill-suited. The ANCOVA assumption that can be particularly problematic when violated is the assumption of independence between treatment and scores on the covariate. In the reading example mentioned earlier, the IQ scores must be independent of treatment, perhaps requiring that we obtain them prior to implementation of the treatment for reading—when it is impossible for the treatment to have affected the IQ scores. The second problem occurs when investigators employ ANCOVA to adjust for initial differences between preexisting groups, such as classrooms. Selecting preexisting *groups*, and then focusing the analysis on the performance of *individuals*, is a clear violation of random assignment procedures. Furthermore, initial biases typically cannot be undone by ANCOVA procedures (e.g., Overall & Woodward, 1977).

Multivariate extensions.   Various multivariate extensions of ANOVA and regression analysis are used by developmental investigators. There follow—in alphabetical order—brief descriptions of the more popular of these extensions, their primary functions or uses, their most common problems, and where interested readers can find out more about them. Beforehand, it is important to note a few similarities among the various multivariate techniques. Most importantly, all of the multivariate procedures apply weights to the participants' scores on the original set of measured variables to form one or more new composite variables; the weights are selected to optimize some function. For example, if the newly constructed composite variable is Y, and the original variables are X_a through X_e with optimum weights a through e, then the composite score for the ith individual is given by

$$Y_i = aX_{ai} + bX_{bi} + cX_{ci} + dX_{di} + eX_{ei}$$

where, for example, X_{ai} is the ith individual's score on variable X_a.

This process is similar to forming the composite variable, total score, for a classroom achievement test. The total score is based on a linear combination of weighted item scores. The item scores may be weighted to maximize individual differences in performance on the test—or an approximation to this, weighting each item 1.0, is more likely used. In multivariate analysis, the weights may be selected, for example, to maximize the correlation between two sets of variables (canonical correlation), to minimize the number of independent dimensions necessary to characterize a set of variables (factor analysis), or to maximize the differences between two or more groups (discriminant analysis).

All multivariate techniques also share a number of common weaknesses. Foremost among these is that they eschew perfectly, or near perfectly, correlated variables. Perfectly correlated variables pose a problem to multivariate analysis called *linear dependency*. Highly correlated variables pose a slightly different problem called *multicollinearity*. Both conditions are undesirable for all forms of multivariate analysis. Second, multivariate procedures require substantial numbers of participants. As the ratio of variables to participants approaches 1.0, the optimizing algorithm used to generate weights increasingly exploits chance relations in the data. As a consequence, the results of the study will not replicate.

Canonical correlation.   The aim of canonical correlation is to explore the interrelations between two sets of variables. It is the multivariate analog of bivariate correlation. Instead of single predictor and criterion variables, canonical correlation is used when sets of predictor and criterion variables are obtained. The technique generates composite scores from a weighted linear combination of the set of predictor variables and of the set of criterion variables; the weights are selected to maximize the correlation between the two composite scores. The linear combinations of variables generated by this procedure are called *canonical variates*; hence, the correlation between canonical variates is called a *canonical correlation*. Following the construction or extraction of the first canonical variate from the predictor and criterion sets of variables and the calculation of their correlation, additional canonical variates may be extracted and correlated. The weights used in forming these subsequent canonical variates are chosen with an additional criterion: The new variates must be independent of the canonical variates already constructed.

Canonical correlation is used when an investigator intends to explore the relations between sets of variables in separate domains; for example, between nursery school children's social interactional behaviors and their performance on cognitive tasks. Unless the ratio of participants to variables in such an investigation is quite large, say 10 to 1, the specific optimum weights used are unlikely to cross-validate in subsequent investigations. Additional information on canonical correlation can be found in Thompson (1984), and in multivariate textbooks by Tabachnick and Fidell (2007) and Stevens (1992).

Discriminant analysis.[17]   The purpose of discriminant analysis is to assign individuals to the appropriate group. Assignments are based on the individual's standing on one or more weighted linear composites of their scores on a set of predictor variables. The weights are selected so that the predictor variables maximize differences between the groups. For example, a discriminant analysis might be used to assign children to popular, neglected, or rejected groups based on composite scores formed by weighting their scores on the scales of the Child Behavior Checklist (CBCL; e.g., Achenbach & Dumenci, 2001). This problem, involving as it does classification into one of three groups, requires the construction of two (one less than the number of groups) composite variables. The composite variables formed in discriminant analysis are called *discriminant functions.* Typical discriminant analysis output provides the weights for the predictor variables that are used in constructing the discriminant functions, that is the weights for the variables that aid in the prediction of group membership. The output also includes information on which category individual children are assigned based on their scores on the discriminant functions, as well as the proportion of children correctly classified. (See standard multivariate texts previously mentioned as well as manuals for standard computer data analysis software such as SPSS; Bryman & Cramer, 2001.)

Factor analysis.   Factor analysis and related techniques such as principal component analysis have as their purpose the discovery of the minimum dimensions underlying a set of variables. Investigators may be interested, for example, in the number of dimensions underlying performance on the subtests of the WISC-R or underlying endorsement of the items included in the CBCL. These dimensions, referred to as factors or components, are constructed by forming weighted linear composites of the original variables (e.g., subtest or item scores). The weights applied to the variables in the construction of each factor vary depending on the factoring technique used. In general, however, the weights are chosen to "explain" the maximum variation in the entire set of variables. Thus, the weights assigned to the variables in the construction of the first factor are chosen so as to maximize the correlations of that factor with the original variables. The weights for the variables in the construction of the second factor are chosen so that factor has the highest correlations with those parts of the original variables not accounted for by the first factor, and so forth.

After factors are extracted, they often are rotated. *Rotation* refers to the transformation of factors by modifying the weights for the variables from which they were constructed. The purpose of rotation is to facilitate description, and hence understanding of the factors

---

[17] Statisticians recommend using logistic regression analysis instead of discriminant function analysis when doing two-group classification (e.g., depressed or not depressed). Discriminant analysis makes two strong assumptions for inference—(1) multivariate normality among the set of predictors for each group on the dependent variable and (2) homogeneity of the within-group covariance matrices—that are rarely met in practice and that are not made in logistic regression (Cohen et al., 2003; Press & Wilson, 1978).

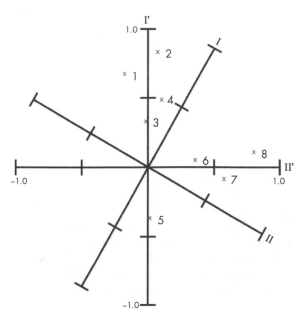

FIGURE 4.14 Illustration of rotation to achieve improved interpretability of factors. The correlations between the original eight variables and the factors, I and II, are indicated by finding the coordinates used to represent the eight variables. For example, Variable 1 (see x associated with 1) has correlations of about +.5 with factor I and −.5 with factor II. The original factors were rotated approximately 30° counterclockwise to form the new factors, I′ and II′. As a result, the five verbal tests (numbered 1 through 5) defined the first rotated factor (I′) and the three quantitative tests (numbered 6 through 8) defined the second rotated factor (II′). Rotation has no effect on the correlations between the variables, but it does change the loadings (correlations) of the variables with the factors. For example, Variable 1 now correlates in excess of .6 with Factor I′, and slightly negatively with factor II′.

extracted from a set of data. In Figure 4.14, the two original factors extracted (I and II) from eight verbal and quantitative tests were rotated (counterclockwise) some 30° to promote understanding of the factors. The original factors (labeled I and II) are hodgepodges of verbal and quantitative abilities; the new factors (labeled I′ and II′) appear to be relatively pure measures of verbal and quantitative skills, respectively. Readers interested in learning more about factor analysis and related techniques can consult the articles by Comrey (1978) and by Rummel (1967), texts by Gorsuch (1983) and McDonald (1985), as well as the multivariate textbooks already noted.

MANOVA.   MANOVA is a straightforward generalization of ANOVA to investigations employing more than one dependent variable. For example, if the Age × Gender × Repeated Assessment problem described in Table 4.21 included two or more DVs, rather than just one DV, MANOVA would be the appropriate method of analysis of the data. Furthermore, the MANOVA summary table would closely resemble in form Part B of Table 4.21, the ANOVA summary table. The primary difference between ANOVA and MANOVA is that the latter forms one or more weighted composites of the DVs that maximize the differences between the levels of the IVs. It is these composite scores, called *discriminant function scores*, that are tested for significance. If two or more discriminant functions are formed, each subsequent discriminant function is orthogonal to (independent of) the previous discriminant functions.

MANOVA has a number of advantages when compared with conducting separate ANOVAs on each dependent variable.

1. MANOVA provides better control over Type I error. Subsequent statistical tests (e.g., ANOVAs) are only conducted if MANOVA indicates that at least one independent variable produces an effect on some linear combination of the dependent variables. (This rule is relaxed when *a priori* predictions are advanced.)
2. MANOVA may detect differences—when a weak effect is distributed over each of a number of correlated dependent variables—that would not be found if a separate ANOVA was conducted on each dependent variable. Thus, in some circumstances, MANOVA may be a more powerful method of analysis than are separate ANOVAs. (However, if the effect is carried by just one DV, MANOVA may be more conservative.)
3. MANOVA has less restrictive assumptions than does the comparable repeated measures ANOVA (Tabachnick & Fidell, 2007).

Other Statistical Techniques

A number of other, newer forms of analysis are available to developmental researchers. Three of these—hierarchical linear modeling (HLM) or multilevel models, structural equation modeling (SEM), and meta-analysis—are sufficiently common and important to deserve mention. A brief explanation of nonlinear regression is also given.

HLM. HLM, also known as multilevel analysis, is a set of regression-like analytic techniques that is particularly well adapted for multistage analysis. Multistage analysis is called for when two or more analytic approaches are combined to address a problem, and two situations encountered by developmental investigators that are likely to require multistage analysis are the analysis of growth and situations in which the number of units of analysis exceeds the number of sampling units.

In the analysis of growth, which prior to multilevel analysis was plagued by problems (see the "Change" subsection under "Seminal Design Issues for Developmental Investigators" and the "Difference scores" subsection under "Types of Scores" above), the first stage in the analysis involves determining a growth function for each participant (see Burchinal & Appelbaum, 1991). These growth functions are based on multiwave assessments, but need not require that each participant be measured on every occasion or on fixed occasions (Hoeksma & Koomen, 1992). In the second stage, the individual growth functions are examined to identify their correlates (e.g., causes or consequences). According to Bryk and Raudenbush (1987), HLM enables investigators to study the structure of individual growth (identify and describe individual growth trajectories), discover the correlates of growth, and also test hypotheses about the effects of experimental treatment on growth curves.

Units of analysis commonly exceed independent sampling units in developmental studies. Consider, for example, an investigation of the relation between friendship status and academic performance when schools are selected that vary, say, in the proximity of classmates' homes to one another and in socioeconomic status (SES). As a result of selection at the level of schools, classrooms are *nested* within schools and children are *nested* within classrooms. This nesting may cause linkages (lack of independence) between respondents' scores, both within schools and within classrooms. HLM (1) provides improved estimates of the relation of friendship status to academic performance by borrowing strength from the fact that similar estimates exist for other schools; (2) allows the testing of how schools varying in the average proximity of classmates' homes to one another and in SES might affect the relation between friendship and academic achievement; and (3) provides partitioning of the relation between friendship and achievement into within- and between-school components.

Although HLM is a powerful general approach for dealing with what have been thorny analytic problems for developmentalists, the technique comes with a set of daunting assumptions regarding the distribution of variables, the structure of the relations between variables, and the metric in which the outcome variables are measured (Bryk & Raudenbush, 1987). According to Raudenbush and Bryk (2002, p. 253), skillful data analysts pay close attention to the assumptions required by their models. They investigate the tenability of assumptions in light of the available data; they consider how sensitive their conclusions are likely to be to violations of these assumptions; and they seek ameliorative strategies when significant violations are discovered. In this regard, a caveat is in order. Hierarchical linear models are relatively new and there are few in-depth studies of the consequences of violating model assumptions. Excellent explanations and tutorials of HLM analysis are available in Cohen et al. (2003), Fitzmaurice, Laird, & Ware (2004), Kristjansson, Kircher, and Webb (2007), Raudenbush and Bryk (2002), Singer and Willett (2003), and Tabachnick and Fidell (2007).

SEM. SEM, structural modeling, linear structural equations, or covariance structural modeling is a multiple regression-like statistical methodology for probing causal models. In contrast to more typical descriptive interpretations of, say, the regression coefficients in a multiple regression analysis, SEM hypothesizes that the coefficients indicate the rate with which the IVs *cause* changes in the DVs. SEM is perhaps most closely associated with the computer program LISREL (linear structural relations), developed by Jöreskog and Sörbom (1983) for estimating the parameters of structural models. However, other approaches to structural model testing are available (e.g., Arbuckle, 1997; Heise, 1975; Kenny, 1979; Ullman & Bentler, 2003).

Structural modeling is particularly attractive to developmentalists. The reasons for this popularity are easily understood. The technique is well adapted for use with nonexperimental data, and it makes its strongest case with multiwave longitudinal data—the kind of data associated traditionally with developmental investigations.[18] In fact, manuscripts using as well as misusing structural modeling increased at such a dramatic rate that a prominent developmental journal, *Child Development*, devoted much of an entire issue "to illuminate the nature and possible applications of this statistical technique to developmental data" (Bronson, 1987). Lists of woes over the misuse of SEM are given by Freedman (1991) and MacCallum (2003).

Structural modeling employs a somewhat different vocabulary than do more traditional forms of design and analysis. In SEM, the variable set is divided into two classes, *exogenous* variables and *endogenous* variables. Exogenous variables are those variables that are hypothesized to produce changes in other (endogenous) variables in the model, but the causes for the exogenous variables themselves are not included in the model. Endogenous variables, in contrast, are presumably changed as a result of other variables in the model. Thus, exogenous variables are always IVs, whereas endogenous variables are DVs, but also can serve as IVs. A variable serving both IV and DV status is sometimes referred to as a mediator variable.

Variables included in some structural models also may be classified as *measured variables* or as *latent variables*. Measured variables (also known as manifest variables), as the name suggests, are variables that are directly assessed; latent variables are estimated—usually by more than one measured variable. As this vocabulary exercise suggests, a structural model (the multiple regression-like part of structural modeling) is often joined with a measurement model (the factor analytic-like part of SEM). When these two models are joined, as in LISREL, a good part of the Greek and English alphabets are required to symbolize the components of the model and their interconnecting equations. Fortunately, models typically

---

[18] SEM and HLM are but two of a number of different approaches to modeling longitudinal (growth) data. See Collins and Sayer (2000) and Raudenbush (2000) for discussions of various approaches to the analysis of growth.

are expressed pictorially, in the form of path diagrams, in addition to being expressed as a series of equations.

A *path diagram* illustrating the structural relations among four variables is displayed in Panel A of Figure 4.15. In path diagrams such as this one, exogenous variables are placed on the far left of the diagram, intervening variables in the middle, and other endogenous variables at the far right. Once the data have been obtained, the path coefficients (correlations and regression coefficients) often are placed on the arrows; the values of the residuals—$(1 - R^2)$ or the proportion of variance in each variable not explained by the model—are included in the ellipses (see McDonald & Ho, 2002). Panel B of Figure 4.15 illustrates the measurement submodel for the Panel A latent variable of child social skills. This latent variable is indexed with three measurement operations: independent observations of the child, teacher ratings, and peer sociometrics. Multiple indexing is a critical aspect of SEM and, in general, is a good research practice.

Each variable in path diagrams that is touched by a single-headed arrow is included as the DV in a structural equation. Each variable attached to the DV by the end of an arrow is included on the right-hand side of the same structural equation as an IV. For example, in the rudimentary model described in Figure 4.15, child social skills would be expressed as a

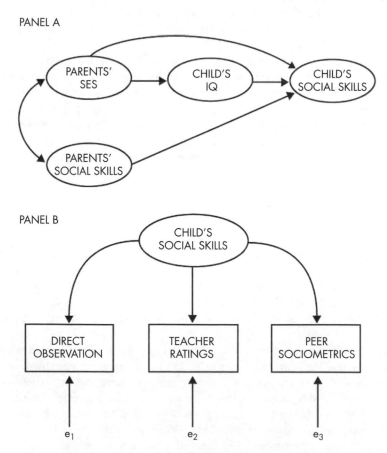

FIGURE 4.15   Path diagrams. Panel A illustrates the structural relations between the exogenous variables, parental SES and social skills, and the endogenous variables of child's IQ (an intervening variable) and social skills. Disturbance components are not included. Panel B illustrates a measurement model for the latent variable, child social skills. e_1, e_2, e_3 indicate error in assessing the latent construct, "child social skill," by means of each of the three measurement operations.

function of child IQ and parental SES and social skills (Panel A), whereas the observational measure of social skill would comprise the DV in an equation including the latent variable of child social skill and error (Panel B).

SEM testing requires a number of reasonably complicated steps or phases. The first step involves formulation of the structural model, in which the hypothesized causal relations between sets of variables are formulated. The second step involves operationalization of the variables and gathering data relevant to the test of the model. Because causes require time to produce their effects, longitudinal data involving a time lag suitable for "capturing" the causal connections stipulated in the model typically are required. After the data have been gathered—and structural modeling requires substantial data, as do all multivariate statistical techniques—they are summarized in a form appropriate for testing the goodness of fit of the model. The summary statistics are then operated on, often with rather complex statistical programs such as LISREL, to produce estimates of the model parameters and tests of statistical significance. One or more of these tests of significance are conducted on the model as a whole. A statistically nonsignificant (typically, chi-square) test indicates that the model adequately *fits* the data, whereas a statistically significant test suggests that the model requires revision—that significant amounts of variability in the data are not accounted for by the model. Statistical tests also are conducted on the individual model components, such as the regression weights relating putative effects to their causes and indicators to their latent variables. For these statistical tests of predicted relations, a nonsignificant test indicates that the subpart of the model tested has been *disconfirmed*—that the expected relation is not reliably different from zero.

It is important to recognize the nature of the causal inferences that can be drawn from confirmation of a structural model. As anyone who has survived an elementary course in statistics has repeatedly heard, correlation does not prove causation. (Nor, it might be added, does any other statistic. The determination of causality is a function of design—and perhaps philosophy of science.) Thus, finding that the predicted correlations between the variables included in the model fit the data increases the credibility of the causal model and the theory on which it was based. This increased credibility resulting from model confirmation assumes, of course, that the model was potentially disconfirmable by the data gathered.

Following testing of the model to determine whether it can be confirmed, or must be disconfirmed, further *exploratory* analyses may be conducted on the model. These analyses are controversial, and are performed to assess how the model might be revised to better fit the empirical results (Overton, 1998, p. 165). The revised model produced as a result of this exploratory work requires additional empirical testing with a fresh sample of data—as does all exploratory model building, no matter which statistical technique provided the means of exploration—to determine whether it will pass a reasonable test of disconfirmation.

SEM is a powerful approach for the analysis of nonexperimental data, but the power comes at some cost. The model requires a careful balance of variables to respondents (some, but by no means all experts suggest not more than [N]$10 - 2$ variables, where N is the number of participants), multiple measures or indicators for its latent variables, appropriate lags between the waves of the longitudinal data that are gathered, and assurance that certain statistical assumptions, including that of linear relations among the variables, are upheld (Freedman, 1991; Hoyle, 2008). Very readable accounts of structural modeling can be found in the special issue of *Child Development* (Bronson, 1987) devoted to that topic (see also McArdle, 2009) and in textbooks (e.g., Bohrnstedt & Knoke, 1994; Pedhazur & Schmelkin, 1991; Ullman, 2007). More technical presentations are available in Ullman and Bentler (2003), Jöreskog and Sörbom (1983), and Kelloway (1998).

Nonlinear regression. Longitudinal studies frequently give rise to nonlinear patterns of change. These nonlinear changes can be seen in situations when change is faster in some periods and slower in others. For example, learning of many skills can be characterized by an *s*-shaped curve: slow initial gain, followed by rapid improvement, and then small gains again until maximum learning is reached (Cudeck & Harring, 2007). A common approach to analyzing nonlinear relations between independent and dependent variables is to linearize the relation by transforming either the independent or dependent variables, or both, and then applying OLS regression. However, this approach is appropriate only when the relation is intrinsically linear (Cohen et al., 2003). When the relation is intrinsically nonlinear, a suitable transformation is not available and nonlinear regression is the most appropriate method of analysis. Logistic regression is one example of nonlinear regression when change or growth is characterized as an *s*-shaped curve. Additional examples of behavioral processes that show nonlinear change and explanations of suitable nonlinear analytic approaches, including hierarchical nonlinear models, are found in Cohen et al. (2003, Chapter 6), Cudeck and Harring (2007), and Fitzmaurice, Davidian, Verbeke, and Molenberghs (2009).

Meta-analysis. Meta-analysis is a systematic, quantitative method of summarizing the results of studies composing a research literature (Curran, 2009; Strube & Hartmann, 1983; Sutton & Higgins, 2008). In the 1970s and 1980s concerns were raised about literature review methods that were less rigorous, systematic, and transparent than the studies they summarized, especially when the research area was characterized by disparate results (Cooper & Hedges, 1994). Unsystematic literature reviews were criticized for their subjectivity, imprecision, and neglect of important information contained in primary studies (Jackson, 1980). These concerns, coupled with the relative explosion of scientific information, suggested the need for better methods of summarizing research literatures.[19]

Meta-analytic techniques serve a variety of functions involved in reviewing a research literature. From the very beginning of operationalizing the review, the techniques include methods for collecting the studies composing the literature systematically to ensure that the "raw data" for the analysis will not be biased (e.g., Hunter, Schmidt, & Jackson, 1982, Chapter 7). The heart of meta-analysis, however, contains the statistical methods for summarizing the results of the primary studies composing the literature. Foremost among these statistical methods are techniques for combining probabilities across studies (Becker, 1994; Rosenthal, 1980b). A number of probability-combining techniques are available, and they all have as their principal purpose determining whether the set of results composing a literature could have arisen by chance. The combination of effect sizes represents another major approach to summarizing results across studies. The methods of determining average effect size assist the reviewer in determining the importance or strength of effect of the findings in a literature. A number of effect size indicators are available for accomplishing this goal (Tatsuoka, 1993), but the correlation coefficient and Cohen's *d* statistic, a standard score variant, are most commonly used for this purpose (Smith, Glass, & Miller, 1980).[20]

---

[19] Cooper and Patall (2009) describe two forms of meta-analysis. The first and more common form analyzes the pooled summary statistics from multiple individual studies and has been called aggregated data (AD) meta-analysis. The second, newer form analyzes the pooled raw data from multiple individual studies or samples and has been variously called individual participant data (IPD) meta-analysis (Cooper & Patall, 2009), integrative data analysis (Curran & Hussong, 2009), and mega-analysis (Sternberg, Baradaran, Abbott, Lamb, & Guterman, 2006). The use of this second form of meta-analysis has grown out of the need for increased collaboration among researchers to share limited resources and may be especially beneficial for developmental science, where long-term longitudinal studies are relatively rare and require years to complete (Curran, 2009; Hoffer & Piccinin, 2009).

[20] The odds ratio (OR) is a third effect size estimate commonly used for meta-analyses of medical treatments and education interventions (Patall & Cooper, 2008). It is the effect size measure of choice for categorical outcomes (Fleiss, 1994).

Beyond the computation of a combined probability and of an average effect size, meta-analysis also provides methods of determining the stability of results. Stability is often assessed using Rosenthal's (1979) fail-safe or file-drawer method. This method estimates the number of unpublished studies with zero effect size that would have to be filed away in the desks of investigators to "wash out" the results of the available studies included in the review.

Finally, because the probability values and effect sizes of the individual studies composing a literature are likely to vary substantially, a number of procedures and strategies have been proposed for identifying those factors associated with variation in outcomes across studies. Potential factors include any number of primary study characteristics that might be coded during the review such as the nature of the sample of participants studied, the methods of operationalizing IVs and DVs, as well as how adequately validity threats were handled in the study. These factors are then treated as IVs (the p-values and effect sizes serve as DVs) in analyses using regression, HLM, or ANOVA techniques, or methods of analysis especially developed for meta-analysis (Hedges & Olkin, 1985; Raudenbush & Bryk, 2002).

Meta-analytic procedures have been reviewed (Bangert-Drowns, 1986)—although, perhaps ironically, using traditional review techniques—and have grown in variety as to require a handbook (Cooper & Hedges, 1994); software for conducting meta-analysis is also available (e.g., Rosenberg, Adams, & Gurevitch, 1997; Sutton & Higgins, 2008). Understandable, technical presentations of meta-analysis are given in a variety of sources, including Cooper (1989), Glass, McGaw, and Smith (1981), Hunter et al. (1982), and Rosenthal (1980a).

Generalized Linear Models

All of the statistical approaches that we have described are special cases of a broad class of regression models collectively known as *generalized linear models*. Generalized linear model theory was developed to bring the analytic techniques applied to quantitative (continuous) and categorical response variables under one general framework (McCullagh & Nelder, 1989; Nelder & Wedderburn, 1972). The models extend the basic concepts of standard regression (ordinary least squares, OLS) and ANOVA to settings where the response variables are discrete and are not assumed to have a normal distribution.

All generalized linear models consist of three components: a random component, a systematic component, and a link function. The random component specifies the type of response variable and its assumed probability distribution. For example, for continuous responses, a normal distribution is assumed; for dichotomous outcomes, such as success/failure or the number of successes out of a fixed number of trials, a binomial distribution is assumed; and for nonnegative counts, such as a cell count in a contingency table, a Poisson distribution is assumed (Agresti, 2007). The systematic component specifies the predictor variables, (e.g., $\beta_0 + \beta_1 X_1$). The link function, $g(\mu)$, specifies a function or transformation that linearly relates the expected value of the response variable, μ, to the predictor variables. The link function also ensures that the values of the predicted scores are within the possible range of observed scores. For example, for count data, the link function is the natural log of the mean, and the form of the generalized linear model is

$$\ln(\hat{\mu}) = \beta_0 + \beta_1 X_1 + \beta_2 X_2 + \ldots + \beta_k X_k$$

This model, the *log-linear model*, specifies that the natural log of the mean, rather than the mean itself, changes linearly with changes in the predictor variables.

Generalized linear models use the method of maximum likelihood, which is not restricted to normality, to fit the model. Maximum likelihood (ML) uses an iterative process that estimates coefficients (and their standard errors) and provides methods for constructing confidence intervals, testing hypotheses, and assessing model fit. All generalized models use the same algorithm for estimating ML parameters (Agresti, 2007). Maximum likelihood and OLS methods yield equivalent estimates when applied to normally distributed continuous data with uncorrelated errors (Fitzmaurice et al., 2004).

Generalized linear models assume that observations are independent. Longitudinal studies, however, violate that critical assumption. Special extensions of generalized linear models, including the method of *generalized estimating equations (GEE)*, have been developed to handle longitudinal and other designs that have nonindependent data (see Agresti, 2007, Chapters 9 & 10; Fitzmaurice et al., 2004, Chapters 10 to 13; Moskowitz & Hershberger, 2002; and Raudenbush & Bryk, 2002, Chapter 10).

Interpreting the Results of Statistical Tests

Developmentalists want to answer three basic questions from their hypothesis-testing research (Kirk, 2003, p. 88): "(1) Is an observed effect real or should it be attributed to chance? (2) If the effect is real, how large is it? And (3) is the effect large enough to be useful?" Unfortunately *only* the first question is answered by a test of statistical significance, but the number of zeros following the decimal in such tests apparently is often used to answer the second and third questions as well. Indeed, as stated by Kirk, null hypothesis statistical testing "distracts us from our real goals: deciding whether data support our scientific hypothesis and are practically significant" (p. 100). For less critical commentaries on null hypothesis statistical testing, see Mulaik, Raju, and Harshman (1997) and Abelson (1997b).

How Large Is It?

Because tests of significance are importantly a function both of the magnitude of the effect and of the sample size—as well as a number of other factors related to power—a statistically significance test cannot be directly interpreted as addressing the question of the size of the effect. Fortunately, however, a substantial number of ancillary statistics have been developed to answer the size question (see, for example, Fleiss, 1994; Rosenthal, 1994). These statistics can be divided into two relatively homogeneous families and one wastebasket "other" category. The homogeneous—and familiar—families are those statistics loosely based on the standardized mean difference statistic (z) and those resembling the correlation coefficient (r). The final wastebasket category contains a variety of types of size estimators—"you name your inferential statistic and we'll provide a size statistic"—and will not be further discussed (see, for example, Kirk, 2003, Table 5.1).

Standardized mean difference-like measures. You will recall from our earlier discussion of z scores that the standardized mean difference describes the signed difference between two means using the standard deviation as the unit of measurement. Consider a two-group design in which the groups have means of 15.2 and 16.4 and the average standard deviation for the two groups is 1.6. The two means differ by .8 (16.4 − 15.2), or by one-half standard deviation units (.8/1.6 = .5). This value of .5 is essentially equal to Cohen's effect-size measure, delta (δ), calculated on these values (Cohen, 1988; Kirk, 2003). Other measures from this effect size family take basically similar form, but differ in detail, such as the method of estimating σ (the population standard deviation) or whether or not corrections for bias are included in the formula.

Cohen provides a set of widely accepted guidelines for interpreting δ, with a value of .2 indicating a small effect, .5 a medium effect, and .8 a large effect (e.g., Cohen, 1992). These guidelines are also useful for determining sample size for a study in the planning stage. If one knows the smallest effect size that is desirable to detect (e.g., medium), the desired likelihood of detecting it (power), and such things as the α-level (e.g., $\alpha = .05$), one can then readily—at least with fairly simple designs—determine how many participants must be recruited to meet those requirements (see, for example, Cohen, 1988; but see Lenth, 2001 for a criticism of this approach).

Correlational measures. Correlational measures of effect size assess the degree of relation between the independent and dependent variables. Moreover, these correlational measures are often presented in their squared form, yielding a proportional overlap between the IV and DV, as in the square of the bivariate (r^2) or multivariate correlation coefficient (R^2). The specific correlational statistic used to assess effect size importantly depends on whether the IV and DV are continuous or categorical, and on the nature of the investigative design and whether it is considered fixed or random. Kirk (2003) suggests that for situations for which fixed-effect ANOVA is employed, omega squared (ω^2) is a commonly used statistic for assessing the strength of association, whereas for random effects designs, rho squared (ρ^2) is more commonly—and appropriately—employed. Both of these squared statistics—as we earlier stated—indicate the proportion of the DV variance that can be attributed to the particular IV. Cohen (1988) also has provided guidelines for interpreting the measures of association: $r^2 = .01$ is a small effect size, $r^2 = .06$ is a medium effect size, and $r^2 = .14$ is a large effect size. Not surprisingly, a number of individuals have provided equations for translating effect size statistics into measures of association and vice versa (e.g., Kirk, 2003).

In interpreting effect size measures it is important to note that a number of critics have discussed their limitations and perturbing factors (e.g., Mitchell & Hartmann, 1981; O'Grady, 1982). These concerns—involving such issues as the effect of restriction of range and unreliability of measures on the interpretation of effect size statistics—are based largely on McNemar's (1969) classic discussion of factors that affect the interpretation of the correlation coefficient.

Confidence intervals. Confidence intervals (CIs) are very useful for evaluating both whether an effect is real and how large it is. Reporting CIs is strongly encouraged because of their superiority to reporting the results of null hypothesis testing alone (e.g, Cumming & Finch, 2005; Kirk, 2003; Nickerson, 2000; Smithson, 2001). Cumming and Finch (2001) list four general ways that CIs are valuable: (1) they give point and interval estimation that is easily understood and facilitate interpretation; (2) they have a link with null hypothesis testing; (3) they support meta-analysis and meta-analytic thinking; (4) they give width information that may be more useful and accessible than statistical power values. The fifth edition of the APA publication manual recommended the following:

> The reporting of confidence intervals . . . can be an extremely effective way of reporting results. Because confidence intervals combine information on location and precision and can often be directly used to infer significance levels, they are, in general, the best reporting strategy. The use of confidence intervals is therefore strongly recommended. (American Psychological Association, 2001, p. 22)

The sixth edition of the publication manual (American Psychological Association, 2010) gave additional guidelines: "whenever possible, provide a confidence interval for each effect size reported to indicate the precision of estimation of the effect size" (p. 34); and "When a table includes point estimates, for example, means, correlations, or regression slopes, it should also, where possible, include confidence intervals" (p. 138).

A CI (e.g., 95% CI) is a calculated interval estimate that surrounds a point estimate and indicates the precision, or likely accuracy, of the point estimate. Whereas a point estimate, such as a mean or effect size, is a single value estimate of a parameter, an interval estimate is a range or band, bounded by an upper and lower end point, within which the parameter is said to lie. The CI is centered on the point estimate and extends a distance, or width, on either side. The width, known as the margin of error, is computed by multiplying the standard error, SE, of the point estimate by the critical values that cut off $\alpha/2$ of the upper and lower tails of a distribution such as the z or t distribution[21] (e.g., $M \pm 1.96 \times SE$, or alternatively $M - 1.96 \times SE < \mu < M + 1.96 \times SE$ for a 95% CI using the z distribution).

Associated with the CI is a confidence level that typically is expressed as a percentage, $100(1 - \alpha)\%$. The confidence level is the probability that an interval estimate, randomly selected from a large number of similarly constructed intervals from independent samples of the same population, includes the population parameter (Fidler & Thompson, 2001).[22] Using a probability statement to interpret a CI can be confusing, however (Nickerson, 2002; see Fidler & Thompson, 2001 for examples of common versus accurate definitions of CIs). Cumming and Finch (2005) recommend that probability statements about individual CIs be avoided since they can be easily misinterpreted. They suggest four alternative interpretations, their top recommendation being "CI is a range of plausible values for μ. Values outside the CI are relatively implausible" (p. 174).

Though investigators may choose any level of confidence, by convention a 95% confidence level, which corresponds with the .05 p-level used in null hypothesis testing, is typically used. All things being equal, the higher the confidence level (e.g., 99%), the wider the CI; the larger the sample size, the narrower the CI and the more precise or accurate the estimate (Kelley & Rausch, 2006).

Additional discussion and instruction on constructing CIs for a variety of models and parameters are given by Cumming and Finch (2001), Fidler and Thompson (2001), and Smithson (2001, 2003). Cumming and Finch (2005) discuss seven rules of inference by eye for interpreting figures with confidence intervals.

---

[21] Confidence intervals for effect sizes expressed in their original units (e.g., $M_1 - M_2$) are constructed as explained above. In contrast, standardized effect sizes, such as Cohen's d, R^2, and η^2, require the critical values from noncentral distributions to construct an accurate CI. CIs constructed using noncentral distributions may not be symmetric around the point estimate and nearly always require iterative estimations that are best done by a computer (Cumming & Finch, 2001; Smithson, 2001).

[22] We can illustrate the correct interpretation of the probability of a CI by deriving the 95% CI for a sample mean in terms of the sampling distribution of the mean from a known population (e.g., Steiger & Fouladi, 1997; see Cumming & Finch, 2001, for an example of deriving a 95% CI for the one-sample t-test). If we take a large number of independent random samples of size N from a normal population with mean μ and standard deviation σ, we will generate a normal distribution of sample means with mean μ and standard deviation (standard error) $\sigma_M = \sigma/\sqrt{N}$. We know that 95% of all possible sample means of size N from the population will fall between -1.96 and 1.96 standard errors of the population mean μ. This fact can be stated as a probability: We know that for all samples of size N from the population the $\Pr(-1.96\sigma_M \le M - \mu \le 1.96\sigma_M) = .95$. We can algebraically manipulate this inequality without changing the correctness of the statement by subtracting M from each of the terms, then multiplying each term by -1, and reversing the inequalities. This gives $\Pr(M - 1.96\sigma_M \le \mu \le M + 1.96\sigma_M) = .95$. That is, over all possible samples, the range between $M - 1.96\sigma_M$ and $M + 1.96\sigma_M$ will include the true mean, μ, 95% of the time. The range of values constitutes the 95% CI for μ. The two end points of the interval are called the 95% confidence limits. It is important to note that the probability statement is not about μ, but about samples. The actual range of numbers making up the CI for a given sample will depend on the sample mean, M. For 95% of the samples, the CI actually will include or "capture" the value of μ; for 5% of the samples, it will not.

Is It Important?

When answered affirmatively, the question of importance in most cases will be accompanied by a significant p value and by a large measure of effect size. But even these two criteria have exceptions: Nonsignificant findings may be suggestively important if they were obtained under particularly adverse conditions of power (e.g., weak design, unreliable measures, shaky manipulations, and few participants); even small effect sizes may be important because they are associated with important theoretical issues. A number of other considerations may determine the importance of an effect, as follows.

1. The relative cost of producing the effect. Even a small effect produced cheaply may be practically important.
2. The minimalist nature of the manipulation. If the manipulation that produced even a small effect was extremely minor (or weak) in nature, it may be important. Prentice and Miller (1992) give numerous illustrations of important effects that were produced from minimalist manipulations in the social psychological literature, including those involving ethnocentrism and mere exposure.
3. The availability of competing treatment. If alternative treatments are not available, even a small effect may be practically important.
4. The intractableness of the DV. Consider a seemingly intractable DV such as the speed with which corpses are pronounced dead. Prentice and Miller (1992) argue that if we found that outcome was influenced by the attractiveness of the corpse—even if only slightly—this would truly be an important illustration of the psychosocial importance of physical attractiveness.

Also see Abelson (1985), Mook (1983), Rosenthal and Rubin (1983), and Yeaton and Sechrest (1981) for additional discussions of the importance issue.

QUALITATIVE RESEARCH METHODS

In this section, we will describe how the qualitative approaches to research differ from the quantitative approach just presented, discuss when the qualitative approaches may be useful, and describe one popular qualitative approach, narrative analysis, as an example. In addition, we will consider how to evaluate the rigor of qualitative studies and entertain the question of whether one should use qualitative methods in combination with quantitative methods.

Qualitative research methods encompass a variety of general approaches. Some of the better known include grounded theory (e.g., Charmaz, 2003; Corbin & Strauss, 2008; Henwood & Pidgeon, 2003), narrative analysis (e.g., Murray, 2003), case study (e.g., Lancy, 2001), discourse analysis (e.g., Antaki, 2008; Potter, 2003; Willig, 2003), and action research (e.g., Fine et al., 2003; Kemmis & McTaggart, 2008). What is common among these approaches is an emphasis on capturing the qualities of a phenomenon through verbal and visual description rather than through statistical analyses (Morrow & Smith, 2000). A variety of data gathering methods is used singly or in combination in qualitative research, including observing and interviewing participants as well as collecting documents and artifacts from or about them (Berg, 2003; Esterberg, 2002). Finally, there are specific strategies for analyzing data gathered, such as grounded theory analysis (e.g., Charmaz, 2003) and narrative analysis (e.g., Murray, 2003). The various approaches, methods, and strategies have unique elements, and unfortunately, a full examination of each is beyond the scope of this chapter. Thus, our present discussion of qualitative research pertains to broader issues common among them. Because narrative analysis is familiar to many developmental scientists, we present it in more detail as an example of a qualitative approach to research.

At the heart of qualitative research lies rich description of the phenomena of interest. Camic, Rhodes, and Yardley (2003b, p. 10) describe the difference between quantitative and qualitative approaches as being akin to the difference between a map and a video:

> A map is extremely useful; it conveys with economy and precision the location of a place and its relationship to other places in terms of proximity and direction. However, even the most detailed map is unable to convey an understanding of what it is like to be at that place. In contrast, a video conveys in vivid detail the constantly changing perspective of the observer. Although this perspective is selective and could not easily be used for navigation, it is able to communicate something of the subjective experience of being there.

Although developmental scientists tend to work with "maps," many appreciate the rich descriptions of "videos." Consider the value of Piaget's interviews with and observations of children (Piaget, 1932/1965; Piaget, Inhelder, & Weaver, 1972/2000). Recall Bowlby's, Mahler's, or Stern's accounts of how relational behavior unfolds between mother and child during the first years of life, and try to imagine their developmental theories without these rich descriptions (Bowlby, 1969/1982; Mahler, Pine, & Bergman, 1975/2000; Stern, 1985). It is no doubt a difficult or impossible task; qualitative information often seems necessary for full comprehension of how individuals change over time.

Given that one acknowledges the epistemological importance of rich description, it is somewhat curious that developmentalists as well as other psychologists tend to favor quantitative methodological and analytic approaches over qualitative approaches (Camic et al., 2003b). It is uncommon to see an exclusively qualitative study presented as the final product in a peer-reviewed developmental science journal. What accounts for this favoritism? Eisner (2003) speculated that psychology's strong positivistic roots continue to shape thinking about what "counts" as science and thus limits what questions psychologists ask and how they go about answering the questions they do ask. Way and Pahl (1999) noted that developmental scientists generally see quantification as a more objective, and thus, a more acceptable means of providing evidence for or against a theory. Overall, psychologists tend to assign qualitative research secondary status by considering it beneficial for obtaining an initial understanding of a topic, theory development, or for illustrative purposes, but not as a finished work (Sciarra, 1999). Also contributing to the bias, training in qualitative research methods is typically not required of undergraduate or graduate students in North American psychology programs (Camic et al., 2003b).

Individuals favoring a qualitative approach reject the tenets of positivism and instead subscribe to idealism, or one of its modern day progenies (e.g., constructivism, interpretivism, hermeneutics). Idealists argue that reality cannot be objectively known, individuals construct their own versions of reality based on their experiences and meanings assigned to those experiences, and investigators' constructions of reality are inseparable from those being investigated (Sciarra, 1999, see also Denzin & Lincoln, 2000). These assumptions lead to different methods of data collection and analysis as well as different ideas about how to evaluate the methodological rigor of research.

When might one consider using qualitative methods?   Some research questions and goals lend themselves particularly well to qualitative methodologies. Camic et al. (2003b) described six reasons for using the qualitative approach.

1. A qualitative approach is often valuable when exploring a topic that few have previously researched. This is probably the most acceptable use for those trained in the positivistic tradition. Qualitative methods allow for theory building and discovery of what is most important about participants' experiences (in contrast to hypothesis testing). For example, Baker and Carson (1999) began interviewing women in substance abuse treatment not anticipating the importance the women would place on their roles as mothers. Upon discovery, however, interview questions about mothering became paramount to their study. Along similar lines, Shadish et al. (2002) stated that qualitative methods are often useful tools for discovering and exploring causal mechanisms prior to designing experimental or quasi-experimental studies of a hypothesis-testing sort.

2. Qualitative methods may be appropriate if one is particularly interested in establishing ecological validity (e.g., Bronfenbrenner, 1979). Qualitative investigators are encouraged to learn about and become part of the real-world context in which their phenomenon occurs to understand it better. For example, Hey (1997) examined adolescent girls' friendships by conducting ethnographic work in schools. Her descriptions primarily come from girls' notes, discourse, and journals gathered in the school setting rather than from rating scales and structured interviews.

3. The qualitative approach tends to emphasize a holistic picture; "microanalysis of parts is always undertaken in the context of a larger whole" (Camic et al., 2003b, p. 9). Qualitative investigators commonly analyze complex relations and inconsistencies to relate the data to larger contexts, such as culture, in ways that are vastly more difficult when one must meet statistical assumptions. For example, a quantitative analyst may treat inconsistent responding by a participant as measurement error, but a qualitative analyst may use those inconsistencies to build a more complex picture of the phenomenon of interest.

4. Qualitative research is quite useful if one is interested in analyzing the subjective meaning participants assign to their experiences. A well-known example in developmental science is Gilligan and colleagues' examination of participants' "voices" as a way to understand identity development (e.g., Gilligan, 1982; see also Gilligan, Spencer, Weinberg, & Bertsch, 2003).

5. Qualitative research allows for an examination of the "aesthetic dimension of human experience" as well as giving the investigator some artistic freedom (Camic et al., 2003b, p. 10). For example, Esterberg (2002) described a study (Becker, 1999) in which the investigator transcribed an individual's narrative into poem-like stanzas so that its circular and repetitive qualities were clearer (see also Gee, 1991, and Gilligan et al., 2003, for similar examples). Artwork was the data in an ethnography focusing on the experience of adolescent pregnancy; Luttrell (2002) collected and analyzed pregnant adolescents' collages as well as theatrical reenactments of their social interactions with peers and parents.

6. Qualitative research may have utility if one is interested in the relationships among participants, participants' relations to their larger society, or the participants' relationship to the researcher and research process. Participatory action research is one example of a qualitative approach that has focused on participants' role in collaborating on or creating research agenda (Fine et al., 2003).

An example of the qualitative approach: Narrative interviews and narrative analysis. Examining the stories individuals tell about themselves is a popular method for understanding development, particularly the processes of identity development and adjustments to life events—see McAdams, Josselson, and Lieblich (2001) for examples. Qualitative investigators refer to these stories as "narratives" (Murray, 2003) or "accounts" (Harvey,

Orbuch, & Weber, 1992). According to Bruner (1990), individuals tell stories to understand their life experiences and to illuminate relations between these experiences. In addition to the stories' content, narrative psychologists are often interested in the stories' structure and function (Murray, 2003).

A narrative is defined by its story-like features. Like stories, narratives have a beginning, middle, and end as well as some type of action. In these ways, they are different from non-narrative answers to questions in structured or unstructured interviews (Esterberg, 2002). Biographical interviews are often the primary method of gathering narratives, although investigators also find individuals' stories in other forms of data, such as observational field notes and personal journals (Esterberg, 2002). Murray (2003) recommended building relationships with participants before collecting their narratives. Participants are less likely to provide good narratives if they do not trust or feel valued.

Biographical interviews tend to be fairly unstructured and participant-driven, but researchers often have some general questions to guide the overall interview process. For example, when gathering the life stories of generative and non-generative African American adults McAdams and Bowman (2001) divided their interview protocol into eight components (life chapters, significant scenes, life challenge, characters, favorite stories, future plot, personal ideology, and life theme). Likewise, Murray (2003) described collecting both life story narratives and more specific, episodic narratives from individuals who experience chronic pain. Murray and colleagues instructed participants to recount specific chronic pain experiences and to provide a more general life history narrative so they could understand participants' chronic pain experiences within the context of their overall life history.

Once narratives are collected, one can analyze different aspects of the stories, including content, structure, and function. Consider the following episodic narrative written by the second author's father:

> In the late 1950s and early 1960s there were hundreds of corner grocery stores and no quick trips [convenience stores]. One of their staple items was candy and small toys for kids. The toys changed with the season—kites in the spring, baseballs in the summer, and Duncan Yo Yo's made of Maple and Birch in the spring. To hype the sales the Duncan company employed Hawaiian, Filipino, and Japanese men about 40 years old who drove from store to store to stock the yo-yo displays. They were in all of the downtown dime stores too. Each week in the spring on a certain day, after school, which was across the street, Gus the Yo-Yo Man would show up. All of the local kids with yo-yos would practice a while and Gus would give them a free, new string. Then they would line up on the curb by the store and he would go down the line announcing each trick he wanted you to do. If you missed the trick, it was quick and simple, Gus shouted, "You're out," and you stepped back. This was a rapid, single elimination process. Towards the end of the school year those of us who had won contests regularly and received patches and yo-yos for our effort were invited to Woolworth's dime store downtown for the "City Championship." Gus showed up, everybody was ushered out into the delivery alley where we lined up against the wall. The elimination began and before long it was down to me and another kid. He went first and missed the "Three-Leaf Clover." I hit it without a problem and the trophy with the yo-yo-headed man was mine. Gus showed me the toughest trick he knew, called "Spider in a Cage," I got on my Schwinn bike and rode home. I lost competitive interest in the yo-yo after that, and yet when some 12- and 13-year-old Scouts had a couple [yo-yos] at the "Order of the Arrow Fall Conclave" in September, I couldn't resist, got one from one of them, and reprised all of the old standards: "Walk the Dog," "Eating Spaghetti," "Around the World," "Rock the Baby," "Over the Falls," and, of course, "Three-Leaf Clover." (narrative taken from Smith, 1996)

Depending on the goals of a study, different aspects of this narrative (and any other narratives collected) can be analyzed. For instance, examining the actual *content* of the story would be appropriate if an investigator is interested in the types of competitive events individuals recall from preadolescence. In general, investigators analyzing narrative content want to know about an individual's experience in the individual's own words. Many times investigators analyze narratives' content with a specific *social context* in mind (Esterberg, 2002). For example, the second author originally framed the story of the yo-yo championship in the context of what it was like to grow up during the 1960s in a working class, Midwestern family.

However, what if an investigator was uninterested in the story of the yo-yo championship itself, but rather interested in how the participant told this story? Then, analyzing the *structure* of the narrative would be appropriate. For example, an investigator might be interested in examining what accounts for a shift in perspective, such as the shift from third-person to first-person perspective in the story above. Alternatively, one might be interested in how the storyteller ends his story by making a connection to a more recent event in his life.[23] Similar to content analysis, one may make connections between the individual's social context (e.g., from a Western culture, being female, being an ethnic minority) and structural elements present in their stories (Murray, 2003).

Finally, rather than focusing on content or structure, qualitative investigators may ask questions about the *function* of the story being told. For example, in the beginning of the yo-yo championship story, the storyteller, now an adult with children of his own, seemingly wants to convey how the world has changed across time ("there were hundreds of corner grocery stores and no quick trips"). In an interesting parallel, at the end of the story the storyteller seemingly wants to convey how a part of him has stayed the same across time ("I couldn't resist, got one from one of them, and reprised all of the old standards"). The storyteller's audience is important to consider when analyzing function; the purpose of the story may change significantly depending on who is listening (Esterberg, 2002). For example, how might the yo-yo championship story be different when told to a stranger rather than to a family member?

Regardless of whether one analyzes content, structure, or function, narrative analysis is a time-consuming process. For this reason, narrative studies typically do not involve large samples (see Kuzel, 1999, for recommendations on sampling). After collecting narratives, qualitative examiners typically transcribe them and read them repeatedly, making decisions about which portions of the narratives to analyze. Sometimes investigators re-transcribe segments into a format that will ease analysis, such as the poetic stanzas described earlier. Once the narratives are in a manageable format, a qualitative investigator can begin formally analyzing the data. Murray (2003) described four analytic approaches for understanding narratives: linguistic (breaking narratives down into their story-like components), literary (examining narratives in terms of their genre or plots), grounded (inductively examining the themes present in narratives), and social contextual (considering the role of context in how narratives are constructed). For the purposes of illustration, we will discuss the steps involved when one uses a linguistic approach.

As first described by Labov (1978) and summarized by Esterberg (2002), one linguistic approach involves segmenting the narratives into six basic parts: abstract, orientation, complicating action, evaluation, results, and coda. The complicating action is essential for a narrative (i.e., something has to happen), but the other elements may or may not be present in any particular narrative. We will describe each of these elements and use the yo-yo championship narrative to illustrate them. The *abstract* lets the audience know a narrative is about to start. Individuals often signal the beginning of a narrative with something like "You won't believe what just happened." The yo-yo story does not contain an abstract, perhaps

---

[23] In developmental psychology literature, McAdams and Bowman (2001) provided another example of structural analysis when examining redemption and contamination sequences in individuals' life stories.

because the narrative was in response to a very specific question rather than an open-ended question. The *orientation* gives the audience background information so that they know the "setting" and main "characters" in the story. For example, in the yo-yo championship narrative, the storyteller describes Gus, the yo-yo man, the basic way in which the yo-yo contests worked, and the context in which they occurred. After the orientation comes the *complicating action*. The complicating action is the main event that happens in the story. In the yo-yo championship narrative, the complicating action is city championship competition. Typically, narratives also contain some sort of *evaluation* component that lets the reader know why they should be interested in what happened. The evaluation component is difficult to pick out in the example of the yo-yo championship story. However, the narrator describes getting a special trophy and learning a difficult yo-yo trick as rewards for winning, relaying to the audience that this is a success story, rather than, for example, a cautionary tale or a conversion story (Esterberg, 2002). The *results* serve as sort of a punch line at the end of the story. Esterberg relates that having a twist at the end of the story is a common practice. This appears to be the case in the yo-yo story; it first appears that the narrator has "retired" from yo-yo tricks, but then the audience finds out he actually has not. Finally, the *coda* lets the audience know the story is finished. In the yo-yo championship story, the storyteller ends by bringing the audience back to his winning yo-yo trick. As Murray (2003, p. 105) related, the linguistic approach "enables the researcher to grasp not only the action core of the narrative account but also the interpretive orientation the participant adopts and the issues that the participant chooses to emphasize and to ignore."

Some qualitative investigators use computer software programs to assist in analyzing qualitative data, such as the narrative data above. More information about computer software options is available in most introductory qualitative methods texts (see also Kelle, 1996). These programs may aid in organizing, segmenting, and coding data. However, be forewarned that much like statistical programs used by quantitative researchers, the software used by qualitative researchers does not replace the investigator's role in data analysis and interpretation (Morrow & Smith, 2000).

Assessing the quality of qualitative studies. There is a longstanding debate among qualitative investigators about how to assess the rigor of qualitative studies (Hammersley, 2008; Merrick, 1999; Willig, 2001). Concepts used in quantitative work, such as reliability and validity, may not be directly applicable when determining the methodological rigor of qualitative work (Merrick, 1999; see Kidder, 1981, for an opposing viewpoint). As stated by Willig (2001), the way in which one evaluates qualitative research needs to be compatible with one's epistemological framework (post-positivist, post-modernist, etc.). For example, if one acknowledges subjectivity in the research process and the construction of knowledge (as the epistemological frameworks above do), assessing inter-rater reliability may be a questionable strategy for determining methodological rigor.

With a post-positivist view in mind, Merrick (1999) described three concepts important to the evaluation of qualitative research: trustworthiness, reflexivity, and representation. *Trustworthiness* is somewhat akin to internal validity in that it is meant to establish the credibility of the qualitative findings. As noted by Merrick (1999), Stiles (1993) described several ways in which qualitative investigators establish trustworthy data. First, they disclose their theoretical orientation so research consumers can better understand their methodological choices and analytic interpretations. Of course, not all consumers will agree with this orientation; however, having it will aid in understanding the investigator's decisions. Elliott, Fischer, and Rennie (1999) called this process "owning one's perspective," whereas Henwood and Pidgeon (1992) considered it a part of "reflexivity" (see the following). Next, investigators should discuss with their readers how they engaged with the research participants and data. Investigators typically need to immerse themselves in their data in intense and prolonged ways, often coming back to the data multiple times, to exhaust the iterative relation between data and interpretation. In addition, qualitative investigators should consider the advantages of triangulating findings with multiple data sources to build a stronger case for their interpretation of the data. Triangulation may increase the likelihood of the data being inconsistent, but these inconsistencies or contradictions sometimes ultimately make sense when a more holistic interpretive approach is employed (Lancy, 2001). Finally, qualitative investigators need to get continual feedback from peers about the research process, their interpretations of data, and their findings. Some may choose to work in peer research teams to ensure they get this feedback (Deutsch, Luttrell, & Dorner, 2004). Debriefing sessions among peer research team members (or just among colleagues) in which the research process and data are discussed provide valuable information to investigators on how they are conceptualizing and representing their phenomenon of interest.

Expanding on concept of *reflexivity*, Merrick (1999) argued that investigators doing good qualitative research contemplate and evaluate their decisions concerning research topic, design, and process as well as introspecting on their personal experiences carrying out the study. The reflective process should ideally occur throughout the life of the study. Reflexivity can be further broken down into three types: personal, functional, and disciplinary (Wilkinson, 1988, as cited in Merrick, 1999). Qualitative investigators demonstrate personal reflexivity when they acknowledge their own background and what effect their experiences might have on the study and its findings. For example, depending on the focus of the study, investigators might consider their age, ethnicity, or marital status as important factors. Functional reflexivity deals with examining the choices made during the research process, such as the decisions on what type of data to gather or from whom to gather it. Finally, disciplinary reflexivity has to do with examiners reflecting on larger issues, such as their assumptions about research methods and science.

Representation, the third concept Merrick (1999) discussed, deals with how investigators share their findings with others (see also Fine, 1994). Investigators need to be sensitive to how they influence what others learn about those whom they have studied. Participants' data, particularly by the time an investigator presents them to the public, contains not only the participants' voices but also the investigator's voice. Acknowledging and explaining possible ways in which the co-construction of data has taken place is encouraged by many qualitative investigators (Merrick, 1999).

A few additional noteworthy concepts are important to assessing rigor in qualitative studies: transferability, independent audit, and negative case analysis. Qualitative investigators often do not discuss external validity or generalizability, but rather the related concept of *transferability* (Merrick, 1999; Henwood & Pidgeon, 1992). Emphasizing the importance of context at all levels (from the specific relation developed between researcher and participants to the relation between these particular participants and culture at large), many using qualitative methods would not expect their results to generalize to a larger population of individuals. However, this does not make their findings useless or meaningless to investigators working in other contexts. Investigators should disclose detailed information about the participants, their participants' background, and the context in which they gathered the data so their audience can make informed decisions about the findings' applicability to other individuals in other contexts (Henwood & Pidgeon, 1992).[24] The principles of the grounded theory of causal inference (Shadish et al., 2002), discussed in the earlier section on quantitative analysis, may help consumers decide on the transferability of qualitative findings.

---

[24] However, this is not to say that two researchers studying the same phenomena in the same context will necessarily arrive at the same results (Eisner, 2003).

Qualitative investigators also discuss the idea of the *independent audit* (Yardley, 2000). Independent audits involve investigators filing all their data, analyses, and other study items in such a way that someone else would see their final product as credible and justified if they were to look through all the materials (regardless of whether it is the only possible product that could have resulted). Evidence of internal consistency, coherence, and documentation of systematic decision-making are key to establishing credibility in an independent audit.[25]

Finally, an understanding of how qualitative investigators conduct their *negative case analysis* is also important to determining the quality of their work. Negative case analysis is the way in which one explores data not fitting with preexisting theory or conceptualizations. Often an inductive process occurs; investigators modify the theory or conceptualization in such a way that all cases fit (McGrath & Johnson, 2003). Qualitative analysts need to describe negative cases and their relation to theory when reporting their findings so consumers understand which parts of theory existed prior to data collection and which emerged through negative case analysis. Hypertypification, the tendency to only see data that fit with preexisting theory or conceptualizations, often results from insufficient immersion with the data and a lack of negative case analysis (Erickson, 1992). When analysts describe how they identified negative cases and subsequently modified theory, they inform consumers of their sensitivity to hypertypification.

Combining qualitative and quantitative methods.[26]   Should qualitative and quantitative methods be used together? Opinions are mixed (see Marecek, 2003, for a good discussion). With their contrasting strengths and weaknesses, it is easy to think the two approaches could potentially complement each other quite nicely and assist in triangulating the phenomenon of interest. However, using the two methods concurrently in the same study or same program of research may be difficult. As articulated earlier, the qualitative approach involves more than just different data collection methods; it has a different epistemological orientation with its own set of assumptions. For example, consider the inherent tensions between objectivity and subjectivity as well as those between the deductive process of hypothesis-testing and the inductive process of negative case analysis.

However, it may be possible for investigators to have multiple epistemologies, acknowledge the strengths and weaknesses of each, and use each without relegating one to secondary status. Lavelli, Pantoja, Hsu, Messinger, and Fogel (2005) provided one example of how to combine quantitative and qualitative approaches harmoniously. Their microgenetic design incorporated both inferential statistics and narrative analysis, resulting in a more extensive understanding of change processes than either methodology could provide independently. Clarke (2003) furnished another illustration of how to use qualitative and quantitative methods in a single study. She statistically demonstrated how social support and education moderate the negative relation between physical disability (due to stroke) and well-being. Then Clarke described the themes present in individuals' accounts of their experiences after having a stroke to elucidate the actual processes by which social support and education moderate the relation. Fine and Elsbach (2000) used six classic social psychological studies as examples to illustrate specific tactics for combining qualitative and quantitative research methods.

Summary.   Qualitative research methods offer investigators not only alternative methods to data collection and analyses, but also alternative epistemological paradigms. With

---

[25] An individual unassociated with the research study may literally carry out an independent audit.

[26] "Mixed method studies" and "mixed model studies" are terms used for studies that combine qualitative and quantitative research methods (Tashakkori & Teddlie, 1998).

qualitative methods, the goal is to illuminate the subjective qualities of a psychological phenomenon rather than trying to quantify it. Investigators accomplish this goal using a wide variety of general approaches, data collection methods, and analytic strategies and evaluate the quality of their studies using alternative criteria, such as trustworthiness, reflexivity, and representation. Readers interested in learning more about qualitative research methods may find the following books useful: Berg (2003), Camic, Rhodes, and Yardley (2003a), Denzin and Lincoln (2000), Esterberg (2002), Flick (2007), Gibbs (2007), Kopala and Suzuki (1999), Lancy (2001), Luttrell (2009), Smith (2003), and Willig (2001). For information about internet-based qualitative and mixed-methods research see Hewson (2008).

ETHICS

Ethics, the field involving the study of right and wrong conduct, seems at first glance to have little relevance to a chapter on the technical aspects of research. However, ethics relates to the conduct of research in the same way as the various aspects of methodology and analysis previously discussed. Every investigator must make a variety of decisions based on ethics during the course of a developmental investigation. Ethical decisions both interact with and determine the methodology and other technical aspects of the research.

International guidelines base research ethics on three general ethical principles:

* *beneficience*—the obligation to maximize research benefits and minimize research harms
* *respect*—the responsibility to ensure that research participation is informed, rational, and voluntary
* *justice*—the obligation to ensure the fair distribution of research benefits and burdens across populations (Fisher & Anushko, 2008).

Perhaps the most general ethical question that every investigator must ask is the following: Should I conduct this research, given its likely contributions in comparison to the risk, discomfort, and inconvenience inflicted or potentially inflicted on those participating in the study? In addition to this overarching ethical question, the investigator must confront numerous other ethical issues concerning participants, their guardians, and research personnel (American Psychological Association, 1982, 1987, 2002a, 2002b).

This section focuses on the ethical issues pertaining to children and their guardians. We describe special ethical problems associated with using children as participants, and the ethical principles for the conduct of research promulgated by the Society for Research in Child Development (SRCD).

Protection of Child Subjects

Commonly, children are participants in developmental research, and their legal status as minors, their level of cognitive development, and their limited experiences may present special ethical problems. Based on these considerations, the SRCD developed a set of principles regarding the conduct of research with children. SRCD first published Principles 1 to 14 in 1990 and added Principles 15 and 16 in 1991. They are located in the Society's annual *Directory of Members* (e.g., SRCD, 2003) and on its website (SRCD, 2007); the annotations below are paraphrases from the standards as well as interpretation of them by the authors.

1. *Non-harmful procedures:* Investigators should not use research procedures that may harm the child, and are obligated to use the least stressful research operation whenever possible. Thompson (1990) reminded investigators to use their knowledge of child development when designing studies; procedures that may be stressful at one age may be less stressful at other ages (e.g., separation from caregivers is probably stressful for young children, but not for adolescents). If investigators introduce stress with their procedures, the anticipated benefits of the study must clearly exceed any risk to the children. If a study is carried out so negligently that nothing can be learned from the results, there is no justification for putting participants though unpleasant experiences (Aronson, Ellsworth, Carlsmith, & Gonzales, 1990). Whenever investigators are in doubt as to the harmful properties of their procedures, they should seek consultation from others. When harmful procedures are proposed, it is important to have careful deliberation by an institutional review board (IRB).

2. *Informed consent and assent:* Investigators working with toddlers and preschool children should make efforts to at least tell the children what will be done, where it will be done, who will be involved, how long their participation will last, whether other children have participated and how they reacted to the research, and whether an incentive will be offered. Then, the children can decide to say "yes" or "no" regarding participation (Miller, 2007). Investigators working with infants and young children should use special effort to explain the research procedures to parents, and should be especially sensitive to any indicators of participants' discomfort because young children are less likely to possess full comprehension of what they are doing or why they are doing it (Abramovitch, Freedman, Thoden, & Nikolich, 1991). Investigators should try to tailor the information they provide based on participants' developmental level. They should also work to minimize coercion because young children sometimes make decisions based on what they think authority figures want them to do (Abramovitch et al., 1991). Investigators should obtain assent from children 7 years of age and older (National Commission for the Protection of Human Subjects, 1977) and possibly for younger children, if they can understand what they will be doing in the study (Bell-Dolan & Wessler, 1994). Informed consent may not be required with certain kinds of observational research conducted in contexts such as supermarkets and playgrounds. Generally, consent need not be obtained if the behaviors studied are naturally occurring ones that are unaffected by the decision to study them; the behaviors are innocuous and are neither revealing nor embarrassing; and the participants are anonymous and certain to remain so (e.g., Miller, 2007, p. 179).

3. *Parental consent:* Investigators should obtain written informed consent from parents or children's legal guardians. Not only should investigators recognize the right of parents and guardians to refuse, but they should also remind them of their right to withdraw permission at any time without penalty.

4. *Additional consent:* Investigators should afford the same rights just mentioned for parents to those who act *in loco parentis*, such as teachers or camp counselors, particularly if their interaction with the child is the focus of study.

5. *Incentives:* Incentives to participate must be fair and must not exceed the range of incentives that the child normally experiences. In particular, incentives should not serve to coerce the child to participate.

6. *Deception:* Some psychologists take the position that deception is never justified with children (e.g., Ferguson, 1978), but this is not a generally accepted position. If deception is used, investigators should satisfy their colleagues that such procedures are warranted. If investigators believe that the deception they employ has the potential to harm, they should apprise participants of the need for deception in a sensitive

and developmentally appropriate manner. Debriefing, which is so critical in research with adults and older children and adolescents, with young children may largely involve providing the children with good feelings about their research participation (Smith, 1967).

7. *Anonymity:* If investigators collect data from institutional records, they should obtain permission from responsible individuals and take precautions to preserve the anonymity of the information contained in these records.

8. *Mutual responsibilities:* Investigators should clarify the responsibilities of all participants in the research enterprise—children, parents, teachers, administrators, and research assistants—at the inception of the study. Investigators should also honor all promises made to parties involved in the research.

9. *Jeopardy:* If an investigator learns of information that jeopardizes a child's well-being during the conduct of a study, he or she has a responsibility to discuss the information with the parents and with experts in the field who may arrange the necessary assistance for the child.

10. *Unforeseen consequences:* If research procedures result in unforeseen negative consequences for child participants, the investigator should take immediate action to ameliorate the untoward effects and should modify the procedures for subsequent participants. If, for example, the procedures instigate negative affect in the child, investigators should institute procedures to reinstate positive feelings immediately.

11. *Confidentiality:* Procedures insuring the confidentiality of participants' responses must be in place. When a possibility exists that others may gain access to research responses, investigators should explain this possibility (along with plans for protecting confidentiality) to participants as part of the procedure of obtaining informed consent.

12. *Informing participants:* The investigator recognizes a duty to inform participants of any misunderstandings, and to report general findings to them in terms appropriate to their understanding. If investigators must withhold information, they should make efforts to ensure that the participants are not damaged by the withheld information.

13. *Reporting results:* Because investigators' comments may carry undue weight, they should exercise caution in reporting results, making evaluative statements, or giving advice to parents, teachers, and the like.

14. *Implications of findings:* Investigators should be particularly mindful of the social, political, and human implications of their research.

15. *Scientific misconduct:* Investigators must refrain from scientific misconduct, including such practices as plagiarism. Plagiarism is the failure to appropriately credit the contributions of others—ranging from "stealing" the studies and research ideas of colleagues and assistants to lesser ethical indiscretions involving the order of authorship and the inclusion of assistants in acknowledgments. The fabrication or falsification of data also constitutes scientific misconduct. This may include fraud or other forms of "scientific embezzlement" (Broad & Wade, 1982; Mahoney, 1976). The Society does not consider unintentional errors or differences in opinion on how to interpret data scientific misconduct. SCRD members guilty of scientific misconduct may be expelled from the Society as well as face other consequences (see APA, 2002a).

16. *Personal misconduct:* Committing a criminal felony may be grounds for expulsion from SRCD. As with scientific misconduct, voting members of the Society's Governing Council make this decision.

It is important to recognize that these principles apply not only to the principal investigator but also to all assistants and technical personnel.

Ethical Issues Not Addressed by SRCD Principles

Investigators' relationships with other researchers, funding agencies, and various special interest groups also involve ethical issues, concerns, and potential conflicts (Dooley, 1990). For example, conflicts of interest may arise when a drug or cigarette company hires researchers to investigate the benefits of the company's products. Clear guidelines are provided for action in these and other related situations, but far fewer safeguards are available—perhaps because breaches of ethics in these areas are thought less likely to produce the shocking moral tragedies of those involving human participants and perhaps because the relevant behaviors are less accessible to public scrutiny. Whatever the case, science is much more dependent on each individual investigator's conscience to move him or her in the direction of ethically correct behavior in these instances. In general, investigators are tasked with "doing good science well" (Fisher & Anushko, 2008, p. 106). The conduct of responsible developmental science depends on investigators' commitment and efforts to act ethically, accompanied by familiarity with national and international regulations, ethics codes, and laws. Doing good science well requires flexibility and sensibility to the research context, the investigator's fiduciary responsibilities, and participant expectations unique to each study (Fisher & Anushko, 2008).

CONCLUSIONS

The advancement of science depends on the quality of substantive questions asked by investigators as well as by the adequacy of the technical means that they employ to answer these questions. This chapter has focused on this technical side of research, including design, measurement, and analysis—as well as ethics. Readers should not expect to be qualified to meet the challenges represented by these technicalities merely as a result of studying this chapter. However, it should have increased their appreciation for this aspect of the research armamentarium and increased their ability to secure the expertness required to become sophisticated consumers and producers of developmental research.

REFERENCES AND SUGGESTED READINGS (▢)

Abelson, R. P. (1985). A variance explanation paradox: When a little is a lot. *Psychological Bulletin*, *97*, 128–132.

Abelson, R. P. (1997a). On the surprising longevity of flogged horses: Why there is a case for the significance test. *Psychological Science*, *8*, 12–15.

Abelson, R. P. (1997b). A retrospective on the significance test ban of 1999 (If there were no significance tests, they would be invented). In L. L. Harlow, S. A. Mulaik, & J. H. Steiger (Eds.), *What if there were no significance tests?* (pp. 117–141). Mahwah, NJ: Lawrence Erlbaum Associates.

Abramovitch, R., Freedman, J. L., Thoden, K., & Nikolich, C. (1991). Children's capacity to consent to participation in psychological research: Empirical findings. *Child Development*, *62*, 1100–1109.

Achenbach, T. M. (1978). *Research in developmental psychology: Concepts, strategies, methods.* New York: Free Press.

Achenbach, T. M., & Dumenci, L. (2001). Advances in empirically based assessment: Revised cross-informant syndromes and new DSM-oriented scales for the CBCL, YSR, and TRF. *Journal of Consulting & Clinical Psychology*, *69*, 699–702.

Agresti, A. (1996). *An introduction to categorical data analysis.* New York: Wiley.

▢ Agresti, A. (2007). *An introduction to categorical data analysis* (2nd ed.). Hoboken, NJ: Wiley.

▢ Alasuutari, P., Bickman, L., & Brannen, J. (Eds.). (2008). *The Sage handbook of social research methods.* London: Sage.

Allport, G. W. (1937). *Personality: A psychological interpretation.* New York: Holt.

American Educational Research Association. (1999). *Standard for educational and psychological testing.* Washington, DC: AERA.

American Psychological Association. (1982). *Ethical principles in the conduct of research with human participants.* Washington, DC: APA.

American Psychological Association. (1987). *Casebook on ethical principles of psychologists.* Washington, DC: APA.

American Psychological Association. (2001). *Publication manual of The American Psychological Association* (5th ed.). Washington, DC: APA.

American Psychological Association. (2002a). Ethical principles of psychologists and code of conduct. *American Psychologist, 57,* 1060–1073.

American Psychological Association. (2002b). Ethical principles of psychologists and code of conduct. Retrieved August 1, 2009, from www.apa.org/ethics/code2002.pdf

American Psychological Association (2010). *Publication manual of the American Psychological Association* (6th ed.). Washington, DC: American Psychological Association.

Anastasi, A. (1958). Heredity, environment, and the question "how"? *Psychological Review, 65,* 197–208.

Anastasi, A. (1988). *Psychological testing* (6th ed.). New York: Macmillan.

Anderson, E. R. (1995). Accelerating and maximizing information from short-term longitudinal research. In J. M. Gottman (Ed.), *The analysis of change* (pp. 139–163). Mahwah, NJ: Lawrence Erlbaum Associates.

Anderson, L. R., & Anger, J. W. (1978). Analysis of variance in small group research. *Personality and Social Psychology Bulletin, 4,* 341–345.

Antaki, C. (2008). Discourse analysis and conversation analysis. In P. Alasuutari, L. Bickman, & J. Brannen (Eds.), *The Sage handbook of social research methods* (pp. 431–446). London: Sage.

Appelbaum, M. I., & Cramer, E. M. (1974). Some problems in the nonorthogonal analysis of variance. *Psychological Bulletin, 81,* 335–343.

Appelbaum, M. I., & McCall, R. B. (1983). Design and analysis in developmental psychology. In P. H. Mussen (Ed.), *Handbook of child psychology: Vol. I. History, theory, and methods* (4th ed., pp. 415–476). New York: Wiley.

Arbuckle, J. L. (1997). *Amos user's guide, Version 3.6.* Chicago: SmallWaters Corporation.

Aronson, E., Ellsworth, P. C., Carlsmith, J. M., & Gonzales, M. H. (1990). *Methods of research in social psychology* (2nd ed.). New York: McGraw-Hill.

Baer, D. M. (1977). Reviewer's comment: Just because it's reliable doesn't mean that you can use it. *Journal of Applied Behavior Analysis, 10,* 117–119.

Bakeman, R., & Gottman, J. M. (1987). Applying observational methods: A systematic view. In J. D. Osofsky (Ed.), *Handbook of infant development* (2nd ed., pp. 818–854). New York: Wiley.

Bakeman, R., & Gottman, J. M. (1997). Observing interaction: An introduction to sequential analysis (2nd ed.). New York: Cambridge University Press.

Baker, P. L., & Carson, A. (1999). I take care of my kids: Mothering practices of substance-abusing women. *Gender and Society, 13,* 347–363.

Baltes, P. B., Lindenberger, U., & Staudinger, U. M. (1998). Life-span theory in developmental psychology. In W. Damon (Series Ed.) & R. M. Lerner (Vol. Ed.), *Handbook of child psychology. Volume 1: Theoretical models of human development* (5th ed., pp. 1029–1143). New York: Wiley.

Baltes, P. B., & Nesselroade, J. R. (1979). History and rationale of longitudinal research. In J. R. Nesselroade & P. B. Baltes (Eds.), *Longitudinal research in the study of behavior and development* (pp. 1–39). New York: Academic Press.

Baltes, P. B., Reese, H. W., & Nesselroade, J. (1988). *Life-span developmental psychology: Introduction to research methods.* Hillsdale, NJ: Lawrence Erlbaum Associates.

Bandura, A. (1997). *Self-efficacy: The exercise of control.* New York: Freeman.

Bangert-Drowns, R. L. (1986). Review of developments in meta-analytic method. *Psychological Bulletin, 99,* 388–399.

Barber, T. X. (1976). *Pitfalls in human research: Ten pivotal points.* New York: Pergamon Press.

Baron, R. M., & Kenny, D. A. (1986). The moderator–mediator distinction in social psychological research: Conceptual, strategic, and statistical considerations. *Journal of Personality and Social Psychology, 51,* 1173–1182.

Barrios, B., & Hartmann, D. P. (1988). Fears and anxieties. In E. J. Mash & L. G. Terdal (Eds.), *Behavioral assessment of childhood disorders* (2nd ed.). New York: Guilford Press.

Baumrind, D. (1991). Effective parenting during the early adolescent transition. In P. A. Cowan & E. M. Hetherington (Eds.), *Advances in family research* (Vol. 2). Hillsdale, NJ: Lawrence Erlbaum Associates.

Becker, B. J. (1994). Combining significance levels. In H. Cooper & L. V. Hedges (Eds.), *The handbook of research synthesis* (pp. 215–230). New York: Sage.

Becker, B. (1999). Narratives of pain in later life and conventions of storytelling. *Journal of Aging Studies, 13,* 73–87.

Bell, R. Q. (1968). A reinterpretation of the direction of effects of socialization. *Psychological Review, 75,* 81–95.

Bell-Dolan, D., & Wessler, A. E. (1994). Ethical administration of sociometric measures: Procedures in use and suggestions for improvement. *Professional Psychology: Research and Practice, 25,* 23–32.

Berg, B. L. (2003). *Qualitative research methods for the social sciences* (5th ed.). Boston: Pearson Allyn & Bacon.

Berk, R. A. (1979). Generalizability of behavioral observations: A clarification of interobserver agreement and interobserver reliability. *American Journal of Mental Deficiency, 83,* 460–472.

Birnbaum, M. H. (2004). Human research and data collection via the internet. *Annual Review of Psychology*, *55*, 803–822.

Bloom, H. S. (2008). The core analytics of randomized experiments for social research. In P. Alasuutari, L. Bickman, & J. Brannen (Eds.), *The Sage handbook of social research methods* (pp. 115–133). London: Sage.

Bohrnstedt, G. W., & Knoke, D. (1994). *Statistics for social data analysis* (3rd ed.). Itasca, IL: F.E. Peacock.

Boivard, J. A., & Embretson, S. E. (2008). Modern measurement in the social sciences. In P. Alasuutari, L. Bickman, & J. Brannen (Eds.), *The Sage handbook of social research methods* (pp. 269–289). London: Sage.

Bollen, K. A. (1989). *Structural equations with latent variable*. New York: Wiley.

Bornstein, M. H., Arterberry, M. E., & Mash, C. (2010). In M. H. Bornstein & M. E. Lamb (Eds.), *Developmental science: An advanced textbook* (6th ed., pp. 303–352). Hove, UK: Psychology Press.

Bornstein, M. H., Hahn, C.-S., Haynes, M., Manian, N., & Tamis-LeMonda, C. S. (2005). New research methods in developmental science: Applications and illustrations. In D. M. Teti (Ed.), *Handbook of research methods in developmental science* (pp. 509–533). Malden, MA: Blackwell.

Bowlby, J. (1969/1982). *Attachment and loss: Vol. 1. Attachment*. New York: Basic Books.

Braybrooke, D. (1987). *Philosophy of the social sciences*. New York: Prentice Hall.

Broad, W. J., & Wade, N. (1982). *Betrayers of the truth*. New York: Simon & Schuster.

Bronfenbrenner, U. (1979). *The ecology of human development*. Cambridge, MA.: Harvard University Press.

Bronson, W. C. (1987). Special section on structural equation modeling: Introduction. *Child Development*, *58*, 1.

Bruner, J. (1990). *Acts of meaning*. Cambridge, MA: Harvard University Press.

Bryk, A. S., & Raudenbush, S. W. (1987). Application of hierarchical linear models to assessing change. *Psychological Bulletin*, *101*, 147–158.

Bryman, A., & Cramer, D. (2001). *Quantitative data analysis with SPSS release 10 for Windows: A guide for social scientists*. New York: Routledge.

Burchinal, M., & Appelbaum, M. I. (1991). Estimating individual developmental functions: Methods and their assumptions. *Child Development*, *62*, 23–43.

Cairns, R. B. (1983). Sociometry, psychometry, and social structure: A commentary on six recent studies of popular, rejected, and neglected children. *Merrill-Palmer Quarterly*, *29*, 429–438.

Cairns, R. B., Bergman, L. R., & Kagan, J. (Eds.). (1998). *Methods and models for studying the individual: Essays in honor of Marian Radke-Yarrow*. Thousand Oaks, CA: Sage.

Camic, P. M., Rhodes, J. E., & Yardley, L. (Eds.). (2003a). *Qualitative research in psychology: Expanding perspectives in methodology and design*. Washington, DC: American Psychological Association.

⊞ Camic, P. M., Rhodes, J. E., & Yardley, L. (2003b). Naming the stars: Integrating qualitative methods into psychological research. In P. M. Camic, J. E. Rhodes, & L. Yardley (Eds.), *Qualitative research in psychology: Expanding perspectives in methodology and design* (pp. 3–15). Washington, DC: American Psychological Association.

Campbell, D. T. (1958). Systematic error on the part of human links in communication systems. *Information and Control*, *1*, 297–312.

Campbell, D. T., & Fiske, D. W. (1959). Convergent and discriminant validation by the multitrait–multimethod matrix. *Psychological Bulletin*, *56*, 81–105.

Campbell, D. T., & Stanley, J. C. (1963). *Experimental and quasi-experimental designs for research*. Chicago: Rand McNally.

Cattell, R. B. (1944). Psychological measurement: Normative, ipsative, interactive. *Psychological Review*, *51*, 292–303.

Cauce, A. M., Ryan, K. D., & Grove, K. (1998). Children and adolescents of color, where are you? Participation, selection, recruitment, and retention in developmental research. In V. C. McLoyd & L. Steinberg (Eds.), *Studying minority adolescents: Conceptual, methodological, and theoretical issues* (pp. 147–166). Mahwah, MJ: Lawrence Erlbaum Associates.

Charmaz, K. (2003). Grounded theory. In J. A. Smith (Ed.), *Qualitative psychology: A practical guide to research methods* (pp. 81–110). Thousand Oaks, CA: Sage.

Christensen, R. (1997). *Log-linear models and logistic regression* (2nd ed.). New York: Springer-Verlag.

Clarke, P. (2003). Towards a greater understanding of the experience of stroke: Integrating quantitative and qualitative methods. *Journal of Aging Studies*, *17*, 171–187.

Cohen, J. (1968). Multiple regression as a general data-analytic system. *Psychological Bulletin*, *70*, 426–443.

Cohen, J. (1988). *Statistical power analysis for the behavioral sciences* (2nd ed.). Hillsdale, NJ: Lawrence Erlbaum Associates.

⊞ Cohen, J. (1990). Things I have learned (so far). *American Psychologist*, *45*, 1304–1312.

⊞ Cohen, J. (1992). A power primer. *Psychological Bulletin*, *112*, 155–159.

Cohen, J., Cohen, P., West, S. S., & Aiken, L. S. (2003). *Applied multiple/correlation analysis for the behavioral sciences* (3rd ed.). Mahwah, NJ: Lawrence Erlbaum Associates.

Cohen, R. J., Montague, P., Nathanson, L. S., & Swerdlik, M. E. (1988). *Psychological testing: An introduction to tests & measurement*. Mountain View, CA: Mayfield.

Cohen, S. H. & Reese, H. W. (Eds.) (1994). *Life-span developmental psychology: Methodological contributions.* Hillsdale, NJ: Lawrence Erlbaum Associates.

Collins, L. M. (2006). Analysis of longitudinal data: The integration of theoretical model, temporal design, and statistical model. *Annual Review of Psychology, 57*, 505–528.

Collins, L. M., & Sayer, A. G. (2000). Modeling growth and change processes: Design, measurement, and analysis for research in social psychology. In H. M. Reis & C. M. Judd (Eds.), *Handbook of research methods in social and personality psychology* (pp. 478–495). New York: Cambridge University Press.

Collins, L. M., & Horn, J. L. (Eds.). (1991). *Best methods for the analysis of change: Recent advances, unanswered questions, future directions.* Washington, DC: American Psychological Association.

Comrey, A. L. (1978). Common methodological problems in factor analytic studies. *Journal of Consulting and Clinical Psychology, 46*, 648–659.

Conover, W. J. (1999). *Practical nonparametric statistics* (3rd ed.). New York: Wiley.

Cook, T. D., & Campbell, D. T. (1979). *Quasi-experimentation: Design and analysis issues for field settings.* Chicago: Rand McNally.

Cook, T. D., & Wong, V. C. (2008). Better quasi-experimental practice. In P. Alasuutari, L. Bickman, & J. Brannen (Eds.), *The Sage handbook of social research methods* (pp. 134–165). London: Sage.

Cooper, H. M. (1989). *Integrating research: A guide for literature reviews.* Newbury Park, CA: Sage.

Cooper, H., & Hedges, L. V. (Eds.). (1994). *The handbook of research synthesis.* New York: Russell Sage Foundation.

Cooper, H., & Patall, E. A. (2009). The relative benefits of meta-analysis conducted with individual participant data versus aggregated data. *Psychology Methods, 14*, 165–176.

Corbin, J., & Strauss, A. (2008). *Basics of qualitative research: Techniques and procedures for developing grounded theory* (3rd ed.). Thousand Oaks, CA: Sage.

Crocker, L., & Algina, A. (1986). *Introduction to classical & modern test theory.* New York: Holt, Rinehart, & Winston.

Cronbach, L. J. (1957). The two disciplines of scientific psychology. *American Psychologist, 12*, 671–684.

Cronbach, L. J., & Furby, L. (1970). How should we measure change—Or should we? *Psychological Bulletin, 74*, 68–80. (Also see Errata, ibid., 1970, *74*, 218.)

Cronbach, L. J., Gleser, G. C., Nanda, H., & Rajaratnam, N. (1972). *The dependability of behavioral measurements.* New York: Wiley.

Cudeck, R., & Harring, J. R. (2007). Analysis of nonlinear patterns of change with random coefficient models. *Annual Review of Psychology, 58*, 615–637.

Cumming, G., & Finch, S. (2001). A primer on the understanding, use, and calculation of confidence intervals that are based on central and noncentral distributions. *Educational and Psychological Measurement, 61*, 532–574.

Cumming, G., & Finch, S. (2005). Inference by eye: Confidence intervals and how to read pictures of data. *American Psychologist, 60*, 170–180.

Curran, P. J. (2009). The seemingly quixotic pursuit of a cumulative psychological science. Introduction to the special issue. *Psychological Methods, 14*, 77–80.

Curran, P. J., & Hussong, A. M. (2009). Integrative data analysis: The simultaneous analysis of multiple data sets. *Psychology Methods, 14*, 81–100.

Darlington, R. B. (1990). *Regression and linear models.* New York: McGraw-Hill.

Delucchi, K. L. (1983). The use and misuse of chi-square: Lewis and Burke revisited. *Psychological Bulletin, 94*, 166–176.

Denzin, N. K., & Lincoln, Y. S. (1994). Introduction: Entering the field of qualitative research. In N. K. Denzin & Y. S. Lincoln (Eds.), *Handbook of qualitative research* (pp. 1–17). Thousand Oaks, CA: Sage.

Denzin, N. K., & Lincoln, Y. S. (2000). *Handbook of qualitative research* (2nd ed.). Thousand Oaks, CA: Sage.

Deutsch, N. L., Luttrell, W., & Dorner, L. M. (2004, March). *Engaging with adolescents: The rewards and challenges of qualitative methods and feminist methodology.* Discussion hour presented at the biennial meeting of the Society for Research on Adolescence, Baltimore.

Dooley, D. (1990). *Social research methods* (2nd ed.). Englewood Cliffs, NJ: Prentice Hall.

Eid, M., & Diener, E. (Eds.) (2006). *Handbook of multimethod measurement in psychology.* Washington, DC: American Psychological Association.

Eisner, E. W. (2003). On the art and science of qualitative research in psychology. In P. M. Camic, J. E. Rhodes, & L. Yardley (Eds.), *Qualitative research in psychology: Expanding perspectives in methodology and design* (pp. 17–29). Washington, DC: American Psychological Association.

Elliott, R., Fischer, C. T., & Rennie, D. L. (1999). Evolving guidelines for publication of qualitative research studies in psychology and related fields. *British Journal for Clinical Psychology, 38*, 215–229.

Embretson, S. E., & Reise, S. P. (2000). *Item response theory for psychologists.* Mahwah, NJ: Lawrence Erlbaum Associates.

Epstein, S., & Brady, E. J. (1985). The person–situation debate in historical and current perspective. *Psychological Bulletin, 98*, 513–537.

Erickson, F. (1992). Ethnographic microanalysis of interaction. In M. D. LeCompte, L. W. Millroy, & J. Preissle (Eds.), *The handbook of qualitative research in education* (pp. 201–225). San Diego, CA: Academic Press.

Esterberg, K. G. (2002). *Qualitative methods in social research.* New York: McGraw-Hill.

Ferguson, L. R. (1978). The competence and freedom of children to make choices regarding participation in research: A statement. *Journal of Social Issues, 34,* 114–121.

Fidell, L. S., & Tabachnick, B. G. (2003). Preparatory data analysis. In J. A. Schinka (Series Ed.) and W. F. Velicer (Vol. Ed.), *Handbook of psychology: Research methods in psychology* (Vol. 2, pp. 115–141). New York: Wiley.

Fidler, F., & Thompson, B. (2001). Computing correct confidence intervals for anova fixed- and random-effects effect sizes. *Educational and Psychological Measurement, 61,* 575–604.

Fine, M. (1994). Working the hyphens: Reinventing self and other in qualitative research. In N. K. Denzin & Y. S. Lincoln (Eds.), *Handbook of qualitative research* (pp. 70–82). Thousand Oaks, CA: Sage.

Fine, M., Torre, M. E., Boudin, K., Bowen, I., Clark, J., Hylton, D., et al. (2003). Participatory action research: From within and beyond prison bars. In P. M. Camic, J. E. Rhodes, & L. Yardley (Eds.), *Qualitative research in psychology: Expanding perspectives in methodology and design* (pp. 173–198). Washington, DC: American Psychological Association.

Fine, G. A., & Elsbach, K. D. (2000). Ethnography and experiment in social psychological theory building: Tactics for integrating qualitative field data with quantitative lab data. *Journal of Experimental Social Psychology, 36,* 51–76.

Fischer, K. W., & Bidell, T. (1998). Dynamic development of psychological structures in action and thought. In W. Damon (Series Ed.) & R. M. Lerner (Vol. Ed.) *Handbook of child psychology. Volume 1: Theoretical models of human development* (5th ed., pp. 467–561). New York: Wiley.

Fisher, C. B., & Anushko, A. E. (2008). Research ethics in social science. In P. Alasuutari, L. Bickman, & J. Brannen (Eds.), *The Sage handbook of social research methods* (pp. 95–109). London: Sage.

Fitzmaurice, G., Davidian, M., Verbeke, G., & Molenberghs, G. (Eds.) (2009). *Longitudinal data analysis.* Boca Raton, FL: Chapman & Hall/CRC.

Fitzmaurice, G. M., Laird, N. M., & Ware, J. H. (2004). *Applied longitudinal analysis.* Hoboken, NJ: Wiley.

Fleiss, J. L. (1975). Measuring agreement between two judges on the presence or absence of a trait. *Biometrics, 31,* 651–659.

Fleiss, J. L. (1994). Measures of effect size for categorical data. In H. Cooper & L. V. Hedges (Eds.), *The handbook of research synthesis* (pp. 245–260). New York: Sage.

Fleiss, J. L., Levin, B., & Paik, M. C. (2003). *Statistical methods for rates and proportions* (3rd ed.). New York: Wiley.

Flick, U. (2007). *Designing qualitative research.* London: Sage.

Franklin, R. D., Allison, D. B., & Gorman, B. S. (Eds.). (1997). *Design and analysis of single-case research.* Mahwah, NJ: Lawrence Erlbaum Associates.

Freedman, D. A. (1991). Statistical models and shoe leather. In P. V. Marsden (Ed.), *Sociological methodology, 1991* (pp. 291–313). Washington, DC: American Sociological Association.

Gardner, W., Hartmann, D. P., & Mitchell, C. (1982). The effects of serial dependency on the use of χ^2 for analyzing sequential data. *Behavioral Assessment, 4,* 75–82.

Gee, J. (1991). A linguistic approach to narrative. *Journal of Narrative and Life History, 1,* 15–39.

Geisser, S., & Greenhouse, S. W. (1958). An extension of Box's results on the use of the *F* distribution in multivariate analysis. *Annals of Mathematical Statistics, 29,* 885–891.

Gelfand, D. M., & Hartmann, D. P. (1984). *Child behavior analysis and therapy* (2nd ed.). New York: Pergamon.

Gibbs, G. (2007). *Analyzing qualitative data.* London: Sage.

Gigerenzer, G., Krauss, S. & Vitouch, O. (2004). The null ritual: What you always wanted to know about significance testing but were afraid to ask. In D. Kaplan (Ed.), *The Sage handbook of quantitative methodology for the social sciences* (pp. 391–408). Thousand Oaks, CA: Sage.

Gilligan, C. (1982). *In a different voice: Psychological theory and women's development.* Cambridge, MA: Harvard University Press.

Gilligan, C., Spencer, R., Weinberg, M. K., & Bertsch, T. (2003). On the listening guide: A voice-centered relational model. In P. M. Camic, J. E. Rhodes, & L. Yardley (Eds.), *Qualitative research in psychology: Expanding perspectives in methodology and design* (pp. 157–172). Washington, DC: American Psychological Association.

Glass, G. V., McGaw, B., & Smith, M. L. (1981). *Meta-analysis in social research.* Beverly Hills, CA: Sage.

Glass, G. V., Peckham, P. D., & Sanders, J. R. (1972). Consequences of failure to meet assumptions underlying the analysis of variance and covariance. *Review of Education Research, 42,* 237–288.

Gorsuch, R. L. (1983). *Factor analysis* (2nd ed.). Hillsdale, NJ: Lawrence Erlbaum Associates.

Gottman, J. M. (Ed.). (1995). *The analysis of change.* Mahwah, NJ: Lawrence Erlbaum Associates.

Graham, J. W. (2009). Missing data analysis: Making it work in the real world. *Annual Review of Psychology, 60,* 549–576.

Graham, J. W., Taylor, B. J., Olchowski, A. E., & Cumsille, P. E. (2006). Planned missing data designs in psychological research. *Psychological Methods, 11,* 323–343.

Guilford, J. P. (1954). *Psychometric methods* (2nd ed.). New York: McGraw-Hill.

Guilford, J. P. (1965). *Fundamental statistics in psychology and education*. New York: McGraw-Hill.

Hammersley, M (2008). Assessing validity in social research. In P. Alasuutari, L. Bickman, & J. Brannen (Eds.), *The Sage handbook of social research methods* (pp. 42–53). London: Sage.

Harlow, L. L. (1997). Significance testing introduction and overview. In L. L. Harlow, S. A. Mulaik, & J. H. Steiger (Eds.), *What if there were no significance tests?* (pp. 1–17) Mahwah, NJ: Lawrence Erlbaum Associates.

Harlow, L. L., Mulaik, S. A., & Steiger, J. H. (Eds.). (1997). *What if there were no significance tests?* Mahwah, NJ: Lawrence Erlbaum Associates.

Harris, C. W. (Ed.) (1963). *Problems in measuring change*. Madison, WI: University of Wisconsin Press.

Hartmann, D. P. (1982a). Assessing the dependability of observational data. In D. P. Hartmann (Ed.), *Using observers to study behavior: New directions for methodology of social and behavioral science* (pp. 51–65). San Francisco: Jossey-Bass.

Hartmann, D. P. (Ed.). (1982b). *Using observers to study behavior: New directions for methodology of behavioral science*. San Francisco: Jossey-Bass.

Hartmann, D. P. (2005). Assessing growth in longitudinal investigations: Selected measurement and design issues. In D. Teti (Ed.), *Handbook of research methods in developmental psychology* (pp. 319–339). Malden, MA: Blackwell.

Hartmann, D. P., & George, T. P. (1999). Design, measurement, and analysis in developmental research. In M. H. Bornstein & M. E. Lamb (Eds.), *Developmental psychology: An advanced textbook* (4th ed., pp. 125–195). Mahwah, NJ: Lawrence Erlbaum Associates.

Hartmann, D. P., & Pelzel, K. (2005). Design, measurement, and analysis in developmental research. In M. H. Bornstein & M. E. Lamb (Eds.), Developmental science: An advanced textbook (5th ed., pp. 103–184). Mahwah, NJ: Lawrence Erlbaum Associates.

Hartmann, D. P., Roper, B. L., & Bradford, D. C. (1979). Some relationships between behavioral and traditional assessment. *Journal of Behavioral Assessment, 1,* 3–21.

Hartmann, D. P., & Wood, D. D. (1990). Observational methods. In A. S. Bellack, M. Hersen, & A. E. Kazdin (Eds.), *International handbook of behavior modification and therapy* (2nd ed., pp. 107–138). New York: Plenum.

Harvey, J. H., Orbuch, T. L., & Weber, A. L. (Eds.). (1992). *Attributions, accounts, and close relationships.* New York: Springer-Verlag.

Hays, W. L. (1988). *Statistics* (4th ed.). Fort Worth, TX: Holt, Rinehart and Winston.

Haynes, S. N., & O'Brien, W. H. (2000). *Principles and practice of behavioral assessment*. New York: Kluwer Academic/Plenum.

Hedges, L. V., & Olkin, I. (1985). *Statistical methods for meta-analysis*. New York: Academic Press.

Heise, D. R. (1975). *Causal analysis*. New York: Wiley.

Henwood, K., & Pidgeon, N. F. (1992). Qualitative research and psychology theorising. *British Journal of Psychology, 83,* 97–112.

Henwood, K., & Pidgeon, N. (2003). Grounded theory in psychological research. In P. M. Camic, J. E. Rhodes, & L. Yardley (Eds.), *Qualitative research in psychology: Expanding perspectives in methodology and design* (pp. 131–155). Washington, DC: American Psychological Association.

Hewson, C. (2008). Internet-mediated research as an emergent method and its potential role in facilitating mixed methods research. In S. N. Hesse-Biber & P. Leavy (Eds.), *Handbook of emergent methods* (pp. 543–570). New York: Guilford.

Hey, V. (1997). *The company she keeps: An ethnography of girls' friendship*. Philadelphia: Open University Press.

Hicks, L. E. (1970). Some properties of ipsative, normative, and forced-choice normative measures. *Psychological Bulletin, 74,* 167–184.

Hochberg, Y. & Tamhane, A. C. (1987). *Multiple comparison procedures*. New York: Wiley.

Hoeksma, J. B., & Koomen, H. M. Y. (1992). Multilevel models in developmental psychological research: Rationales and applications. *Early Development and Parenting, 1*(3), 157–167.

Hoffer, S. M., & Piccinin, A. M. (2009). Integrative data analysis through coordination of measurement and analysis protocol across independent longitudinal studies. *Psychology Methods, 14,* 150–164.

Hoffman, L. W. (1991). The influence of the family environment on personality: Accounting for sibling differences. *Psychological Bulletin, 1991,* 187–203.

Hollander, M. (1999). *Nonparametric statistical methods* (2nd ed.). New York: Wiley.

House, A. E., House, B. J., & Campbell, M. B. (1981). Measures of interobserver agreement: Calculation formulas and distribution effects. *Journal of Behavioral Assessment, 3,* 37–57.

Hothorn, T., Bretz, F., & Westfall, P. (2008). Simultaneous inference in general parametric models. *Biometrical Journal, 50,* 346–363.

Hoyle, R. H. (2008). Latent variable models of social research data. In P. Alasuutari, L. Bickman, & J. Brannen (Eds.), *The Sage handbook of social research methods* (pp. 395–413). London: Sage.

Hsu, J. C. (1996). *Multiple comparisons: Theory and methods*. London: Chapman & Hall.

Huck, S. W., & Sandler, H. M. (1979). *Rival hypotheses: Alternative interpretations of data based conclusions*. New York: Harper & Row.

Huitema, B. E. (1980). *The analysis of covariance and alternatives*. New York: Wiley.

Hunt, J. M. (1961). *Intelligence and experience*. New York: Ronald Press.

Hunter, J. E., Schmidt, F. L., & Jackson, G. B. (1982). *Meta-analysis: Cumulating research findings across studies*. Beverly Hills, CA: Sage.

Iwata, B. A., Bailey, J. S., Fuqua, R. W., Neef, N. A., Page, T. J., & Reid, D. H (Eds.) (1989). *Methodological and conceptual issues in applied behavior analysis: 1968–1988*. Lawrence, KS: Society for the Experimental Analysis of Behavior.

Jackson, G. B. (1980). Methods for integrative reviews. *Review of Educational Research, 50*, 438–460.

Johnston, J. M., & Pennypacker, H. S. (1993). *Strategies and tactics of behavioral research* (2nd ed.). Hillsdale, NJ: Lawrence Erlbaum Associates.

Jöreskog, K. G., & Sörbom, D. (1983). *Lisrel V and Lisrel VI: Analysis of linear structural relationships by maximum likelihood and least squares methods* (2nd ed.). Uppsala, Sweden: University of Uppsala Department of Statistics.

Judd, C. M., & McClelland, G. H. (1989). *Data analysis: A model-comparison approach*. New York: Harcourt Brace Jovanovich.

Judd, C. M., McClelland, G. H., & Culhane, S. E. (1995). Data analysis: Continuing issues in the everyday analysis of psychological data. *Annual Review of Psychology, 46*, 433–465.

Kahneman, D. (1965). Control of spurious association and the reliability of the controlled variable. *Psychological Bulletin, 64*, 326–329.

Kazdin, A. E. (1980). *Research design in clinical psychology*. New York: Harper & Row.

Kelle, U. (Ed.). (1996). *Computer-aided qualitative data analysis: Theory, methods and practice*. Thousand Oaks, CA: Sage.

Kelley, K., & Maxwell, S. (2008). Sample size planning with applications to multiple regression: Power and accuracy for omnibus and targeted effects. In P. Alasuutari, L. Bickman, & J. Brannen (Eds.), *The Sage handbook of social research methods* (pp. 166–192). London: Sage.

Kelloway, E. K. (1998). *Using LISREL for structural equation modeling: A researcher's guide*. Thousand Oaks, CA: Sage Publications.

Kelley, K., & Rausch, J. R. (2006). Sample size planning for the standardized mean difference: Accuracy in parameter estimation via narrow confidence intervals. *Psychological Methods, 11*, 363–385.

Kemmis, S., & McTaggart, R. (2008). Participatory action research. Communicative action and the public sphere. In N. K. Denzin & Y. S. Lincoln (Eds.), *Strategies of qualitative inquiry* (3rd ed., pp. 271–330). Thousand Oaks, CA: Sage.

Kennedy, J. J. (1992). *Analyzing qualitative data: Log-linear analysis for behavioral research* (2nd ed.). New York: Praeger.

Kenny, D. A. (1979). *Correlation and causality*. New York: Wiley.

Kenny, D. A., & Judd, C. M. (1986). Consequences of violating the independence assumption in analysis of variance. *Psychological Bulletin, 99*, 422–431.

Kerig, P. K., & Lindahl, K. M. (Eds.). (2001). *Family observational coding systems: Resources for systemic research*. Mahwah, NJ: Lawrence Erlbaum Associates.

Kidder, L. H. (1981). Qualitative research and quasi-experimental frameworks. In M. B. Brewer & B. E. Collins (Eds.), *Scientific inquiry and the social sciences* (pp. 226–256). San Francisco: Jossey-Bass.

Kirk, R. E. (1995). *Experimental design: Procedures for the behavioral sciences* (3rd ed.). Pacific Grove, CA: Brooks/Cole.

Kirk, R. E. (2003). The importance of effect magnitude. In S. F. Davis (Ed.), *Handbook of research methods in experimental psychology* (pp. 83–105). Malden, MA: Blackwell.

Knight, G. P., & Hill, N. E. (1998). Measurement equivalence in research involving minority adolescents. In V. C. McLoyd & L. Steinberg (Eds.), *Studying minority adolescents: Conceptual, methodological, and theoretical issues* (pp. 183–210). Mahwah, NJ: Lawrence Erlbaum Associates.

Knoke, D., & Burke, P. J. (1980). *Log-linear models*. Beverly Hills, CA: Sage.

Kopala, M., & Suzuki, L. A. (Eds.). (1999). *Using qualitative methods in psychology*. Thousand Oaks, CA: Sage.

Kraemer, H. C., & Jacklin, C. N. (1979). Statistical analysis of dyadic social behavior. *Psychological Bulletin, 86*, 217–224.

Kratochwill, T. R., & Levin, J. R. (Eds.). (1992). *Single-case research design and analysis: New directions for psychology and education*. Hillsdale, NJ: Lawrence Erlbaum Associates.

Kraut, R., Olson, J., Banaji, M., Bruckman, A., Cohen, J., & Couper, M. (2004). Psychological research online: Report of board of scientific affairs' advisory group on the conduct of research on the internet. *American Psychologist, 59*, 105–117.

Kristjansson, S. D., Kircher, J. C., & Webb, A. K. (2007). Multilevel models for repeated measures research designs in psychophysiology: An introduction to growth curve modeling. *Psychophysiology, 44*, 728–736.

Kuhn, T. S. (1970). *The structure of scientific revolutions* (2nd ed.). Chicago: University of Chicago Press.

Kuzel, A. J. (1999). Sampling in qualitative inquiry. In B. F. Crabtree & W. L. Miller (Eds.), *Doing qualitative research* (2nd ed., pp. 33–46). Thousand Oaks, CA: Sage.

Labov, W. (1978). Crossing the gulf between sociology and linguistics. *American Sociologist, 13*, 93–103.

Lancy, D. F. (2001). *Studying children and schools: Qualitative research traditions.* Prospect Heights, IL: Waveland.

Landis, J. R., & Koch, G. G. (1979). The analysis of categorical data in longitudinal studies of development. In J. R. Nesselroade & P. B. Baltes (Eds.), *Longitudinal research in the study of behavior and development* (pp. 233–261). New York: Academic Press.

Larzelere, R. E., & Mulaik, S. A. (1977). Single-sample tests for many correlations. *Psychological Bulletin, 84*, 557–569.

Lavelli, M., Pantoja, A. P. F., Hsu, H.-C., Messinger, D., & Fogel, A. (2005). Using microgenetic designs to study developmental change processes. In D. M. Teti (Ed.), *Handbook of research methods in developmental science* (pp. 40–65). Malden, MA: Blackwell.

Lenth, R. V. (2001). Some practical guidelines for effective sample size determination. *American Statistician, 55*, 187–193.

Lerner, R. M. (1998). The life course and human development. In W. Damon (Series Ed.) and R. M. Lerner (Vol. Ed.), *Handbook of child psychology. Volume 1: Theoretical models of human development* (5th ed., pp. 1–24). New York: Wiley.

Lewis, D., & Burke, C. J. (1949). The use and misuse of the chi-square test. *Psychological Bulletin, 46*, 433–489.

Lewis, D., & Burke, C. J. (1950). Further discussion of the use and misuse of the chi-square test. *Psychological Bulletin, 47*, 347–355.

Lipsey, M. W. (1990). *Design sensitivity: Statistical power for experimental research.* Newbury Park, CA: Sage

Little, R. J., & Rubin, D. B. (1987). *Statistical analysis with missing data.* New York: Wiley.

Luttrell, W. (2002). *Pregnant bodies, fertile minds: Gender, race, and the schooling of pregnant teens.* London: Routledge.

Luttrell, W. (Ed.). (2009). *Qualitative educational research: Readings in reflexive methodology and transformative practice.* London: Routledge.

MacCallum, R. C. (2003). 2001 presidential address: Working with imperfect models. *Multivariate Behavioral Research, 38*, 113–139.

MacKinnon, D. P., Fairchild, A. J., & Fritz, M. S. (2007). Mediation analysis. *Annual Review of Psychology, 58*, 593–614.

Magidson, J., & Vermunt, J. K. (2004). Latent class models. In D. Kaplan (Ed.) *The Sage handbook of quantitative methodology for the social sciences* (pp. 175–198). Thousand Oaks, CA: Sage.

Mahler, M. S., Pine, F., & Bergman, A. (1975/2000). *The psychological birth of the human infant: Symbiosis and individuation.* New York: Basic Books.

Mahoney, M. J. (1976). *Scientist as subject: The psychological imperative.* Cambridge, MA: Ballinger Publication Company.

Marecek, J. (2003). Dancing through minefields: Toward a qualitative stance in psychology. In P. M. Camic, J. E. Rhodes, & L. Yardley (Eds.), *Qualitative research in psychology: Expanding perspectives in methodology and design* (pp. 49–69). Washington, DC: American Psychological Association.

Maritz, J. S. (1995). *Distribution-free statistical methods* (2nd ed.). New York: Chapman & Hall.

Maxwell, S. E., Kelley, K., & Rausch, J. R. (2008). Sample size planning for statistical power and accuracy in parameter estimation. *Annual Review of Psychology, 59*, 537–563.

McAdams, D. P., & Bowman, P. J. (2001). Narrating life's turning points: Redemption and contamination. In D. P. McAdams, R. Josselson, & A. Lieblich (Eds.), *Turns in the road: Narrative studies of lives in transition* (pp. 3–34). Washington, DC: American Psychological Association.

McAdams, D. P., Josselson, R., & Lieblich, A. (Eds.). (2001). *Turns in the road: Narrative studies of lives in transition.* Washington, DC: American Psychological Association.

McArdle, J. J. (2009). Latent variable modeling of difference and changes with longitudinal data. *Annual Review of Psychology, 60*, 577–605.

McCall, R. B. (1977). Challenges to a science of developmental psychology. *Child Development, 48*, 333–344.

McCullagh, P., & Nelder, J. A. (1989). *Generalized linear models* (2nd ed.). London: Chapman & Hall.

McDonald, R. P. (1985). *Factor analysis and related methods.* Hillsdale, NJ: Lawrence Erlbaum Associates.

McDonald, R. P., & Ho, M. H. R. (2002). Principles and practice in reporting structural equation analyses. *Psychological Methods, 7*, 64–82.

McGrath, J. E., & Johnson, B. A. (2003). Methodology makes meaning: How both qualitative and quantitative paradigms shape evidence and its interpretation. In P. M. Camic, J. E. Rhodes, & L. Yardley (Eds.), *Qualitative research in psychology: Expanding perspectives in methodology and design* (pp. 31–48). Washington, DC: American Psychological Association.

McGuire, W. J. (1969). Suspiciousness of experimenter's intent. In R. Rosenthal & R. L. Rosnow (Eds.), *Artifact in behavioral research* (pp. 13–57). New York: Academic Press.

McNemar, Q. (1969). *Psychological statistics* (4th ed.). New York: Wiley.

Meehl, P. E. (1978). Theoretical risks and tabular asterisks: Sir Karl, Sir Ronald, and the slow progress of soft psychology. *Journal of Consulting and Clinical Psychology, 46*, 806–834.

Meng, X., Rosenthal, R., & Rubin, D. B. (1992). Comparing correlated correlation coefficients. *Psychological Bulletin, 111*, 172–175.

Merrick, E. (1999). An exploration of quality in qualitative research: Are "reliability" and "validity" relevant? In M. Kopala & L. A. Suzuki (Eds.), *Using qualitative methods in psychology* (pp. 25–36). Thousand Oaks, CA: Sage.

Messick, S. (1983). Assessment of children. In P. Mussen (Ed.), *Handbook of child psychology: Vol. 1. History, theory, and methods* (4th ed., pp. 477–526). New York: Wiley.

Messick, S. (1994). Foundations of validity: Meaning and consequences in psychological assessment. *European Journal of Psychological Assessment, 10*, 1–9.

Miller, S. A. (2007). *Developmental research methods* (3rd ed.). Thousand Oaks, CA: Sage.

Mischel, W., & Peake, P. K. (1983). Analyzing the construction of consistency in personality. In M. M. Page (Ed.), *Personality—Current theory & research: 1982 Nebraska symposium on motivation* (pp. 233–262). Lincoln, NE: University of Nebraska Press.

Mitchell, C., & Hartmann, D. P. (1981). A cautionary note on the use of omega squared to evaluate the effectiveness of behavioral treatments. *Behavioral Assessment, 3*, 93–100.

Mook, D. G. (1983). In defense of external invalidity. *American Psychologist, 38*, 379–387.

Morrison, D. F. (2000). *Multivariate statistical methods* (3rd ed.). New York: McGraw-Hill.

Morrison, D. E., & Henkel, R. E. (Eds.). (1970). *The significance test controversy*. Chicago: Aldine.

Morrow, S. L., & Smith, M. L. (2000). Qualitative research for counseling psychology. In S. D. Brown & R. W. Lent (Eds.), *Handbook of counseling psychology* (3rd ed., pp. 119–230). New York: Wiley.

Moskowitz, D. S. & Hershberger, S. L. (Eds.). (2002). *Modeling intraindividual variability with repeated measures data: Methods and applications*. Mahwah, NJ: Lawrence Erlbaum Associates.

Mulaik, S. A., Raju, N. S., & Harshman, R. A. (1997). There is a time and place for significance testing. In L. L. Harlow, S. A. Mulaik, & J. H. Steiger (Eds.), *What if there were no significance tests?* (pp. 65–115). Mahwah, NJ: Lawrence Erlbaum Associates.

Murray, M. (2003). Narrative psychology and narrative analysis. In P. M. Camic, J. E. Rhodes, & L. Yardley (Eds.), *Qualitative research in psychology: Expanding perspectives in methodology and design* (pp. 95–112). Washington, DC: American Psychological Association.

National Commission for the Protection of Human Subjects. (1977). *Report and recommendations: Research involving children*. Washington, DC: U.S. Government Printing Office.

Neher, A. (1967). Probability pyramiding, research error and the need for independent replication. *Psychological Record, 17*, 257–262.

Neisser, U., Boodoo, G., Bouchard, T. J., Jr., Boykin, A. W., Brody, N., Ceci, S. J., et al. (1996). Intelligence: Knowns and unknowns. *American Psychologist, 51*, 77–101.

Nelder, J. A., & Wedderburn, R. W. M. (1972). Generalized linear models. *Journal of the Royal Statistical Society: Series A (General), 135*, 370–384.

Nesselroade, J. R., & Baltes, P. B. (Eds.). (1979). *Longitudinal research in the study of behavior and development*. New York: Academic Press.

☐ Nickerson, R. S. (2000). Null hypothesis significance testing: A review of an old and continuing controversy. *Psychological Methods, 5*, 241–301.

Nunnally, J. C. (1978). *Psychometric theory* (2nd ed.). New York: McGraw-Hill.

☐ Nunnally, J. C., & Bernstein, I. H. (1994). *Psychometric theory* (3rd ed.). New York: McGraw-Hill.

O'Brien, R. G., & Castelloe, J. (2007). Sample-size analysis for traditional hypothesis testing: Concepts and issues. In A. Dmitrienko, C. Chuang-Stein, & R. D'Agostino (Eds.), *Pharmaceutical statistics using SAS: A practical guide* (pp. 237–271). Cary, NC: SAS.

O'Grady, K. E. (1982). Measures of explained variance: Cautions and limitations. *Psychological Bulletin, 92*, 766–777.

Overall, J. E., & Woodward, J. A. (1977). Nonrandom assignment and the analysis of covariance. *Psychological Bulletin, 84*, 588–594.

Overton, W. F. (1998). Developmental psychology: Philosophy, concepts, and methodology. In W. Damon (Series Ed.) & R. M. Lerner (Vol. Ed.), *Handbook of child psychology. Volume 1: Theoretical models of human development* (5th ed., pp. 107–188). New York: Wiley.

Ozer, D. J. (1985). Correlation and the coefficient of determination. *Psychological Bulletin, 97*, 307–315.

Pampel, F. C. (2000). *Logistic regression: A primer*. Thousand Oaks, CA: Sage.

Parsonson, B. S., & Baer, D. M. (1978). The analysis and presentation of graphic data. In T. R. Kratochwill (Ed.), *Single subject research: Strategies for evaluating change* (pp. 101–165). New York: Academic Press.

Patall, E. A., & Cooper, H. (2008). Conducting a meta-analysis. In P. Alasuutari, L. Bickman, & J. Brannen (Eds.), *The Sage handbook of social research methods* (pp. 536–554). London: Sage.

Patterson, G. R. (1993). Orderly change in a stable world: The antisocial trait as a chimera. *Journal of Consulting and Clinical Psychology*, *61*, 911–919.

Pedhazur, E. J., & Schmelkin, L. P. (1991). *Measurement, design, and analysis: An integrated approach*. Hillsdale, NJ: Lawrence Erlbaum Associates.

Piaget, J. (1932/1965). *The moral judgment of the child*. New York: Free Press.

Piaget, J., Inhelder, B., & Weaver, H. (1972/2000). *The psychology of the child*. New York: Basic Books.

Popper, K. (1959). *The logic of scientific discovery*. New York: Basic Books.

Potter, J. (2003). Discourse analysis and discursive psychology. In P. M. Camic, J. E. Rhodes, & L. Yardley (Eds.), *Qualitative research in psychology: Expanding perspectives in methodology and design* (pp. 73–94). Washington, DC: American Psychological Association.

Prentice, D. A., & Miller, D. T. (1992). When small effects are impressive. *Psychological Bulletin*, *12*, 160–164.

Press, S. J., & Wilson, S. (1978). Choosing between logistic regression and discriminant analysis. *Journal of the American Statistical Association*, *73*, 699–705.

Raudenbush, S. W. (2000). Comparing personal trajectories and drawing causal inferences from longitudinal data. *Annual Review of Psychology*, *52*, 501–525.

Raudenbush, S. W. & Bryk, A. S. (2002). Hierarchical linear models: Applications and data analysis methods (2nd ed.). Thousand Oaks, CA: Sage.

Reips, U.-D. (2006). Web-based methods. In M. Eid & E. Diener (Eds.), *Handbook of multimethod measurement in psychology* (pp. 73–85). Washington, DC: American Psychological Association.

Reiss, R. D. (1989). *Approximate distributions of order statistics: With applications to nonparametric statistics*. New York: Springer-Verlag.

Ribisl, K. M., Walton, M., Mowbray, C. T., Luke, D. A., Davidson, W. S., & Bootsmiller, B. J. (1996). Minimizing participant attrition in panel studies through the use of effective retention and tracking strategies: Review and recommendations. *Evaluation and Program Planning*, *19*, 1–25.

📖 Rindskopf, D. (2004). Trends in categorical data analysis: New, semi-new, and recycled ideas. In D. Kaplan (Ed.) *The Sage handbook of quantitative methodology for the social sciences* (pp. 137–149). Thousand Oaks, CA: Sage.

Rogosa, D. (1988). Myths about longitudinal research. In K. W. Schaie, R. T. Campbell, W. Meredith, & S. C. Rawlings (Eds.), *Methodological issues in aging research* (pp. 171–209). New York: Springer.

Rosenberg, M. S., Adams, D. C., & Gurevitch, J. (1997). *Metawin: Statistical software for meta-analysis with resampling tests*. Sunderland, MA: Sinauer.

Rosenthal, R. (1979). The "file-drawer problem" and tolerance for null results. *Psychological Bulletin*, *85*, 185–193.

Rosenthal, R. (Ed.). (1980a). *Quantitative assessment of research domains*. San Francisco: Jossey-Bass.

Rosenthal, R. (1980b). Summarizing significance levels. In R. Rosenthal (Ed.), *Quantitative assessment of research domains* (pp. 33–46). San Francisco: Jossey-Bass.

Rosenthal, R. (1994). Parametric measures of effect size. In H. Cooper & L. V. Hedges (Eds.), *The handbook of research synthesis* (pp. 231–244). New York: Sage.

Rosenthal, R., & Rosnow, R. L. (Ed.). (1969). *Artifact in behavioral research*. New York: Academic Press.

Rosenthal, R., & Rosnow, R. (1985). *Contrast analysis: Focused comparisons in the analysis of variance*. New York: Cambridge University Press.

Rosenthal, R., & Rubin, D. (1983). A note on percent of variance explained as a measure of the importance of effects. *Journal of Applied Social Psychology*, *9*, 395–396.

Rummel, R. J. (1967). Understanding factor analysis. *Journal of Conflict Resolution*, *XI*, 444–480.

Schafer, J. L., & Graham, J. W. (2002). Missing data: Our view of the state of the art. *Psychological Methods*, *7*, 147–177.

Schaie, K. W. (1965). A general model for the study of developmental problems. *Psychological Bulletin*, *64*, 92–107.

Schaie, K. W., & Caskie, G. I. L (2005). Methodological issues in aging research. In D. M. Teti (Ed.), *Handbook of research methods in developmental science* (pp. 21–39). Malden, MA: Blackwell.

Sciarra, D. (1999). The role of the qualitative researcher. In M. Kopala & L. A. Suzuki (Eds.), Using qualitative methods in psychology (pp. 37–48). Thousand Oaks, CA: Sage.

Shadish, W. R. (1986). Planned critical multiplism: Some elaborations. *Behavioral Assessment*, *8*, 75–103.

Shadish, W. R., & Cook, T. D. (2009). The renaissance of field experimentation in evaluation interventions. *Annual Review of Psychology*, *60*, 607–629.

📖 Shadish, W. R., Cook, T. D., & Campbell, D. T. (2002). *Experimental and quasi-experimental designs for generalized causal inference*. Boston: Houghton Mifflin.

Shonkoff, J. P., & Phillips, D. A. (Eds.). (2000). *From neurons to neighborhoods: The science of early childhood development*. Washington, DC: National Academy Press.

Silva, F. (1993). *Psychometric foundations and behavioral assessment*. Newbury Park, CA: Sage.

Singer, J. D., & Willett, J. B. (2003). *Applied longitudinal data analysis: Modeling change and event occurrence*. New York: Oxford University Press.

Skitka, L. J., & Sargis, E. G. (2006). The internet as psychological laboratory. *Annual Review of Psychology*, *57*, 529–555.

Smith, J. A. (Ed.). (2003). *Qualitative psychology: A practical guide to research methods*. Thousand Oaks, CA: Sage.

Smith, K. E. (1996). *Changing times: My father's life from 1960 to 1970*. Unpublished manuscript, University of Idaho, Moscow, ID.

Smith, M. B. (1967). Conflicting values affecting behavioral research with children. *American Psychologist*, *22*, 377–382.

Smith, M. L., Glass, G. V., & Miller, T. I. (1980). *The benefits of psychotherapy*. Baltimore: Johns Hopkins University Press.

Smithson, M. (2001). Correct confidence intervals for various regression effect sizes and parameters: The importance of noncentral distributions in computing intervals. *Educational and Psychological Measurement*, *61*, 605–632.

📖 Smithson, M. (2003). *Confidence intervals*. Thousand Oaks, CA: Sage.

Society for Research in Child Development. (2003). *Directory of members*. Chicago: SRCD.

Society for Research in Child Development. (2007). SRCD ethical standards for research with children: Updated by the SRCD Governing Council, March 2007. Retrieved July 9, 2009, from www.srcd.org/index2.php?option=com_content&do_pdf=1&id=68

Solomon, R. L., & Lessac, M. S. (1968). A control group design for experimental studies of developmental processes. *Psychological Bulletin*, *70*, 145–150.

Steiger, J. H., & Fouladi, R. T. (1997). Noncentrality interval estimation and the evaluation of statistical models. In L. L. Harlow, S. A. Mulaik, & J. H. Steiger (Eds.), *What if there were no significance tests?* (pp. 221–257). Mahwah, NJ: Lawrence Erlbaum Associates.

Steiger, J. H., & Ward, L. M. (1987). Factor analysis and the coefficient of determination. *Psychological Bulletin*, *101*, 471–474.

Stern, D. N. (1985). *The interpersonal world of the infant*. New York: Basic Books.

Sternberg, K. J., Baradaran, L. P., Abbott, C. B., Lamb, M. E., & Guterman, E. (2006). Type of violence, age, and gender differences in the effects of family violence on children's behavior problems: A mega-analysis. *Developmental Review*, *26*, 89–112.

Stevens, J. (1992). *Applied multivariate statistics for the social sciences* (2nd ed.). Hillsdale, NJ: Lawrence Erlbaum Associates.

Stiles, W. B. (1993). Quality control in qualitative research. *Clinical Psychology Review*, *13*, 593–618.

Strayer, F. F., Verissimo, M., Vaughn, B. E., & Howes, C. (1995). A quantitative approach to the description and classification of primary social relationships. In E. Waters, B. E. Vaughn, G. Posada, & K. Kondo-Ikemura (Eds.), Caregiving, cultural, and cognitive perspectives on secure-base behavior and working models: New growing points of attachment theory and research. *Monographs of the Society for Research in Child Development*, *60*, 49–70.

Strube, M. J., & Hartmann, D. P. (1983). Meta-analysis: Techniques, applications, and functions. *Journal of Consulting and Clinical Psychology*, *51*, 14–27.

Suen, H. K., & Ary, D. (1989). *Analyzing quantitative behavioral observation data*. Hillsdale, NJ: Lawrence Erlbaum Associates.

Sutton, A. J., & Higgins, J. P. T. (2008). Recent developments in meta-analysis. *Statistics in Medicine*, *27*, 625–650.

Tabachnick, B. G., and Fidell, L. S. (2007). *Using multivariate statistics* (5th ed.). Boston: Pearson.

Tamhane, A. C. (2009). *Statistical analysis of designed experiments: Theory and applications*. Hoboken, NJ: Wiley.

Tashakkori, A., & Teddlie, C. (1998). *Mixed methodology: Combining qualitative and quantitative approaches*. Thousand Oaks, CA: Sage.

Tatsuoka, M. (1993). Effect size. In G. Keren & C. Lewis (Eds.), *A handbook for data analysis in the behavioral sciences: Methodological issues* (pp. 461–479). Hillsdale, NJ: Lawrence Erlbaum Associates.

📖 Teti, D. (Ed.). (2005). *Handbook of research methods in developmental science*. Malden, MA: Blackwell.

Thomas, L., & Krebs, C. J. (1997). A review of statistical power analysis software. *Bulletin of the Ecological Society of America*, *78*, 128–139.

Thompson, B. (1984). *Canonical correlation analysis: Uses and interpretation*. Beverly Hills, CA: Sage.

Thompson, R. A. (1990). Vulnerability in research: A developmental perspective on research risk. *Child Development*, *61*, 1–16.

Toothaker, L. E. (1991). *Multiple comparisons for researchers*. Newbury Park, CA: Sage.

Tukey, J. W. (1977). *Exploratory data analysis*. Reading, MA: Addison-Wesley.

Tversky, A., & Kahneman, D. (1971). Belief in the law of small numbers. *Psychological Bulletin*, *76*, 105–110.

Ullman, J. B. (2007). Structural equation modeling. In B. G. Tabachnick & L. S. Fidell, *Using multivariate statistics* (5th ed., pp. 676–780). New York: Pearson.

Ullman, J. B., & Bentler, P. M. (2003). Structural equation modeling. In J. A. Schinka (Series Ed.) & W. F. Velicer (Vol. Ed.), *Handbook of psychology: Research methods in psychology* (Vol. 2, pp. 607–634). New York: Wiley.

Valsiner, J. (Ed.). (1986). *The individual subject and scientific psychology*. New York: Plenum Press.

Way, N., & Pahl, K. (1999). Friendship patterns among urban adolescent boys: A qualitative account. In M. Kopala & L. A. Suzuki (Eds.), *Using qualitative methods in psychology* (pp. 145–161). Thousand Oaks, CA: Sage.

Webber, S. J., & Cook, T. D. (1972). Subject effects in laboratory research: An examination of subject roles, demand characteristics, and valid inference. *Psychological Bulletin, 77,* 273–295.

West, S. (Ed.). (1983). Personality and prediction: Nomothetic and idiographic approaches. *Journal of Personality, 51* (No. 3, whole).

Westfall, P. H., Tobias, R. D., Rom, D., Wolfinger, R. D., & Hochberg, Y. (1999). *Multiple comparisons and multiple tests using SAS*. Cary, NC: SAS.

Wickens, T. D. (1989). *Multiway contingency tables analysis for the social sciences*. Hillsdale, NJ: Lawrence Erlbaum Associates.

Widaman, K. F., & Reise, S. P. (1997). Exploring the measurement invariance of psychological instruments: Applications in the substance use domain. In K. J. Bryant, M. Windle, & S. G. West (Eds.), *The science of prevention: Methodological advances from alcohol and substance abuse research* (pp. 281–324). Washington, DC: American Psychological Association.

Wilkinson, L., & the Task Force on Statistical Inference. (1999). Statistical methods in psychology journals: Guidelines and explanations. *American Psychologist, 54,* 594–604.

Wilkinson, S. (1988). The role of reflexivity in feminist psychology. *Women's Studies International Forum, 11,* 493–502.

Willett, J. B. (1988). Questions and answers in the measurement of change. In E. Z. Rothkopf (Ed.), *Review of research in education 15: 1988–89* (pp. 345–422). Washington, DC: American Educational Research Association.

Willett, J. B. (1989). Some results on reliability for the longitudinal measurement of change: Implications for the design of studies of individual growth. *Educational and Psychological Measurement, 49,* 587–602.

Willett, J. B. (1994). Measurement of change. In T. Husen and T. N. Postlewaite (Eds.), The international encyclopedia of education (2nd ed., pp. 671– 678). Oxford, UK: Pergamon Press. Retrieved October 19, 2009, from http://gseacademic.harvard.edu/~willetjo/pdffiles/Willett1994.pdf

Willett, J. B., & Singer, J. D. (2004). Discrete-time survival analysis. In D. Kaplan (Ed.), *The Sage handbook of quantitative methodology for the social sciences* (pp. 199–211). Thousand Oaks, CA: Sage.

Willig, C. (2001). *Introducing qualitative research in psychology: Adventures in theory and method*. Philadelphia: Open University Press.

Willig, C. (2003). Discourse analysis. In J. A. Smith (Ed.), *Qualitative psychology: A practical guide to research methods* (pp. 159–183). Thousand Oaks, CA: Sage.

Wohlwill, J. F. (1970). The age variable in psychological research. *Psychological Review, 77,* 49–64.

Wohlwill, J. F. (1973). *The study of behavioral development*. New York: Academic Press.

Yardley, L. (2000). Dilemmas in qualitative health research. *Psychology and Health, 15,* 215–228.

Yeaton, W., & Sechrest, L. (1981). Meaningful measures of effect. *Journal of Consulting and Clinical Psychology, 49,* 766–767.

PERSONALITY AND INDIVIDUAL DEVELOPMENT IN SOCIAL CONTEXT

❖ 5 ❖

THE INDIVIDUAL CHILD: TEMPERAMENT, EMOTION, SELF, AND PERSONALITY

Ross A. Thompson and Abby C. Winer
University of California, Davis
Rebecca Goodvin
Western Washington University

INTRODUCTION

This chapter is concerned with the unique qualities that develop to distinguish the individual child from others, the qualities that contribute to the growth of personality. The goal is to understand what the child brings to the social world from the very beginning that marks developing individuality. It is important to note, however, that "the individual child" does not really exist except in the mind of the theorist. From the moment of conception throughout life, a person's growth is constituted by the influences of others, beginning with the quality of prenatal care and continuing in the variety of social influences that guide developing thoughts, emotions, and personality throughout adulthood. Nor do developing people come as empty entities to these interactions. They bring with them temperamental predispositions, unfolding emotional capacities, and developing self-awareness that individualize each transaction with the social world. In this regard, considering "the individual child" involves asking what developing people bring to their encounters with family members, peers, the school, and community.

Why focus on developing temperament, emotion, and self in the construction of personality? One reason is that these three early-emerging attributes establish young children's individuality to others—and to themselves. Temperament forms the initial bedrock of personality development through the dispositions by which young infants first exert a unique influence on others around them, and become recognized by others as distinct individuals. Emotion is an important way that individuality is developmentally broadened and deepened as emerging capacities for emotional expression, understanding, and regulation contribute to the growth of personality. Self is important for how it organizes emergent personality processes around a changing, yet consistent, core of self-perceived personhood. This trio of emerging capacities helps to define individuality from the beginning of life. Another reason is that temperament, emotion, and self each reflects an interaction between emergent intrinsic capacities and the influences of the social world. In this ongoing dynamic between nature and nurture, personality takes shape, and each developing child becomes a unique actor in a complex social world.

The development of temperament is considered first, in the next section. We address the defining features that distinguish temperament from moods or emotions, and then consider the core dimensions of temperamental individuality. Then we summarize research findings concerning the stability of temperament over time and its relation to personality features, especially in relation to new research in **molecular genetics** on the biological foundations of temperament. This leads to a broader discussion of how temperament develops, and the influence of temperament in the growth of behavior and personality. Emotional development is profiled in the section that follows. Definitional issues are again considered first. Because emotions are so complex, our discussion then turns to the question, "what is emotional development the development of?" In answering this question, the psychobiological foundations of emotion; the growth of emotion perception and understanding; empathy; emotion and the growth of self-understanding; emotional **display rules**; and **emotion regulation** are each profiled, along with the growth of emotion in close relationships. The last major section considers the development of self. Not surprisingly, we first consider "what is 'self'?" and the various dimensions of self-awareness and self-understanding that emerge developmentally. We then offer a developmental outline of how the self emerges in infancy, early childhood, middle childhood, adolescence, and adulthood. In a concluding section, we relate the developmental processes discussed in this chapter to the growth of personality. Throughout this chapter, we consider for each topic the importance of culture, emerging new research questions, and methods of study.

TEMPERAMENT

Beginning shortly after birth, a child's individuality is manifested primarily in temperament. The child's dominant mood, adaptability, activity level, persistence, threshold for distress (or happiness), self-regulation, and other characteristics are important because of the influence they have on others, and because they constitute the foundations of personality growth. Parents and other caregivers devote considerable effort to identifying, accommodating to, and sometimes modifying the temperamental features of young children. Parents also understand that, to the extent that we can see in the baby the person-to-be, we see in temperament the personality-to-be. Most parents are fascinated by their child's temperamental individuality because it distinguishes their child in ways that foreshadow, they believe, the growth of personality dispositions. Developmental research into temperament has been motivated by the same interests. What is temperament and its core features? How consistent over time are temperamental characteristics, and do they constitute the basis for personality development? How does temperament influence development—and how does temperament itself develop over time?

Defining Temperament

Temperament concerns the early emerging, stable individuality in a person's behavior, and this is what distinguishes temperamental individuality from more transient moods, emotions, or other influences on the developing child. More specifically, temperament is defined as constitutionally based individual differences in behavioral characteristics, especially those reflecting reactivity and self-regulation, that are relatively consistent across situations and over time (Goldsmith et al., 1987; Rothbart & Bates, 2006). Encompassed within this definition are several important points.

First, temperamental characteristics are *constitutional* in nature. Temperament is biologically based and derives from the interaction of genetic predispositions, maturation, and experience. The biological foundations of temperament are multifaceted. Individual differences in temperamental qualities associated with emotionality, activity, and other characteristics are strongly heritable (Caspi & Shiner, 2006; Goldsmith, 2002; Plomin, DeFries,

Craig, & McGuffin, 2003). Molecular genetics research has implicated several common genetic polymorphisms with temperament and personality characteristics. These include polymorphisms in the dopamine D4 receptor (DRD4), which is associated with novelty seeking and impulsivity, and the serotonin transporter promoter region (5HTTLPR), which is associated with negative emotionality and harm avoidance (Ebstein, Benjamin, & Belmaker, 2000). Genetic individuality is, in turn, expressed in many physiological systems, including individual differences in the reactivity of subcortical and sympathetic nervous system structures (Kagan & Fox, 2006), neuroendocrine functioning (Gunnar & Davis, 2003; Gunnar & Vasquez, 2006), cerebral asymmetry (Fox, Schmidt, & Henderson, 2000), parasympathetic regulation (Porges, 2007; Porges, Doussard-Roosevelt, & Maiti, 1994), attentional processes in the central nervous system (Rothbart, 2007; Rothbart, Posner, & Kieras, 2006), and many other psychobiological processes (see Martin & Fox, 2006, and Rothbart & Bates, 2006 for reviews).

Many of these features of biological individuality emerge very early in life, and thus influence developing social, emotional, and other dispositional qualities in the child. Although it is common to assume that the biological foundations of temperament account for the stability of temperamental attributes over time, it is important to remember that these biological foundations are also developing systems whose maturation may change the nature or organization of temperament. The early months and years of life witness not only the budding of behavioral individuality, in other words, but also the rapid growth and consolidation of neurological, neuroendocrine, neocortical, and other biological systems on which temperament is based. As a consequence, the 3-year-old is biologically much different from the newborn, and these biological differences contribute to developmental changes in temperamental qualities. Emotional reactivity, for example, is manifested within the context of far more organized behavioral capabilities in the older child, and the self-control of a 3-year-old is greater than it is just after birth—but less than it will be at age 6—which further alters emotional reactivity (Eisenberg & Morris, 2002; Rothbart et al., 2006).

Furthermore, experiences can also modify biological functioning in ways that influence temperament. This is seen most clearly in how early experiences of social adversity heighten biological stress reactivity in young children, such as how neglectful or abusive care can alter cortisol levels and other aspects of biological stress responding, causing children to become more temperamentally wary and irritable (Ashman & Dawson, 2002; Wiik & Gunnar, 2009). Supportive relationships can buffer stress reactivity, however, as when children who are temperamentally reactive to threat or danger are able to respond in a physiologically more adaptive manner in the presence of a sensitive caregiver (Nachmias, Gunnar, Mangelsdorf, Parritz, & Buss, 1996). These examples illustrate the fundamental interaction of biology and experience in the growth of temperament and its developmental influences.

A second defining feature is that temperament is expected to be *relatively stable* over time. That is, individual differences in temperamental characteristics are stable: A child who is dispositionally more cheerful than peers in infancy should, as a preschooler, still be more cheerful than age-mates. We should not expect temperamental characteristics to be rigidly stable in developing persons, but they should show greater stability than do other behavioral attributes. Studying the stability of temperament over time poses theoretical as well as methodological challenges, however. Theoretically, under what circumstances are temperamental attributes likely to be stable over time, and when is discontinuity more likely? Are there developmental phases when temperament is more likely to be modifiable, for instance, and does the quality of an individual's transactions with the social environment, such as parent–child relationships, influence the stability of temperament? Are some individuals more susceptible to changes in temperament than others? We shall consider later in greater detail these theoretical issues.

Methodologically, temperamental characteristics are inferred from behavior, but a person's behavior changes substantially with development. Growth of this kind makes the study of stability or change in temperament a difficult task. An infant with a high activity level manifests this attribute quite differently from a comparable preschooler or adolescent, for example, and high activity level is also likely to mean different things to other people in that child's world (it may be an amusing characteristic to the parents of an infant, but an irritating attribute to a preschool teacher seeking to manage a group of children). Using developmentally appropriate indicators, it is tricky to assess the same temperamental characteristic in an individual over time, but the failure to do so can contribute to a misestimation of the stability of temperament.

Third, temperament *interacts with the environment* as an influence on development. Although it is common to think of temperament as having a direct and specific influence on developing capacities such as attachment, sociability, and adjustment, it is more often true that its influence is mediated by environmental characteristics, such as the demands and stresses of the child's home, the sensitivity and adaptability of social partners, and the manner in which temperament guides the child's choices of activities in the environment as well as interpretations of those experiences. Several studies have shown, for example, that the quality of parental care interacts with early temperament to shape later physiological and behavioral outcomes associated with temperament (Crockenberg, Leerkes, & Lekka, 2007; Porter, Wouden-Miller, Silva, & Porter, 2003; Sheese, Voelker, Rothbart, & Posner, 2007). This is true even for children with "difficult" temperaments, because the consequences of temperamental difficulty are mediated by the ways in which temperament can be expressed in social contexts (in constructive or inappropriate ways), the reactions of other people, and the values of the culture concerning normative behavior. The fact that temperament interacts with environmental influences should not be surprising because development is complex and is rarely guided by one or a few primary influences. Any temperamental attribute can yield diverse developmental trajectories depending on the context in which temperament is perceived and interpreted, and other influences on the same trajectories.

Temperament also interacts with the environment because of how temperament is construed in light of cultural values and beliefs (Bornstein, 1995). Differences in how children's characteristics are conceptualized arise from cultural variation in how particular temperamental characteristics are valued (Cole & Dennis, 1998; Cole & Packer, Chapter 3, this volume; Harwood, Miller, & Irizarry, 1995). Shy and inhibited behavior is viewed much differently, and is associated with different parenting practices, in North American and Chinese families, for example, with inhibition associated with warm, accepting parenting in traditional areas of China but with punitiveness in Canada (Chen et al., 1998). Likewise, Japanese mothers are reported to value levels of proximity-seeking and fussiness in their infants that US mothers find problematic or indicative of developmental problems (Rothbaum, Weisz, Pott, Miyake, & Morelli, 2000).

Dimensions of Temperament

Another way of answering the question "what is temperament?" is to identify the primary dimensions of temperament. In what ways is temperamental individuality typically expressed? Temperament theorists vary somewhat in their answers to this question (Goldsmith et al., 1987; Rothbart & Bates, 2006). To Thomas, Chess, and their colleagues—who emphasized that temperament defines the stylistic component (the "how") of behavior rather than the content (the "what") of behavior—temperament is expressed in characteristics such as the *rhythmicity* of biological functions, *approach* to or *withdrawal* from new stimuli, *adaptability, distractability, activity level, quality of mood, persistence* or *attention span, intensity of reaction,* and *sensory threshold of responsiveness* (Chess & Thomas, 1986; Thomas & Chess, 1977; Thomas, Chess, & Birch, 1968). To Rothbart and her colleagues, temperamental individuality includes broad dimensions such as *negative affectivity, surgency/extraversion*, and **effortful control** as well as specific temperament features such as *soothability* and *activity* (see Rothbart & Bates, 2006). Buss and Plomin (1984) portrayed temperament in terms of variability in three dimensions: *activity level, emotionality*, and *sociability*.

There are some common themes in these alternative conceptualizations of temperament (see Table 5.1). Each regards activity level as a distinctive temperamental quality (to Rothbart, as a component of surgency), primarily owing to its salience and its broad influence on behavior. Each views self-regulation as important to temperamental variability because of how differences in regulatory capacities influence behavior, attention, impulsivity, and emotional expression. In addition, variations in positive and negative emotionality figure prominently in each formulation. Indeed, Goldsmith and Campos (1982) defined temperament as individual differences in the expression of the primary emotions, such as happiness, sadness, distress, fear, and anger. It is interesting that emotionality is such an important part of how temperament is conceptualized because this feature of temperament reflects the centrality of emotion to the behavioral variability that we can observe in infants and young children, whose proneness to distress, soothability, and smiling and laughter are extremely important to caregivers. Of course, temperament is different from emotion because it is more multidimensional and more enduring than are transient emotional states, but it is unmistakable that both immediate

TABLE 5.1
Temperament Dimensions as Described by Developmental Temperament Researchers

Common Dimensions	Rothbart & Bates[1]	Thomas & Chess[2]	Buss & Plomin
Emotion[3]	*Negative affectivity* Frustration Fear Discomfort Sadness Soothability	*Quality of mood*	*Emotionality*
Self-regulation[4]	*Effortful control* Attentional control Inhibitory control Perceptual sensitivity Low-intensity pleasure	*Rhythmicity* Approach/Withdrawal Adaptability Distractability Persistence–Attention span Sensory threshold of responsiveness	
Activity level	*Extraversion/surgency* Activity Shyness (low) High-intensity pleasure Smiling & laughter Impulsivity Positive anticipation Affiliation	*Activity level* Intensity of reaction	*Activity level* Sociability

[1] Rothbart and Bates identify three broad temperament dimensions, along with specific features of temperament reflecting variability in each dimension.
[2] Thomas, Chess, and their colleagues believed that these specific dimensions of temperament could be integrated into three broad temperament types: "easy," "slow to warm up," and "difficult."
[3] Goldsmith and Campos (1982) proposed a theory of temperament that defined temperament as individual differences in the arousal and expression of the primary emotions.
[4] Kagan (2002) focuses on behavioral inhibition as a core temperament dimension, which reflects the self-regulatory features of temperament.

emotional expressions and the more enduring emotion-related features of temperament are salient features of early behavior.

Moreover, early temperamental distress proneness, soothability, and positive emotionality are also salient as developmental precursors to later personality features such as extraversion, agreeableness, neuroticism, conscientiousness, shyness, and aggressiveness. Indeed, the emotional features of early temperament make it easy to see the conceptual overlap between infancy/childhood temperament and the structure of adult personality, and this connection adds credence to the view that temperament constitutes an important foundation for personality development (Caspi & Shiner, 2006).

Emotional dispositions are also central to the conceptualization of temperamental "*difficulty*." Temperamental difficulty is a profile that includes predominantly negative mood, frequent and intense negative emotional behavior, irregularity, poor adaptability, and demandingness (Bates, 1980, 1987; Chess & Thomas, 1986; Thomas et al., 1968). (Its counterpart, *easy* temperament, is characterized by generally positive mood, soothability, regularity, and adaptability.) The concept of difficult temperament implies that particular constellations or profiles of temperamental attributes may be "greater than the sum of their parts" because they have a more significant impact on social relationships and behavioral adjustment than do individual dimensions taken alone. Consistent with the characteristics of difficultness, several researchers have found that infants with a difficult temperamental profile are more likely than others later in development to exhibit externalizing difficulties (such as aggression and conduct problems) and internalizing difficulties (such as anxiety) (Bates, Bayles, Bennett, Ridge, & Brown, 1991; Keily, Bates, Dodge, & Pettit, 2001; see Rothbart & Bates, 2006). These associations may occur because difficult temperament renders a child more vulnerable to later behavior problems, but they may also occur because temperamental difficulty influences the social relationships that also shape personality growth and the emergence of externalizing and internalizing difficulties.

A very different approach to temperamental difficulty, however, has been proposed by Belsky (Belsky, 2005; Belsky, Bakermans-Kranenburg, & van IJzendoorn, 2007), who argues that negative temperamental characteristics render children more susceptible to positive as well as negative environmental influences. This **differential susceptibility hypothesis** argues that the association of difficult temperament with later behavioral problems is not owing to continuity in intrinsic vulnerability, but because difficult children are more likely to be affected by negative environmental influences around them (such as frustrated parenting). However, research suggests that children with difficult temperament are also more susceptible to positive parenting influences than are children with easier temperamental qualities, suggesting that temperament may influence how much children are affected by the social environment (Gallagher, 2002). These processes require further study.

Another way of understanding temperamental profiles is to conceptualize temperament as revealing fundamental variability in *reactivity* and *self-regulation* (Rothbart & Bates, 2006; Rothbart, Ellis, & Posner, 2004). Reactive features of temperament reflect how easily a person becomes aroused to respond to events, and can be observed in the rate of onset, speed of escalation, persistence, and intensity of emotional reactions, as well as variability in activity level, attention span, and sensory threshold. Self-regulatory features of temperament are revealed in how reactivity is modulated, and can be observed in effortful control, inhibition of responding (as in soothability), orienting, and adaptability. One advantage of the conceptualization of temperament in terms of reactivity and self-regulation is that it mirrors the dynamic interaction between excitatory and inhibitory nervous system processes, and thus better enables researchers to map the psychobiological components of temperamental individuality (Kagan & Fox, 2006; Rothbart & Bates, 2006; Rothbart et al., 2004). This approach also enables theorists to see the range of temperamental attributes in terms of two broad aspects of behavioral responding that characterize people throughout life, because individual differences in reactivity and self-regulation remain important throughout the life course.

Different theoretical views of the dimensions of temperament have methodological implications, of course. Temperament can be measured in various ways, but each approach has interpretive problems as well as advantages (Bates, 1987; Rothbart & Goldsmith, 1985). Parents are likely to have considerable insight into the temperamental attributes of offspring because of their long-term knowledge of the child's behavior in many different circumstances, and parent-report temperament questionnaires are inexpensive and convenient to use. But parents may be biased informants in various ways: Their relationships with offspring, their personality characteristics, and their efforts to present their children (and themselves) in a positive light can each skew temperament reports. There is currently vigorous debate concerning the suitability of using parent-report temperament questionnaires and the extent to which these measures can be made more valid (compare Kagan & Fox, 2006, with Rothbart & Bates, 2006).

Laboratory and naturalistic observations of temperament-related behavior in children have their own strengths and weaknesses. Direct observations by unacquainted observers are more objective, and laboratory studies enable researchers to control more precisely the conditions in which children are studied. But observational approaches are expensive and time-consuming, are limited (by practical and ethical considerations) in the range of circumstances in which children are studied, and cannot easily enable repeated assessments in different situations of the same temperamental attributes (comparable to how parent-report measures index temperamental variability over a range of situations). The result may be a comparatively distorted or incomplete portrayal of temperament. Consequently, some researchers recommend a multimethod strategy in which parent-report and observational assessments of temperament are used convergently and in which the unique and shared variance of each measure can be studied (see Bornstein, Gaughran, & Segui, 1991, and Kochanska, 1995, for illustrations of such a strategy).

Stability of Temperamental Qualities, and Prediction of Later Behavior

Is it true that we see in temperament the foundations of later personality? Or are temperamental attributes observed early in life rather pliable and changing over time? Embedded within these superficially straightforward questions are more difficult queries (see Bornstein, 1998, for a thoughtful discussion of different meanings of stability and continuity in behavior). Can the same temperamental attribute be measured at different ages using age-appropriate measures? If so, is there a strong association between comparable measures of temperament at each age (i.e., does a child rank similarly among peers on the same temperamental quality at different ages)? Does temperament at an earlier age predict other relevant later behavior, such as personality attributes, in the same person? If so, does the strength of prediction depend on the age at which temperament is initially assessed?

The answers to these questions depend, not surprisingly, on the specific temperament dimensions of interest, along with other developmental considerations (see Caspi & Shiner, 2006, Rothbart & Bates, 2006, and Shiner & Caspi, 2003, for reviews of this research in which the following account is based). Several general conclusions seem warranted.

First, measures of temperament obtained neonatally or in the initial months of life are only weakly or inconsistently associated with later assessments of the same temperament dimensions. This is true, for example, of distress proneness, activity level, and attention. The instability of individual differences in these dimensions of temperament should not be surprising in view of how significantly the infant is changing during the first year as psychobiological systems progressively mature. The generalized distress response of the newborn gradually becomes more differentiated to distinguish anger/frustration and fear, for example, as the infant's appraisal capacities and neurophysiological systems mature (Buss & Goldsmith, 1998). Later in the first year, inhibition begins to appear (illustrated in the wariness that 9-month-olds often show to a stranger) that further alters the child's negative reactivity, and may also affect activity level (Thompson & Limber, 1990). At the same time, neocortical maturation underlies changes in attentional processes that result in greater voluntary control over visual attention and changes in temperamental qualities such as attention span (Rothbart et al., 2004). Taken together, the rapid pace of developmental change in the first year means that the biological systems that express temperament are themselves changing, and these changes likely contribute to the instability of individual differences in temperament during this period. A temperamental characteristic such as attention span is a psychobiologically more mature behavior in a 3-year-old than in a 6-month-old, and the developing neuro-biological, perceptual, and cognitive systems associated with temperament likely reorganize developing individuality.

Second, greater short-term stability in certain temperament dimensions begins to be observed after the first year, and sometimes earlier. Characteristics such as **behavioral inhibition**, positive emotionality, effortful control, and even activity level show moderate stability in repeated assessments over periods of several months or sometimes years when they are carefully measured in age-appropriate ways (or based on parent reports using developmentally appropriate questions). Moreover, these early assessments of temperament sometimes predict later personality characteristics. Kagan, Snidman, Kahn, and Townsley (2007) found, for example, that groups of infants who were distinguished by their emotional reactions to novelty were also different in adolescence: Infants who were highly reactive, for example, were found to be dour and anxious about the future as adolescents. In another study, Bosquet and Egeland (2006) provided a description of how these kinds of long-term influences may occur through the ways that early temperament contributes to a developmental cascade of intervening influences leading to adolescent anxious symptomatology. In their study, early differences in reactivity and regulation predicted emotion regulation problems in preschool that foreshadowed, in turn, childhood anxiety problems in a cumulation of emotional risks over time. However, associations between temperament assessments and long-term behavioral outcomes are weaker or inconsistent in most other studies, suggesting that aspects of developing individuality remain fairly pliable across childhood. In many respects, developing individuality has not yet become consolidated.

Third, there is increasing evidence for longer-term associations between temperament and later behavior after the second year of life. Sometimes these long-term associations are quite impressive. In a sample of over 800 children in New Zealand studied every 2 years from early childhood to young adulthood, Caspi and his colleagues have found significant associations between temperamental qualities at age 3 and personality traits at ages 21 and 26 (Caspi et al., 2003; Newman, Caspi, Silva, & Moffitt, 1997; see also Caspi & Silva, 1995). Young children who were temperamentally "undercontrolled" (impulsive, irritable, distractable) were more likely to show externalizing behavioral problems in adolescence and lower levels of adjustment and greater interpersonal conflict in early adulthood. By contrast, young children who were temperamentally inhibited were, as young adults, more likely to be rated as cautious and restrained but showed adequate adjustment. These impressive consistencies in individual characteristics indicate that childhood temperament can have long-term correlates in later personality growth. Not all studies show such strong continuities, however, and such findings are not apparent for all children (see, e.g., Pfeifer, Goldsmith, Davidson, & Rickman, 2002). Considerably more research is required to discover why these continuities between temperament and later personality exist for some children, but not for others. Some theoretical proposals are presented in the next section.

Why does temperament have greater predictive power after infancy? One reason may be that some of the psychobiological foundations of temperament have become consolidated (although many continue to mature throughout childhood) and are having enduring influences on personality development. Once many of the core neurobehavioral bases of temperament have become organized during the early years, in other words, temperamental individuality is expressed more consistently. Another reason may be that other concurrent developmental processes help to consolidate temperamental individuality after infancy. As we shall see, the preschooler is an increasingly self-aware, intentional child who is developing a more complex self-image and whose choices of friends, activities, and settings are guided, in part, by an emerging sense of self. That sense of self is likely to be grounded in temperamental individuality. For instance, young children who begin to perceive themselves as more shy will choose friends with similar characteristics, participate in certain activities (such as dyadic play) in which they feel comfortable in preference to other activities requiring leadership or public performance, and become increasingly perceived by others in ways that are consistent with their self-perception as shy or inhibited. Because this sense of self is influenced by temperamental characteristics, it may contribute to the integration of temperamental characteristics with the development of personality and the consolidation of behavioral individuality in the years to come. Finally, the perceptions of others are also important contributors to the consolidation of temperamental individuality. By the time a young child reaches the toddler and preschool years, caregivers, childcare teachers, peers, siblings, and others have likely developed stable perceptions of what the child is like that influence how they respond to her or him. In doing so, they help to reinforce and consolidate the behavioral characteristics they perceive.

Taken together, temperament research shows that the stability of temperament, and its prediction to later behavioral attributes, is contingent. Some researchers believe that temperament is more likely to be stable within, but not between, major periods of developmental change and reorganization, such as the transition from infancy to early childhood (Goldsmith et al., 1987). Others argue that temperament will become increasingly stable, and predictive, with increasing age because of the ways that developing self-understanding, social awareness, intentionality, social comparison, and other changes make children increasingly aware of their individual characteristics and capable of acting on this realization (Caspi & Silva, 1995; Shiner & Caspi, 2003). These two views are not, of course, inconsistent approaches, and each helps to explain why early temperament is sometimes not very predictive of later individuality. Despite this, theorists concur, temperament becomes a foundation for personality as temperamental attributes become developmentally consolidated and incorporated into a stable personality structure.

Temperament and Development

Temperamental dispositions do not always foreshadow later personality. Sometimes change rather than continuity over time is more apparent. Understanding why this is so requires appreciating the dynamic interaction of temperamental characteristics with other developmental influences in personality growth, particularly from the social environment, and how this interaction shapes behavioral individuality. Temperament researchers have several ways of portraying this developmentally interactive process.

First, a child's temperamental profile may mesh well, or poorly, with the requirements and opportunities of the child's social setting. Consequently, the influence of temperament on personality or adjustment depends on the "goodness of fit" between temperament and environmental demands. Chess and Thomas (1986; Thomas & Chess, 1977) originated this concept in describing the developmental outcomes of difficult temperament. As they argued, temperamental difficulty need not contribute to later behavior problems if the social and physical environment is accommodated to the child's needs and characteristics. When parents are tolerant and understanding, for example, and opportunities for constructively channeling temperamental qualities are provided (e.g., frequent flexible self-chosen options rather than no choices in activities), difficult temperament can lead to more positive, adaptive personality attributes. By contrast, even children who are temperamentally easy will likely develop behavioral problems if they live in settings where demands are excessive and developmentally inappropriate, and partners are cold and insensitive. The same process of environmental "match" or "mismatch" applies to other temperamental attributes, such as activity level, negative or positive emotionality, or attention span. In each case, the accommodation of the environment to the child's unique characteristics foreshadows better adjustment than the failure of social partners to recognize and adapt to the child's temperamentally based needs. This is one of the reasons why sensitive, responsive parenting is such an important predictor of positive personality outcomes in children and a buffer of the negative effects of early poor adjustment (Thompson, 2006a).

It is important to remember, however, that a child's environment changes significantly over time in ways that can also influence temperament–environment goodness-of-fit. As children mature, for example, parents, teachers, and other adults increasingly expect more competent, self-controlled behavior, children enter into settings (such as preschool and school) that require compliance, initiative, and cooperation, and children increasingly participate with adults in circumstances (such as church, concerts, and other events) in which they must understand and enact socially appropriate behavior. Environmental expectations thus become less flexible and less amenable to some children's temperamental profiles over time, consistently with the normative expectations of the culture (Bornstein, 1995). These changes in social expectations may also include divergent expectations for gender-appropriate conduct, such that boys and girls find environmental demands differentially amenable to their behavioral styles. As a consequence, a particular temperamental profile may fit well with environmental demands and opportunities at one age (e.g., low persistence or attention span in infancy), but provide a poor fit later (e.g., the same characteristics during the school years). In this way, the temperament–environment match is a developmentally dynamic one, and this dynamic is likely to influence the stability of temperamental attributes over time as well as their relations to later personality.

Second, a child's temperamental profile may influence how the child interacts with people and settings. This can occur in several ways (Scarr & McCartney, 1983; Shiner & Caspi, 2003). For one, a child's behavioral style may *evoke* certain reactions from others, such as how a child with a temperamentally sunny disposition naturally elicits smiles and interest from peers and adults. These positive social reactions are likely, in turn, to influence the child's development and the growth of personality attributes (such as sociability) much differently from the reactions evoked by a child with a more negative temperamental profile. For another, a child's behavioral style may guide that person's *preferences* for partners, settings, and activities. For example, someone with a high activity level is more likely to participate in sports with other active people than a person with a low activity level for whom more sedentary activities and partners are more comfortable. These choices also influence development because they channel the range of opportunities and challenges that children are likely to encounter to those that accord with their dispositional characteristics. Furthermore, children's behavioral styles may influence how they *alter* their social environments. For example, a child with a difficult temperamental profile may have a stronger influence on other people than a child with a more inhibited or adaptable style.

Over time, of course, children and youth become progressively more capable of choosing their partners and settings to harmonize with their personal preferences. By the time of adulthood they can often create lifestyles that are consistent with their personality styles in the choices they have made of marital partner, occupation, residence, hobbies, and other activities. This is one reason, therefore, that temperamental and personality dispositions tend to become more consolidated over time: People increasingly choose partners and create lifestyles with characteristics that are compatible with their own. However, many people are incapable of exercising this kind of choice, especially when they encounter unexpected misfortune or have limited resources or options (such as in poverty) with which to exercise choice. In these circumstances, especially when the environmental demands are out of sync with temperamental attributes, we might expect poorer adjustment (and less stability in personality attributes) because of the difficulties presented by a mismatched, unaccommodating, or unexpectedly changing environment.

Third, a child's temperamental profile may influence how that person perceives, experiences, interprets, and thinks about life events (Rothbart & Bates, 2006; Shiner & Caspi, 2003; Wachs & Gandour, 1983). This can begin quite early. A 1-year-old with a positive, outgoing disposition is likely to regard the approach of an unfamiliar but friendly adult much differently than a temperamentally inhibited infant, and will feel greater interest and curiosity (rather than fear) when encountering a new setting (such as a peer's playroom). Children's different responses in these and similar circumstances may have broader consequences for the growth of social skills, the emergence of peer relationships, and intellectual development. Temperament may also be an important influence on how a child interprets and responds to the parent. Kochanska (1993, 1995) argues, for example, that **conscience** develops differently for young children who differ in temperamental fearfulness. Conscience develops best for temperamentally fearful children when their mothers use gentle, nonassertive discipline practices in a manner that avoids overstressing their offspring. By contrast, for temperamentally non-fearful children conscience is best predicted by a secure attachment to the mother and the positive, shared partnership it helps to create between them. Temperamental qualities cause the two types of young children to perceive and respond to their mothers' discipline practices in different ways. It is also possible that temperament influences thinking and information processing more broadly, especially in light of the importance of emotion and attentional persistence to an individual's capacities to concentrate, remember, and reason competently at all ages.

Temperament is likely to interact with environmental influences in other ways as well. Temperamental qualities may enhance a person's vulnerability to intrinsic or extrinsic stressors and, in doing so, contribute to the development of maladjustment or dysfunction. Alternatively, temperamental attributes may provide buffers against the stressors that might occur by strengthening resiliency, such as that provided by positive mood, adaptability, and greater self-regulation (Rothbart & Bates, 2006). Or temperament may enhance or diminish a person's sensitivity to all kinds of environmental influences, whether positive or negative (Belsky, 2005; Belsky et al., 2007). In each of these profiles of temperament–environment interactions, it is clear that the developmental trajectories yielded by a particular temperamental profile depend not only on temperamental attributes, but also on the nature of environmental demands and opportunities. In a sense, these formulations converge on the conclusion that temperament causes people to experience the world in distinct ways (Wachs, 1992).

Temperament: Conclusion and Future Directions

Contemporary research on temperament offers conclusions that differ markedly from traditional portrayals. By contrast with traditional formulations that temperament emerges early, is highly consistent across situations and over time because of its psychobiological origins, and is directly tied to the growth of personality, current research underscores that temperament is a biologically based but developmentally evolving feature of behavior. For this reason, temperamental attributes become increasingly more consistent over time as temperamental individuality is enveloped into the network of self-perceptions, behavioral preferences, and social experiences that together shape developing personality. Moreover, contemporary research shows that, although temperament may have direct effects on behavior and development, temperament more commonly interacts with environmental influences to shape development in complex ways.

These conclusions remind us of the complexity of human development and of the multifaceted ways that temperament influences emergent individuality. They also help to explain why we commonly consider infant or child temperament, but rarely conceive of adult temperament. By adulthood, personality has fully developed to include many features of self-understanding, social dispositions, behavioral style, attributional processes, and other facets that incorporate, elaborate, and extend initial temperamental dispositions.

Future directions in temperamental research will be enlivened by methodological advances, particularly in the field of molecular genetics, which enables researchers to identify specific gene polymorphisms and study how their behavioral correlates interact with environmental characteristics. Just as temperamental research has underscored the importance of temperament–environment transactions in behavioral development, molecular genetics is highlighting the pervasiveness of gene–environment interactions. As a practical illustration, researchers found that a program designed to improve maternal sensitivity to young children with behavioral problems worked best for children with a gene polymorphism (DRD4 7-repeat) that is associated with problem behavior, aggression, and hyperactivity (Bakermans-Kranenburg, van IJzendoorn, Pijilman, Mesman, & Juffer, 2008). Genetic vulnerability in the child interacted with the environmental intervention to alter behavioral outcomes for young children (see Figure 5.1). Molecular genetics research will also play a role in studying the effects of gene–gene interactions on behavioral development, which are likely to be especially important for complex behaviors such as temperament. The influence of one gene may depend on the presence or absence of another gene or genes (Ebstein et al., 2000; see Lakatos et al., 2003, for an example), and better understanding of these interactions will contribute to understanding genetic and environmental risk processes.

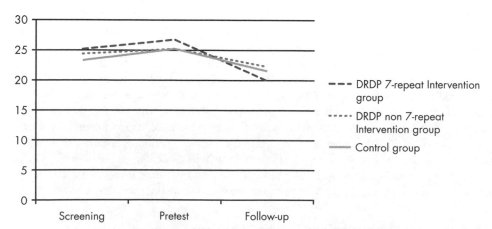

FIGURE 5.1   Summary of findings from Bakermans-Kranenburg et al. (2008), illustrating the interaction of genes (i.e., the DRD4 7-repeat gene polymorphism, associated with problem behavior and hyperactivity) and environment (i.e., a program designed to improve maternal sensitivity) in children's behavior (represented by arbitrary units on the y-axis) at the follow-up assessment. Children with the DRD4 7-repeat polymorphism responded more positively to the program than did children without the polymorphism, or children in the control group.

Current researchers are also devoting considerable attention to the interactive and mediated influences of temperamental processes on development. For example, early temperamental vulnerability interacts with harsh parenting in the development of conduct disorders in young children (see Owens & Shaw, 2003; Shaw, Miles, Ingoldsby, & Nagin, 2003). This highlights one of the important applications of temperamental theory and research to the field of developmental psychopathology as researchers are better understanding how temperamental individuality confers unique vulnerabilities, and strengths, on children in their encounters with supportive or stressful social environments. In all, this means that one can no longer append a parent-report temperament measure to a research design and, by doing so, create a temperament study. Instead, contemporary developmental research on temperament is examining theoretically sophisticated questions based on temperament theory using multiple methods that are well suited to the developmental samples and questions under study.

EMOTION

Emotions also shape our experience of the world, and they exercise a pervasive influence throughout the life span. By contrast with temperamental variability, however, the effects of emotional reactions can be enduring or brief, transcontextual or situationally specific. Moreover, emotional experience changes considerably with development and includes a rich variety of basic and complex feelings that far surpass the range of temperamental variability in mood. Emotions are also complexly tied to other developmental processes. Emotional development is associated with psychobiological maturation, self-understanding and the understanding of others, the child's growing capacities to appraise people and environments, social interaction and self-control, and the awareness of social rules and social conventions.

We take for granted that emotions are part of everyday life. But consider how much emotional experience changes over the life course. It is easy to see in infancy the extremes of emotional arousal, from raucous crying to exuberant delight, that are minimally regulated by the child and sometimes uncontrollable except through the sensitive intervention of caregivers. In infants the raw, basic experience of emotion is readily apparent, but the infant is also sensitive to the emotions of others and strives to comprehend their meaning. For the preschooler, basic emotions that have been present from early in life have become supplemented by self-conscious emotions, such as pride, guilt, shame, and embarrassment, that reflect evaluations of the self (see Table 5.2). Emotional experiences are also thought about, discussed with parents and peers, and frequently enacted in sociodramatic play. The preschooler is more self-aware emotionally and has begun to understand the causes and consequences of emotional experiences and the influence of emotions on social interaction.

By middle childhood, children have become more reflective and strategic in their emotional lives. Emotions can be more effectively regulated through cognitive means (such as using distracting thoughts) as well as behavioral strategies (such as fleeing a distressing situation), and emotions can be intentionally hidden through display rules that dissemble genuine feelings. But children of this age are also capable of genuine empathy and greater emotional understanding than ever before. In adolescence, it appears as if the emotional swings of infancy have reappeared, but the emoter is now a psychologically more complex individual who reflects on the unique origins of personal emotional experience, is acutely sensitive to the psychological bases of emotion in others (especially peers), and can feel strongly in response to symbolic (e.g., music, narrative) as well as direct elicitors of emotion.

Does emotional development continue into adulthood? Yes, but the character of its development changes. Rather than witnessing the unfolding of new, psychologically more complex emotional experiences, adults often seek to create personal lifestyles that are emotionally

TABLE 5.2
Basic and Self-Conscious Emotions in Development

	Basic Emotions	Self-conscious Emotions
Examples	• Happiness • Sadness • Fear • Interest • Anger • Disgust • Surprise	• Pride • Guilt • Shame • Embarrassment
Origins	Biologically deeply rooted in the human species	Arousal depends on social values and expectations
Universal?	Strongest evidence that these are universal for humans	Unclear whether self-conscious emotions are all culturally universal
Development	Appear at birth or early in infancy	Develop late in the second and the third year of life

Sources: Izard (1991), Izard & Ackerman (2000), Lewis & Michalson (1983).

satisfying, predictable, and manageable through their choices of occupation, partners, and other activities. In other words, adults strive to construct their lives to incorporate emotional experiences that are personally desirable, and this strategy may include career choices that promise the satisfactions and challenges of productive labor, personal choices such as making (and breaking) marital ties and the pleasures (and turmoil) of childrearing, and leisure choices that offer the excitement of musical, artistic, athletic, or other creative pursuits. Of course, not all succeed in doing so, especially when their economic conditions do not permit much choice in life decisions. Adults also become skillful at managing the expression of their personal feelings to accord with their social circumstances and personal goals. Although new capacities for emotion may emerge (e.g., poignancy), the theme of emotional development in adulthood is the adaptive integration of emotional experience into satisfying daily life and successful relationships with others. This is one reason why adults seem emotionally more stable and predictable—and, sometimes, less animated—than children or adolescents.

This developmental survey not only underscores the changing tapestry of emotional experience, but also highlights the relation between emotional development and the growth of personality. At each stage of life, new capacities for emotional experience, expression, and understanding contribute to personality development as they help to organize and express developing individuality. In this respect, emotional growth is an important part of the growth of personality from infancy through later life. Furthermore, in tracing the influence of emotion in development, it is increasingly clear that emotional development is shaped by cultural beliefs about emotion. From parents' reactions to their infants' emotional displays to everyday views of what constitutes mature emotionality in adulthood, cultural values influence the salience of particular emotions, the significance accorded emotional life, and the specific ways that emotion influences personality development.

Defining Emotion

But what is emotion? The question almost begs an answer because of the ubiquity of emotion in everyday experience. Each person is intimately acquainted with the visceral reactions (rapid heart rate, sweaty palms), subjective experience (inability to concentrate, infusion or depletion of energy), cognitive appraisals (of threat, the unexpected, goal achievement), facial expressions, and other familiar constituents of emotions that we linguistically demarcate as fear, anger, joy, distress, guilt, or other feelings.

Our common-sense view is that emotions are organized categorically because our subjective, physiological, and cognitive experiences of emotions, such as sadness, anger, disgust, and joy, are so different. This view has deep roots within developmental emotions research (see, for example, Izard, 1991; Izard & Ackerman, 2000; Lewis & Michalson, 1983). But this view has been increasingly questioned. Researchers examining emotion in different cultures point out that the manner in which we commonly conceptualize different emotions reflects the linguistic distinctions of English-speaking people and are different for people from different cultural and linguistic systems (Lutz, 1988). Others argue that our emotional lives are constituted not by a succession of qualitatively distinct emotions but rather by subtly nuanced blends of a broad variety of emotional states that range in dynamic and intensive qualities according to our interactions with the surrounding world (Thompson, 1990).

As a result, most emotion theorists have adopted a **functionalist approach** (Saarni, Campos, Camras, & Witherington, 2006) that emphasizes the role of emotion in goal attainment in everyday experience, as reflected in the following definition: "Emotion is thus the person's attempt or readiness to establish, maintain, or change the relation between the person and his or her changing circumstances, on matters of significance to that person" (Saarni et al., 2006, p. 227). By defining emotion in very broad terms of person–environment transactions that matter to the person, emotion is associated with goal-attainment, as well as with social relationships, situational appraisals, action tendencies, self-understanding, self-regulation, and a variety of other developmentally changing processes. The range of emotion is not confined to a specific set of categories defined by their linguistic delineation (although functionalist theorists talk of "emotion families" that share common characteristics), but is considerably broader because of how emotion is conceptualized in different social and cultural groups based on the nature of typical person–environment transactions. The definition of emotion is thus more open-ended in functionalist accounts. To be sure, the openness in how emotion is regarded from a functionalist perspective introduces considerably greater ambiguity into theory and research on emotional growth (e.g., are hunger, effort, arrogance, and indifference also emotions?), and it is unclear what (if any) features distinguish emotion from other motivational states or from personality processes. But by linking emotion to an individual's goals, developmental researchers have found the functionalist perspective valuable for understanding emotional development in the context of the increasingly complex, sophisticated interactions of the child with a changing social world.

What is Emotional Development the Development of?

We can easily observe the changes that occur in emotion with increasing age. A toddler rages at the collapse of a block tower while an adult purses his lips while figuring out alternative ways around a blocked goal. But what accounts for growth in emotionality? Emotional development incorporates many features of psychological growth, making this topic an especially integrative field of study (Denham, 1998). These include the psychobiological foundations of emotion, developing capacities for perceiving emotion in others, emotional understanding, the development of empathy, the growth of self-understanding, mastery of emotional display rules, and developing capacities for emotion regulation. The story of emotional development is how these different features of emotion mature and become integrated in shaping emotional experience and its expression.

Neurobiological foundations. In light of the preceding discussion of the psychobiological foundations of temperament, it is unsurprising that emotional development is also based on neurophysiological, neuroendocrine, and other biological processes that change rapidly in infancy and childhood (LeDoux, 2000; Panksepp, 1998). As a biologically ancient feature of human functioning, emotion is rooted in primitive regions of the brain such as the limbic system, especially the amygdale, which is often regarded as the "emotion center" of the brain (Johnson, 2010). But because it is involved in the most complex aspects of human behavior, emotion is also guided by some of the most sophisticated regions of the cerebral cortex, especially the evolutionarily newer prefrontal cortex (Davidson, Fox, & Kalin, 2007). Moreover, emotional reactions are also influenced by hormones and **neurotransmitters** regulated by a variety of brain areas (Gunnar & Vasquez, 2006). This makes an apparently simple emotional reaction a surprisingly complex psychobiological event, and there are significant developmental changes in these neurobiological processes that affect emotional behavior. For example, the unpredictable swings of arousal of the neonate become progressively more modulated and controllable in infancy as maturational advances occur in adrenocortical activation and in parasympathetic regulation (Gunnar & Davis, 2003; Porges et al., 1994). With later developing functional connections between subcortical and frontal systems regulating emotion, furthermore, enhanced capacities for emotion regulation emerge in the childhood years (Lewis & Todd, 2007; Ochsner & Gross, 2007).

Emotion perception.   Another important facet of emotional development is the capacity to accurately perceive emotion in others. This is an early emerging phenomenon: Even 5-month-olds can discriminate and categorize facial expressions of smiling (Bornstein & Arterberry, 2003). By the end of the first year and early in the second, infants have become capable of discerning the emotional meaning underlying many adult facial and vocal expressions and of incorporating this meaning into their interpretation of the adult's behavior in a phenomenon called "social referencing" (Saarni et al., 2006). When an infant encounters an unfamiliar person or object, for instance, the sight of the adult's reassuring smile or terrified look (especially if it is accompanied by appropriate vocalizations and other behavior) influences the child's tendency to approach or withdraw. The baby appropriately "reads" the meaning of the adult's emotional expression and its relevance to the unfamiliar event. In later months, this basic capacity for accurate perception of emotional signals is supplemented by a more acute awareness of the meaning of the emotional signal. By the end of the second year, for example, toddlers seem to be more consciously aware of the subjectivity of emotional experience: Another person can feel differently than oneself (Repacholi & Gopnik, 1997). As a consequence, parents begin to witness their toddlers intervening in the emotions of others by comforting a distressed peer or teasing a sibling.

Emotional understanding.   With further conceptual growth, understanding of emotion becomes incorporated into young children's broader knowledge about the psychological states of others. Consistent with the expansion of their naive "theory of mind," for example, 2- to 3-year-olds understand that emotion is associated with the fulfillment of desires, and 4- to 5-year-olds appreciate the more complex linkages between emotions and thoughts, beliefs, and expectations (Bartsch & Wellman, 1995; Thompson & Lagattuta, 2006; Wellman, 2002). This broadening psychological understanding richly expands children's conceptualization of emotion because it enables young children to appreciate how emotion is linked to the satisfaction or frustration of desires (which vary in different people) and to beliefs (which may be incorrect, such as the child who mistakenly thinks that her lunch bag contains a delectable dessert when in fact her father forgot to include it).

In middle childhood, children begin to conceive of emotional processes, such as how emotional intensity gradually dissipates over time, how specific emotions are related to antecedent causes, and how personal background, experiences, and personality can yield unique emotional reactions (see review by Thompson, 1990). Somewhat later, by about age 9 or 10, children begin to understand how multiple emotions can be simultaneously evoked by the same event, such as feeling happy and scared when performing before a group (Donaldson & Westerman, 1986). Later, adolescents better appreciate the complex psychological causes of emotion in relational experience, self-reflection, and existential concerns (Harter, 2006; Harter & Monsour, 1992). It is easy to see how these advances in emotional understanding are relevant to children's growing self-awareness and to the growth of personality because of how they offer insight into experiences of ambivalence, emotional self-control (and lacking emotional control), relationships, and psychological conflict.

The development of emotion understanding also reflects the influences of cultural beliefs about emotion. Because of how emotions are perceived and interpreted to young children by parents and others, children from different cultures derive different understandings of the antecedent causes of emotion and the appropriate emotions to experience and express in different social situations. Cole and her colleagues, for example, have identified cultural differences in children's understanding of appropriate emotional responses to difficult inter-personal situations, such as whether negative emotions should be revealed and whether shame or anger is an acceptable response, consistent with broader differences in interpersonal beliefs between individualist and collectivist cultures (Cole & Tamang, 1998; Cole & Tan, 2007). Emotion understanding is thus shaped by both the local (e.g., familial) and the broader (e.g., cultural) contexts in which children live.

By what processes do children acquire this expanding understanding of emotion? Along with the influences of developing intellectual capacities and social experience (especially with peers), researchers note that everyday conversations between young children and their parents provide potent opportunities to learn about emotion (Lagattuta & Wellman, 2002; Thompson, 2006b; Thompson, Laible, & Ontai, 2003). This is especially so in cultures that accord significance to discussing emotional experiences. As children begin to share their experiences and observations with caregivers in simple accounts (beginning almost from the time they can talk), parents elaborate, inquire, interpret, and otherwise clarify the child's accounts in ways that contribute to the growth of emotional understanding (Denham, 1998; Dunn, 1994; Thompson, 2006b). Thus when a young preschooler observes his older sister arriving home from school in tears, his inquiry about why this was so can provide a conversational forum for learning about emotion and its causes. In acting thus, of course, adults not only clarify but also socialize emotional knowledge, conveying expectations about appropriate emotional behavior and the causes and consequences of emotional displays (Thompson et al., 2003; Thompson & Meyer, 2007).

In this way, norms and expectations concerning emotion are explicitly communicated to children through conversation. However, the messages that children receive about the causes of emotion, the consequences of emotional displays, and the value of particular emotions depend on both cultural context and the personal characteristics of the child. For example, Fivush's (1994, 1998) research indicates that lessons about emotion differ based on the gender of the child. With girls, parents discuss more sadness than anger, attribute emotions to social-relational causes (e.g., sadness is caused when someone else is hurt), and resolve negative emotions through reassurance and reconciliation. Parents conversing with boys discuss anger more often than sadness, attribute emotions to autonomous causes (e.g., sadness is caused by losing a toy), and are less likely to discuss resolution of negative emotions. Cultural differences also exist in emotion-related beliefs and in parents' inclusion of emotion in conversation, which alters the opportunities for children to learn about emotion in this manner. Mullen and Yi (1995), for example, found that in conversation about past events with their 3-year-old children, US mothers referred to their child's and others' thoughts and feelings nearly twice as often as Korean mothers.

Empathy and emotional contagion.   The growth of emotion perception and emotional understanding also enhances the child's vicarious sensitivity to the emotions of others. Young infants often respond resonantly to the emotions they perceive in others—fussing when they hear another person crying, for instance (Sagi & Hoffman, 1976)—but these early episodes of emotional contagion are not truly empathic because the baby has no real comprehension of the circumstances provoking another's feelings. With the rapid growth in emotional understanding that occurs in early childhood, however, young children can respond with genuine empathy (as well as a variety of other emotional reactions) to another's anguish. In everyday circumstances as well as in experimental contexts, toddlers are observed to react with concerned attention to the sight and sound of the mother's distress (Zahn-Waxler, 2000; Zahn-Waxler & Radke-Yarrow, 1990), and empathic responses increase in sophistication and scope in the years that follow. Early empathic responding is sometimes (although not consistently) accompanied by prosocial initiatives, such as efforts to comfort the distressed person, but with increasing age empathy becomes somewhat more reliably associated with helping behavior as well as with other prosocial initiatives, although empathy remains motivationally complex (Eisenberg, Spinrad, & Sadovsky, 2006). Taken together, the growth of empathy reflects children's developing affective as well as cognitive awareness of the emotional experiences of others, as well as the changing role of interpersonal emotion in social relationships.

Emotion and the growth of self-understanding.   Emotional growth is also closely tied to the development of self-understanding, which we consider in greater detail in the section that follows. A major advance in emotional growth occurs during the late second and third years of life, when young children become more physically and psychologically self-aware (reflected in verbal self-references and efforts to "do it myself") and, at the same time, show emerging reactions of pride, guilt, shame, embarrassment, and other self-conscious emotions (Lagattuta & Thompson, 2007; Thompson, 2006a). Thus, the simple joy of success becomes accompanied by looking and smiling to an adult and calling attention to the feat (pride), and in response to conspicuous attention toddlers increasingly respond with smiling, gaze aversion, and self-touching (embarrassment). These responses reflect new emotional capacities built on new forms of self-awareness.

The emergence of self-conscious evaluative emotions such as pride and shame during the third year depends not only on the growth of self-awareness, however, but also on young children's appreciation of standards of conduct and the ability to apply those standards to an evaluation of their own behavior (Thompson, Meyer, & McGinley, 2006). Feelings of pride derive from the realization of an accomplishment that is personally meaningful, and likewise guilt is elicited when one violates a significant standard of conduct. The capacities to understand behavioral standards and apply them personally are slowly developing, and young children initially rely on parental evaluations as the basis for their feelings of pride, guilt, or shame in their behavior (Stipek, 1995). Indeed, it is common to find young preschoolers checking back regularly with the parent as they work on a challenging task or are engaged in misbehavior, and the adult's subsequent emotional response—combined with verbal comments underscoring the evaluative standard ("You worked hard at that puzzle!")—significantly shapes the child's own.

In this regard, therefore, the development of self-conscious emotions such as pride, shame, and guilt has a complex connection to the growth of self-understanding. These emotional capacities depend on a young child's self-awareness, but the circumstances in which they are elicited provide important cues to the child concerning self-worth and its association with the child's fidelity to specific standards of achievement or morality. Furthermore, the importance of these evaluative standards to the child, and the feelings associated with compliance or misbehavior, are also tied to the warmth and security of the parent–child relationship (Thompson, 2006a, 2008). These themes are considered in greater detail below.

Understanding and use of display rules. Emotions are intrinsically social, and one aspect of emotional development is understanding and applying social rules for the display of emotion in social settings (see Table 5.3). A person is supposed to show delight when opening a gift, even if it is undesirable (especially in the presence of the gift-giver), and one is not supposed to laugh at a defeated opponent or at someone who takes an unexpected spill on a slippery sidewalk. People use emotional "display rules" to mask the expression of true feelings with a more appropriate emotional expression to protect self-esteem, avoid hurting others' feelings, and preserve relationships. Young children clearly do not fully share this awareness, which is why they commonly reject undesirable gifts and act in other socially inappropriate ways. Although they begin to manage their emotional expressions to protect the feelings of others as young as age 4 (Banerjee, 1997; Cole, 1986), it is not until they reach middle childhood that they can conceptualize the meaning of emotional display rules and their purposes (Jones, Abbey, & Cumberland, 1998; Saarni, 1999). Their grasp of the meaning, application, and importance of display rules for emotional behavior increases significantly in the years that follow. As it does so, children make a remarkable discovery: Emotional appearance is not necessarily emotional reality. What others show is not necessarily what they feel. People may deliberately seek to deceive concerning their true feelings. And most important, one can disguise one's own true feelings and thus retain the privacy of emotional experience.

As a social phenomenon, display rules are susceptible to the same cultural and contextual variability as other features of emotional development. Thus, cultural values differ significantly concerning the importance of dissembling one's emotions to others. Cole's work in Nepal suggests that there are important conventions, different from those of the United States, for displaying both positive and negative emotions, and these are recognized by children as young as age 6 (Cole & Tamang, 1998; Cole & Tan, 2007). Even within Western cultures the display rules conveyed to boys and girls differ. It is more appropriate for girls than for boys, for example, to display feelings of sadness or fear (Fivush, 1994).

TABLE 5.3
Display Rules for Emotional Expressions

Rule	Definition	Application
MAXIMIZE	Enhancing the expression of an emotion that you actually feel	• A young child cries more loudly after a fall when a caregiver is present • An adult expresses far more delight at a pleasant gift than he or she actually feels
MINIMIZE	Reducing the expression of an emotion that you actually feel	• A child or adolescent seems not to care very much after losing a competitive game • An adult shows mild dismay when receiving disappointing news in the presence of others
NEUTRALIZE	Showing no emotional expression at all even though you are feeling aroused	• A child puts on a "poker face" despite being teased by a sibling • An adult has an immobile, expressionless face when being reprimanded by an authority
MASK	Replacing the expression of emotion that you feel with the opposite emotional expression	• A child expresses delight when opening a disappointing gift in the presence of the gift-giver • An adult smiles and congratulates a coworker who has achieved recognition that the adult envies

Source: Ekman, 2003; Ekman & Friesen, 1975.

Emotion regulation. Emotion regulation concerns the management of emotional experience. In contrast to display rules, which regulate emotional expressions, strategies of emotion regulation influence emotion itself (Cole, Martin, & Dennis, 2004; Eisenberg & Morris 2002; Thompson, 1990, 1994). There are many reasons why people of all ages seek to change their emotional experience. People seek to regulate their emotions to feel better under stress (managing negative emotions and increasing feelings of happiness or well-being), think better (managing any kind of strong emotion), act courageously (curtailing feelings of fear or anxiety), enhance motivation (sometimes by accentuating guilt), elicit support (by focusing on personal distress or anxiety), affirm relationships (by enhancing sympathetic or empathetic feelings for another), and for other reasons. Understanding emotion regulation thus requires appreciating the diverse personal goals underlying regulatory efforts. Sometimes these goals are self-evident: Children and adults manage emotions when striving to cope with difficult circumstances. But these goals are also shaped by the social context: Competent emotion regulation may be best observed, for example, when a young child loudly protests a bully's provocations when adults are nearby, but quietly tolerates this abuse when adults are absent (Thompson, 1994). In this regard, processes of emotion regulation—such as the use of display rules—are social and cultural, and it is unsurprising that skills in emotion regulation are related to social competence in children (e.g., Gilliom, Shaw, Beck, Schonberg, & Lukon, 2002).

Emotion regulation is social also because the earliest forms of emotion regulation are the efforts of caregivers to manage the emotions of their young offspring. Parents do so by directly intervening to soothe or pacify the child, and also do so in other ways, such as by regulating the emotional demands of familiar settings such as home and daycare (often in accord with their perceptions of the child's temperamental strengths and vulnerabilities), altering the child's construal of emotionally arousing experiences (acting enthusiastically while going on a Ferris wheel or taking a trip to the dentist), and coaching children on expectations or strategies for emotional management (Garner & Spears, 2000; Spinrad, Stifter, Donelan-McCall, & Turner, 2004). With growing maturity, however, emotions become internally managed in increasingly sophisticated ways (Thompson, 1990, 1994). Whereas the newborn infant may cry uncontrollably, the toddler can seek assistance from others, the preschooler can talk about her feelings and their causes, the school-age child can redirect attention, reconceptualize the situation, and use other deliberate cognitive strategies to manage feelings, the adolescent can use personally effective means of regulating emotion (such as playing meaningful music or talking to a close friend), and the adult can alter schedule, responsibilities, and activities to change emotional demands. The growth of these intrinsic capacities for emotion regulation is thus built on advances in emotional understanding (discussed earlier) and self-understanding (discussed later) that enable developing persons to better understand the personal causes and consequences of emotional arousal, and devise increasingly sophisticated and effective means of managing emotion.

This portrayal of the growth of emotion regulation suggests that skills of emotion management increase with age as the result of brain maturation, greater emotion understanding, and enhanced experience. But the developmental story is more complex (Thompson, Lewis, & Calkins, 2008). One reason is that neurobiologically there is a continuing interaction between lower emotion centers (such as the amygdala) and higher regulatory centers (such as the prefrontal cortex) such that they are mutually influential (Lewis & Todd, 2007; Ochsner & Gross, 2007; Quirk, 2007). The prefrontal cortex exerts inhibitory influence over the amygdala, for example, but the amygdala also constrains cortical processing in the prefrontal cortex according to emotional meanings that have been previously established. As a practical matter, this means that emotion regulation at any age is colored by emotional biases that have become incorporated into nervous system processes through genetic influences (e.g., Ebstein et al., 2000), experience (such as early chronic exposure to stress), or their interaction. In one study, for example, 2-year-olds who were behaviorally identified as emotionally inhibited or uninhibited were later studied as adults, and neuroimaging analyses were conducted as they viewed novel faces. The findings revealed heightened amygdala activation in the inhibited group of adults when viewing novel (vs. familiar) faces, but no differences in the uninhibited group (Schwartz, Wright, Shin, Kagan, & Rauch, 2003; see also Kagan et al., 2007). Although more longitudinal research is needed, these findings suggest that a strong biological bias toward fearful reactions to unfamiliar events based in limbic system thresholds may color emotional processes to maturity, despite the growth of higher cortical inhibitory systems. The same may be true when early experiences (such as physical abuse) introduce similar biases into the brain's emotional processing. Pollak and his colleagues have found, for example, that children with a history of maltreatment showed lower perceptual thresholds for identifying angry facial and vocal expressions in adults that were complemented by lower activational thresholds in brain regions governing focused attention when viewing these faces (Pollak, 2008; Pollak & Kistler, 2002; Pollak, Klorman, Thatcher, & Cicchetti, 2001). Experiences of abuse had altered brain functioning with respect to alertness to cues of interpersonal threat.

The growth of emotion regulation is important because it reflects both the significance of developing self-control over basic emotional reactions and also the complexity of the processes underlying emotional arousal. For this reason, and also because of its practical and therapeutic implications (see Luby & Belden, 2006; Thompson, 2000), study of the growth of emotion regulation remains one of the most vigorous areas of developmental emotions research.

Emotion and Relationships

Contemporary research on emotional development shows that emotions are not just internal experiences with outward expression, but are deeply influenced by the social contexts in which they occur. As functionalist emotion theorists note, the person–environment transactions of significance to an individual are usually social, and relationships influence not only emotion elicitation but also strategies for managing emotional experience and its expression. The social context is also crucial to the growth of emotion perception and emotional understanding by which children develop an appreciation of the meaning of emotion to themselves and others, and emotional development is further enlivened by the vicarious experiences of empathy and emotional contagion. A child's skills in emotion perception, understanding, and self-regulation are, in turn, significant influences on the child's social acceptance and social competence (Denham et al., 2003). In one study, multiple measures of preschoolers' emotional competence predicted their social competence with peers a year later, and also partially mediated the influence on social competence of a secure attachment (Denham, Blair, Schmidt, & DeMulder, 2002; see Figure 5.2). Emotional competence was measured, in this study, as individual differences in emotion regulation and emotion understanding. It is, in short, impossible to conceptualize emotional development except with reference to the social conditions that add meaning to emotional behavior throughout life.

The most important feature of the social context is, of course, the close relationships on which people depend for support. This is especially true during the early years of life, when a child's attachment to caregivers provides an emotional context of security and reassurance, or insecurity and uncertainty, that colors self-perception and understanding of others (Thompson, 2006a). Close relationships influence emotional development because they shape many of the conditions in which young children experience, understand, and interpret emotion in the context of everyday social interaction, shared conversations, coping support, instruction and modeling, and a variety of other social influences on emotional development

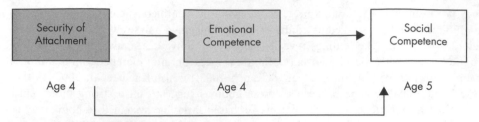

FIGURE 5.2 Summary of findings from Denham et al. (2002), showing the importance of emotional competence to the development of social competence in preschoolers. Multiple measures of emotional competence directly predicted social competence a year later, and also partially mediated the influence of a secure parent–child attachment.

(Gottman, Katz, & Hooven, 1997; Laible & Thompson, 2007). Even more fundamentally, parent–child relationships color emotional development through children's developing expectations of support and sensitivity (or lack of it), the construals of emotionally relevant situations that are shaped by the adult's attributional style, and the emotional demands of these relationships on the developing person (see Figure 5.3).

Unfortunately, these relational influences are sometimes most clearly apparent in disturbed parent–child relationships when the consequences of emotional turmoil in the home for early emotional development are evident (Thompson & Calkins, 1996; Thompson, Flood, & Goodvin, 2006; Thompson & Goodman, 2010). Young offspring of parents with affective disorders such as depression are at heightened risk of problems with emotion and emotional regulation, for example, because of the caregiver's limited accessibility as a source of emotional support, and the adult's parenting practices that enhance the child's feelings of responsibility and helplessness (Goodman & Gotlib, 1999). As a result, the offspring of a depressed caregiver become overinvolved in the parent's affective problems, unduly obligated to buttress the parent's emotional state, and feeling inappropriately guilty when their efforts inevitably fail. Children from homes characterized by marital conflict show a heightened sensitivity to distress and anger that is manifested in insecurity and diminished coping

You didn't like that he was bouncing your guy off the game, and that made you really mad.

It's hard when you feel so angry. You're going "AAAH, he's bouncing my guy off there!" Right?

It makes you sad thinking about it, doesn't it?

You know, after you stopped the game, the other guys said, "You know, Joey wasn't really doing so bad." You thought you were losing, but you weren't.

FIGURE 5.3 Excerpt from a mother's conversation with her 5-year-old about a recent emotional experience, illustrating one of the ways that experience of close relationships contributes to emotion understanding.

capacities when adults argue between themselves (Cummings & Davies, 1996; Davies & Woitach, 2008). From the preschool years onward, these children also become overinvolved in their parents' emotional conflicts and have difficulty managing the strong emotions these conflicts arouse in them (Sturge-Apple, Davies, Winter, Cummings, & Schermerhorn, 2008). Maltreating mothers are less aware of their children's feelings and less competent at helping their children cope with emotionally arousing situations, which contributes to the emotional difficulties of their offspring (Shipman & Zeman, 2001). At times, the quality of parenting interacts with young children's genetic vulnerability to either enhance children's risk of developing self-regulatory problems or buffer them against these difficulties (Kochanska, Philibert, & Barry, 2009). The sensitivity and support provided by close relationships are required for children to develop in an emotionally healthy manner. Unfortunately, these studies also illustrate how emotional processes in the home can contribute to the intergenerational transmission of emotional problems from parent to offspring.

Emotion: Conclusion and Future Directions

Understanding how significantly social relationships influence emotional experience underscores the complexity of emotion and its development, and constitutes an important direction for future research. Contrary to the view that emotion is the outward expression of an internal subjectivity, research highlights that the elicitors of emotion, the meaning of emotional arousal, and the understanding of emotional experience and its expression are each deeply social processes. This research is important also for understanding the role of emotion in personality development. Because the emotions with which infants and young children begin to understand themselves and others and communicate with partners are socially instigated and construed, personality is founded on the shared meanings associated with emotion in a particular culture.

As is true in the study of temperament, developmental emotions research is also advancing through genetically informed research designs that enable scientists to understand the hereditary foundations to emotional responding, and by neurobiological research that permits greater insight into the areas of the brain relevant to emotion activation and emotion regulation. It is easy to read these research literatures and conclude that these represent the "nature" of emotional development whereas studies of social influences reflect its "nurture." But as research on temperament has also shown, dichotomizing biological and social influences on developing individuality is scientifically obsolete as research, earlier reviewed, increasingly demonstrates that gene–environment interactions are important, as are the influences of experiences on brain development. In each case, emotional growth is the result of the dynamic interaction over time of biology and experience.

This conclusion is also true of the development of emotion regulation, which will also continue to provoke future research in this field. It is not difficult to understand why, in light of the importance of emotion regulation to the development of social competence and emotional well-being, and the relevance of emotion regulation to understanding problems in developmental psychopathology—such as conduct disorders, depression, and aggressive behavior—and their remediation. But research increasingly shows that emotion regulation is a more complicated developmental process than is often assumed, involving a deeper interaction between the "activational" and the "regulatory" features of emotion. As this interaction is further studied, it will likely lead to more insightful ways of understanding the origins of affective psychopathology in childhood as well as promising treatment interventions.

SELF

As mature people, it is almost impossible to conceive of life without a sense of self. The integrated perception of "me" at the center of all of life experience seems natural and inevitable. But if we stop to consider all that "self" encompasses, it is apparent that this concept is considerably more complex than our intuitive experience suggests, and that the development of self is a multifaceted process that extends throughout life. Moreover, because the sense of self organizes and integrates our experience of who we are in the context of changing life events, it provides an essential foundation to personality development. Studying the growth of self is thus an essential developmental task, and (as we shall see) requires methods that are as diverse as are the different facets of "self."

What is "Self"?

At the core of "self" is, of course, the sense of *subjective self-awareness*. This is the perception of self as an actor, perceiver, emoter, thinker, and experiencer in the midst of all of which one is consciously aware. It is the "I-self" that, to William James (1890) and his followers (Harter, 2006), denotes the uniquely personal experience of life, in contrast to the "me-self" that constitutes the various characteristics that can be objectively known about a person by others. Subjective self-awareness develops very early in life and provides a foundation for the growth of self.

But there is more. Self also includes *self-representation*: who you think you are. This includes physical self-recognition, assigning categorical labels to the self (for gender, racial or ethnic identity, age, and the like), attributing characterological qualities to self (such as shy, friendly, bright, or strong-willed), and understanding how self-relevant processes function (such as thinking, feeling, and motivation). These forms of physical and psychological self-definition provide the basis for perceiving similarities and differences between self and other people, applying social constructions of psychological attributes (such as gender) to the self, gaining insight into the causes and motives underlying one's behavior, making ingroup–outgroup differentiations, self-management, and creating a self-concept. Although self-representation expands and is refined considerably throughout life as self-awareness assumes progressively more complex and differentiated features, the development of self-representation also begins quite early. Long before the second birthday, for example, toddlers are capable of recognizing their physical mirror image (Lewis & Brooks-Gunn, 1979), have begun to use language for simple self-description (Stern, 1985), and can identify basic emotional states in themselves (Bretherton, Fritz, Zahn-Waxler, & Ridgeway, 1986). By contrast, it is not until later childhood and adolescence that children begin to perceive themselves as members of societal groups and can evaluate ingroup–outgroup distinctions (Killen, Lee-Kim, McGlothlin, & Stangor, 2002).

Another feature of self is *autobiographical personal narrative* by which the recollections of specific events in the past are integrated because of their personal meaning and relation to the self (Nelson & Fivush, 2004). Although young children are fairly proficient at recalling general events in the immediate past, it is not until after age 3 that **autobiographical memory** emerges, and most adults cannot recall events of their lives prior to this age (Howe & Courage, 1993; Welch-Ross, 1995). Autobiographical memory differs from general event recall because of the sense of self that is central to the narrative account, organizing and giving meaning to the events that are remembered. One reason for the relatively late emergence of autobiographical personal narrative, therefore, is that the kind of self-knowledge required to instill past events with personal meaning does not begin to emerge until after the third birthday (Howe & Courage, 1993, 1997; Nelson & Fivush, 2004).

A fourth aspect of self consists of the variety of *self-evaluations* that color self-representations and become integrated into the self-concept and self-image (Cole et al., 2001; Harter, 2006). Self-evaluations often derive from the internalization of others' evaluations, but they also arise from the quality of personal self-regard and developing capacities for self-understanding (Stipek, 1995). A temperamentally shy child living in a society that values assertion and extraversion may increasingly view this characteristic as a liability, for example, as she becomes more aware of the difficulties posed by shyness in socializing with others. These self-evaluations guide how personal characteristics (or the self as a whole) come to be colored as strengths or weaknesses, benefits or liabilities, desirable or undesirable. As we shall see, it is likely that rudimentary ways of perceiving the self as good or bad develop in a nonlinguistic form in the initial 2 years of life, but these self-evaluations become considerably more multifaceted, incisive, nuanced, and differentiated in the years to come.

Finally, another emergent aspect of self is the *social self*—that is, the self primarily regarded in a social context. Although the sense of self is continuously influenced by social interactions and relationships (especially with parents), it is not until around the second birthday that young children begin to be interested and concerned with how their behavior is perceived by caregivers (Lagattuta & Thompson, 2007; Stipek, 1995). This is the beginning of more complex processes by which the self is oriented to its social context. In the years that follow, for example, social comparison processes will become an important facet of self-evaluation (Frey & Ruble, 1990), children and adolescents will be concerned with managing their self presentation through self-monitoring strategies (Snyder, 1987), and adolescents will realize that they have "multiple selves" that are suited to the expectations and demands of different social situations—and they will sometimes wonder which is their "true self" (Harter & Monsour, 1992).

Although these different facets of the "self" are not independent, conceptually disentangling them allows insight into two features of the development of self that might otherwise remain unrecognized. First, the growth of self begins surprisingly early but is an extraordinarily complex, and therefore extended, developmental process. Although some sense of self exists from very early in the first year, self-awareness is qualitatively different for infants, young children, adolescents, young adults, and older people because of the changes in self-representation, autobiographical personal narrative, and self-evaluative processes that occur over time. Asking when "the self" develops is, in this sense, a meaningless question.

Second, the developing self is the core of developing individuality and of the growth of personality. The sense of self provides coherence and organization to personal experience through the feeling of subjective self-awareness and the self-representations through which experience is interpreted (Sroufe, 1996; Stern, 1985). It offers the realization of temporal continuity between personal past, present experience, and expectations for the future through autobiographical narrative and a continuing self-concept (Moore & Lemmon, 2001). It provides a means of self-understanding and thus contributes also to understanding other people through the recognition of how one is similar to, as well as different from, others (Harter, 2006). In these ways, the developing self, like temperament and emotional growth, provides an essential scaffold to the developing personality.

These features of the self develop within the context of cultural beliefs about the nature of self. Thus, although children universally distinguish themselves from others and assign categorical labels to who they are, the nature and characteristics of self that children identify, and what children value (or devalue) about themselves depend on the culture context in which they live. These cultural views of the self are developed quite early. Mothers from the United States emphasize their preschool offspring's autonomy much more in conversation and social interaction than do Japanese mothers, for example, although there are also social class differences in maternal behavior within the US (Dennis, Cole, Zahn-Waxler, & Mizuta, 2002;

Wiley, Rose, Burger, & Miller, 1998). These socialization differences are already reflected in the autobiographical narratives of children from Western and non-Western cultures (Han, Leichtman, & Wang, 1998; Wang, 2004). Such cultural differences in conceptions of the self are important because Western ideas are inherent in how self-development is conceptualized and studied in contemporary psychology, and offer a reminder that the self is socially constructed in somewhat different ways throughout the world (Thompson & Virmani, 2009).

Methods of Developmental Study

As this discussion of the multifaceted features of the self suggests, researchers rarely strive to study the developing "self" in a comprehensive fashion. Rather, they study the growth of elements of self: self-descriptive statements, autobiographical memory, self-esteem, and other self-system processes. This means that research methods must be carefully developed to index the specific self-related processes of interest, as well as being suitable to the ages of the children under study. Researchers use different empirical tools for studying the growth of autobiographical memory (involving, for example, guided recall of events in the recent or distant past in conversation with the mother, with particular attention to the child's self-referential statements) than they use to investigate developmental changes in self-esteem (in which affective self-regard is assessed, often in response to carefully designed interview questions) or young children's self-descriptions. Each is a component of the developing "self," but each must be evaluated using methods that are specific to the particular domain of the self that is of special interest.

Studying the developing "self" is challenging also because the focus of empirical inquiry is on a young person's self-perceptions, and thus research methods often depend on self-report. The development of appropriate self-report measures for children of different ages can be challenging. Developmental scientists have long known, for example, that the conceptual capabilities of toddlers and preschoolers can be underestimated because of their limited capacities to verbalize their own thoughts and understanding, so researchers in this field have had to be creative in developing procedures to assess developing self-awareness in very young children who may not yet have the words to express what they think or feel. This can involve ingenious strategies of story construction (Emde, Wolfe, & Oppenheim, 2003), puppets (Measelle, Ablow, Cowan, & Cowan, 1998), or other procedures to elucidate what young children know and think about themselves. Researchers' success in doing so has helped to reveal that young children think of themselves more complexly and with greater psychological insight than was earlier believed. Even more striking is research on infants' self-recognition enlisting nonverbal methods that require babies to discriminate the effects of their own actions from those of others (Rochat & Striano, 2002). Creative methods are, in short, necessary in this field.

A Developmental Outline of the Self

There is considerable interest in the growth of the self because of the insights it affords into the emergence of personality. Moreover, because the experience of self provides a window into what a person finds rewarding or unpleasant, how he or she is motivated, and how personal experiences are construed, understanding the growth of self offers insights into individual differences in many other developmental processes.

Infancy. In traditional formulations, the newborn enters the world in a state of psychological disorganization or in a condition of psychological undifferentiation from the caregiver. In either case, the newborn was believed to be poorly prepared for the development of a sense of self. Current views emphasize, by contrast, that young infants have surprising cap-abilities for assembling, from isolated everyday experiences, the consistent frame of reference that eventually develops into subjective self-awareness (Gergely, 2007; Meltzoff, 2007). As they are physically handled, move and touch things, respond to social interaction, and experi-ence assorted visceral sensations, young infants progressively acquire a sense of physical self-awareness related to the functioning of their bodies. As they act on social and nonsocial objects (especially those that respond contingently), the experience of agency contributes to a dawning awareness of volition and its consequences. As they experience varieties of emotion, especially in response to social interaction, the sense of subjectivity is enriched and further consolidated. These experiences contribute to the development of a basic experience of the subjective self within the first 6 to 8 months of life.

After this, the self grows dramatically. By the end of the first year, self-awareness in relation to interpersonal (or intersubjective) events has emerged with the infant's dawning realization that others are also subjective entities who have viewpoints that are different from, and potentially can be shared with, the self (Tomasello & Rakoczy, 2003). Self-awareness is revealed in behavior as diverse as protocommunicative acts (sounds to others that signal intention or desire), efforts to achieve **joint attention** (when the baby reaches from a high chair to a desired toy, for example, while making urgent sounds and maintaining eye contact with the caregiver), striving to reengage social interaction after a period of inattention, and social referencing (Rochat & Striano, 2002; Tomasello & Rakoczy, 2003). In these and other ways, young infants reveal an implicit awareness that others have subjective states (such as attention and emotion) that can be altered by the child's efforts. Well before the second birthday, infants also become capable of physical self-recognition when presented with their mirror images (Lewis & Brooks-Gunn, 1979). They touch self-referentially when looking at themselves in the mirror (see Figure 5.4).

Late in the second year and early in the third, toddlers show indications of early self-representation in their verbal self-reference, such as using their names or referring to "me" (Bates, 1990) and in their use of simple emotion terms to describe their internal experiences (Bretherton et al., 1986). Other indications of emerging self-representation are assertions of competence, such as insisting on "do it myself" (Bullock & Lutkenhaus, 1988; Stipek, Gralinski, & Kopp, 1990), identifying the self by gender and in other ways (Ruble, Martin, & Berenbaum 2006), and the emergence of self-conscious emotions such as pride, embarrass-ment, and guilt (Lagattuta & Thompson, 2007). During this time, toddlers are also acquiring a sensitivity to standards and their applications to the self (Kochanska, Aksan, Prisco, & Adams, 2008), showing early signs of conscience (Thompson et al., 2006), and beginning to exercise self-control (Kopp & Wyer, 1994). Young children in the second and third years are, in short, experiencing rapidly expanding self-awareness and self-representation.

FIGURE 5.4 In infancy, playful responding to one's mirror image evolves, by the end of the second year, to self-referential touching that reflects the child's self-recognition in the mirror image.

The growth of self occurs because of changes within the child, and also because of relational influences. The organization and continuity of early experience provide the basis for emerging self-awareness. This organization derives from how parents structure the baby's experience around routines that are manageable, repetitive, and predictable, so that the baby becomes capable of anticipating events that will occur. Caregivers also offer social interactive experiences that are emotionally salient and reciprocal, so that the baby's social initiatives and responses have meaningful and contingent consequences (Thompson, 2006a). In providing experiences with these characteristics, sensitive caregivers offer the structure and consistency that enable a sense of self to become organized. Caregivers also provide opportunities in social interaction for infants to learn about the different subjective viewpoints that people possess, and to practice the skills for gaining access to these alternative subjectivities (through gestural and vocal communication, social referencing, and in other ways) (Tomasello & Rakoczy, 2003). Later, as self-representations begin to take shape, social interactions with caregivers shape the conditions in which toddlers feel proud or shameful, the competencies that they seek to exercise independently or with assistance, and the ways that they begin to identify and represent themselves as well as other people (Lagattuta & Thompson, 2007; Stipek, 1995). In this respect, consistent with classic theories of the self (e.g., Mead, 1934), young children begin to regard themselves through the lens of others' regard for them (i.e., the "looking glass self").

Unfortunately, not all caregivers provide a sensitive relational context for the development of positive or healthy self-regard. As self-representations begin to take shape in the second and third years of life, a parent's inappropriate expectations, belittling judgments, or impatience can contribute to negative self-regard, expressed in young children's shame or avoidance, even before a young child has mastered the linguistic capabilities for expressing self-regard (Kelley & Brownell, 2000). Indeed, it is possible that the roots of negative self-representations begin even earlier, in the manner in which infants learn to expect either positive and supportive assistance or more abrupt or negative interactions with their caregivers during everyday episodes of social play, caregiving routines, and the relief of distress. In one study, the mother's report of parenting stress and depressive symptomatology was associated with young children's negative self-concept, but a secure mother–child attachment was associated with positive self-concept in the same children (Goodvin, Meyer, Thompson, & Hayes, 2008). It is for this reason that many developmental researchers regard a secure parent–infant attachment as a crucial foundation for the growth of healthy self-regard because of its influence on the young child's developing self-representations or, in the words of some attachment theorists, **internal working models** of the self (Thompson, 2006a).

Early childhood. These "working models" become further elaborated and consolidated in the relational experiences of early childhood. This occurs because of significant growth in young children's self-representations during the preschool years. During this period, children acquire an expanded appreciation of psychological states in themselves and others, incorporating an increasing understanding of people's intentions, goals, emotions and desires, and later of thoughts, beliefs, and expectations, into their rudimentary "theory of mind" (Wellman, 2002). An expanding comprehension of internal psychological states not only assists young children in comprehending the thoughts and emotions of others, but also in understanding themselves and their own feelings and thinking. This development is reflected in how they describe themselves. Young children rely primarily on concrete, observable features in their spontaneous self-descriptions (e.g., "I am big, I can run fast, and can count to 100"), but they can also use psychological trait terms ("I am naughty sometimes, but good with adults") when describing themselves (Eder, 1989, 1990; Measelle et al., 1998). Although young children's use of trait terms such as "good" and "naughty" lacks the rich meaning inherent in how older people use these concepts, these self-descriptions are like personality traits in that they show stability over time and are similar to how others (such as their mothers) describe them (Brown, Mangelsdorf, Agathen, & Ho, 2008; Eder & Mangelsdorf, 1997). Even a preschooler's use of a concrete feature, such as describing herself/himself as a girl or boy, is accompanied by a basic understanding of the psychological attributes and stereotypes associated with being male or female (Ruble et al., 2006). Preschoolers are, in short, beginning to acquire increasingly complex and multidimensional self-representations based on how they perceive their physical (including temperamental qualities) and psychological characteristics (Brown et al., 2008; Marsh, Ellis, & Craven, 2002; Measelle, John, Ablow, Cowan, & Cowan, 2005) (see Table 5.4).

These self-representations are strongly influenced by how children believe they are regarded by others. Indeed, one of the hallmarks of early childhood is preschoolers' growing concern with how they are seen by the significant people in their lives (Lagattuta & Thompson, 2007; Stipek, 1995; Thompson et al., 2006). When they are engaged in misbehavior or tackling challenging tasks, for instance, young children are sensitive to the implicit or explicit standards of conduct that are reflected in parental evaluations of their behavior. They often anticipate positive parental responses (and seek to avoid negative reactions) before they occur, and incorporate parental standards into their own self-evaluations. Parental values, expectations, and beliefs are transmitted in many other contexts also. As noted earlier, for instance, everyday conversations between young children and their parents are a forum for meaningful lessons about behavioral expectations, emotional reactions, causal attributions, and the self in the context of the shared recall of the day's events. Consider, for example, the following brief conversation between a young child and his mother about an event earlier in the morning (Dunn & Brown, 1991, p. 97):

Child: Eat my Weetabix. Eat my Weetabix. Crying.
Mother: Crying, weren't you? We had quite a battle. "One more mouthful, Michael."
           And what did you do? You spat it out!
Child: (*Pretends to cry*)

Embedded within this short, shared recollection about a breakfast dispute are significant messages from the mother about the causal sequence of events, the reason for Michael's distress, and culpability for perceived misbehavior. These messages to the child are also

TABLE 5.4
Early Psychological Self-Representations in Preschoolers

4½- to 7½-year-olds[1]	4- and 5-year-olds[2]	5½-year-olds[3]	4- and 5-year-olds[4]
Academic competence	Timidity	Self-control	Self-concept in
Achievement motivation	Agreeableness	Self-acceptance via achievement	terms of:
Social competence	Negative affect	Self-acceptance via affiliation	• physical
Peer acceptance	Positive self-concept		appearance
Depression–anxiety			• peers
Aggression–hostility			• parents
			• verbal
			• math

[1] Measelle et al. (1998).
[2] Brown et al. (2008); Goodvin et al. (2008) (each research group used the same dimensions, although Goodvin and colleagues also identified positive self-concept).
[3] Eder (1990).
[4] Marsh et al. (2002).

lessons about the self, of course. By the mother's account, Michael's crying resulted from uncooperative behavior (by contrast with good boys, who cooperate) that resulted in his crying, whereas Michael's initial representation of the morning's confrontation likely focused instead on his mother's insistence about eating unpleasant breakfast cereal. In discussing everyday events like these with young children, similar lessons about the self are implicitly transmitted by caregivers in how they structure, elaborate, and clarify the child's simple representations of daily experience.

Furthermore, many developmental researchers believe that early, shared recountings of daily experiences with an adult also provide the basis for autobiographical personal narrative (Miller, 1994; Nelson & Fivush, 2004; Welch-Ross, 1995). It is easy to see why. By instilling an interpretive framework organized with reference to the child, caregivers structure the shared recounting of personal experiences in a manner that reinstantiates and consolidates recall, and also underscores the personal significance of events for the child. This makes events more memorable and helps to integrate them into a network of representations of events that are knit together because of their relevance to self. Indeed, parents' use of rich emotional language for highlighting the personal significance of events in conversations with their young children is associated with children's early self-concept development (Bird & Reese, 2006; Welch-Ross, Fasig, & Farrar, 1999).

Autobiographical memory does not begin to emerge until after the third birthday because prior to this time, young children have limited self-knowledge, are insufficiently self-aware psychologically to represent events autobiographically, and also have minimal capabilities for conversing meaningfully with parents (Nelson & Fivush, 2004; Reese, 2002; Welch-Ross, 1995). Furthermore, children's capacity to conceptualize the self as enduring over time may not develop until early in the fourth year (Povinelli & Simon, 1998). Once these abilities have developed, shared conversations with caregivers provide an important foundation to the growth of autobiographical memory. This means that children's autobiographical personal narratives—or, put differently, their emergent "working model" of the self—are likely to incorporate the moral values, causal attributions, emotional inferences, and perceptions of the child that caregivers incorporate into their shared recollections of the child's experiences (Thompson, 2006a). A parent who regards the young child as mischievous, rambunctious, cautious, or moody is likely to instill these perceptions into the shared recounting of the day's events, and these characteristics are likely, in turn, to be incorporated into the child's self-representations. At later ages, as children become mnemonically more skilled, they are less reliant on shared conversations with parents to retain autobiographical events, but for younger children the influence of these conversations is powerful. It is unsurprising, therefore, that young children's psychological self-representations are similar to how their mothers regard them (Brown et al., 2008; Eder & Mangelsdorf, 1997). But as a consequence, some young children are vulnerable to incorporating the negative or demeaning judgments of their caregivers.

In general, most young children have a positive view of their competencies (Wigfield, Eccles, Schiefele, Roeser, & Davis-Kean, 2006). Young children perceive themselves as capable in many things, confidently predicting success even when they have failed, and maintaining sunny expectations for the future (Harter & Pike, 1984). One reason is that young children have difficulty distinguishing between their desired and their actual performance and, believing that ability can be changed with increased effort, do not easily recognize the limits in their capabilities (Stipek, 1984). Another reason is that preschoolers do not spontaneously enlist social comparison to evaluate their performance against the behavior of others, but instead evaluate their skills against what they were capable of accomplishing at an earlier age (Frey & Ruble, 1990). By the standard of temporal comparison, of course, most young children can feel positive and optimistic about their capabilities. However, when social comparison information is made salient to them, even children as young as 4½ may knowingly use this information to evaluate their own competence (Butler, 1998). Their sunny self-regard does not last long, however. There is a progressive decline in children's judgments of their own competencies as they proceed through the primary grades (Wigfield et al., 2006).

Middle childhood. Self-understanding changes considerably in the school years as children develop more differentiated, realistic, and sophisticated forms of self-representation and self-evaluation. One reason this occurs is the growth of spontaneous social comparison enlisted into self-evaluation. In middle childhood, children spontaneously and more thoughtfully compare their capabilities and attributes with those of their peers to determine how well they "measure up" (Frey & Ruble, 1990; Pomerantz, Ruble, Frey, & Greulich, 1995). Because few children excel in all aspects, social comparison fosters a more differentiated awareness of personal strengths and weaknesses—the realization, for example, that someone may be skilled at sports, have difficulty with math, but be average in social popularity (Cole et al., 2001). Social comparison processes are fostered by the intellectual competencies that emerge during this period of life (Case, 1991), and also by the social conditions of middle childhood. Schools increasingly use comparative performance-based evaluations (in contrast with the rewards in preschool for simply trying), and in clubs, athletic groups, and other gatherings children are organized into age-stratified groups that better enable them to compare their capabilities with those of their peers (Wigfield et al., 2006).

Social and temporal comparison processes, together with expanding cognitive capabilities, have important consequences for children's developing self-understanding in middle childhood. They contribute to more complex and sophisticated self-evaluations. In contrast to the comparatively general positive self-regard of preschoolers, older children's self-descriptions include a more balanced assessment of personal strengths and weaknesses. Distinguishing among various domains of competency—such as academic achievement, athletic prowess, peer popularity, physical appearance, behavioral conduct, and, somewhat later, romantic appeal and job competence—children view themselves as having desirable and/or undesirable qualities in each of many different domains (Cole et al., 2001; Harter, 2006). Children also see themselves in the context of the multiple roles they assume in middle childhood as family member, student, teammate, club member, and other roles, and in relation to the various identities they assume as Asian, Jewish, female, middle-class, and so forth (Harter, 2006). In middle childhood, children also become increasingly aware that differences in ability are not easily changed, and can constrain potential achievement (Dweck, 2002; Pomerantz & Saxon, 2001). They are thus better able to use past performance and personal self-awareness as a guide to more accurately predicting how well they will perform.

Self-esteem in certain domains begins to decline during the school years because of children's more realistic and self-critical self-assessments and the influence of social comparison. Children's perceptions of their physical and intellectual competencies, for example, decline progressively throughout the school years (Eccles, Wigfield, Harold, & Blumenfeld, 1993; Wigfield et al., 2006; but see Cole et al., 2001, for different conclusions). These declines are for both boys and girls, although depending on the domain, rates of decline vary somewhat by gender (Jacobs, Lanza, Osgood, Eccles, & Wigfield, 2002). A decline in academic self-esteem is perhaps inevitable in light of the unrealistic optimism of the preschool years, but it helps to explain why individual differences in self-confidence and their motivational implications become so important in middle childhood (Dweck, 2002). By contrast, other facets of self-esteem, such as children's perceptions of their social competence, rise rather than decline throughout middle childhood (Cole et al., 2001). As these diverse changes in self-concept reflect, older children have a better understanding of personality traits as internal dispositions that are manifested in diverse behavior, and begin to perceive themselves as persons with complex personalities.

The emergence of social comparison and other social influences on developing self-understanding reveals also the growth of the social self, as children increasingly perceive themselves in terms of a complex social context. In middle childhood, children become more adept at self-presentation: managing how they appear before others. With respect to emotions, for example, children acquire considerably greater understanding and apply this insight to developing skills of emotion regulation and in using emotional display rules to dissemble their true feelings in the presence of others (Saarni, 1999). Children know how to act appropriately in different social situations and have the self-control to do so, whether remaining quiet at a concert, looking attentively in class, or adopting an easy-going demeanor with friends. The increasingly self-conscious enactment of socially appropriate behaviors on the stage of public regard reflects the greater insight of older children into their social selves, and provides a foundation for further advances in self-understanding of adolescence.

Adolescence and beyond.   The intellectual capacity for abstract thought flourishes during adolescence, and abstract thought enables teenagers to think of themselves and others much differently than before (Collins & Steinberg, 2006). They can reflect on discrepancies as well as consistencies within their profile of personality characteristics, and ponder what these discrepancies mean for the integrity of who they are (Harter, 2006). They can appreciate the different personae they appear to be in different social situations, and wonder which (if any) reveals their "true self" (Harter & Monsour, 1992). They can contrast their personal characteristics with the attributes of an idealized self, and worry over whether the gap will ever be narrowed (Markus & Nurius, 1986). As one teenager put it, "I'd like to be friendly and tolerant all of the time. That's the kind of person I want to be, and I'm disappointed when I'm not" (Harter, 1990).

Adolescents can also reflect on the life experiences that have contributed to their unique personalities, and believe that nobody else has the same personal outlook that they do. They can ponder how others regard them and experience considerable self-consciousness that derives from assuming that others view them with the same critical scrutiny with which they regard themselves. They can also begin wondering about the roles and responsibilities they will assume as adults, and in doing so begin the process of forging an occupational, religious, political, and sexual identity (Erikson, 1968; Kroger, 1993). Gender identity intensifies, along with teenagers' self-segregation into gender-typed activities and interests (Ruble et al., 2006). The burgeoning capacities for abstract thought, together with the social circumstances of adolescence and the psychobiological changes associated with puberty, can foster significant changes in self-understanding, self-evaluation, and the social self (Collins & Steinberg, 2006). They can also make adolescence a period of introspection, disturbing self-criticism, and pain as well as pleasure at the new forms of self-awareness that emerge. These challenges can invite anxious self-reflection, bold experimentation, or both. Indeed, two reasons that adolescents report for engaging in "false self" behavior, besides the effort to ensure acceptable self-presentation to significant others, are that others devalue who they truly are and to experiment with different roles and different possible selves (Harter, Marold, Whitesell, & Cobbs, 1996).

The effort to "discover" or "find" oneself in adolescence derives not necessarily from deficiencies in prior self-understanding but rather from the new questions about the self that are raised by new forms of self-awareness, as well as new social roles and circumstances. The psychobiological changes of puberty mean that teenagers are perceiving themselves, and are being perceived by others, less as children and more like young adults, and these changes in how they are regarded by others can introduce welcomed as well as confusing revisions in self-perception depending on the timing of puberty and its meaning to the teenager. At the same time, adolescents are departing from childhood roles (their schools are larger, classes more impersonal, expectations more stringent, teachers more authoritarian; see Wigfield et al., 2006) and are beginning to enter into adult roles and activities (in an after-school job, in classes that teach job skills or prepare for college, and in exploring romantic and sexual relationships). Given how much one's physical appearance and social context are bedrocks to personal identity at any stage of life, it is unsurprising that these rather dramatic pubertal and role-related changes can provoke significant questions about the self in adolescence.

It might be expected that with the onset of these psychobiological, cognitive, and con-textual changes in early adolescence, self-esteem declines. But the story of adolescence is similar to middle childhood: Self-esteem changes in various ways for different domains of self-perceived competence, such as academic, social, and athletic (Cole et al., 2001). Consistent with their experience at earlier ages, adolescents can benefit from positive, supportive parent-ing that incorporates acceptance and approval, permitted self-expression, and behavioral guidelines that are rationally discussed (Collins & Steinberg, 2006; Grolnick, 2003). Indeed, contrary to popular stereotypes about the teenage years, parents remain important to adoles-cents' self-esteem even as peers also become important, partly because of parents' centrality to the teenager's life experience.

As many of the psychological, psychobiological, and social transitions of early adolescence are consolidated and accommodated, teenagers increasingly look to young adulthood with goals and plans that they are working to achieve. To be sure, the "who am I?" questions that are inaugurated in adolescence are rarely answered with any certainty or completeness by the close of the teenage years. Issues of identity, multiple selves, and the dissonance between actual and ideal selves continue to be explored in early adulthood, and may be reevoked much later in life as the result of significant life changes (e.g., divorce, job loss, personal injury). By contrast with the adolescent's initial encounter with these questions about self, however, the adult can approach these issues as familiar if nagging concerns, having crystallized a sense of self in the choices of occupation, marital partner, and lifestyle that both reflect and help to define who you are, and in the other life circumstances that provide stability and consistency to daily experience. In this respect, the sense of self is more reliable in adulthood because, having engaged in the explorations of the teenage years, the adult has made choices and commitments that (to a greater or lesser extent) are satisfactory, and that provide a founda-tion for occupation, family, and other pursuits of life.

Self: Conclusion and Future Directions

A sense of self is such a familiar part of individuality and self-regard that it is easy to forget how painstakingly self-understanding is constructed through infancy, childhood, and ado-lescence. Moreover, a sense of self is such a central frame of reference for personal experience that it is easy to neglect how much it is a product of social influences. These influences begin with the quality of care an infant receives, continue with how autobiographical self-awareness is constructed through conversation, and extend even to the discovery of self in the context of adolescent peer relationships. This is important especially when we appreciate that a sense of self is a core feature of personality development. Personality derives, in part, from how people create a sense of themselves from personal self-reflection and self-awareness, and also by looking in the mirror of others' regard for them.

Cultural practices provide an envelope within which the self develops from birth through-out life, and future research will devote greater attention to the intersection between cultural values, family practices, and the development of self (Thompson & Virmani, 2009). All of the social influences on the development of self discussed above are culturally colored, and this begins early in the different experiences of contingent social play that help to create a sense of subjective self-awareness in infancy, to the different opportunities afforded for mirror self-recognition, to the incentives and support for developing skills in self-management, to parents' expressed and implied evaluations of children's conduct (see Keller, 2007; Rogoff, 2003). Cultural practices further influence the development of self in how parents converse with their children about everyday experiences, emphasizing the child's feelings, the lessons of experience, or responsible conduct depending on the cultural context (Wang & Fivush, 2005; Wang, Leichtman, & Davies, 2000). To the extent that the development of self is socially constructed, culture will receive increased attention as an important part of that constructive context.

The importance of culture is also reflected in the cultural diversity of children growing up in the United States. In light of the remarkable increase in racial and ethnic diversity, attention to the development of self, ethnic and racial identity, cultural identity development, and acculturation processes as part of the development of self will require increased research attention (Quintana, 2007, 2008). Research findings suggest that for children of immigrants, for example, the manner in which children fit into the broader community—and the community, in turn, fits into the dominant American society—can significantly determine the extent of acculturative stress they experience, including stress related to self-understanding and identity (Zhou, 1997). Attention to cross-cultural and within-culture diversity in the development of self will contribute to a broader appreciation of the social determinants of how children come to understand who they are, and the influence of developing self-awareness on personality growth.

CONCLUSIONS

Although the newborn enters the world as a biologically unique individual, temperamental individuality provides only the most basic core of personality development. As capacities for emotional responding and understanding subsequently unfold, temperamental qualities become elaborated and integrated into a broader network of capabilities. And as a nascent sense of self and self-understanding also develop, temperament becomes incorporated into how the child experiences the self, how others perceive the child, and how self-understanding emerges from the interaction of these processes.

Personality development encompasses, of course, a broader range of influences than just temperament, emotion, and self-awareness. This discussion has touched on many of these additional contributors to personality growth. Personality is shaped by significant relationships, especially those with the mother, father, and other primary caregivers, who provide an emotional context of security and support (or, alternatively, insecure uncertainty) in which confidence, self-esteem, sociability, and empathy (or their opposites) can emerge (Thompson, 2006a). Personality is also forged by broader social experiences, such as with peers in the school and neighborhood, the socioeconomic conditions of the family that shape life challenges and opportunities, and the cultural norms and beliefs that envelop all of these processes, which remind us that the development of "the individual child" is a theoretical abstraction. Personality development is also shaped by the emergence of conscience and moral understanding, social cognition and its influence on social behavior, and the emergence of gender identity that also infuse the growth of emotion and of self. In a sense, personality development is an inclusive construct that incorporates the variety of psychobiological, conceptual, social, and contextual influences that self-organize to constitute developing individuality through the life course.

In focusing on temperament, emotion, and self, however, we have considered three of the earliest foundations to developing individuality that provide a basis for personality growth and the elaboration of personality in the years following infancy (Caspi & Shiner, 2006). With the foundation in place in the initial years of life, personality unfolds and becomes individually refined, consolidated, and strengthened in many ways (Caspi & Shiner, 2006; Thompson, 1988). Personality influences how experiences are construed and interpreted by people, and thus how they respond to social and nonsocial events, and the reciprocal effects they have on future development. Personality influences the choices of social partners, activities, and environmental settings, and the opportunities and challenges these choices pose for further growth. Personality influences the resiliency and vulnerabilities that all individuals experience in their encounters with stressful and everyday life events, as well as the resources people have for coping. Personality influences self-construction and the multifaceted ways that individuals perceive themselves in their current life circumstances in light of how they understand their personal past, their current dispositions, and their needs and desires. In these and many other ways, therefore, personality develops but also mediates between the individual and the social and nonsocial world, and the interaction between personality and the social context affects growth in many developmental domains, and shapes the further growth of personality.

Developing individuality is thus both exceedingly personal—touching at the heart of our sense of self—and socially constituted. This is true at the beginning of life, and throughout the life course. It is in this manner that we experience ourselves as unique actors in the social world, but sharing much in common with those with whom we live life.

REFERENCES AND SUGGESTED READINGS (⬚)

Ashman, S. B., & Dawson, G. (2002). Maternal depression, infant psychobiological development, and risk for depression. In S. H. Goodman & I. H. Gotlib (Eds.), *Children of depressed parents* (pp. 37–58). Washington, DC: American Psychological Association.

Bakermans-Kranenburg, M. J., van IJzendoorn, M. H., Pijlman, F. T. A., Mesman, J., & Juffer, F. (2008). Experimental evidence for differential susceptibility: Dopamine D4 receptor polymorphism (DRD4 VNTR) moderates intervention effects on toddlers' externalizing behavior in a randomized controlled trial. *Developmental Psychology*, *44*, 293–300.

Banerjee, M. (1997). Hidden emotions: Preschoolers' knowledge of appearance–reality and emotion display rules. *Social Cognition*, *15*, 107–132.

⬚ Bartsch, K., & Wellman, H. M. (1995). *Children talk about the mind*. New York: Oxford University Press.

Bates, E. (1990). Language about me and you: Pronomial reference and the emerging concept of self. In D. Cicchetti & M. Beeghly (Eds.), *The self in transition* (pp. 165–182). Chicago: University of Chicago Press.

Bates, J. E. (1980). The concept of difficult temperament. *Merrill-Palmer Quarterly*, *29*, 299–319.

Bates, J. E. (1987). Temperament in infancy. In J. D. Osofsky (Ed.), *Handbook of infant development* (2nd ed., pp. 1101–1149). New York: Wiley.

Bates, J. E., Bayles, K., Bennett, D. S., Ridge, B., & Brown, M. M. (1991). Origins of externalizing behavior problems at eight years of age. In D. Pepler & K. Rubin (Eds.), *Development and treatment of childhood aggression* (pp. 93–120). Hillsdale, NJ: Lawrence Erlbaum Associates.

Belsky, J. (2005). Differential susceptibility to rearing influences: An evolutionary hypothesis and some evidence. In B. Ellis & D. Bjorklund (Eds.), *Origins of the social mind: Evolutionary psychology and child development* (pp. 139–163). New York: Guilford.

Belsky, J., Bakermans-Kranenburg, M. J., & van IJzendoorn, M. H. (2007). For better and for worse: Differential susceptibility to environmental influences. *Current Directions for Psychological Science*, *16*, 300–304.

Bird, A., & Reese, E. (2006). Emotional reminiscing and the development of an autobiographical self. *Developmental Psychology*, *42*, 613–626.

Bornstein, M. H. (1995). Form and function: Implications for studies of culture and human development. *Culture & Psychology*, *1*, 123–137.

Bornstein, M. H. (1998). Stability in mental development from early life: Methods, measures, models, meanings and myths. In F. Simion & G. Butterworth (Eds.), *The development of sensory, motor and cognitive capacities in early infancy: From perception to cognition* (pp. 301–332). Hove, UK: Psychology Press.

Bornstein, M. H., & Arterberry, M. E. (2003). Recognition, discrimination, and categorization of smiling by 5-month-old infants. *Developmental Science, 6*, 585–599.

Bornstein, M. H., Gaughran, J. M., & Segui, I. (1991). Multimethod assessment of infant temperament: Mother questionnaire and mother and observer reports evaluated and compared at five months using the Infant Temperament Measure. *International Journal of Behavioral Development, 14*, 131–151.

Bosquet, M., & Egeland, B. (2006). The development and maintenance of anxiety symptoms from infancy through adolescence in a longitudinal sample. *Development and Psychopathology, 18*, 517–550.

Bretherton, I., Fritz, J., Zahn-Waxler, C., & Ridgeway, D. (1986). Learning to talk about emotions: A functionalist perspective. *Child Development, 57*, 529–548.

Brown, G. L., Mangelsdorf, S. C., Agathen, J. M., & Ho, M. (2008). Young children's psychological selves: Convergence with maternal reports of child personality. *Social Development, 17*, 161–182.

Bullock, M., & Lutkenhaus, P. (1988). The development of volitional behavior in the toddler years. *Child Development, 59*, 664–674.

Buss, A. H., & Plomin, R. (1984). *Temperament: Early developing personality traits*. Hillsdale, NJ: Lawrence Erlbaum Associates.

Buss, K. A., & Goldsmith, H. H. (1998). Fear and anger regulation in infancy: Effects on the temporal dynamics of affective expression. *Child Development, 69*, 359–374.

Butler, R. (1998). Age trends in the use of social and temporal comparison for self-evaluation: Examination of a novel developmental hypothesis. *Child Development, 69*, 1054–1073.

Camras, L. A. (2000). Surprise! Facial expressions can be coordinative motor structures. In M. Lewis & I. Granic (Eds.), *Emotion, development, and self-organization* (pp. 100–124). New York: Cambridge University Press.

Case, R. (1991). Stages in the development of the young child's first sense of self. *Developmental Review, 11*, 210–230.

Caspi, A., Harrington, H., Milne, B., Amell, J. W., Theodore, R. F., & Moffitt, T. E. (2003). Children's behavioral styles at age 3 are linked to their adult personality traits at age 26. *Journal of Personality, 71*, 495–513.

Caspi, A., & Shiner, R. L. (2006). Personality development. In W. Damon & R. M. Lerner (Eds.), N. Eisenberg (Vol. Ed.), *Handbook of child psychology, Vol. 3: Social, emotional and personality development* (6th ed., pp. 300–365). New York: Wiley.

Caspi, A., & Silva, P. A. (1995). Temperamental qualities at age three predict personality traits in young adulthood: Longitudinal evidence from a birth cohort. *Child Development, 66*, 486–498.

Chen, X., Hastings, P. D. Rubin, K. H., Chen, H., Cen, G., & Stewart, S. L. (1998). Child-rearing attitudes and behavioral inhibition in Chinese and Canadian toddlers: A cross-cultural study. *Developmental Psychology, 34*, 677–686.

Chess, S., & Thomas, A. (1986). *Temperament in clinical practice*. New York: Guilford.

Cole, D. A., Maxwell, S. E., Martin, J. M., Peeke, L. G., Seroczynski, A. D., Tram, J. M., et al. (2001). The development of multiple domains of child and adolescent self-concept: A cohort sequential longitudinal design. *Child Development, 72*, 1723–1746.

Cole, P. (1986). Children's spontaneous control of facial expression. *Child Development, 57*, 1309–1321.

Cole, P. M., & Dennis, T. A. (1998). Variations on a theme: Culture and the meaning of socialization practices and child competence. *Psychological Inquiry, 9*, 276–278.

Cole, P. M., Martin, S. E., & Dennis, T. A. (2004). Emotion regulation as a scientific construct: Methodological challenges and directions for child development research. *Child Development, 75*, 317–333.

Cole, P. M., & Tamang, B. L. (1998). Nepali children's ideas about emotional displays in hypothetical challenges. *Developmental Psychology, 34*, 640–646.

Cole, P. M., & Tan, P. Z. (2007). Emotion socialization from a cultural perspective. In J. E. Grusec & P. D. Hastings (Eds.), *Handbook of socialization: Theory and research* (pp. 516–542). New York: Guilford.

Collins, W. A., & Steinberg. L. (2006). Adolescent development in interpersonal context. In W. Damon & R. M. Lerner (Eds.), N. Eisenberg (Vol. Ed.), *Handbook of child psychology, Vol. 3: Social, emotional, and personality development* (6th ed., pp. 1003–1067). New York: Wiley.

Crockenberg, S. C., Leerkes, E. M., & Lekka, S. K. (2007). Pathways from marital aggression to infant emotion regulation: The development of withdrawal in infancy. *Infant Behavior & Development, 30*, 97–113.

Cummings, E. M., & Davies, P. (1996). *Children and marital conflict*. New York: Guilford.

Davidson, R. J., Fox, A., & Kalin, N. H. (2007). Neural bases of emotion regulation in nonhuman primates and humans. In J. J. Gross (Ed.), *Handbook of emotion regulation* (pp. 47–68). New York: Guilford.

Davies, P. T., & Woitach, M. J. (2008). Children's emotional security in the interparental relationship. *Current Directions in Psychological Science, 17*, 269–274.

Denham, S. (1998). *Emotional development in young children*. New York: Guilford.

Denham, S. A., Blair, K. A., DeMulder, E., Levitas, J., Sawyer, K., Auerbach-Major, S., et al. (2003). Preschool emotional competence: Pathway to social competence. *Child Development, 74*, 238–256.

Denham, S., Blair, K., Schmidt, M., & DeMulder, E. (2002). Compromised emotional competence: Seeds of violence sown early? *American Journal of Orthopsychiatry, 72*, 70–82.

Dennis, T. A., Cole, P. M., Zahn-Waxler, C., & Mizuta, I. (2002). Self in context: Autonomy and relatedness in Japanese and U.S. mother–preschool dyads. *Child Development, 73*, 1803–1817.

Donaldson, S. K., & Westerman, M. A. (1986). Development of children's understanding of ambivalence and causal theories of emotion. *Developmental Psychology, 22*, 655–662.

Dunn, J. (1994). Changing minds and changing relationships. In C. Lewis & P. Mitchell (Eds.), *Children's early understanding of mind* (pp. 297–310). Hove, UK: Lawrence Erlbaum Associates.

Dunn, J., & Brown, J. (1991). Relationships, talk about feelings, and the development of affect regulation in early childhood. In J. Garber & K. A. Dodge (Eds.), *The development of emotion regulation and dysregulation* (pp. 89–108). New York: Cambridge University Press.

Dweck, C. S. (2002). The development of ability conceptions. In A. Wigfield & J. S. Eccles (Eds.), *Development of achievement motivation* (pp. 57–88). San Diego, CA: Academic.

Ebstein, R. P., Benjamin, J., & Belmaker, R. H. (2000). Personality and polymorphism of genes involved in aminergic neurotransmission. *European Journal of Pharmacology, 410*, 205–214.

Eccles, J. S., Midgley, C., Wigfield, A., Buchanan, C. M., Reuman, D., Flanagan, C., et al. (1993). Development during adolescence: The impact of stage–environment fit on young adolescents' experiences in schools and in families. *American Psychologist, 48*, 90–101.

Eccles, J. S., Wigfield, A., Harold, R. D., & Blumenfeld, P. (1993). Age and gender differences in children's self- and task perceptions during elementary school. *Child Development, 64*, 830–847.

Eder, R. A. (1989). The emergent personologist: The structure and content of 3½-, 5½-, and 7½-year-olds' concepts of themselves and other persons. *Child Development, 60*, 1218–1228.

Eder, R. A. (1990). Uncovering children's psychological selves: Individual and developmental differences. *Child Development, 61*, 849–863.

Eder, R. A., & Mangelsdorf, S. C. (1997). The emotional basis of early personality development: Implications for the emergent self-concept. In R. Hogan & S. Briggs (Eds.), *Handbook of personality psychology* (pp. 209–240). Orlando, FL: Academic Press.

Eisenberg, N. & Morris, A. S. (2002). Children's emotion-related regulation. In R. Kail (Ed.), *Advances in child development and behavior* (Vol. 30, pp. 190–229). San Diego, CA: Academic.

Eisenberg, N., Spinrad, T. L., & Sadovsky, A. (2006). Empathy-related responding in children. In M. Killen & J. Smetana (Eds.), *Handbook of moral development* (pp. 517–549). Mahwah, NJ: Lawrence Erlbaum Associates.

Ekman, P. (2003). *Emotions revealed*. New York: Times Books.

Ekman, P., & Friesen, W. (1975). *Unmasking the face*. Englewood Cliffs, NJ: Prentice Hall.

Emde, R. N., Wolfe, D. P., & Oppenheim, D. (2003). *Revealing the inner worlds of young children: The MacArthur Story Stem Battery and parent–child narratives*. New York: Oxford University Press.

Erikson, E. H. (1968). *Identity, youth, and crisis*. New York: Norton.

Fivush, R. (1994). Constructing narrative, emotion, and self in parent–child conversations about the past. In U. Neisser & R. Fivush (Eds.), *The remembering self* (pp. 136–157). Cambridge, UK: Cambridge University Press.

Fivush, R. (1998). Gendered narratives: Elaboration, structure, and emotion in parent–child reminiscing across the preschool years. In C. P. Thompson & D. J. Herrmann (Eds.), *Autobiographical memory: Theoretical and applied perspectives* (pp. 79–103). Mahwah, NJ: Lawrence Erlbaum Associates.

Fox, N. A., Schmidt, L. A., & Henderson, H. A. (2000). Developmental psychophysiology: Conceptual and methodological perspectives. In J. T. Cacioppo, L. G. Tassinary, & G. G. Berntson (Eds.), *Handbook of psychophysiology* (2nd ed., pp. 665–686). New York: Cambridge University Press.

Frey, K. S., & Ruble, D. N. (1990). Strategies for comparative evaluation: Maintaining a sense of competence across the life span. In R. J. Sternberg & J. Kolligian, Jr. (Eds.), *Competence considered* (pp. 167–189). New Haven, CT: Yale University Press.

Gallagher, K. C. (2002). Does child temperament moderate the influence of parenting on adjustment? *Developmental Review, 22*, 623–643.

Garner, P. W., & Spears, F. M. (2000). Emotion regulation in low-income preschoolers. *Social Development, 9*, 246–264.

Gergely, G. (2007). The social construction of the subjective self: The role of affect-mirroring, markedness, and ostensive communication in self-development. In L. Mayes, P. Fonagy, & M. Target (Eds.), *Developmental science and psychoanalysis: Integration and innovation* (pp. 45–88). London: Karnac Books.

Gilliom, M., Shaw, D. S., Beck, J. E., Schonberg, M. A., & Lukon, J. L. (2002). Anger regulation in disadvantaged preschool boys: Strategies, antecedents, and the development of self-control. *Developmental Psychology, 38*, 222–235.

Goldsmith, H. H. (2002). Genetics of emotional development. In R. J. Davidson, K. R. Scherer, & H. H. Goldsmith (Eds.), *Handbook of affective sciences*. New York: Oxford University Press.

Goldsmith, H. H., Buss, A. H., Plomin, R., Rothbart, M. K., Thomas, A., Chess, S., et al. (1987). Roundtable: What is temperament? Four approaches. *Child Development, 58*, 505–529.

Goldsmith, H. H., & Campos, J. J. (1982). Toward a theory of infant temperament. In R. N. Emde & R. J. Harmon (Eds.), *The development of attachment and affiliative systems* (pp. 161–193). New York: Plenum.

Goodman, S. H., & Gotlib, I. H. (1999). Risk for psychopathology in the children of depressed mothers: A developmental model for understanding mechanisms of transmission. *Psychologial Review*, *106*, 458–490.

Goodvin, R., Meyer, S., Thompson, R. A., & Hayes, R. (2008). Self-understanding in early childhood: Associations with attachment security, maternal perceptions of the child, and maternal emotional risk. *Attachment & Human Development*, *10*(4), 433–450.

Gottman, J. M., & Katz, L. F., & Hooven, C. (1997). *Meta-emotion: How families communicate emotionally*. Mahwah, NJ: Lawrence Erlbaum Associates.

Grolnick, W. S. (2003). *The psychology of parental control*. Mahwah, NJ: Lawrence Erlbaum Associates.

Gunnar, M. R., & Davis, E. P. (2003). Stress and emotion in early childhood. In R. M. Lerner & M. A. Easterbrooks (Eds.), *Handbook of psychology, Vol. 6: Developmental Psychology* (pp. 113–134). New York: Wiley.

Gunnar, M. R., & Vasquez, D. (2006). Stress neurobiology and developmental psychopathology. In D. Cicchetti & D. Cohen (Eds.), *Developmental psychopathology, Vol. 1: Developmental neuroscience* (2nd ed., pp. 533–577). New York: Wiley.

Han, J. J., Leichtman, M. D., & Wang, Q. (1998). Autobiographical memory in Korean, Chinese, and American children. *Developmental Psychology*, *34*, 701–713.

Harter, S. (1990). Causes, correlates and the functional role of global self-worth: A life-span perspective. In R. J. Sternberg & J. Kolligian, Jr. (Eds.), *Competence considered* (pp. 67–98). New Haven, CT: Yale University Press.

Harter, S. (2006). The self. In W. Damon & R. M. Lerner (Eds.), *Handbook of child psychology, Vol. 3: Social, emotional and personality development* (6th ed., pp. 505–570). New York: Wiley.

Harter, S., Marold, D. B., Whitesell, N. R., & Cobbs, G. (1996). A model of the effects of parent and peer support on adolescent false self behavior. *Child Development*, *67*, 360–374.

Harter, S., & Monsour, A. (1992). Developmental analysis of conflict caused by opposing attributes in the adolescent self-portrait. *Developmental Psychology*, *28*, 251–260.

Harter, S. & Pike, R. (1984). The pictorial scale of perceived competence and social acceptance for young children. *Child Development*, *55*, 1969–1982.

Harwood, R. L., Miller, J. G., & Irizarry, N. L. (1995). *Culture and attachment*. New York: Guilford.

Howe, M. L., & Courage, M. L. (1993). On resolving the enigma of infantile amnesia. *Psychological Bulletin*, *113*, 305–326.

Howe, M. L., & Courage, M. L. (1997). The emergence and early development of autobiographical memory. *Psychological Review*, *104*, 499–523.

Izard, C. E. (1991). *The psychology of emotions*. New York: Plenum.

Izard, C. E., & Ackerman, B. (2000). Motivational, organizational, and regulatory functions of discrete emotions. In M. E. Lewis & J. M. Haviland-Jones (Eds.), *Handbook of emotions* (2nd ed.). New York: Guilford.

Jacobs, J. E., Lanza, S., Osgood, D. W., Eccles, J. S., & Wigfield, A. (2002). Changes in children's self-competence and values: Gender and domain differences across grades one through twelve. *Child Development*, *73*, 509–527.

James, W. (1890). *The principles of psychology*. New York: Henry Holt.

Johnson, M. H. (2010). Developmental neuroscience, psychophysiology, and genetics. In M. H. Bornstein & M. E. Lamb (Eds.), *Developmental science: An advanced textbook* (6th ed., pp. 201–240). Hove, UK: Psychology Press.

Jones, D. C., Abbey, B. B., & Cumberland, A. (1998). The development of display rule knowledge: Linkages with family expressiveness and social competence. *Child Development*, *69*, 1209–1222.

Kagan, J. (2002). Behavioral inhibition as a temperamental category. In R. J. Davidson, K. R. Scherer, & H. H. Goldsmith (eds.), *Handbook of affective sciences* (pp. 320–331). New York: Oxford University Press.

Kagan, J., & Fox, N. A. (2006). Biology, culture, and temperamental biases. In W. Damon & R. M. Lerner (Eds.), *Handbook of child psychology, Vol. 3: Social, emotional and personality development* (6th ed., pp. 167–225). New York: Wiley.

Kagan, J., Snidman, N., Kahn, V., & Townsley, S. (2007). The preservation of two infant temperaments into adolescence. *Monographs of the Society for Research in Child Development*, *72*, 1–75.

Keily, M. K., Bates, J. E., Dodge, K. A., & Pettit, G. S. (2001). Effects of temperament on the development of externalizing and internalizing behaviors over 9 years. In F. Columbus (Ed.), *Advances in psychology research* (Vol. 6, pp. 255–288). Hauppauge, NY: Nova Science Publishers.

Keller, H. (2007). *Cultures of infancy*. Mahwah, NJ: Lawrence Erlbaum Associates.

Kelley, S. A., & Brownell, C. (2000). Mastery motivation and self-evaluative affect in toddlers: Longitudinal relations with maternal behavior. *Child Development*, *71*, 1061–1071.

Killen, M., Lee-Kim, J., McGlothlin, H., & Stangor, C. (2002). How children and adolescents evaluate gender and racial exclusion. *Monographs of the Society for Research in Child Development*, *67*.

Kochanska, G. (1993). Toward a synthesis of parental socialization and child temperament in early development of conscience. *Child Development*, *64*, 325–347.

Kochanska, G. (1995). Children's temperament, mothers' discipline, and security of attachment: Multiple pathways to emerging internalization. *Child Development*, *66*, 597–615.

Kochanska, G., Aksan, N., Prisco, T. R., & Adams, E. E. (2008). Mother–child and father–child mutually responsive orientation in the first 2 years and children's outcomes at preschool age: Mechanisms of influence. *Child Development*, *79*, 30–44.

Kochanska, G., Philibert, R. A., & Barry, R. A. (2009). Interplay of genes and early mother–child relationship in the development of self-regulation from toddler to preschool age. *Journal of Child Psychology and Psychiatry*, *50*, 1331–1338.

Kopp, C. B., & Wyer, N. (1994). Self-regulation in normal and atypical development. In D. Cicchetti & S. L. Toth (Eds.), *Disorders and dysfunctions of the self. Rochester Symposium on Developmental Psychopathology* (Vol. 5, pp. 31–56). Rochester, NY: University of Rochester Press.

Kroger, J. (1993). Ego identity: An overview. In J. Kroger (Ed.), *Discussions on ego identity* (pp. 3–20). Hillsdale, NJ: Lawrence Erlbaum Associates.

Lagattuta, K., & Thompson, R. A. (2007). The development of self-conscious emotions: Cognitive processes and social influences. In R. W. Robins & J. Tracy (Eds.), *Self-conscious emotions* (2nd ed., pp. 91–113). New York: Guilford.

Lagattuta, K. H., & Wellman, H. M. (2002). Differences in early parent–child conversations about negative versus positive emotions: Implications for the development of emotion understanding. *Developmental Psychology*, *38*, 564–550.

Laible, D. J., & Thompson, R. A. (2007). Early socialization: A relational perspective. In J. Grusec & P. Hastings (Eds.), *Handbook of socialization* (pp. 181–207). New York: Guilford.

Lakatos, K., Nemoda, Z., Birkas, E., Ronai, Z., Kovacs, E., Ney, K., et al. (2003). Association of D4 dopamine receptor gene and serotonin transporter promoter polymorphisms with infants' response to novelty. *Molecular Psychiatry*, *8*, 90–97.

LeDoux, J. E. (2000). Emotion circuits in the brain. *Annual Review of Neuroscience*, *23*, 155–184.

Lewis, M. D. (1997). Personality self-organization: Cascading constraints on cognition–emotion interaction. In A. Fogel, M. C. Lyra & J. Valsiner (Eds.), *Dynamics and indeterminism in developmental and social processes* (pp. 193–216). Mahwah, NJ: Lawrence Erlbaum Associates.

Lewis, M., & Brooks-Gunn, J. (1979). *Social cognition and the acquisition of self*. New York: Plenum.

Lewis, M., & Michalson, L. (1983). *Children's emotions and moods*. New York: Plenum.

Lewis, M. D., & Todd, R. M. (2007). The self-regulating brain: Cortical–subcortical feedback and the development of intelligent action. *Cognitive Development*, *22*, 406–430.

Luby, J. L., & Belden, A. C. (2006). Mood disorders: Phenomenology and a developmental emotional reactivity model. In J. L. Luby (Ed.), *Handbook of preschool mental health* (pp. 209–230). New York: Guilford.

Lutz, C. (1988). *Unnatural emotions: Everyday sentiments on a Micronesian atoll and their challenge to Western theory*. Chicago: University of Chicago Press.

Markus, H., & Nurius, P. (1986). Possible selves. *American Psychologist*, *41*, 954–969.

Marsh, H. W., Ellis, L. A., & Craven, R. G. (2002). How do preschool children feel about themselves? Unraveling measurement and multidimensional self-concept structure. *Developmental Psychology*, *38*, 376–393.

Martin, J. N., & Fox, N. A. (2006). Temperament. In K. McCartney & D. Phillips (Eds.), *Blackwell handbook of early childhood development* (pp. 126–146). Oxford, UK: Blackwell.

Mead, G. H. (1934). *Mind, self, and society*. Chicago: University of Chicago Press.

Measelle, J. R., Ablow, J. C., Cowan, P. A., & Cowan, C. P. (1998). Assessing young children's views of their academic, social, and emotional lives: An evaluation of the self-perception scales of the Berkeley Puppet Interview. *Child Development*, *69*, 1556–1576.

Measelle, J. R., John. O. P., Ablow, J. C., Cowan, P. A., & Cowan, C. P. (2005). Can children provide coherent, stable, and valid self-reports on the Big Five dimensions? A longitudinal study from ages 5 to 7. *Journal of Personality and Social Psychology*, *89*, 90–106.

Meltzoff, A. (2007). "Like me": A foundation for social cognition. *Developmental Science*, *10*, 126–134.

Miller, P. J. (1994). Narrative practices: Their role in socialization and self-construction. In U. Neisser & R. Fivush (Eds.), *The remembering self: Construction and accuracy in the self-narrative* (pp. 158–179). New York: Cambridge University Press.

Moore, C., & Lemmon, K. (2001). *The self in time: Developmental perspectives*. Mahwah, NJ: Lawrence Erlbaum Associates.

Mullen, M. K., & Yi, S. (1995). The cultural context of talk about the past: Implications for the development of autobiographical memory. *Cognitive Development*, *10*, 407–419.

Nachmias, M., Gunnar, M., Mangelsdorf, S., Parritz, R., & Buss, K. (1996). Behavioral inhibition and stress reactivity: The moderating role of attachment security. *Child Development*, *67*, 508–522.

Nelson, K., & Fivush, R. (2004). The emergence of autobiographical memory: A social cultural developmental theory. *Psychological Review*, *111*, 486–511.

Newman, D. L., Caspi, A., Silva, P. A., & Moffitt, T. E. (1997). Antecedents of adult interpersonal functioning: Effects of individual differences in age 3 temperament. *Developmental Psychology*, *33*, 206–217.

Ochsner, K. N., & Gross, J. J. (2007). The neural architecture of emotion regulation. In J. J. Gross (Ed.), *Handbook of emotion regulation* (pp. 87–109). New York: Guilford.

Ontai, L. L., & Thompson, R. A. (2002). Patterns of attachment and maternal discourse effects on children's emotion understanding from 3- to 5-years of age. *Social Development*, *11*, 433–450.

Owens, E. B., & Shaw, D. S. (2003). Predicting growth curves of externalizing behavior across the preschool years. *Journal of Abnormal Child Psychology*, *31*, 575–590.

Panksepp, J. (1998). *Affective neuroscience*. London: Oxford University Press.

Pfeifer, M., Goldsmith, H. H., Davidson, R. J., & Rickman, M. (2002). Continuity and change in inhibited and uninhibited children. *Child Development*, *73*, 1474–1485.

Plomin, R., DeFries, J. C., Craig, I. W., & McGuffin, P. (Eds.) (2003). *Behavioral genetics in the postgenomic era*. Washington, DC: American Psychological Association.

Pollak, S. D. (2008). Mechanisms linking early experience and the emergence of emotions: Illustrations from the study of maltreated children. *Current Directions in Psychological Science*, *17*, 370–375.

Pollak, S. D., & Kistler, D. J. (2002). Early experience is associated with the development of categorical representations for facial expressions of emotion. *Proceedings of the National Academy of Sciences of the United States of America*, *99*, 9072–9076.

Pollak, S. D., Klorman, R., Thatcher, J. E., & Cicchetti, D. (2001). P3b reflects maltreated children's reactions to facial displays of emotion. *Psychophysiology*, *38*, 267–274.

Pomerantz, E. M., Ruble, D. N., Frey, K. S., & Greulich, F. (1995). Meeting goals and confronting conflict: Children's changing perceptions of social comparison. *Child Development*, *66*, 723–738.

Pomerantz, E. M., & Saxon, J. L. (2001). Conceptions of ability as stable and self-evaluative processes: A longitudinal examination. *Child Development*, *72*, 152–173.

Porges, S. W. (2007). The polyvagal perspective. *Biological Psychology*, *74*, 116–143.

Porges, S. W., Doussard-Roosevelt, J. A., & Maiti, A. K. (1994). Vagal tone and the physiological regulation of emotion. In N. A. Fox (Ed.), Emotion regulation: Behavioral and biological considerations. *Monographs of the Society for Research in Child Development*, *59* (Serial no. 240), 167–186.

Porter, C. L., Wouden-Miller, M., Silva, S. S., & Porter, A. E. (2003). Marital harmony and conflict: Linked to infants' emotional regulation and cardiac vagal tone. *Infancy*, *4*, 297–307.

Povinelli, D. J., & Simon, B. B. (1998). Young children's understanding of briefly versus extremely delayed images of self: Emergence of the autobiographical stance. *Developmental Psychology*, *34*, 188–194.

Quintana, S. M. (2007). Racial and ethnic identity: Developmental perspectives and research. *Journal of Counseling Psychology*, *54*, 259–270.

Quintana, S. M. (2008). Racial perspective taking ability: Developmental, theoretical, and empirical trends. In S. M. Quintana and C. McKown (Eds.), *Handbook of race, racism, and the developing child* (pp. 16–36). New York: Wiley.

Quirk, G. J. (2007). Prefrontal–amygdala interactions in the regulation of fear. In J. J. Gross (Ed.), *Handbook of emotion regulation* (pp. 27–46). New York: Guilford.

Reese, E. (2002). Social factors in the development of autobiographical memory: The state of the art. *Social Development*, *11*, 124–142.

Repacholi, B., & Gopnik, A. (1997). Early reasoning about desires: Evidence from 14- and 18-month-olds. *Developmental Psychology*, *33*, 12–21.

Rochat, P., & Striano, T. (2002). Who's in the mirror? Self–other discrimination in specular images by four- and nine-month-old infants. *Child Development*, *73*, 35–46.

Rogoff, B. (2003). *The cultural nature of human development*. New York: Oxford University Press.

Rothbart, M. K. (2007). Temperament, development, and personality. *Current Directions in Psychological Science*, *16*, 207–212.

Rothbart, M. K., & Bates, J. E. (2006). Temperament. In W. Damon & R. M. Lerner (Eds.), *Handbook of child psychology, Vol. 3: Social, emotional and personality development* (6th ed., pp. 99–166). New York: Wiley.

Rothbart, M. K., Ellis, L. K., & Posner, M. I. (2004). Temperament and self-regulation. In R. F. Baumeister & K. D. Vohs (Eds.), *Handbook of self-regulation* (pp. 357–370). New York: Guilford.

Rothbart, M. K., & Goldsmith, H. H. (1985). Three approaches to the study of infant temperament. *Developmental Review*, *5*, 237–260.

Rothbart, M. K., Posner, M. I., & Kieras, J. (2006). Temperament, attention, and the development of self-regulation. In K. McCartney & D. Phillips (Eds.), *The Blackwell handbook of early childhood development* (pp. 328–357). London: Blackwell.

Rothbaum, F., Weisz, J., Pott, M., Miyake, K., & Morelli, G. (2000). Attachment and culture: Security in the United States and Japan. *American Psychologist*, *55*, 1093–1104.

Ruble, D. N., Martin, D. L., & Berenbaum, S. A. (2006). Gender development. In W. Damon & R. M. Lerner (Eds.), *Handbook of child psychology, Vol. 3: Social, emotional and personality development* (6th ed., pp. 858–932). New York: Wiley.

Saarni, C. (1999). *The development of emotional competence*. New York: Guilford.

Saarni, C., Campos, J. J., Camras, L., & Witherington, D. (2006). Emotional development: Action, communication, and understanding. In W. Damon & R. M. Lerner (Eds.), *Handbook of child psychology, Vol. 3: Social, emotional and personality development* (6th ed., pp. 226–299). New York: Wiley.

Sagi, A., & Hoffman, M. L. (1976). Empathic distress in the newborn. *Developmental Psychology, 12*, 175–176.

Scarr, S., & McCartney, K. (1983). How people make their own environments: A theory of genotype–environment effects. *Child Development, 54*, 424–435.

Schwartz, C., Wright, C., Shin, L., Kagan, J., & Rauch, S. (2003). Inhibited and uninhibited infants "grown up": Adult amygdalar response to novelty. *Science, 300*, 1952–1953.

Shaw, D. S., Miles, G., Ingoldsby, E. M., & Nagin, D. S. (2003). Trajectories leading to school-age conduct problems. *Developmental Psychology, 39*, 189–200.

Sheese, B. E., Voelker, P. M., Rothbart, M. K., & Posner, M. I. (2007). Parenting quality interacts with genetic variation in dopamine receptor D4 to influence temperament in early childhood. *Development and Psychopathology, 19*, 1039–1046.

Shiner, R., & Caspi, A. (2003). Personality differences in childhood and adolescent: Measurement, development, and consequences. *Journal of Child Psychology and Psychiatry, 44*, 2–32.

Shipman, K. L., & Zeman, J. (2001). Socialization of children's emotion regulation in mother–child dyads: A developmental psychopathology perspective. *Development and Psychopathology, 13*, 317–336.

Snyder, M. (1987). *Public appearances, private realities: The psychology of self-monitoring.* New York: Freeman.

Spinrad, T. L., Stifter, C. A., Donelan-McCall, N., & Turner, L. (2004). Mothers' regulation strategies in response to toddlers' affect: Links to later emotion self-regulation. *Social Development, 13*, 40–55.

Sroufe, L. A. (1996). *Emotional development.* New York: Cambridge University Press.

Stern, D. N. (1985). *The interpersonal world of the infant.* New York: Basic Books.

Stipek, D. (1984). Young children's performance expectations: Logical analysis or wishful thinking? In J. Nicholls (Ed), *The development of achievement motivation* (pp. 33–56). Greenwich, CT: JAI Press.

Stipek, D. (1995). The development of pride and shame in toddlers. In J. P. Tangney & K. W. Fischer (Eds.), *Self-conscious emotions* (pp. 237–252). New York: Guilford.

Stipek, D., Gralinski, J. H., & Kopp, C. B. (1990). Self-concept development in the toddler years. *Developmental Psychology, 26*, 972–977.

Sturge-Apple, M. L., Davies, P. T., Winter, M. A., Cummings, E. M., & Schermerhorn, A. (2008). Interparental conflict and children's school adjustment: The explanatory role of children's internal representations of interparental and parent–child relationships. *Developmental Psychology, 44*, 1678–1690.

Thomas, A., & Chess, S. (1977). *Temperament and development.* New York: Brunner/Mazel.

Thomas, A., Chess, S., & Birch, H. G. (1968). *Temperament and behavior disorders in children.* New York: New York University Press.

Thompson, R. A. (1988). Early development in life-span perspective. In P. B. Baltes, D. L. Featherman, & R. M. Lerner (Eds.), *Life-span development and behavior*, Vol. 9 (pp. 129–172). Hillsdale, NJ: Lawrence Erlbaum Associates.

Thompson, R. A. (1989). Causal attributions and children's emotional understanding. In C. Saarni & P. Harris (Eds.), *Children's understanding of emotion* (pp. 117–150). New York: Cambridge University Press.

Thompson, R. A. (1990). Emotion and self-regulation. In R. A. Thompson (Ed.), *Socioemotional development. Nebraska Symposium on Motivation* (Vol. 36, pp. 367–469). Lincoln, NE: University of Nebraska Press.

Thompson, R. A. (1994). Emotion regulation: A theme in search of definition. In N. A. Fox (Ed.), The development of emotion regulation and dysregulation: Biological and behavioral aspects. *Monographs of the Society for Research in Child Development, 59*, 25–52.

Thompson, R. A. (1998). Empathy and its origins in early development. In S. Braten (Ed.), *Intersubjective communication and emotion in early ontogeny* (pp. 144–157). New York: Cambridge University Press.

Thompson, R. A. (2000). Childhood anxiety disorders from the perspective of emotion regulation and attachment. In M. W. Vasey & M. R. Dadds (Eds.), *The developmental psychopathology of anxiety* (pp. 160–182). Oxford, UK: Oxford University Press.

Thompson, R. A. (2006a). The development of the person: Social understanding, relationships, conscience, self. In W. Damon & R. M. Lerner (Eds.), *Handbook of child psychology, Vol. 3: Social, emotional and personality development* (6th ed., pp. 24–98). New York: Wiley.

Thompson, R. A. (2006b). Conversation and developing understanding: Introduction to the special issue. *Merrill-Palmer Quarterly, 52*(1), 1–16.

Thompson, R. A. (2008). Early attachment and later development: Familiar questions, new answers. In J. Cassidy & P. R. Shaver (Eds.), *Handbook of attachment* (2nd ed., pp. 348–365). New York: Guilford.

Thompson, R. A., & Calkins, S. (1996). The double-edged sword: Emotional regulation for children at risk. *Development and Psychopathology, 8*, 163–182.

Thompson, R. A., Flood, M. F., & Goodvin, R. (2006). Social support and developmental psychopathology. In D. Cicchetti & D. Cohen (Eds.), *Developmental psychopathology, Vol. III: Risk, disorder, and adaptation* (2nd ed., pp. 1–37). New York: Wiley.

Thompson, R. A., & Goodman, M. (2010). Development of emotion regulation: More than meets the eye. In A. Kring & D. Sloan (Eds.), *Emotion regulation and psychopathology* (pp. 38–58). New York: Guilford Press.

Thompson, R. A., & Lagattuta, K. (2006). Feeling and understanding: Early emotional development. In K. McCartney & D. Phillips (Eds.), *The Blackwell handbook of early childhood development* (pp. 317–337). Oxford, UK: Blackwell.

Thompson, R. A., Laible, D. J., & Ontai, L. L. (2003). Early understanding of emotion, morality, and the self: Developing a working model. In R. V. Kail (Ed.), *Advances in child development and behavior* (Vol. 31, pp. 137–171). San Diego, CA: Academic.

Thompson, R. A., Lewis, M., & Calkins, S. D. (2008). Reassessing emotion regulation. *Child Development Perspectives, 2*(3), 124–131.

Thompson, R. A., & Limber, S. (1990). "Social anxiety" in infancy: Stranger wariness and separation distress. In H. Leitenberg (Ed.), *Handbook of social and evaluation anxiety* (pp. 85–137). New York: Plenum.

Thompson, R. A. & Meyer, S. (2007). The socialization of emotion regulation in the family. In J. Gross (Ed.), *Handbook of emotion regulation* (pp. 249–268). New York: Guilford.

Thompson, R. A., Meyer, S., & McGinley, M. (2006). Understanding values in relationship: The development of conscience. In M. Killen & J. Smetana (Eds.), *Handbook of moral development* (pp. 267–297). Mahwah, NJ: Lawrence Erlbaum Associates.

Thompson, R. A. & Virmani, E. A. (2009). Self and personality. In M. H. Bornstein (Ed.), *Handbook of cultural developmental science* (pp. 175–187). Mahwah, NJ: Lawrence Erlbaum Associates.

Tomasello, M., & Rakoczy, H. (2003). What makes human cognition unique? From individual to shared to collective intentionality. *Mind & Language, 18*, 121–147.

Wachs, T. D. (1992). *The nature of nurture.* Newbury Park, CA: Sage.

Wachs, T. D., & Gandour, M. J. (1983). Temperament, environment, and six-month cognitive–intellectual development: A test of the organismic specificity hypothesis. *International Journal of Behavioral Development, 6*, 135–152.

Wang, Q. (2004). The emergence of cultural self-constructs: Autobiographical memory and self-description in European American and Chinese Children. *Developmental Psychology, 40*, 3–15.

Wang, Q., and Fivush, R. (2005). Mother–child conversations of emotionally salient events: Exploring the functions of emotional reminiscing in European-American and Chinese families. *Social Development, 14*, 473–495.

Wang, Q., Leichtman, M., and Davies, K. (2000). Sharing memories and telling stories: American and Chinese mothers and their 3-year-olds. *Memory, 8*, 159–178.

Welch-Ross, M. K. (1995). An integrative model of the development of autobiographical memory. *Developmental Review, 15*, 338–365.

Welch-Ross, M. K., Fasig, L. G., & Farrar, M. J. (1999). Predictors of preschoolers' self-knowledge: Reference to emotion and mental states in mother–child conversation about past events. *Cognitive Development, 14*, 401–422.

Wellman, H. M. (2002). Understanding the psychological world: Developing a theory of mind. In U. Goswami (Ed.), *Blackwell handbook of childhood cognitive development* (pp. 167–187). Oxford, UK: Blackwell.

Wigfield, A., Eccles, J. S., Schiefele, U., Roeser, R. W., & Davis-Kean, P. (2006). Development of achievement motivation. In W. Damon & R. M. Lerner (Eds.), *Handbook of child psychology, Vol. 3: Social, emotional and personality development* (6th ed., pp. 933–1002). New York: Wiley.

Wiik, K. L., & Gunnar, M. R. (2009). Development and social regulation of stress neurobiology in human development: Implications for the study of traumatic memories. In J. Quas & R. Fivush (Eds.), *Stress and memory development: Biological, social and emotional considerations* (pp. 256–277). New York: Oxford University Press.

Wiley, A. R., Rose, A. J., Burger, L. K., & Miller, P. J. (1998). Constructing autonomous selves through narrative practices: A comparative study of working-class and middle class families. *Child Development, 69*, 833–847.

Zahn-Waxler, C. (2000). The development of empathy, guilt, and internalization of distress: Implications for gender differences in internalizing and externalizing problems. In R. J. Davidson (Ed.), *Anxiety, depression, and emotion* (pp. 222–265). New York: Oxford University Press.

Zahn-Waxler, C., & Radke-Yarrow, M. (1990). The origins of empathic concern. *Motivation and Emotion, 14*, 107–130.

Zhou, M. (1997). Growing up American: The challenge confronting immigrant children and children of immigrants. *Annual Review of Sociology, 23*, 63–95.

❖ 6 ❖

THE ROLE OF PARENT–CHILD RELATIONSHIPS IN CHILD DEVELOPMENT

Michael E. Lamb
Cambridge University
Charlie Lewis
Lancaster University

INTRODUCTION

Within accounts of personality development and **socialization** over the past century, the central role of parent–child relationships has been emphasized with great consistency. Freud's (e.g., 1940) emphasis on the importance of early parent–child relationships and his conclusion that children's experiences in early life can have lasting influences on later life have been especially influential, with a focus on the infant–mother relationship especially prominent in his later work. In many respects, these concerns resonated in the theoretical debates that characterized the second half of the twentieth century. During this period, many scholars switched their allegiance from psychoanalytic theory to a perspective based on **attachment theory**, which itself reflected the integration of psychoanalytic, cybernetic, and ethological theory and therefore nicely exemplified the forces that have helped shape the emergence of developmental science. Within the broader debate between perspectives inspired by psychoanalysis and learning theory, which stressed the primacy of observable patterns of interaction (for a history, see Maccoby, 1992), attachment theory has become the dominant perspective on parent–child relationships, in part because it has accommodated the emerging cognitivist paradigm (the assumption that psychology should focus on mental processes) that has become popular (Carpendale & Lewis, 2006).

The concept of attachment is essentially relational, however, and thus contrasts with contemporary drives to locate human cognition solely within the individual (Overton, 2006). The theory holds that attachments develop out of interactions within dynamic relationships, with individuals' experiences of different relationships making up their grasp of the social world. Three related issues have also drawn increasing attention from developmental psychologists over the past 40 years or so. First, there has been increasing sensitivity to claims that the family is a system in which children influence their parents (Bell, 1968; Danziger, 1971; Lewis & Rosenblum, 1974) as much as parents "socialize" children, and that each part of the system must be understood with reference to the other parts. This has become a dominant theme in contemporary research (McHale, 2007).

Secondly, it has long been recognized that parenting and child development do not take place in a social vacuum. Parents and children interact within a complex system of influences that extend far beyond the household. For example, many infants in industrialized countries spend time in day care from a much earlier age than they did 20 years ago (Lamb & Ahnert, 2006). A few bold researchers, following Bronfenbrenner's (1979) exhortations, have even attempted to view the family in the context of a network of social relationships extending from the child's immediate relationships (such as those with care providers) into communities and the culture at large (e.g., Lamb, 1999b; Pence, 1988).

Thirdly, researchers have made extensive efforts recently to identify the role of **behavior genetics** in understanding parent–child relationships and their effects. Although it emerged in the 1930s, the behavioral genetics approach has become increasingly visible over the past quarter century (Plomin, DeFries, McClearn, & McGuffin, 2000). Researchers in this tradition use comparisons between monozygotic and dizygotic twins or between adopted and non-adopted children to distinguish genetic influences from the effects of both shared and non-shared environmental factors. In childhood, attention has been focused on behavior problems (Moffitt, 2005), especially aggression, and personality development, with researchers such as Deater-Deckard (2000) suggesting that parental responsiveness and affective engagement between parents and children have a genetic component. Such findings and arguments make a compelling case for taking account of the complexities of formative interactions between genes and environmental factors. In a longitudinal study, for example, O'Connor, Neiderhiser, Reiss, Hetherington, and Plomin (1998) compared adoptees at genetic risk for antisocial behavior because their biological mothers had such histories with those not obviously at risk. The researchers found that children at risk for antisocial behavior were treated more negatively by their adoptive parents and that the levels of parental negativity were correlated with the children's levels of behavior problems, even when the children's genetic predispositions were taken into account.

Such provocative findings ensure that the behavior genetics approach to the study of individual differences will remain prominent among researchers, especially because recent analyses assume no incompatibility with the traditional psychological perspectives that still predominate (see Collins, Maccoby, Steinberg, Hetherington, & Bornstein, 2000, for a discussion). At the same time, the literature on parenting has always had its dissenters. Over the past decade, for example, Judith Harris' (1995, 1998) "group socialization" theory has forced us to reconsider the influence of parents on their children's development, by arguing that the peer group has a dominant role. Current analyses continue to reflect on whether and how child care experiences influence children's psychosocial development (Belsky et al., 2007) and are more receptive to the idea that there is great plasticity in the genetic factors that channel development (Belsky, 1997; Belsky & Pluess, 2009).

Partly as a result of the these conceptual developments, the past 20 years has witnessed an explosion of research on the effects of parenting, taking account of some of the complexities of development. No contemporary account of parenting can easily isolate substantial formative associations between individual "determinants" and outcomes:

> In current socialization studies, simple first-order correlations between parenting characteristics and child outcomes are seldom relied on. Indeed, sometimes they are not even reported. Instead, multivariate analyses are used to investigate such questions as whether a given aspect of parenting has different effects on different kinds of children or in families living in different circumstances; or whether different aspects of parenting have independent, additive effects, whether they are interchangeable, or whether they interact so that the effects of one depend on the level of another. (Maccoby, 2000, pp. 6–7)

The analyses hinted at use of mediational analyses within longitudinal research so that the effects of different potential factors can be seen to influence jointly the developmental process (see, e.g., Criss, Shaw, Moilanen, Hitchings, & Ingoldsby, 2009). These new statistical approaches that have been made accessible to psychologists include multilevel (O'Connor, Dunn, Jenkins & Rashbash, 2006), structural equation (e.g., Schudlich & Cummings, 2007), and hierarchical modeling (e.g., Elgar, Mills, McGrath, Waschbusch, & Brownridge, 2007) techniques. These procedures, in turn, allow ever more complex models to be formulated, often (quite wrongly) led by the data rather than by good psychological theory.

Because so many diverse factors shape contemporary research on parenting, it is difficult to summarize what we know about parents' influences on their children's development. It is often noted that there is no "unifying theory" of parenting (e.g., O'Connor, 2002), as if such a theory were possible! Indeed, the diversity of extant perspectives either reflects the complex nature of parenting and its influences on child development or indicates that the field is still in its infancy and has yet to develop a fully fledged and comprehensive theory, as O'Connor suggests. Our task in this chapter is to summarize the major themes that animate and motivate current and future work, recognizing at the outset that psychoanalytic theorizing has clearly influenced current research, theory, and clinical practice, and has helped promote and preserve the multidisciplinary scholarship and research that has been so influential. We begin by examining current portrayals of parent–infant relationships, using attachment theory as a secure base from which to incorporate complementary perspectives. Thereafter, we turn to relationships between preschool-age, elementary school-age, and adolescent children and their parents, discussing the mechanisms by which these relationships are gradually transformed in the course of development. One major message here is that parenting is a dynamic construct—parents relate to babies in fundamentally different ways than parents relate to adolescents—and that such changes in parenting must be mapped. Systemic factors are emphasized throughout by comparing the parenting styles and influences of mothers and fathers. This allows us only to hint at the complexity of the family system—a fuller account would consider, in addition, the influences of siblings, grandparents, and care providers, but this is beyond the scope of our chapter.

A final section of the chapter examines the broader societal factors that affect the adequacy or quality of the relationships between parents and their children, and their impact on child development. In this context, we discuss the possible impact of parent and child gender, sociocultural and socioeconomic variations, divorce and single parenthood, and family violence.

ATTACHMENT THEORY: A FRAMEWORK FOR UNDERSTANDING PARENT–INFANT RELATIONSHIPS

All major theories of emotional development have discussed the development of attachments, but the most influential explanation was provided by John Bowlby (1969), a psychoanalyst who was impressed by ethological theories regarding the early emotional communication between infants and their parents. Bowlby's attachment theory emphasized the way that the infant's innate capacity to emit signals to which adults are biologically predisposed to respond fostered the development of attachments.

Bowlby's theory built on the assumption that the behavioral propensities of infants and parents must be considered in the context of the environment in which our species evolved. In that "environment of evolutionary adaptedness," the survival of infants depended on their ability to maintain proximity to protective adults. Unlike many other species, however, young humans are unable to move closer to or follow adults for several months; they are even incapable of clinging to adults to maintain contact. Human infants must instead rely on signals to entice adults to approach them. For these signals to be effective, adults must be predisposed to respond. The best example of such a *prepotent* signal is the infant cry, which is very effective in attracting adults to approach, pick up, and soothe the crying infant.

Bowlby (1969) described four phases in the development of parent–infant attachments:

1. the newborn phase of indiscriminate social responsiveness (the first one or two months)
2. the phase of discriminating sociability (the second to the seventh months)
3. "maintenance of proximity to a discriminated figure by means of locomotion as well as signals" (from the seventh month through the second year)
4. the phase of goal-corrected partnership (the third year on).

Phase 1: Indiscriminate Social Responsiveness of Newborns (Birth through One or Two Months)

This phase is marked by the development of a repertoire of signals by the infant. Infant cries have a markedly arousing effect on those who hear them: Typically, adults are motivated to relieve the cause of the baby's distress via physiological mechanisms that have long been recognized (e.g., Frodi et al., 1978; Murray, 1979). The most common response to crying is to pick up the infant (Bell & Ainsworth, 1972), and the most effective way of quieting a distressed infant is to hold him or her (Korner & Thoman, 1970, 1972). This illustrates Bowlby's assumption that both infants and adults have biologically determined behavioral predispositions that serve to maximize the infant's chances of survival. Crying is the first example of a class of behaviors labeled *attachment behaviors* by Bowlby. The defining or common characteristic of these behaviors is that they all serve to bring the baby close to protective and caring adults. In the early months, this goal is achieved by getting adults to approach the infant, but responsibility later shifts.

A second potent attachment behavior enters the baby's repertoire in the second month of life—smiling. Like crying, smiling is a signal that affects adults' behavior. However, smiles are effective because they encourage adults to *stay near* and continue interacting with the baby—both find the interaction *pleasant*—whereas cries encourage adults to *approach* the baby in order to terminate a signal that they find *aversive* (Ambrose, 1961; Frodi, Lamb, Leavitt, & Donovan, 1978a).

From birth, therefore, the baby is capable of affecting his or her environment and the people in it, although babies use proximity-promoting signals indiscriminately in this phase. They are satisfied with anyone who responds to their smiles, cries, and other signals, and they do not yet show any preferences for particular people. This is not surprising, because babies do not yet have the capacity to discriminate among or recognize individuals. Toward the end of this phase, the relevant perceptual and cognitive capacities develop, and babies start to recognize people in varied contexts, preferring those with whom they have most consistent interaction. This defines the transition to the second phase of attachment development.

Phase 2: Discriminating Sociability (One or Two Months through Six or Seven Months)

Although Bowlby (1969) suggested that the second phase began in the second or third month of life, infants are able to discriminate visually among people much earlier than this using auditory, visual, olfactory, and kinesthetic cues (Lamb, Bornstein, & Teti, 2002). Very young infants recognize their mothers' faces and also identify them by voice or smell but, of course, this does not imply that they realize that these are different characteristics of the same person (Bushnell, Sai & Mullin, 1989; Field, Cohen, Garcia, & Greenberg, 1984). We do not know when infants develop multimodal concepts of people and thus realize that when they hear their mothers' voices, for example, they will see their mothers' faces if they open their eyes.

Once babies can recognize familiar people, they can start to exhibit preferences among them. Presumably because infants associate particular people with pleasurable experiences (e.g., feeding, cuddling, rocking, play) and the relief of distress from early on, or because familiarity (other things being equal) tends to produce positive feelings, babies soon prefer to interact with familiar people.

During this phase of development, babies are far more coordinated behaviorally than they were earlier. Their arousal level is much less variable, and they spend more time in alert states (Emde & Robinson, 1979). Parent–infant play becomes more frequent, and in many Western cultures face-to-face games become sources of delight for both adults and infants. In early interactions of this sort, the adult assumes major responsibility for keeping the interaction going; the baby coos, smiles, or sticks out his or her tongue and the adult responds with a similar action (Kaye & Marcus, 1981). From repeated experiences of this type, however, the baby seems to learn three things: the rule of *reciprocity* (namely, that in social interaction, partners take turns acting and reacting to the other's behavior); *effectance* (his or her behavior can affect the behavior of others in a consistent and predictable fashion) and *trust* (the caretaker can be counted on to respond when signaled). These concepts are learned not only in the course of face-to-face interactions but also in the interactions centered on infant distress and adults' attempts to soothe them (Lamb, 1981a, 1981b), and their acquisition is a major step in the process of becoming social. Once infants realize that their cries (and later their smiles and coos) elicit predictable responses from others, they begin to develop a coherent view of the social world and perceive themselves as individuals who can significantly affect others. The degree to which babies feel confident of their predictions regarding the behavior of others—that is, their degree of trust or faith in the reliability of specific people—determines the security of their attachment relationships. Obviously, individual differences in the level of trust or perceived effectance each infant develops depend in part on individual differences in the responsiveness of the adults with whom the baby interacts (see below).

Phase 3: Attachments—Specific, Enduring, Affective Bonds (Seven to Twenty-Four Months)

By seven months of age, infants clearly understand and respect the rule of reciprocity in their interactions. Intentional social behavior is also possible. The beginning of Phase 3 is marked by two major behavioral changes. First, the baby now starts to protest (by crying) when left by one of the people to whom he or she is attached—*separation protest*—which signifies the baby's concern about the departure and present whereabouts of an attachment figure. Second, the baby is now able to move from place to place without assistance and this opens up a wealth of opportunities for exploration and allows the infant to assume an increasingly active role in achieving and maintaining proximity to attachment figures. Ainsworth, Blehar, Waters, and Wall (1978) label this as *the* attachment phase, because the proximity of the parent becomes a key concern and the quality of the infant's interactions plays a crucial role in the construction of self (Bowlby, 1969)—a topic discussed below, as well as by Thompson, Winer, and Goodvin in Chapter 5 of this volume.

Phase 4: Goal-Correlated Partnerships (Twenty-Four to Thirty Months Onward)

For Bowlby (1969), the next major transition occurs at the beginning of the third year of life, although infants become increasingly sophisticated in their abilities to behave intentionally, communicate linguistically, and respond appropriately in a variety of different contexts in the intervening months. As they grow older, children initiate more of their interactions and are therefore respondents in proportionately fewer of them. They can tolerate increasing distance from attachment figures, and become increasingly adept at interacting with peers and unfamiliar adults. For Bowlby, the major qualitative transformation involves the capacity for elementary role taking and the ability to take the parents' needs into account when interacting with them.

Measuring Attachment Relationships

As explained earlier, infants come to trust or count on the adults who respond consistently to their signals; in Bowlby's terminology, differences in the adults' responsiveness shape the child's *internal working models* of them. Not all adults are equivalently responsive or sensitive, however, and so infants should differ with respect to the amount of trust they feel, and thus the way they behave. To explore this question, Ainsworth developed a procedure—the Strange Situation—for assessing the *security of infant–adult attachment* (Ainsworth et al., 1978). The procedure has seven episodes, designed to expose infants to increasing levels of stress in order to observe how they organize their attachment behaviors around their parents when distressed by being in an unfamiliar environment, the entrance of an unfamiliar adult, and brief separations from the parent (Table 6.1).

According to attachment theory, infants should be able to use attachment figures as secure bases from which to explore the novel environment. The stranger's entrance should lead infants to inhibit exploration and draw a little closer to their parents, at least temporarily. In response to their parents' departure, infants should attempt to bring them back by crying or searching, and by limiting exploration and affiliation. Following their parents' return, infants should seek to reengage in interaction and, if distressed, perhaps ask to be cuddled and comforted. The same responses should occur, with somewhat greater intensity, following the second separation and reunion. In fact, this is precisely how about 65% of the infants studied in the United States behave in the Strange Situation (Teti & Teti, 1996; Thompson, 1998). Following the practices of Ainsworth and her colleagues, these infants are regarded as securely attached (they are also called Type B) because their behavior conforms to theoretical predictions about how babies should behave in relation to attachment figures.

By contrast, some infants seem unable to use their parents as secure bases from which to explore, and they are called insecure. Some are distressed by their parents' absence, and behave ambivalently on reunion, both seeking contact and interaction and angrily rejecting it when it is offered. These infants are conventionally labeled insecure–resistant or ambivalent (Type C). They typically account for about 15% of the infants in American research samples (Teti & Teti, 1996; Thompson, 1998). A third group of infants seem little concerned by their parents' absence. Instead of greeting their parents on reunion, they actively avoid interaction and ignore their parents' bids. These infants are said to exhibit insecure–avoidant attachments (Type A), and they typically constitute about 20% of the infants in American samples (Teti &

TABLE 6.1
The Strange Situation Procedure

Episode	Persons Present	Entrances and Exits
1	Parent and child	
2	Parent, stranger, and child	Stranger enters
3	Stranger and child	Parent departs
4	Parent and child	Stranger departs
5	Child	Parent departs
6	Stranger and child	Stranger enters
7	Parent and child	Parent enters; stranger departs

Teti, 1996; Thompson, 1998). Main and her colleagues have also described a fourth group of infants whose behavior is "disoriented" and/or "disorganized" (Type D; Main & Solomon, 1990). These infants simultaneously display contradictory behavior patterns, manifest incomplete or undirected movements, and appear confused or apprehensive about approaching their parents. These infants may be similar in some respects to infants in all three of the other groups, although they tend to be overrepresented in the insecure sub-groups.

Attachment theorists have emphasized the role played by prior infant–mother interactions in shaping these patterns of behavior, which are believed to reflect internal working models shaped by those earlier interactions. There is general support for the notion that sensitive or responsive parenting—that is, nurturant, attentive, nonrestrictive parental care—and synchronous infant–mother interactions are associated with secure infant behavior in the Strange Situation, and this appears to be true of US-based samples as well as samples from cultures outside the United States (De Wolff & van IJzendoorn, 1997; Posada et al., 1999; Thompson, 1998). The mothers of infants who behave in either insecure–avoidant or insecure–resistant fashions manifest less socially desirable patterns of behavior: They may overstimulate or understimulate, fail to make their behaviors contingent on infant behavior, appear cold or rejecting, and sometimes act ineptly. Similar proportions of infants fall into the major categories when assessed interacting with their fathers (Lamb & Lewis, 2010).

Because there is much variability in these results, it is difficult to identify precisely what aspects of parental behavior are important. Some studies identify warmth but not sensitivity, some patterning of stimulation but not warmth or amount of stimulation, and so forth. There is a general belief, however, that insecure–avoidant attachments are associated with intrusive, overstimulating, rejecting parenting, whereas insecure–resistant attachments are linked to inconsistent, unresponsive parenting (Belsky, 1999; De Wolff & van IJzendoorn, 1997). Certainly, programs that make parents more sensitive to their infants do increase the likelihood that those infants will be securely attached (Bakermans-Kranenburg, van IJzendoorn & Juffer, 2003). Although the antecedents of disorganized attachments are less well established, disorganized attachments are more common among abused and maltreated infants and among infants exposed to other pathological caretaking environments (Lyons-Ruth & Jacobvitz, 1999; Teti, Gelfand, Messinger, & Isabella, 1995; for a meta-analysis, see Baer & Martinez, 2006) and may be consequences of parental behaviors that infants find frightening or disturbing (Main & Hesse, 1990; Schuengel, Bakermans-Kranenburg, van IJzendoorn, & Blom, 1999).

To Whom Do Attachments Form?

According to Bowlby, the consistency of an adult's presence and availability during a sensitive period—the first six postnatal months—determines whom the baby will become attached to. If there were no consistent caretaker over this period (as might occur in institutions such as hospitals, for example), the baby would not form an attachment. Ainsworth and Bowlby proposed that most babies have a hierarchy of attachment figures and that their primary caretakers—usually their mothers—become primary attachment figures before any other relationships are formed (Bretherton & Munholland, 1999). Once infants have this foundation, Ainsworth and Bowlby argued, the infants may (and often do) form relationships with others—for example, fathers and older siblings. Obviously, these individuals must regularly spend some minimum amount of time with infants if attachments are to form, but unfortunately we do not know what this minimum level is.

Adult–infant interaction is also important in determining whether infant–adult attachments will form, because infants become attached to those persons whom they associate, over time, with consistent, predictable, and appropriate responses to their signals and needs. The importance of quality of interaction rather than quantity is underscored by the evidence that babies become attached to both of their parents even though most continue to spend much less time with their fathers than with their mothers (Lamb, 2002a; Lamb & Lewis, 2010). In stress-free situations such as the home, babies show no consistent preference for one parent. When stress occurs—whether occasioned by fatigue, the threat or reality of separation, or the entry of a stranger—proximity-seeking attachment behaviors increase and are directed toward whichever parent is with the baby. Research in the 1970s suggested that even with little contact between fathers and their babies, infants become attached to their fathers, although when both parents were present, babies between the ages of 10 and 18 months typically turned to their mothers preferentially when distressed (Lamb, 1976a, 1976c). Such findings confirm that mothers tend to be the primary attachment figures of young infants, and that infants nevertheless become attached to their fathers and mothers at about the same time, contrary to Bowlby's prediction.

Research suggests that even with little contact between fathers and their babies, infants become attached to their fathers.

In many cultures, including the USA and the UK, mothers and fathers interact with babies in distinctly different ways. A detailed analysis of videotaped records of face-to-face play between parents and very young infants (two- to six-month-olds) showed that fathers provided more unpredictable, less rhythmic, and less containing stimulation (both physical and vocal) than mothers did (Yogman, 1981). Naturalistic home observations of older infants and their parents yielded similar findings (Lamb, 1976b). For example, triadic interactions between parents and their 11–15-month-olds showed that mothers seemed set on maintaining the interaction, while fathers show more positive affect (Lindsey & Caldera, 2006). Similarly, Borke, Lamm, Eickhorst and Keller (2007) found that German fathers tended to engage in a more "distal" style of interaction whereas mothers were more proximal (i.e., they used bodily contact).

Fathers are also more likely to engage in physically stimulating or unpredictable types of play than are mothers (Lamb, 1976b, 1977a), while mothers are more likely to initiate games like pat-a-cake and peek-a-boo, or to engage in bouts of play mediated by toys. Importantly, these differences in the types of play are not evident in all social and cultural contexts (Lamb, 1977b, 2002a), suggesting that they reflect social aspects of the parents' roles, rather than intrinsic or biological factors.

Level of Contact, Sensitivity and Attachments

The evidence suggests that, across a variety of cultural settings, about two-thirds of the attachments to either parent are rated secure (e.g., Ahnert, Pinquart & Lamb, 2006; Diener, Mangelsdorf, McHale, & Frosch, 2002; Lamb, Hwang, Frodi, & Frodi, 1982). Most studies, such as that of Monteiro et al. (in press) using an attachment Q-sorting technique, show few differences in the average levels of infant–mother and infant–father security. Yet even today mothers and fathers often spend very different amounts of time with their infants (Korman & Lewis, 2001; Lewis, 1986). This raises an interesting question: How much contact is required to establish a secure attachment and what it is about that contact that is important, particularly given the recent shift towards greater paternal involvement (O'Brien, 2005; Pleck & Masciadrelli, 2004)?

How infants form secure, insecure, and disorganized relationships with their attachment figures has been central to discussion of attachments since the development of the theory. Much emphasis has been placed on the role of **parental sensitivity** (see, e.g., Ainsworth et al., 1978), although others have used terms such as "affect attunement" (Jonsson & Clinton, 2006; Stern, Hofer, Haft, & Dore, 1985), "affect mirroring" (Fonagy, Gergely, Jurist, & Target, 2002), responsiveness (Bornstein, Tamis-LeMonda, Hahn, & Haynes, 2008), and "mutual responsivity" (Kochanska, Aksan, Prisco, & Adams, 2008). In a recent study, Barry, Kochanska, and Philibert (2008) reported that children with a genetic risk for maladaptive development (a short allele in the 5-HTTLPR polymorphism linked to serotonin uptake) had insecure attachments at 15 months if their mothers had been less sensitive, but secure attachments if mothers had earlier been more sensitive. Such results complement other findings showing that the responsivity of parents to their infants' distress at six months predicts both social competence and behavior problems two and a half years later (Leerkes, Blankson, & O'Brien, 2009). We must avoid assuming that the direction of influence simply runs from parent to child (Papousek, 2007), however; each participant affects the other. For example, Pauli-Pott and Mertesacker (2009) found that highly positive maternal affect accompanied by positive affect in the infant at 4 months of age predicted secure relationships in the Strange Situation at 18 months, but when accompanied by negative or neutral infant affect, positive maternal affect predicted later insecure attachment.

As far as fathers are concerned, it seems reasonable to assume that individual differences in paternal sensitivity influence the security of infant–father attachment just as individual differences in maternal sensitivity influence the security of infant–mother attachment (see above). Notaro and Volling (1999), however, found no significant associations between assessments of American mother- and father–infant attachment in the Strange Situation, and near contemporaneous measures of parental responsiveness in a brief (3-minute) session. These findings were consistent with an earlier report that measures of father–infant interaction at home when infants were 6 and 9 months of age were unrelated to the security of infant–father attachment in the Strange Situation at 12 months (Volling & Belsky, 1992) and with Rosen and Rothbaum's (1993) observation that measures of both maternal and paternal behavior were weakly associated with later assessments of attachment security in the Strange Situation. By contrast, Brown, Mangelsdorf, Wong, Shigeto, & Neff, (2009) also reported stability between 1 and 3 years in the security of infant–father attachment, while Goossens and Van IJzendoorn (1990) reported that the sensitivity of fathers in a free-play session was correlated with near-contemporaneous assessments of infant–father attachment in a sample of Dutch fathers, and a meta-analysis of eight studies concerned with the association between paternal sensitivity and the quality of infant–father attachment in the Strange Situation revealed a small but statistically significant association (Van IJzendoorn & DeWolff, 1997) that was significantly weaker than the association between maternal sensitivity and the security of infant–mother attachment (Van IJzendoorn & DeWolff, 1997). Differential patterns of influence for mothers and fathers are evident in mediational analyses (Kochanska et al., 2008) and up to the age of three (Lindsey, Cremeens, Colwell, & Caldera, 2009).

The reasons for such differences between parents are not clear. Cox, Owen, Henderson, and Margand (1992) found that American fathers who were more affectionate, spent more time with their 3-month-olds, and had more positive attitudes were more likely to have infants who were securely attached to them 9 months later. Caldera, Huston, and O'Brien (1995) likewise reported that American infants were more likely to appear insecure in the Strange Situation at 18 months when their fathers appeared more detached in a semi-structured laboratory setting 12 months earlier. Further, Van IJzendoorn (1995) reported an association between the security of infant–father attachment and the Dutch fathers' representation of their own childhood attachments. It could be that the relative amounts of time spent by fathers are important as well, making today's more involved fathers more influential than their predecessors. Such associations raise intriguing questions about whether and how attachment styles in infancy prepare the child for later social-cognitive skills.

Predictive Validity of Attachment Styles in Infancy

The association between Strange Situation behavior and styles of interaction with others has been well documented (Berlin & Cassidy, 1999; Kerns, 1996; Sroufe, 1996; Teti, 2005). Babies with secure attachments to their mothers are later more cooperatively playful than insecure infants when interacting with friendly strangers or peers. Other researchers have examined the relation between Strange Situation classifications and aspects of later achievement motivation in children, reporting that secure infant–mother attachments at 12 or 18 months are associated with superior problem-solving abilities in a variety of stressful and challenging contexts in the preschool years. In particular, children who were securely attached to their mothers as infants persisted longer and more enthusiastically in cognitively challenging situations than did children who had insecure attachments (Frankel & Bates, 1990; Grossmann, Grossmann, & Zimmerman, 1999; Sroufe, 1983). Secure infants also seem to be more resilient and robust when stressed or challenged and appear more socially competent and independent when they later enter preschool (Teti & Teti, 1996). Insecure attachment in infancy, particularly of the disorganized/disoriented type (D), is associated with elevated rates of antisocial and externalized behavior problems in later childhood (Lyons-Ruth, Easterbrooks, & Davidson, 1997; Shaw, Owens, Vondra, & Keenan, 1996).

The effects of infant–father attachment on subsequent behavior have also been studied. Sagi, Lamb, and Gardner (1986) reported that the security of both mother– and father–infant attachment on Israeli kibbutzim was associated with indices of the infants' sociability with strangers: Securely attached infants were more sociable than insecure–resistant infants. Earlier, Lamb et al. (1982) reported that Swedish infants who were securely attached to their fathers were more sociable with strangers, and Main and Weston (1981) found that the security of both mother–infant and father–infant attachments affected American infants' responses to an unfamiliar person (dressed as a clown). Belsky, Garduque, and Hrncir (1984) reported that the security of both attachment relationships, but especially the infant–mother attachment, affected executive capacity, an index of cognitive performance, in a sample of American toddlers.

The results of other studies suggest that infant–mother attachments may have greater and more consistent predictive power than infant–father attachments. Main, Kaplan, and Cassidy (1985) reported that earlier and concurrent assessments of mother–child attachment had greater impact on children's attachment-related responses than earlier and concurrent assessments of child–father attachment. Similar results were reported by Suess, Grossmann, and Sroufe (1992), who studied associations between parent–infant attachment security and the quality of German children's later interactions with peers. Interestingly, although the parents' sensitivity toward their 12-month-olds did not predict later behavior problems in one study (Benzies, Harrison, & Magill-Evans, 1998), Verschueren and Marcoen (1999) reported that the security of child–mother attachments had a greater effect on the positive self-perceptions of 5- and 6-year-olds than did child–father attachments, whereas the security of child–father attachments best predicted whether or not the children would have behavior problems. In both studies, the beneficial effects of secure attachments to one parent partially but not completely offset the adverse effects of insecure attachment to the other, and we might expect the same to be true in infancy. By contrast, Steele, Steele, Croft, and Fonagy (1999) found that the ability of British 6-year-olds to read affective expressions in cartoons was predicted by the security of infant–mother attachments 5 years earlier, but not by infant–father attachments at 18 months or by the parents' feelings of attachment during pregnancy. Later in this chapter, we discuss in greater depth the longer term formative implications of infant–parent attachments.

Attachment within the Family System: Infants, Mothers and Fathers

At the start of the chapter, we emphasized the increasingly popular claim that a full under-standing of parenting must take into consideration the system of family relationships and not only individual relationships, and we need to include the role of physiological processes within this system. New fathers interact with their newborns in the same ways as mothers do (Rödholm & Larsson, 1982). Indeed their attentiveness is matched by similar changes in hormonal levels (decreased levels of testosterone and estradiol, coupled with increasing levels of cortisol and prolactin) around the time of their infants' births (Storey, Walsh, Quinton, & Wynne-Edwards, 2000). The female hormone estrogen seems to make younger women more sensitive to "cuteness" in infants than either men or menopausal women (Sprengelmeyer et al., 2009). Fathers also experience postnatal mood swings that may well have biological foundations (Ramchandani, Stein, Evans, O'Connor, & the ALSPAC Study Team, 2005). Such findings might provide a biological explanation for the association between the way expectant parents interact with dolls during pregnancy and their later interactions with infants and toddlers (Favez et al., 2006).

However, it is important to note that "biological parenthood" does not necessarily yield stronger attachments. Indeed, IVF and biological fathers in Sweden showed similar patterns of "prenatal attachment", and the stronger these feelings the easier it was for these men to adjust to early parenthood (Hjelmstedt & Collins, 2008). In stably cohabiting families, fathers' reports of attachment to their infants are also consistent over time (Condon, Corkindale, & Boyce, 2008).

Another influence on the family system is the gender of the participants. Fagot and Kavanagh (1993) reported that both parents found interaction with insecurely attached infants less pleasant, and both tended to become less involved in interactions with insecurely attached boys, a factor that may explain the greater likelihood of behavior problems among boys. Interestingly, fathers had unusually high levels of interaction with insecure–avoidant girls, who received the fewest directive instructions from their mothers. Schoppe-Sullivan, Diener, Mangelsdorf, Brown, McHale, and Frosch (2006) provided further evidence of the complementarity of parental roles. They found that, although fathers and mothers were similarly sensitive to their one-year-old sons, mothers appeared more sensitive to daughters than fathers were and less sensitive to sons than to daughters. At the same time, the fathers were more sensitive to sons when their partners were less sensitive. The complexity of the underlying associations was underscored by Gable, Crnic, and Belsky (1994), who reported robust correlations among marital quality, the quality of parent–child relationships, and child outcomes in a study of 2-year-olds. Infants characterized by negative emotionality early in the first year tended to become more positive when they had active, sensitive, and happily married mothers, whereas some infants became more negative when their fathers were dissatisfied with their marriages, insensitive, and uninvolved in their children's lives (Belsky, Fish, & Isabella, 1991). Davis, Schoppe-Sullivan, Mangelsdorf, and Brown (2009) also found that the infant's temperament influenced the quality of parenting, particularly those aspects shared between the two parents.

Clearly, attachments cannot be treated in isolation from other factors, particularly the relationship between the parents. In a study of 20-month-olds, for example, Easterbrooks and Goldberg (1984) found that the children's adaptation was promoted by both the amount of paternal involvement and, more importantly, the quality or sensitivity of their fathers' behavior. By contrast, the security of neither infant–mother nor infant–father attachment predicted the adjustment at age five of infants reared on traditional kibbutzim (those with central dormitories for children) in Israel, although, in keeping with the ecological model described earlier, the security of the infant–caretaker relationship did predict later behavior (Oppenheim, Sagi, & Lamb, 1988).

Lamb and his colleagues (Lamb, Thompson, Gardner, & Charnov, 1985; Thompson, 1998) have emphasized that the degree of **predictive validity** from measures of attachment security is far from perfect, regardless of whether the child–mother or child–father attachment is studied. Rather, the predictive relationship between Strange Situation behavior in infancy and subsequent child behavior is found only when there is stability in caretaking arrangements and family circumstances that seem to maintain stability in patterns of parent–child inter-action subsequently reflected in similar patterns of Strange Situation behavior. This raises the interesting question: Is the prediction of adjustment over time attributable to individual differences in the quality of early infant–parent attachments, or is it attributable to the con-tinuing quality of child–parent interactions over time? The latter would imply that the quality of early relationships was predictively valuable not because it caused later differences directly, but because it presaged later differences in the quality of relationships that in turn support continuing differences in the child's behavior. In other words, early interactions may shape the initial internal working models that are believed to guide behavior but these internal working models are continually updated and revised in light of later interactions. Such a pattern of findings would place the locus of stability in continuing parent–child interactions rather than in some characteristic of the child fixed by formative interactions with parents early in life. We return to these issues later in the chapter when discussing the long-term implications of individual differences in the quality of early child–parent relationships.

A GRADUAL ENTRANCE INTO THE SOCIAL WORLD: THE PRESCHOOL AND SCHOOL YEARS

The years between infancy and the child's entry into formal educational settings are marked by dramatic developmental changes. Seven areas of change—physical and locomotor growth, language, impulse control, social-cognitive understanding, conceptions of the self, cognitive executive processes, and the desire for autonomy—characterize the years between infancy and school and have significant effects on the nature and quality of parent–child relationships (Maccoby, 1984). Importantly, the transition from infancy to early childhood brings a dra-matic change in the roles of parents because physical, mental, and language development makes new behavioral capacities possible and facilitates the comprehension of more complex parental communication. From the end of infancy, the amount of child care performed by parents also declines progressively (DeLuccie, 1996; Galinsky, 1999). Toward the end of the second year of life, therefore, parents increasingly attempt to shape their children's social lives by directly encouraging children to behave in appropriate ways and discouraging them from inappropriate and socially proscribed behavior. The ability to conceptualize symbolically facilitates another important process—**observational learning**. Initial discussions of the process emphasized the need for observers to store a model's behavior in memory and then recall it for subsequent performance in order for this form of learning to be effective (Bandura, 1969, 1977). More recent theory encompasses not only observational learning but also the system of interactions and relationships, drawing on cognitive models of development and social factors such as attachments (Bandura, 1986, 1997).

The Preschool Child's Understanding of Social Relationships

Research until the 1980s emphasized the preschool child's continuing egocentrism. Over the past 20 years, however, many researchers have studied the understanding of social relationships in terms of the ability to predict others' actions or thoughts using the false belief paradigm in which the child has to make a judgment about another person's beliefs when that person's behavior suggests that he or she has a different conception of reality. In such situations, preschoolers recognize the other's perspective—albeit in a relatively immature manner—by the age of four (Wellman, Cross, & Watson, 2001). Although there is heated controversy about the origins of these skills (see Lewis & Carpendale, 2010, for an introduction), it is likely that the ability to "read minds" emerges gradually in the course of everyday social interaction, particularly with parents and other family members. Thus, 3- to 4-year-olds typically perform better in false belief tests (Figure 6.1) when they have more siblings (Jenkins & Astington, 1996; Lewis et al., 1996; Perner et al., 1994), particularly older siblings (Ruffman et al., 1998). This "sibling effect" suggests that family factors affect the emergence of these perspective-taking skills. The more contact that preschoolers have with extended family members, particularly more socially proficient relatives such as older cousins, uncles, and aunts, the earlier they acquire such skills (Lewis et al., 1996). Presumably, the quality of

FIGURE 6.1 False-belief test.

interaction between parents and children also predicts the speed at which children come to understand such important aspects of their social world.

Three types of evidence support this hypothesis. In infancy, first of all, children learn how to understand social interactions in the course of everyday experiences, particularly those that involve teasing and shared attention (Reddy, 2003; Tomasello, 1999). Second, variations in parenting style are correlated with differences in the development of **social cognition** (Astington, 1996; Ruffman, Perner, & Parkin, 1999; Sabbagh & Seamans, 2008; Vinden, 2001), indicating that parents stage-manage the toddler's and preschooler's gradual entry into both social interactions and social understanding. For example, Ruffman et al. (1999) found that children scored higher on tests of false belief when their parents dealt with disciplinary events by asking their children to reflect on the victims' feelings. Similarly, maternal talk about the mind and cooperative sibling interaction in the third year predict the age of acquisition of mental state reasoning (Dunn, Brown, & Beardsall, 1991; Dunn, Brown, Slomkowski, Tesla, & Youngblade, 1991). Third, factors within the attachment relationship itself predict concurrent and later psychosocial functioning, as assessed in the child's developing ability to understand mental states (Fonagy & Target, 1997; Hobson, 2002; Meins, 1999). Early evidence of an association between attachment and social understanding in infancy was reported by Bretherton, Bates, Benigni, Camaioni, and Volterra (1979), who found that securely attached 12-month-olds had been more likely to point at objects and look to see whether the parent was looking (known as "proto-declarative" pointing) a month earlier. Securely attached children also did better on diverse "**theory of mind**" tasks (Fonagy, Redfern & Charman, 1997; Symons & Clark, 2000), whereas children who were securely attached at one year of age were more likely to pass a false belief task at 4 years (Meins, 1997) and more complex mind reading tests at 5 years (Meins, Fernyhough, Russell, & Clarke-Carter, 1998).

What accounts for the correlation between secure attachment and more skilled social understanding? Following Bretherton et al. (1979), Fonagy and Target (1997) suggested that there is a close association between the ability to understand that people have mental states and the earlier self-representational skills presumed by the internal working model construct. Fonagy and Target suggested that conceptually related "reflective" functions serve as a basis of later social understanding, emerging as a natural consequence of generalizations from the attachment relationships with parents. Meins (1999; Meins, Fernyhough, Fradley, & Tuckey, 2001; see also Ereky-Stevens, 2008) suggested that the parent's communication style is crucial to this transmission. Describing parents who treat their children as "persons" with thoughts and feelings as "mindminded," Meins argued that such parents tend to "treat their infants as individuals with minds, rather than merely entities with needs that must be met" (1999, p. 332), exposing infants and toddlers to more talk about psychological constructs. From this perspective, exposure to mental state language and secure attachment are highly intertwined. Thus, mothers' language about 5-month-olds' minds (but not mindminded language about other people) predicted the children's false belief performance at age four (Meins et al., 2002). In this way, social understanding is acquired while children learn about and within social relationships (Carpendale & Lewis, 2010).

These links between attachment and later social understanding are surely influenced by the interactional processes that we discussed earlier. For example, "mind-mindedness" is mediated by the processes identified earlier: sensitivity of parents to their infants (Laranjo, Bernier, & Meins, 2008; Ontai & Thompson, 2008), "joint engagement" with their toddlers (Nelson, Adamson & Bakeman, 2008) or responsiveness (Ensor & Hughes, 2008) to their preschoolers' behaviors and later utterances. However, the picture is more complicated. There is cross-cultural evidence that some of the patterns addressed above do not generalize to other settings. For example, Lewis, Huang, and Rooksby (2006) did not find associations between parental styles, family size (interactions with cousins because few families had more than one child) and false belief in mainland China.

Do Mothers and Fathers Differentially Socialize Boys and Girls?

Other than parental attachments and/or the use of forms of language that allow the children to enter into more complex social relationships, are there other identifiable influences on the development of social understanding? Gender has a pervasive influence on socialization in general, and parent–child interaction in particular (Fagot, 1995; Ruble & Martin, 1998), although researchers have documented surprisingly few differences in the ways in which boys and girls are treated by their parents during the first years of life (Lytton & Romney, 1991; Russell & Saebel, 1997; Siegel, 1987). For example, Lytton and Romney's meta-analysis of 172 studies involving over 27,000 children revealed only one consistent difference between mothers and fathers—a significant, but small, tendency for fathers to encourage the use of sex-typed toys more than mothers did. Otherwise, there were insufficient data to support the claim that mothers and fathers differentially affect their children's sex-role development. Lytton and Romney further reported that, beyond the preschool years, the similarities between the behavior of mothers and fathers increased. Later research has confirmed this pattern. For example, French fathers tended to be more directive in play with toddlers than were mothers (Labrell, 1994), but by 42 months, fathers no longer challenged their children more than mothers did (Labrell, Deleau, & Juhel, 2000). Similarly, early differences in parent–child language (Gleason, 1975; Rowe, Coker, & Pan, 2004) are not clearly echoed in patterns of parent–child communication in the preschool period (Pellegrini, Brody & Stoneman, 1987; Welkowitz, Bond, Feldman & Tota, 1990), although preschool teachers seem to convey powerful but subtle sex-differentiating signals to young children (Leaper, 2002; Maccoby, 1998).

Researchers typically observe mothers and fathers in the same context, which may not be equivalently representative of the settings in which they typically interact with their children. Different settings impose different constraints on parents (Lewis & Gregory, 1987; Ross & Taylor, 1989), and most researchers do not sample contexts in a way that would allow them to determine whether some contexts magnify or minimize parental styles or have different effects depending on the parents' styles. This tendency on the part of researchers is likely to obscure discernible differences between the behavior of mothers and fathers, although the results of a few studies suggest that such differences exist in the preschool period. In one recent study, for example, Lindsey and Mize (2001) examined parent–child and child–peer dyads in "pretend" and "physical play" sessions. Not only did mothers engage in more pretend play with their daughters while father–son dyads specialized in physical play, but patterns of parent–child pretend and physical play also predicted the amounts of the same type of play with peers. Similarly, Hagan and Kuebli (2007) explored the way parents assisted their preschoolers on a balance beam. They found that mothers were equally attentive to children of either sex, but fathers were particularly protective of their daughters in this context. Future research needs to examine such subtle differences between parents.

Even in the preschool period, children in a variety of cultures clearly differentiate between the roles of mothers and fathers. For example, Raag and Rackliff (1998) introduced pre-schoolers to a laboratory play room in which a range of sex-neutral and sex-stereotyped toys were laid out, and then asked the children which toys they and their parents thought it was appropriate to play with. Many boys, particularly those who had chosen sex-stereotypical toys, stated that their fathers would consider cross-sex toy play to be "bad." Thus fathers were believed by sons, but not daughters, to have more restrictive rules of conduct than mothers did. By their entry into school, furthermore, children appear to have highly stereotyped views of parental roles. Domestic work is widely described as the mother's prerogative whereas bread winning is seen as the province of fathers throughout the school years (Hartley, 1960; Langford, Lewis, Solomon, & Warin, 2001; Williams, Bennett, & Best, 1975). Interviews with over 800 5- to 15-year-olds in four societies revealed that these beliefs persisted into middle childhood and adolescence (Goldman & Goldman, 1983). Such differences suggest that maternal and paternal styles, while hard to discern in observational studies, may have strong effects on preschoolers, perhaps because they perceive subtle nuances in parental behavior or social stereotypes which underpin sex role differences.

Future research is needed to explore how mothers and fathers influence their preschoolers' development. We need more longitudinal research that straddles the boundaries of social interactions between parents and children and the latter's "cognitive" development. In an exemplary study of this sort, LaBounty, Wellman, Olson, Lagattuta, & Liu (2008) reported that mothers' emotional expressiveness with 3½-year-olds was related to the children's later (5 years) grasp of emotions, whereas fathers' use of "causal explanatory" language in conversation predicted their children's concurrent and later "theory of mind" understanding.

The School-Age Child

Few researchers have focused on parent–child relationships involving children between six and twelve years of age. The school years have been a focus of active research in the past two decades, but researchers have typically emphasized either the roles played by mothers and fathers or the parents' overall parenting styles. In this section, we briefly compare mothers and fathers before describing some fundamental dimensions of parenting.

As their children grow older, mothers continue to spend more time with their children than fathers do (Collins & Russell, 1991; Pleck & Masciadrelli, 2004). When observed together, however, mothers and fathers initiate activities with equal frequency (Noller, 1980), and there are broad similarities in their reactions to their children's play and cognitive styles (Bronstein, 1984). Individual patterns of paternal closeness are relatively stable over time during middle childhood, and there are discernible parental styles in this period (Herman & McHale, 1993). Most research on socialization during this phase has been concerned with the influences of peers, teachers, and educational institutions on children's adjustment (see Eccles and Roeser, Chapter 8, and Rubin and his colleagues, Chapter 7, this volume). Those researchers who have examined parent–child relationships during the elementary school years have focused on achievement and achievement motivation or on the competition between parental and peer influences, rather than on the association between the quality of parent–child relationships and aspects of children's socioemotional development. Parents remain influential and affectively salient throughout this period and into adolescence, however. Interactions with parents allow children to practice, rehearse, and refine skills that later facilitate interactions with peers (MacDonald & Parke, 1984; Parke et al., 2002, 2004). Furthermore, as peers become more important at the end of middle childhood, parents continue to remain central; their role is transformed rather than usurped (Buhrmeister & Furman, 1990; Collins, Harris, & Susman, 1995; Lamborn & Steinberg, 1993; Oosterwegel & Oppenheimer, 1993).

Styles of Parenting in Middle Childhood

Due in part to advances in children's cognitive skills and abilities, school-aged children need less intensive and more subtle monitoring and exert more self-control than younger children. Most parents and professionals, however, believe that parents must continue to assume directive roles, allowing children to express emotions fully, making important norms salient, and setting appropriate limits when necessary (Greenberg & Speltz, 1988). Parental monitoring is still valuable; Crouter, MacDermid, McHale, and Perry-Jenkins (1990) found that less well-monitored boys received lower grades at school than children whose parents monitored them more closely. Successful parents are therefore sensitive to the changing needs of growing children, gradually increasing the children's involvement in such family decisions as the allocation of responsibilities and household chores (Goodnow, 1996). Parent–child relationships continue to be recalibrated and redefined as parents become increasingly involved in anticipatory guidance and emotional support. Parents continue to promote emotional stability by serving as "secure bases," despite the fact that their children begin to shield their emotional and social lives from their parents' view. Conflicts over behavioral control are replaced by a concern with achievement and industriousness, with an explicit focus on helping children make the transition to adult roles. Both parents and children play important roles in the redefinition of their relationships.

As Maccoby (1984, 1992) has argued, "coordination" and "co-regulation" rather than bidirectional patterns of influence increasingly characterize parent–child relationships in middle childhood. Based on new methods of monitoring, guiding, and supporting their children, parents reinforce children's understanding of moral standards, although there is more concern with equity and fairness in the parent–child relationship during middle childhood than there was earlier. Consequently, effective socialization increasingly involves monitoring children rather than directing them (Baumrind, 1991; Hetherington & Clingempeel, 1992).

Parents adjust their demands during middle childhood in accordance with the expectation that, by the time children reach adolescence, they should approach adult standards of behavior. Compared with parents of younger children, for example, parents of school-aged children are less inclined to use physical coercion with their children and are more apt to appeal to their self-esteem or to their sense of humor, and seek to arouse their guilt (Maccoby, 1984, 1992). Verbal mediation of control replaces physical control and this transition affects children's behavior: When mothers rely on reasoning and suggestions, children tend to negotiate, whereas when mothers use direct maternal strategies, children tend to be defiant (Kuczynski, Kochanska, Radke-Yarrow, & Girnius-Brown, 1987). Advances in cognitive development enable children to understand the legitimacy of parental authority (Damon, 1983). Recent theoretical analyses have stressed the need to consider the bidirectional influences of parent–child relationships and the wider contexts in which they take place (Kuczynzki, 2003).

During this phase, the manner in which children interact with their parents also changes. School-aged children do not express anger toward their parents as openly and as often as they did when they were younger, and they are less likely to whine, yell, and hit. In part, this is because parents of school-aged children are less concerned with promoting autonomy and establishing daily routines and more concerned with children's industriousness and achievement. Recent sociological analyses of family communication styles point to a shift towards family "democracy" over successive generations (e.g., Beck & Beck-Gernsheim, 1995; Giddens, 1998). Whereas education was considered to be the responsibility of the schools a generation ago, contemporary parents worry about the extent to which they should become involved in their children's school work (Solomon, Warin & Lewis, 2002), whether they should require children to do chores, what standards of performance they should demand, and the extent to which they should monitor their children's social life (Maccoby, 1984). Anticipatory guidance of the child, monitoring of the child's activities, expressions of affection, and parental teaching during this phase all serve to prevent behavior problems (Holden, 1995; Holden & Miller, 1999). It is not just that children with disengaged parents are more socially incompetent, irresponsible, immature, and alienated from their families; they also have poorer relationships with peers and perform more poorly at school (Baumrind 1991; Patterson, Reid, & Dishion, 1992; Rubin et al., Chapter 7, this volume). Clearly, parental involvement plays an important role in the development of both social and cognitive competence in children, whereas a lack of parental monitoring is strongly associated with the risk of delinquent behavior (Andrews & Dishion, 1994).

According to Freud, the superego begins to become dominant in middle childhood, and, as a result, children become preoccupied with mastering adult standards of behavior. Children want to meet their parents' expectations and feel distressed when they fail, although they may blame the distress on their parents or themselves. This ambiguity may mark the beginning of the intrapersonal and interpersonal conflict that becomes prominent during adolescence (Freud, 1958). As discussed below, however, most research casts doubt on the psychoanalytic depiction of adolescence as a period of significant intrapersonal and interpersonal conflict.

Baumrind's Model of Parental Styles

Some of the most influential research on the ways in which specific childrearing patterns were associated with particular child outcomes was initiated by Baumrind in the 1960s (Baumrind, 1967, 1971, 1973, 1975, 1991; Baumrind & Black, 1967). Baumrind distinguished four patterns of **parenting**, which she labeled **authoritarian, authoritative**, permissive, and nonconformist. According to Baumrind, authoritarian parents value obedience and recommend forceful imposition of the parents' will, permissive parents believe that parents should be nonintrusive but available as resources, whereas nonconformist parents, although opposed to authority, are "less passive and exert more control than permissive parents" (Baumrind, 1975, p. 14). Between the extremes represented by authoritarian and permissive parents fall authoritative parents, who encourage independence and attempt to shape their preschoolers' behavior using rational explanation.

According to Baumrind, authoritative parents are sensitive to and facilitate their children's changing sense of self. Furthermore, by allowing themselves to learn from their children, authoritative parents maximize their positive impact, teaching their children, as authoritarian and permissive parents do not, that social competence emerges within a context of interpersonal give-and-take. Although authoritative parents strive to foster independence, they also inculcate a value system characterized by conformity to cultural and societal norms by balancing the use of both reasoning and punishment.

Authoritative parents, by contrast, value self-assertion, wilfulness, and independence, and foster these goals by assuming active and rational parental roles. Baumrind (1967, 1972) explained that the children of authoritative parents are socially responsible because their parents clearly communicate realistic demands that are intellectually stimulating while generating moderate amounts of tension.

Mothers, Fathers, and Cultural Influences on Parenting Styles

Attempts to compare mothers' and fathers' approaches to parenting have yielded inconclusive findings. Baumrind's analysis underscores the need to study parents' philosophies of childrearing, but Baumrind focused on parents rather than mothers and/or fathers, and she has not explored why parents adopt the strategies they do. Studying the parents of 305 Australian preschoolers, Russell and his colleagues (1998) found that mothers were more likely to identify with the authoritative style of parenting, whereas fathers were more likely to describe themselves as either authoritarian or permissive. Parents were also more often identified with the authoritarian perspective when the child under discussion was a son. These patterns of evidence suggest that we need to consider both the children's impact on the parents' childrearing beliefs and the reasons why mothers and fathers may have differing philosophies, because these may well be colored by the divergent roles they assume in the

Authoritative parents inculcate a value system characterized by conformity to cultural and societal norms by balancing the use of reasoning and punishment.

family. Of course, this assertion needs to be explored empirically in a wide variety of cultural and subcultural settings.

Although authoritative parents foster a sense of independence in their children, they also inculcate a value system characterized by conformity to cultural and societal norms by balancing the use of reasoning and punishment. Many researchers have confirmed Baumrind's original conclusion that firm and responsive parenting seems to promote greater cooperation, less delinquency, and higher social and cognitive competence in children. However, further research into comparisons of different cultural contexts has complicated the picture. In African American families, authoritarian parenting, particularly if associated with physical punishment, may not increase the level of behavior problems, suggesting that the pattern of findings reported by Baumrind is culture-specific (Baumrind, 1972). In addition, Baumrind has yet to document the developmental processes by which authoritative parents facilitate their children's socialization (Darling & Steinberg, 1993).

In the past two decades, however, other researchers have greatly enriched our understanding of socialization processes (Bugental & Goodnow, 1998), with family systems analysts such as Patterson (1976, 1982) documenting the processes by which parents and children shape one another's behavior. For example, some parents unwittingly train their children to use negative gestures manipulatively while others both fail to extinguish their children's undesirable behaviors and may even foster conduct problems (Andrews & Dishion, 1994). **Conduct disordered** teenagers also elicit coercive behavior from adults (Patterson et al., 1992). These insights have been useful in the development of intervention programs designed to help parents exercise more effective control over their children's and adolescents' behavior (Andrews & Dishion, 1994).

MacKinnon(-Lewis) and her colleagues (MacKinnon, Lamb, Belsky, & Baum, 1990; MacKinnon-Lewis, Lamb, Arbuckle, Baradaran, & Volling, 1992; MacKinnon-Lewis et al., 1994; MacKinnon-Lewis, Volling, Lamb, Hattie, & Baradaran, 2001) have also built on Patterson's work, demonstrating that the behavior of both parents and children is affected by their expectations or attributions about one another, and that both attributions and behavioral tendencies are influenced by the dyad's history of interactions. Studies such as these illustrate the role of cognitions in family socialization; values and beliefs are increasingly viewed as both motivators and interpretive lenses through which parents and children of all ages view one another, and analysis of the cognitive facets of parent–child socialization is increasingly prominent (Bugental & Goodnow, 1998).

Parental behaviors and children's cognitive constructions of the world are filtered through the same attachment lens that influences earlier development, with some studies suggesting gender differences in the patterns of attachment. For example, Diener, Isabella, Behunin, and Wong (2008) found that 6- to 10-year-old American boys reported more secure attachments to fathers than to mothers, whereas the reverse was true of girls. Other researchers reported more secure child–mother than child–father attachments (Booth-LaForce et al., 2006). Such patterns have their social and cognitive correlates and sequelae. In keeping with the findings on preschoolers, maternal and paternal closeness are independently related to peer-rated adjustment and perceived self-competence in American 10-year-olds (Rubin et al., 2004). Such findings complement earlier ones in which attachment security with both parents is associated with various indices of positive friendship qualities among preadolescents (Lieberman, Doyle, & Markiewicz, 1999).

Both parents also influence their children's early educational aspirations. Booth-LaForce et al. (2006) found that secure attachments related to superior self-perceived academic competence especially when children had secure attachments to both parents. Martin, Ryan and Brooks-Gunn (2007) likewise found that mothers' and fathers' support for their two-year-olds independently predicted their children's language and arithmetic scores just before school entry at the age of five. Further, fathers who are supportive in their preschoolers' interactions have offspring who do better on cognitive and language assessments (Cabrera, Shannon & Tamis-LeMonda, 2007). The same holds true in the school years. Most research on educational attainment suggests that the levels of parental conversation and parental limit setting affect achievement, with no clear differences between mothers and fathers (e.g., Scott, 2004).

In two large studies, however, Flouri and Buchanan (2004) found that British children with more involved fathers had higher IQs at 7 years of age. Belsky et al. (2008) found that parents' support for their children's independent thinking was related to reading and arithmetic at 6 to 8 years, particularly in boys. In addition, however, fathers' support for independent thinking best predicted changes over this age range. This is consistent with evidence that fathers exert demands on their children, particularly their sons, in the subjects they especially value, such as physics or mathematics (Crowley, Callanan, Tenenbaum, & Allen, 2001; Tenenbaum & Leaper, 2003). When fathers become involved in school activities, this contributes unique variance to their children's educational perfomance (McBride, Schoppe-Sullivan, & Ho, 2005).

Of course, this does not mean that fathers make unique contributions to development in middle childhood. In interpreting longitudinal evidence, Lewis, Newson and Newson (1982) argued that such correlations are more likely to reflect a range of factors, particularly about the relationship between the parents. Recent evidence supports this view. For example, the link between paternal involvement and child outcomes is linked with the quality of the father–mother relationship (Goldman, 2005) as well as to factors outside the family such as the parents' employment patterns (Gottfried, Gottfried, & Bathurst, 2002). We return to these issues later in the chapter.

The Individual's Construction of Relationships: Internal Working Models

Although most of the research on parent–child attachments has concentrated on the interactions between parents and their infants within the reunion episode of the Strange Situation, many theorists have examined the changing nature and function of parent–child attachment relationships, reasoning that these continue to develop and change in ways that require continued coordination and integration as maturing individuals adapt to their changing social contexts (see Greenberg, Cicchetti, & Cummings, 1990; Sroufe, 1988, 1996). As mentioned earlier, ideas within cognitive science concerning the importance of self-representations (e.g., Mandler, 1985), led attachment theorists to propose that infants and young children construct "internal working models" in the course of early interactions that reflect their experience of the self in these relationships and guide their behavior in later relationships (Bowlby, 1969, 1973, 1988; Bretherton, 1990, 1991, 1993). Although internal working models continue to be formed during and after early childhood, maintaining continuity in individual developmental pathways, there exists wide variation across individuals in the degree to which working models reflect the individual's own experiences, as well as his or her cognitive, linguistic, and behavioral skills (Bowlby, 1973).

Internal working models represent children's conceptions of attachment figures as reflected in their interactions and in the feedback they receive from their parents. Working models influence overt demonstrations of attachment behavior as children grow older, but attachment behavior becomes more subtle with age because older children are more capable of evaluating the intentions, motives, and behaviors of attachment figures. Crittenden (1990, 1992, 1994) has further proposed that individuals acquire multiple working models associated with different memory systems. In what she terms the dynamic maturation model of attachment, she argues that we need to consider simultaneously both attachments and the way family processes affect the impact of parental styles on children's internal working models (Crittenden, 2006; Crittenden & Dallos, 2009). These are particularly sensitive to conflict and parental neglect.

The internal working model construct has become central to explanations of the role played by attachment relationships in children's social relationships and individual psychosocial functioning over time. Main, Kaplan, and Cassidy (1985) suggested that emotional openness in discussing imagined parent–child separations and conversations with parents reflected aspects of children's mental representations of relationships with their parents. Specifically, those children who were securely attached at 12 months provided accounts that appeared more coherent, elaborate, and emotionally open at 6 years of age, whereas those children who were insecurely attached at 12 months were more likely to offer sad, irrational, or bizarre responses later, or else were completely silent. Slough (1988) reported similar results. Using a story completion task, furthermore, Cassidy (1988) found that children who behaved securely on reunion with their mothers represented themselves positively in interviews and were better able to acknowledge less than perfect aspects of the self than children who behaved insecurely.

ADOLESCENCE

One prediction of attachment theory is that there will be transgenerational continuities in attachment styles. Main and her colleagues (George, Kaplan, & Main, 1985; Main & Goldwyn, 1994) developed the adult attachment interview (AAI) to assess adults' ability to integrate early memories of their relationships with parents into overarching working models of relationships. According to Main, these working models fall into one of three categories, with adults classified as *autonomous* (free to evaluate their early attachment relationships), *dismissive* of their attachment relationships, or *preoccupied* with their attachment relationships. According to Kobak and Sceery (1988), adolescents in the secure or autonomous group were rated by their peers as more ego resilient, less anxious, and less hostile. These adolescents reported little distress and high levels of social support, whereas those in the dismissive group were rated low on ego resilience and high on hostility by their peers, with whom they had distant relationships. Adolescents in the preoccupied group were viewed as less ego resilient and more anxious by their peers, and they reported higher levels of personal distress and family support than those in the dismissive group. Steinberg (1990) has hypothesized that securely attached adolescents may be more likely than dismissive or preoccupied adolescents to renegotiate healthy relationships with their parents successfully. Autonomous adults appeared more sensitively responsive to their infants than adults in the dismissive and preoccupied groups, and their children were more likely to be securely attached (see van IJzendoorn, 1995, for a review). As mentioned earlier, for example, British mothers' and fathers' perceptions during pregnancy of their attachments to their own parents predicted the security of their infants' later attachments to them (Fonagy, Steele & Steele, 1991; Steele, Steele, & Fonagy, 1996).

These studies on the associations between individual internal working models and parent–child relationships suggest that secure children, adolescents, and adults who see attachment figures as well as themselves as primarily good, though not perfect, are able to communicate with ease, tend to have flexible interpersonal styles, express empathy for others, and discuss attachment relationships coherently without idealizing them.

Many psychologists have made note of qualitative and functional transformations in parent–child relationships in adolescence (Collins, 1990; Hauser et al., 1987; Hill, 1988; Parke & Buriel, 1998; Shulman & Seiffge-Krenke, 1997), with children shifting their dependence first to same-sex and then to opposite-sex peers, while continuing the processes of self-differentiation and individuation which become the major themes of development in adolescence (Collins, 1990; Grotevant, 1998; Hill & Holmbeck, 1987; Steinberg, 1988, 1990). As with previous phases of development, research comparing mothers and fathers reveals few differences between mothers' and fathers' interactional styles (Russell & Saebel, 1997; Silverberg, Tennenbaum, & Jacob, 1992), although parent–adolescent relationships are increasingly marked by self-assertion, distance, and conflict. Steinberg (1987) found that early maturing sons and daughters reported more conflict with their mothers than later maturing children, although these processes may take a different form and have different meaning in mother–child and father–child relationships. The effects of puberty are frequently confounded with the effects of other age-related changes such as the transition from elementary to middle or from middle to high school (Collins & Russell, 1991; Simmons & Blyth, 1987), but whatever their relative importance, the biological, social, and cognitive changes associated with puberty all make early adolescence a critical transitional period during which youngsters are expected to consolidate their knowledge of the norms and roles of adult society and, at least in Western industrialized societies, begin to become emotionally and economically independent of their parents (Grotevant, 1998).

Baumrind (1991) noted that parents of adolescents tend to use increasingly complex variations of the basic patterns described above when faced with the unique challenges and changes characteristic of the adolescent period. She concluded that:

> Adolescents' developmental progress is held back by directive, officious, or unengaged practices and facilitated by reciprocal, balanced interactions characteristic of . . . authoritative . . . parents. Directive parents who are authoritarian generate internalizing problem behaviors and are less successful at curtailing drug use. Directive parents who are not authoritarian effectively promote positive competence. (p. 753)

Similarly, Dornbusch, Ritter, Leiderman, Roberts, and Fraleigh (1987) found that adolescents with authoritative parents had higher grades in school than adolescents whose parents were

Parent–adolescent relationships are increasingly marked by self-assertion, distance, and conflict.

rated authoritarian or permissive. The relationship between parental styles and school performance, however, may be mediated by adolescent psychosocial maturity, work orientation, and socioemotional adjustment (Steinberg, Elmen, & Mounts, 1989). Studies of the links between attachments and peer relationships also show clear links in adolescence. For example, Dykas, Ziv and Cassidy (2008) found that 17-year-olds rated as securely attached on the AAI were seen by their contemporaries as more prosocial and less aggressive.

Mothers, Fathers, and Adolescents

Researchers have also described some interesting differences between the ways in which mothers and fathers relate to male and female adolescents (Collins & Russell, 1991; Steinberg, 1987, 1990). Collins and Russell focused on three dimensions of parent–child relationships in middle-class families: interactions (measured by frequency, extent and structure), affect (indexed by the degree of positive affect, closeness, and cohesion), and cognition (indexed by discrepancies between parents' and children's perceptions of their relationships). They concluded that, as in infancy, mothers engage in more frequent interaction with children in middle childhood and adolescence (especially interactions involving caretaking and routine family tasks) than fathers do, and that most father–child interactions involve play, recreation, and goal-oriented actions and tasks (see also Lamb, 1997; Montemayor & Brownlee, 1987; Russell & Russell, 1987). When dyadic and systemic aspects of parent–adolescent relationships are examined (Larson & Richards, 1994; Steinberg, 1990), mothers appear to engage in more shared activities with daughters than with sons, although both relationships are marked by relatively high levels of both closeness and discord. Fathers, by contrast, tend to be more engaged with their sons, have little contact with daughters, and generally have more distant relationships with their children than mothers do (Hosley & Montemayor, 1997; Montemayor & Brownlee, 1987; Youniss & Ketterlinus, 1987). Mothers and fathers become equivalently involved in activities related to their children's scholastic and extracurricular performance and achievement (Youniss & Smollar, 1985), however, and both parents continue to engage in frequent nurturant caretaking (Russell & Russell, 1987). In most interactional domains, in fact, the differences between mothers and fathers are neither as large nor as consistent as many theorists have hypothesized (Lamb, 1997) although adolescents in North America (Hosley & Montemayor, 1997) and Britain (Langford et al., 2001) consistently report being closer to their mothers than to their fathers. Adolescents believe that their mothers know them better than their fathers do, and, although they care about both mothers and fathers, daughters are more likely than sons to differ with parents regarding the degree of closeness

(Langford et al., 2001, Hosley & Montemayor, 1997; Youniss & Ketterlinus, 1987). Korean daughters see their fathers as distant and controlling (Rohner & Pettengill, 1985).

Because fathers spend less time with, have fewer conversations with, and are less affectively salient to their adolescent children, one might expect them to be less influential. Consistent with this, daughters report being relatively uninfluenced by their fathers (Larson & Richards, 1994) and even sons feel that mothers provide more support than fathers do (Youniss & Smollar, 1985). On the other hand, there is clear evidence that some fathers have positive influences on their children's academic performance (Chen, Liu, & Li, 2000) and achievement, particularly in sports (Jodl, Michael, Malanchuk, Eccles, & Sameroff, 2001). One recent analysis of almost 1300 Taiwanese eighth graders found that their attachments to their mothers and fathers independently predicted differences in their psychosocial adjustment (Liu, 2008). In addition, Phares (1996, 1997) concluded a review of the literature on child psychopathology by noting that fathers have powerful direct and indirect effects on their children's adjustment. For example, Brennan, Hammen, Katz, and Le Brocque (2002) reported that maternal and paternal depression had additive adverse effects on adolescents' adjustment, and maternal depression had a more reliable effect on adolescents when the fathers were substance abusers.

As in earlier years, of course, some patterns of influence in adolescence are quite complex and indirect. In an observational study, for example, Gjerde (1986) found that mother–son interactions were less stormy when fathers were present than when mothers and sons were observed alone, whereas father–son interactions were of poorer quality in triadic than in dyadic settings. Parents and adolescents may view their interaction quite differently as well. Noller and Callan (1988) videotaped 41 mother–father–adolescent triads discussing the adolescents' behavior and then had trained observers, the interactants, and members of other mother–father–child triads rate the degree of anxiety, dominance, involvement, and friendliness shown by each of the interactants. The ratings made by the experts were very similar to those made by members of other families. Interactants rated other members of their families more negatively than they rated themselves, although the ratings by participating and non-participating parents were more divergent than ratings by adolescents who were and were not involved.

Both Gjerde's and Noller and Callan's studies illustrate innovative techniques for studying parent–adolescent relationships, and underscore the importance of obtaining data from multiple informants. Further amplifying this point, Sternberg and her colleagues (Sternberg et al., 1993; Sternberg, Lamb, & Dawud-Noursi, 1998; Sternberg, Lamb, Guterman, & Abbott 2006b) showed that mothers' and adolescents' views of children's behavior problems varied depending on the informants' experiences and perspectives.

Tensions in the Parent–Adolescent Relationship

Tension is inevitable as parents try to maintain attachments and dependency while teenagers strive for independence. Until the mid-1970s, in fact, adolescence was viewed as a period during which parental influence was gradually usurped by the influence of the peer group as a result of intergenerational conflict over values, norms, and behavior (Coleman, 1961). Research on parent–adolescent relationships was largely influenced by psychoanalysts such as Anna Freud (1958) who believed that the biological changes associated with puberty cause emotional distress which in turn leads to rebelliousness and family conflict in the context of a second Oedipal constellation (see also Blos, 1979; Josselson, 1980; Sebald, 1977). These normative processes allegedly drove an emotional wedge between adolescents and their parents and this in turn was believed to facilitate the successful transition from childhood to adulthood. In fact, Anna Freud thought that adolescents who had close respectful relationships with their parents were probably at greatest risk for later psychopathology, a hypothesis that has not been supported empirically (Steinberg, 1990). Indeed, the notion that adolescence is typically characterized by conflict and turmoil rather than by closeness and harmony has been replaced by the realization that most children make the transition to adulthood without significant ego instability. Large-scale surveys show that the vast majority of adolescents continue to rely on their parents for advice, support, and emotional intimacy (Maccoby & Martin, 1983; McGrellis, Henderson, Holland, Sharpe, & Thomson, 2000; Noller & Callan, 1986; Offer, Ostrov, & Howard, 1981), suggesting that parent–adolescent relationships are marked by increasing interdependence and mutuality rather than by detachment and conflict. In contrast to the traditional "storm and stress" model, Coleman and Hendry (1990) theorized that adolescence is a phase of development in which, as with every other stage, individuals come to terms with successive shifts—in parental, peer, and heterosexual relationships.

Solomon, Warin, Lewis, and Langford (2002) explored the ways in which family members describe the patterns of closeness and responsibility between adolescents and their parents, noting that, in a gesture of intergenerational solidarity, many parents (especially mothers) and teenagers describe each other as friends or "mates." Such patterns echo McGrellis et al.'s (2000) large survey of British teenagers in which parents, particularly mothers, were listed high on the adolescents' list of "heroes"—consistently above sports, TV, and pop idols. However, the detailed interviews and qualitative analyses performed by Solomon and his colleagues indicated that these reports obscured underlying paradoxes and contradictions in parent–adolescent relationships as the partners strived for mutuality. As an extreme example, some parents, particularly mothers, reported that they would let their young teenagers go into town on the bus to meet friends, but might follow in their car to ensure their safety. Or, they might allow their children to spend many hours with their boyfriends/girlfriends, but check their teenager's diaries to ensure that they were not sexually active.

Although parent–adolescent relationships are not typically characterized by conflict and turmoil, there is a significant amount of minor but persistent conflict between parents and adolescents (Collins, 1991, 1997; Holmbeck & O'Donnell, 1991; Smetana, 1995), which reaches a peak in mid-adolescence and then declines (Offer et al., 1981; Steinberg, 1981). It has been estimated that families with adolescent children on average argue approximately twice a week (Montemayor, 1983), but this bickering or quarrelling over everyday issues (school work, chores, quarrels with siblings, personal hygiene and grooming, activities, friends, and mundane disobedience) is rarely severe enough to interfere with the development of healthy parent–adolescent relationships and seldom escalates into conflict (Acock & Bengtson, 1978; Youniss & Smollar, 1985). Steinberg (1990) estimated that conflict severe enough to yield a drastic deterioration in the quality of family relationships occurs in only about 5% to 10% of families. The types of issues that are the focus of family arguments change little from preadolescence through late adolescence (Hosley & Montemayor, 1997; Smetana, 1989), although disputes over household responsibilities become more frequent in late adolescence whereas disputes about academic performance peak in early adolescence with the transition to junior high school (Hamburg, 1985).

Preadolescents and adolescents seldom dispute parents' authority to make rules although they argue that parents should not impose such rules unilaterally, and should not have such low expectations of their abilities to comply (Damon, 1977; Hunter, 1984). Perhaps, therefore, family conflicts facilitate communication and adolescent autonomy by promoting open discussions of the parents' reasons and adolescents' protests over their parents' unilateral authority and demands (Youniss, 1989; Youniss & Smollar, 1985). The fact that children contest the basis of their parents' authority also underscores the fact that parent–adolescent conflict may be interpreted differently by parents and children (Larson & Richards, 1994). Parents are more likely to offer conventional interpretations of conflict whereas adolescents are more likely to interpret conflict in terms of personal jurisdiction (Smetana, 1988, 1989, 1995).

Summary

The preadolescent and adolescent periods mark the beginning of the biological changes associated with puberty which parallel transformations in the quality and meaning of parent–child relationships. Self-differentiation and individuation are linked to children's growing sexuality, and they may bring distance and conflict to parent–child relationships. Unfortunately, researchers studying the transformations of relationships during this period have not yet successfully disentangled the effects of puberty from the effects of contemporaneous role transitions.

During adolescence, children are expected to consolidate and apply their knowledge about the roles and rules of adult society, begin to achieve emotional and economic independence from parents, and complete the biological and physical changes that began in the pre-adolescent period. Psychoanalysts such as Anna Freud believe that intrapsychic forces associated with a "second Oedipal" event, interacting with the biological changes associated with pubertal development, disrupt emotional functioning, thereby producing adolescent rebelliousness and intrafamilial strife. This view has been challenged by the results of large-scale surveys showing no widespread psychopathology among adolescents, with only about 5% to 10% of families experiencing a dramatic decline in the quality of parent–child relationships during adolescence. Contrary to the psychoanalytic view, furthermore, adolescents do not become disengaged from their parents; instead parent–child relationships are qualitatively and functionally transformed. Some scholars have hypothesized that adolescents increasingly distance themselves from their parents, with the result that parent–offspring relationships are increasingly marked by self-assertion and conflict over family decisions. Other social scientists have suggested that parent–child relationships characterized by unilateral authority become parent–adolescent relationships marked by cooperative negotiations (mutuality), emotional closeness, and continuing parental support and influence.

THE LONGER VIEW: PARENTS' INFLUENCES ON TEENAGERS AND YOUNG ADULTS

It is relatively difficult to conduct longitudinal research following individuals into adulthood because families may move, or may not be eager for repeated contact with researchers, but the few existing studies have yielded interesting patterns. For a start, the "children" in these families appear to learn from particular experiences in the teenage years. For example, adults' feelings about their relationships and peer interactions are positively correlated with their experiences of parental care in the adolescent years (Burns & Dunlop, 1998), a finding that is consistent with findings showing continuities between adults' attachment feelings in pregnancy and their children's behavior in the Strange Situation (see above). Early paternal involvement also predicts adult children's feelings of satisfaction in spousal relationships and self-reported parenting skills (Franz, McClelland, & Weinberger, 1991). Likewise, fathers' expressions of hostility towards their 16-year-olds and the extent to which they undermined their teenagers' autonomy predicted the degree of hostility and low ego-resiliency reported in the "child" by close friends at age 25 (Allen, Hauser, O'Connor, & Bell, 2002). Measures of teenager–mother hostility also predicted adjustment at age 25.

Other researchers have examined paternal involvement in children's lives in relation to both concurrent parent–child measures and the children's later psychosocial functioning. For example, Lewis, Newson, and Newson (1982) found that the reported involvement of British fathers in two-parent households at ages 7 and 11 predicted the children's performance in national examinations at age 16 as well as whether or not they had a criminal record by age 21. Likewise, in their analyses of data from the UK National Child Development Study, Flouri and Buchanan (2002a, 2002b) have reported a variety of positive predictive associations between patterns of paternal involvement and later indices (when the "children" were 33 years of age) of psychosocial adjustment even when a range of possible mediating factors (e.g., gender, parental socioeconomic status (SES), family structure, parental mental health, maternal involvement) were controlled. Maternally reported father-involvement at age 7 predicted the child's self-reported closeness to father at 16 and lower levels of police contact as reported by the child's mother and teacher (Flouri & Buchanan, 2002a). This in turn predicted marital satisfaction and diminished psychological distress at age 33 (Flouri & Buchanan, 2002b). At the same time, self-reported closeness to mother at age 16 predicted only marital satisfaction 17 years later. Furthermore, Koestner, Franz, and Weinberger (1990) reported significant associations between paternal involvement at age five and the children's feelings when they were in their early thirties—more than 25 years later. Similarly, Franz, McClelland, Weinberger, and Peterson (1994) re-contacted children initially studied by Sears, Maccoby and Levin (1957) and reported that "Over a period of 36 years, the children of warm, affectionate fathers, and boys with warm mothers and less stressful childhood years were more likely to be well adjusted adults who, at age 41, were mentally healthy, coping adequately, and psychosocially mature" (p. 141). Results such as these suggest that, in the long term, patterns of father–child closeness might be crucial predictors of later psychosocial adjustment although the patterns of maternal and paternal influence remain to be explored in depth.

These longitudinal studies relied predominantly on maternal reports of early paternal involvement and warmth, however, and we must be cautious in inferring paternal influences from these data, particularly as marital closeness is a strong predictor of children's psychological well-being as well (Cummings, Goeke-Morey, & Raymond, 2004; Davies & Cummings, 1994; Grych & Fincham, 1990). It could be that maternal reports of high paternal involvement reflect something else, such as family harmony or the mother's own psychological well-being, and this would explain why levels of paternal involvement are often unrelated to contemporaneous indices of adjustment. For example, Israeli teenagers' academic performance was related to their descriptions of maternal, but not paternal, involvement (Feldman, Guttfreund, & Yerushalmi, 1998).

Further work needs to be conducted to tease apart the reasons for these links between paternal relationships with children and later psychological functioning. At present, the evidence seems to suggest that some features of father–child relationships might be more influential than expected given the amounts of time men in two-parent households typically spend with their children. It could be that paternal influences are epiphenomenal—involved men might for example have better adjusted adult children because 50% of their genetic make-up is shared. The theoretical debates summarized at the start of the chapter underscore the need to avoid simplistic interpretations of associations that are likely to be complex as well as simplistic comparisons between father-present and father-absent families.

On the other hand, although it is clear that some fathers (like mothers) can have adverse effects on their children's adjustment, on balance the literature shows positive effects of paternal involvement with children. For example, Sarkadi, Kristiansson, Oberklaid, and Bremberg (2008) conducted a systematic review of 24 longitudinal studies involving 22,300 children; 22 reported significant paternal influences on child development. Of these, 21 recorded "positive" influences and only one negative. Although in some studies the paternal effect was no longer significant when SES was controlled, and factors such as cohabitation were most important, the authors concluded that paternal involvement appears to affect the frequency both of behavior problems in boys and of psychological problems in girls. Paternal involvement was related to decreased delinquency and economic disadvantage in low SES families and showed a general association with enhanced cognitive development.

How do these effects of fathering work? Clearly, we need sophisticated models that take account of the complexities of factors in the family and social systems, including each parent's psychosocial adjustment, their relationship, wider social processes and the child's own developmental status. In an exemplary study, Boyce and his colleagues (2006) found that the effects of paternal involvement in infancy on behavior problems at the age of nine were moderated by measures of the children's psycho-physiological sensitivity at the age of seven. Children with high autonomic reactivity who had experienced both low father involvement in infancy and maternal depression later had the most pronounced problems.

DIVERSITY IN FAMILY PATTERNS AND RELATIONSHIPS

In this final section, we aim to illustrate the need for researchers to address the issue of diversity more completely by briefly describing research on cultural variation, the effects of divorce and single parenting, and the effects of family violence on children and adolescents. The research on single parent and divorcing families underlines not only the importance of parenting relationships in children's development, but also the factors that influence these so poignantly—the relationship between parents, economic and social factors that influence the family system and, importantly, the ways in which these factors change continuously through time. Family violence is discussed because the research has identified some important themes that are relevant to our broader understanding of family influences on child and adolescent development.

Cultural and Subcultural Variation

Despite the multicultural nature of contemporary societies, most information on the socio-emotional development of children has been derived from studies of white, middle-class North Americans. Ethnocentricity in developmental science has limited the generalizability and universality of developmental principles and norms, while restricting our understanding of the variations in human behavior and experiences across cultures and subcultures (Bornstein, 2009). It is all too easy to make assumptions about the similarities and differences between family types and members of different ethnic groups. Social scientists frequently assume, for example, that most households include two adult parents living with their children, although it has long been clear that such households are in the minority (Lamb, 1999b; Rapoport, Rapoport, & Strellitz, 1975).

Researchers are also somewhat blind to ethnic differences, particularly given the dramatic international migration that took place in the second half of the twentieth century. For example, more than 30% of all young Americans today come from minority backgrounds and ethnic minority families constitute the fastest growing segment of the US population (Cabrera & Garcia Coll, 2004; Parke & Buriel, 1998; Roopnarine, 2004). African Americans make up an increasing proportion of the total population of young people in the USA, while the numbers of Hispanic youths and of children born to immigrants are growing rapidly. In addition, children in the United States are increasingly likely to grow up in poverty, which has harmful effects on the nature and quality of parent–child relationships (Brooks-Gunn, Britto, & Brady, 1999; Duncan & Brooks-Gunn, 1997). Conditions of family hardship, for example, are associated with less responsive, patient, and nurturant parental behavior toward children and adolescents (Brooks-Gunn & Chase-Lansdale, 1995; Lempers, Clark-Lempers & Simons,

1989; Osofsky, Hann, & Peebles, 1993; Tamis-Lemonda & McFadden, 2010). Because socio-economic and sociocultural factors appear to have such a powerful effect on the processes and outcomes of socialization (Parke & Buriel, 1998), there have been increasing demands by social scientists to include culture and cultural experiences as critical variables in research on human development. Recent years have witnessed increased attention to African American (McHale et al., 2006) and Latin American (Cabrera, Shannon, West, & Brooks-Gunn, 2006) parenting on the part of researchers. This research has elucidated differences between African American, European American, and Latino American families (Foster & Kalil, 2007; Roopnarine, Fouts, Lamb, & Lewis-Elligan, 2005; Fouts, Roopnarine, & Lamb, 2007; Fouts et al., in press; Vogel, Bradley, Raikes, Boller, & Shears,, 2006), but most researchers have focused on problems in development (Coley & Medeiros, 2007) and there is sill insufficient analysis of normative family patterns, let alone the cultural diversity around the world (Bornstein, 2009), particularly because the effects of culture and ethnicity are often confounded with the effects of SES and poverty (Tamis LeMonda & McFadden, 2010).

Even though their practices deviate massively from those that characterize industrialized countries, studies of child care among hunter-gatherers, such as the !Kung, Bofi, or Aka, have also contributed significantly to our understanding of the causes of variation in child rearing practices. In these countries, for example, the amount of child care performed by fathers varies depending on the availability of other care providers (Konner, 2005; Hewlett, 1987, 2005; Hewlett & MacFarlan, 2010). More generally, Hrdy's (2005; see also Lamb & Ahnert, 2006) examination of "allo-mothering" underscores not only the extent to which allo-mothering is nearly universal but also how the identity of "allo-mothers" varies as individuals opportunistically exploit the human resources available to them.

Forest dwelling hunter-gatherers such as the Aka and the Bofi are characterized by extremely egalitarian norms and minimal gender differentiation, whereas hunter-gatherers such as the Hadza of East Africa are more gender stratified and, not coincidentally, not characterized by equivalently high levels of paternal participation in child care (Marlowe, 2005). Paternal participation in infant care is also lower among agricultural groups in Africa than among the forest hunter-gatherers such as the Aka and Bofi, although fathers in these cultures begin providing care, guidance, and tutelage to their offspring much earlier in development than Western fathers became involved in childcare in the middle part of the twentieth century.

The physical and social ecologies occupied by these African groups and by parents in industrialized societies are dramatically different, yet the relevant research shows that variability, change, adaptability, and opportunism are key features when we examine parenting (perhaps especially fathering) and child care in cross-cultural and/or historical perspective (Hewlett & Macfarlan, 2010).

The significance of sociocultural factors is also evident in research on parental disciplinary styles. Steinberg and Darling (1994; Steinberg, Darling & Fletcher, 1995), for example, found that although authoritative rearing was always beneficial or at least not harmful and that disengaged parenting was always harmful or at least not beneficial, the impact of parenting style varied across sociocultural groups. Authoritative parenting was beneficial and neglectful parenting was disadvantageous for European American and Latin youth, but authoritarian parenting was more advantageous for Asian American adolescents and more disadvantageous for European American adolescents than for adolescents in the other groups.

Few researchers have compared parent–adolescent relationships in different countries. Kroger (1985) found that American, New Zealand, and British adolescents from Grades 6, 8, 10, and 12 all had similar attitudes towards parental authority. Although American girls of all ages felt more favorably about their parents, girls in New Zealand, who had positive attitudes toward their parents in the early grades, became less positive as they grew older. Feldman and her colleagues (Feldman & Rosenthal, 1991; Feldman, Rosenthal, Mont-Reynaud, Leung, & Lau, 1991) found that although Hong Kong Chinese adolescents reported more misbehavior and expected to achieve behavioral autonomy later that did Australian and American youth, levels of misconduct and expectations of behavioral autonomy were related in similar ways to family environments and adolescent values in Chinese and Western cultures. More studies of this sort may be especially informative as we seek to distinguish the effects of broad cultural factors from the effects of parental socialization strategies. Recent studies of parenting and child development among immigrants promise to be especially informative in this regard (see Lamb & Bougher, 2009, for a brief review of some recent research on this topic).

Divorce and Single Parenthood

Although the rates of divorce have leveled recently, about half of the children in the United States and northern Europe are still likely to experience the separation of their parents before they reach adulthood (Amato, in press). Interestingly, geographical and/or cultural factors influence the contact between parents and their children after their parents' divorce. In North America, many children lose meaningful contact with their fathers, whereas in the geographically more compact UK, in which the term "custody" was abolished over a decade ago, children usually reengage with their fathers to some (often limited) degree after an initially difficult period (Maclean & Eekelaar, 1997). Nevertheless, common sense and scientific research tell us that the experience of divorce and continuing parental separation are experiences likely to have psychological costs, demonstrably with respect to psychosocial adjustment, behavior and achievement at school, educational attainment, employment trajectories, income generation, involvement in antisocial and even criminal behavior, and the ability to establish and maintain intimate relationships. Controversy and ideology bedeviled acknowledgment and analysis of these costs in the 1970s and 1980s, but there is substantial consensus today that children are better off psychologically and developmentally in two- rather than single-parent families (Amato, in press; see also Malloy, Lamb, and Katz, Chapter 9, this volume) and that the effects of father loss due to the parents' separation/divorce are greater and more reliable than the effects of father absence due to paternal death (Amato & Keith, 1991; Maier & Lachman, 2000).

The first challenge, of course, was to determine why these differences emerge. Whereas social scientists and commentators such as Biller (1981, 1993) and Blankenhorn (1995) proposed that child adjustment was adversely affected when children lacked father figures in their lives, most social scientists questioned this interpretation both because it failed to acknowledge the many other salient and potentially harmful conditions or events experienced by children whose parents do not live together and because it cannot account for the diversity of responses to separation and divorce (Lamb, 1999b, 2002b; Lamb & Kelly, 2009). Notwithstanding group differences between children in single- and two-parent families, only a minority of children in single-parent families are maladjusted; the majority evince no psychopathology or behavioral symptoms, whether or not they experience psychic pain (Emery, 1999; Hetherington & Kelly, 2002).

A variety of factors account for individual differences in children's adjustment following the divorce/separation of their parents (Lamb, 2002a; Lamb & Kelly, 2009), as Malloy and her colleagues explain in Chapter 9. Typically, first of all, single parenthood is associated with a variety of social and financial stresses with which custodial parents must cope, largely on their own. Second, because single mothers need to work more extensively outside the home than married mothers do, parents spend less time with children in single-parent families and the levels of supervision and guidance are lower and less reliable than in two-parent families (Hetherington & Kelly, 2002; McLanahan, 1999). Thirdly, divorce commonly disrupts one of the child's most important and enduring relationships, that with his or her father (Lamb & Kelly, 2009). Children's well-being is significantly enhanced when their relationships with nonresidential fathers are positive and when nonresident fathers are actively engaged in their lives (Fabricius, Braver, Diaz, & Velez, 2010). (Positive relationships with custodial mothers were also beneficial, of course.) Finally, conflict between parents commonly precedes, emerges during, or increases during the separation and divorce processes, and often continues beyond them (Cummings, Merrilees, & Ward George, 2010; Kelly, 2000).

The level of involvement and quality of relationships between both parents and their children, the level of conflict between the two parents, and the socioeconomic circumstances in which children reside all affect adjustment to divorce/single parenthood and in the absence of intensive and reliable longitudinal data, it is often difficult either to discern causal relationships unambiguously or to establish the relative importance of different factors. For example, child adjustment, paternal involvement in decision-making, the level of high-quality contact children have with non-custodial parents and the amount of child support received are all correlated (Amato & Gilbreth, 1999; Braver & O'Connell, 1998; Braver et al., 1993; Furstenberg & Cherlin, 1991; McLanahan & Sandefur, 1994; Seltzer, 1991, 1994, 1998; Zill & Nord, 1996), making it difficult to determine which factor is most important.

Family Violence

Surprising as it may seem, most incidents of serious and less physical violence in the United States and other industrial nations occur among family members in the home (Straus & Gelles, 1986, 1990; Straus, Gelles, & Steinmetz, 1980). Because no standardized data collection techniques or consensual definitions exist, however, estimates of the prevalence of child maltreatment in the US vary between 200,000 and 4 million cases per year, with as many as 1 million cases of "serious abuse" and 2,000 to 5,000 fatalities per year (Finkelhor & Dziuba-Leatherman, 1994; Sedlak & Broadhurst, 1996; Straus & Gelles, 1990). In addition, the parents of 10% to 30% of the children in the US treat one another violently (Geffner & Pagelow, 1990; Hughes & Luke, 1998; Straus & Gelles, 1986, 1990), often in the presence of their children (Hughes, Parkinson & Vargo, 1989; O'Brien, John, Margolin, & Erel, 1994). Various factors (such as the child's age, gender, and sociodemographic status) are related to the reported incidence of domestic violence, as is the source of information about the reported abuse (Sternberg & Lamb, 1999).

The consequences of domestic violence are pervasive, although no single behavioral or emotional characteristics are common to abused children, and other aspects of the child's environment may be highly influential (Emery, 1989). In addition, many of the earlier studies had particularly severe methodological problems (such as the failure to include appropriate comparison groups, or to obtain objective measures of the violence, or children's adjustment) and researchers still commonly fail to document all possible types of family violence in the studies they conduct (National Research Council, 1993). In comparison with non-abused children, abused children of all ages manifest many psychological deviations, but there is no one-to-one relation between incidents and symptoms (Ammerman, Cassisi, Herson, & Van Hasselt, 1986; Cicchetti, in press; Emery & Billings, 1998). In addition to possible neurodevelopmental and psychological impairment (Lynch & Roberts, 1982; Oates, Peacock, & Forrest, 1984), socioemotional and psychological damage is also common. Social learning theorists contend that physical abuse leads to later aggression because aggressive responses are frequently modeled and often have desirable consequences (Dodge, Bates, & Pettit, 1990; Emery, 1989). Not surprisingly, maltreated children have poor relations with peers (Dodge et al., 1990; Dodge, Pettit, & Bates, 1994; George & Main, 1979; Salzinger, Feldman, Hammer, & Rosario, 1993; Wolfe & Mosk, 1983) with whom they behave aggressively (Bousha &

Twentyman, 1984; Dodge et al., 1990; Egeland & Sroufe, 1981; George & Main, 1979; Kaufman & Cicchetti, 1989; Price & Van Slyke, 1991), suffer from deficits in social cognition (Barahal, Waterman, & Martin, 1981), lack empathy (Main & George, 1985), appear depressed (Kazdin, Moser, Colbus, & Bell, 1985; Sternberg et al., 1993), and perform poorly on cognitive tasks and in school (Eckenrode, Laird, & Doris, 1993; Hoffman-Plotkin & Twentyman, 1984; Kendall-Tackett & Eckenrode, 1996). Abused children are also more likely to manifest aggressive, non-compliant acting-out (Pianta, Egeland, & Erickson, 1989; Sternberg et al., 1993). Abused children may become overly attentive to hostile cues, mis-interpreting the behavior of others and responding with aggression (Dodge et al., 1990; Price & Van Slyke, 1991) and to develop insecure attachments (Carlson, Cicchetti, Barnett, & Braumwald, 1989; Crittenden, 1988; Crittenden & Ainsworth, 1989; Lamb, Gaensbauer, Malkin, & Shultz, 1985) because they have come to see the world as a threatening place, although most abused children remain attached to abusive parents and see positive aspects to their relationships (Sternberg et al., 1994, 2005). Abused and neglected children are also more likely than are matched controls to be arrested for delinquency, to become adult criminals, and to exhibit violent criminal behavior (Widom, 1989, 1994). Not all abused or neglected children suffer these negative consequences, however, although researchers have yet to discern why some adolescents are more resilient than others. Factors such as age of onset and seriousness of abuse and neglect probably play a role in determining long-term outcomes (Sternberg, Baradaran, Abbott, Lamb, & Guterman, 2006a). On the other hand, there is increasing evidence that children can be affected adversely by family violence even when they "merely" witness violence and are not themselves directly assaulted or neglected (Holden, Geffner, & Jouriles, 1998).

CONCLUSIONS

Thanks in large part to Freud's insightful focus on the formative significance of parent–child relationships, students of social and personality development have studied these relationships throughout much of the past century. Over time, they have come to place less emphasis on the "critical" importance of early experiences and relationships, choosing instead to view relationships at various stages of the lifespan as significant, albeit changing, aspects of the formative social environment. As we have noted in this chapter, the focal contents of parent–child relationships change as children grow older and, presumably, as their parents mature as well. Initially, parents provide a context in which children learn that their behaviors have consequences, developing conceptions of their own effectance and trust in others' reliable responsiveness. Thereafter, parents instill standards of behavior and self-control, before becoming foils for their children's pursuit of independence and autonomy as adolescence unfolds. Needless to say, parents differ in their ability to respond sensitively to their children's individual needs and characteristics, and in the way in which they strive to discipline and socialize their children. These differences affect the quality of parent–child relationships and may in turn have long-term influences on children's behavior and adjustment, although their relative importance, in the context of the many other influential events children experience, remain to be determined. Certainly, researchers today see parent–child relationships as dynamic systems that vary in quality depending on individual, familial, societal, and cultural circumstances.

Although some research topics (especially parent–infant and, to a lesser extent, parent–adolescent relationships) have been very well studied, others (e.g., "parenting" young adults or children in middle childhood) have been relatively neglected. The need to address these topics remains. Much current scholarship is focused on connections among previously unrelated areas. For example, Parke and his colleagues (2002, 2004) have made extensive efforts to unravel the patterns of influence between the family and peer systems, having shown that they are highly interrelated. At the same time, researchers in the behavioral genetics and social learning traditions have combined forces to examine the complexity of interactions between genetic and social factors (Hetherington, Bridges, & Insabella, 1998). Only by combining approaches in this manner will we obtain a broader understanding of the ways in which parents shape their children's development.

Although we have made considerable progress in our attempts to understand the complexities of parenting, three key issues will need especially close attention in the immediate future. First, there are many gaps in our understanding of research methods. As O'Connor (2002) suggests, reliance on diverse methods is virtuous, but brings with it particular problems, especially when different methods produce incompatible results! Second, we persist in treating "parenting" as "mothering," because mothers continue to take the major role in child care and socialization and are more available to study, whereas research continues to suggest that we should distinguish father–child and mother–child relationships and their influences. Finally, as Hay and Nash (2002) and Lamb (1999b) pointed out, we continue to assume that the "traditional" nuclear family is the blueprint against which all other types of family should be compared—usually unfavorably. The challenge for future research is to acknowledge that psychologists tend to focus rather narrowly on households typical of their white, predominantly Anglo-Saxon backgrounds, even though such families are in the minority, and that their studies poorly reflect and represent the diversity and complexity of contemporary family life.

REFERENCES AND SUGGESTED READINGS (□)

Acock, A. C., & Bengtson, V. L. (1978). On the relative influence of mothers and fathers: A covariance analysis of political and religious socialization. *Journal of Marriage and the Family, 40*, 519–530.

Ahnert, L., Pinquart, M., & Lamb, M. E. (2006). Security of children's relationships with nonparental care providers: A meta-analysis. *Child Development, 74*, 664–679.

Ainsworth, M. D. S., Blehar, M. C., Waters, E., & Wall, S. (1978). *Patterns of attachment: A psychological study of the strange situation.* Hillsdale, NJ: Lawrence Erlbaum Associates.

Allen, S. M., Hauser, S. T., O'Connor, T. G., & Bell, K. L. (2002). Prediction of peer-rated adult hostility from autonomy struggles in adolescent–family interactions. *Development and Psychopathology, 14*, 123–137.

Amato, P. R. (1993). Children's adjustment to divorce: Theories, hypotheses, and empirical support. *Journal of Marriage and the Family, 55*, 23–38.

Amato, P. R. (2000). Diversity within single-parent families. In D. H. Demo, K. R. Allen, & M. A. Fine (Eds.), *Handbook of family diversity* (pp. 149–172). Oxford, UK: Oxford University Press.

Amato, P. R., & Gilbreth, J. G. (1999). Nonresident fathers and children's well-being: A meta-analysis. *Journal of Marriage & the Family, 61*, 557–573.

Amato, P. R., & Keith, B. (1991). Parental divorce and the well-being of children: A meta-analysis. *Psychological Bulletin, 110*, 26–46.

Amato, P. R., & Rezac, S. J. (1994). Contact with nonresidential parents, interparental conflict, and children's behavior. *Journal of Family Issues, 15*, 191–207.

Amato, P. R., & Sobelewski, J. M. (2004). The effects of divorce on fathers and children: Nonresidential father and stepfathers. In M. E. Lamb (Ed.), *The role of the father in child development* (4th ed., pp. 341–367). New York: Wiley.

Ambrose, J. A. (1961). The development of the smiling response in early infancy. In B. M. Foss (Ed.), *Determinants of infant behavior* (pp. 179–196). London: Methuen.

Ammerman, R. T., Cassisi, J. E., Herson, M., & Van Hasselt, V. B. (1986). Consequences of physical abuse and neglect in children. *Clinical Psychology Review, 6*, 291–310.

Andrews, D. W., & Dishion, T. J. (1994). The microsocial structure underpinnings of adolescent problem behavior. In R. D. Ketterlinus & M. E. Lamb (Eds.), *Adolescent problem behaviors: Issues and research* (pp. 187–207). Hillsdale, NJ: Lawrence Erlbaum Associates.

Astington, J. W. (1996). What is theoretical about the child's understanding of mind? A Vygotskian view of its development. In P. Carruthers & P. K. Smith (Eds.), *Theories of theories of mind* (pp. 184–199). Cambridge, UK: Cambridge University Press.

Baer, J., & Martinez, C. D. (2006). Child maltreatment and insecure attachment: A meta-analysis. *Journal of Reproductive & Infant Psychology*, 24, 187–197.

Bakermans-Kranenburg, M. J., van IJzendoorn, M. H., & Juffer, F. (2003). Less is more: Meta-analyses of sensitivity and attachment interventions in early childhood. *Psychological Bulletin*, 129, 195–216.

Bandura, A. (1969). *Principles of behavior modification*. New York: Holt, Rinehart, & Winston.

Bandura, A. (1977). Self-efficacy: Toward a unifying theory of behavioral change. *Psychological Review*, 84, 191–215.

Bandura, A. (1986). *Social foundations of thought and action: A social cognitive theory*. Englewood Cliffs, NJ: Prentice Hall.

Bandura, A. (1997). *Self-efficacy: The exercise of control*. New York: Freeman.

Barahal, R. M., Waterman, J., & Martin, H. P. (1981). The social cognitive development of abused children. *Journal of Consulting and Clinical Psychology*, 49, 508–516.

Barry, R. A., Kochanska, G., & Philibert, R. A. (2008). G–E interaction in the organization of attachment: mothers' responsiveness as a moderator of children's genotypes. *Journal of Child Psychology and Psychiatry*, 49, 1313–1320.

Baumrind, D. (1967). Child care practices anteceding three patterns of preschool behavior. *Genetic Psychology Monographs*, 75, 43–88.

Baumrind, D. (1971). Current patterns of parental authority. *Developmental Psychology Monographs*, 4, 1–103.

Baumrind, D. (1972). An exploratory study of socialization effects on black children: Some black–white comparisons. *Child Development*, 43, 261–267.

Baumrind, D. (1973). The development of instrumental competence through socialization. In A. Pick (Ed.), *Minnesota symposia on child psychology* (Vol. 7, pp. 3–46). Minneapolis, MN: University of Minnesota.

Baumrind, D. (1975). *Early socialization and the discipline controversy*. Morristown, NJ: General Learning.

Baumrind, D. (1991). Parenting styles and adolescent development. In R. M. Lerner, A. C. Petersen, & J. Brooks-Gunn (Eds.), *Encyclopedia of adolescence* (Vol. 2, pp.746–758). New York: Garland Publishing.

Baumrind, D., & Black, A. E. (1967). Socialization practices associated with dimensions of competence in preschool boys and girls. *Child Development*, 38, 291–327.

Beck, U., & Beck-Gernsheim, E. (1995). *The normal chaos of love*. Cambridge, UK: Polity.

Bell, R. Q. (1968). A reinterpretation of the direction of effects in studies of socialization. *Psychological Review*, 75, 81–95.

Bell, S. M., & Ainsworth, M. D. (1972). Infant crying and maternal responsiveness. *Child Development*, 43, 1171–1190.

Belsky, J. (1997). Variation in susceptibility to rearing influence: An evolutionary argument. *Psychological Inquiry*, 8, 182–186.

Belsky, J. (1999). Interactional and contextual determinants of attachment security. In J. Cassidy & P. R. Shaver (Eds.), *Handbook of attachment: Theory, research, and clinical applications* (pp. 249–264). New York: Guilford Press.

Belsky, J., Booth-LaForce, C., Bradley, R., Brownell, C. A., Burchinal, M., Campbell, S. B., et al. (2008). Mothers' and fathers' support for child autonomy and early school achievement. *Developmental Psychology*, 44, 895–907.

Belsky, J., Fish, M., & Isabella, R. A. (1991). Continuity and discontinuity in infant negative and positive emotionality: Family antecedents and attachment consequences. *Developmental Psychology*, 27, 421–431.

Belsky, J., Garduque, L., & Hrncir, E. (1984). Assessing performance, competence, and executive capacity in infant play: Relations to home environment and security of attachment. *Developmental Psychology*, 20, 406–417.

⧉ Belsky, J., & Pluess, M. (2009). The nature (and nurture?) of plasticity in early human development. *Perspectives on Psychological Science*, 4, 345–351.

Belsky. J., Vandell, D. L., Burchinal, M., Clarke-Stewart, K., McCartney, K., & Owen, M. T. (2007). Are there long-term effects of early child care? *Child Development*, 78, 681–701.

Benzies, K. M., Harrison, M. J., & Magill-Evans, J. (1998). Impact of marital quality and parent–infant interaction on preschool behavior problems. *Public Health Nursing*, 15, 35–43.

Berlin, L. J., & Cassidy, J. (1999). Relations among relationships: Contributions from attachment theory and research. In J. Cassidy & P. R. Shaver (Eds.), *Handbook of attachment: Theory, research, and clinical applications* (pp. 688–712). New York: Guilford Press.

Biller, H. B. (1981). Father absence, divorce, and personality development. In M. E. Lamb (Ed.), *The role of the father in child development* (2nd ed., pp. 489–552). New York: Wiley.

Biller, H. B. (1993). *Fathers and families: Paternal factors in child development*. Westport, CT: Auburn House.

Blankenhorn, D. (1995). *Fatherless America*. New York: Basic Books.

Blos, P. (1979). *The adolescent passage*. New York: International Universities Press.

Booth-LaForce, C., Oh, W., Kim, A., Rubin, K. H., Rose-Krasnor, L., & Burgess, K. (2006). Attachment, self-worth, and peer-group functioning in middle childhood. *Attachment and Human Development*, 8, 309–325.

Borke, J., Lamm, B., Eickhorst, A., & Keller, H. (2007). Father–infant interaction, paternal ideas about early child care, and their consequences for the development of children's self-recognition. *Journal of Genetic Psychology*, 168, 365–379.

Bornstein, M. H. (Ed.) (2009). *Handbook of cultural developmental science*. New York: Psychology Press.

Bornstein M. H., Tamis-LeMonda C. S., Hahn C. S., & Haynes, O. M. (2008). Maternal responsiveness to young children at three ages: Longitudinal analysis of a multidimensional, modular, and specific parenting construct. *Developmental Psychology, 44,* 867–874.

Bousha, D. M., & Twentyman, C. T. (1984). Mother–child interactional style in abuse, neglect, and control groups: Naturalistic observations in the home. *Journal of Abnormal Psychology, 93,* 106–144.

Bowlby, J. (1969). *Attachment and loss: Vol. 1. Attachment.* New York: Basic Books.

Bowlby, J. (1973). *Attachment and loss: Vol. 2. Separation: Anxiety and anger.* New York: Basic Books.

Bowlby, J. (1988). *A secure base: Parent–child attachment and healthy human development.* New York: Basic Books.

Boyce, W. T., Essex, M. J., Alkon, A., Goldsmith, H. H., Kraemer, H. C., & Kupfer, D. J. (2006). Early father involvement moderates biobehavioral susceptibility to mental health problems in middle childhood. *Journal of the American Academy of Child and Adolescent Psychiatry, 45,* 1510–1520.

Braver, S. H., Wolchik, S. A., Sandler, I. N., Fogas, B. S., & Zvetina, D. (1991). Frequency of visitation by divorced fathers: Differences in reports by fathers and mothers. *American Journal of Orthopsychiatry, 61,* 448–454.

Braver, S. L., & O'Connell, E. (1998). *Divorced dads: Shattering the myths.* New York: Thatcher Putnam.

Braver, S. L., Wolchik, S. A., Sandler, I. N., Sheets, V. L., Fogas, B., & Bay, R.C. (1993). A longitudinal study of noncustodial parents: Parents without children. *Journal of Family Psychology, 7,* 9–23.

Brennan, P. A., Hammen, C., Katz, A. R., & Le Brocque, R. M. (2002). Maternal depression, paternal psychopathology, and adolescent diagnostic outcomes. *Journal of Consulting & Clinical Psychology, 70,* 1075–1085.

Bretherton, I. (1990). Open communication and internal working models: Their role in the development of attachment relationships. In R. A. Thompson (Ed.), *Socioemotional development* (pp. 57–114). Lincoln, NE: University of Nebraska.

Bretherton, I. (1991). Pouring new wine into old bottles: The social self as internal working model. In M. R. Gunnar & L. Λ. Sroufe (Eds.), *Self process and development: Minnesota symposia on child psychology* (Vol. 23, pp. 1–41). Hillsdale, NJ: Lawrence Erlbaum Associates.

Bretherton, I. (1993). From dialogue to internal working models: The co-construction of self relationships. In C. A. Nelson (Ed.), *Memory and affect in development* (pp. 237–263). Hillsdale, NJ: Lawrence Erlbaum Associates.

Bretherton, I., Bates, E., Benigni, L., Camaioni, L., & Volterra, V. (1979). Relations between cognition, communication, and quality of attachment. In E. Bates (Ed.), *The emergence of symbols: Cognition and communication in infancy* (pp. 223–269). New York: Academic Press.

Bretherton, I., & Munholland, K. A. (1999). Internal working models in attachment relationships: A construct revisited. In J. Cassidy & P. R. Shaver (Eds.), *Handbook of attachment: Theory, research, and clinical applications* (pp. 89–111). New York: Guilford Press.

Bronfenbrenner, U. (1979). Contexts of child rearing: Problems and prospects. *American Psychologist, 34,* 844–850.

Bronstein, P. (1984). Differences in mothers' and fathers' behaviors toward children: A cross-cultural comparison. *Developmental Psychology, 20,* 995–1003.

Brooks-Gunn, J., Britto, P. R., & Brady, C. (1999). Struggling to make ends meet: Poverty and child development. In M. E. Lamb (Ed.), *Parenting and child development in "nontraditional" families* (pp. 279–304). Mahwah, NJ: Lawrence Erlbaum Associates.

Brooks-Gunn, J., & Chase-Lansdale, P. L. (1995). Adolescent parenthood. In M. H. Bornstein (Ed.), *Handbook of parenting* (pp. 113–150). Hillsdale, NJ: Lawrence Erlbaum Associates.

Brown, G. L., Mangelsdorf, S. C., Wong, M. S., Shigeto, A. & Neff, C. (2009, April). *Fathering and father–child attachment across the first three years: Stability and longitudinal links.* Poster presented at the Society for Research in Child Development, Denver, CO.

Bugental, D. B., & Goodnow, J. S. (1998). Socialization processes. In W. Damon & N. Eisenberg (Eds.), *Handbook of child psychology: Vol. 3. Social, emotional and personality development* (5th ed., pp. 289–463). New York: Wiley.

Buhrmeister, D. P., & Furman, W. C. (1990). Perceptions of sibling relationships during middle childhood and adolescence. *Child Development, 61,* 1387–1398.

Burns, A., & Dunlop, R. (1998). Parental divorce, parent–child relations, and early adult relationships: A longitudinal Australian study. *Personal Relationships, 5,* 393–407.

Bushnell, I. W. R., Sai, F., & Mullin, J. T. (1989). Neonatal recognition of the mother's face. *British Journal of Developmental Psychology, 7,* 3–15.

Cabrera, N., & Garcia Coll, C. (2004). Latino fathers: Uncharted territory in need of much exploration. In M. E. Lamb (Ed.), *The role of the father in child development* (4th ed., pp. 98–120). Hoboken, NJ: Wiley.

Cabrera, N. J., Shannon, J. D., & Tamis-LeMonda, C. S. (2007). Fathers' influence on their children's cognitive and emotional development: From toddlers to pre-K. *Journal of Applied Developmental Science, 11,* 208–213.

Cabrera, N. J., Shannon, J. D., West, J., & Brooks-Gunn, J. (2006). Parental interactions with Latino infants: Variation by country of origin and English proficiency. *Child Development, 77,* 1190–1207.

Caldera, Y. M., Huston, A. C., & O'Brien, M. (1995). *Antecedents of father–infant attachment: A longitudinal study.* Paper presented at the Society for Research in Child Development, Indianapolis, IN.

Carlson, V., Cicchetti, D., Barnett, D., & Braunwald, K. G. (1989). Finding order in disorganization: Lessons from research on maltreated infants' attachment to their caregivers. In D. Cicchetti & V. Carlson (Eds.), *Child maltreatment: Theory and research on the causes and consequences of child abuse and neglect* (pp. 494–528). New York: Cambridge University Press.

Carpendale, J. I. M., & Lewis, C. (2006). *How children develop social understanding.* Oxford, UK: Blackwell.

Carpendale, J. I. M., & Lewis, C. (2010). The development of social understanding: A relational perspective. In W. Overton & R. M. Lerner (Eds.), *The handbook of lifespan developmental psychology* (Vol. 1). Chichester, UK: Wiley.

Cassidy, J. (1988). Child–mother attachment and the self in six-year-olds. *Child Development, 59,* 121–134.

Chen, X., Liu, M., & Li, D. (2000). Parental warmth, control and indulgence and their relations to adjustment in Chinese children. *Journal of Family Psychology, 14,* 401–409.

Clarke-Stewart, K. A., & Hayward, C. (1996). Advantages of father custody and contact for the psychological well-being of school-age children. *Journal of Applied Developmental Psychology, 17,* 239–270.

Coleman, J. C., & Hendry, L. (1990). *The nature of adolescence* (2nd ed.). London: Routledge.

Coleman, J. S. (1961). *The adolescent society: The social life of the teenager and its impact on education.* New York: Basic Books.

Coley, R. L., & Medeiros, B. L. (2007). Reciprocal longitudinal relations between nonresident father involvement and adolescent delinquency, *Child Development, 78,* 132–147.

Collins, W. A. (1990). Parent–child relationships in the transition to adolescence: Continuity and change in interaction, affect, and cognition. In R. Montemayor, G. R. Adams, & T. Gullotta (Eds.), *From childhood to adolescence: A transitional period? Advances in adolescent development.* (Vol. 2, pp. 85–106). Beverly Hills, CA: Sage.

Collins, W. A. (1991). Shared views and parent–adolescent relationships. In R. L. Paikoff (Ed.), *Shared views in the family during adolescence: New directions for child development* (Vol. 51, pp. 103–110). San Francisco: Jossey-Bass.

Collins, W. A. (1997). Relationships and development during adolescence: Interpersonal adaptation to individual change. *Personal Relationships, 4,* 1–14.

Collins, W. A., Harris, M. L., & Susman, A. (1995). Parenting during middle childhood. In M. H. Bornstein (Ed.), *Handbook of parenting* (Vol. 1, pp. 65–89). Mahwah, NJ: Lawrence Erlbaum Associates.

Collins, W. A., Maccoby, E. E., Steinberg, L., Hetherington, E. M., & Bornstein, M. H. (2000). Contemporary research on parenting: The case for nature and nurture. *American Psychologist, 55,* 218–232.

Collins, W. A., & Russell, G. (1991). Mother–child and father–child relationships in middle childhood and adolescence: A developmental analysis. *Developmental Review, 11,* 99–136.

Condon, J. T., Corkindale, C. K., & Boyce, P. (2008). Assessment of postnatal paternal–infant attachment: Development of a questionnaire instrument. *Journal of Reproductive and Infant Psychology, 26,* 195–210.

Cooksey, E. C. (1997). Consequences of young mothers' marital histories for children's cognitive development. *Journal of Marriage and the Family, 59,* 245–261.

Cooksey, E. C., & Fondell, M. M. (1996). Spending time with his kids: Effects of family structure on fathers' and children's lives. *Journal of Marriage and the Family, 58,* 693–707.

Cox, M. J., Owen, M. T., Henderson, V. K., & Margand, N. A. (1992). Prediction of infant–father and infant–mother attachment. *Developmental Psychology, 28,* 474–483.

Criss, M., Shaw, D. S., Moilanen, K. L., Hitchings, J. E., & Ingoldsby, E. M. (2009). Family, neighborhood, and peer characteristics as predictors of child adjustment: A longitudinal analysis of additive and mediation models. *Social Development, 18,* 511–535.

Crittenden, P. M. (1988). Relationship at risk. In J. Belsky & T. J. Nezworski (Eds.), *Clinical implications of attachment* (pp. 136–176). Hillsdale, NJ: Lawrence Erlbaum Associates.

Crittenden, P. M. (1990). Internal representational models of attachment relationships. *Infant Mental Health Journal, 11,* 259–277.

Crittenden, P. M. (1992). Treatment of anxious attachment in infancy and early childhood. *Development and Psychopathology, 4,* 575–602.

Crittenden, P. M. (1994). Peering into the black box: An exploratory treatise on the development of self in young children. In D. Cicchetti & S. L. Toth (Eds.), *Disorders and dysfunctions of the self* (pp. 79–148). Rochester, NY: University of Rochester.

Crittenden, P. M. (2006). A dynamic-maturational model of attachment. *Australian and New Zealand Journal of Family Therapy, 27,* 105–115.

Crittenden, P. M., & Ainsworth, M. D. S. (1989). Child maltreatment and attachment theory. In D. Cicchetti & V. Carlson (Eds.), *Child maltreatment: Theory and research on the causes and consequences of child abuse and neglect* (pp. 432–463). New York: Cambridge University Press.

Crittenden, P. M., & Dallos, R. (2009). All in the family: Integrating attachment and family systems theories. *Clinical Child Psychology & Psychiatry, 14,* 389–409.

Crouter, A. C., MacDermid, S. M., McHale, S. M., & Perry-Jenkins, M. (1990). Parental monitoring and perceptions of children's school performance and conduct in dual- and single-earner families. *Developmental Psychology, 26,* 649–657.

Crowley, K., Callanan, M. A., Tenenbaum, H. R., & Allen, E. (2001). Parents explain more often to boys than to girls during shared scientific thinking. *Psychological Science, 12*, 258–261.

Cummings, E. M., & Davies, P. T. (1994). *Children and marital conflict: The impact of family dispute and resolution.* New York and London: Guilford.

Cummings, E. M., Goeke-Morey, M. C., & Raymond, J. (2004). Fathers in family context: Effects of marital quality and marital conflict. In M. E. Lamb (Ed.), *The role of the father in child development* (4th ed., pp. 196–221). Hoboken, NJ: Wiley.

Cummings, E. M., Merrilees, C. E., & Ward George, M. (2010). Fathers, marriages and families: Revisiting and updating the framework for fathering in family context. In M. E. Lamb (Ed.), *The role of the father in child development* (5th ed., pp. 154–176). Hoboken, NJ: Wiley.

Cummings, E. M., & O'Reilly, A. W. (1997). Fathers in family context: Effects of marital quality on child adjustment. In M. E. Lamb (Ed.), *The role of the father in child development* (3rd ed., pp. 49–65). New York: Wiley.

Damon, W. (1977). Measurement and social development. *Counseling Psychologist, 6*, 13–15.

Damon, W. (1983). *Social and personality development.* New York: Norton.

Danziger, K. (1971). *Socialization.* Hamondsworth, UK: Penguin.

Darling, N., & Steinberg, L. (1993). Parenting style context: An integrative model. *Psychological Bulletin, 113*, 487–496.

Davies, P. T., & Cummings, E. M. (1994). Marital conflict and child adjustment: An emotional security hypothesis. *Psychological Bulletin, 116*, 387–411.

Davis, E., Schoppe-Sullivan, S. J., Mangelsdorf, S. C., & Brown, G. L. (2009). The role of infant temperament in stability and change in coparenting behavior across the first year of life. *Parenting: Science and Practice, 9*, 143–159.

Deater-Deckard, K. (2000). Parenting and child behavioral adjustment in early childhood: A quantitative genetic approach to studying family processes. *Child Development, 71*, 468–484.

DeLuccie, M. (1996). Predictors of paternal involvement and satisfaction. *Psychological Reports, 79*, 1351–1359.

De Wolff, M. S., & van IJzendoorn, M. H. (1997). Sensitivity and attachment: A meta-analysis on parental antecedents of infant attachment. *Child Development, 68*, 571–591.

Diener, M. L., Isabella, R. A., Behunin, M. G., & Wong, M. S. (2008). Attachment to mothers and fathers during middle childhood: Associations with child gender, grade, and competence. *Social Development, 17*, 84–101.

Diener, M., Mangelsdorf, C., McHale, J., & Frosch, C. (2002). Infants' behavioral strategies for emotion regulation with fathers and mothers: Associations with emotional expressions and attachment quality. *Infancy, 5*, 151–172.

Dodge, K. A., Bates, J. E., & Pettit, G. S. (1990). Mechanisms in the cycle of violence. *Science, 250*, 1678–1683.

Dodge, K. A., Pettit, G. S., & Bates, J. E. (1994). Effects of physical maltreatment on the development of peer relations. *Development and Psychopathology, 6*, 43–55.

Dornbusch, S. M., Ritter, R. L., Liederman, H., Roberts, D., & Fraleigh, M. (1987). The relation of parenting style to adolescent school performance. *Child Development, 58*, 1244–1257.

Downey, D. B. (1994). The school performance of children from single-mother and single-father families: Economic or interpersonal deprivation? *Journal of Family Issues, 15*, 129–147.

Duncan, G., & Brooks-Gunn, J. (Eds.). (1997). *Consequences of growing up poor.* New York: Russell Sage Foundation.

Dunn, J., Brown, J., & Beardsall, L. (1991). Family talk about feeling states and children's later understanding of others' emotions. *Developmental Psychology, 27*, 448–455.

Dunn, J., Brown, J., Slomkowski, C., Tesla, C., & Youngblade, L. (1991). Young children's understanding of other people's feelings and beliefs: Individual differences and their antecedents. *Child Development, 62*, 1352–1366.

Dykas, M. J., Ziv, Y., & Cassidy, J. (2008). Attachment and peer relations in adolescence. *Attachment & Human Development, 10*, 123–141.

Easterbrooks, M. A., & Goldberg, W. A. (1984). Toddler development in the family: Impact of father involvement and parenting characteristics. *Child Development, 55*, 740–752.

Eckenrode, J., Laird, M., & Doris, J. (1993). School performance and disciplinary problems among abused and neglected children. *Developmental Psychology, 29*, 53–62.

Egeland, B., & Sroufe, L. A. (1981). Attachment and early maltreatment. *Child Development, 52*, 44–52.

Elgar, F. J., Mills, R. S. L., McGrath, P. J., Waschbusch, D. A., & Brownridge, D. A. (2007). Maternal and paternal depressive symptoms and child maladjustment: The mediating role of parental behavior. *Journal of Abnormal Child Psychology, 35*, 943–955.

Emde, R. N., & Robinson, J. (1979). The first two months: Recent research in developmental psychology and the changing view of the newborn. In J. Noshpitz & J. Call (Eds.), *Basic handbook of child psychiatry.* New York: Basic Books.

Emery, R. E. (1989). Family violence. *American Psychologist, 44*, 312–329.

Emery, R. E. (1994). *Renegotiating family relationships: Divorce, child custody, and mediation.* New York: Guilford.

Emery, R. E. (1999). *Marriage, divorce, and children's adjustment* (2nd ed.). Thousand Oaks, CA: Sage Publications.

Emery, R. E., & Billings, L. L. (1998). An overview of the nature, causes, and consequences of abusive family relationships. *American Psychologist, 53*, 121–135.

Ensor, R., & Hughes, C. (2008). Content or connectedness? Mother–child talk and early social understanding. *Child Development, 79*, 201–216.

Ereky-Stevens, K. (2008). Associations between mothers' sensitivity to their infants' internal states and children's later understanding of mind and emotion. *Infant and Child Development, 17*, 527–543.

Fabricius, W. V., Braver, S. L., Diaz, P., & Velez, C. F. (2010). Custody and parenting time: Links to family relationships and well-being after divorce. In M. E. Lamb (Ed.), *The role of the father in child development* (5th ed., pp. 201–240). Hoboken, NJ: Wiley.

Fagot, B. I. (1995). Parenting boys and girls. In M. H. Bornstein (Ed.), *Handbook of parenting* (Vol. 1, pp. 163–183). Mahwah, NJ: Lawrence Erlbaum Associates.

Fagot, B. I., & Kavanagh, K. (1993). Parenting during the second year: Effects of children's age, sex and attachment classification. *Child Development, 64*, 258–271.

Favez, N., Frascarolo, F., Carneiro, C., Montfort, V., Corboz-Warnery, A. & Fivaz-Depeursinge, E. (2006). The development of the family alliance from pregnancy to toddlerhood and children outcomes at 18 months. *Infant and Child Development, 15*, 59–73.

Feldman, R., Guttfreund, D., & Yerushalmi, H. (1998). Parental care and intrusiveness as predictors of the abilities–achievement gap in adolescence. *Journal of Child Psychology & Psychiatry & Allied Disciplines, 39*, 721–730.

Feldman, S. S., & Rosenthal, D. A. (1991). Age expectations of behavioral autonomy in Hong Kong, Australian, and American youth: The influence of family variables and adolescents' values. *International Journal of Psychology, 26*, 1–23.

Feldman, S. S., Rosenthal, D. A., Mont-Reynaud, R., Leung, K., & Lau, S. (1991). Ain't misbehavin': Adolescent values and family environments as correlates of misconduct in Australia, Hong Kong, and the United States. *Journal of Research on Adolescence, 1*, 109–134.

Field, T. M., Cohen, D., Garcia, R., & Greenberg, R. (1984). Mother–stranger face discrimination by the newborn. *Infant Behavior and Development, 7*, 19–25.

Finkelhor, D., & Dziuba-Leatherman, J. (1994). Children as victims of violence: A national survey. *Pediatrics, 91*, 413–420.

Flouri, E., & Buchanan, A. (2002a). Father involvement in childhood and trouble with the police in adolescence: Findings from the 1958 British cohort. *Journal of Interpersonal Violence, 17*, 689–701.

Flouri, E., & Buchanan, A. (2002b). What predicts good relationships with parents in adolescence and partners in adult life: Findings from the 1958 British birth cohort. *Journal of Family Psychology, 16*, 186–198.

Flouri, E., & Buchanan, A. (2004). Early fathers' and mothers' involvement and child's later educational outcomes. *British Journal of Educational Psychology, 74*, 141–153.

Fonagy, P., Gergely, G., Jurist, E., & Target, M. (2002). *Affect regulation, mentalization, and the development of the self*. New York: Other Press.

Fonagy, P., Redfern, S., & Charman, T. (1997). The relationship between belief–desire reasoning and a projective measure of attachment security (SAT). *British Journal of Developmental Psychology, 15*, 51–61.

Fonagy, P., Steele, H., & Steele, M. (1991). Maternal representations of attachment during pregnancy predict the organization of infant–mother attachment at one year of age. *Child Development, 62*, 891–905.

Fonagy, P., & Target, M. (1997). Attachment and reflective function: Their role in self-organization. *Development and Psychopathology, 9*, 679–700.

Foster, E. M., & Kalil, A. (2007). Living arrangements and children's development in low-income white, black, and Latino families. *Child Development, 78*, 1657–1674.

Fouts, H., Roopnarine, J. L., & Lamb, M. E. (2007). Social experiences and daily routines of African-American infants in different socioeconomic contexts. *Journal of Family Psychology, 21*, 655–664.

Frankel, K. A., & Bates, J. E. (1990). Mother–toddler problem solving: Antecedents in attachment, home behavior, and temperament. *Child Development, 61*, 810–819.

Franz, C. E., McClelland, D. C., & Weinberger, J. (1991). Childhood antecedents of conventional social accomplishment in midlife adults: A 36-year prospective study. *Journal of Personality & Social Psychology, 60*, 586–595.

Franz, C. E., McClelland, D. C., Weinberger, J., & Peterson, C. (1994). Parenting antecedents of adult adjustment: A longitudinal study. In C. Perris, W. A. Arrindell, & M. Eisemann (Eds.), *Parenting and psychopathology* (pp. 127–144). New York: Wiley.

Freud, A. (1958). Adolescence. *Psychoanalytic Study of the Child, 13*, 255–278.

Freud, S. (1940). *An outline of psychoanalysis*. New York: Norton.

Frodi, A. M., Lamb, M. E., Leavitt, L. A., & Donovan, W. L. (1978a). Fathers' and mothers' responses to infant smiles and cries. *Infant Behavior and Development, 1*, 187–198.

Frodi, A. M., Lamb, M. E., Leavitt, L. A., Donovan, W. L., Neff, C., & Sherry, D. (1978b). Fathers' and mothers' responses to the faces and cries of normal and premature infants. *Developmental Psychology, 14*, 490–498.

Furstenberg, F. F., Jr., & Cherlin, A. J. (1991). *Divided families: What happens to children when parents part*. Cambridge, MA: Harvard University Press.

Gable, S., Crnic, K., & Belsky, J. (1994). Coparenting within the family system: Influences on children's development. *Family Relations: Journal of Applied Family & Child Studies, 43*, 380–386.

Gadsden, V. L. (1999). Black families in intergenerational and cultural perspective. In M. E. Lamb (Ed.), *Parenting and child development in "nontraditional" families* (pp. 221–246). Mahwah, NJ: Lawrence Erlbaum Associates.

Galinsky, E. (1999). *Ask the children: What America's children really think about paternal employment.* New York: Morrow.

Geffner, R., & Pagelow, M. D. (1990). Victims of spouse abuse. In R. T. Ammerman & M. Hersch (Eds.), *Treatment of family violence* (pp. 113–135). New York: Wiley.

George, C., Kaplan, N., & Main, M. (1985). *Adult attachment interview.* Unpublished manuscript, University of California, Berkeley.

George, C., & Main, M. (1979). Social interactions of young abused children: Approach, avoidance, and aggression. *Child Development, 50*, 306–318.

Giddens, A. (1998). *The third way.* Cambridge, UK: Polity.

Gjerde, P. F. (1986). The interpersonal structure of family interaction settings: Parent–adolescent relations in dyads and triads. *Developmental Psychology, 22*, 297–304.

Gleason, J. B. (1975). Fathers and other strangers: Men's speech to young children. In D. P. Dato (Ed.), *Language and linguistics* (pp. 289–297). Washington, DC: Georgetown University Press.

Goldman, J. D. C., & Goldman, R. J. (1983). Children's perceptions of parents and their roles: A cross-national study in Australia, England, North America and Sweden. *Sex Roles, 9*, 791–812.

Goldman, R. (2005). *Fathers' involvement in their children's education.* London: National Family and Parenting Institute.

Goodman, G. S., Emery, R. E., & Haugaard, J. J. (1998). Developmental psychology and law: Divorce, child maltreatment, foster care, and adoption. In W. Damon, I. Siegel, & A. Renninger (Eds.), *Handbook of child psychology: Vol. 4. Child psychology in practice* (5th ed., pp. 775–875). New York: Wiley.

Goodnow, J. J. (1996). From household practices to parents' ideas about work and interpersonal relationships. In S. Harkness & C. Super (Eds.), *Parents' cultural belief systems* (pp. 313–344). New York: Guilford.

Goossens, F. A., & van IJzendoorn, M. H. (1990). Quality of infants' attachments to professional caregivers: Relation to infant–parent attachment and day-care characteristics. *Child Development, 61*, 832–837.

Gottfried, A. E., Gottfried, A. W., & Bathurst, K. (2002). Maternal and dual earner employment status and parenting. In M. H. Bornstein (Ed.), *Handbook of parenting* (Vol. 2, pp. 207–230). Mahwah, NJ: Lawrence Erlbaum Associates.

Greenberg, M. T., Cicchetti, D., & Cummings, E. M. (Eds.). (1990). *Attachment in the preschool years: Theory, research, and intervention.* Chicago: University of Chicago Press.

Greenberg, M. T., & Speltz, M. (1988). Attachment and the ontogeny of conduct problems. In J. Belsky & T. J. Nezworski (Eds.), *Clinical implications of attachment* (pp. 177–218). Hillsdale, NJ: Lawrence Erlbaum Associates.

Grossmann, K. E., Grossmann, K., & Zimmermann, P. (1999). A wider view of attachment and exploration: Stability and change during the years of immaturity. In J. Cassidy & P. R. Shaver (Eds.), *Handbook of attachment: Theory, research, and clinical applications* (pp. 760–786). New York: Guilford.

Grotevant, H. D. (1998). Adolescent development in family contexts. In W. Damon & N. Eisenberg (Eds.), *Handbook of child psychology: Vol. 3. Social, personality, and emotional development* (5th ed., pp. 1097–1149). New York: Wiley.

Grych, J. H., & Fincham, F. D. (1990). Marital conflict and children's adjustment: A cognitive–contextual framework. *Psychological Bulletin, 108*, 267–290.

Hagan, L. K., & Kuebli, J. (2007). Mothers' and fathers' socialization of preschoolers' physical risk taking. *Journal of Applied Developmental Psychology, 28*, 2–14.

Hamburg, B. A. (1985). Early adolescence: A time of transition and stress. *Journal of Early Adolescence, 78*, 158–167.

Hanson, T. L., McLanahan, S. S., & Thomson, E. (1996). Double jeopardy: Parental conflict and stepfamily outcomes for children. *Journal of Marriage & the Family, 58*, 141–154.

Harris, J. R. (1995). Where is the child's environment? A group socialization theory of development. *Psychological Review, 102*, 458–489.

Harris, J. R. (1998). The *nurture assumption: Why children turn out the way they do.* Glencoe, IL: Free Press.

Hartley, R. (1960). Children's concepts of male and female roles. *Merrill-Palmer Quarterly, 6*, 83–91.

Hauser, S., Book, B., Houlihan, J., Powers, S., Weiss-Perry, B., Follansbee, D., et al. (1987). Sex differences within the family: Studies of adolescent and parent family interactions. *Journal of Youth and Adolescence, 16*, 199–220.

Hay, D., & Nash, A. (2002). Social development in different family arrangements. In P. K. Smith & C. Hart (Eds.), *Blackwell handbook of childhood social development* (pp. 238–261). Oxford, UK: Blackwell.

Herman, M. A., & McHale, S. M. (1993). Coping with parental negativity: Links with parental warmth and marital adjustment. *Journal of Applied Developmental Psychology, 14*, 121–130.

Herzog, E., & Sudia, C. E. (1973). Children in fatherless families. In B. M. Caldwell & H. N. Ricciuti (Eds.), *Review of child development research* (Vol. 3, pp. 141–232). Chicago: University of Chicago Press.

Hetherington, E. M., Bridges, M., & Insabella, G. M. (1998). What matters? What does not? Five perspectives on the association between marital transitions and children's adjustment. *American Psychologist, 53*, 167–184.

Hetherington, E. M., & Clingempeel, G. (1992). Coping with marital transitions. *Monographs of the Society for Research in Child Development, 57* (Serial No. 227).

Hetherington, E. M., & Henderson, S. H. (1997). Fathers in stepfamilies. In M. E. Lamb (Ed.), *The role of the father in child development* (3rd ed., pp. 212–226). New York: Wiley.

Hetherington, E. M., & Kelly, J. (2002). *For better or for worse: Divorce reconsidered.* New York: Norton.

Hetherington, E. M., & Stanley-Hagan, M. M. (1999). Stepfamilies. In M. E. Lamb (Ed.), *Parenting and child development in "nontraditional" families.* (pp. 137–159). Mahwah, NJ: Lawrence Erlbaum Associates.

Hewlett, B. S. (1987). Intimate fathers: Patterns of paternal holding among Aka pygmies. In M. E. Lamb (Ed.), *The father's role: Cross-cultural perspectives* (pp. 295–330). Hillsdale, NJ: Lawrence Erlbaum Associates.

Hewlett, B. S. (2005). Who cares for hunter-gatherer children? In B. S. Hewlett & M. E. Lamb (Eds.), *Hunter-gatherer childhoods* (pp. 175–176). New Brunswick, NJ: Aldine/Transaction.

Hewlett, B. S., & MacFarlan, S. J. (2010). Fathers' roles in hunter-gatherer and other small-scale cultures. In M. E. Lamb (Ed.), *The role of the father in child development* (5th ed., pp. 413–434). Hoboken, NJ: Wiley.

Hill, J. (1988). Adapting to menarche: Familial control and conflict. In M. Gunnar (Ed.), *Minnesota symposium on child psychology* (Vol. 21, pp. 43–77). Hillsdale, NJ: Lawrence Erlbaum Associates.

Hill, J., & Holmbeck, G. N. (1987). Familial adaptation to biological change during adolescence. In R. M. Lerner & T. Foch (Eds.), *Biological–psychological interactions in early adolescence: A life-span perspective* (pp. 207–223). Hillsdale, NJ: Lawrence Erlbaum Associates.

Hjetmstedt, A., & Collins, A. (2008). Psychological functioning and predictions of relationships in IVF fathers and controls. *Scandinavian Journal of Caring Science, 22*, 72–78.

Hobson, P. (2002). *The cradle of thought: Explorations of the origins of thinking.* London: Macmillan.

Hoffman-Plotkin, D., & Twentyman, C. T. (1984). A multimodal assessment of behavioral and cognitive deficits in abused and neglected preschoolers. *Child Development, 55*, 794–802.

Holden, G. W. (1995). Parental attitudes towards childrearing. In M. H. Bornstein (Ed.), *Handbook of parenting* (Vol. 3, pp. 359–392). Mahwah, NJ: Lawrence Erlbaum Associates.

Holden, G. W., Geffner, R., & Jouriles, E. W. (Eds.). (1998). *Children exposed to marital violence: Theory, research, and applied issues.* Washington, DC: American Psychological Association.

Holden, G. W., & Miller, P. C. (1999). Enduring and different: A meta-analysis of the similarity in parents' child rearing. *Psychological Bulletin, 125*, 223–254.

Holmbeck, G. N., & O'Donnell, K. (1991). Discrepancies between perceptions of decision making behavioral autonomy. In R. Paikoff (Ed.), *Shared views in the family during adolescence: New directions for child development* (pp. 51–69). San Francisco: Jossey-Bass.

Hosley, C. A., & Montemayor, R. (1997). Fathers and adolescents. In M. E. Lamb (Ed.), *The role of the father in child development* (3rd ed., pp. 162–178). New York: Wiley.

Hrdy, S. B. (2005). Comes the child before man: How cooperative breeding and prolonged post weaning dependence shaped human potential. In B. S. Hewlett & M. E. Lamb (Eds.), *Hunter-gatherer childhoods* (pp. 65–91). New Brunswick, NJ: Transaction/Aldine.

Hrdy, S. B. (2009). *Mothers and others.* Cambridge, MA: Harvard University Press.

Hughes, H. M., & Luke, D. A. (1998). Heterogeneity of adjustment among children of battered women. In G. W. Holden, R. Geffner, & E. W. Jouriles (Eds.), *Children exposed to marital violence: Theory, research, and applied issues* (pp. 185–221). Washington, DC: American Psychological Association.

Hughes, H. M., Parkinson, D. L., & Vargo, M. C. (1989). Witnessing spouse abuse and experiencing physical abuse: A "double whammy"? *Journal of Family Violence, 4*, 197–209.

Hunter, F. T. (1984). Socializing procedures in parent–child and friendship relations during adolescence. *Developmental Psychology, 20*, 1092–1099.

Isaacs, M. B., & Leon, G. H. (1988). Remarriage and its alternatives following divorce: Mother and child adjustment. *Journal of Marital & Family Therapy, 14*, 163–173.

Jarvis, P. A., & Creasey, G. L. (1991). Parental stress, coping, and attachment in families with an 18-month-old infant. *Infant Behavior & Development, 14*, 383–395.

Jenkins, J. M. (2000). Marital conflict and children's emotions: The development of an anger organization. *Journal of Marriage and the Family, 62*, 723–736.

Jenkins, J. M., & Astington, J. W. (1996). Cognitive factors and family structure associated with theory of mind development in young children. *Developmental Psychology, 32*, 70–78.

Jodl, K. M., Michael, A., Malanchuk, O., Eccles, J. S., & Sameroff, A. (2001). Parents' roles in shaping early adolescents' occupational aspirations. *Child Development, 72*, 1247–1265.

Johnson, J. R. (1994). High conflict divorce. *Future of Children, 4*, 165–182.

Johnston, J. R., Kline, M., & Tschann, J. M. (1989). Ongoing postdivorce conflict: Effects on children of joint custody and frequent access. *American Journal of Orthopsychiatry, 59*, 576–592.

Jonsson, C.-O., & Clinton, D. (2006). What do mothers attune to during interactions with their infants? *Infant and Child Development*, *15*, 387–402.

Josselson, R. (1980). Ego development in adolescence. In J. Adelson (Ed.), *Handbook of adolescent psychology* (pp. 188–210). New York: Wiley.

Jouriles, E. N., Norwood, W. D., McDonald, R., Vincent, J. P., & Mahoney, A. (1996). Physical violence and other forms of marital aggression: Links with children's behavior problems. *Journal of Family Psychology*, *10*, 223–234.

Katz, L. F., & Gottman, J. M. (1993). Patterns of marital conflict predict children's internalizing and externalizing behaviors. *Developmental Psychology*, *29*, 940–950.

Kaufman, J., & Cicchetti, D. (1989). Effects of maltreatment of school-age children's socioemotional development: Assessments in a day-camp setting. *Developmental Psychology*, *4*, 516–524.

Kaye, K., & Marcus, J. (1981). Infant imitation: The sensory-motor agenda. *Developmental Psychology*, *17*, 258–265.

Kazdin, A. E., Moser, J., Colbus, D., & Bell, R. (1985). Depressive symptoms among psychically abused and psychiatrically disturbed children. *Journal of Abnormal Psychology*, *94*, 298–307.

Kelly, J. B. (2000). Children's adjustments in conflicted marriage and divorce: A decade review of research. *Journal of the American Academy of Child and Adolescent Psychiatry*, *39*, 963–973.

Kendall-Tackett, K. A., & Eckenrode, J. (1996). The effects of neglect on academic achievement and disciplinary problems: A developmental perspective. *Child Abuse & Neglect*, *20*, 161–169.

Kerns, K. A. (1996). Individual differences in friendship quality: Links to child–mother attachment. In W. M. Bukowski, W. W. Hartup, & A. F. Newcomb (Eds.), *The company they keep: Friendship in childhood and adolescence* (pp. 137–157). New York: Cambridge University Press.

Kiernan, K. E. (2006). Non-residential fatherhood and child involvement: Evidence from the Millennium Cohort Study. *Journal of Social Policy*, *35*, 651–669.

Kobak, R., & Sceery, A. (1988). Attachment in late adolescence: Working models, affect regulation, and representation of self and others. *Child Development*, *59*, 135–146.

Kochanska, K., Aksan, N., Prisco, T. R., & Adams E. E. (2008). Mother–child and father–child mutually responsive orientation in the first 2 years and children's outcomes at preschool age: Mechanisms of influence. *Child Development*, *79*, 30–44.

Koestner, R., Franz, C., & Weinberger, J. (1990). The family origins of empathic concern: A 26-year longitudinal study. *Journal of Personality & Social Psychology*, *58*, 709–717.

Konner, M. (2005). Hunter-gatherer infancy and childhood: The !Kung and others. In B. S. Hewlett & S. E. Lamb (Eds.), *Hunter-gatherer childhoods: Evolutionary, developmental and cultural perspectives*. New Brunswick, NJ: Aldine/Transaction.

Korman, M., & Lewis, C. (2001). Mothers' and fathers' speech to infants: Explorations of the complexity of context. In M. Almgren et al. (Eds.), *Research on child language* (pp. 431–453). Somerville, MA: Cascadilia Press.

Korner, A. F., & Thoman, E. G. (1970). Visual alertness in neonates as evoked by maternal care. *Journal of Experimental Child Psychology*, *10*, 67–78.

Korner, A. F., & Thoman, E. G. (1972). The relative efficacy of contact and vestibular–proprioceptive stimulation in soothing neonates. *Child Development*, *43*, 443–453.

Kroger, J. (1985). Relationships during adolescence: A cross-national study of New Zealand and United States teenagers. *Journal of Adolescence*, *8*, 47–56.

Kuczynski, L. (2003). Beyond directionality: Bilateral conceptual frameworks for studying dynamics in parent–child relations. In L. Kuczynski (Ed.), *Handbook of dynamics in parent–child relations* (pp. 3–24). Thousand Oaks, CA: Sage.

Kuczynski, L., Kochanska, G., Radke-Yarrow, M., & Girnius-Brown, O. (1987). A developmental interpretation of young children's noncompliance. *Developmental Psychology*, *23*, 799–806.

LaBounty, J., Wellman, H. M., Olson, S., Lagattuta, K., & Liu, D. (2008). Mothers' and fathers' use of internal state talk with their young children. *Social Development*, *17*, 757–775.

Labrell, F. (1994). A typical interaction behavior between fathers and toddlers: Teasing. *Early Development and Parenting*, *3*, 125–130.

Labrell, F., Deleau, M., & Juhel, J. (2000). Father's and mother's distancing strategies towards toddlers. *International Journal of Behavioral Development*, *24*, 356–361.

Lamb, M. E. (1976a). Effects of stress and cohort on mother– and father–infant interaction. *Developmental Psychology*, *12*, 435–443

Lamb, M. E. (1976b). Interactions between eight-month-old children and their fathers and mothers. In M. E. Lamb (Ed.), *The role of the father in child development* (1st ed., pp. 307–328). New York: Wiley.

Lamb, M. E. (1976c). Twelve-month-olds and their parents: Interaction in a laboratory playroom. *Developmental Psychology*, *12*, 237–244.

Lamb, M. E. (1977a). The development of mother–infant and father–infant attachments in the second year of life. *Developmental Psychology*, *13*, 637–648.

Lamb, M. E. (1977b). Father–infant and mother–infant interaction in the first year of life. *Child Development*, *48*, 167–181.

Lamb, M. E. (1981a). Developing trust and perceived effectance in infancy. In L. P. Lipsitt (Ed.), *Advances in infancy research* (Vol. 1, pp. 101–130). Norwood, NJ: Ablex.

Lamb, M. E. (1981b). The development of social expectation in the first year of life. In M. E. Lamb & L. R. Sherrod (Eds.), *Infant social cognition* (pp. 155–175). Hillsdale, NJ: Lawrence Erlbaum Associates.

Lamb, M. E. (1997). The development of father infant relationships. In M. E. Lamb (Ed.), *The role of the father in child development* (3rd ed., pp. 104–120, 332–342). New York: Wiley.

Lamb, M. E. (1999a). Noncustodial fathers and their impact on the children of divorce. In R. A. Thompson & P. R. Amato (Eds.), *The post-divorce family: Research and policy issues* (pp. 105–125). Thousand Oaks, CA: Sage.

Lamb, M. E. (Ed.) (1999b). *Parenting and child development in "nontraditional" families*. Mahwah, NJ: Lawrence Erlbaum Associates.

Lamb, M. E. (2002a). Infant–father attachments and their impact on child development. In C. S. Tamis-LeMonda & N. Cabrera (Eds.), *Handbook of father involvement* (pp. 93–118). Mahwah, NJ: Lawrence Erlbaum Associates.

Lamb, M. E. (2002b). Nonresidential fathers and their children. In C. S. Tamis-LeMonda & N. Cabrera (Eds.), *Handbook of father involvement* (pp. 169–184). Mahwah, NJ: Lawrence Erlbaum Associates.

Lamb, M. E., & Ahnert, L. (2006). Nonparental child care: Context, concepts, correlates, and consequences. In W. Damon et al. (Eds.), *Handbook of child psychology* (Vol. 4, 6th ed., pp. 950–1016). Hoboken, NJ: Wiley.

Lamb, M. E., Bornstein, M. H., & Teti, D. M. (2002). *Development in infancy* (4th ed.). Mahwah, NJ: Lawrence Erlbaum Associates.

Lamb, M. E., & Bougher, L. D. (2009). How does migration affect mothers' and fathers' roles within their families? Reflections on some recent research. *Sex Roles, 60*, 611–614.

Lamb, M. E., Gaensbauer, T. J., Malkin, C. M., & Shultz, L. (1985). The effects of abuse and neglect on security of infant–adult attachment. *Infant Behavior and Development, 8*, 35–45.

Lamb, M. E., Hwang, C. P., Frodi, A. M., & Frodi, M. (1982). Security of mother and father–infant attachment and its relation to sociability with strangers in traditional and nontraditional Swedish families. *Infant Behavior & Development, 5*, 355–367.

Lamb, M. E., & Kelly, J. B. (2009). Improving the quality of parent–child contact in separating families with infants and young children: Empirical research foundations. In R. M. Galatzer-Levy, L. Kraus, & J. Galatzer-Levy (Eds.), *The scientific basis of child custody decisions* (2nd ed., pp. 187–214). Hoboken, NJ: Wiley.

Lamb, M. E., & Lewis, C. (2010). The development and significance of father–child relationships in two-parent families. In M. E. Lamb (Ed.), *The role of the father in child development* (5th ed.). Chichester, UK: Wiley.

Lamb, M. E., Thompson, R. W., Gardner, E. L., & Charnov, E. L. (1985). *Infant–mother attachment: The origins and development significance of individual differences in Strange Situation behavior*. Hillsdale, NJ: Lawrence Erlbaum Associates.

Lamborn, S. D., & Steinberg, L. (1993). Emotional autonomy redux: Revisiting Ryan and Lynch. *Child Development, 64*, 483–499.

Langford, W., Lewis, C., Solomon, Y. & Warin, J. (2001). *Family understandings: Closeness, authority and independence in families with teenagers*. London: Family Policy Study Centre & Joseph Rowntree Foundation.

Laranjo, J., Bernier, A., & Meins, E. (2008). Associations between maternal mind-mindedness and infant attachment security: Investigating the mediating role of maternal sensitivity, *Infant Behavior and Development, 31*, 688–695.

Larson, R., & Richards, M. H. (1994). *Divergent realities: The emotional lives of mothers, fathers, and adolescents*. New York: Basic Books.

Leaper, C. (2002). Parenting girls and boys. In M. Bornstein (Ed.), *Handbook of parenting: Children and parenting* (2nd ed., Vol. 1, pp. 189–225). Mahwah, NJ: Lawrence Erlbaum Associates.

Leerkes, E. M., Blankson, A. N. & O'Brien, M. (2009). Differential effects of maternal sensitivity to infant distress and nondistress on social–emotional functioning. *Child Development, 80*, 762–775.

Lempers, J. D., Clark-Lempers, D., & Simons, R. L. (1989). Economic hardship, parenting, and distress in adolescence. *Child Development, 60*, 25–39.

Lewis, C. (1986). *Becoming a father*. Milton Keynes, UK: Open University Press.

Lewis, C., & Carpendale, J. I. M. (2010). Social cognition. In P. K. Smith & C. Hart (Eds.), *The handbook of social development* (2nd ed.). Oxford, UK: Blackwell.

Lewis, C., Freeman, N. H., Kyriakidou, C., Maridaki-Kassotaki, K., & Berridge, D. (1996). Social influences on false belief access: Specific sibling influences or general apprenticeship? *Child Development, 67*, 2930–2947.

Lewis, C., & Gregory, S. (1987). Parents' talk to their infants: The importance of context. *First Language, 7*, 201–216.

Lewis, C., Huang, Z. & Rooksby, M. (2006). Chinese preschoolers' false belief understanding: Is social knowledge underpinned by parental styles, social interactions or executive functions? *Psychologia, 49*, 252–266.

Lewis, C., Newson, J., & Newson, E. (1982). Father participation throughout childhood. In N. Beail & J. McGuire (Eds.), *Fathers: Psychological perspectives* (pp. 174–793). London: Junction.

Lewis, M. & Rosenblum, L. (Eds.) (1974). *The effect of the infant on its caregiver*. New York: Wiley.

Leyendecker, B., & Lamb, M. E. (1999). Latino families. In M. E. Lamb (Ed.), *Parenting and child development in "nontraditional" families* (pp. 247–262). Mahwah, NJ: Lawrence Erlbaum Associates.

Lieberman, M., Doyle, A. B., & Markiewicz, D. (1999). Developmental patterns in security of attachment to mother and father in late childhood and early adolescence: Associations with peer relations. *Child Development, 70*, 202–213.

Lindsey, E. W., & Caldera, Y. M. (2006). Mother–father–child triadic interaction and mother–child dyadic interaction: Gender differences within and between contexts. *Sex Roles, 55*, 511–521.

Lindsey, E. W., Campbell, J., MacKinnon-Lewis, C., Frabutt, J. M., & Lamb, M. E. (2002). Marital conflict and boys' peer relationships: The mediating role of mother–son emotional reciprocity. *Journal of Family Psychology, 16*, 466–477.

Lindsey, E. W., Colwell, M. J., Frabutt, J. M., Chambers, J. C., & MacKinnon-Lewis, C. (2008). Mother–child dyadic synchrony in European American and African American families during early adolescence. *Merrill-Palmer Quarterly, 54*, 289–315.

Lindsey, E. W., Cremeens, P. R., Colwell, M. J., & Caldera, Y. M. (2009). The structure of parent–child dyadic synchrony in toddlerhood and children's communication competence and self-control. *Social Development, 18*, 375–396.

Lindsey, E. W., & Mize, J. (2001). Contextual differences in parent–child play: Implications for children's gender role development. *Sex Roles, 44*, 155–176.

Liu, Y.-L. (2008). An examination of three models of the relationships between parental attachments and adolescents' social functioning and depressive symptoms. *Journal of Youth & Adolescence, 37*, 941–952.

Lynch, M., & Roberts, J. (1982). *Consequences of child abuse.* London: Academic Press.

Lyons-Ruth, K., Easterbrooks, M. A., & Davidson, C. C. (1997). Infant attachment strategies, infant mental lag, and maternal depressive symptoms: Predictors of internalizing and externalizing problems at age 7. *Developmental Psychology, 33*, 681–692.

Lyons-Ruth, K., & Jacobvitz, D. (1999). Attachment disorganization: Unresolved loss, relational violence, and lapses in behavioral and attentional strategies. In J. Cassidy & P. R. Shaver (Eds.), *Handbook of attachment: Theory, research, and clinical applications* (pp. 520–554). New York: Guilford.

Lytton, H., & Romney, D. M. (1991). Parents' differential socialisation of boys and girls: A meta-analysis. *Psychological Bulletin, 109*, 267–296.

Maccoby, E. (1984). Middle childhood in the context of the family. In W. A. Collins (Ed.), *Development during middle childhood: The years from six to twelve* (pp. 184–239). Washington, DC: National Academy of Sciences.

Maccoby, E. E. (1992). The role of parents in the socialization of children: A historical overview. *Developmental Psychology, 28*, 1006–1017.

Maccoby, E. E. (1998). *The two sexes: Growing up apart, coming together.* Cambridge, MA: Harvard University Press.

Maccoby, E. E. (2000). Parenting and its effects on children: On reading and misreading behavior genetics. *Annual Review of Psychology, 51*, 1–27.

Maccoby, E. E., & Martin, J. (1983). Socialization in the context of the family: Parent–child interaction. In P. H. Mussen & E. M. Hetherington (Eds.), *Handbook of child psychology: Vol. 4. Socialization, personality, and social development* (4th ed., pp. 1–101). New York: Wiley.

MacDonald, R. H., & Parke, R. D. (1984). Bridging the gap: Parent–child play interaction and peer competence. *Child Development, 55*, 1265–1277.

MacKinnon, C., Lamb, M. E., Belsky, J., & Baum, C. (1990). An affective–cognitive model of mother–child aggression. *Development and Psychopathology, 2*, 1–14.

MacKinnon-Lewis, C., Lamb, M. E., Arbuckle, B., Baradaran, L. P., & Volling, B. (1992). The relationship between biased maternal and filial attributions and the aggressiveness of their interactions. *Development and Psychopathology, 2*, 1–14.

MacKinnon-Lewis, C., Volling, B. L., Lamb, M. E., Dechman, K., Rabiner, D., & Curtner, M. E. (1994). A cross-contextual analysis of children's social competence: From family to school. *Developmental Psychology, 30*, 325–333.

MacKinnon-Lewis, C., Volling, B. L., Lamb, M. E., Hattie, J., & Baradaran, I. (2001). A longitudinal examination of the associations between mothers' and children's attributions and their aggression. *Development and Psychopathology, 13*, 69–81.

Maclean, M., & Eekelaar, J. (1997). *The parental obligation: A study of parenthood across households.* Oxford, UK: Hart.

Maier, E. H., & Lachman, M. E. (2000). Consequences of early parental loss and separation for health and well-being in midlife. *International Journal of Behavioral Development, 24*, 183–189.

Main, M., & George, C. (1985). Response of abused and disadvantaged toddlers to distress in age mates: A study in the day care setting. *Developmental Psychology, 21*, 407–412.

Main, M., & Goldwyn, R. (1994). *Adult attachment classification system.* Unpublished manuscript, University of California, Berkeley.

Main, M., & Hesse, E. (1990). Parents' unresolved traumatic experiences are related to infant disorganized attachment status: Is frightened and/or frightening parental behavior the linking mechanism? In M. T. Greenberg, D. Cicchetti, & E. M. Cummings (Eds.), *Attachment in the preschool years: Theory, research, and intervention* (pp. 161–182). Chicago: University of Chicago Press.

Main, M., Kaplan, N., & Cassidy, J. (1985). Security in infancy, childhood, and adulthood: A move to the level of representation. In I. Bretherton & E. Waters (Eds.), Growing points of attachment theory and research. *Monographs of the Society for Research in Child Development, 50* (1/2, Serial No. 209), 66–104.

Main, M., & Solomon, J. (1990). Procedures for identifying infants as disorganized/disoriented during the Ainsworth Strange Situation. In M. T. Greenberg, D. Cicchetti, & E. M. Cummings (Eds.), *Attachment in the preschool years: Theory, research, and intervention* (pp. 121–160). Chicago: University of Chicago Press.

Main, M., & Weston, D. R. (1981). Security of attachment to mother and father: Related to conflict behavior and the readiness to establish new relationships. *Child Development, 52*, 932–940.

Mandler, G. (1985). *Cognitive psychology: An essay in cognitive science*. Hillsdale, NJ: Lawrence Erlbaum Associates.

Marlowe, F. W. (2005). Who tends Hadza children? In B. S. Hewlett & M. E. Lamb (Eds.), *Hunter-gatherer childhoods* (pp. 177–190). New Brunswick, NJ: Aldine/Transaction.

Martin, A., Ryan, R. M., & Brooks-Gunn, J. (2007). The joint influence of mother and father parenting on child cognitive outcomes at age 5. *Early Childhood Research Quarterly, 22*, 423–439.

McAdoo, H. P. (1993). Ethnic families: Strengths that are found in diversity. In H. P. McAdoo (Ed.), *Ethnic families: Strength in diversity* (pp. 3–14). Newbury Park, CA: Sage.

McBride, B. A., Schoppe-Sullivan, S. J., & Ho, M. H. (2005). The mediating role of fathers' school involvement on student achievement. *Journal of Applied Developmental Psychology, 26*, 201–216.

McGrellis, S., Henderson, S., Holland, J., Sharpe, S., & Thomson, R. (2000). *Beyond the moral maze: A quantitative study of young people's values*. London: Tuffnell.

McHale, J. P. (2007) When infants grow up in multiperson relationship systems. *Infant Mental Health Journal, 28*, 370–392.

McHale, S. M., Crouter, A. C., Kim, J. Y., Burton, L. M., Davis, K. D., Dotterer, A. M., et al. (2006). Mothers' and fathers' racial socialization in African American families: Implications for youth. *Child Development, 77*, 1387–1402.

McLanahan, S. S. (1999). Father absence and the welfare of children. In E. M. Hetherington (Ed.), *Coping with divorce, single parenting, and remarriage: A risk and resiliency perspective* (pp. 117–145). Mahwah, NJ: Lawrence Erlbaum Associates.

McLanahan, S. S., & Sandefur, G. (1994). *Growing up with a single parent: What hurts, what helps?* Cambridge, MA: Harvard University Press.

McLanahan, S., & Teitler, J. (1999). The consequences of father absence. In M. E. Lamb (Ed.), *Parenting and child development in "nontraditional" families* (pp. 83–102). Mahwah, NJ: Lawrence Erlbaum Associates.

McNeal, C., & Amato, P. R. (1998). Parents' marital violence: Long-term consequences for children. *Journal of Family Issues, 19*, 123–139.

Meins, E. (1997). Security of attachment and maternal tutoring strategies: Interaction within the zone of proximal development. *British Journal of Developmental Psychology, 15*, 129–144.

Meins, E. (1999). Sensitivity, security and internal working models: Bridging the transmission gap. *Attachment & Human Development, 1*, 325–342.

Meins, E., Fernyhough, C., Fradley, E., & Tuckey, M. (2001). Rethinking maternal sensitivity: Mothers' comments on infants' mental processes predict security of attachment at 12 months. *Journal of Child Psychology and Psychiatry, 42*, 637–648.

Meins, E., Fernyhough, C., Russell, J., & Clark-Carter, D. (1998). Security of attachment as a predictor of symbolic and mentalising abilities: A longitudinal study. *Social Development, 7*, 1–24.

Meins, E., Fernyhough, C., Wainwright, R., Das Gupta, M., Fradley, E., & Tuckey, M. (2002). Maternal mind-mindedness and attachment security as predictors of theory of mind understanding. *Child Development, 73*, 1715–1726.

Moffitt, T. E. (2005). The new look of behavioral genetics in developmental psychopathology: Gene–environment interplay in antisocial behaviors. *Psychological Bulletin, 131*, 533–554.

Monteiro, L., Verissimo, M., Vaughn, B. E., Santos, A. J., Torres, N., & Fernandes, M. (in press). The organization of children's secure base behaviour in two parent Portuguese families and father's participation in child related activities. *European Journal of Developmental Psychology*.

Montemayor, R. (1983). Parents and adolescents in conflict: All families some of the time and some families most of the time. *Journal of Early Adolescence, 3*, 83–103.

Montemayor, R., & Brownlee, J. (1987). Fathers, mothers, and adolescents: Gender based differences in parental roles during adolescence. *Journal of Youth and Adolescence, 16*, 281–291.

Murray, A. D. (1979). Infant crying as an elicitor of parental behavior: An examination of two models. *Psychological Bulletin, 86*, 191–215.

National Research Council. (1993). *Understanding child abuse and neglect*. Washington, DC: National Academy.

Nelson, P. B., Adamson, L. B., & Bakeman, R. (2008). Toddlers' joint engagement experience facilitates preschoolers' acquisition of theory of mind. *Developmental Science*, *11*, 840–845.

Noller, P. (1980). Cross-gender effect in two-child families. *Developmental Psychology*, *16*, 159–160.

Noller, P., & Callan, V. J. (1986). Adolescent and parent perceptions of family cohesion and adaptability. *Journal of Adolescence*, *9*, 97–106.

Noller, P., & Callan, V. J. (1988). Understanding parent–adolescent interactions: Perceptions of family members and outsiders. *Developmental Psychology*, *24*, 707–714.

Notaro, P. C., & Volling, B. L. (1999). Parental responsiveness and infant–parent attachment: A replication study with fathers and mothers. *Infant Behavior & Development*, *22*, 345–352.

Oates, K., Peacock, A., & Forrest, D. (1984). The development of abused children. *Developmental Medicine and Child Neurology*, *26*, 649–659.

O'Brien, M. (2005). *Shared caring: Bringing fathers into the frame*. Manchester, UK: Equal Opportunities Commission.

O'Brien, M., John, R. S., Margolin, G., & Erel, O. (1994). Reliability and diagnostic efficacy of parents' reports regarding children's exposure to marital aggression. *Violence and Victims*, *9*, 45–62.

O'Connor, T. G. (2002). The effects of parenting reconsidered: Findings, challenges and applications. *Journal of Child Psychology and Psychiatry*, *43*, 555–572.

O'Connor, T. G., Dunn, J., Jenkins, J. M., & Rasbash, J. (2006). Predictors of between-family and within-family variation in parent–child relationships. *Journal of Child Psychology and Psychiatry*, *47*, 498–510.

O'Connor, T. G., Neiderhiser, J. M., Reiss, D., Hetherington, E. M., & Plomin, R. (1998). Genetic contributions to continuity, change, and co-occurrence of antisocial and depressive symptoms in adolescence. *Journal of Child Psychology & Psychiatry & Allied Disciplines*, *39*, 323–336.

Offer, D., Ostrov, E., & Howard, K. (1981). *The adolescent: A psychological self-portrait*. New York: Basic Books.

Ontai, L. L., & Thompson, R. A. (2008). Attachment, parent–child discourse and theory-of-mind development. *Social Development*, *17*, 47–60.

Oosterwegel, A., & Oppenheimer, L. (1993). *The self-system: Developmental changes between and within self-concepts*. Hillsdale, NJ: Lawrence Erlbaum Associates.

Oppenheim, D., Sagi, A., & Lamb, M. E. (1988). Infant–adult attachments on the kibbutz and their relation to socioemotional development 4 years later. *Developmental Psychology*, *24*, 427–433.

Osofsky, J. D., Hann, D. M., & Peebles, C. (1993). Adolescent parenthood: Risks and opportunities for parent and infants. In C. Zeanah (Ed.), *Handbook of infant mental health* (pp. 106–119). New York: Guilford.

Overton, W. F. (2006). Developmental psychology: Philosophy, concepts, methodology. In W. Damon & R. M. Lerner (Series Eds.) and R. M. Lerner (Volume Ed.), *Handbook of child psychology: Vol. 1. Theoretical models of human development* (6th ed., pp. 18–88). Hoboken, NJ: Wiley.

Papousek, M. (2007). Communication in early infancy: An arena of intersubjective learning. *Infant Behavior and Development*, *30*, 258–266.

Parke, R. D., & Buriel, R. (1998). Socialization in the family: Ethnic and ecological perspectives. In W. Damon & N. Eisenberg (Eds.), *Handbook of child psychology: Vol. 3. Social, emotional, and personality development* (5th ed., pp. 463–552). New York: Wiley.

Parke, R. D., Dennis, J., Flyr, M., Morris, K. L., Killian, C., McDowell, D. J., et al. (2004). Fathering and children's peer relationships. In M. E. Lamb (Ed.), *The role of the father in child development* (4th ed., pp. 32–57). New York: Wiley.

Parke, R. D., Simpkins, S. D., McDowell, D. J., Kim, M., Killian, C., Dennis, J., et al. (2002). Relative contributions of families and peers to children's social development. In P. K. Smith & C. Hart (Eds.), *Blackwell handbook of childhood social development* (pp. 156–177). Oxford, UK: Blackwell.

Patterson, G. R. (1976). The aggressive child: Victim and architect of a coercive system. In L. A. Hamelynch, L. C. Handy, & E. J. March (Eds.), *Behavior modification and families* (pp. 267–316). New York: Brunner/Mazel.

Patterson, G. R. (1982). *Coercive family processes*. Eugene, OR: Castalia.

Patterson, G. R., Reid, J. B., & Dishion, T. J. (1992). *A social learning approach IV: Antisocial boys*. Eugene, OR: Castalia.

Pauli-Pott, U., & Mertesacker, B. (2009). Affect expression in mother–infant interaction and subsequent attachment development. *Infant Behavior & Development*, *32*, 208–215.

Pellegrini, A. D., Brody, G. H., & Stoneman, Z. (1987). Children's conversational competence with their parents. *Discourse Processes*, *10*, 93–106.

Pence, A. R. (Ed.) (1988). *Ecological research with children and families: From concepts to methodology*. New York: Teachers College Press.

Perner, J., Ruffman, T., & Leekam, S. R. (1994). Theory of mind is contagious: You catch it from your sibs. *Child Development*, *65*, 1228–1238.

Phares, V. (1996). *Fathers and developmental psychopathology*. New York: Wiley.

Phares, V. (1997). Psychological adjustment, maladjustment, and father–child relationships. In M. E. Lamb (Ed.), *The role of the father in child development* (3rd ed., pp. 261–283). New York: Wiley.

Pianta, R., Egeland, B., & Erickson, M. F. (1989). The antecedents of maltreatment: Results of the Mother–Child Interaction Research Project. In D. Cicchetti & V. Carlson (Eds.), *Child maltreatment: Theory and research on the causes and consequences of child abuse and neglect* (pp. 203–253). New York: Cambridge University Press.

Pleck, E. (2004). The dimensions of fatherhood: A history of the good dad–bad dad complex. In M. E. Lamb (Ed.), *The role of the father in child development* (4th ed., pp. 32–57). New York: Wiley.

Pleck, J. H., & Masciadrelli, B. P. (2004). Paternal involvement by U.S. residential fathers: Levels, sources and consequences. In M. E. Lamb (Ed.), *The role of the father in child development* (4th ed., pp. 222–270). New York: Wiley.

Plomin, R., DeFries, J. C., McClearn, G. E., & McGuffin, P. (2000). *Behavioral genetics* (4th ed.). New York: Worth.

Posada, G., Jacobs, A., Carbonell, O. A., Alzate, G., Bustamante, M. R., & Arenas, A. (1999). Maternal care and attachment security in ordinary and emergency contexts. *Developmental Psychology*, *35*, 1379–1388.

Price, J. M., & Van Slyke, D. (1991, April). *Social information processing patterns and social adjustment of maltreated children*. Paper presented to the Society for Research in Child Development, Seattle, WA.

Raag, T., & Rackliff, C. L. (1998). Preschoolers' awareness of social expectations of gender: Relationships to toy choices. *Sex Roles*, *38*, 685–700.

Ramchandani, P., Stein, A., Evans, J., O'Connor, T. G., & the ALSPAC Study Team (2005). Paternal depression in the postnatal period and child development: A prospective population study. *The Lancet*, *365*, 3201–3205.

Rapoport, R., Rapoport, R., & Strellitz, Z. (1975). *Fathers, mothers and others*. London: Routledge.

Reddy, V. (2003). On being the object of attention: Implications for self–other consciousness. *Trends in Cognitive Sciences*, *7*, 397–402.

Rödholm, M., & Larsson, K. (1982). The behavior of human male adults at their first contact with a newborn. *Infant Behavior and Development*, *5*, 121–130.

Rohner, R. P., & Pettengill, S. M. (1985). Perceived parental acceptance–rejection and parental control among Korean adolescents. *Child Development*, *56*, 524–528.

Roopnarine, J. L. (2004). African American and African Caribbean fathers: Level, quality and meaning of involvement. In M. E. Lamb (Ed.), *The role of the father in child development* (4th ed., pp. 58–97). Hoboken, NJ: Wiley.

Roopnarine, J. L., Fouts, H. N., Lamb, M. E., & Lewis-Elligan T. Y. (2005). Mothers' and fathers' behaviors toward their 3–4 month-old infants in low-, middle-, and upper-socioeconomic African American families. *Developmental Psychology*, *41*, 723–731.

Rosen, K. S., & Rothbaum, F. (1993). Quality of parental caregiving and security of attachment. *Developmental Psychology*, *29*, 358–367.

Ross, H., & Taylor, H. (1989). Do boys prefer daddy or his physical style of play? *Sex Roles*, *20*, 23–33.

Rowe, M. L., Coker, D., & Pan, B. A. (2004). A comparison of fathers' and mothers' talk to toddlers in low-income families. *Social Development*, *13*, 278–291.

Rubin, K. H., Coplan, R. J., Chen, X., Buskirk, A. A., & Wojslawowicz, J. C. (2004). Peer relationships in childhood. In M. H. Bornstein & M. E. Lamb (Eds.), *Developmental science: An advanced textbook* (5th ed., pp. 469–512). Mahwah, NJ: Lawrence Erlbaum Associates.

Ruble, D. N., & Martin, C. L. (1998). Gender development. In W. Damon and N. Eisenberg (Eds.), *Handbook of child psychology: Vol. 3. Social, emotional, and personality development* (5th ed., pp. 933–1016). New York: Wiley.

Ruffman, T., Perner, J., Naito, M., Parkin, L., & Clements, W. A. (1998). Older (but not younger) siblings facilitate false belief understanding. *Developmental Psychology*, *34*, 161–174.

Ruffman, T., Perner, J., & Parkin, L. (1999). How parenting style affects false belief understanding. *Social Development*, *8*, 395–411.

Russell, A., Aloa, V., Feder, Y., Glover, A., Miller, H., & Palmer, G. (1998). Sex-based differences in parenting styles in a sample with preschool children. *Australian Journal of Psychology*, *50*, 89–99.

Russell, G., & Russell, A. (1987). Mother–child and father–child relationships in middle childhood. *Child Development*, *58*, 1573–1585.

Russell, A., & Saebel, J. (1997). Mother–son, mother–daughter, father–son, and father–daughter: Are they distinct relationships? *Developmental Review*, *17*, 111–147.

Sabbagh, M. A., & Seamans, E. L. (2008). Intergenerational transmission of theory-of-mind. *Developmental Science*, *11*, 354–360.

Sagi, A., Lamb, M. E., & Gardner, W. (1986). Relations between Strange Situation behavior and stranger sociability among infants on Israel kibbutzim. *Infant Behavior & Development*, *9*, 271–282.

Salzinger, S., Feldman, R., Hammer, M., & Rosario, M. (1993). The effects of physical abuse on children's social relationships. *Child Development*, *64*, 169–187.

Sarkadi, A., Kristiansson, R., Oberklaid, F., & Bremberg, S. (2008). Fathers' involvement and children's developmental outcomes: A systematic review of longitudinal studies. *Acta Paediatrica*, *97*(2), 153–158.

Schoppe-Sullivan, S. J., Diener, M. L., Mangelsdorf, S. C., Brown, G. L., McHale, J. L., & Frosch, C. A. (2006). Attachment and sensitivity in family context: The roles of parent and infant gender. *Infant & Child Development*, *15*, 367–385.

Schudlich, T. D. D. R., & Cummings, E. M. (2007). Parental dysphoria and children's adjustment: Marital conflict styles, children's emotional security, and parenting as mediators of risk. *Journal of Abnormal Child Psychology*, *35*, 627–639.

Schuengel, C., Bakermans-Kranenburg, M., van IJzendoorn, M. H., & Blom, M. (1999). Unresolved loss and infant disorganization: Links to frightening maternal behavior. In J. Solomon & C. George (Eds.), *Attachment disorganization* (pp. 71–94). New York: Guilford.

Scott, J. (2004). Family, gender and educational attainment in Britain: A longitudinal study. *Journal of Comparative Family Studies*, *35*, 565–589.

Sears, R. R., Maccoby, E. E., & Levin, H. (1957). *Patterns of child rearing*. Palo Alto, CA: Stanford University.

Sebald, H. (1977). *Adolescence: A social psychological analysis* (2nd ed.). Englewood Cliffs, NJ: Prentice Hall.

Sedlak, A. J., & Broadhurst, D. D. (1996). *Third national incidence study of child abuse and neglect: Final report*. Washington, DC: US Department of Health and Human Services.

Seltzer, J. A. (1991). Relationships between fathers and children who live apart: The father's role after separation. *Journal of Marriage & the Family*, *53*, 79–101.

Seltzer, J. A. (1994). Consequences of marital dissolution for children. *Annual Review of Sociology*, *20*, 235–266.

Seltzer, J. A. (1998). Men's contributions to children and social policy. In A. Booth & A. C. Crouter (Eds.), *Men in families: When do they get involved? What difference does it make?* (pp. 303–314). Hillsdale, NJ: Lawrence Erlbaum Associates.

Shaw, D. S., Owens, E. B., Vondra, J. I., & Keenan, K. (1996). Early risk factors and pathways in the development of early disruptive behavior problems. *Development & Psychopathology*, *8*, 679–699.

Shulman, S., & Seiffge-Krenke, I. (1997). *Fathers and adolescents: Developmental and clinical perspectives*. London: Routledge.

Siegel, A. U. (1987). Are sons and daughters more differently treated by fathers than by mothers? *Developmental Review*, *7*, 183–209.

Silverberg, S. B., Tennenbaum, D. L., & Jacob, T. (1992). Adolescence and family interaction. In V. B. Van Hasselt & M. Hersen (Eds.), *Handbook of social development: A lifespan perspective* (pp. 347–370). New York: Plenum.

Simmons, R. G., & Blyth, D. A. (1987). *Moving into adolescence: The impact of pubertal change and school context*. New York: Aldine DeGruyter.

Simons, R. L. & Associates (1996). *Understanding differences between divorced and intact families: Stress, interaction, and child outcome*. Thousand Oaks, CA: Sage.

Slough, N. (1988). *Assessment of attachment in five-year-olds: Relationship among separation, the internal representation, and mother–child functioning*. Unpublished doctoral dissertation, University of Washington, Seattle.

Smetana, J. G. (1988). Adolescents' and parents' conceptions of parental authority. *Child Development*, *59*, 321–335.

Smetana, J. G. (1989). Adolescents' and parents' reasoning about actual family conflicts. *Child Development*, *60*, 1052–1067.

Smetana, J. G. (1995). Context, conflict, and constraint in adolescent–parent authority relationships. In M. Killen & D. Hart (Eds.), *Morality in everyday life: Developmental perspectives* (pp. 225–255). Cambridge, UK: Cambridge University Press.

Solomon, Y., Warin, J. & Lewis, C. (2002). Helping with homework? Homework as a site of tension for parents and teenagers. *British Educational Research Journal*, *28*, 603–622.

Solomon, Y., Warin, J., Lewis, C. & Langford, W. (2002). Intimate talk between parents and their teenage children: Democratic openness of covert control. *Sociology*, *36*, 965–983.

Sprenglemeyer, R., Perrett, D. I., Fagan, E. C., Coinwell, R. E., Lobmaier, J. S., Sprengelmeyor, A., et al. (2009). The cutest little baby face: A hormonal link to sensitivity to cuteness in infant faces. *Psychological Science*, *20*, 149–154.

Sroufe, L. A. (1983). Individual patterns of adaptation from infancy to preschool. In M. Perlmutter (Ed.), *Development and policy concerning children with special needs* (pp. 41–83). Hillsdale, NJ: Lawrence Erlbaum Associates.

Sroufe, L. A. (1988). The role of infant–caregiver attachment in development. In J. Belsky & T. J. Nezworski (Eds.), *Clinical implications of attachment* (pp. 18–40). Hillsdale, NJ: Lawrence Erlbaum Associates.

Sroufe, L. A. (1996). *Emotional development*. Cambridge, UK: Cambridge University Press.

Steele, H., Steele, M., Croft, C., & Fonagy, P. (1999). Infant–mother attachment at one year predicts children's understanding of mixed emotions at six years. *Social Development*, *8*, 161–178.

Steele, H., Steele, M., & Fonagy, P. (1996). Associations among attachment classifications of mothers, fathers, and their infants. *Child Development*, *67*, 541–555.

Steinberg, L. (1981). Transformation in family relationships at puberty. *Developmental Psychology*, *17*, 833–840.

Steinberg, L. (1987). Impact of puberty on family relations: Effects of pubertal status and pubertal timing. *Developmental Psychology*, *23*, 451–460.

Steinberg, L. (1988). Reciprocal relations between parent–child distance and pubertal maturation. *Developmental Psychology*, *24*, 122–128.

Steinberg, L. (1990). Interdependence in the family: Autonomy, conflict, and harmony in the parent–adolescent relationships. In S. S. Feldman & G. Elliott (Eds.), *At the threshold: The developing adolescent* (pp. 255–276). Cambridge, MA: Harvard University Press.

Steinberg, L. D., & Darling, N. E. (1994). The broader context of social influence in adolescence. In R. K. Silbereisen & E. Todt (Eds.), *Adolescence in context* (pp. 25–45). New York: Springer-Verlag.

Steinberg, L. D., Darling, N. E., & Fletcher, A. C. (1995). Authoritative parenting and adolescent development: An ecological journey. In P. Moen, G. H. Elder, & K. Luscher (Eds.), *Examining lives in context* (pp. 423–466). Washington, DC: American Psychological Association.

Steinberg, L., Elmen, J. D., & Mounts, N. S. (1989). Authoritative parenting, psychosocial maturity, and academic success among adolescents. *Child Development, 60,* 1424–1436.

Stern, D. N., Hofer, L., Haft, W., & Dore, J. (1985). Affect attunement: The sharing of feeling states between mother and infant by means of inter-modal fluency. In T. Field, & N. Fox (Eds.), *Social perception in infants* (pp. 249–268). Norwood, NJ: Ablex.

Sternberg, K. J., Baradaran, L., Abbott, C. B., Lamb, M. E., & Guterman, E. (2006a). Type of violence, age, and gender differences in the effects of family violence on children's behavior problems: A mega analysis. *Developmental Review, 26,* 89–112.

Sternberg, K. J., & Lamb, M. E. (1999). Violent families. In M. E. Lamb (Ed.), *Parenting and child development in "nontraditional" families* (pp. 305–325). Mahwah, NJ: Lawrence Erlbaum Associates.

Sternberg, K. J., Lamb, M. E., & Dawud-Noursi, S. (1998). Understanding domestic violence and its effects: Making sense of divergent reports and perspectives. In G. W. Holden, R. Geffner, & E. W. Jouriles (Eds.), *Children exposed to family violence* (pp. 121–156). Washington, DC: American Psychological Association.

Sternberg, K. J., Lamb, M. E., Greenbaum, C., Cicchetti, D., Dawud, D., Cortes, R. M., et al. (1993). Effects of domestic violence on children's behavior problems and depression. *Developmental Psychology, 29,* 44–52.

Sternberg, K. J., Lamb, M. E., Greenbaum, C., Dawud, S., Cortes, R. M., & Lorey, F. (1994). The effects of domestic violence on children's perceptions of their perpetrating and nonperpetrating parents. *International Journal of Behavioral Development, 17,* 779–795.

Sternberg, K. J., Lamb, M. E., Guterman, E., & Abbott, C. B. (2006). Effects of early and later family violence on children's behavior problems and depression: A longitudinal, multi-informant perspective. *Child Abuse and Neglect, 30,* 283–306.

Sternberg, K. J., Lamb, M. E., Guterman, E., Abbott, C. B., & Dawud-Noursi, S. (2005). Adolescents' perceptions of attachments to their mothers and fathers in families with histories of domestic violence: A longitudinal perspective. *Child Abuse and Neglect, 29,* 853–869.

Storey, A. E., Walsh, C. J., Quinton, R. L., & Wynne-Edwards, R. E. (2000). Hormonal correlates of paternal responsiveness in new and expectant fathers. *Evolution and Human Behavior, 21,* 79–95.

Straus, M. A., & Gelles, R. J. (1986). Change in family violence from 1975–1985. *Journal of Marriage and the Family, 48,* 465–479.

Straus, M. A., & Gelles, R. J. (1990). How violent are American families? Estimates from the national family violence resurvey and other studies. In M. A. Straus & R. J. Gelles (Eds.), *Physical violence in American families* (pp. 95–108). New Brunswick, NJ: Transaction Books.

Straus, M. A., Gelles, R. J., & Steinmetz, S. (1980). *Behind closed doors: Violence in the American family.* New York: Doubleday/Anchor.

Suess, G. J., Grossmann, K. E., & Sroufe, L. A. (1992). Effects of infant attachment to mother and father on quality of adaptation in preschool: From dyadic to individual organisation of self. *International Journal of Behavioral Development, 15,* 43–65.

Symons, D. K., & Clark, S. E. (2000). A longitudinal study of mother–child relationships and theory of mind in the preschool period. *Social Development, 9,* 3–23.

Tamis-LeMonda, C. S., & McFadden, K. E. (2010). Fathers from low-income backgrounds: Myths and evidence. In M. E. Lamb (Ed.), *The role of the father in child development* (5th ed., pp. 296–318). Hoboken, NJ: Wiley.

Tenenbaum, H. R., & Leaper, C. (2003). Parent–child conversations about science: The socialization of gender inequities? *Developmental Psychology, 39,* 34–47.

Teti, D. M. (Ed.) (2005). *Handbook of research methods in developmental psychology.* Oxford, UK: Blackwell.

Teti, D. M., Gelfand, D. M, Messinger, D. S., & Isabella, R. (1995). Maternal depression and the quality of early attachment: An examination of infants, preschoolers, and their mothers. *Developmental Psychology, 31,* 364–376.

Teti, D. M., & Teti, L. O. (1996). Infant–parent relationships. In N. Vanzetti & S. Duck (Eds.), *A lifetime of relationships* (pp. 77–104). Belmont, CA: Brooks/Cole.

Thompson, R. A. (1998). Early sociopersonality development. In W. Damon & N. Eisenberg (Eds.), *Handbook of child psychology: Vol. 3. Social, emotional, and personality development* (5th ed., pp. 25–104). New York: Wiley.

Tomasello, M. (1999). *The cultural origins of human cognition.* Cambridge, MA: Harvard University Press.

van IJzendoorn, M. H. (1995). The association between adult attachment representations and infant attachment, parental responsiveness, and clinical status: A meta-analysis on the predictive validity of the Adult Attachment Interview. *Psychological Bulletin, 113,* 404–410.

van IJzendoorn, M. H., & Juffer, F. (2006). Meta-analytic evidence for massive catch-up and plasticity in physical, socio-emotional, and cognitive development. *Journal of Child Psychology & Psychiatry, 47*, 1228–1245.

van IJzendoorn, M. H., & De Wolff, M. S. (1997). In search of the absent father–meta-analysis of infant–father attachment: A rejoinder to our discussants. *Child Development, 68*, 604–609.

Verschueren, K., & Marcoen, A. (1999). Representation of self and socioemotional competence in kindergartners: Differential and combined effects of attachment to mother and father. *Child Development, 70*, 183–201.

Vinden, P. G. (2001). Parenting attitudes and children's understanding of mind. A comparison of Korean American and Anglo-American families. *Cognitive Development, 16*, 793–809.

Vogel, C. A., Bradley, R. H., Raikes, H. H., Boller, K., & Shears, J. K. (2006). Relation between father connectedness and child outcomes. *Parenting: Science and Practice, 6*, 189–209.

Volling, B. L., & Belsky, J. (1992). Infant, father, and marital antecedents of infant–father attachment security in dual-earner and single-earner families. *Journal of Behavioral Development, 15*, 83–100.

Welkowitz, J., Bond, R. N., Feldman, L., & Tota, M. E. (1990). Conversational time patterns and mutual influence in parent–child interactions: A time series approach. *Journal of Psycholinguistic Research, 19*, 221–243.

Wellman, H. M., Cross, D., & Watson, J. (2001). Meta-analysis of theory of mind development: The truth about false belief. *Child Development, 72*, 655–684.

Widom, C. S. (1989). The cycle of violence. *Science, 244*, 160–166.

Widom, C. S. (1994). Childhood victimization and risk for adolescent problem behaviors. In M. E. Lamb & R. D. Ketterlinus (Eds.), *Adolescent problem behaviors* (pp. 127–164). Hillsdale, NJ: Lawrence Erlbaum Associates.

Williams, J., Bennett, S., & Best, D. (1975). Awareness and expression of sex stereotypes in young children. *Developmental Psychology, 11*, 635–642.

Wolfe, D. A., & Mosk, M. D. (1983). Behavioral comparisons of children from abusive and distressed families. *Journal of Consulting and Clinical Psychology, 51*, 702–708.

Yogman, M. (1981). Games fathers and mothers play with their infants. *Infant Mental Health Journal, 2*, 241–248.

Youniss, J. (1989). Parent–adolescent relationships. In W. Damon (Ed.), *Child development today and tomorrow* (pp. 379–392). Hoboken, NJ: Jossey-Bass.

Youniss, J., & Ketterlinus, R. D. (1987). Communication and connectedness in mother and father–adolescent relationships. *Journal of Youth and Adolescence, 16*, 265–280.

Youniss, J., & Smollar, J. (1985). *Adolescent relations with mothers, fathers, and friends.* Chicago: University of Chicago Press.

Zill, N., & Nord, C. W. (1996). *Causes and consequences of involvement by non-custodial parents in their children's lives: Evidence from a national longitudinal study.* Paper presented to the National Center on Fathers and Families Roundtable, New York.

PEER RELATIONSHIPS IN CHILDHOOD

Kenneth H. Rubin
University of Maryland
Robert Coplan
Carleton University
Xinyin Chen
University of Western Ontario
Julie Bowker
University at Buffalo, the State University of New York
Kristina L. McDonald
University of Maryland

INTRODUCTION

An early view of the development of adaptive and maladaptive behaviors during childhood and adolescence suggested that such outcomes stemmed largely from the quality of the child's relationship with his or her parents and from the types of socialization practices that the parents engaged in. This primary focus on the developmental significance of the parent–child relationship and of parenting practices was proposed early by Freud (1933) in his theory of psychosexual development, by Sears, Maccoby, and Levin (1957) in their seminal research on the significance of discipline variability and social learning, and by Bowlby (1958) in his influential writings on the long-term developmental importance of the mother–infant attachment relationship. Without denying the veracity of these claims, it is nevertheless the case that adjustment and maladjustment in childhood stem from a wide variety of sources including genetic and biological underpinnings and social influences other than parents. For example, children and adolescents spend enormous amounts of time, both in and out of home, relating to and interacting with many other people of potential influence. These significant others include their siblings, teachers or out-of-home caregivers, and peers. Children's **peers** are the focus of the present chapter.

To examine the significance of peers in children's lives, this chapter is organized as follows. We begin with a discussion of the theory that has brought the study of peers to its present status. Next, we describe normative patterns of peer interaction from infancy through late childhood and early adolescence. In the following section, we review the literature on children's **friendships**; we examine what it is that draws children together as friends and the qualitative dimensions of children's behavior displayed during interaction with friends. Next, we describe the functions of the peer group, the processes involved in peer group formation, and peer group norms and organization. This section leads to a discussion of the correlates, proximal determinants, and consequences of being accepted or rejected by the peer group. The distal processes (e.g., family factors, cultural factors) by which children become accepted or rejected by their peers are described in another section. Our chapter concludes with a discussion of some of the directions that future research might produc-tively follow.

The purpose of this chapter is to describe the nature and significance of children's peer relationships. It is our intention to argue that such relationships represent contexts within which a significant degree of adaptive development occurs, and that without the experience of normal peer relationships, maladaptive development is likely to follow.

THEORETICAL PERSPECTIVES ON PEER RELATIONSHIPS RESEARCH

The theoretical groundwork for modern research on children's peer relationships can be traced back over 75 years. Piaget (1932) suggested that children's relationships with peers could be clearly distinguished from their relationships with adults. Adult–child relationships could be construed as being asymmetrical and falling along a vertical plane of dominance and power assertion. Children normally accept adults' rules, not necessarily because they understand them, but rather because obedience is required. By contrast, children's relation-ships with peers were portrayed as being balanced, egalitarian, and as falling along a more or less horizontal plane of power assertion and dominance. It was within the context of peer interaction that Piaget believed children could experience opportunities to examine conflict-ing ideas and explanations, to negotiate and discuss multiple perspectives, and to decide to compromise with or to reject notions held by peers. Piaget influenced a good deal of con-temporary research concerning children's peer relationships, particularly regarding relations among how children think about their social worlds (social-cognition), their social behaviors, and the quality of their peer relationships (e.g., Rose-Krasnor & Denham, 2009).

Another early theoretical perspective on peer relationships stems from the writings of Sullivan (1953). Like Piaget, Sullivan believed that the concepts of mutual respect, equality, and reciprocity developed from peer relationships. Sullivan, however, emphasized the signifi-cance of "special" relationships—chumships and friendships—for the emergence of these concepts. In the early school years, whether friends or not, Sullivan thought children were basically insensitive to their peers. During the juvenile years (late elementary school), how-ever, children were thought to be able to recognize and value each other's personal qualities; as a consequence, peers gained power as personality shaping agents. Sullivan's theory has proved influential in terms of the contemporary study of children's friendships (e.g., Vitaro, Boivin, & Bukowski, 2009) as well as in understanding loneliness as a significant motivational force in development and adjustment (e.g., Asher & Paquette, 2003).

Building on the turn-of-the-century notions of Cooley (1902), George Herbert Mead (1934) developed a third influential theory in which he suggested that the ability to reflect on the *self* developed gradually over the early years of life, primarily as a function of peer play and peer interaction. This theoretical position has been highly influential in contemporary research concerning relations between the quality of children's peer relationships and the organization of the self-system (e.g., Boivin & Hymel, 1997).

Learning and social learning theory is yet another approach that has guided current research on children's peer relationships. The basic tenet of the social learning approach to development is that children learn about their social worlds, and how to behave within these contexts, through direct peer tutelage and observation of peers "in action" (Bandura & Walters, 1963). From this perspective, peers are viewed as behavior control and behavior change agents for each other. In this regard, children punish or ignore non-normative social behavior and reward or reinforce positively those behaviors viewed as culturally appropriate and competent.

Ethological theory has also provided a novel and substantial influence on the study of children's peer relationships. From an ethological perspective, it is argued that there is a relation between biology and the ability to initiate, maintain, or disassemble particular relationships. It is a central tenet of ethological theory that social behavior and organizational structure are limited by biological constraints, and that they serve an adaptive evolutionary function (Hinde & Stevenson-Hinde, 1976). A basic focus of contemporary human ethological research has been the provision of detailed descriptions of the organization and structure of social behaviors and groups (Vaughn & Santos, 2009). Moreover, with the assumption that behavior is best understood when observed in natural settings, ethological theory has had a major impact on how children's peer interactions and relationships are studied.

Finally, there is the *group socialization theory* of Harris (1995, 1999, 2009). In a series of literature reviews, Harris challenged the view that primarily their parents mold children's personalities; rather, in her view, the peer group plays a more significant role in personality and social development. Briefly, she proposed that, once children find themselves outside the home, they take on the norms prevalent in the groups within which they spend their time . . . and, for the most part, those groups comprise other children! Drawing from social psychological perspectives on the significance of group norms (a motivation to "fit in"), in-group biases and out-group hostilities, and social cognitive views of group processes, she argued that children's identities develop primarily from their experiences within peer groups. Although Harris' view that parents and such dyadic relationships as friendship are relatively unimportant for individual development has drawn many criticisms (e.g., Collins, Maccoby, Steinberg, Hetherington, & Bornstein, 2000), publication of her work could have met with unanimous applause on the parts of those researchers who have attempted to demonstrate the significance of peer interactions, relationships, and groups for normal and abnormal development. For decades, theorists, researchers, and policy makers who have cited the primacy of parenting and the parent–child relationship have challenged those who have attempted to establish the significance of children's peer experiences. With Harris' counterchallenge, a gauntlet was thrown down—researchers must now begin to address some central questions about the causal roles that genes, biology, family, and peers play in child and adolescent adjustment and maladjustment.

THE DEVELOPMENTAL COURSE OF PEER INTERACTION

Infancy and the Toddler Period

Not surprisingly, children become increasingly interactive and competent at initiating and maintaining social exchanges as they grow older. What might be surprising is how very young children are when they can be first observed to engage in socially directed behaviors toward peers.

Given obvious motoric, cognitive, and verbal limitations, one might not expect much peer interaction when observing young infants. Indeed, Buhler (1935), in one of the first studies of peer interaction in infancy, suggested that prior to 6 months, babies were fairly oblivious to each other's presence. However, there is now reason to believe that the social awareness of very young infants has been grossly underestimated. For example, Eckerman (1979) reported that infants as young as 2 months of age are aroused by the presence of peers and engage in mutual gaze. Other signs of socially oriented interest during the first half-year of life include smiling, vocalizing, and reaching toward peers (Fogel, 1979). By 6 to 9 months, infants direct looks, vocalizations, and smiles at one another—and often return such gestures in kind (Hay, Pederson, & Nash, 1982).

Babies show signs of socially oriented interest such as smiling and reaching towards peers from the age of 2 months.

These socially oriented behaviors increase steadily with age over the first year of life. Moreover, the tendency to *respond* to social overtures increases dramatically during the last quarter of the first year (Jacobson, 1981). Responses are often in the form of imitative acts, focused on objects. Mueller and Silverman (1989) argued that these imitations represent the first evidence of shared meanings between peers, an important precursor for cooperative peer activities. Despite the apparent sociability of the infant, it seems fairly clear that social interaction with peers occurs relatively rarely and that when interactive bouts do occur, they are not for lengthy periods of time.

During the second year, toddlers take giant steps in advancing their social repertoires (Brownell & Kopp, 2007). With the emergence of locomotion and the ability to speak (Adolph & Berger, 2010; MacWhinney, 2010), social interchanges become increasingly complex. From the somewhat unpredictable social response sequences observed between infants, interactive exchanges and sequences in the toddler period can be characterized as more predictable, complex, coordinated, and lengthy (Ross & Conant, 1992; Verba, 1994). These interactions typically take the form of simple "games," which are marked by reciprocal imitative acts and the emergence of turn-taking (Howes, 1988; Ross, Lollis, & Elliot, 1982; Warneken, Chen, & Tomasello, 2006). Hay and Cook (2007) argued that these prototypical social games are characterized by a "playful, nonliteral quality" (p. 103) that distinguishes them from more "literal" interaction (e.g., interpersonal conflict). Importantly, by the toddler period, children are more likely to socially imitate peers than to imitate adults (Ryalls, Gull, & Ryalls, 2000).

The Preschool Years

The major social interactive advance in the third year of life is the ability for children to share symbolic meanings through social pretense (Howes & Matheson, 1992). Children begin to spontaneously take on complementary roles, none of which "matches" their real-world situations, and to agree on the adoption of these imaginary roles within a rule-governed context. These remarkable accomplishments can be seen in the peer play of many 24- to 48-month-olds. The ability to share meaning during pretense has been referred to as *intersubjectivity* (Trevarthen, 1979). Goncu (1993) reported a systematic change in the intersubjective quality of the social interchanges of 3- versus 4½-year-olds. For example, the social interactions of older preschoolers involve longer sequences and turns and incorporate a more coordinated agreement among partners in terms of the roles, rules, and themes of pretend play.

In summary, despite the advances noted above, it is clearly the case that when infants and toddlers are brought together in social groups, they spend most of their time alone, or near or watching others, and *not* in coordinated, complex social exchanges.

Social participation. In 1932, Parten described six sequential **social participation** categories: unoccupied behavior, solitary play, onlooker behavior (the child observes others but does not participate in the activity), parallel play (plays beside but not with other children), associative play (plays and shares with others), and cooperative play (social play in which there is a defined division of labor). Parten concluded that children between the ages of 2 and 5 engage in increasing frequencies of associative and cooperative play and in decreasing frequencies of idle, solitary, and onlooker behavior. Parten's social participation scale and her findings dominated the literature concerning children's play and sociability for almost 50 years. Yet her database derived from a sample of only 40 children attending a single university laboratory preschool. Furthermore, conclusions based on her data were simplistic. For example, the 3-year-old preschooler was characterized as a solitary or parallel player and the 5-year-old was described as spending the most time in associative or cooperative play.

A more critical reading of Parten's study suggests a more complex set of conclusions. To begin with, children at all ages engage in unoccupied, onlooking, solitary, parallel, and group play activities (Howes & Matheson, 1992). Even at 5 years, children spend less of their free play time in classroom settings interacting with others than being alone or near others. Moreover, the major developmental changes in the play of preschoolers concern the cognitive maturity of their solitary, parallel, and group interactive activities (Rubin, Watson, & Jambor, 1978). Solitary-sensorimotor behaviors become increasingly rare over the preschool years, and the relative frequency of solitary-construction or exploration remains the same. Furthermore, the only types of social interactive activity to increase with age are sociodramatic play and games-with-rules. Taken together, the extant data reveal *age differences* only for particular forms of solitary and group behaviors.

Other early developmental differences. There are developmental differences not only on the prevalence or level of social participation, but also on the nature (e.g., prosocial versus aggressive) of social interaction. On the prosocial side, helping and sharing behaviors with peers are observed to increase from the early toddler to the early preschool years (Benenson, Markovits, Roy, & Denko, 2003; Eisenberg, Fabes, & Spinrad, 2006). This is likely a result of increasing social-cognitive and affective perspective-taking abilities. A more sophisticated understanding of how others think and feel promotes the development of empathy, which may in turn lead to more prosocial behaviors (Vaish, Carpenter, & Tomasello, 2009). This also facilitates more "mature" peer interactions. For example, Brownell, Ramani, and Zerwas (2006) reported age-related changes in children's social understanding and cooperation over the first three years of life. Whereas coordinated activities between younger toddlers were sporadic and more likely to be coincidental in nature, during the second year children were considerably more skilled at cooperating towards a common goal.

Finally, throughout the preschool years, children also demonstrate age-related increases in social-communicative competence (Goldstein, Kaczmarek, & English, 2002). For example, from toddlerhood to preschool-age, children develop the ability to use gestures to represent absent objects and to explicitly coordinate roles in pretend play (Sawyer, 1997). Moreover, older preschool age children direct more speech to their peers than do their younger counterparts and their communication with peers is more likely to include indirect (i.e., declaratives, interrogatives, inferred requests) than direct (imperatives) requests (Garvey, 1984). Genyue

Sharing behavior increases from the early toddler to the early preschool years.

and Lee (2007) described the emergence of *flattery* behavior between the ages of 3 and 6 years, with older preschoolers appropriately moderating their display of such behavior in keeping with the familiarity and presence/absence of the intended target. However, regardless of age, two-thirds of preschoolers' socially directed speech is comprehensible and has a successful outcome (Levin & Rubin, 1983). These data raise questions concerning Piaget's assumption that the speech of preschoolers is characterized primarily by egocentric utterances.

Notwithstanding these increases in prosocial and sociable behaviors, preschoolers' interactions with peers also evolve in terms of more negative social interchanges. For example, although aggression tends to decline overall from toddlerhood to the preschool years (particularly instrumental aggression such as fights over toys and possessions; NICHD Early Child Care Research Network, 2001), an increasing proportion of aggression becomes *hostile* in intent. This may be due to preschoolers' increased understanding of social motives and peer intentions (e.g., Lee & Cameron, 2000), which may also contribute toward an accompanying increase in social-cognitively "advanced" forms of *social* and *relational* aggression (Crick, Casas, & Mosher, 1997).

Development beyond the Preschool Period

In middle childhood, children's interactions with peers become increasingly complex and multifaceted. In many respects, these developments can be attributed to continued advances in the abilities to understand and appreciate others' thoughts, intentions, and emotions (Izard, 2009; Selman & Schultz, 1990). Thus, social communicative competence continues to improve with age, and children become more adept at establishing shared meanings with their peers (Goldstein et al., 2002). Continued improvement in **social skills** allows for children to more competently achieve their social goals and resolve interpersonal dilemmas (Rubin & Rose-Krasnor, 1992). Furthermore, with age children become better able to engage in rule-governed competitive games (Hartup, Brady, & Newcomb, 1983). Finally, there continue to be age-related increases in altruistic behavior from early to middle and late childhood (Eisenberg et al., 2006).

In summary, we have described the developmental progression of children's interactive skills with peers. These skills aid children to initiate and maintain dyadic relationships with non-familial others. These special dyadic relationships have been posited to serve many adaptive functions throughout the childhood and adolescent years; indeed, throughout life! We turn now to a discussion of children's friendships.

CHILDREN AND THEIR FRIENDS

The establishment and maintenance of close friendships with peers represent challenging yet rewarding endeavors throughout childhood. In childhood, however, the constituent factors associated with friendship formation and maintenance vary with age; indeed, the very meaning of friendship undergoes developmental change. In the following sections we discuss the functions of friendship, children's changing understandings of friendship, prevalence and stability of friendship during childhood and adolescence, issues of friendship measurement, the friendship formation processes, similarities between friends, children's interactive behaviors with friends and non-friends, gender-related issues in children's friendships, children without friends, and friendship and adjustment. An overriding theme is the significance of friendship in children's psychosocial development.

Functions of Friendship

A friendship is a close, mutual, and voluntary dyadic relationship. This definition distinguishes friendship from such peer-group level constructs as popularity, which refers to the experience of being liked or accepted by or well-known among one's peers. Defining features of friendship include reciprocity and a feeling of perceived equality between individuals. In its simplest definition, *reciprocity* refers to the return of like behavior and affection between partners and is an essential component of any definition of friendship.

Friendships in childhood serve to (1) provide support, self-esteem enhancement, and positive self-evaluation; (2) provide emotional security; (3) provide affection and opportunities for intimate disclosure; (4) provide intimacy and affection; (5) offer consensual validation of interests, hopes, and fears; (6) provide instrumental and informational assistance; (7) promote the growth of interpersonal sensitivity; and (8) offer prototypes for later romantic, marital, and parental relationships (Newcomb & Bagwell, 1995; Sullivan, 1953). Perhaps the most important function of friendship is to offer children an extra-familial base of security from which they may explore the effects of their behaviors on themselves, their peers, and their environments.

From a developmental perspective, Parker and Gottman (1989) argued that friendship serves different functions for children at different points in their development. For the *young child*, friendship serves to maximize excitement and amusement levels in play, and helps to organize behavior in the face of arousal. In *middle childhood*, friendships aid in acquiring knowledge about behavioral norms and help children learn the skills necessary for successful self-presentation and impression management. These skills become crucial in middle childhood when anxiety about peer relationships develops. Finally, in *adolescence*, friendships serve to assist individuals in their quest for self-exploration and identity formation and to help them integrate logic and emotions.

Children's Conceptions of Friendship

One of the most productive areas of developmental inquiry has been the study of how children think about and define friendship. In general, friendship conceptions have been assessed by asking children such questions as "What is a best friend?" or "What do you expect from a best friend?" In response to these questions and others, children of all ages describe best-friendships as relationships that are characterized by reciprocity or mutual "give and take" (Hartup & Stevens, 1999). Beyond this general agreement about the importance of reciprocity, however, developmental differences exist in children's conceptions of friendship. For instance, during early and middle childhood (7 to 8 years), children describe friends as companions who live nearby, have nice toys, and share the child's expectations about play activities (Bigelow & LaGaipa, 1980). During late childhood (10 to 11 years) shared values and rules become more important, and friends are expected to stick up for, and be loyal to, each other. Finally, by early adolescence (11 to 13 years), friends are seen as sharing similar interests, making active attempts to understand each other, and willing to engage in intimate self-disclosure (Schneider & Tessier, 2007). Taken together, it appears that children's understanding of friendship become increasingly sophisticated and their expectations become increasingly linked to intimacy with age.

Why do such developmental changes occur? Selman and Schultz (1990) argued that the key to developmental change in children's friendship conceptions is *perspective taking* ability. Young children do not yet realize that other people feel or think about things differently from themselves. As children grow older, they gradually take on the viewpoints of others, moving from egocentrism to a mutual perspective. As a final step, children/adolescents are able to mentally stand outside of the social system comprising their social interactions and relationships and to view themselves and their relationships with others from the perspective of someone who is not involved in the relationship, that is from a "third person perspective". This shift in how children "see" themselves and others is thought to be manifested in their understanding of friendships.

Other researchers have argued that children's friendship expectations develop in conjunction with the child's understanding of reciprocity (e.g., Youniss, 1980). Young children who believe that their own contribution toward a friendship is the most important are more likely to understand friendship in terms of momentary interactions and how they themselves are affected. By adolescence, friendship is perceived as an ongoing relationship, and friends are people on whom children can count for continuing understanding and intimate social support. In contrast, Berndt (1981) argued that friendship conceptions represent the cumulative assimilation of basically unrelated themes or dimensions, such as commonalities in play interests and self-disclosure. According to Berndt, children do not abandon initial notions about play and mutual association when they eventually recognize the importance of intimacy and loyalty.

Although the jury is still out in terms of what may be the underlying mechanisms by which the understanding of friendships develops, speculation is plausible. Essentially, children's conceptions about friendship reflect their own transitions from the world of the concrete to the world of the abstract. What children may require and desire in a friendship develops as a function of their growing understanding of the world and in conjunction with their own expanding social needs. Beginning in early childhood, the social world is increasingly cognitively differentiated. Eventually, children begin to realize that a friendship can serve potentially as both a resource and a context that differ from the conditions that exist with non-friends.

The Prevalence and Stability of Friendship

Perspectives on the development of children's friendship conceptions generate several predictions about the nature of such friendships at various ages, along with how children will behave in the company of their friends. For example, it would be consistent with these perspectives if children's friendships were seen to demonstrate more stability, prosocial responding, psychological similarity, and intimate personal knowledge over time and age. As it happens, most children and adolescents have at least one mutual friend (Hartup & Stevens, 1999). Beginning in the elementary school years, children's friendships are identified by way of friendship nominations. For example, children may be asked to nominate their "best" three same-gender friends in their class, grade, and school. The *mutuality* of nominations is then evaluated; thus, a child who receives a reciprocal best friendship nomination is considered to have a mutual best friend. According to Parker and Asher (1993), approximately 75% to 80% of children have at least one mutual *best* friendship, although prevalence varies across studies due to variability in the measurement of "best" friendship (e.g., when the number of best friendship nominations permitted differs; Berndt & McCandless, 2009).

Identifying a child's friends is not as easy a task as one may surmise. Simply asking a child to name her or his best friend(s) may lead to the production of a socially desirable response or the unilateral choice of a partner who does not reciprocate the friendship nomination. Furthermore, the child may misinterpret the "meaning" of a friend, and may provide an overinclusive set of responses (e.g., by naming "chums" or "acquaintances" rather than a "best friend"). Historically, most peer relationships researchers have limited friendship nominations to same-gender friends "in your class" or "in your grade" primarily because the majority of children only nominate same-gender, same-grade, and same-school peers as their best friends (Hartup & Stevens, 1999). But growing evidence that a sizable number of children and adolescents have friends from outside-school contexts (neighborhood, different school, sports team, out of town, online, and so forth; e.g., Mesch & Talmud, 2007) and who are of the other gender, and that these friendships can strongly influence adjustment (e.g., Chan & Poulin, 2007; Kiesner, Poulin, & Nicotra, 2003; Poulin & Pedersen, 2007), has led to a recent shift toward relaxing these friendship nomination restrictions in studies of child and adolescent friendships.

Once mutual friendships are formed, friendships at all ages show remarkable stability. During the preschool years, two-thirds of children who identify one another as friends do so again 4 to 6 months later (Gershman & Hayes, 1983). Berndt and Hoyle (1985) found an increase in the stability of mutual friendships from age 5 years (50%) to age 10 years (75%), but not from age 10 years to age 14 years. In fact, it has been consistently found that only half of all young adolescent friendships are stable across one academic school year (Bowker, 2004; Wojslawowicz Bowker, Rubin, Burgess, Booth-LaForce, & Rose-Krasnor, 2006). This lack of increased stability during early adolescence can be accounted for by two factors. To begin with, friendships tend to become more exclusive with age—as such, children may allow some friendships to dissolve. As well, as children approach puberty, rapid changes in interests, and varying rates of development may result in a period of change in friendships choices (Berndt, 1985; Bowker, 2004). However, the trend toward increased stability in friendships continues into older age (Cairns, Leung, Buchanan, & Cairns, 1995). There is also evidence suggesting that boys are more likely than girls to have stable same-gender (Benenson & Christakos, 2003; Hardy, Bukowski, & Sippola, 2002) and other-gender friendships (Chan & Poulin, 2007). Multi-context friendships (friendships that comprise individuals who interact both inside and outside of school) also appear to be more stable than single-context friendships (Chan & Poulin, 2007).

Similarities between Friends

What are some of the factors that influence the formation of children's friendships? A facile first response is that age and gender are important magnets that pull children together. In addition, friends tend to be of the same ethnic background (Aboud & Mendelson, 1996). Thus, from an early age, children are attracted to and choose friends who are like themselves in *observable* characteristics. For example, it has been reported that children are attracted to peers whose behavioral tendencies are similar to their own (Rubin, Lynch, Coplan, Rose-Krasnor, & Booth, 1994). Greater behavioral similarities exist between friends than non-friends, and children share friendships with other children who resemble themselves in terms of prosocial and delinquent/antisocial behaviors (Haselager, Hartup, van Lieshout, & Riksen Walraven, 1998; Popp, Laursen, Kerr, Burk, & Stattin, 2008), shyness and internalized distress (e.g., Hogue & Steinberg, 1995; Rubin, Wojslawowicz, Rose-Krasnor, Booth-LaForce, & Burgess, 2006b), popularity and acceptance (Kupersmidt, DeRosier, & Patterson, 1995), peer group difficulties (e.g., victimization; Bowker et al., 2009), academic achievement and motivation (Altermatt & Pomerantz, 2003), and hobbies or interests (e.g., Selfhout, Branje, ter Bogt, & Meeus, 2009). In addition to similarity in behavior and peer group functioning, friends are more similar in their targets for aggression than nonfriends (Card & Hodges, 2006).

Similarity has been associated not only with friendship formation (Kupersmidt et al., 1995), but also with friendship maintenance. For instance, by adolescence, stable friendship pairs, in comparison to those members of friendships that dissolve, are more likely to be similar to each other in their *attitudes* about school and academic aspirations; the use of drugs and alcohol; and that which is considered to be normal teen behavior (e.g., Urberg, Degirmencioglu, & Piligrim, 1997; Vitaro, Tremblay, Kerr, Pagani, & Bukowski, 1997).

Behaviors between Friends

Friends interact with each other differently than do non-friends. In general, children of all ages engage in more talk, task orientation, cooperation, positive affect, and effective conflict management during social interactions with friends than with non-friends (Hartup, 1996; Simpkins & Parke, 2002). In this regard, friendship is not only a social and positive relational context, but it also provides for the expression and regulation of affect (Parker & Gottman, 1989).

From a developmental perspective, children as young as 3½ years direct more social overtures, engage in more social interaction, and play in more complex ways with friends than with non-friends (Doyle, 1982). Preschool-aged friends tend to be more cooperative with each other during play (Charlesworth & LaFreniere, 1983), and 4th and 5th grade friends demonstrate greater play sophistication (e.g., positive fantasy play, negotiation) when interacting with their friends than with non-friends (Simpkins & Parke, 2002). By adolescence, friend/non-friend behavioral differences are even stronger than in middle childhood or the early preschool years. Altruistic acts, particularly generosity, cooperation, and helpfulness between friends, increase with age and continue well into adolescence (Berndt, 1985; Windle, 1994).

Research involving **conflict** between friends and non-friends is somewhat contradictory. Friends differ from non-friends not only by engaging in more friendly interactions, but also by demonstrating more quarreling, active hostility (assaults and threats) and reactive hostility (refusals and resistance) between pairs. For example, Hartup and his colleagues (Hartup & Laursen, 1995; Hartup, Laursen, Stewart, & Eastenson, 1998) observed that nursery school children engaged in more conflicts overall with their friends than with neutral associates. Simpkins and Parke (2002) also reported greater levels of negative affect and guilty coercion within dyads of friends than non-friends. Most likely, these findings can be attributed to the fact that friends spend more time actually interacting with each other than do non-friends.

There are important differences, however, in the ways in which friends and non-friends *resolve* conflicts that arise, and in what the outcomes of those conflicts are likely to be. For example, friends, as compared with non-friends, make more use of negotiation and disengagement, relative to standing firm, in their resolution of conflicts. In terms of conflict outcomes, friends are more likely to reach equitable resolutions (Newcomb & Bagwell, 1995) and agreements (Tomada, Schneider, & Fonzi, 2002). Thus, although the amount of conflict is greater between friends than non-friends, friends resolve conflicts in ways that help ensure that their relationships persist beyond the conflict and continue into the future (Laursen, Hartup, & Keplas, 1996).

In summary, children appear to behave differently in the company of friends than non-friends. When interacting with friends, children engage in more prosocial behaviors as well as more conflicts than when with non-friends. These conflicts are more likely to be resolved through negotiation, and the outcomes are usually equitable and involve mutual agreement. The differences described suggest that children view friendship as a unique context, separate and qualitatively different from their experiences with non-friends.

Gender-Related Issues

There appear to be some similarities in the ways that boys and girls think about friendship; for example, both boys and girls emphasize that they depend on friends for company, approval, and support (Craft, 1994). However, gender differences emerge when boys and girls are asked the question "What do you expect from a good friend?" Girls tend to respond by referring to that which they may *receive* from a good friend; boys emphasize *reciprocity*, or provisions that they expect to receive from, as well as give to, a friend (Craft, 1994). Differences also are revealed when children are asked to describe their same-gender peers. Girls often describe them as being nice. In contrast, boys are more likely to describe their male classmates in terms of their interests; fighting, artistic, and athletic abilities; goofiness; and academic performance (Benenson, 1990). These findings provide some support for the proposition that boys are more concerned with status within the peer group, whereas girls are more concerned with friendship and affiliations.

Studies of children's friendships also reveal gender differences in the *quality* of boys' and girls' friendships. Girls report more intimate exchange, conflict resolution, validation and caring, and help and guidance within their friendships than do boys (Parker & Asher, 1993; Rubin et al., 2004). These findings might be explained by girls' greater orientation toward dyadic relationships. Girls may be more emotionally invested in their friendships, which in turn, may help to foster intimacy and feelings of closeness. Gender differences are not typically found, however, in levels of relationship satisfaction (Parker & Asher, 1993; Rose & Rudolph, 2006), suggesting that the abovementioned positive features of friendship may carry different "meaning" for boys and girls (Rose, Swenson, & Robert, 2009). And there is growing evidence that girls' friendships can be psychologically stressful relationship experiences. For instance, girls report greater distress when imagining the termination of their friendships than do boys (Benenson & Christakos, 2003). Also, girls report more **co-rumination**, or intimate self-disclosure done in a "ruminative" fashion (e.g., negative dwelling on emotionally charged and intimate everyday occurrences and feelings), within their friendships than do boys (Rose, 2002), which in turn, is concurrently and predictively associated with **internalizing problems** (Rose, 2002; Rose, Carlson, & Waller, 2007).

One of the main gender differences in friendships is that girls report more intimate exchange than boys.

Children without Friends

Some children may be unsuccessful in their attempts to make friends. Indeed, researchers have found that approximately 15% to 20% of children and young adolescents are *friendless*, or without any mutual friends (Parker & Asher, 1993; Parker & Seal, 1996). Importantly, a similar percentage of youth have been found to be consistently or *chronically* friendless (Wojslawowicz Bowker et al., 2006). Friendless children may lack social skills or may demonstrate behaviors that their peers judge to be unattractive (Parker & Seal, 1996). Regardless of the reason for friendlessness, however, children without mutual friends report more loneliness than do children with mutual friendships (e.g., Parker & Seal, 1996; Parker & Asher, 1993), and chronic friendlessness has been associated with increasing internalizing difficulties and peer victimization (Ladd & Troop-Gordon, 2003; Wojslawowicz Bowker et al., 2006) Moreover, Bagwell, Newcomb, and Bukowski (1998) found that being without a mutual friend during the 5th grade was a negative predictor of feelings of general self-worth during adulthood.

It should be noted that children who are *rejected* by their peers are not necessarily friendless (Cairns, Cairns, Neckerman, Gest, & Gariepy, 1988). Relatedly, not all highly and average accepted children have mutual friendships (Parker & Asher, 1993). This leads to a number of interesting questions regarding the possible effects of having a close friendship. Laursen, Bukowski, Aunola, and Nurmi (2007) found, for example, that initial social isolation predicted increases in internalizing and **externalizing problems** and initial internalizing and externalizing problems predicted increases in isolation, *but only for those children who did not have a mutual friendship*. Thus, a single close friend may serve to alleviate the negative "costs" of being disliked and isolated by the majority of one's peers.

Friendship and Adjustment

Considerable evidence has accumulated that having a friend can promote or support positive adjustment, particularly during potentially stressful times of transition and peer difficulty (e.g., Berndt & Keefe, 1995). For example, as children make the transition into elementary school, those who enter school with a mutual friend report higher levels of school satisfaction and academic interest than those children who begin the school years without a friend. Hodges and colleagues found that simply having a mutual best friend protected youth from the internalizing and externalizing "costs" of peer victimization (Hodges, Boivin, Vitaro, & Bukowski, 1999).

The associations between friendship and adjustment, however, are more complex when the stability and quality of the friendship is considered, along with the characteristics of the best friend. In one study, Berndt, Hawkins, and Jiao (1999) found that ratings of sociability and leadership increased across the transition from elementary to middle school, but only for those children who had high-quality, stable friendships. Behavior problems were found to increase from sixth to seventh grade only for those children who had stable friendships with children who had behavior problems themselves. Furthermore, having a high-quality, positive friendship has been linked to positive psychological well-being (Berndt & Keefe, 1995). But results from a few studies suggest that there may also be a "dark" side to some high-quality friendships (Bowker & Rubin, 2009; Rose, 2002; Rose et al., 2007). For instance, Rose and colleagues found that co-rumination is associated with both positive friendship quality and such emotional difficulties as anxiety and depression. Taking such findings together, it appears critical to consider more than one friendship "factor" in studies of friendship and adjustment.

Friendship and shy/withdrawn children.   Children who are shy, socially wary, and anxious might be expected to have difficulties forming and maintaining friendships. After all, social timidity may preclude opportunities to establish friendships to begin with, and social skills deficits associated with social wariness may prove to inhibit the formation and maintenance of friendship over time. However, no differences have been reported in the proportions of friendship prevalence and friendship stability for shy/withdrawn children relative to non-shy/non-withdrawn children. For example, the prevalence of best friendships among *young* socially withdrawn children is not significantly different from that among non-withdrawn children (Ladd & Burgess, 1999), and approximately 60% of withdrawn 8-, 9-, and 10-year-olds have reciprocated friendships, a percentage that is nearly identical to that of non-withdrawn age-mates (Schneider, 1999; Rubin et al., 2006b). Rubin and colleagues also found that withdrawn children were as likely as non-withdrawn children to have a stable best friendship during late childhood and early adolescence (Rubin et al., 2006b). It appears that social withdrawal and shyness are individual characteristics that do not influence the formation, prevalence, and maintenance of friendship in childhood.

Beyond prevalence and stability, however, there is some evidence that the friendship experiences of many shy/withdrawn children may be less than positive relationship experiences. For example, there is some evidence that withdrawn children tend to form friendships with similarly withdrawn and victimized peers, and that their friendships are relatively poor in relationship quality (Rubin et al., 2006b; Schneider, 1999). These findings suggest a "misery loves company" scenario for withdrawn children and their best friends. One may conjure up images of victimized friends coping poorly in the world of peers ... images reflected in recent newspaper and television accounts of peer victimization and its untimely consequences. In support of this notion, having a withdrawn friend has been associated with increased social withdrawal across the middle school transition (Oh et al., 2008). Yet *any* mutual best friendship, even if it is a "miserable" one, but especially if it is stable (Oh et al., 2008), may help withdrawn children navigate difficult times of transition and school change (Rubin et al., 2004).

Friendship and externalizing children.   Similar to shy/withdrawn children, those who act "against" their social worlds through **aggression**, opposition, and impulsivity also do *not* have difficulty *forming* friendships. Although they tend to be more disliked than other children (Newcomb, Bukowski, & Pattee, 1993), the majority of aggressive children have a mutual best friendship and are as likely as well-adjusted children to have mutual friends (e.g.,Vitaro, Brendgen, & Tremblay, 2000).

Aggression, however, seems to be negatively related to friendship stability (e.g., Hektner, August, & Realmuto, 2000), a finding that is not too surprising considering the adverse nature of aggression. Moreover, aggressive children have friends who are more aggressive or their relationships are more confrontational and antisocial in quality (Dishion, Andrews, & Crosby, 1995; Dishion, Eddy, Haas, Li, & Spracklen, 1997). High levels of relational aggression (e.g., threatening friendship withdrawal) *within* the friendship, and high levels of exclusivity, jealousy, and intimacy characterize the friendships of relationally aggressive children. In contrast, overtly aggressive children direct their overt aggression *outside* their friendship dyads, and report low levels of intimacy (Grotpeter & Crick, 1996).

Perhaps alarmingly, it has been reported that aggressive behaviors become more acceptable to peers and attractive with age (e.g., Bukowski, Sippola, & Newcomb, 2000), and more strongly associated with perceived popularity (Cillessen & Mayeux, 2004). Moreover, it is well known that a child's association with deviant friends and peers often leads to subsequent behavioral and social difficulties (Berndt & Keefe, 1995; Dishion, McCord, & Poulin, 1999). As such, researchers would do well to examine the processes by which aggressive behavior becomes increasingly acceptable and whether friendship serves to exacerbate difficulties rather than ameliorate them during the late childhood and early adolescent years.

Summary

Most children have at least one friend. Children become friends with other children who are like themselves in terms of "surface" characteristics and behavioral characteristics, and, during the adolescent years, with others who share similar attitudes, opinions, and values. Children's *conceptions* of friendship progress from the concrete to the abstract with age, and this change is reflected in their behavior with their friends. With age, children's friendships demonstrate more stability, more reciprocal altruism, and more intimate personal knowledge. Friends engage in qualitatively different types of interactions than non-friends at all ages, and the characteristics of these interactions can be used to describe and predict the friendship formation process. Children who are in the process of becoming friends are more likely to communicate clearly, self-disclose more often, and resolve conflicts more effectively than children who do not become friends. Although conflict often occurs within friendships, friends resolve conflicts in ways that *enhance* the likelihood that the relationship will persist or continue. There are also notable gender differences in the qualities of boys' and girls' friendships, and research on children who are without mutual best friends supports the hypothesis that friendship plays a significant role in social development by providing children with settings and contexts within which to learn about themselves, their peers, and the world around them.

CHILDREN'S GROUPS

Thus far, we have emphasized developmental trends in social interaction and the significance of dyadic peer relationships. However, children also spend a large proportion of their time in formal and informal group settings where membership is not defined solely by friendship. In the following sections we explore the structural and functional characteristics of the peer group, the processes that are involved in group formation, and group norms and organization.

The Peer Group as a Social Context

It is not uncommon to see groups of preschool children playing together in the classroom, the schoolyard, or the neighborhood. When children of this young age are observed together, for the most part, their behaviors are independently oriented, and their concerns are with their own immediate ends (Isaacs, 1933). Somewhere in middle childhood, however, a change occurs. This change can be characterized as a transformation from a *group of peers* to a *peer group*.

Peer groups usually range in size from three to over 10 children, with an average of five or six members, and mostly comprise same-gender peers (Chen, Chang, & He, 2003a; Kindermann, McCollom, & Gibson, 1995). In childhood, relatively small and intimate cliques predominate. However, children's involvements in cliques tend to decline in adolescence, whereas affiliation with larger crowds becomes a salient feature of adolescent social life (e.g., Brown, Eicher & Petrie, 1986). These developmental shifts may result from broader changes in social-cognitive abilities and social-ecological conditions. Whereas young children may seek support from intimate groups as a source of psychological dependence in an effort to establish personal autonomy from parents, adolescents may strive to acquire a sense of identity in a peer context with different lifestyles and value systems (Brown, 1990). Moreover, with increasing age, more sophisticated social skills allow adolescents to maintain extensive and different types of peer relationships.

There are mixed findings in the literature concerning gender differences in group characteristics. Although some researchers have reported that boys are more likely than girls to engage in group activities and that boys' groups are larger than girls' groups (Benenson, Apostoleris & Parnass, 1997; Maccoby, 1995; Ruble & Martin, 1998; Thorne & Luria, 2001), others have failed to find significant gender differences in the extensivity of peer networks (e.g., Cairns et al., 1995; Tarrant, 2002).

Insofar as the *nature* of the peer group is concerned, some researchers (e.g., Strayer & Strayer, 1976) have argued that the characteristics of a group can be represented by the additive effects of a specific behavior (e.g., dominance) from each member on each other member. It has also been argued that the group may develop on the basis of dyadic social relationships and thus may be best conceived of as an aggregation of relationships (e.g., Hinde, 1987). Nevertheless, many researchers have agreed that the characteristics of a group are emergent, that is, not reducible to the characteristics of the individuals who compose the group (Cairns & Cairns, 1994; Chen, Chen, & Kaspar, 2001). Unlike such dyadic social relationships as friendship, the peer group represents a social context that is developed through the collective functioning of members based on group norms and values (Brown, 1990; Cairns & Cairns, 1994). Children in the group are "tied together" and, at the same time, constrained by common interests and group norms. As a result, the "character" of the group may serve to guide how children react to various tasks and thus function as a context for social interactions and individual behaviors (Brown, 1990).

Peer Group Functions

In peer group interactions, children learn a variety of specific skills that are required for group functioning. Fine (1987) argued that peer groups teach children (1) how to engage in cooperative activity aimed at collective rather than individual goals; (2) about social structures; (3) the skills associated with leading and following others; (4) the control of hostile impulses towards fellow members; and (5) to mobilize aggression in the service of group loyalty by directing it towards "outsiders". In addition, social networks and emotional connections that children establish and maintain with other members may constitute a major source of social support for children to cope with stress and adjustment difficulties (Hartup, 1992). In short, frequent contact, common activities and interpersonal affective connectedness among group members may make children's groups a strong socialization influence (Kindermann, 1993).

It has been argued that whereas experiences with friends may be specific to dyadic social situations, peer groups may have pervasive impact on individual social, emotional, and behavioral functioning and adjustment in larger social settings. Findings from empirical research are consistent with these arguments (e.g., Cairns & Cairns, 1994; Chen, Chang, Liu, & He, 2008; Kindermann, McCollom, & Gibson, 1995). For example, whereas natural peer groups might be formed based on children's motivational factors, the profile of peer networks significantly predicts subsequent changes in individual motivation in school (Kindermann, 1993). Similar findings have been reported concerning the contributions of peer groups to such matters as school drop-out, teenage pregnancy, and delinquency (e.g., Cairns & Cairns, 1994; Chen et al., 2001; Dekovic, Engels, Shirai, De Kort, & Anker, 2002; Kiesner, Poulin, & Nicotra, 2003; Xie, Cairns & Cairns, 2001).

Cliques and Crowds

According to Brown (1990), there are two main types of peer groups: *cliques* and *crowds*. Whereas cliques are relatively smaller friendship-based groups, crowds are reputation-based collectives of similarly stereotyped individuals who are defined by the primary attitudes or activities their members share. Clique activities are often represented by relatively intensive interactions and emotional involvement of group members. Crowds are more loosely organized and less intimate than cliques; members of a crowd may not even interact with one another. However, crowds often grant adolescents an identity embedded within a larger social structure. In high school, identifiable crowds include "normals," "jocks," "brains," "populars," "greasers," "partyers," "loners," and "druggies" (Brown, Mounts, Lamborn, & Steinberg, 1993). For example, "jocks" are very involved in athletics and tend to be popular; "brains" worry about their grades and have marginal standing with peers; and "druggies" do poorly in school, are hostile towards authority figures, and engage in risky health behaviors such as unsafe sex and binge drinking (Eccles & Roeser, Chapter 8, this volume; La Greca, Prinstein, & Fetter, 2001).

Crowd membership is an important contributor to an adolescent's social functioning because of its influence on social contacts and relationships with peers. For example, the stigma that is placed on members of a particular crowd channels adolescents into relationships and dating patterns with those sharing a similar crowd label. These negative reputations may prevent adolescents from exploring new identities and discourages a shift to other crowd memberships. There is evidence that the stigma associated with some large peer groups or crowds influences the judgments that adolescents form about their peers (Horn, 2003). Consistent with the findings from research focused on individuals' aggressive reputations and social cognitions (e.g., Dodge, 1980), Horn (2003) found that adolescents are biased in their use of reputational or stereotypical information about particular groups, especially when presented with ambiguous situations. It is likely that these crowd-specific evaluations help to perpetuate group stereotypes and the structure of peer groups within a school.

Methodological Issues in the Study of Peer Groups

Until recently, the measurement or quantification of peer groups was difficult, if not ineffective. Traditionally, researchers relied on self-report data by asking children or young adolescents to create a list of their closest friends or group members. This single-informant approach raised psychometric concerns with regard to the reliability and validity of the data.

Assessing peer groups.   Two techniques, social network analysis (SNA, Richards, 1995) and the social cognitive map (SCM, Cairns, Gariepy, & Kindermann, 1989) were introduced to assess peer groups. SNA is based on friendship nominations. Children are typically asked to list up to 10 friends with whom they hang out most often in the school. Through the analysis of a computer program, NEGOPY (Richards, 1995), clusters of students who report having relatively high contact with one another are identified. NEGOPY can detect group members, liaisons, dyads, and isolates based on patterns of friendship links and the strengths of the links; participants are assigned membership in one of the social network positions. *Group members* are those individuals who belong to a rather exclusive social group that comprises at least three individuals who have most (>50%) of their links with other members in the same group and who are all connected by some paths entirely within the group. *Liaisons* are individuals who have friendships with group members, but are not group members themselves. *Dyads* are individuals who have one reciprocated friendship link, either to each other or to another individual. These individuals do not belong to a group *per se*, but have mutual friendships. Finally, *isolates* are those children who have no reciprocated friendships. It should be noted that because SNA is based on friendship (either reciprocal or non-reciprocal) links, groups identified through the program represent *friendship networks*.

Compared with SNA, the "composite social cognitive map" (SCM) technique, developed by Cairns et al. (1989), assesses peer groups more directly. Children are first asked "Are there people in school who hang around together a lot? Who are they?" To ensure that the respondents include themselves, a follow-up question is asked: "What about you? Do you hang around together a lot with a group? Who are these people you hang around with?" Children are expected to report on groups about which they are most knowledgeable. Based on the reports of all participants, a matrix is constructed from the number of occasions that any two persons co-occurred in the same group. Specifically, each participant's group-membership profile is first generated based on the frequencies of nominations of group membership with every other child in the class. Then a profile similarity index is derived by correlating pairs of individual group-membership profiles. Children with similar group-membership profiles are clustered into the same group (Cairns & Cairns, 1994).

This latter methodology offers several advantages. To begin with, not all children are required as respondents in order to obtain an accurate representation of naturally occurring peer groups. Obtaining nominations from half of the children in a particular setting seems to be sufficient. As well, the examination of individual connectedness provides information beyond public consensus about rejected or popular children. Popular children are not necessarily popular in all social groups, and "social maps" provide a vehicle to determine this aspect of peer groups.

Examining the contextual effect of the peer group.   Researchers have used multilevel modeling to examine the significance of the peer group for individual social behaviors and school performance in several studies (Espelage, Holt, & Henkel, 2003; Ryan, 2001). Chen et al. (Chen, Chang, & He, 2003; Chen et al., 2008), for example, investigated group effects on social functioning and academic achievement in Chinese children. Individual-level relations between academic achievement and social functioning might be *mediated* and facilitated by the group context. By providing a social context for the selection and socialization processes (e.g., establishing the group profile and reputation, mutual regulation based on group norms), the peer group served to promote the formation of relations between academic achievement and social functioning. Moreover, depending on specific group norms, peer group functioning might *moderate* the relations between individual academic achievement and social adjustment. Compared with their counterparts in other groups, for example, children who had academic difficulties and were affiliated with low-achieving groups were more likely to display social problems. The low-achieving groups exacerbated social and behavioral problems of academically poor children and placed them at heightened risk for maladaptive social development. High-achieving groups, however, served a buffering function that protected academically poor children from developing social problems. As a result, academically weak children in high-achieving groups developed fewer social problems than their counterparts in low-achieving groups.

Summary

Peer groups offer children a unique context for learning about themselves and others (see Vaughn & Santos, 2009 for a review). Children's initial dyadic experiences with friends assist them in acquiring the appropriate social skills necessary for peer acceptance. Once children are accepted by their peers, a variety of different cliques is formed, and members are afforded the opportunity to explore the group setting. Sometimes adolescents assume membership in "crowds." Through membership in cliques and crowds adolescents learn about common goals, cooperation, the complex interrelationships that make up a group's structure, and importantly, social skills and qualities that are required for effective functioning in a collective context. Cliques and crowds offer distinct social opportunities to adolescents. The former provides a context for adolescents to test and develop values and roles in the absence of adult monitoring; the latter offers extra-familial support in the development of a sense of self.

PEER ACCEPTANCE, REJECTION, AND PERCEIVED POPULARITY

The experience of being liked and accepted by the peer group-at-large is known as **peer acceptance** and the experience of being disliked by peers has been termed **peer rejection**. The construct of **perceived popularity**, or who it is that children think are "popular," cool, central, or highly visible, has gained research attention with the acknowledgment that children who are perceived by the larger peer group to be popular may not always be well-liked by the larger peer group (e.g., Merten, 1997; Parkhurst & Hopmeyer, 1998). In the following sections, we examine the methods used by researchers to assess acceptance, rejection, and perceived popularity within the peer group. We also describe findings concerning the possible determinants of peer acceptance, rejection, and perceived popularity and the outcomes that persistent difficulties with peers may entail.

Assessing the Quality of Children's Peer Relationships

There are myriad procedures designed to assess the quality of children's peer relationships (see Asher & McDonald, 2009 and Cillessen, 2009 for more descriptions). Basically, these procedures can be subdivided into categories corresponding to two questions: "Is the child liked?" and "What is the child like?" (Parker & Asher, 1987). To answer these questions, researchers have relied on several sources of information concerning the valence and nature of children's peer interactions, including parents, clinicians, and archival data. However, the most common sources employed have involved children, teachers, and direct behavioral observations. Children are excellent informants about who it is in their peer group that has qualitatively good or poor relationships. As "insiders," peers recognize and identify characteristics of children and their relationships that are ultimately relevant in the determination of the child's social status and integration within the peer group. Moreover, the judgments of peers are based on many extended and varied experiences with those being evaluated. For example, as "insiders" peers are privy to low frequency, but psychologically significant events (e.g., a punch in the nose or taking someone's valued possession), which lead to the establishment and maintenance of particular social reputations. Finally, peer assessments of children's behaviors and relationships represent the perspectives of many observers with whom the target child has had a variety of relationships (Rubin, Bukowski, & Parker, 2006a). Taken together, it is not surprising that most contemporary research concerning the quality, the correlates, and the determinants of children's peer relationships is dominated by peer assessment methodology.

Like peers, teachers may provide useful and rich data concerning low frequency social exchanges that contribute to the quality of a child's peer relationships. One advantage that teacher assessments have over peer assessments is that the data collection process is much more efficient and less time consuming. Classroom time is not necessary to gather the assessment data. A second advantage is that teachers may prove to be more objective than peers in their assessments of social behavior. Teachers are not part and parcel of the group structure or behavioral schemes being evaluated; thus, they may be valuable, objective sources of information. However, teachers may bring with them an "adultomorphic" perspective that carries with it value judgments about social behaviors that might differ from those of children. As well, their judgments may be biased by their relations with children and children's gender (e.g., Ladd & Profilet, 1996).

Assessments of Peer Acceptance

Sociometric nominations trace their origins through Moreno (1934), who originally used it to examine attraction and repulsion within the peer group. Coie, Dodge, and Coppotelli (1983) furthered Moreno's work, creating a method of assessment still widely used today. This method of assessing **sociometric popularity** and rejection is to have children nominate three to five peers whom they "like" and "dislike." From these nominations children are categorized into status groups based on the number of positive and negative nominations they received from peers. To control for class size, nominations are standardized within each classroom (or grade). Usually, only same-gender nominations are used to control for the opposite gender negative biases that occur in childhood.

Based on these nominations, children are classified into five sociometric categories. Children who receive many "like" and few "dislike" nominations are labeled (sociometrically) *popular*, those who receive many "like" and many "dislike" nominations are *controversial*. The other categories are *rejected* (liked by few and disliked by many), *neglected* (liked by few and disliked by few), and *average* (near the midrange of liked and disliked nominations). Over the years, researchers have found that the more extreme sociometric classifications are moderately stable over time; popular children tend to remain popular, and rejected children tend to remain rejected, although this stability declines over longer intervals (e.g., Cillessen, Bukowski, & Haselager, 2000). However, when one examines the relation between peer rejection and associated negative outcomes, a significant amount of variance remains unexplained. Recent work has explored the construct of "classification strength" to increase the sensitivity of sociometric measurement (DeRosier & Thomas, 2003). Classification strength refers to the degree to which a child falls within a prescribed status group. For example, classification strength would distinguish between children in the same status group by differentiating between borderline-rejected and extremely rejected children. DeRosier and Thomas's (2003) work indicates that using classification strength results in greater concurrent validity with sociobehavioral adjustment.

A second method to capture peer acceptance is a rating-scale measure. Rating-scale methods involve children rating each of their classmates (or a randomly selected group of grade-mates) on a scale (e.g., 1 = *not at all* to 5 *very much*) of how much they like to play or work with that person. This method can be used to yield a continuous indicator of peer acceptance or to classify children into groups based on low, average, or high acceptance. An advantage of rating-scale measures is that each child in a class or grade receives an equal number of ratings rather than information just being gathered on the prominent or salient children, as may be the case when nominations are used.

Similar to the measurement of peer acceptance and rejection, perceived popularity is often measured with peer nominations. Researchers have asked children to nominate peers they believe to be most popular and peers they believe to be least popular (e.g., Cillessen & Mayeux, 2004; Rose, Swenson, & Waller, 2004). As with the sociometric nominations technique, nominations of peer-perceived popularity are standardized and children are assigned to one of three possible groups: popular, unpopular, or average (all others). Other researchers have measured a similar construct to perceived popularity by asking teachers to nominate students who they believe are "popular" and have many friends (Rodkin, Farmer, Pearl, &

Van Acker, 2000, 2006). Those who have simultaneously examined sociometric popularity and peer-perceived popularity have found that these two types of measurement may identify distinct groups of children and that correlations between acceptance and perceived popularity are moderate to strong (Cillessen & Mayeux, 2004; Hawley, 2003; LaFontana & Cillessen, 2002; Parkhurst & Hopmeyer, 1998; Vaillancourt & Hymel, 2006). When examining the sociometrically assessed *controversial* group in terms of perceived popularity, results differ by study. Parkhurst and Hopmeyer (1998) found that children identified as controversial were the most likely group to be labeled as popular by a peer-perception measure. However, LaFontana and Cillessen (1999) found that controversial children were more likely to be perceived as "average." All in all, it seems that traditional assessments of likeability may portray different pictures than do peer group perceptions of popularity.

Despite its "popularity" as a measurement tool, the use of sociometric techniques carries with it some potential disadvantages. For example, some researchers have suggested that the use of sociometric nominations and ratings may be ethically problematic. The use of negative nomination measures may implicitly sanction negative judgments about peers and lead children to view disliked peers even more negatively (Bell-Dolan, Foster, & Sikora, 1989). To address this issue, Iverson, Barton, and Iverson (1997) conducted interviews with 10- and 11-year-olds regarding their reactions to completing group-administered sociometric nominations. Some children reported that a few of the low-status peers were talked about "behind their backs" but that these negative comments were never revealed to the low-status children. However, no child reported having hurt feelings or having knowledge of anyone else having hurt feelings. Iverson and colleagues maintain that sociometric assessments do not breach the ethical condition of minimal risk of harm—harm not greater than children might encounter in daily life.

Sociometric techniques have other limitations, such as practicality. Sociometric assessments are most often made in schools, because this is where children spend a majority of their time in the company of peers (Eccles & Roeser, Chapter 8, this volume). However, obtaining consent from everyone involved (i.e., school administrators, parents, teachers, children) is often difficult. If children nominate a classmate who has not agreed to participate, researchers are ethically bound not to use the data. Thus, for a researcher to obtain an accurate picture of a school's social structure there is strong need to obtain consent from a large majority of the school-attending children.

Nevertheless, a great deal can be learned about normative child development through the use of sociometric techniques and the simultaneous assessment of social behavior. The methods designed to identify the behavioral characteristics of children are examined below.

Assessment of Child Behaviors

Peer assessments of social behavior.   In general, peer assessment procedures involve asking children to nominate peers on the basis of a variety of behavioral roles or character descriptions provided (e.g., "Who in your class is a good leader?", "Who gets into fights?", or "Who likes to play alone?"). Nominations received from peers are summed in various ways to provide indices of a child's typical social behavior or reputation within the peer group (Asher & McDonald, 2009). A commonly used peer assessment technique is the *Revised Class Play* (Masten, Morison, & Pellegrini, 1985) and its subsequent adaptations (e.g., Rubin et al., 2006b). Factor analysis of children's nominations using these measures has yielded dimensions of aggression, shyness/withdrawal, exclusion/victimization, sociability-leadership, and prosocial behaviors.

As mentioned above, the use of peers as informants carries with it many advantages, the most important of which may be that peers can identify children who engage in behaviors that are salient to other children but too infrequent or too subtle for researchers to observe with any reliability (Rubin et al., 2006a). However, a disadvantage of peer assessments involves potential reputational biases (Hymel, Wagner, & Butler, 1990b). In this regard, even though a child's behaviors may change over time, her "reputation" may persist with peers. In particular, reputations are likely to be influenced by infrequent but salient events (e.g., aggressive outbursts, social gaffes). In addition, peer ratings are affected by the characteristics of the "rater," including behavioral reputation, peer status, age, and liking of the target (Younger & Boyko, 1987).

Finally, the *type* of behavior being described appears to impact on peer nominations and ratings. For example, peer assessments of sociability and aggression are more stable than those of social withdrawal (e.g., Moskowitz, Schwartzman, & Ledingham, 1985). From very early in childhood, aggression is viewed as deviant and unacceptable. Social withdrawal, however, is not viewed negatively by peers until the later years of childhood (e.g., Younger, Gentile, & Burgess, 1993). Consequently, the instability of peer assessments of social withdrawal may be attributed to the inability of young children to conceptualize these behaviors accurately.

Teacher assessments of social behavior. It is not uncommon for researchers to request teachers to assess the social and emotional characteristics of their students. Many standardized measures exist at present. Generally, these measures can be broken down into several socioemotional clusters or factors that fall along dimensions of positive child behaviors, aggression, hyperactivity, and anxiety (Coplan & Rubin, 1998; Ladd & Profilet, 1996).

Relations between teacher and peer assessments of children's social behavior are quite strong, especially concerning aggression and sociability (Ledingham, Younger, Schwartzman, & Bergeron, 1982). The relations between teacher and peer assessments of behavior increase from early to late childhood, but more so for externalizing behaviors than for internalizing behaviors (Hymel, Rubin, Rowden, & LeMare, 1990a). The increased correspondence between peer- and teacher-derived ratings of social withdrawal with age also mirrors the age-related increase in the association between peer rejection and social withdrawal (Rubin & Mills, 1988; Younger et al., 1993).

Behavioral observations of social behavior. Behavioral observations represent the standard against which all other forms of social behavioral assessment must be measured. In this regard, a "true" face-valid picture of aggression, withdrawal, or socially competent behavior is probably best captured from observations of children in naturalistic settings. Laboratory or analog methods are also useful for carefully observing socially important behaviors that may be hard to capture or may occur less frequently in natural settings (e.g., Hubbard, 2001; McDonald, Putallaz, Grimes, Kupersmidt, & Coie, 2006; Putallaz & Wasserman, 1990). From these observations, age and gender "norms" can be established for the production of particular forms of social behavior. From these "norms," procedures may be developed to identify children who deviate from their age-mates or from children of the same gender.

Several observational taxonomies have been developed to assess the frequency of occurrence of various behavior styles, relationship roles, and levels of social competence. For example, Rubin (2001) developed the *Play Observation Scale* (POS), a norm-based time-sampling procedure to assess free play behaviors in early and middle childhood. During free play (either in a class or in a laboratory play room), behaviors with and without peers are coded on a checklist that includes the cognitive play categories of functional-sensorimotor, exploratory, constructive, dramatic, and games-with-rules behaviors nested within the abovementioned social participation categories of solitary, parallel, and group activities

(Figure 7.1). In addition, overt and relational aggression, rough-and-tumble play, unoccupied and onlooker behaviors, and conversations with peers are recorded. Observational procedures such as the *Play Observation Scale* are useful in targeting children whose behaviors (e.g., aggression, social withdrawal) deviate from age-group norms. Additionally such procedures can be used to validate peer and teacher assessments of children's social behavior.

Play Observation Scale Coding Sheet (2001)

Name of Child:_____   ID_____   Cohort___   Age___

Free Play Session _____

Time Sample

	:10	:20	:30	:40	:50	:60
uncodable						
out of room						
transitional						
unoccupied						
onlooker						
Solitary Behaviors:						
Occupied						
Constructive						
Exploratory						
Functional						
Dramatic						
Games						
Parallel Behaviors:						
Occupied						
Constructive						
Exploratory						
Functional						
Dramatic						
Games						
Group Behaviors:						
Occupied						
Constructive						
Exploratory						
Functional						
Dramatic						
Games						
Peer Conversation						
Double Coded Behaviors:						
Anxious Behaviors						
Hovering						
Aggression						
Rough-and-Tumble						

Conversation/Interacting With: 1_____ 2_____ 3_____ 4_____ 5_____ 6_____

FIGURE 7.1   The play observation scale coding sheet used by Rubin (2001).

Unfortunately, several factors conspire against the use of observational methodology. To begin with, observations are time-, energy-, and money-consuming. Whereas peer and teacher assessments can be conducted in minutes or hours, observations can require weeks or months of data collection. Second, as children get older, it becomes increasingly difficult to observe them during "free play"—although technological advances in remote audiovisual recording have allowed researchers to observe children's interactions and conversations from afar (e.g., Asher, Rose, & Gabriel, 2001; Pepler & Craig, 1995). Finally, observations may be reactive; for example, children who are aware that they are being observed may behave in atypical manners, perhaps suppressing negative behaviors or increasing the production of prosocial behaviors.

To summarize, many different methods have been used to assess children's functioning in their peer group. Sociometric techniques are useful indications of how children feel about a specific child, that is, "Is the child liked?" This does not, however, inform us about the behaviors associated with, or contributing to, these assessments. Conversely, assessments and behavioral observations of children's social behaviors describe "what the child is like" but fail to inform us about their standing in the peer group. In the following section, we examine relations between peer acceptance and children's social behaviors.

CORRELATES AND DETERMINANTS OF PEER ACCEPTANCE

Which children are liked or disliked by peers? What are these children like? These two questions have been subjected to countless studies for more than half a century (e.g., Bonney, 1942; Northway, 1944). From the start, we must issue two cautions. Because many of the data on these questions stem from correlational studies, one must not assume that the behaviors associated with peer acceptance or rejection necessarily *cause* children's social status. Second, not all correlates and potential causes of peer acceptance and rejection are behavioral in nature. For example, sociometric popularity is positively associated with academic competence, physical attractiveness, and having a good sense of humor (e.g., Daniels & Leaper, 2006); it is negatively associated with having an uncommon name (see Hartup, 1983, for a relevant review). Importantly, however, physical appearance and uncommon names are not particularly strong correlates of peer acceptance. The variables most highly associated with status in the peer group include children's social behaviors and their ways of thinking about social phenomena.

Behavioral Correlates of Peer Acceptance

If one is to accept the classification scheme currently in vogue *vis-à-vis* the study of children's peer relationships, one might expect to find different and distinct behaviors associated with popular, rejected, neglected, and average peer status. However, the reality is that membership in each of the sociometrically classified groups may be acquired in a multitude of ways.

Sociometrically popular children are generally prosocial, skilled at initiating and maintaining qualitatively positive relationships, and are assertive and named as leaders by peers (e.g., Asher & McDonald, 2009; Chen & Tse, 2008; Gazelle, 2008; Pakaslahti, Karjalainen, & Keltikangas-Jarvinen, 2002; Tomada & Schneider, 1997). When entering new peer situations, popular children are more likely than members of other sociometric status groups to consider the frame of reference common to the ongoing playgroup and to establish themselves as sharing in this frame of reference (Putallaz & Wasserman, 1990). It is as if they ask themselves "What's going on?" and "How can I fit in?" Sociometrically popular children are also less likely to draw unwarranted attention to themselves when entering ongoing playgroups.

That is, they do not talk exclusively or arrogantly about themselves and their own social goals or desires, and they do not disrupt ongoing group activities (Dodge, Schlundt, Schocken, & Delugach, 1983). When entering playgroups, and during other social activities, sociometric-ally popular children speak clearly and respond contingently to the social overtures of others (Black & Logan, 1995). In short, sociometrically popular children appear to be socially competent.

Children *perceived* as popular are characteristically dominant but otherwise are not as easily "summed up." Indeed, perceived popularity has been linked to a varied list of charac-teristics. For example, perceived popularity has been associated with both physical and relational aggression, the latter of which is intended to harm relationships and friendships, especially for older children (Cillessen & Mayeux, 2004; Rose et al., 2004), as well as prosocial behavior (Cillessen & Mayeux, 2004; LaFontana & Cillessen, 2002). Perceived popularity has also been associated with having a good sense of humor, academic competence, athletic ability, being attractive, and being stylish and wealthy (Vaillancourt & Hymel, 2006). *Contro-versial* children display a combination of positive and negative social behaviors, perhaps because they may be the same children perceived as popular (see above).

To understand the discrepant characteristics that are related to being perceived as popular, researchers have investigated whether there may be separate and distinct groups of perceived popular children. Researchers have found two such groups: "model" and "tough" children (Rodkin et al., 2000, 2006). "Model" children are perceived as being "cool" and at the same time are academically competent, physically skilled, sociable, and not rated as aggressive by teachers. "Tough" children are also perceived as "cool" but are highly aggressive and physic-ally competent. Rubin (2002) also distinguished between these groups of children by applying the labels of "popular-as-decent" and "popular-as-dominant."

Relations between forms of aggression and perceived popularity have been investigated, as the causal nature between status and aggression are questioned. Examinations of these associations reveal that relational aggression may be more central than physical or overt aggression to the establishment and maintenance of perceived popularity. In a longitudinal investigation of acceptance, perceived popularity, and aggression, Cillessen and Mayeux (2004) found evidence to suggest that children who are perceived as popular subsequently increase their use of relational aggression. They hypothesize that relational aggression may serve as a means to maintain social prominence during adolescence, especially for girls (Cillessen & Mayeux, 2004; Rose et al., 2004). Furthermore, Rose et al. (2004) found that the association between overt aggression and perceived popularity was fully explained through the association of both constructs with relational aggression.

Neglected children have been shown to interact with their peers less frequently than average children, and to be less sociable and less aggressive, disruptive, and negative than other children, including those in the average group (Coie & Dodge, 1988). Neglected children have often been characterized as shy and withdrawn (e.g., Coie & Kupersmidt, 1983; Dodge, Murphy, & Buchsbaum, 1984), yet this is still up for debate (Rubin, LeMare, & Lollis, 1990). Although, as indicated, neglected children appear to interact with peers less frequently than do other children, no consistent evidence has emerged to suggest that neglected children display the psychological and emotional characteristics of social anxiety and extreme social wariness that are concomitants of social withdrawal. Furthermore, many researchers have failed to find sociometrically neglected children to be more withdrawn than average children (e.g., Rubin, Chen, & Hymel, 1993).

In summary, few behaviors have been found to be distinctive of sociometrically neglected children. Indeed, neglected children appear to be low on nearly every dimension of behavior (see Newcomb et al., 1993). Significantly, this sociometric classification is also relatively unstable, even over short periods (e.g., Newcomb & Bukowski, 1984). Furthermore, the defining characteristic of this group—a lack of "noticeability"—makes it very difficult to obtain good peer assessments of their behaviors. With this in mind, the fact that there appear to be few strong associations between neglected status and specific behaviors is unsurprising.

Rejected children are also quite heterogeneous in their behavioral characteristics. The most commonly cited correlate of peer *rejection* is aggression. Three forms of aggression appear to be associated clearly and strongly with sociometric rejection—instrumental aggression, bullying, and relational aggression. Instrumental aggression is directed at others for the purpose of obtaining desired objects, territories, or privilege. Bullying is directed toward the harming (or the threatening thereof), either physically or verbally, of particular intimidated victims (Olweus, 1993). As noted above, the goal of relational aggression is to manipulate or disrupt relationships and friendships, and its form can be overt or covert, but is usually covert (Archer & Coyne, 2005; Crick et al., 1997). Social aggression has also been linked with peer rejection; social aggression has been defined as aggression meant to manipulate group acceptance and damage others' social standing (Galen & Underwood, 1997). Regardless of type of aggression and regardless of type of measurement (peer ratings, observations, teacher ratings) aggression is highly correlated with peer dislike (Crick et al., 1997; Haselager, Cillessen, Van Lieshout, Riksen-Walraven, & Hartup, 2002; McNeilley-Choque, Hart, Robinson, Nelson, and Olsen, 1996).

Most of the data we have described above are correlational. In two studies, however, Dodge (1983) and Coie and Kupersmidt (1983) observed the interactions of *unfamiliar* peers with one another. These interactions took place over several days. Gradually some of the children became popular while others were rejected. The behaviors that most clearly predicted peer rejection were instrumental and reactive aggression. Crick (1996) has obtained similar results over the course of a school year.

Not all aggressive children are rejected. Aggressive children make up only 40% to 50% of the rejected group. Newcomb and colleagues (1993) proposed that aggression may not necessarily lead to peer rejection if it is balanced by a set of positive qualities that facilitate interactions and positive relations with other children. When aggressive behavior co-occurs with disruptive, hyperactive, or inattentive and immature behavior it is more likely to be associated with rejection than when it does not (e.g., Miller-Johnson, Coie, Maumary-Gremaud, Bierman, & The Conduct Problems Prevention Research Group, 2002). Furthermore, with increasing age, it appears as if aggression becomes decreasingly associated with rejection, especially among boys (e.g., Sandstrom & Coie, 1999). The negative association between physical aggression and peer acceptance decreases in strength as children progress through junior high school (Cillessen & Mayeux, 2004), perhaps as children form groups with similar peers (Cairns et al., 1988) or as they develop more differentiated views of their social world (Rubin et al., 2006a).

Socially anxious, timid, and withdrawn children have likewise been reported as rejected. Withdrawn children make up 10% to 20% of the rejected group (e.g., Parkhurst & Asher, 1992; Volling, MacKinnon-Lewis, Rabiner, & Baradaran, 1993), but peer rejection, in this case, may depend on the form of withdrawal displayed and, as mentioned previously, the age of the child. Solitary-passive behavior comprises solitary exploratory and/or constructive activity in the company of others; this activity appears relatively benign in early childhood, but becomes increasingly associated with peer rejection with increasing age (Rubin & Mills, 1988). Solitary-active behavior comprises solitary sensorimotor activity and/or dramatic play in the company of others (Coplan, Rubin, Fox, Calkins, & Stewart, 1994) and is associated with rejection throughout childhood (Rubin & Mills, 1988). Lastly, social reticence comprises behaviors such as watching others from afar and avoiding activity altogether (Coplan et al., 1994) and may reflect internalized feelings of social anxiety (Rubin, Coplan, & Bowker, 2009).

Reticence appears to elicit peer rejection and exclusion, *in vivo*, from very early through late childhood (Gazelle & Ladd, 2003; Hart et al., 2000; Stewart & Rubin, 1995).

There are also gender differences in how social withdrawal is related to peer rejection. Socially withdrawn boys are more likely to be rejected than similarly behaved girls (Coplan, Gavinsky-Molina, Lagace-Seguin, & Wichmann, 2001; Gazelle, 2008; Gazelle & Ladd, 2003), perhaps because withdrawn behaviors violate male gender norms (Caspi, Elder, & Bem, 1988). However, Gazelle (2008) found that this gender difference did not hold if children were attention-seeking or aggressive in addition to being anxious and solitary. Agreeable anxious-solitary and normative anxious-solitary girls were less rejected than their male counterparts; however, if children were disruptive or aggressive in addition to being anxious and solitary, they were equally likely to be rejected by peers, regardless of gender. It would appear that any form of social behavior considered deviant from normalcy is likely to be associated with peer rejection. The extant studies have been carried out mostly in Western cultures. Given that "normalcy" may have different definitions in non-Western cultures, it may be that the behaviors associated with peer rejection in the West are not those typically associated with rejection in other cultures. We discuss this possibility, especially as it relates to social withdrawal, in a later section.

Social Cognitive Correlates of Peer Acceptance

Researchers have hypothesized that the ways in which children interpret and process information about their social worlds play a causal role in determining their social behaviors (Crick & Dodge, 1994; Lemerise & Arsenio, 2000), and in turn, peer acceptance and/or rejection. An example of how social cognition may be implicated in establishing particular types of peer relationships is taken from a **social information-processing** model described by Rubin and Rose-Krasnor (1992). These authors speculated that when children face an interpersonal dilemma (e.g., making new friends or acquiring an object from someone else), their thinking follows a particular sequence. First, children may select a *social goal*. This entails establishing a representation of the desired *end state* of the problem solving process. Second, they *examine the task environment*; this involves reading and interpreting all the relevant social cues. For example, boys and girls are likely to produce different solutions when faced with a social dilemma involving same-gender as opposed to opposite-gender peers (Rubin & Krasnor, 1986). As well, the social status, familiarity, and age of the participants in the task environment are likely to influence the child's goal and strategy selection (Krasnor & Rubin, 1983). Third, they *access and select strategies*; this process involves generating possible plans of action for achieving the perceived social goal and choosing the most appropriate one for the specific situation. Fourth, they *implement the chosen strategy*. Finally, it is proposed that children *evaluate the outcome of the strategy*; this step involves assessing the situation to determine the relative success of the chosen course of action in achieving the social goal. If the initial strategy is unsuccessful, the child may repeat it, or select and enact a new strategy, or abandon the situation entirely. Crick and Dodge (1994) proposed a similar social-cognitive model designed to account for *aggression* in children. This model consists of six stages, namely, (1) encoding of social cues; (2) interpreting of encoded cues; (3) clarifying goals; (4) accessing and generating potential responses; (5) evaluating and selecting responses; and (6) enacting chosen responses. The social competence model is outlined in Figure 7.2.

Lemerise and Arsenio (2000) integrated *emotional* experiences into the Crick and Dodge (1994) social information-processing model. For example, aggressive children's emotional reactions to problematic social situations might include frustration or anger; anxious/withdrawn children may react with fear. These emotions, in turn, may influence the information that is attended to and the information that is recalled. This mood-congruent information

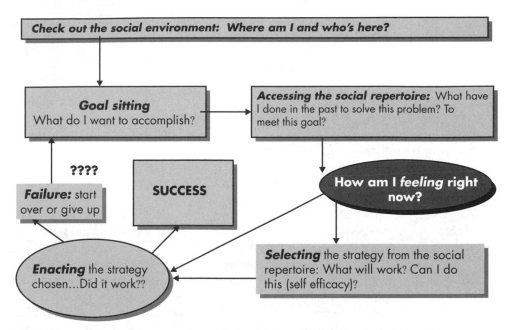

FIGURE 7.2   An information processing model of social competence and social problem solving.

processing might reinforce aggressive children's social schemas or "working models" that the social world is hostile or withdrawn children's notions that the social world is fear inducing. These emotional responses may explain, in part, why aggressive and withdrawn children respond in predictable ways to negative events befalling them.

Aggressive-rejected children demonstrate characteristic deficits or qualitative differences in performance at various stages of these models. They are more likely than their non-aggressive and more popular counterparts to assume malevolent intent when they are faced with negative circumstances, even when the social cues are ambiguous (e.g., Dodge et al., 2003; Orobio de Castro, Veerman, Koops, Bosch, & Monshouwer, 2002). When selecting social goals, rejected children tend to have motives that undermine, rather than establish or enhance, their social relationships. For example, their goals might comprise "getting even" with or "defeating" their peers (e.g., Rabiner & Gordon, 1992; Rose & Asher, 1999). In contrast, sociometrically popular children believe that negotiation and compromise will help them reach their social goals while simultaneously maintaining positive relationships with peers (Hart, DeWolf, Wozniak, & Burts, 1992; Hart, Ladd, & Burleson, 1990; Rose & Asher, 1999; Troop-Gordon & Asher, 2005).

As noted above, children must have access to a broad repertoire of strategies to meet their social goals. Researchers have found that aggressive and rejected children have smaller strategic repertoires, generate more hostile or dominant strategies, and generally assess these strategies differently from their non-aggressive or nonrejected peers (e.g., Chung & Asher, 1996; Dodge & Price, 1994). For example, they are more inclined to select solutions as agonistic or bribe strategies, and they are less likely than their non-aggressive or more popular counterparts to suggest prosocial strategies in response to social problems concerning object acquisition or friendship initiation (e.g., Crick, Grotpeter, & Bigbee, 2002; Orobio de Castro et al., 2002). Furthermore, aggressive children are more likely to view aggression as a viable or appropriate response (e.g., Erdley & Asher, 1998) and anticipate greater rewards for aggressive behavior (Boldizar, Perry, & Perry, 1989; Perry, Perry, & Rasmussen, 1986).

During interviews, young *withdrawn* children suggest during interviews that they would use more adult-dependent and non-assertive social strategies to solve their interpersonal dilemmas (Rubin, 1982). Examining their attributions, withdrawn children are also more likely than aggressive or comparison children to feel as if they will fail in social situations and to attribute their social failures to dispositional characteristics rather than to external circumstances (Wichmann, Coplan, & Daniels, 2004).

Also of relevance to understanding how social cognitions are related to peer acceptance is the construct of **rejection sensitivity**, the tendency to defensively expect, readily perceive, and overreact to rejection (Downey, Lebolt, Rincon, & Freitas, 1998). Rejection sensitivity has been defined as the tendency to defensively expect, readily perceive, and overreact to rejection (Downey et al., 1998). It is typically assessed by presenting children with hypothetical scenarios and asking them how nervous or angry they would feel and how much they expect to be rejected in each situation. Downey and colleagues have hypothesized that expectations of rejection that are accompanied by anger may lead to aggressive behavior with peers and that (nervous or) anxious expectations of rejection may lead to internalizing or anxious behaviors with peers. In support of this hypothesis, Downey et al. (1998) found that angry expectations of rejection were positively associated with teacher-rated aggression and negatively linked with social competence. Furthermore, child and adolescent anxious expectations have been linked with social anxiety and social withdrawal (London, Downey, Bonica, & Paltin, 2007). Longitudinal evidence also suggests that peer rejection predicts increases in rejection sensitivity over time (Sandstrom, Cillessen, & Eisenhower, 2003); however, research on the processes by which peer rejection and rejection sensitivity are linked across time is currently in its infancy.

Thus, the social-cognitive profiles of rejected withdrawn and aggressive children are quite distinct. The latter group is likely to interpret ambiguous social stimuli as hostile and threatening, misattribute blame to others, and respond with inappropriate anger-aggravated hostility. There can be no doubt why such cognition-behavior sequences are associated with peer rejection. Withdrawn children are more likely to generate adult-dependent strategies and unassertive strategies, as well as blame themselves for their social failures. Social dilemmas may evoke emotionally anxious-fearful reactions in withdrawn children; their inability to regulate and overcome their wariness is thought to result in an unassertive, submissive social problem solving style.

Cognitions and Feelings about the Self and Peer Acceptance

Do children feel and think better about themselves when they experience positive peer relationships? Is there a relation between negative self-perceptions and peer rejection? These important questions have attracted much research attention.

Perceived social competence was first defined and assessed by Harter (1998) as an index of children's awareness of their own peer acceptance or social skillfulness. In general, children with higher perceived social competence tend to be more popular with peers, and there is also a trend for the magnitude of this relation to increase with age (Ladd & Price, 1986).

Rejected children think more poorly of their own social competencies than do their more popular age-mates. Longitudinal evidence shows that being rejected in school predicts later negative social self-concept (Hymel et al., 1990a; Ladd & Troop-Gordon, 2003). It may also be that negative self-perceptions predict increases in peer rejection (Salmivalli & Isaacs, 2005), although it is likely that peer rejection and negative self-perceptions mutually reinforce one another. However, this general association may be true only for that group of rejected children described as anxious-withdrawn, submissive, sensitive, and/or wary (e.g., Boivin & Hymel, 1997). As indicated above, withdrawn children display a pattern of self-defeating attributions for social situations (i.e., they attribute their social failures to stable and internal causes and their social successes to unstable and external causes; Rubin & Krasnor, 1986; Wichmann et al., 2004). In contrast, rejected-aggressive children do not report thinking poorly about their social relationships with peers; indeed, rejected-aggressive children appear to overestimate their social competence and peer acceptance (Boivin, Poulin, & Vitaro, 1994; Zakriski & Coie, 1996). These findings are in keeping with the results of studies concerning extremely withdrawn and extremely aggressive children; it is only the former group that reports having difficulty with their social skills and peer relationships (Rubin et al., 1993).

Self-efficacy is the degree to which children believe they can successfully perform behaviors that are necessary for achieving desired outcomes (Bandura, 1977). In general, positive correlations have been found between children's social self-efficacy perceptions and positive sociometric nomination scores (Wheeler & Ladd, 1982). Aggressive and socially withdrawn children differ with regard to their perceived social self-efficacy. First, aggressive and non-aggressive children do not differ from each other concerning their self-efficacy perceptions of prosocial behaviors; aggressive children, however, report higher efficacy for enacting verbally and physically aggressive acts than do their peers (Erdley & Asher, 1996). In contrast, withdrawn children report lower efficacy for enacting verbally and physically aggressive behaviors relative to peers (Quiggle, Garber, Panak, & Dodge, 1992).

It should not be surprising to learn that children who feel socially incompetent, and who believe that others dislike them, come to develop feelings of isolation and loneliness. Indeed, researchers have consistently reported that it is only the sociometrically rejected group that discloses strong feelings of loneliness relative to average and popular children; neglected children are no more lonely or dissatisfied with their social circumstances than sociometrically average children (Asher & Wheeler, 1985). Chronic peer rejection may also lead to increases in loneliness over time (Burks, Dodge, & Price, 1995). Importantly, only rejected-submissive/timid/withdrawn children report being lonelier than their more accepted peers; rejected-aggressive children do not express negative feelings in this regard. These relations have been found throughout childhood (Boivin & Hymel, 1997; Cassidy & Asher, 1992; Crick & Ladd, 1993) and early adolescence (Parkhurst & Asher, 1992).

The data described above lead to two clear conclusions. First, rejected children internalize their social difficulties with peers; they report that they are less competent, less efficacious, and less satisfied *vis-à-vis* their social skills and peer relationships. Second, this conclusion is more likely for that subset of rejected children who can be described as withdrawn, timid, or submissive.

Finally, it may be that having a good friend can go a long way in preventing the development of negative feelings about one's social life. For example, friendship *quality* is associated with indices of psychosocial adjustment and functioning, such as self-esteem (Berndt, 1996; Rubin et al., 2009). These data help to explain the finding that rejected-aggressive children do not report difficulties with the self-system. Although classmates generally dislike this group, aggressive children tend to affiliate with others like them (Cairns & Cairns, 1991). The social support available to them, albeit from a deviant subgroup, may buffer aggressive children from developing negative self-perceptions and loneliness.

In summary we have described the characteristics of sociometrically popular, rejected, neglected, controversial, and perceived popular children. Of these groups, only rejected, controversial, and perceived popular children appear to have substantive behavioral problems. Furthermore, the difficulties associated with peer rejection appear to differ markedly from those who are characteristically aggressive and those who are submissive, wary, and withdrawn. Rejected-*aggressive* children can best be characterized as behaviorally hostile and as having a limited social-cognitive repertoire insofar as resolving their interpersonal problems is concerned. Indeed, they believe that they can "get things done" (meet their social goals) by behaving in an aggressive manner. Furthermore, they do not seem to understand that their behaviors lead others to dislike them; they do not report feeling poorly about their social skills or relationships. Rejected-*withdrawn* children, by contrast, can best be characterized as behaviorally submissive and as thinking and feeling poorly about themselves and their social relationships; they also suffer feelings of isolation and loneliness. Given these characterizations, it behooves us to ask whether peer rejection can be used as a "red flag" to identify children who may be at risk for developing negative psychological "outcomes" as adolescents or adults. We address this question in the following section.

OUTCOMES OF PEER RELATIONSHIPS DIFFICULTIES

There is some debate among researchers as to the "causal" nature implied by the relations typically reported between peer rejection and psychological maladjustment. For example, it is possible that underlying behavioral tendencies that may account for children being rejected by peers (i.e., aggression) also contribute toward later negative outcomes (i.e., juvenile delinquency). In this regard, the experience of peer rejection itself does not actually lead to adjustment difficulties. However, results from a series of recent longitudinal studies have provided compelling support for the notion that peer rejection itself provides a unique contribution toward later maladjustment.

Peer Rejection and Externalizing Problems

Results of longitudinal studies have indicated that peer rejection in childhood is associated with a wide range of **externalizing problems** in adolescence, including delinquency, conduct disorder, attentional difficulties, and substance abuse (Kupersmidt & Coie, 1990). These findings are not particularly surprising given the well-established link between aggression and peer rejection, and especially given that aggressive-rejected children are more likely to remain rejected over time.

However, other studies have indicated that *early* peer rejection provides a unique increment in the prediction of later antisocial outcomes, even when controlling for previous levels of aggression and externalizing problems (e.g., Ladd & Burgess, 2001; Miller-Johnson et al., 2002; Miller-Johnson, Coie, Maumary-Gremaud, Lochman, & Terry, 1999; Wentzel, 2003). For example, Laird, Jordan, Dodge, Pettit, and Bates (2001) followed 400 children from early childhood through to adolescence. They reported that peer-rated sociometric rejection at ages 6 to 9 years predicted externalizing problems in adolescence, even when controlling for the stability of externalizing problems over this age period.

The development of new statistical and methodological techniques has also allowed researchers to deconstruct the relation between peer rejection and subsequent maladjustment. For example, Dodge and colleagues (2003) reported that peer rejection predicted longitudinal "growth" in aggression over time (controlling for original levels of aggression) from early to middle childhood, and from middle childhood to adolescence. These researchers also found a developmental pathway in which peer rejection led to more negative information processing patterns (i.e., hostile cue interpretation), which in turn led to increased aggression. Additionally, Prinstein and La Greca (2004) found that girls' childhood aggression predicted later substance use and sexual risk behavior, but only for those girls who were disliked or rejected in junior high school. Given that changes in peer acceptance tend to precede changes in aggression over time, but not vice versa (Haselager et al., 2002), one can begin to understand the truly *transactional* nature of the relation between peer rejection and the development of externalizing problems over time.

Peer Rejection and Internalizing Problems

Results from a growing number of studies have indicated that anxious withdrawal is contemporaneously and predictively associated with **internalizing problems** across the lifespan, including low self-esteem, anxiety problems, loneliness, and depressive symptoms (e.g., Coplan, Prakash, O'Neil, & Armer, 2004; Coplan, Arbeau, & Armer, 2008; Crozier, 1995; Gest, 1997; Prior, Smart, Sanson, & Oberklaid, 2000). Rubin and colleagues followed a group of children from kindergarten (age 5 years) to the ninth grade (age 15 years). They reported that withdrawal in kindergarten and Grade 2 predicted self-reported feelings of depression, loneliness, and negative self-worth, and teacher ratings of anxiety in the fifth grade (age 11 years; Hymel et al., 1990a; Rubin & Mills, 1988). In turn, social withdrawal in the fifth grade predicted self-reports of loneliness, depression, negative self-evaluations of social competence, feelings of not belonging to a peer group that could be counted on for social support, and parental assessments of internalizing problems in the ninth grade (Rubin, Chen, McDougall, Bowker, & McKinnon, 1995a).

Researchers have also begun to explore the *unique* role of peer rejection in the prediction of internalizing problems. For example, in a longitudinal study following 405 children from kindergarten to Grade 7, Kraatz-Keily, Bates, Dodge, and Pettit (2000) reported that peer rejection predicted increases in both internalizing and externalizing problems over time. Relatedly, Gazelle and Ladd (2003) found that shy-anxious kindergarteners who were also excluded by peers displayed a greater stability in anxious solitude through the fourth grade. Anxious-solitary children who were not excluded by peers displayed decreased anxious solitude over time. In this regard, there appears to be a dialectic or transactional relation between anxious-solitude and rejection (Rubin et al., 2009).

In understanding the link between peer rejection and psychosocial adjustment, it may also be important to consider the role of children's *perceptions* of their *own* peer rejection. Children's perceived rejection has been associated with increases in depression over time (e.g., Kistner, Balthazor, Risi, & Burton, 1999). Moreover, Sandstrom, Cillessen, and Eisenhower (2003) found that children's self-appraisal of peer rejection was associated with increased internalizing and externalizing problems even after controlling for actual peer rejection. Thus, children's *beliefs* that they are rejected may play an influential role in the development of psychosocial maladjustment.

Summary

In this section, we presented evidence that supported the premise that peer rejection can directly cause such negative outcomes as internalizing and externalizing problems. Furthermore, believing that one is rejected by the peer group can also affect negative outcomes. As we have already noted, two major causes of peer rejection are the demonstration of aggressive and withdrawn behavior. The display of socially competent behavior protects children from peer rejection. Thus, it would appear important to understand the underlying causes of both competent and incompetent social behavior and, based on this information, develop prevention and intervention programs that may protect children from peer rejection and its negative consequences. We consider the developmental origins of children's peer relationships and social skills in the following section.

ORIGINS OF CHILDREN'S PEER RELATIONSHIPS AND SOCIAL SKILLS

By now, it should be obvious that children's peer relationships and social skills are of central importance to their experience of everyday life. Popular and socially competent children feel and think well of themselves, and they fare better in school than their less popular and skilled age-mates. Rejected children tend to lead less successful lives, both academically and personally.

It seems reasonable to ask questions about the origins of children's peer relationships and social skills. There is growing evidence that biological or dispositional factors (e.g., child temperament) directly and indirectly impact on the quality of children's peer relationships. The social well-being of children also appears to be influenced by parent–child relationships and parents' socialization beliefs and behaviors. Here we review dispositional, parenting, and ecological factors that have been associated with children's peer relationships.

Temperament and Peer Relationships

Temperament can be broadly defined as the biological basis for the affective arousal, expression, and regulatory components of personality (Goldsmith et al., 1987). Variability in these components contributes to differences in individual personality characteristics, and is associated with a wide range of developmental outcomes (see Wachs & Kohstamm, 2001). There is compelling evidence to suggest that child temperament plays a particularly powerful role in children's social interactions with peers. For example, in a longitudinal study from early childhood to adolescence, Prior and colleagues (2000) reported that almost half the variation in children's social skills could be explained by temperamental traits.

Researchers have focused on three broad groups of temperamental traits that appear to be differentially associated with children's social functioning in the peer group. The first of these is related to *resistance to control* (sometimes labeled *manageability*). These characteristics encompass lack of attention, low agreeableness, and strong attention to rewarding stimuli. These "difficult to manage" children tend to be boisterous and socially immature, and unresponsive to parents' and teachers' attempts to modulate their activities (Bates, 2001). In the peer group, such children tend to have poorer social skills, and are more likely to "act out" and display other externalizing problems (Coplan, Bowker, & Cooper, 2003; Fabes et al., 1999; Patterson & Sanson, 1999).

The second broadly defined group of temperamental traits that has been related to children's peer relationships concerns *negative affect* (sometimes labeled *reactivity*) and includes negative emotional reactivity and difficulty-to-regulate or difficulty-to-control affect. Children who are highly reactive and poorly regulated are easily angered, frustrated, and provoked by peers, and do not adequately control the expression of these negative emotions. These children tend to have poorer social skills, and display both internalizing and externalizing problems (Eisenberg et al., 2001; Guerin, Gottfried, & Thomas, 1997; Rubin, Burgess, Dwyer, & Hastings, 2003). Clearly, these constellations of dispositionally based behaviors mark children for peer rejection.

There is also some indication that emotion regulation may be a risk/protective factor in the relation between children's sociability and social adjustment. Rubin, Coplan, Fox, and Calkins (1995b) reported that temperamentally *sociable* children who lacked emotion regulatory control were disruptive and aggressive among peers, yet their sociable counterparts who could regulate their emotions were socially competent. Dispositionally unsociable children, who were good emotion regulators, appeared to suffer no ill effects of their lack of social behavior. These children were productive engagers of constructive and exploratory play when in the peer group. Unsociable children who were poor emotion regulators, however, demonstrated anxious and wary behaviors and were more behaviorally reticent in a peer play setting. Furthermore, these unsociable, poor emotion-regulating children were viewed by parents as having more internalizing problems than their age-mates. Thus, preschoolers who are emotionally dysregulated appear to behave in ways that will result in peer rejection, regardless of sociability. Moreover, difficulties in **emotion regulation** can contribute toward the development of both internalizing and externalizing problems.

Finally, the third group of temperamental traits constitutes shyness/inhibition and involves wary responses to social situations and novelty. Temperamentally shy children may want to play with other children, but tend to refrain from talking and interacting with peers because of social fear and anxiety (Coplan et al., 2004; Henderson, Marshall, Fox, & Rubin, 2004; Rubin, Burgess, & Hastings, 2002). With peers, shy children display less socially competent and prosocial behaviors, employ less positive coping strategies, and are more likely to develop anxiety problems (see Rubin, Bowker, & Kennedy, 2009 for a review). Moreover, as noted above, shy and socially withdrawn children become increasingly rejected and victimized by peers over time (Gazelle & Rudolph, 2004).

Parenting and Peer Relationships

Children usually grow up living with their parents and one or more siblings. Moreover, their families bring with them societal and cultural expectations and values, and stressors and supports that must assuredly influence children's social repertoires. Parents serve at least three roles or functions in the child's development of social competence and qualitatively positive peer relationships. First, parent–child interaction represents a context within which many competencies necessary for social interaction with others develop. Second, the parent–child relationship provides a safety net permitting the child the freedom to examine the features of the social universe, thereby enhancing the development of social skills. Third, it is within the parent–child relationships that the child begins to develop expectations and assumptions about interactions and relationships with other people (Booth-LaForce & Kerns, 2009).

Parent–child attachment relationships precede peer relationships, and because this is normally the case, formative experiences in the family may play an important role in influencing the development of peer relationships (e.g., Booth-LaForce & Kerns, 2009). *Attachment theory* has provided a framework and a methodology for making predictions from parent–child relationships to peer relationships. According to attachment theorists, parents who are able and willing to recognize their infants' or toddlers' emotional signals, to consider their children's perspectives, and to respond promptly and appropriately according to their children's needs help their children develop a belief system that incorporates the parent as one who can be relied on for protection, nurturance, comfort, and security (Belsky & Cassidy, 1995). A sense of trust in relationships results from the secure infant/toddler–parent bond. Furthermore, the child forms a belief that the self is competent and worthy of positive response from others.

The securely attached young child feels secure, confident, and self-assured when introduced to novel settings; this sense of felt security fosters the child's exploration of the social environment. Exploration of the social milieu leads to peer interaction and play, which, in turn, leads to the development of skills essential for the establishment and maintenance of positive peer relationships. Alternatively, the insecurely attached child believes that interpersonal relationships are rejecting or neglectful. Such conceptions of relationships are thought to result in the child's attempting to strike out aggressively at peers or avoid peer interaction; both of these behavioral styles preclude the child from the benefits of peer interaction.

There are, in fact, considerable data documenting the relations between the quality of infant–parent attachment relationships and the quality of children's social interactions with peers throughout the first 5 years of life (see Booth-LaForce & Kerns, 2009 for a review). For example, insecure-avoidant (A) babies later exhibit more hostility, anger, and distancing and aggressive behavior in preschool settings than their secure (B) counterparts (e.g., Egeland, Pianta, & O'Brien, 1993). Insecure-ambivalent (C) infants are more whiney, easily frustrated, and socially inhibited at 2 years than their secure age-mates (e.g., Fox & Calkins, 1993; Spangler & Schieche, 1998). Insecure-disorganized-disoriented (D) attachment status in infancy predicts the subsequent display of aggression among preschool and elementary school peers (e.g., Lyons-Ruth, Easterbrooks, & Cibelli, 1997). Finally, research also indicates that infants with secure attachment histories are later more popular and socially competent in the peer group in elementary school than their insecurely attached peers (see Booth-LaForce & Kerns, 2009 and Sroufe, Egeland, Carlson, & Collins, 2005 for reviews).

Studies of the contemporaneous relations between attachment and children's social behaviors and relationships support the longitudinal data just described. For example, in early and middle childhood as well in early adolescence, youngsters who experience a secure relationship with their mothers have been found to be more popular, sociable, and competent with peers than their insecure counterparts, whereas those who are insecure exhibit more aggressive and/or withdrawn behaviors (Booth-LaForce et al., 2006; Granot & Mayseless, 2001; Rose-Krasnor, Rubin, Booth, & Coplan, 1996).

In support of the notion that the child's *internal working model* provides substance for his or her social cognitions and behaviors, Cassidy, Scolton, Kirsh, and Parke (1996) found that children assessed as securely attached at 3½ years of age provided more prosocial responses to negative events and had more positive representations than insecure children about peer intentions during ambiguous negative acts when they were 10 years old. In concert with attachment theory, the authors speculated that securely attached children develop representations of their mothers as sensitive and responsive, and thus are unlikely to do something that would intentionally harm them. These internal representations guide children to develop similar conceptions of their peers.

Finally, given that the parent–child attachment relationship is a *dyadic* one, it would suggest that the dyadic friendship relationships of securely attached children should differ from those of insecurely attached children. Support for this notion stems from studies in which children with secure attachment relationships, in contrast to those with insecure attachments, are found (1) to report having one or more good friends; (2) to indicate fewer problems with peers such as being ridiculed or excluded from group activities; (3) to have fewer negative and asynchronous friendships; and (4) to be capable of establishing and maintaining close and intimate friendships with peers (Kerns, Klepac, & Cole, 1996; McElwain & Volling, 2004; Lieberman, Doyle, & Markiewicz, 1999; Rubin et al., 2004).

Parenting Behaviors and Peer Relationships

Parents may influence the development of social behaviors, and ultimately, the quality of their children's peer relationships by (1) providing opportunities for their children to have contact with peers; (2) monitoring their children's peer encounters when necessary; (3) coaching their children to deal competently with interpersonal peer-related tasks; and (4) disciplining unacceptable, maladaptive peer-directed behaviors (Parke, Burks, Carson, Neville, & Boyum, 1994; Parke & O'Neill, 1999; Pettit & Mize, 1993). For example, Ladd and Golter (1988) reported that mothers who arranged child–peer engagements had preschoolers who (1) had a larger number of playmates; (2) had more consistent play companions in their informal non-school networks; and (3) were better liked by peers. Mothers who initiated peer activities were likely to have children who spent more time playing in peers' homes; this variable was associated with peer acceptance (Ladd, Hart, Wadsworth, & Golter, 1988). Furthermore, parents who initiated peer opportunities for their children were more likely to have children

Parenting behavior affects a child's peer relationships; parents who provide opportunities for peer contact help their children to initiate and manage their own peer relationships.

who were socially competent (Kerns, Cole, & Andrews, 1998; Ladd & Hart, 1992). From these findings, it would appear that parents' provision of opportunities for peer inter-action help empower their children with the abilities to initiate and manage their own peer relationships.

Parents also regularly monitor, supervise, and coach their children during peer activities. Lack of parental monitoring has generally been linked to children's externalizing behavior difficulties and adolescent delinquency (Barber, 2002). Furthermore, children whose parents rely on indirect rather than direct monitoring of their peer contacts are less hostile towards others (Ladd & Golter, 1988). Moreover, children whose mothers and fathers offer advice on how to manage their social dilemmas are viewed by parents and teachers as socially com-petent (McDowell, Parke, & Wang, 2003). And mothers' over- as well as under-involvement in orchestrating and monitoring peer contacts is detrimental to children's social success, at least among boys (Ladd & Hart, 1992).

Mothers of more popular children are more active and effective in supervising their children's peer-related behaviors during free play than mothers of less well accepted children. Furthermore, mothers of less popular children suggest that they would coach their children to be more avoidant in response to hypothetical problems involving peers, whereas mothers of more popular children encourage their children to employ positive and assertive strategies for handling interpersonal problems involving peers (Finnie & Russell, 1988).

In summary, when parents provide their children with opportunities to play with peers, coach their children through difficulties with peers, and facilitate their children's peer inter-actions, their children are more popular among their age-mates.

With respect to parental behaviors much of the research on parenting and peer relation-ships has focused on the importance of two dimensions of parenting: warmth and control. Warmth typically denotes parental behaviors such as praise, encouragement, physical affec-tion, physical and psychological availability, and approval. Control has been defined as con-sistent enforcement of rules accompanied by an ability to make age-appropriate demands on the child. Parents of unpopular and/or peer-rejected children have been reported to use inept, harsh, and authoritarian disciplinary and socialization practices more frequently than those of their more popular counterparts (e.g., Bierman & Smoot, 1991). These findings seem to hold for preschoolers and elementary schoolers. Alternatively, parents of popular and socially competent children use more feelings-oriented reasoning and induction, warm control, and more positivity during communication (Mize & Pettit, 1997).

As noted above, children's behaviors influence the extent to which they may be accepted or rejected by peers. In this regard, studies that simply correlate parenting behaviors and cognitions with peer acceptance appear to miss a "step" in the link between these two phenomena. However, researchers who study links between parenting and children's social behaviors provide the information necessary to understand the links between parenting and peer acceptance. For example, with regard to the socialization of socially incompetent behaviors, parents who may be characterized as physically punitive, cold, rejecting, overly critical, and inconsistent in their discipline practices have children who behave aggressively during peer interaction (e.g., Dishion, 1990; Dishion & Patterson, 2006). In this regard, parents who are cold, rejecting, and punitive provide substantive models of hostility to their children (Patterson, 1983). Researchers have also consistently shown that parents of aggressive children inadvertently reinforce aggressive and impulsive behaviors (Dishion & Patterson, 2006). Importantly, it is not only cold, hostile, authoritarian parenting that promotes childhood aggression. Parents of aggressive children have also been found to be emotionally neglectful and lacking in responsiveness (Greenberg, Speltz, & Deklyen, 1993). Thus, parental permissiveness, indulgence, and lack of supervision appear connected to children's demonstrating aggressive behavior in the peer group (see Rubin & Burgess, 2002, for a review). Taken together, punitive, rejecting, cold, and overly permissive parenting behaviors are associated with, and predictive of, childhood aggression, which in turn is associated with, and predictive of, peer rejection.

Research concerning parenting behaviors and styles associated with social withdrawal (the other major behavioral correlate of peer rejection) focus on overcontrol and overprotection (see Hastings, Nuselovici, Rubin, & Cheah, 2010 for a review). Parents who use high power assertive strategies and who place many constraints on their children's independence and exploration appear to hinder the development of social competence and interaction with peers (Degnan, Henderson, Fox, & Rubin, 2008). Furthermore, children who are socially withdrawn are on the receiving end of parental overcontrol and overprotection (Hane, Cheah, Rubin, & Fox, 2008). There is also some evidence to suggest that parents may inadvertently exacerbate childhood shyness and social anxiety by modeling or reinforcing children's socially anxious behaviors (e.g., Barrett, Dadds, & Rapee, 1996).

CULTURE AND PEER RELATIONSHIPS

What we know about the development and correlates, causes, and outcomes of children's social behaviors and relationships is constrained by the cultures in which we study these phenomena (Cole & Packer, Chapter 3, this volume). The vast majority of the published data on children's peer experiences are derived from studies conducted in North America and Western Europe. Simply put, we know very little about the development and significance of peer acceptance, rejection, and friendship in non-Western cultures. Among the many aspects of socioemotional and cognitive functioning in human development, children's experiences in the peer group are perhaps most sensitive to **cultural influences** (Hinde, 1987). Children's behaviors in the peer context, peer evaluations and responses in interactions, the formation and function of peer relationships, and the organization of peer groups are likely to be culture-bound because they are often directed by cultural conventions, norms, and values (Chen & French, 2008).

Cultural influence may be reflected in children's peer interaction styles, peer acceptance and rejection, friendships and social networks. At the *behavioral* level, socialization pressures resulting from cultural endorsement and constraint may be directly associated with the prevalence and development of specific behaviors such as cooperation (Domino, 1992), compliance

(Chen et al., 2003), and emotional expressivity (e.g., Schneider, 1998). At the *overall peer acceptance* level, cultural value systems determine, to a great extent, standards for peer acceptance and rejection of children who are prototypically assertive (Chen, Li, Li, Li, & Liu, 2000) and aggressive (Casiglia, Lo Coco & Zappulla, 1998) among their peers. Finally, the functional roles that children's *friendships* and *peer groups* fulfill may vary across culture (e.g., French, Jansen, Rianasari, & Setiono, 2003; French, Setiono, & Eddy, 1999). For example, whereas the enhancement of self-esteem is regarded as particularly significant among friends in Western cultures, it is not highly appreciated among children in other cultures (e.g., China; Chen, Kaspar, Zhang, Wang, & Zheng, 2004). Similarly, whereas group affiliation is viewed in Western cultures as fulfilling individual psychological needs, such as the development of self-identity and enhancement of feelings about self-worth (Sullivan, 1953), Chinese culture places great emphasis on the role of the peer group to socialize members in appropriate *collective* behavior. In this regard, Eastern cultures may pay more attention to the *nature* of peer group networks ("good" or "bad" in terms of the consistency between group goals and activities and collectivistic orientations) than to individual functioning (Chen et al., 2008).

A central issue concerning cultural influence on peer interactions and relationships is the role of cultural norms and values in defining the "meanings" of social behaviors. Culture may not only affect the development and prevalence of particular social behaviors, but may also provide guidance for social judgment and evaluation of those behaviors that serve as a basis of social acceptance and rejection (Chen & French, 2008). Specifically, cultural patterns, especially those concerning socialization goals and expectations, are likely to affect group and individual beliefs, attitudes, and value systems. For example, one important socialization goal in Western cultures is the development of individual autonomy, assertiveness, and independence. These characteristics are highly emphasized during social interaction (Triandis, 1990). In contrast, social connectedness, interdependence, and conformity are valued social characteristics in most Asian and Latino collectivistic cultures (Greenfield, 1994). These different cultural beliefs and norms provide a frame of reference for the social evaluation of adaptive and maladaptive behaviors (Bornstein, 1995). Social evaluations may, in turn, affect how children interpret and react to each other's behaviors, and eventually determine whether a child is accepted by peers or the types of relationships the child develops with others.

The argument that different cultures draw different meanings from given social behaviors and interaction patterns in different ways has received empirical support in a series of cross-cultural studies by Chen and colleagues (Chen et al., 1998; Chen, Chen, Li, & Wang, 2009). Consistent with the findings of Western researchers, the frequent display of prosocial and cooperative behaviors was positively associated with peer acceptance and teacher-rated competence; the frequent display of aggressive or disruptive behavior was related to peer rejection in Chinese children (Chen, Rubin, & Li, 1995). In China, however, aggressive children experience feelings of loneliness and depression; this is not typically the case among aggressive children in North America (Chen et al., 1995). This finding may emanate from the strict prohibition of disruptive and aggressive behavior among Chinese children; students who display such deviant behaviors are often publicly criticized and even humiliated by teachers and peers in Chinese schools.

The role of culture as a context is also evident in the social interpretations of shy-inhibited behavior. In the Western literature, the display of shy, socially inhibited behavior is thought to derive from an approach–avoidance conflict in social situations; thus, socially withdrawn, restrained behaviors are taken to reflect internal fearfulness and a lack of social confidence (see Rubin et al., 2003). Children who display shy-inhibited behavior are believed to be socially incompetent, immature, and maladaptive in cultural contexts within which individual characteristics of assertiveness, expressiveness, and competitiveness are valued and encouraged (Triandis, 1990). However, shy-inhibited behavior is considered an indication of accomplishment and maturity in traditional Chinese culture; shy, wary, and inhibited children are perceived as well-behaved and understanding (e.g., Chen, in press; Luo, 1996). The social and cultural endorsement of their behavior is likely to help shy-sensitive children obtain social support and develop self-confidence in social situations. Accordingly, it has been found that whereas shy-inhibited children in Canada and the United States experience social and psychological difficulties, shy children in China are accepted by peers, well adjusted to the school environment, and less likely than others to report loneliness and depression (e.g., Chen, Rubin, Li, & Li, 1999). In an observational study, for example, when shy-inhibited children made initiations to their peers, they were likely to receive positive, supportive responses such as approval, cooperation, and compliance in China, but negative responses such as rejection and neglect in Canada (Chen, DeSouza, Chen, & Wang, 2006). Moreover, peers were more likely to voluntarily initiate positive interactions such as sharing and helping behaviors with shy children in China than in Canada. These findings indicate the significance of cultural norms for the development of social behaviors and peer relationships.

In summary, cross-cultural studies, especially those conducted in China and other Asian countries, have indicated that some behaviors viewed as maladaptive and abnormal in Western cultures are viewed as adaptive and acceptable therein. Peer acceptance is associated with behaviors that are viewed as acceptable within a culture, and behaviors regarded as culturally maladaptive are associated with peer rejection. Unfortunately, there has been little work, longitudinal or otherwise, in which researchers have examined the distal predictors (e.g., temperament, family factors) that may help explain cultural differences in the prediction and long-term outcome of peer acceptance and rejection. Such studies would enrich our knowledge of the cultural "meanings" of children's social behaviors and relationships.

CONCLUSIONS

In this chapter, we have reviewed literature concerning children's peer relationships. It should be clear that experiences garnered by children in the peer group and with their friends represent significant development phenomena. Thus, children who are accepted by peers and who have qualitatively rich friendships appear to fare better, throughout childhood, than children who are rejected and excluded by the peer group or who are lacking in friendship.

In this chapter, we have attempted to document those factors responsible, in part, for children's peer and friendship status. Influences include such intraindividual factors as temperament, emotion regulation, and social cognitive prowess as well as such interindividual factors as family relationships (e.g., attachment), quality of parenting style experienced, and cultural norms and values.

Although we have learned a great deal about the significance of children's peer interactions, relationships, and groups, there remain some rather interesting and important questions to address. For example, little research has focused on individual differences in the extent to which very young children (toddlers) demonstrate socially competent and incompetent behavior. Indeed, what does competent social behavior look like at age one or two? We indicated that by the end of the second year of life toddlers are able to engage in complementary and reciprocal interactive behaviors with peers. But do individual differences in such behaviors predict social competence, peer acceptance, and the ability to make and keep friends in later years? If dispositional and socialization factors vary in infancy, it seems likely that individual differences in social skills may be present in the second and third years of life—differences that may predict and/or lead to adaptation to the developmental milestone of preschool or kindergarten entry.

In this chapter we also presented a brief overview of the significance of children's friendships. We indicated that children's friendships serve a variety of functions including the provision of emotional and social support. We noted that children's ideas about friendship become increasingly abstract with age. Furthermore, children's friendships are posited to play an increasingly important role with age. Yet little is known about when it is in childhood that friendship can first serve as a promoter or inhibitor of adaptation or as a buffer against the ill-effects of parental or peer neglect or rejection. This issue of the functional significance of friendship may prove very helpful in planning intervention programs for children who demonstrate poorly developed social skills and peer relationships as early as the preschool years.

We indicated that from as early as 3 years of age, children's groups can be characterized by stable and rigid dominance hierarchies. The main function of these hierarchies appears to be to reduce conflict and aggression among peer group members. In the early years of childhood, the most dominant members of the peer group are the most popular and most highly imitated in their peer group. Yet dominance status in these earliest years of childhood is gained through consistent victory in interpersonal conflict. The route to dominance status in the middle and later years of childhood is, as yet, uncharted. It remains to be seen whether the relations between dominance status and peer acceptance remain consistent throughout childhood. Indeed, is it the case that dominance status, as assessed in early childhood, predicts perceived power and popularity when children move into middle school? This is a time when many of those perceived as popular are also viewed by peers as somewhat aggressive, assertive, and as boastful "show-offs." The early origins of young adolescent perceived popularity, dominance, and leadership represent areas that require the attention of researchers.

The topic of children's peer relationships has caught the attention of the lay public. Not a day goes by without a major newspaper, magazine article, or even films appearing on such matters as popularity, rejection, friendship, bullying, conflict, meanness, and peer pressure. With the eyes of the public attending to such matters, it remains up to the researcher to provide the consumer with a research-based picture of the roles played by the peer group in childhood and adolescence. It would be timely, indeed, to offer policy makers and educators the suggestion that "no child left behind" movements in public schools should incorporate children's social skills and relationships into the academic curriculum. After all, if children are rejected or victimized by peers in their schools, they may find it rather difficult to concentrate on learning to read, write, or solve mathematical problems (Wentzel & Asher, 1995; Wentzel, McNamara-Barry, & Caldwell, 2004). If children are lacking friends in school, or if they are lacking in social skills, what is the likelihood that they would feel comfortable working on group projects? Children's peer interactions, relationships, and groups are not only relevant insofar as psychological and emotional adjustment is concerned; they are clearly important entities as children attempt to make their ways through their everyday lives.

ACKNOWLEDGMENTS

This chapter was supported by National Institute of Mental Health grant 1R01MH58116 to Kenneth H. Rubin.

REFERENCES AND SUGGESTED READINGS (▢)

Aboud, F., & Mendelson, M. (1996). Determinants of friendship selection and quality: Developmental perspectives. In W. Bukowski & A. Newcomb (Eds.), *The company they keep: Friendship in childhood and adolescence* (pp. 87–112). Cambridge, UK: Cambridge University Press.

Adler, P. A., Kless, S. J., & Adler, P. (1992). Socialization to gender roles: Popularity among elementary school boys and girls. *Sociology of Education*, *65*, 169–187.

Adolph, K. E., & Berger, S. E. (2010). Physical and motor development. In M. H. Bornstein & M. E. Lamb (Eds.), *Developmental science: An advanced textbook* (6th ed., pp. 241–302). Hove, UK: Psychology Press.

Altermatt, E., & Pomerantz, E. (2003). The development of competence-related and motivational beliefs: An investigation of similarity and influence among friends. *Journal of Educational Psychology*, *95*(1), 111–123.

Archer, J., & Coyne, S. M. (2005). An integrated review of indirect, relational, and social aggression. *Personality and Social Psychology Review*, *9*, 212–230.

Asher, S. R., & McDonald, K. L. (2009). The behavioral basis of acceptance, rejection, and perceived popularity. In K. H. Rubin, W. M. Bukowski, & B. Laursen (Eds.), *Handbook of peer interactions, relationships, and groups* (pp. 232–248). New York: Guilford Press.

Asher. S. R., & Paquette, J. (2003). Loneliness and peer relations in childhood. *Current Directions in Psychological Science*, *12*, 75–78.

Asher, S. R., Rose, A. J., & Gabriel, S. W. (2001). Peer rejection in everyday life. In M. R. Leary (Ed.), *Interpersonal rejection* (pp. 105–142). New York: Oxford University Press.

Asher, S. R., & Wheeler, V. A. (1985). Children's loneliness: A comparison of rejected and neglected peer status. *Journal of Consulting and Clinical Psychology*, *53*, 500–505.

Bagwell, C. L., Newcomb, A. F., & Bukowski, W. M. (1998). Preadolescent friendship and peer rejection as predictors of adult adjustment. *Child Development*, *69*, 140–153.

Bandura, A. (1977). *Social learning theory*. Englewood Cliffs, NJ: Prentice Hall.

Bandura, A., & Walters, R. H. (1963). *Social learning and personality development*. New York: Holt, Rinehart, & Winston.

Barber, B. K. (2002). *Intrusive parenting: How psychological control affects children and adolescents*. Washington, DC: American Psychological Association.

Barrett, P. M., Dadds, M. R., & Rapee, R. M. (1996). Family treatment of childhood anxiety disorders: A controlled trial. *Journal of Consulting and Clinical Psychology*, *64*, 333–342.

Bates, J. E. (2001). Adjustment style in childhood as a product of parenting and temperament. In T. D. Wachs & G. A. Kohstamm (Eds.), *Temperament in context* (pp. 173–200). Mahwah, NJ: Lawrence Erlbaum Associates.

Bell-Dolan, D., Foster, S., & Sikora, D. (1989). Effects of sociometric testing on children's behavior and loneliness in school. *Developmental Psychology*, *25*, 306–311.

Belsky, J., & Cassidy, J. (1995). Attachment: Theory and evidence. In M. L. Rutter, D. F. Hay, & S. Baron-Cohen (Eds.), *Developmental principles and clinical issues in psychology and psychiatry* (pp. 373–402). Oxford, UK: Blackwell.

Benenson, J. F. (1990). Gender differences in social networks. *Journal of Early Adolescence*, *10*, 472–495.

Benenson, J. F., Apostoleris, N. H., & Parnass, J. (1997). Age and sex differences in dyadic and group interaction. *Developmental Psychology*, *33*, 538–543.

Benenson, J. F., & Christakos, A. (2003). The greater fragility of females' versus males' closest same-sex friendships. *Child Development*, *74*, 1123–1129.

Benenson, J. F., Markovits, H., Roy, R., & Denko, P. (2003). Behavioural rules underlying learning to share: Effects of development and context. *International Journal of Behavioural Development*, *27*, 116–121.

Berndt, T. J. (1981). Relations between social cognition, nonsocial cognition, and social behavior: The case of friendship. In J. H. Flavell & L. Ross (Eds.), *Social cognitive development* (pp. 176–199). Cambridge, UK: Cambridge University Press.

Berndt, T. J. (1985). Prosocial behavior between friends in middle childhood and early adolescence. *Journal of Adolescence*, *5*, 307–313.

Berndt, T. J. (1996). Friendship quality affects adolescents' self esteem and social behavior. In W. M. Bukowski, A. F. Newcomb, & W. W. Hartup (Eds.), *The company they keep: Friendship during childhood and adolescence*. New York: Cambridge University Press.

Berndt, T. J., Hawkins, J. A., & Jiao, Z. (1999). Influences of friends and friendships on adjustment to junior high school. *Merrill-Palmer Quarterly*, *45*, 13–41.

Berndt, T. J., & Hoyle, S. G. (1985). Stability and change in childhood and adolescent friendships. *Developmental Psychology*, *21*, 1007–1015.

Berndt, T. J., & Keefe, K. (1995). Friends' influence on adolescents' adjustment to school. *Child Development*, *66*, 1313–1329.

Berndt, T. J., & McCandless, M. A. (2009). Methods of investigating children's relationships with friends. In K. H. Rubin, W. M. Bukowski, & B. Laursen (Eds.), *Handbook of peer interactions, relationships, and groups* (pp. 63–81). New York: Guilford Press.

Bierman, K. L., & Smoot, D. L. (1991). Linking family characteristics with poor peer relations: The mediating role of conduct problems. *Journal of Abnormal Child Psychology*, *19*, 341–356.

Bigelow, B. J., & LaGaipa, J. J. (1980). The development of friendship values and choice. In H. Foot & A. Chapman (Eds.), *Friendship and social relations in children* (pp. 15–44). New Brunswick, NJ: Transaction.

Black, B., & Logan, A. (1995). Links between communication patterns in mother–child, father child, and child–peer interactions and children's social status. *Child Development, 66,* 255–271.

Boivin, M., & Hymel, S. (1997). Peer experiences and social self-perceptions: A sequential model. *Developmental Psychology, 33,* 135–145.

Boivin, M., Poulin, F., & Vitaro, F. (1994). Depressed mood and peer rejection in childhood. *Development and Psychopathology, 6,* 483–498.

Boldizar, J. P., Perry, D. G., & Perry, L. C. (1989). Outcome values and aggression. *Child Development, 60,* 571–579.

Bonney, M. E. (1942). A study of social status on the second grade level. *Journal of Genetic Psychology, 60,* 271–305.

Booth-LaForce, C., & Kerns, K. A. (2009). Family influences on children's peer relationships. In K. H. Rubin, W. Bukowski, & B. Laursen (Eds.), *Peer interactions, relationships, and groups* (pp. 508–530). New York: Guilford Press.

Booth-LaForce, C., Oh, W., Kim, A. H., Rubin, K. H., Rose-Krasnor, L., & Burgess, K. (2006). Attachment, self-worth, and peer-group functioning in middle childhood. *Attachment & Human Development, 8,* 309–325.

Bornstein, M. H. (1995). Form and function: Implications for studies of culture and human development. *Culture and Psychology, 1*(1), 123–138.

Bowker, A. (2004). Predicting friendship stability during early adolescence. *Journal of Early Adolescence, 24,* 85–112.

Bowker, J., Fredstrom, B., Rubin, K., Rose-Krasnor, L., Booth-LaForce, C., & Laursen, B. (2009). *Distinguishing those children who form new best friends from those who do not.* Unpublished manuscript.

Bowker, J. C., & Rubin, K. H. (2009). Self-consciousness, friendship quality, and internalizing problems during early adolescence. *British Journal of Developmental Psychology, 19,* 249–268.

Bowlby, J. (1958). The nature of the child's tie to his mother. *International Journal of Psychoanalysis, 39,* 350–373.

Brendgen, M., Little, T. D., & Krappmann, L. (2000). Rejected children and their friends: A shared evaluation of friendship quality? *Merrill-Palmer Quarterly, 46* (1), 45–70.

Brown, B. B. (1990). Peer groups and peer cultures. In S. S. Feldman & G. R. Elliott (Eds.), *At the threshold* (pp. 171–196). Cambridge, MA: Harvard University Press.

Brown, B. B., Eicher, S. A., & Petrie, S. (1986). The importance of peer group ("crowd") affiliation in adolescence. *Journal of Adolescence, 9,* 73–96.

Brown, S. B., Mounts, N., Lamborn, S. D., & Steinberg, L. (1993). Parenting practices and peer group affiliation in adolescence. *Child Development, 64,* 467–482.

Brownell, C. A. & Kopp, C. B. (2007). *Socioemotional development in the toddler years: Transitions and transformations.* New York: Guilford Press.

Brownell, C. A., Ramani, G. B., & Zerwas, S. (2006). Becoming a social partner with peers: Cooperation and social understanding in one- and two-year-olds. *Child Development, 77,* 803–821.

Buhler, C. (1935). *From birth to maturity: An outline of the psychological development of the child.* London: Routledge & Kegan Paul.

Bukowski, W. M., Sippola, L. K., & Newcomb, A. F. (2000). Variations in patterns of attraction to same- and other-sex peers during early adolescence. *Developmental Psychology, 36*(2), 147–154.

Burks, V. S., Dodge, K. A., & Price, J. M. (1995). Models of internalizing outcomes of early rejection. *Development & Psychopathology, 7,* 683–695.

Cairns, R. B., & Cairns, B. D. (1991). Social cognition and social networks: A developmental perspective. In D. J. Pepler & K. H. Rubin (Eds.), *The development and treatment of childhood aggression* (pp. 249–278). Hillsdale, NJ: Lawrence Erlbaum Associates.

Cairns, R. B., & Cairns, B. D. (1994). *Lifelines and risks: Pathways of youth in our time.* Cambridge, UK: University Press.

Cairns, R. B., Cairns, B. D., Neckerman, H. J., Gest, S., & Gariepy, J. L. (1988). Peer networks and aggressive behavior: Peer support or peer rejection? *Developmental Psychology, 24,* 815–823.

Cairns, R. B., Gariepy, J. L., & Kindermann, T. (1989). *Identifying social clusters in natural settings.* Unpublished manuscript, University of North Carolina at Chapel Hill.

Cairns, R. B., Leung, M. C., Buchanan, L. & Cairns, B. (1995). Friendships and social networks in childhood and adolescence: Fluidity, reliability, and interrelations. *Child Development, 66,* 1330–1345.

Card, N., & Hodges, E. (2006). Shared targets for aggression by early adolescent friends. *Developmental Psychology, 42,* 1327–1338.

Casiglia, A. C., Lo Coco, A., & Zappulla, C. (1998). Aspects of social reputation and peer relationships in Italian children: A cross-cultural perspective. *Developmental Psychology, 34,* 723–730.

Caspi, A., Elder, G. H., Jr., & Bem, D. J. (1988). Moving away from the world: Life-course patterns of shy children. *Developmental Psychology, 24,* 824–831.

Cassidy, J., & Asher, S. R. (1992). Loneliness and peer relations in young children. *Child Development, 63,* 350–365.

Cassidy, J., Scolton, K. L., Kirsh, S. J., & Parke, R. D. (1996). Attachment and representations of peer relationships. *Developmental Psychology, 32,* 892–904.

Chan, A. & Poulin, F. (2007). Monthly changes in the composition of friendship networks in early adolescence. *Merrill-Palmer Quarterly*, *53*(4), 578–602.

Charlesworth, W. R., & LaFreniere, P. (1983). Dominance, friendship, and resource utilization in preschool children's groups. *Ethology and Sociobiology*, *4*, 175–186.

Chen, X. (in press). Shyness-inhibition in childhood and adolescence: A cross-cultural perspective. In K. H. Rubin & R. Coplan (Eds.), *The development of shyness and social withdrawal*. New York: Guilford Press.

Chen, X., Chang, L., & He, Y. (2003a). The peer group as a context: Mediating and moderating effects on the relations between academic achievement and social functioning in Chinese children. *Child Development*, *74*, 710–727.

Chen, X., Chang, L., Liu, H., & He, Y. (2008). Effects of the peer group on the development of social functioning and academic achievement: A longitudinal study in Chinese children. *Child Development*, *79*, 235–251.

Chen, X., Chen, H., & Kaspar, V. (2001). Group social functioning and individual socio-emotional and school adjustment in Chinese children. *Merrill-Palmer Quarterly*, *47*, 264–299.

Chen, X., Chen, H., Li, D., & Wang, L. (2009). Early childhood behavioral inhibition and social and school adjustment in Chinese children: A 5-year longitudinal study. *Child Development*, *80*, 1692–1704.

Chen, X., DeSouza, A., Chen, H., & Wang, L. (2006). Reticent behavior and experiences in peer interactions in Canadian and Chinese children. *Developmental Psychology*, *42*, 656–665.

Chen, X. & French, D. (2008). Children's social competence in cultural context. *Annual Review of Psychology*, *59*, 591–616.

Chen, X., Hastings, P., Rubin, K. H., Chen, H., Cen, G., & Stewart, S. L. (1998). Childrearing attitudes and behavioral inhibition in Chinese and Canadian toddlers: A cross-cultural study. *Developmental Psychology*, *34*, 677–686.

Chen, X., Kaspar, V., Zhang, Y., Wang, L., & Zheng, S. (2004). Peer relationships among Chinese and North American boys: A cross-cultural perspective. In N. Way & J. Chu (Eds.), *Adolescent boys in context* (pp. 197–218). New York: New York University Press.

Chen, X., Li, D., Li, Z., Li, B., & Liu, M. (2000). Sociable and prosocial dimensions of social competence in Chinese children: Common and unique contributions to social, academic and psychological adjustment. *Developmental Psychology*, *36*, 302–314.

Chen, X., Rubin, K. H., & Li, B. (1995) Social and school adjustment of shy and aggressive children in China. *Development and Psychopathology*, *7*, 337–349.

Chen, X., Rubin, K. H., Li, B., & Li, Z. (1999). Adolescent outcomes of social functioning in Chinese children. *International Journal of Behavioural Development*, *23*, 199–223.

Chen, X., Rubin, K. H., Liu, M., Chen, H., Wang, L., Li, D., et al. (2003b). Compliance in Chinese and Canadian toddlers. *International Journal of Behavioral Development*, *27*, 428–436.

Chen, X. & Tse, H. C. (2008). Social functioning and adjustment in Canadian-born children with Chinese and European backgrounds. *Developmental Psychology*, *44*, 1184–1189.

Chung, T., & Asher, S. R. (1996). Children's goals and strategies in peer conflict situations. *Merrill-Palmer Quarterly*, *42*, 125–147.

Cillessen, A. H. N. (2009). Sociometric methods. In K. Rubin, W. Bukowski, & B. Laursen (Eds.), *Handbook of peer interactions, relationships, and groups* (pp. 82–99). New York: Guilford Press.

Cillessen, A., Bukowski, W., & Haselager, G. (2000). Stability of sociometric categories. *New Directions for Child and Adolescent Development*, *88*, 75–93.

Cillessen, A. H. N., & Mayeux, L. (2004). From censure to reinforcement: Developmental changes in the association between aggression and social status. *Child Development*, *75*, 147–163.

Coie, J. D. & Dodge, K. A. (1988). Multiple sources of data on social behavior and social status. *Child Development*, *59*, 815–829.

Coie, J. D. & Dodge, K. A. (1998). Aggression and anti-social behavior. In N. Eisenberg (Ed.), *Handbook of child psychology: Social, emotional, and personality development* (5th ed., pp. 779–862). New York: Wiley.

Coie, J. D., Dodge, K. A., & Coppotelli, H. (1983). Continuities and changes in children's social status: A five-year longitudinal study. *Merrill-Palmer Quarterly*, *29*, 261–282.

Coie, J. D., & Krehbiehl, G. (1984). Effects of academic tutoring on the social status of low-achieving, socially rejected children. *Child Development*, *55*, 1465–1478.

Coie, J. D., & Kupersmidt, J. (1983). A behavioral analysis of emerging social status in boys' groups. *Child Development*, *54*, 1400–1416.

Collins, W., Maccoby, E. E, Steinberg, L., Hetherington, E. M., & Bornstein, M. H. (2000). Contemporary research on parenting: The case for nature and nurture. *American Psychologist*, *55*, 218–232.

Cooley, C. H. (1902). *Human nature and the social order*. New York: Scribner.

Coplan, R. J., Arbeau, K. A., & Armer, M. (2008). Don't fret, be supportive! Maternal characteristics linking child shyness to psychosocial and school adjustment in kindergarten. *Journal of Abnormal Child Psychology*, *36*, 359–371.

Coplan, R. J., Bowker, A., & Cooper, S. (2003). Parenting stress, child temperament, and social adjustment in preschool. *Early Childhood Research Quarterly*, *18*, 376–395.

Coplan, R. J., Gavinsky-Molina, M. H., Lagace-Seguin, D., & Wichmann, C. (2001). When girls versus boys play alone: Gender differences in the associates of nonsocial play in kindergarten. *Developmental Psychology*, *37*, 464–474.

Coplan, R. J., Prakash, K., O'Neil, K., & Armer, M. (2004). Do you "want" to play? Distinguishing between conflicted-shyness and social disinterest in early childhood. *Developmental Psychology*, *40*, 244–258.

Coplan, R. J., & Rubin, K. H. (1998). Exploring and assessing non-social play in the preschool: The development and validation of the Preschool Play Behavior Scale. *Social Development*, *7*, 72–91.

Coplan, R. J., Rubin, K. H., Fox, N. A., Calkins, S. D., & Stewart, S. L. (1994). Being alone, playing alone, and acting alone: Distinguishing among reticence and passive and active solitude in young children. *Child Development*, *65*, 129–137.

Craft, A. (1994). Five and six year-olds' views of friendship. *Educational Studies*, *20*(2), 181–194.

Crick, N. R. (1996). The role of overt aggression, relational aggression, and prosocial behavior in the prediction of children's future social adjustment. *Child Development*, *67*, 2317–2327.

Crick, N. R., Casas, J. F., & Mosher, M. (1997). Relational and overt aggression in preschool. *Developmental Psychology*, *33*, 579–588.

Crick, N. R., & Dodge, K. A. (1994). A review and reformulation of social information-processing mechanisms in children's social adjustment. *Psychological Bulletin*, *115*, 74–101.

Crick, N. R., Grotpeter, J. K., & Bigbee, M. A. (2002). Relationally and physically aggressive children's intent attributions and feelings of distress for relational and instrumental peer provocations. *Child Development*, *73*(4), 1134–1142.

Crick, N. R., & Ladd, G. W. (1993). Children's perceptions of their peer experiences: Attributions, loneliness, social anxiety, and social avoidance. *Developmental Psychology*, *29*(2), 244–254.

Crozier, W. R. (1995). Shyness and self-esteem in middle childhood. *British Journal of Educational Psychology*, *65*, 85–95.

Daniels, E. & Leaper, C. (2006). A longitudinal investigation of sport participation, peer acceptance, and self-esteem among adolescent girls and boys. *Sex Roles*, *55*, 878–880.

Degnan, K. A., Henderson, H. A., Fox, N. A., & Rubin, K. H. (2008). Predicting social wariness in middle childhood: The moderating roles of childcare history, maternal personality and maternal behavior. *Social Development*, *17*, 471–487.

Dekovic, M., Engels, R. C. M. E., Shirai, T., De Kort, G., & Anker, A. L. (2002). The role of peer relations in adolescent development in two cultures: The Netherlands and Japan. *Journal of Cross-Cultural Psychology*, *33*, 577–595.

DeRosier, M. E., & Thomas, J. M. (2003). Strengthening sociometric prediction: Scientific advances in the assessment of children's peer relations. *Child Development*, *74*, 1379–1392.

DeSouza, A., & Chen, X. (2002, July). *Social initiative and responses of shy and non-shy children in China and Canada*. Presented at the Biennial Conference of the International Society for the Study of Behavioral Development (ISSBD), Ottawa, Canada.

Dishion, T. J. (1990). The family ecology of boys' peer relations in middle childhood. *Child Development*, *61*, 874–892.

Dishion, T. J., Andrews, D. W., & Crosby, L. (1995). Antisocial boys and their friends in early adolescence: Relationship characteristics, quality, and interactional process. *Child Development*, *66*, 139–151.

Dishion, T. J., Eddy, M., Haas, E., Li, F., & Spracklen, K. (1997). Friendships and violent behavior during adolescence. *Social Development*, *6*(2), 207–223.

Dishion, T. J., McCord, J., & Poulin, F. (1999). When interventions harm: Peer groups and problem behavior. *American Psychologist*, *54*(9), 755–764.

Dishion, T. J., & Patterson, G. R. (2006). The development and ecology of antisocial behavior. In D. Cicchetti & D. J. Cohen (Eds.), *Developmental psychopathology, Vol. 3: Risk, disorder, and adaptation* (pp. 503–541). New York: Wiley.

Dodge, K. A. (1980). Social cognition and children's aggressive behavior. *Child Development*, *51*, 162–170.

Dodge, K. A. (1983). Behavioral antecedents of peer social status. *Child Development*, *54*, 1386–1399.

Dodge, K. A., Lansford, J., Burks, V., Bates, J. E., Pettit, G., Fontaine, R., et al. (2003). Peer rejection and social information-processing factors in the development of aggressive behavior problems in children. *Child Development*, *74*, 374–393.

Dodge, K. A., Murphy, R. R., & Buchsbaum, K. (1984). The assessment of intention-cue detection skills in children: Implications for developmental psychopathology. *Child Development*, *55*, 163–173.

Dodge, K. A., & Price, J. M. (1994). On the relation between social information processing and socially competence behavior in early school-aged children. *Child Development*, *65*, 1385–1397.

Dodge, K. A., Schlundt, D. G., Schocken, I., & Delugach, J. D. (1983). Social competence and children's social status: The role of peer group entry strategies. *Merrill-Palmer Quarterly*, *29*, 309–336.

Domino, G. (1992). Cooperation and competition in Chinese and American children. *Journal of Cross-Cultural Psychology, 23*, 456–467.

Downey, G., Lebolt, A., Rincon, C., & Freitas, A. L. (1998). Rejection sensitivity and children's interpersonal difficulties. *Child Development, 69*, 1074–1091.

Doyle, A. (1982). Friends, acquaintances, and strangers: The influence of familiarity and ethnolinguistic background on social interaction. In K. H. Rubin & H. S. Ross (Eds.), *Peer relations and social skills in childhood.* New York: Springer-Verlag.

Eckerman, C. O. (1979). The human infant in social interaction. In R. Cairns (Ed.), *The analysis of social interactions: Methods, issues, and illustrations* (pp. 163–178). Hillsdale, NJ: Lawrence Erlbaum Associates.

Egeland, B., Pianta, R., & O'Brien, M. A. (1993). Maternal intrusiveness in infancy and child maladaptation in early school years. *Development & Psychopathology, 5*(3), 359–370.

Eisenberg, N., Cumberland, A., Spinrad, T. L., Fabes, R. A., Shepard, S. A., Reiser, M., et al. (2001). The relations of regulation and emotionality to children's externalizing and internalizing problem behavior. *Child Development, 72*, 1112–1134.

Eisenberg, N., Fabes, R. A., & Spinrad, T. L (2006). Prosocial development. In W. Damon & R. M. Lerner (Series Ed.) & N. Eisenberg (Vol. Ed.), *Handbook of child psychology: Vol. 3. Social, emotional, and personality development* (6th ed., pp. 646–718). New York: Wiley.

Erdley, C. A., & Asher, S. R. (1996). Children's social goals and self-efficacy perceptions as influences on their responses to ambiguous provocation. *Child Development, 67*, 1329–1344.

Espelage, D. L., Holt, M. K., & Henkel, R. R. (2003). Examination of peer-group contextual effects on aggression during early adolescence. *Child Development, 74*, 205–220.

Fabes, R.A., Eisenberg, N., Jones, S., Smith, M., Guthrie, I., Poulin, R., et al. (1999). Regulation, emotionality, and preschoolers' socially competent peer interactions. *Child Development, 70*, 432–442.

Fine, G. A. (1987). *With the boys: Little league baseball and preadolescent culture.* Chicago: University of Chicago Press.

Finnie, V., & Russell, A. (1988). Preschool children's social status and their mothers' behavior and knowledge in the supervisory role. *Developmental Psychology, 24*, 789–801.

Fogel, A. (1979). Peer- vs. mother-directed behavior in 1- to 3-month old infants. *Infant Behavior and Development, 2*, 215–226.

Fox, N. A. & Calkins, S. (1993). Relations between temperament, attachment, and behavioral inhibition: Two possible pathways to extroversion and social withdrawal. In K. H. Rubin & J. Asendorpf (Eds.), *Social withdrawal, inhibition, and shyness in childhood* (pp. 81–100). Chicago: University of Chicago Press.

Franzoi, S. L., Davis, M. H., & Vasquez-Suson, K.A. (1994). Two social worlds: Social correlates and stability of adolescent status groups. *Journal of Personality and Social Psychology, 67*, 462–473.

French, D. C., Jansen, E. A., Rianasari, M., & Setiono, K. (2003). Friendships of Indonesian children: Adjustment of children who differ in friendship presence and similarity between mutual friends. *Social Development, 12*, 605–621.

French, D. C., Setiono, K., & Eddy, J. M. (1999). Bootstrapping through the cultural comparison minefield: Childhood social status and friendship in the United States and Indonesia. In W. A. Collins & B. Laursen (Eds.). *Relationships as developmental contexts: Minnesota symposium on child psychology* (Vol. 30, pp. 109–131). Hillsdale, NJ: Lawrence Erlbaum Associates.

Freud, S. (1933). *New introductory lectures on psychoanalysis.* New York: Norton.

Furman, W., Simon, V., Shaffer, L., & Bouchey, H. A. (2002). Adolescents' working models and styles for relationships with parents, friends, and romantic partners. *Child Development, 73*, 241–255.

Galen, B. R. & Underwood, M. K. (1997). A developmental investigation of social aggression among children. *Developmental Psychology, 33*, 589–600.

Garvey, C. (1984). Children's talk. Cambridge, MA: Harvard University Press.

Gazelle, H. (2008). Behavioral profiles of anxious solitary children and heterogeneity in peer relations. *Developmental Psychology, 44*, 1604–1624.

Gazelle, H., & Ladd, G. W. (2003). Anxious solitude and peer exclusion: A diathesis-stress model of internalizing trajectories in childhood. *Child Development, 74*, 257–278.

Gazelle, H., & Rudolph, K. D. (2004). Moving toward and away from the world: Social approach and avoidance trajectories in anxious solitary youth. *Child Development, 75*, 1–21.

Genyue, F., & Lee, K. (2007). Social grooming in the kindergarten: The emergence of flattery behavior. *Developmental Science, 10*, 255–265.

Gershman, E. S., & Hayes, D. S. (1983). Differential stability of reciprocal friendships and unilateral relationships among preschool children. *Merrill-Palmer Quarterly, 29*, 169–177.

Gest, S. D. (1997). Behavioral inhibition: Stability and association with adaptation from childhood to early adulthood. *Journal of Personality and Social Psychology, 72*, 467–475.

Goldsmith, H. H., Buss, A., Plomin, R., Rothbart, M. K., Thomas, A., Chess, S., et al. (1987). What is temperament? Four approaches. *Child Development, 58*, 505–529.

Goldstein, H., Kaczmarek, L. A., & English, K. M. (2002). *Promoting social communication: Children with developmental disabilities from birth to adolescence*. Baltimore: Brookes.

Goncu, A. (1993). Development of intersubjectivity in the dyadic play of preschoolers. *Early Childhood Research Quarterly, 8*, 99–116.

Granot, D., & Mayseless, O. (2001). Attachment security and adjustment to school in middle childhood. *International Journal of Behavioral Development, 25*(6), 530–541.

Greenberg, M. T., Speltz, M. L., and Deklyen, M. (1993). The role of attachment in the early development of disruptive behavior problems. *Development and Psychopathology, 5*, 191–213.

Greenfield, P. M. (1994). Independence and interdependence as developmental scripts: Implications for theory, research, and practice. In P. M. Greenfield & R. R. Cocking (Eds.), *Cross-cultural roots of minority child development* (pp. 1–40). Hillsdale, NJ: Lawrence Erlbaum Associates.

Grotpeter, J. K., & Crick, N. R. (1996). Relational aggression, overt aggression, and friendship. *Child Development, 67*, 2328–2338.

Guerin, D. W., Gottfried, A. W., & Thomas, C. W. (1997). Difficult temperament and behavior problems: A longitudinal study from 1.5 to 12 years. *International Journal of Behavioural Development, 21*, 71–90.

Hane, A. A., Cheah, C. S. L., Rubin, K. H., & Fox, N. A. (2008). The role of maternal behavior in the relation between shyness and social withdrawal in early childhood and social withdrawal in middle childhood. *Social Development, 17*, 795–811.

Hardy, C. L., Bukowski, W. M., & Sippola, L. K. (2002). Stability and change in peer relationships during the transition to middle-level school. *Journal of Early Adolescence, 22*(2), 117–142.

Harris, J. R. (1995). Where is the child's environment? A group socialization theory of development. *Psychological Review, 102*(3), 458–489.

Harris, J. R. (1999). How to succeed in childhood. In S.J. Ceci & W. Williams (Eds.), The nature–nurture debate: The essential readings (pp. 84–95). Malden, MA: Blackwell.

Harris, J. R. (2009). *The nurture assumption: Why children turn out the way they do*. New York: Free Press.

Hart, C. H., DeWolf, M. D., Wozniak, P., & Burts, D. C. (1992). Maternal and paternal disciplinary styles: Relations with preschoolers' playground behavioral orientations and peer status. *Child Development, 63*, 879–892.

Hart, C. H., Ladd, G. W., & Burleson, B. R. (1990). Children's expectations of the outcomes of social strategies: Relations with sociometric status and maternal disciplinary styles. *Child Development, 61*, 127–137.

Hart, C. H., Yang, C., Nelson, L. J., Robinson, C. C., Olsen, J. A., Nelson, D. A., et al. (2000). Peer acceptance in early childhood and subtypes of socially withdrawn behaviour in China, Russia and the United States. *International Journal of Behavioral Development, 24*, 73–81.

Harter, S. (1998). The development of self-representations. In N. Eisenberg (Ed), *Handbook of child psychology: Social, emotional, and personality development* (5th ed., pp. 553–618). New York: Wiley.

Hartup, W. W. (1983). Peer relations. In E. M. Hetherington (Ed.), *Handbook of child psychology: Vol. 4. Socialization, personality and social development* (4th ed., pp. 103–196). New York: Wiley.

Hartup, W. W. (1992). Social relationships and their developmental significance. *American Psychologist, 44*, 120–126.

Hartup, W. W. (1996). The company they keep: Friendships and their developmental significance. *Child Development, 67*, 1–13.

Hartup, W. W., Brady, J. E., & Newcomb, A. F. (1983). Social cognition and social interaction in childhood. In E. T. Higgins, D. N. Ruble, & W. W. Hartup (Eds.), *Social cognition and social development*. New York: Cambridge University Press.

Hartup, W. W., & Laursen, B. (1995). Conflict and context in peer relations. In C. H. Hart (Ed.), *Children on playgrounds*. Ithaca, NY: State University of New York Press.

Hartup, W. W., Laursen, B., Stewart, M. A., & Eastenson, A. (1998). Conflicts and the friendship relations of young children. *Child Development, 69*, 1590–1600.

Hartup, W. H., & Stevens, N. (1999). Friendships and adaptation across the life span. *Current Directions in Psychological Science, 8*, 76–79.

Haselager, G. J. T., Cillissen, H. N., Van Lieshout, C. F. M., Riksen-Walraven, J. M. A., & Hartup, W. W. (2002). Heterogeneity among peer-rejected boys across middle childhood: Developmental pathways of social behavior. *Child Development, 73*, 446–456.

Haselager, G. J. T., Hartup, W. M., van Lieshout, C. F. M., & Riksen-Walraven, J. M. (1998). Similarities between friends and nonfriends in middle childhood. *Child Development, 69*(4), 1198–1208.

Hastings, P. D., Nuselovici, J. N., Rubin, K. H., & Cheah, C. S. L. (2010). Shyness, parenting, and parent–child relationships. In K. H. Rubin & R. J. Coplan (Eds), *The development of shyness and social withdrawal in childhood and adolescence* (pp. 107–130). New York: Guilford.

Hawley, P. H. (2003). Prosocial and coercive configurations of resource control in early adolescence: A case for the well-adapted Machiavellian. *Merrill-Palmer Quarterly, 49*, 279–309.

Hay, D. F. & Cook, K. V. (2007). The transformation of prosocial behavior from infancy to childhood. In

C. A. Brownell & C. B. Kopp (Eds.), *Socioemotional development in the toddler years: Transitions and transformations* (100–131). New York: Guilford Press.

Hay, D. F., Pederson, J., & Nash, A. (1982). Dyadic interaction in the first year of life. In K. H. Rubin & H. S. Ross (Eds.), *Peer relationships and social skills in childhood*. New York: Springer-Verlag.

Hektner, J. M., August, G. J., & Realmuto, G. M. (2000). Patterns and temporal changes in peer affiliation among aggressive and nonaggressive children participating in a summer school program. *Journal of Clinical Child Psychology*, *29*(4), 603–614.

Henderson, H. A., Marshall, P. J., Fox, N. A., & Rubin, K. H. (2004). Psychophysiological and behavioral evidence for varying forms and functions of nonsocial behavior in preschoolers. *Child Development*, *75*, 251–263.

Hinde, R. A. (1987). *Individuals, relationships and culture*. Cambridge, UK: Cambridge University Press.

Hinde, R. R. & Stevenson-Hinde, J. (1976). Toward understanding relationships: Dynamic stability. In P. Bateson & R. Hinde (Eds.), *Growing points in ethology* (pp. 451–479). Cambridge, UK: Cambridge University Press.

Hodges, E. V. E., Boivin, M., Vitaro, F., & Bukowksi, W. M. (1999). The power of friendship protection against an escalating cycle of peer victimization. *Developmental Psychology*, *35*(1), 94–101.

Hogue, A., & Steinberg, L. (1995). Homophily of internalized distress in adolescent peer groups. *Developmental Psychology*, *31*(6), 897–906.

Horn, S. (2003). Adolescents' reasoning about exclusion from social groups. *Developmental Psychology*, *39*(1), 71–84.

Howes, C. (1988). Peer interaction of young children. *Monographs of the Society for Research in Child Development*, *53* (No. 217).

Howes, C., & Matheson, C. C. (1992). Sequences in the development of competent play with peers: Social and social-pretend play. *Developmental Psychology*, *28*, 961–974.

Hubbard, J. A. (2001). Emotion expression processes in children's peer interaction: The role of peer rejection, aggression, and gender. *Child Development*, *72*, 1426–1438.

Hubbard, J. A., Dodge, K. A., Cillessen, A. H. N., Coie, J. D., & Schwartz, D. (2001). The dyadic nature of social information processing in boys' reactive and proactive aggression. *Journal of Personality and Social Psychology*, *80*, 268–280.

Hymel, S., Rubin, K. H., Rowden, L., & LeMare, L. (1990a). Children's peer relationships: Longitudinal predictions of internalizing and externalizing problems from middle to late childhood. *Child Development*, *61*, 2004–2021.

Hymel, S., Wagner, E., & Butler, L. (1990b). Reputational bias: View from the peer group. In S. R. Asher & J. Coie (Eds.), *Peer rejection in childhood* (pp. 156–186). Cambridge, UK: Cambridge University Press.

Isaacs, S. (1933). *Social development in young children: A study of beginnings*. London: Routledge.

Iverson, A. M., Barton, E. A., & Iverson, G. L (1997). Analysis of risk to children participating in a sociometric task. *Developmental Psychology*, *33*, 104–112.

Izard, C. E. (2009). Emotion theory and research: Highlights, unanswered questions, and emerging issues. *Annual Review of Psychology*, *60*, 1–25.

Jacobson, J. L. (1981). The role of inanimate objects in early peer interaction. *Child Development*, *52*, 618–626.

Kerns, K. A., Cole, A. K., & Andrews, P. B. (1998). Attachment security, parent peer management practices, and peer relationships in preschoolers. *Merrill-Palmer Quarterly*, *44*, 504–522.

Kerns, K. A., Klepac, L., & Cole, A. (1996). Peer relationships and preadolescents' perceptions of security in the child–mother relationship. *Developmental Psychology*, *33*, 703–710.

Kiesner, J., Poulin, F., & Nicotra, E. (2003). Peer relations across contexts: Individual–network homophily and network inclusion in and after school. *Child Development*, *74*(5), 1328–1343.

Kindermann, T. A. (1993). Natural peer groups as contexts for individual development: The case of children's motivation in school. *Developmental Psychology*, *29*, 970–977.

Kindermann, T. A., McCollom, T. L., & Gibson, E., Jr. (1995). Peer networks and students' classroom engagement during childhood and adolescence. In K. Wentzel & J. Juvonen (Eds.), *Social motivation: Understanding children's school adjustment*. New York: Cambridge University Press.

Kistner, J., Balthazor, M., Risi, S., & Burton, C. (1999). Predicting dysphoria from actual and perceived acceptance in childhood. *Journal of Clinical Child Psychology*, *28*, 94–104.

Kraatz-Keily, M., Bates, J. E., Dodge, K. A., & Pettit, G. S. (2000). A cross-domain analysis: Externalizing and internalizing behaviors during 8 years of childhood. *Journal of Abnormal Child Psychology*, *28*, 161–179.

Krasnor, L., & Rubin, K. H. (1983). Preschool social problem solving: Attempts and outcomes in naturalistic interaction. *Child Development*, *54*, 1545–1558.

Kupersmidt, J. B., & Coie, J. D. (1990). Preadolescent peer status, aggression, and school adjustment as predictors of externalizing problems in adolescence. *Child Development*, *61*, 1350–1362.

Kupersmidt, J., DeRosier, M., & Patterson, C. (1995). Similarity as the basis for children's friendships: The roles of sociometric status, aggressive and withdrawn behavior, academic achievement and demographic characteristics. *Journal of Social and Personal Relationships*, *12*, 439–452.

Ladd, G. W., & Burgess, K. B. (1999). Charting the relationship trajectories of aggressive, withdrawn, and aggressive/withdrawn children during early grade school. *Child Development*, *70*(4), 910–929.

Ladd, G. W., & Burgess, K. B. (2001). Do relational risks and protective factors moderate the linkages between childhood aggression and early psychological and school adjustment? *Child Development, 72*, 1579–1601.

Ladd, G. W., & Golter, B. (1988). Parents' initiation and monitoring of children's peer contacts: Predictive of children's peer relations in nonschool and school settings? *Developmental Psychology, 24*, 109–117.

Ladd, G. W., & Hart, C. H. (1992). Creating informal play opportunities: Are parents' and preschoolers' initations related to children's competence with peers? *Developmental Psychology, 28*, 1179–1187.

Ladd, G. W., Hart, C. H., Wadsworth, E. M., & Golter, B. S. (1988) Preschoolers' peer networks in nonschool settings: Relationship to family characteristics and school adjustment. In S. Salzinger, J. Antrobus, & M. Hammer (Eds.), *Social networks of children, adolescents, and college students*. Hillsdale, NJ: Lawrence Erlbaum Associates.

Ladd, G. W., & Price, J. M. (1986). Promoting children's cognitive and social competence: The relation between parents' perceptions of task difficulty and children's perceived and actual competence. *Child Development, 57*, 446–460.

Ladd, G. W., & Profilet, S. M. (1996). The child behavior scale: A teacher report measure of young children's aggressive, withdrawn, and prosocial behaviors. *Developmental Psychology, 32*, 1008–1024.

Ladd, G. W., & Troop-Gordon, W. (2003). The role of chronic peer difficulties in the development of children's psychological adjustment problems. *Child Development, 74*, 1344–1367.

Laird, R. D., Jordan, K. Y., Dodge, K. A., Pettit, G. S., & Bates, J. E. (2001). Peer rejection in childhood, involvement with antisocial peers in early adolescence, and the development of externalizing behavior problems. *Development and Psychopathology, 13*, 337–354.

LaFontana, K. M., & Cillessen, A. H. N. (1998). The nature of children's stereotypes of popularity. *Social Development, 7*, 301–320.

LaFontana, K. M., & Cillessen, A. H. N. (1999). Children's interpersonal perceptions as a function of sociometric and peer-perceived popularity. *Journal of Genetic Psychology, 160*, 225–242.

LaFontana, K. M., & Cillessen, A. H. N. (2002). Children's perceptions of popular and unpopular peers: A multimethod assessment. *Developmental Psychology, 38*, 635–647.

La Greca, A., Prinstein, M., & Fetter, M. (2001). Adolescent peer crowd affiliation: Linkages with health-risk behaviors and close friendships. *Journal of Pediatric Psychology, 26*(3), 131–143.

Langlois, J. H., & Stephan, C. W. (1981). Beauty and the beast: The role of physical attraction in peer relationships and social behavior. In S. S. Brehm, S. M. Kassin, & S. X. Gibbans (Eds.), *Developmental social psychology: Theory and research* (pp. 152–168). New York: Oxford University Press.

Laursen, B., Bukowski, W., Aunola, K., & Nurmi, J. (2007). Friendship moderates prospective associations between social isolation and adjustment problems in young children. *Child Development, 78*, 1395–1404.

Laursen, B., Hartup, W. W., & Keplas, A. L. (1996). Towards understanding peer conflict. *Merrill-Palmer Quarterly, 42*, 76–102.

Ledingham, J., Younger, A., Schwartzman, A., & Bergeron, G. (1982). Agreement among teacher, peer and self-ratings of children's aggression, withdrawal and likeability. *Journal of Abnormal Child Psychology, 10*, 363–372.

Lee, K., & Cameron, A. (2000). Extracting truthful information from lies: Emergence of the expression–representation distinction. *Merrill-Palmer Quarterly, 46*, 1–20.

Lemerise, E. A., & Arsenio, W. F. (2000). An integrated model of emotion processes and cognition in social information processing. *Child Development, 71*, 107–108.

Levin, E., & Rubin, K. H. (1983). Getting others to do what you wanted them to do: The development of children's requestive strategies. In K. Nelson (Ed.), *Child language* (Vol. 4). Hillsdale, NJ: Lawrence Erlbaum Associates.

Lieberman, M., Doyle, A., & Markiewicz, D. (1999). Developmental patterns in security of attachment to mother and father in late childhood and early adolescence: Associations with peer relations. *Child Development, 70*(1), 202–213.

London, B., Downey, G., Bonica, C., & Paltin, I. (2007). Social causes and consequences of rejection sensitivity. *Journal of Research on Adolescence, 17*, 481–506.

Luo, G. (1996). *Chinese traditional social and moral ideas and rules*. Beijing, China: The University of Chinese People Press.

Lyons-Ruth, K., Easterbrooks, M. A., & Cibelli, C. D. (1997). Infant attachment strategies, infant mental lag, and maternal depressive symptoms: Predictors of internalizing and externalizing problems at age 7. *Developmental Psychology, 33*(4), 681–692.

Maccoby, E. E. (1995). The two sexes and their social systems. In P. Moen, G. H. Elder, Jr., & K. Luescher (Eds.), *Examining lives in context: Perspectives on the ecology of human development* (pp. 347–364). Washington, DC: American Psychological Association.

MacWhinney, B. (2010). Language development. In M. H. Bornstein & M. E. Lamb (Eds.), *Developmental science: An advanced textbook* (6th ed., pp. 389–424). Hove, UK: Psychology Press.

Masten, A. S., Morison, P., & Pellegrini, D. S. (1985). A Revised Class Play method of peer assessment. *Developmental Psychology, 3*, 523–533.

McDonald, K. L., Putallaz, M., Grimes, C. L., Kupersmidt, J. B., & Coie, J. D. (2006). Girl talk: Gossip, friendship, and sociometric status. *Merrill-Palmer Quarterly, 53*, 381–411.

McDowell, D. J., Parke, R. D., & Wang, S. (2003). Differences between mothers' and fathers' advice-giving style and content: Relations with social competence and psychological functioning in middle childhood. *Merrill-Palmer Quarterly, 49*, 55–76.

McElwain, N. L., & Volling, B. L. (2004). Attachment security and parental sensitivity during infancy: Associations with friendship quality and false belief understanding at age four. *Journal of Social and Personal Relationships, 21*, 639–667.

McNeilley-Choque, M. K., Hart, C. H., Robinson, C. C., Nelson, L. J., & Olsen, S. F. (1996). Overt and relational aggression on the playground: Correspondence among different informants. *Journal of Research in Childhood Education, 11*, 47–67.

Mead, G. H. (1934). *Mind, self, and society*. Chicago: University of Chicago Press.

Merten, D. E. (1997). The meaning of meanness: popularity, competition, and conflict among junior high school girls. *Sociology of Education, 70*, 175–191.

Mesch, G., & Talmud, I. (2007). Similarity and the quality of online and offline social relationships among adolescents in Israel. *Journal of Research on Adolescence, 17*, 455–466.

Miller-Johnson, S., Coie, J. D., Maumary-Gremaud, A., Bierman, K. & The Conduct Problems Prevention Research Group (2002). Peer rejection and aggression and early starter models of conduct disorder. *Journal of Abnormal Child Psychology, 30*, 217–230.

Miller-Johnson, S., Coie, J., Maumary-Gremaud, A., Lochman, J., & Terry, R. (1999). Relationship between childhood peer rejection and aggression and adolescent delinquency severity and type among African-American youth. *Journal of Emotional and Behavioral Disorders, 7*, 137–146.

Mize, J., & Pettit, G. S. (1997). Mother's social coaching, mother–child relationship style, and children's peer competence: Is the medium the message? *Child Development, 68*(2), 312–332.

Moreno, J. L. (1934). *Who shall survive? A new approach to the problem of human inter-relations*. Washington, DC: Nervous and Mental Disease Publishing Co.

Moskowitz, D. S., Schwartzman, A. E., & Ledingham, J. E. (1985). Stability and change in aggression and withdrawal in middle childhood and early adolescence. *Journal of Abnormal Psychology, 94*, 30–41.

Mueller, E., & Silverman, N. (1989). Peer relations in maltreated children. In D. Cicchetti & V. Carlson (Eds.), *Child mistreatment: Theory and research on the causes and consequences of child abuse and neglect* (pp. 529–578). New York: Cambridge University Press.

Newcomb, A. F. & Bagwell, C. (1995). Children's friendship relations: A meta-analytic review. *Psychological Bulletin, 117*, 306–347.

Newcomb, A. F. & Bukowski, W. M. (1984). A longitudinal study of the utility of social preference and social impact sociometric classification schemes. *Child Development, 55*, 1434–1447.

Newcomb, A. F., & Bukowski, W. M., & Pattee, L. (1993). Children's peer relations: A meta-analyic review of popular, rejected, neglected, controversial, and average sociometric status. *Psychological Bulletin, 113*, 99–128.

NICHD Early Child Care Research Network (2001). Child care and children's peer interaction at 24 and 36 months: The NICHD study of early child care. *Child Development, 72*, 1478–1500.

Northway, M. L. (1944). Outsiders: A study of the personality patterns of children least acceptable to their age mates. *Sociometry, 7*, 10–25.

Oh, W., Rubin, K. H., Bowker, J. C., Booth-LaForce, C., Rose-Krasnor, L., & Laursen, B. (2008). Trajectories of social withdrawal from middle childhood to early adolescence. *Journal of Abnormal Child Psychology, 36*(4), 553–566.

Olweus, D. (1993) Victimization by peers: Antecedents and long-term outcomes. In K. H. Rubin & J. B. Asendorf (Eds.), *Social withdrawal, inhibition, and shyness in childhood*. Hillsdale, NJ: Lawrence Erlbaum Associates.

Orobio de Castro, B., Veerman, J. W., Koops, W., Bosch, J. D., & Monshouwer, H. J. (2002). Hostile attribution of intent and aggressive behavior: A meta-analysis. *Child Development, 73*(3), 916–934.

Pakaslahti, L., Karjalainen, A., & Keltikangas-Jarvinen, L. (2002). Relationships between adolescent prosocial problem-solving strategies, prosocial behaviour, and social acceptance. *International Journal of Behavioral Development, 26*, 137–144.

Parke, R. D., Burks, V. M., Carson, J. L., Neville, B., & Boyum, L.A. (1994). Family–peer relationships: A tripartite model. In R. D. Parke & S. G. Kellam (Eds.), *Exploring family relationships with other social contexts*. Hillsdale, NJ: Lawrence Erlbaum Associates.

Parke, R. D., & O'Neil, R. (1999). Social relationships across contexts: Family–peer linkages. In W. A. Collins & B. Laursen (Eds.), *Minnesota symposium on child psychology* (Vol. 30, pp. 211–239). Hillsdale, NJ: Lawrence Erlbaum Associates.

Parker, J. G., & Asher, S. R. (1987). Peer relations and later personal adjustment: Are low-accepted children at risk? *Psychological Bulletin, 102*, 357–389.

Parker, J. G., & Asher, S. R. (1993). Friendship and friendship quality in middle childhood: Links with peer group acceptance and feelings of loneliness and social dissatisfaction. *Developmental Psychology, 29*, 611–621.

Parker, J. G., & Gottman, J. M. (1989). Social and emotional development in a relational context: Friendship interaction from early childhood to adolescence. In T. J. Berndt & G. W. Ladd (Eds.), *Peer relations in child development* (pp. 15–45). New York: Wiley-Interscience.

Parker, J. G., & Seal, J. (1996). Forming, losing, renewing, and replacing friendships: Applying temporal parameters to the assessment of children's friendship experiences. *Child Development, 67,* 2248–2268.

Parkhurst, J. T., & Asher, S. R. (1992). Peer rejection in middle school: Subgroup differences in behavior, loneliness, and interpersonal concerns. *Developmental Psychology, 28,* 231–241.

Parkhurst, J. T., & Hopmeyer, A. (1998). Sociometric popularity and peer-perceived popularity: Two distinct dimensions of peer status. *Journal of Early Adolescence, 18,* 125–144.

Parten, M. B. (1932). Social participation among preschool children. *Journal of Abnormal and Social Psychology, 27,* 243–269.

Patterson, G. R. (1983). Stress: A change agent for family process. In N. Garmezy & M. Rutter (Eds.), *Stress, coping, and development in children* (pp. 235–264). Baltimore: Johns Hopkins University Press.

Patterson, G., & Sanson, A. (1999). The association of behavioral adjustment to temperament, parenting and family characteristics among 5-year-old children. *Social Development, 8,* 293–309.

Pepler, D. J., & Craig, W. (1995). A peek behind the fence: Naturalistic observations of aggressive behavior with remote audiovisual recording. *Developmental Psychology, 31,* 548–553.

Perry, D. G., Perry, L. C., & Rasmussen, P. (1986). Cognitive social learning mediators of aggression. *Child Development, 57,* 700–711.

Pettit, G. S., & Mize, J. (1993). Substance and style: Understanding the ways in which parents teach children about social relationships. In S. Duck (Ed.), *Learning about relationships* (pp. 118–151). Newbury Park, CA: Sage.

Piaget, J. (1932). *The moral judgment of the child.* Glencoe, IL: Free Press.

Popp, D., Laursen, B., Kerr, M., Burk, W., & Stattin, H. (2008). Modeling homophily over time with an actor–partner interdependence model. *Developmental Psychology, 44,* 1028–1039.

Poulin, F., & Pedersen, S. (2007). Developmental changes in gender composition of friendship networks in adolescent girls and boys. *Developmental Psychology, 43*(6), 1484–1496.

Prinstein, M. J., & La Greca, A. M. (2004). Childhood rejection, aggression, and depression as predictors of adolescent girls' externalizing and health risk behaviors: A six-year longitudinal study. *Journal of Consulting and Clinical Psychology, 72,* 103–112.

Prior, M., Smart, D., Sanson, A., & Oberklaid, F. (2000). Does shy-inhibited temperament in childhood lead to anxiety problems in adolescence? *Journal of the American Academy of Child and Adolescent Psychiatry, 39,* 461–468.

Putallaz, M., & Wasserman, A. (1990). Children's entry behaviors. In S. R. Asher & J. D. Coie (Eds.), *Peer rejection in childhood.* New York: Cambridge University Press.

Quiggle, N., Garber, J., Panak, W., & Dodge, K. A. (1992). Social-information processing in aggressive and depressed children. *Child Development, 63,* 1305–1320.

Rabiner, D., & Gordon, L. (1992). The coordination of conflicting social goals: Differences between rejected and nonrejected boys. *Child Development, 63,* 1344–1350.

Raudenbush, S. W., & Bryk, A. S. (2002). *Hierarchical linear models: Applications and data analysis methods.* Thousand Oaks, CA: Sage.

Richards, W. D. (1995). *NEGOPY 4.30 manual and user's guide.* Burnaby, Canada: Simon Fraser University.

Rodkin, P. C., Farmer, T. W., Pearl, R., & Van Acker, R. (2000). Heterogeneity of popular boys: Antisocial and prosocial configurations. *Developmental Psychology, 36,* 14–24.

Rodkin, P. C., Farmer, T. W., Pearl, R., & Van Acker, R. (2006). They're cool: Social status and peer group supports for aggressive boys and girls. *Social Development, 15,* 175–204.

Rose, A. J. (2002). Co-rumination in the friendships of girls and boys. *Child Development, 73,* 1830–1843.

Rose, A. J., & Asher, S. R. (1999). Children's goals and strategies in response to conflicts within a friendship. *Developmental Psychology, 35,* 69–79.

Rose, A. J., Carlson, W., & Waller, E. M. (2007). Prospective associations of co-rumination with friendship and emotional adjustment: Considering the socioemotional trade-offs of co-rumination. *Developmental Psychology, 43*(4), 1019–1031.

Rose, A. J., & Rudolph, K. D. (2006). A review of sex differences in peer relationship processes: Potential trade-offs for the emotional and behavioral development of girls and boys. *Psychological Bulletin, 132,* 98–131.

Rose, A., Swenson, L., & Robert, C. (2009). Boys' and girls' motivations for refraining from prompting friends to talk about problems. *International Journal of Behavioral Development, 33,* 178–184.

Rose, A., Swenson, L., & Waller, E. (2004). Overt and relational aggression and perceived popularity: Developmental differences in concurrent and prospective relations. *Developmental Psychology, 40,* 378–387.

Rose-Krasnor, L., & Denham, S. (2009). Social and emotional competence in early childhood. In K. H. Rubin, W. Bukowski, & B. Laursen (Eds.), *Peer interactions, relationships, and groups* (pp. 162–179). New York: Guilford Press.

Rose-Krasnor, L., Rubin, K. H., Booth, C. L., and Coplan, R. (1996). Maternal directiveness and child attachment security as predictors of social competence in preschoolers. *International Journal of Behavioral Development*, *19*, 309–325.

Ross, H. S., & Conant, C. L. (1992). The social structure of early conflict: Interactions, relationships, and alliances. In C. U. Shantz & W. W. Hartup (Eds.), *Conflict in child and adolescent development*. Cambridge, UK: Cambridge University Press.

Ross, H. S., Lollis, S. P., & Elliot, C. (1982). Toddler–peer communication. In K. H. Rubin & H. S. Ross (Eds.), *Peer relationships and social skills in childhood*. New York: Springer-Verlag.

Rubin, K. H. (1982). Social and social-cognitive developmental characteristics of young isolate, normal and sociable children. In K. H. Rubin & H. S. Ross (Eds.), *Peer relationships and social skills in childhood* (pp. 353–374). New York: Springer-Verlag.

Rubin, K. H. (2001). *The Play Observation Scale (POS)*. University of Maryland, College Park. Available from author.

Rubin, K. H. (2002). *The friendship factor: Helping our children navigate their social world—and why it matters for their success and happiness*. New York: Viking Penguin.

Rubin, K. H., Bowker, J., & Kennedy, A. (2009). Avoiding and withdrawing from the peer group in middle childhood and early adolescence. In K. H. Rubin, W. Bukowski, & B. Laursen (Eds.), *Handbook of peer interactions, relationships, and groups* (pp. 303–321). New York: Guilford Press.

Rubin, K., Bukowski, W., & Parker, J. (2006a). Peer interactions, relationships, and groups. In W. Damon, R. Lerner, & N. Eisenberg (Eds.,) *Handbook of child psychology: Vol. 3. Social, emotional, and personality development* (6th ed., pp. 571–645). New York: Wiley.

Rubin, K. H. & Burgess, K. (2002). Parents of aggressive and withdrawn children. In M. Bornstein (Ed.), *Handbook of parenting* (2nd ed., Vol. 1, pp. 383–418). Hillsdale, NJ: Lawrence Erlbaum Associates.

Rubin, K. H., Burgess, K. B., Dwyer, K. D., & Hastings, P. (2003). Predicting preschoolers' externalizing behaviors from toddler temperament, conflict, and maternal negativity. *Developmental Psychology*, *39*, 164–176.

Rubin, K. H., Burgess, K. B., & Hastings, P. D. (2002). Stability and social–behavioral consequences of toddlers' inhibited temperament and parenting behaviors. *Child Development*, *73*, 483–495.

Rubin, K. H., Cheah, C. S. L., & Fox, N. (2001). Emotion regulation, parenting and display of social reticence in preschoolers. *Early Education & Development*, *12*, 97–115.

Rubin, K. H., Chen, X., & Hymel, S. (1993). Socioemotional characteristics of withdrawn and aggressive children. *Merrill-Palmer Quarterly*, *39*, 518–534.

Rubin, K. H., Chen, X., McDougall, P., Bowker, A., & McKinnon, J. (1995a). The Waterloo Longitudinal Project: Predicting internalizing and externalizing problems in adolescence. *Development and Psychopathology*, *7*, 751–764.

Rubin, K. H., Coplan, R. J., & Bowker, J. C. (2009). Social withdrawal in childhood. *Annual Review of Psychology*, *60*, 141–171.

Rubin, K. H., Coplan, R. J., Fox, N. A., & Calkins, S. (1995b). Emotionality, emotion regulation, and preschoolers' social adaptation. *Development and Psychopathology*, *7*, 49–62.

Rubin, K. H., Dwyer, K. M., Booth, C. L., Kim, A. H., Burgess, K. B., & Rose-Krasnor, L. (2004) Attachment, friendship, and psychosocial functioning in early adolescence. *Journal of Early Adolescence*, *24*, 326–356.

Rubin, K. H., & Krasnor, L. R. (1986). Social-cognitive and social behavioral perspectives on problem solving. In M. Perlmutter (Ed.), *Cognitive perspectives on children's social and behavioral development. The Minnesota symposia on child psychology* (Vol. 18, pp. 1–68). Hillsdale, NJ: Lawrence Erlbaum Associates.

Rubin, K. H., LeMare, L. & Lollis, S. (1990). Social withdrawal in childhood: Developmental pathways to peer rejection. In S. Asher & J. Coie (Eds.), *Peer rejection in childhood*. New York: Cambridge University Press (pp. 217–249).

Rubin, K. H., Lynch, D., Coplan, R., Rose-Krasnor, L., & Booth, C. L. (1994). "Birds of a feather . . .": Behavioral concordances and preferential personal attraction in children. *Child Development*, *65*, 1778–1785.

Rubin, K. H., & Mills, R. S. L. (1988). The many faces of social isolation in childhood. *Journal of Consulting and Clinical Psychology*, *6*, 916–924.

Rubin, K. H. & Rose-Krasnor, L. (1992). Interpersonal problem solving. In V. B. Van Hassat & M. Hersen (Eds.), *Handbook of social development* (pp. 283–323). New York: Plenum.

Rubin, K. H., Watson, K., & Jambor, T. (1978). Free play behaviors in preschool and kindergarten children. *Child Development*, *49*, 534–536.

Rubin, K. H., Wojslawowicz, J. C., Rose-Krasnor, L., Booth-LaForce, C., & Burgess, K. B. (2006b). The best friendships of shy/withdrawn children: Prevalence, stability, and relationship quality. *Journal of Abnormal Child Psychology*, *34*, 139–153.

Ruble, D. N., & Martin, C. L. (1998). Gender development. In N. Eisenberg (Ed.), *Handbook of child psychology: Vol 3. Social, emotional, and personality development* (pp. 933–1016). New York: Wiley.

Ryalls, B. O., Gull, R. E., & Ryalls, K. R. (2000). Infant imitation of peer and adult models: Evidence for a peer model advantage. *Merrill-Palmer-Quarterly*, *46*, 188–202.

Ryan, A. M. (2001). The peer group as a context for the development of young adolescent motivation and achievement. *Child Development*, *72*, 1135–1150.

📖 Salmivalli, C. & Isaacs, J. (2005). Prospective relations among victimization, rejection, friendlessness, and children's self- and peer-perceptions. *Child Development, 76*(6), 1161–1171.

Sandstrom, M. J., Cillessen, A. H. N., & Eisenhower, A. (2003). Children's appraisal of peer rejection experiences: Impact on social and emotional adjustment. *Social Development, 12*, 530–550.

Sandstrom, M. J., & Coie, J. D. (1999). A developmental perspective on peer rejection: Mechanisms of stability and change. *Child Development, 70*, 955–966.

Sawyer, R. K. (1997). *Pretend play as improvisation: Conversation in the preschool classroom.* Mahwah, NJ: Lawrence Erlbaum Associates.

Schneider, B. H. (1998). Cross-cultural comparison as doorkeeper in research on the social and emotional adjustment of children and adolescents. *Developmental Psychology, 34*, 793–797.

Schneider, B. (1999). A multimethod exploration of the friendships of children considered socially withdrawn by their school peers. *Journal of Abnormal Child Psychology, 27*, 115–123.

Schneider, B., & Tessier, N. (2007). Close friendship as understood by socially withdrawn, anxious early adolescents. *Child Psychiatry & Human Development, 38*(4), 339–351.

Sears, R. R., Maccoby, E., & Levin, H. (1957). *Patterns of child rearing.* White Plains, NY: Peterson.

Selfhout, M., Branje, S., ter Bogt, T., & Meeus, W. H. J. (2009). The role of music preferences in early adolescents' friendship formation and stability. *Journal of Adolescence, 32*, 95–107.

Selman, R.L. (1980). *The growth of interpersonal understanding.* New York: Cambridge University Press.

Selman, R. & Schultz, L. (1990). *Making a friend in youth: Developmental theory and pair therapy.* Chicago: University of Chicago Press.

📖 Simpkins, S., & Parke, R. (2002). Do friends and nonfriends behave differently? A social relations analysis of children's behavior. *Merrill-Palmer Quarterly, 48*, 263–283.

Spangler, G., & Schieche, M. (1998). Emotional and adrenocortical responses of infants to the strange situation: The differential function of emotional expression. *International Journal of Behavioral Development, 22*, 681–706.

Sroufe, L. A., Egeland, B., Carlson, E. A., & Collins, W. A. (2005). Placing early attachment experiences in developmental context. In K. E. Grossmann, K. Grossmann, & E. Waters (Eds.), *Attachment from infancy to adulthood* (pp. 48–70). New York: Guilford Press.

Stewart, S. L. & Rubin, K. H. (1995). The social problem solving skills of anxious-withdrawn children. *Development and Psychopathology, 7*, 323–336.

📖 Strayer, F. F. & Santos, A. J. (1996). Affiliative structures in preschool peer groups. *Social Development, 5*, 117–130.

Strayer, F. F., & Strayer, J. (1976). An ethological analysis of social agonism and dominance relations among preschool children. *Child Development, 47*, 980–989.

Sullivan, H. S. (1953). *The interpersonal theory of psychiatry.* New York: Norton.

Tarrant, M. (2002). Adolescent peer groups and social identity. *Social Development, 11*, 110–123.

Thorne, B., & Luria, Z. (2001). Sexuality and gender in children's daily worlds. In J. M. Henslin (Ed.), *Down to earth sociology: Introductory readings* (11th ed., pp. 156–167). New York: The Free Press.

Tomada, G., & Schneider, B. H. (1997). Relational aggression, gender, and peer acceptance: Invariance across culture, stability over time, and concordance among informants. *Developmental Psychology, 33*, 601–609.

Tomada, G., Schneider, B., & Fonzi, A. (2002). Verbal and nonverbal interactions of four- and five-year-old friends in potential conflict situations. *Journal of Genetic Psychology, 163*, 327–339.

Trevarthen, C. (1979). Communication and cooperation in early infancy: A description of primary intersubjectivity. In M. Bullowa (Ed.), *Before speech* (pp. 321–347). Cambridge, UK: Cambridge University Press.

Triandis, H. C. (1990). Cross-cultural studies of individualism and collectivism. *Nebraska Symposium on Motivation* (Vol. 37, pp. 41–133). Lincoln, NE: University of Nebraska Press.

Troop-Gordon, W. P., & Asher, S. R. (2005). Modifications in children's goals when encountering obstacles to conflict resolution. *Child Development, 76*, 568–582.

Urberg, K. A., Degirmencioglu, S. M., & Pilgrim, C. (1997). Close friend and group influence on adolescent cigarette smoking and alcohol use. *Developmental Psychology, 33*, 834–844.

Vaillancourt, T., & Hymel, S. (2006). Aggression and social status: The moderating roles of sex and peer-valued characteristics. *Aggressive Behavior, 32*, 396–408.

Vaish, A., Carpenter, M., & Tomasello, M. (2009). Sympathy through affective perspective taking and its relation to prosocial behavior in toddlers. *Developmental Psychology, 45*(2), 534–543.

Vaughn, B. E., & Santos, A. J. (2009). Structural descriptions of social transactions among young children: Affiliation and dominance in preschool groups. In K. H. Rubin, W. Bukowski, & B. Laursen (Eds.), *Handbook of peer interactions, relationships, and groups* (pp. 195–214). New York: Guilford Press.

Verba, M. (1994). The beginnings of collaboration in peer interaction. *Human Development, 37*, 125–139.

Vitaro, F., Boivin, M., & Bukowski, W. M. (2009). The role of friendship in child and adolescent psychosocial development. In K. H. Rubin, W. Bukowski, & B. Laursen (Eds.), *Peer interactions, relationships, and groups* (pp. 568–588). New York: Guilford Press.

Vitaro, F., Brendgen, M., & Tremblay, R. (2000). Influence of deviant friends on delinquency: Searching for moderator variables. *Journal of Abnormal Child Psychology*, *28*, 313–325.

Vitaro, F., Tremblay, R. E., Kerr, M., Pagani, L., & Bukowski, W. M. (1997). Disruptiveness, friends' characteristics, and delinquency in early adolescence: A test of two competing models of development. *Child Development*, *68*, 676–689.

Volling, B. L., MacKinnon-Lewis, C., Rabiner, D., & Baradaran, L. P. (1993). Children's social competence and sociometric status: Further exploration of aggression, social withdrawal, and peer rejection. *Development and Psychopathology*, *5*, 459–483.

Wachs, T. D., & Kohstamm, G. A. (2001). *Temperament in context*. Mahwah, NJ: Lawrence Erlbaum Associates.

Warneken, F., Chen, F., & Tomasello, M. (2006). Cooperative activities in young children and chimpanzees. *Child Development*, *77*, 640–663.

Wentzel, K. R. (2003). Sociometric status and adjustment in middle school: A longitudinal study. *Journal of Early Adolescence*, *23*, 5–28.

Wentzel, K. R., & Asher, S. R. (1995). The academic lives of neglected, rejected, popular, and controversial children. *Child Development*, *66*, 754–763.

Wentzel, K. R., McNamara-Barry, C., & Caldwell, K. A. (2004). Friendships in middle school: Influences on motivation and school adjustment. *Journal of Educational Psychology*, *96*(2), 195–203.

Wheeler, V. A., & Ladd, G. W. (1982). Assessment of children's self-efficacy for social interactions with peers. *Developmental Psychology*, *18*, 795–805.

Wichmann, C., Coplan, R. J., & Daniels, T. (2004). The social cognitions of socially withdrawn children. *Social Development*, *13*, 377–392.

Windle, M. A. (1994). A study of friendship characteristics and problem behaviors among middle adolescents. *Child Development*, *65*, 1764–1777.

Wojslawowicz Bowker, J. C., Rubin, K. H., Burgess, K. B., Booth-LaForce, C., & Rose-Krasnor, L. (2006). Behavioral characteristics associated with stable and fluid best friendship patterns in middle childhood. *Merrill-Palmer Quarterly*, *52*(4), 671–693.

Xie, H., Cairns, B. D., & Cairns, R. B. (2001). Predicting teen motherhood and teen fatherhood: Individual characteristics and peer affiliations. *Social Development*, *10*, 488–511.

Younger, A. J., & Boyko, K. A. (1987). Aggression and withdrawal as social schemas underlying chidlren's peer perceptions. *Child Development*, *58*, 1094–1100.

Younger, A., Gentile, C., & Burgess, K. (1993). Children's perceptions of social withdrawal: Changes accross age. In K. H. Rubin & J. Asendorpf (Eds.), *Social withdrawal, inhibition, and shyness in childhood*. Hillsdale, NJ: Lawrence Erlbaum Associates.

Youniss, J. (1980). *Parents and peers in social development: A Piaget–Sullivan perspective*. Chicago: University of Chicago Press.

Zakriski, A. L., & Coie, J. D. (1996). A comparison of aggressive-rejected and nonaggressive-rejected children's interpretations of self-directed and other-directed rejection. *Child Development*, *67*, 1048–1070.

❖ 8 ❖

SCHOOL AND COMMUNITY INFLUENCES ON HUMAN DEVELOPMENT

Jacquelynne S. Eccles
University of Michigan
Robert W. Roeser
Portland State University

INTRODUCTION

In 1979, Bronfenbrenner published the first of a series of works charging developmental psychology with the need to study human development from more naturalistic and contextual points of view. He stressed that humans develop within a set of embedded physical and sociocultural contexts of influence beginning with their own biological make-up and ending with the political/historical contexts into which they are born and raised. Bronfenbrenner emphasized that we cannot understand human development without understanding the multidimensional forces that operate across time both within and across these levels of influence—biological, psychological, social, cultural, economic, and political. Although it is true that children are most directly influenced by their immediate relationships and face-to-face interactions with other human beings, particularly their parents, siblings, extended family members, friends, peers and teachers, these proximal human relationships are nonetheless shaped by more distal social, cultural, economic, and political forces in the contemporary societal context. For example, workplace experiences affect parents' mental health and economic resources, which in turn affect parenting behaviors and child outcomes (e.g., Whitbeck et al., 1997). Similarly, neighborhoods structure the types of opportunities and risks children are exposed to whenever they leave their home, and thereby, to the extent their parents adapt their parenting behaviors to the neighborhood environment outside of the home, also affect parent–child interactions in the home (e.g., Furstenberg, Cook, Eccles, Elder, & Sameroff, 1999). Finally, schools are elaborate multilevel institutions that influence children's academic, social–emotional and behavioral development in a wide variety of ways—ranging from teacher influences on student **achievement** associated with the quality of instruction, to physical influences on student mood and motivation associated with the school building itself in terms of noise, light, cleanliness, and overcrowding, to peer influences on students' behavioral conduct based on the social composition of a school's student body (e.g., Rutter & Maughan, 2002).

Since 1979, there has been growing interest in the influences of these extra-familial contexts of human development. Researchers have begun looking at of the contributions of neighborhoods, communities, religious institutions and schools, as well as larger, political, societal, cultural, and historical forces, on young people's academic, social–emotional and behavioral

361

development. In this chapter, we focus on two of these contexts: schools and community-based settings (such as churches, synagogues or mosques; playgrounds; afterschool clubs; and neighborhood streets). Young people spend many of their waking hours in such settings, and this is increasingly true as they move into adolescence. Although these extra-familial settings afford opportunities and present various risks for healthy development, they have been researched less than the family by developmental scientists until relatively recently. As a result, much of the current work on how school and community settings influence child and adolescent development has been done by scholars from a broad range of disciplines outside of developmental psychology, including educational psychology, sociology, anthropology, applied linguistics, history, and so on. We draw on a variety of these disciplinary resources in this chapter. This kind of interdisciplinary perspective on the role of schools and community settings in child and adolescent development is a necessary dimension of the kind of ecologically oriented and culturally and historically informed developmental science that Bronfenbrenner outlined.

We focus first on schools, because they occupy a central place in the developmental agenda set forth for children in almost every nation of the world. Thus, in the majority of nations, from the time children first enter school in early or middle childhood until they complete their formal education sometime in adolescence, children and youth spend more time in schools than in any other context outside their homes. By virtue of their central role in lives of children and families, schools are increasingly playing a role in the education of children and youth not only in terms of the traditional "three Rs" of reading, writing and arithmetic, but also in terms of moral and character development, the cultivation of motivation to learn and a desire for lifelong learning, the promotion of social–emotional skills and well-being, and the prevention and remediation of emotional–behavioral problems (Greenberg et al., 2003; Roeser & Eccles, 2000).

Exploring all the possible ways in which educational institutions influence the various domains of child and adolescent development is beyond the scope of a single chapter. Instead, we present a developmental systems framework for conceptualizing the context of schooling, and provide a set of examples of pathways of influence by which the multilevel and multidimensional nature of the context of school can influence child and adolescent development. Specifically, we focus on three normative developmental moments when the influences of various dimensions of the context of school on students' motivation, achievement, and well-being are most evident: the transitions into elementary (ages 5–10), middle (ages 10–14), and high school (ages 14–18). We begin this section by describing schools as multilevel social organizations that can influence children's cognitive, socio-emotional, and behavioral development through organizational, social, and instructional processes that operate at several different levels of the overall *school system*. These levels range from the immediate, very proximal relationships between students, tasks, and teachers in the classroom; to quasi-proximal influences in terms of principals and school boards in setting school-level policies; to distal national level policies mandating particular kinds of assessments and funding structures for schools. After providing a descriptive account of these various levels of the school system, we present three examples of how chains of causal processes can operate across multiple levels of the school system to influence students' daily experiences of teaching and learning in school and, thereby, their longer-term educational lifepaths as they enter and pass through elementary and secondary school and beyond (Roeser & Peck, 2003). The first example focuses on the transition into elementary school, the second on the transition from elementary school into either junior high school or middle school, and the third on the transition into high school. In these examples, we try to highlight the important reciprocal relations that exist between students and the people and conditions of their school environments (e.g., Skinner & Belmont, 1993). We also discuss how different students, characterized by different profiles of personal and socioeconomic risks and assets, fare differentially across these **school transitions**. We focus on schools in the first section of this chapter.

In addition to schools, we also focus on community and neighborhoods as central contexts of human development. Developmental science's interest in community and neighborhood influences has evolved more recently than its interest in schools. Prior to about two decades ago, it was rare to find an article on neighborhood influences in any of the major developmental psychology journals. Since that time, there has been a dramatic rise in their prevalence. Much of this increase reflected initial concerns with children growing up in poverty. In 1987, a sociologist, William Julius Wilson, published an influential book, *The Truly Disadvantaged*, which spotlighted the potential role of neighborhood effects on human development. Since then, various interdisciplinary teams of researchers have initiated large-scale projects to study the impact of neighborhood and community forces on human development. We summarize the results of this work in the second part of this chapter.

We end the chapter with a discussion of how both school and community contexts can affect child and adolescent development through their structuring of peer groups and social networks more generally, and through affordances for participation in organized activities that impart skills, meaning, and satisfying relationships. Schools and communities have a large influence on the nature of the peers with whom individuals spend the most time. Schools also structure the nature of these interactions through grouping and instructional practices. We elaborate on these influences. We also summarize the indirect influence of schools and communities on children's and adolescents' involvement in community-based and after-school extracurricular activities. Children and adolescents also spend a great deal of time out of school. As they get older, much of this time is spent outside the home. Does it matter what they do during this time? Does participating in organized activities such as team sports, volunteer service, or faith-based organizations influence development? How? We summarize emerging theory and research evidence regarding these questions towards the end of the chapter.

SCHOOLS AS CENTRAL CONTEXTS OF DEVELOPMENT

What constitutes the developmental context of schooling? Drawing on developmental contextual perspectives (e.g., Bronfenbrenner, 1979; Ford & Lerner, 1992; Sameroff, 1983), we conceptualize the context of schooling as one that bridges between the macro-levels of society and culture that shape the practice of education from afar, and the middle levels and micro-levels of the school as an organization, its *classrooms* and the people that inhabit these settings whose daily acts of leadership, teaching, and social interaction affect children's learning and development in immediate ways (Cole, 1996). Figure 8.1 depicts the school environment as encompassing such a span of interdependent contexts spanning from the very macro (e.g., national educational policies) to the very micro (design of particular academic tasks) in relation to a given child within the school system. This descriptive model of the context of schooling is guided by seven basic assumptions derived from developmental systems thinking, as follows.

1. The context of schooling involves a complex nested social system, characterized by multiple levels of structure and organization and associated with particular kinds of processes aimed at shaping acts of leadership, teaching and learning.
2. It is the complex configurations of factors across levels, operating through both indirect and direct chains of effects involving people, resources, and educational practices, that exert important influences on children's academic, socioemotional, and behavioral development.

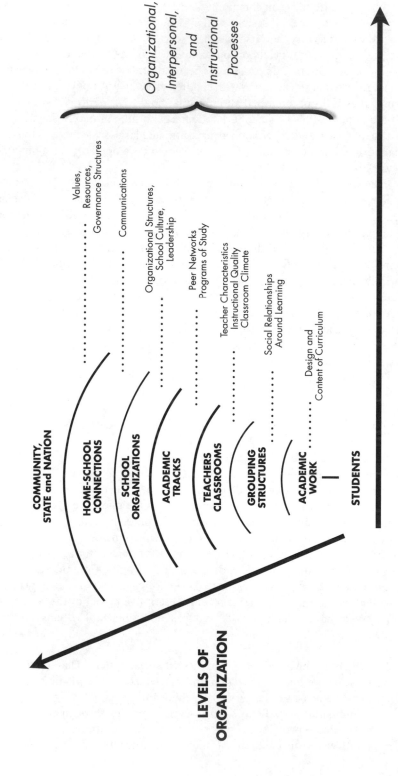

FIGURE 8.1   Model of the context of schooling.

3. The kinds of structures and processes associated with the school system "develop" from both the first-person perspective of, and a third-person perspective on, the growing child as he or she moves through the various institutions that compose the system (elementary, middle, and high schools).

4. The study of human development in contexts such as schools today requires a focus on cultural diversity and the fact that young people from different racial, ethnic, linguistic, and socioeconomic backgrounds face different kinds of barriers and opportunities with respect to education.

5. As whole persons encompassing social, emotional, moral, behavioral and cognitive–intellectual dimensions of being, humans both learn and are affected by acts of teaching and learning across multiple dimensions—not just the cognitive/intellectual one.

6. School socialization effects are mediated to some significant degree by young people's subjective perceptions of their developmental contexts as well as by their own **agentic** behavior that co-constitutes these contexts in ways that feed back to shape their own development.

7. Education in free and democratic societies is not only about enculturation and a trajectory of increasing participation of cultural ways of knowing, feeling and doing; it is also ideally about the development of qualities of mindful awareness and concern for others that allow for freedom of thought, creativity, harmonious relations among diverse peoples, and myriad forms of social and personal renewal (Roeser & Peck, 2009). In the next section, we elaborate on these assumptions.

Assumption 1: The Context of Schooling Involves Multiple Nested Levels of Organization Generically Called a "School System"

From the location of the school within macro-level government systems characterized by laws and the educational policies of the nation, state, and local school district, "down" to the micro-level of the classroom and the social dynamics between teachers and students from different ethnic and racial backgrounds, the context of schooling in human development can be conceptualized as a multilevel system characterized by an array of political, cultural, economic, organizational, interpersonal, and instructional processes that both directly and indirectly shape the development of educators and students alike (Sarason, 1990; Zalantino & Sleeman, 1975). The different levels of context of schooling can be conceptualized as moving out from the child in a series of temporally and spatially "larger" contexts with their associated processes and webs of influence (see Figure 8.1). Examples of such nested contexts and their related causal processes include the nature of academic work (Level 1); the structure of classroom activities and groups (Level 2); the quality of teachers' professional preparation, their classroom pedagogy and the **classroom climate** (Level 3); the existence of academic tracks composed of particular types of students and teachers (Level 4); the nature of school organizational structure and culture (Level 5); the presence or absence of linkages between schools and other institutions in the local community (home, community-based organizations; Level 6), and location of the school within district, state, and national governance systems (Level 7). Thus, understanding the context of schooling requires considerable interdisciplinary expertise in order to address the complexity of these seven interdependent levels of school systems and to assess the influences of such complexity on child and youth outcomes. It also requires the measurement of both "etic" and "emic" features of the context of schooling to capture both the tacit and tangible dimensions of these nested levels (Roeser, Urdan, & Stephens, 2009).

Assumption 2: Causal Chains of Influence Operate Within and Across Levels of the Context of Schooling to Affect Child and Adolescent Development

From a developmental science perspective, complex causal chains of effect across multiple levels and involving various organizational, interpersonal and instructional resources and practices are usually necessary to understand a "school effect" on student outcomes (Rutter & Maughan, 2002). For example, imagine a situation in which, due to concerns about equity in achievement among students from different socioeconomic backgrounds, a superintendent mandates that all schools in the district implement a new, equity-producing pedagogical practice called cooperative learning (district level). Principals in this district would presumably then organize their teachers to learn the new pedagogical technique (school level) and to apply it in their classrooms (classroom level). If it were implemented well, all children within classrooms in this school would be seen working in groups (group level) on fairly complex, conceptual problems for which cooperative techniques were designed (academic work level; e.g., Cohen & Lotan, 1997). Research suggests this would lead to increases in self-esteem, inter-ethnic relationships, and achievement among the children, especially for those of low ability or status (student level; Stevens & Slavin, 1995). In contrast, if the policy were implemented in a way that did not prepare the teachers adequately to implement cooperative learning techniques properly in the classroom, it could harm teachers and students by creating groups that actually reinforce preexisting status differences among students as well as peer segregation of students along socioeconomic lines. Such an outcome might affect not only students, but also teachers. It could, hypothetically, undermine their sense of **efficacy** with regard to effectively teaching students with varying abilities and statuses (Cohen & Lotan, 1997) and thereby lead to diminishing efforts to do so over time (e.g., Tschannen-Moran, Woolfolk Hoy, & Hoy, 1998).

As a second example, consider the influences on both teachers and students that the No Child Left Behind policy, originally designed to increase teacher accountability for student learning and enhance student performance in the core subjects, has actually had (e.g., No Child Left Behind (NCLB) legislation; Nichols & Berliner, 2007). Frustrated with the relatively poor performance of many of America's children compared to children in other modern societies, NCLB was put into place with the goal of holding schools, teachers, and students responsible for greater gains in learning as assessed by standardized tests. It was hoped that by enacting an accountability regime involving frequent and ongoing testing, by providing testing results to parents, and by tying the test results to a series of incentives and punishments for schools, the policy would motivate principals, teachers, parents, and students to work together towards academic improvement. Testing has now been in place since 2003, and there is little evidence of any marked improvements in the performance of America's students on standardized achievement tests in math, reading, and science (Nichols & Berliner, 2007, 2008). Why? How can a developmental science perspective help to analyze this situation? What are the complex webs and chains of causal influences that may lie behind the results of NCLB as an educational policy?

A developmental perspective on this policy focuses attention on issues of context and how well policy-mandated changes might affect the context of schooling, as well as how well those contexts meet or fail to meet the needs and goals of those involved—in this case, teachers and students (e.g., Boyce et al., 1998). For instance, there is growing evidence that mandated testing has a number of unintended negative effects on teachers and students. At the most basic level, high-stakes testing puts extraordinary pressure on teachers to teach to the test and sometimes even engage in less than ethical practices to insure student success on such tests (Berliner, 2003). That is, some teachers, under pressure, act in ways that are actually contrary to their professional ideals. The power of situations in this regard, as social psychology has repeatedly demonstrated, is considerable (Ross & Nisbett, 1981). Furthermore, mandated testing often leads to the use of particular classroom instructional methods such as drill and practice on test-like items; and that such practices, necessary to address national mandates as assessed by standardized multiple choice tests, are often at odds with teachers' own preferred instructional strategies and assessment practices (Ball, 2002; Nichols & Berliner, 2007). This discrepancy between the kinds of teaching that are mandated through the testing system and related incentives and punishments of NCLB, and the intrinsic desires of teachers themselves with regard to teaching and assessment practices, may lead to diminished motivation for teachers to do this work in the short term and the long term (Deci & Ryan, 2002). Such a dampening of teacher enthusiasm could, in turn, adversely affect students' own motivation, effort, and achievement in the classroom (Brophy, 1988). In this example, one can see how a motivational and developmental science lens on schooling can begin to disclose insights into how a well-intended mandate from the nation, state, or district can have both intended and unintended consequences for teacher and student behavior.

Assumption 3: The Structures, Processes, and Webs of Influence Associated With the Context of Schooling Change Across Development

From both a first-person and a third-person perspective, we can say that the structures and processes of the school system develop as children move into and progress through elementary school, middle school, high school, and on to post-secondary educational settings. That is, not only are children developing, but so too is the whole nature of the context of schooling that they experience over time. The inclusion of a time dimension along the bottom of Figure 8.1 emphasizes this point. For example, Eccles and her colleagues (1993) documented a cluster of grade-related changes in various organizational, social, and instructional processes in schools as students transition from elementary to middle school. They found, for instance, that school size increases, the closeness of relationships between teachers and students declines, and social comparison and competition become more prevalent motivational strategies in classrooms. These changes have been linked to declines in young people's motivation to learn and well-being as they move into and through secondary-school environments in a variety of developmental studies now (see Roeser et al., 2009). Understanding the interaction of different school features on children at different ages of development is a critical component of a developmental science approach to understanding the role of schooling in human development (Eccles & Roeser, 2009; Finn, 2006; Perry & Weinstein, 1998).

Assumption 4: The Study of Development in School Contexts is also the Study of Cultural Diversity and Issues of Equity in Education

Currently, the school-aged population in the US (ages 5 to 18 years) is growing and includes approximately 49 million individuals (Sable & Garofano, 2007). Since 1965, the number of Asian- and Latin-American immigrants to the United States has steadily increased (National Research Council, 1997). These ongoing trends, in conjunction with variations in birth rates among different ethnic populations, have had the effect of increasing the racial, ethnic, and linguistic diversity of the school-aged population in the US (National Center for Education Statistics (NCES), 2005). Racially and ethnically, the school-aged population today is approximately 57% European-American; 20% Latin-American; 17% African-American; 5% Asian-American/Pacific-Islander; and 1% Native American (Sable & Garofano, 2007). The percentage of Latin-American students increased rapidly since the early 1990s and is expected to continue to rise over the next decade. Culturally and linguistically, approximately one in five in the school-aged population is either an immigrant or the child of recent immigrants

(Garcia, Jensen, & Cuellar, 2006; Suarez-Orozco & Saurez-Orozco, 2001); and one in five speak a language other than English (mostly Spanish) in their homes (NCES, 2006). These "new Americans" are primarily from Latin America, Asia and the Caribbean—particularly Mexico, followed by the Philippines, Vietnam, the Dominican Republic, and China (Camarota & McArdle, 2003).

Racial, ethnic, and linguistic background, as well as immigrant generational status, intersects with poverty in the lives of school-aged children and adolescents. Data show that European-American and Asian-American children and adolescents are the least likely to grow up in poverty, regardless of their (immigrant) generational status. In contrast, between a quarter and a third of all African-Americans and Native Americans, and over a third of Latin Americans (especially Mexican immigrants and children of immigrants) between the ages of 5 and 18 years old grow up in poverty in the US today (NCES, 2005).

Due to factors such as poverty and its correlates, data also show ongoing achievement gaps between young people from different racial, ethnic, linguistic and socioeconomic backgrounds. Despite impressive gains over the past 30 years, for example, African-American children continue to score less well on achievement tests than their European-American counterparts (Wigfield et al., 2006). Latin-American and Native-American students have shown less educational progress over the decades compared to European-Americans and still achieve at lower levels, whereas Asian-Americans perform at levels comparable to or exceeding those of Whites (NCES, 2007). For instance, Asian-Americans are much more likely to complete advanced placement courses in math and science before high-school graduation that European-Americans, who in turn were more likely to do so than their African-, Latin-, and Native-American peers (NCES, 2007).

Of particular concern today is the educational progress of native and foreign-born children and youth of Mexican descent. Latinos, especially those with familial roots in Mexico, are the largest and most rapidly growing ethnic "minority" group in the United States. Because of their rapid growth, the aggregate level of education of Latin Americans will strongly affect the quality of the future labor force, as well as future demand for public services (Vernez, Abrahamse & Quigley, 1996). Unfortunately, immigrants from Mexico and the next generation experience downward assimilation in the United States due to factors such as low human capital, negative cultural contexts of reception, and curtailed educational attainments (Portes & Rumbaut, 2001). Mexican immigrants are the least likely of all immigrants to attend high school or college, and the same is true for the native-born same-ethnic peers (Slavin & Calderon, 2001). Furthermore, among those who do enroll in post-secondary education, Mexican-descent youth are overrepresented in those who attend 2-year community colleges (Kao & Thompson, 2003).

Differences in school resources: The issue of educational equity is an important part of the study of schooling and development.

In summary, statistics on the demographic composition of the school-aged population, as well as those on differences in educational outcomes among different sub-groups, highlight that an inquiry into the role of schools as early and long-term contexts of child and adolescent development is also an inquiry into cultural diversity in human development. Such an inquiry is also necessarily about significant and longstanding issues of inequality in educational opportunities and outcomes for young people from different racial, ethnic, and socioeconomic backgrounds. Attention to issues of cultural diversity, and issues of educational equity, are an important, if oftentimes implicit, part of the study of schooling and development (Entwisle, Alexander, & Olson, 1997).

Assumption 5: Acts of Teaching and Learning Involve and Affect "Whole Persons"

Acts of teaching and learning are inherently social, emotional, moral, behavioral, and cognitive affairs, simultaneously (Noddings, 2005a; Shulman, 2005). In short, teacher and learning involve whole persons (Roeser & Galloway, 2002). Additionally, good teaching has a lot in common with good parenting and the kind of security for exploration and learning that effective parents afford their young. In both cases, more capable adults need to provide the younger learner with both a safe social–emotional base from which they can start out and return to in times of uncertainty, and scaffolded opportunities for exploration and autonomous skill development that, when feeling safe, the young can take advantage of in the service of learning (Wentzel, 2002). This breadth of the goals in education is illustrated in Table 8.1, where we list various aims of educational training and the kinds of developmental outcomes one would expect to see in the students if these skills are taught effectively. This assumption implies that the social, emotional, and moral dimensions of the teaching and the overall context of schooling need to be made explicit and measured as key components of school and classroom environments (e.g., Jennings & Greenberg, 2009; Pianta & Hamre, 2009; Roeser, Urdan, & Stephens, 2009). In addition, the social, emotional, and moral outcomes of schooling, in addition to cognitive intellectual ones, need to be made explicit and studied in future research studies as well (e.g., Mind and Life Educational Research Network (submitted);

TABLE 8.1
Non-subject matter aims and outcomes of education involving "whole children" and "whole adolescents"

Domains and Skills	Motive Dispositions	Action Tendencies
Self-regulation		
Emotion regulation	Self-control and resilience	Behavioral inhibition and recovery
Attention regulation	Will power and stick-to-itiveness	Behavioral focus and persistence
	Self-confidence and efficacy	Behavioral initiative and persistence
Prosociality		
Social skills	Cooperation and conscientiousness	Helping and rule-abiding behavior
Conflict resolution skills	Agreeableness	Civil behavior
Mindful awareness		
Self-awareness	Personal responsibility and curiosity	Moral living and lifelong learning
Social awareness	Social responsibility and empathy	Contributions to community
Cultural awareness	Mutual respect and openmindedness	Non-discrimination/celebration of diversity
Global awareness	Universal responsibility and compassion	Contributions to peaceful world change

Noddings, 2005b; Roeser et al., 2009). In summary, the holistic conceptualization of both educational contexts and outcomes in terms of multiple domains of development (e.g., the intellectual, the social, the moral, and the emotional) is an important valued-added perspective that developmental science can add to the study of schooling and its influences on human development.

Assumption 6: Children Co-construct Their Educational Lifepaths Through School by Making Meaning of Schools in Subjective Ways and Through Their Own Agency and Characteristics

Another assumption of a developmental science approach to schooling is that the socialization effects of schooling are mediated to some degree by young people themselves through their subjective perceptions, agentic actions, and evocative characteristics. First, young people shape their own school experiences based on their subjective perceptions of the socialization context and socializing agents in schools. The assumption is that children and adolescents appraise and make meaning of their developmental contexts in terms of how well they "fit" or are "mismatched" with fundamental biological, psychological, and social needs (Boyce et al., 1998; Eccles & Midgley, 1989; Roeser, Eccles, & Strobel, 1998b). Depending on how well the instructional and interpersonal features of school contexts "fit with" or are "mismatched" with the needs of students at various ages, and to the extent that students perceive such fits or mismatches, the theory predicts either positive or negative changes in motivation, well-being and behavior, respectively (Eccles & Roeser, 2009). Of course, students' perceptions are biased or shaped by their previous domain-relevant experiences, so this form of memory-appraisal of present-action sequence forms one way in which students "create" their own developmental life-space.

Another mechanism by which students contribute to their own development in school is through their intrinsic curiosity, competence motivation, exploratory behaviors, and **agency** in general (Deci & Ryan, 2002). Organisms are active in their own development from the very beginnings of life, and to talk about school effects without an understanding of the transactional nature of such effects is to explore only half of the picture. The notion of person–environment transactions in the determination of achievement and educational lifepaths more generally remains a challenging but important theoretical approach to the study of schooling (e.g., Roeser et al., 2002b).

A third way in which students contribute to their own development in schools is through their evocative characteristics, including both physical (e.g., attractiveness) and personality-based (e.g., extraversion) characteristics, which, by either intentionally or unintentionally eliciting certain kinds of reactions from others, can contribute to the nature of the socializing context and its reciprocal effects on the person (e.g., Caspi & Roberts, 2001).

Although there is a rather large research literature examining the unidirectional effects of "contexts on kids," relatively few studies attend to understanding the conjoint role that students, their perceptions, their own agentic acts, and their evocative characteristics, in conjunction with the nature of their physical and social environments in school, play in their own learning and development there (e.g., Skinner & Belmont, 1993). Understanding such person–environment contributions to educational lifepaths is a clear goal of a developmental science perspective on schooling (Eccles & Midgley, 1989, Roeser & Peck, 2003; Rutter & Maughan, 2002). As Boyce and colleagues (1998) put it with regard to the study of development and psychopathology—and the same applies to the study of development and education—the next phase of research needs to attend to both "the actual *transactions* between children and contexts and the *transduction* of contextual influences into pathways of biological mediation" (p. 143; emphasis in original).

Education in free and democratic societies is not only about enculturation and a trajectory of increasing participation of cultural ways of knowing, feeling and doing; it is also ideally about the development of qualities of mindful awareness and concern for others.

Assumption 7: Education is About Cultural Ways of Knowing *and* Qualities of Awareness

In addition to socializing young people in culturally sanctioned ways of thinking and feeling (i.e., *civic education*) and scaffolding their development of knowledge and disciplined ways of knowing (i.e., *subject-matter education*), we propose that public education in free and democratic societies necessarily ought to be in places that educate for mindful awareness and related volitional modes of attending, thinking, feeling, perceiving, acting, and interacting. The means by which the public education system can do this we term *contemplative education* (Roeser & Peck, 2009). Whereas the cultivation of civic-mindedness and the acquisition of subject-matter knowledge are essential outcomes of education related to sociocultural participation, the cultivation of awareness and willful self-regulation are preconditions for deep learning, freedom of thought, creativity, harmonious social relationships, and myriad forms of personal and social renewal.

In the next section, we describe the various levels and associated processes that comprise the context of schooling (see Figure 8.1) and provide some examples of research linking these various levels and processes to aspects of children's academic, social–emotional, and behavioral development. After this, we summarize what we know about developmental changes in these various aspects of schooling as children progress through different school types (elementary, middle, and high school), as well as how such changes influence aspects of children's and adolescents' development.

LEVELS OF THE CONTEXT OF SCHOOLING

Level 1: Academic Work

The nature of the academic work students are asked to do is at the heart of their school experience. At a fundamental level, the nature of school work affects not only what children may come to know about themselves and the world, but also their capacities to pay attention (e.g., listening to stories), their interests and passions, and their morals and ethics (Dewey, 1902; Doyle, 1983). Two key aspects of academic work that can influence students' emotional, cognitive, and moral development are (a) the content of the curriculum in terms of its intellectual substance and its consideration of global social–historical realities (e.g., Noddings, 2005a, 2005b; Partnership for 21st Century Skills, 2008; Zins, Weissberg, Wang, & Walberg, 2004); and (b) the design of instruction in terms of scaffolding knowledge development, and also in terms of its capacity to cultivate interest, meaningfulness, challenge, and deep cognitive, emotional, and behavioral engagement with the material (Blumenfeld, 1992; Blumenfeld, Mergendoller, & Swartout, 1987).

Both the content and the design of academic tasks can be conceptualized in terms of their relative attunement or mismatch with the developmental needs and capacities of students of a particular age and social background, and the needs of society at a particular time in history. Some evidence supports the notion that academic work that is meaningful to the developmental and historical reality of children's experience promotes motivation to learn and helps to "bond" young people with the institution of school (e.g., Burchinal, Roberts, Zeisel, & Rowley, 2008; Roeser, Eccles & Sameroff, 2000). Curricula that represent the "voices," images, role models, and historical experiences of traditionally underrepresented groups may be particularly important for helping students from such groups to identify with school and success in school, and for students from the majority cultural group to develop a broader understanding of the diversity, as well as the experiences and contributions, of minority groups in history (Ball, 2002; Fine, 1991; Graham & Taylor, 2002; Romo & Falbo, 1996; Valencia, 1991). The challenge of providing curricula that address developmentally and historically meaningful topics to a diverse and large school population is a central and ongoing challenge in education in the United States and many developed nations today (Meier, 2008). For instance, studies show that boredom in school, low interest, and perceived irrelevance of the curriculum are associated with diminished engagement and learning and, for some, can be part of the reason for withdrawing from school (Assor, Kaplan, & Roth, 2002; Eccles, 1983; Finn, 2006; Jackson & Davis, 2000; Larson & Richards, 1989; National Research Council and Institute of Medicine (NRC/IOM), 2004; Newmann, Wehlage, & Lamborn, 1992).

Although there exist many innovative curriculum movements today that are reinvigorating the teaching of subject matter (e.g., the Facing History and Ourselves Project: Sleeper & Strom, 2006), we want to draw attention to one emerging movement that aims to provide a new kind of curriculum into public school education: the **social–emotional learning** movement (SEL; Elias et al, 1997). SEL programs focus on teaching content and skills related to learning in five core "non-subject matter" domains: self-awareness, social awareness, responsible decision-making, self-management, and relationship management (Collaborative for Academic, Social, and Emotional Learning, 2003). Reviews and meta-analyses of social and emotional learning programs delivered in classrooms provide evidence that SEL programs can prevent substance abuse (Gottfredson & Wilson, 2003), antisocial behavior (Wilson, Gottfredson, & Najaka, 2001) and mental health problems (Durlak & Wells, 1997). Furthermore, a recent meta-analysis (Durlak, Weissberg, Taylor & Dymnicki, in press) examined the outcomes of over 250 experimental studies of social and emotional learning programs for all students. Of the 27 programs that examined indicators of academic achievement at the post-intervention period, students receiving SEL programs showed significant and meaningful improvements on achievement test performance; the effect was equivalent to approximately a 10 percentage point gain on achievement testing. Further, program students were significantly more likely to attend school, less likely to be disciplined for misbehavior, and received better grades. Thus, evidence is accruing to suggest that by broadening the academic curriculum to include social–emotional learning, dividends for behavioral, social–emotional, and intellectual development can be achieved.

In addition to the "what is taught" in schools, the "how things are taught," including the design of academic tasks, also can influence children's motivation, engagement, and learning (Ball, 2002; Blumenfeld, 1992; Deci & Ryan, 2002; Fredricks, Blumenfeld, & Paris, 2004). Choosing materials that provide an appropriate level of challenge for a given class, designing learning activities that require diverse cognitive operations (e.g., opinion, following routines, memory, comprehension), structuring lessons so they build on each other in a systematic fashion, using multiple representations of a given problem, and explicitly teaching children strategies that assist in learning (e.g., asking oneself if one has understood what was just read) are but a few of the design features that can "scaffold" learning and promote interest, engagement and learning. Work on the role of interest in learning, engagement, and intrinsic motivation highlights the important role of the design of academic tasks in this regard (Renninger, 2000). Increased interest is associated with greater engagement in the task and higher levels of mastery of the material (Fredricks et al., 2004; Renninger, 2000; Wigfield, Eccles, Schiefele, Roeser, & Davis-Kean, 2006). Even more importantly, interesting tasks increase intrinsic motivation to do well (Deci & Ryan, 2002) and increase the likelihood that students develop a strong personal identity as a committed school student (Eccles, 2009). Thus, at this level of analysis, one can see that the nature of academic work plays a central role in a chain of related educational outcomes, including task interest to task engagement, to mastery and learning, to intrinsic motivation to learn, to identification of oneself as a learner who is bonded to school.

From a developmental perspective, there is evidence that the content and design of academic work may not change over time in ways that reflect the increasing cognitive sophistication, diverse life experiences, and identity-linked motivational needs of children and adolescents as they move from the elementary into the secondary-school years (Eccles, 2009; Wigfield et al., 2006). As one indication, middle-school children report the highest rates of boredom when doing schoolwork, especially passive work (e.g., listening to lectures) and in particular classes such as social studies, mathematics, and science (Larson, 2000; Larson & Richards, 1989). Academic work becomes less, rather than more, complex in terms of the cognitive demands as children move from elementary to junior high school (Juvonen, 2007; Juvonen, Le, Kaganoff, Augustine, & Constant, 2004). It may be that declines in children's motivation during the transition to secondary school in part reflect academic work that lacks challenge and meaning commensurate with children's cognitive and emotional needs (Eccles & Midgley, 1989). For instance, Roeser, Eccles, and Sameroff (1998) found that curricular meaningfulness, as perceived by middle-school students, was a positive predictor of longitudinal changes in their valuing of and commitment to school from the beginning to the end of middle school. The findings showed that the more meaningful students found their work in English, science, and social studies, the more they valued their education and learning over time. Efforts at middle-school reform also support this hypothesis: Adolescents' motivation to learn is maintained and does not decline when secondary schools introduce more challenging and developmentally and historically meaningful academic work (Eccles, Wigfield, & Schiefele, 1998; Jackson & Davis, 2000; Lee & Smith, 2001).

In sum, although research in this area is still relatively sparse, some evidence shows that as children develop cognitively and emotionally, and as they begin to take a greater interest in understanding the world and their identity within that world, schools often provide repetitive, low-level tasks that are unimaginative in content and design. This seems particularly true in an age in which learning is increasingly seen as synonymous with performance on multiple choice standardized tests. The nature of these changes in academic work is likely to undermine motivation in most children, as well as to exacerbate motivational and behavioral difficulties in those children who had trouble with academic work earlier in their development during elementary school (see Roeser, Eccles, & Freedman-Doan, 1999). In addition, although more evidence is needed here as well, there is some indication that teaching children about social and emotional issues may be an important new addition to classroom curriculum in the twenty-first century.

LEVEL 2: GROUPS AND ACTIVITY STRUCTURES

The next level of the context of schooling that can influence child and adolescent development concerns the social structure of learning activities in the classroom. Classroom instruction is delivered through different grouping and activity structures, including whole-group instruction, individualized instruction, and small-group instruction. Groups are often formed on the basis of children's ability level; alternatively, groups can be formed from students representing a diverse array of abilities brought together in a cooperative work arrangement (Oakes, 2005; Stevens & Slavin, 1995). Thus, some classroom grouping strategies are associated with individualistic activity structures, in which individuals work alone and their behavior is independent of others; other foster social comparison in which there is competition; and still others foster collaboration and cooperation. In these ways, different classroom social structures communicate quite different implicit messages about relationships with others, the goals of learning, and children's abilities—messages that, in turn, influence children's perceptions of students' own academic competence and social acceptability, as well as their perceptions of the characteristics of their classmates (Roseth, Johnson, & Johnson, 2008).

Different group structures also elicit different patterns of teacher behaviors and peer group associations. For instance, research has shown that the use of either whole-class instruction or within-class ability groups can highlight ability differences among students, can lead to increased social comparison by students and teachers, and can make salient differential teacher treatment of high and low achievers in the classroom (Oakes, 2005; Wigfield et al., 2006). When this happens, activity structures in the classroom are serving to reinforce rather than disrupt achievement status hierarchies, differentiated competence beliefs between low and high achievers, and friendship selection patterns based primarily on similarities in academic abilities. Given the equation of achievement with intelligence and worth in American society (Covington, 2000), low-ability children often show diminished self-perceptions of competence and feelings of self-worth in classrooms where status differences are made salient by the kinds of activity structures and teaching strategies described above (Oakes, 2005; Rosenholtz & Simpson, 1984). Research also indicates that children positioned as "low ability" in the classroom are more likely perceived by their classmates as less desirable friends than their high-achieving peers (Karweit & Hansell, 1983). In this case, activity structures are exerting influences on the formation of social networks or patterns of social isolation among students. We say more about these processes later when we discuss ability **tracking**.

The use of collaborative or cooperative groups is a popular alternative to either whole-group, ability-grouped, or individualized instruction at the elementary-school level. Stevens and Slavin (1995) concluded that cooperative learning techniques in which students work in small groups and receive rewards or recognition based on group performance lead to increases in student achievement, self-esteem, and social acceptance among students of different social statuses and ethnic backgrounds. With proper instruction in the social skills necessary for group work, cooperative groups can provide numerous "niches" for students with different strengths to participate in the learning process, can increase the amount of social support and reinforcement available in the classroom for learning complex material, can increase contact among students of different abilities and, thus, can foster a broader network of friendship patterns in the classroom and fewer instances of social isolation (Roseth et al., 2008).

From a developmental perspective, the use of whole-group and within-class ability-grouped instruction increases in frequency as children progress from elementary to middle and high school. Within-class ability grouping in reading is widespread even in the early grades; the use of between-class ability grouping in mathematics, English, and science classes increases considerably as children move into and through secondary school (Feldlaufer, Midgley, & Eccles, 1988; Eccles, et al., 1993, 1998; NRC/IOM, 2004). At the same time, the use of both individualized instruction and cooperative grouping declines. This is a good example of a change in educational environment that is mismatched with the needs of youth. A recent meta-analysis of over eight decades of research on approximately 17,000 early adolescents from 11 different countries showed that higher achievement and more positive peer relationships were associated with cooperative rather than competitive or individualistic activity structures in the middle-school classroom (Roseth et al., 2008). We discuss the implications of these grade-related changes in activity structures further below when we address the transition into secondary school.

LEVEL 3: TEACHERS, INSTRUCTION, AND CLASSROOM CLIMATE

The next level of the context of school that is important to consider in developmental research is that of teachers and their beliefs and pedagogical practices, as well as the social and instructional atmosphere of the classroom they create through their presence and practice. With regard to the kinds of teacher beliefs that are consequential for their pedagogical decisions, practices, and interpersonal behavior in the classroom, teachers' professional identity beliefs about themselves as a teacher, as well as their pedagogical beliefs about the kinds of teaching practices that work best in motivating and supporting learning, are important (Roeser, Marachi, & Gehlbach, 2002a). Due in part to these beliefs and the actions they motivate and regulate, the hypothesis is that teachers create particular kinds of classroom learning environments for and with students. Dimensions of learning environments have historically been conceptualized in terms of the order and management of the classroom, the nature of social relationships among peers and between teachers and students, and the instructional climate in terms of ways of motivating learning, providing instruction and support for student learning, and giving feedback to students (Moos, 1979). In the next section, we provide examples of research on key processes operating at the level of teacher identity and pedagogical beliefs, instructional practices, and the classroom climate as a whole that have, independently and interdependently, been shown to affect children's and adolescents' development in school.

Teacher Professional Identity and Pedagogical Beliefs

Social cognitive and sociocultural approaches to the study of teaching and learning have demonstrated the important role that teachers' beliefs play in shaping their pedagogical decisions and strategies in the classroom (Calderhead, 1996; Shulman, 2005). The kinds of beliefs that have been found to motivate teachers' instructional decisions and interpersonal behavior in the classroom include their efficacy beliefs regarding their teaching and interpersonal capabilities, their instructional goals and styles of managing classrooms and motivating students, and the kinds of expectations and beliefs that teachers may have about individual—or even groups of—students they teach, and their views about what it means and takes to "learn" something. More recently, scholars have begun to examine how teachers' social–emotional competencies are also key determinants of their behavior in the classroom (Jennings & Greenberg, 2009).

Efficacy for teaching beliefs.   Teachers' efficacy beliefs regarding their ability to perform the core tasks of teaching—managing a classroom, teaching for understanding and assisting students who need additional support, and maintaining emotional balance while doing these—are key processes affecting not only teaching-related behaviors in the classroom, but also the regulation of emotion and well-being. Tschannen-Moran, Woolfolk Hoy, and Hoy (1998), for instance, found that teachers' efficacy beliefs were positively related to their investment of effort in teaching, their persistence in working with students with academic difficulties, and their willingness to experiment with new teaching strategies. Other studies have shown that when teachers hold high generalized expectations for student learning and students perceive these expectations, students achieve more and experience a greater sense of competence as learners (Ashton, 1985; Brophy, 2004; Eccles et al., 1998; Lee & Smith, 2001; Midgley, Feldlaufer, & Eccles, 1989; NRC/IOM, 2004, Weinstein, 1989). Unfortunately, as we discuss later, the proportion of teachers with a high sense of teacher efficacy decreases as children move from elementary into secondary school. In addition, the proportion of teachers with a strong sense of teaching efficacy is lower in schools that educate a predominance of poor and minority children (Darling-Hammond, 1997; Eccles et al., 1993; Juvonen, 2007; Juvonen et al., 2004; NRC/IOM, 2004; Roeser & Midgley, 1997).

With respect to emotional well-being and regulation, Roeser and Midgley (1997) found that elementary-school teachers who felt more efficacious with regard to their ability to successfully teach all of their students also reported less stress in dealing with the emotional–behavioral problems that some of their students displayed in their classrooms. This makes sense because efficacy indexes confidence to be successful at a task given current resources and supports (Bandura, 1994), whereas stress results when environmental challenges overcome individuals' ability to cope given current resources and supports (Folkman & Lazarus, 1984). Self-efficacy beliefs and subjective stress go hand-in-glove.

Role beliefs.   Teachers' beliefs about what their professional role entails are another important component of their professional identities. Two common role definitions that teachers identify with are that of the "academic instructor" (oriented toward teaching academic content) and that of the "socializer" (oriented toward addressing children's social–emotional and behavioral needs; fosterer of the "good citizen"). In a study of 98 elementary-school teachers, Brophy (1988, 2004) found that an endorsement of the "instructor" role was critical for teachers' ability to ensure student achievement, but that some of the most effective teachers were those who blended an academic with a socializing focus. In addition, he found that teachers who saw themselves primarily as "instructors" responded much more negatively to those students who were under-achievers, academically unmotivated, or disruptive during learning activities than to the other students in the class; in contrast, "socializers" responded most negatively to either the hostile aggressive and defiant students or the children who thwarted the teachers' efforts to form close personal relationships. In this study, one can see how different role beliefs are associated with both instructional outcomes and interpersonal processes in the classroom, insofar as role beliefs seem to index the kinds of sensitivities teachers have to being "triggered" emotionally in the classroom.

Differential expectations for student success.   Another set of teacher beliefs that have been studied in relation to student outcomes is the differential expectations that teachers have regarding the likelihood of success of different students within the same classroom. Most of the studies linking differential teacher expectations to either their own behaviors or to their students' achievement and motivation have been done under the rubric of teacher expectancy effects. The issue is whether teacher expectancies about different students' prospects for success, and the related differential patterns of student interaction that can flow from these expectancies, translate into levels of student achievement that "live up" or "live down" to the teachers' initial expectancies (Rosenthal, 1974). In developmental science, this kind of "self-fulfilling prophecy" is an example of how hypothesized "interactional continuity," operating here through differential teacher expectancies and related behavior that reinforces students' present ability level, can influence students' achievement trajectories in school over time (Caspi & Roberts, 2001).

The history of research in this area has been controversial and contested, but it appears that teacher-expectancy effects depend on whether teachers structure activities differently for, and interact differently with, high- and low-expectancy students, as well as on whether the students perceive these differences (Jussim, Eccles, & Madon, 1996; Weinstein, 1989). A great deal of the work on teacher-expectancy effects has focused on differential treatment related to gender, ethnic group, and/or social class. Most of this work has investigated the potential undermining effects of low teacher expectations on girls (for mathematics and science), on minority children (for all subject areas), and on children from lower social class family backgrounds (again for all subject areas) (Eccles & Wigfield, 1985; Jussim et al., 1996; Parsons, Kaczala, & Meece, 1982; Rists, 1970).

Weinstein (1989) and her colleagues, for instance, found that both high- and low-achieving students report perceiving differential teacher treatment of students on the basis of ability in most elementary-school classrooms. High achievers are seen by students of all ability levels as receiving higher expectations, more opportunities to participate in class, and more choice about work, whereas low achievers are seen as receiving more negative feedback, more control, and more feedback concerning work completion and following rules. The greater the perceived differential treatment in a classroom, the greater is the impact that teachers' expectations will have on achievement and children's self-perceptions of competence (Weinstein, 1989). Observational studies of teacher behavior validate these perceptions: Teachers often do treat high and low achievers differently in these ways (Brophy, 1988; NRC/IOM, 2004).

Other work, however, suggests that teacher expectancy effects may not be as negative as once believed. For the effect to be of great concern, one needs to demonstrate that it has a negative biasing effect (i.e., that teachers' expectations lead to changes in motivation and performance over time beyond what would be expected given knowledge of the characteristics of the specific students; Jussim et al., 1996; Jussim, Palumbo, Chatman, Madon, & Smith, 2000; Madon et al., 2001). Evidence for such negative biasing effects is minimal in the short run. Much of the association between teacher expectations for individual students and subsequent student motivation and performance reflects the "accurate" association between teacher expectations and student characteristics, such as prior achievement levels and behavioral patterns (Jussim et al., 1996; Madon et al., 2001). In addition, not all teachers respond to their expectations with behaviors that undermine the motivation and performance of the low-expectancy students. Some teachers respond to low expectations with increased instructional and motivational efforts for particular students and succeed in increasing both student motivation and learning (Goldenberg, 1992). Nonetheless, small but consistent teacher expectancy effects over time can have a large cumulative effect on students' motivation and achievement (Jussim et al., 1996; Smith, Jussim, & Eccles, 1999), particularly if these effects begin in kindergarten and the first grade (Entwisle & Alexander, 1993). Finally, Jussim et al. (1996) found that girls, low-socioeconomic status students, and minority students are more susceptible to these effects than European American, middle-class boys.

Weiner (1991) and Graham (1991) studied a slightly different aspect of within-classroom variations in the teacher–student interaction linked to teacher expectancy effects. Weiner (1991) hypothesized that teachers' emotional reactions may convey their expectations to students. Specifically, it was hypothesized that teachers may display pity in providing negative feedback to those students for whom they have low expectations. In contrast, it was hypothesized that teachers would display anger in providing negative feedback to those students for whom they have high expectations. Such a difference in effect could underlie teacher expectancy effects. Graham (1991) investigated this hypothesis by manipulating bogus instructors' emotional reactions to experimental participants' (learners') performance on a laboratory task: "Instructors" who showed pity and offered excessive help, for example, produced "learners" who either attributed their "failures" to lack of ability and lowered their expectations for success (Graham & Barker, 1990) or engaged in a variety of behaviors (e.g., making excuses for their poor performance) designed to maintain the learners' sense of self-worth (Covington, 1992). Similarly, Parsons, Kaczala, and Meece (1982) demonstrated that, when praise is used in a way that conveys low teacher expectations (i.e., patronizing praise for low-level successes), it undermines junior high-school students' confidence in their abilities as well as their expectations for success. In contrast, when overt criticism conveys high teacher expectations (i.e., when the teacher uses public criticism only with high-performing students to protect the low-performing students' egos), high rates of criticism are associated with higher than predicted confidence in one's ability.

Researchers such as Steele and Aronson (Aronson & Steele, 2005; see Nisbett, 2008, for a review) have linked perceptions of differential expectations, particularly for African-American students, to school disengagement and disidentification (the separation of one's self-esteem from all forms of school-related feedback). Steele and Aronson argue that when African-American students believe that teachers and other adults have negative **stereotypes** of African-American children's academic abilities and this belief is made salient, the African-American students' performance anxieties increase and their academic confidence decreases, which, in turn, lead them to disidentify with the school context to protect their self-esteem. It is interesting that other studies using the same theoretical notions and experimental techniques have shown that Asian-American students believe that teachers and adults expect them to perform very well and that belief leads Asian students to perform better on tests when their ethnicity is made salient (Shih, Pittinsky, & Ambady, 1999). Furthermore in very similar studies, Shih and her colleagues have found that Asian-American females perform better on tests of math ability when their Asian identity is made salient and worse on the same tests when their female identity is made salient (Ambady, Shih, Kim & Pittinsky, 2001; Shih et al., 1999).

Researchers interested in the relatively poor academic performance of adolescents from some ethnic groups have suggested another classroom-based experience linked to teachers' expectations, beliefs, and prejudices: **discrimination**, specifically, the impugning of one's intellectual ability based on ethnicity, race, or gender (Brody et al., 2006; Chavous, Rivas-Drake, Smalls, Griffin, & Cogburn, 2008; Fordham & Ogbu, 1986; Garcia Coll et al., 1996; Graham & Taylor, 2002; Ruggiero & Taylor, 1995; Roeser et al., 1998a; Wong, Eccles, & Sameroff, 2003). Two types of discrimination have been discussed: (1) anticipation of future discrimination in the labor market, which might be seen as undermining the long-term benefits of education (Fordham & Ogbu, 1986), and (2) the impact of daily experiences of discrimination in school and other settings that can affect mental health and academic motivation (Chavous et al., 2008; Sellers, Caldwell, Schmeelk-Cine & Zimmerman, 2003; Roeser et al., 1998a; Wong et al., 2003). Both types have been shown to adversely affect the development of ethnic-minority adolescents.

For instance, in a 2-year longitudinal analysis of African-American early adolescents across seventh to ninth grade of junior high, Wong et al. (2003) found that adolescents who perceived more incidents of racial discrimination with teachers, school staff, and classmates in Grade 8 also showed declines in their academic self-concept and teacher-reported grades and increases in their self-reported psychological distress for Grade 7 to Grade 9. Furthermore, they found that African-American youth who had a positive connection to their ethnic group showed less of a decline in school motivation, achievement, and well-being over time in relation to level of perceived discrimination. In this sample, anticipated future discrimination appeared to motivate the youth to do their very best so that they would be maximally equipped to deal with future discrimination. Similarly, in a study of Puerto Rican 13- to 14-year-old early adolescents, Szalacha et al. (2003) found that adolescents who perceived more incidents of racial discrimination with classmates, store clerks, teachers, and neighbors also reported lower global self-worth. Several researchers have pointed out that the impact of experiences of racism may be particularly salient during middle childhood and early adolescence as children begin to solidify their ethnic identities and are often exposed to more heterogeneous student populations in terms of ethnic, religion, and other social categories (Rowley, Burchinal, Roberts, & Zeisel, 2008; Wong et al., 2003).

In a large study of Asian, Mexican, and Central and South American immigrant high-school students growing up in major metropolitan areas of the United States, Portes and Rumbaut (2001) found that a majority of youth in their sample reported feeling discriminated against at school and in other settings. The major sources of this perceived discrimination were European-American classmates, teachers, and neighbors. Such experiences were associated with greater feelings of depression among the youth in the study.

Rosenbloom and Way (2004) also studied the dynamics of discrimination in multiracial urban high schools. Asian-American students reported harassment by peers, whereas African-American and Latin-American students were more likely to report discrimination by adults such as teachers. The authors linked the experiences of discrimination among different groups: when teachers preferred Asian-American students and saw "model minority," the African-American and Latino adolescents resented this differential teacher treatment and thus harassed the Asian-American students.

One interesting finding is beginning to emerge for this work on discrimination: it appears that when youth have a strong positive ethnic identity, it has protective effects against the potential aversive effects of daily experiences of ethnic discrimination. Several researchers have found that those African-American youth who have strong and positive ethnic identities are much less negatively affected by experiences of racial discrimination than their less strongly identified peers (Burchinal et al., 2008; Chavous et al., 2003; Harris-Britt, Valrie, Kurtz-Costes, & Rowley, 2007; Wong et al., 2003). Thus, educating for diversity and redressing discrimination are two goals that educators might pursue in their efforts to reduce the persistent ethnic group differences in school achievement.

Pedagogical Goals

Another key set of cognitions that are associated with teachers' classroom behavior concerns their beliefs about the purposes or goals of instruction and learning in school (e.g., Covington, 2000). **Achievement goal theory** is a social–cognitive approach to the study of motivated behavior in achievement settings that posits that cognitive *purposes* or goals organize the quality of individual's attention, emotion, cognition, and consequently, behavior during teaching or learning (Ames, 1992; Maehr & Midgley, 1996). Ames (1992) has used goal theory to describe how mastery- or performance-oriented classrooms can emerge from the goals that teachers hold implicitly about the purposes of learning and related ways of teaching and motivating learning. Specifically, Ames linked teachers' pedagogical goals to the ways that teachers use time in their classrooms; distribute authority; recognize, group and evaluate students; and design classroom tasks. She focused on two particular achievement goals that teachers can espouse that then shape their pedagogical practice—a relative ability or a mastery goal orientation (Roeser, Midgley, & Urdan, 1996). These two goal orientations are hypothesized to lead to two different patterns of instruction.

The first pattern, called a "relative ability-goal orientation," is one in which teachers believe that the goal of learning is demonstrating one's abilities, especially relative to others. Grouping by ability, differential rewards for high achievers, public evaluative feedback, academic competitions, and other practices promoting the notion that academic success means out-performing others and proving one's superior ability are practices employed by such teachers that are consistent with this goal orientation (Ames, 1992; Midgley, 2002). Unfortunately, most youth, by definition, are not "the best" and thus may not receive rewards and recognition in classrooms that emphasize relative ability. We know that in ability-oriented classrooms, children are more likely to use low-level strategies to learn, experience more anxiety and negative affect, and devote attentional resources to making themselves look smarter or avoiding looking dumber than other students rather than learning the material (Ames, 1992; Midgley, 2002). Urdan, Midgley, and Anderman (1998) found that fifth grade teachers' reports of their performance-oriented approaches to instruction (e.g., helping students see how their performance compares to others, pointing out students who do well academically as models for other students) were positively associated with students' reported use of self-handicapping in the classroom (purposefully withdrawing effort in order to protect self-worth). This study and others suggest that children who lack confidence in their academic competence are particularly vulnerable in such environments (Covington, 2000). Although few studies have looked at this, it seems plausible that learned helpless responses to academic failure, the avoidance of engaging in work, negative emotional experiences, and stereotype threat effects are more likely to beset low-ability students in ability-focused environments (Dweck, 2002; Roeser, 2004).

On the other hand, some teachers hold the view that mastery, self-improvement, and progressive skill development are the valued ends of learning in the classroom. These beliefs "show through" in terms of greater efforts to acknowledge individual effort and improvement regardless of a child's current ability level, provisions of choice and collaborative work in which social comparison and status differences are de-emphasized, and more teacher talk to students about the idea that mastering new content, learning from mistakes, and continuing to try despite setbacks are more highly valued hallmarks of learning and being successful (e.g., Turner et al., 2002). For example, using observational data, Meece (1991) found that upper elementary teachers in classrooms rated by students as more mastery-oriented than other classrooms were more likely to promote meaningful learning, adapt instruction to the developmental levels and interests of students, support student autonomy and peer collaboration, and emphasize the intrinsic value of learning. Other studies have shown that ninth grade teachers' self-reported mastery-oriented approaches to instruction (e.g., stressing to students the importance of understanding work and not just memorizing it, making an effort to provide students with work that has meaning in their everyday lives) were positively associated with students' aggregate perceptions of their classrooms as mastery-oriented. These aggregate perceptions were related, in turn, to lower incidences of student-reported disruptive behavior in the classroom. Mastery-oriented pedagogical practices have also been linked to reductions in students' concerns about their ability relative to peers and the feelings of self-consciousness, anxiety, or disenfranchisement that can accompany such concerns (Assor, Vansteenkiste, & Kaplan, 2009; Maehr & Midgley, 1996; Midgley, 2002; Murayama & Elliot, 2009; NRC/IOM, 2004; Roeser et al., 1996). In addition, mastery-focused classrooms can foster children's use of deeper processing strategies to learn, positive affective around learning, and more of an intrinsic, task-mastery-oriented motivation approach to learning in the students (Covington, 2000).

For developmental changes in teachers' professional identity, beliefs, and goals, grade-level changes have been documented for all of these types of teacher beliefs. For example, grade-level differences in teachers' efficacy beliefs regarding their ability to teach and influence all of the students in their classes have been found. Midgley, Feldlaufer, and Eccles (1989a) showed that teachers in junior high-school environments feel less efficacious than their colleagues who teach in elementary-school settings. These results are not surprising due to the larger number of students, the lack of extended contact with students during the day, and the content-focused educational training that secondary teachers experience in comparison to their elementary-school colleagues. Nonetheless, this decline in teacher efficacy can have a major impact on child development, particularly for the low-performing children. As discussed more fully later in this chapter, students' experiencing a decline in their teachers' sense of efficacy as they transition into secondary school is associated with declines in aspects of motivation and school engagement. Early adolescents need role models who provide supportive feedback about their ability to be successful academically. If teachers do not feel particularly efficacious in relation to their teaching, their students are likely to lose confidence in their ability to learn.

There are also grade-related differences in teachers' role beliefs. Compared to teachers in elementary-school settings, teachers in secondary-school settings see their role more in relation to content instruction than to socialization (McPartland, 1990). This difference likely reflects two factors: First, secondary teachers' education is more focused on particular content areas than on child development. Second, aspects of teachers' work in secondary schools such as departmentalization by academic discipline and large student loads also promote a focus on academic content issues rather than individual mental health concerns. Similarly, Roeser et al. (2002a) found that secondary-school teachers are less likely to endorse the notion that students' mental health concerns are part of the teacher role than elementary-school teachers. An important implication of such findings is that, at a time when adolescents need academic and socioemotional guidance and support from both parents and non-parental adults (i.e., during early adolescence), teachers may be less likely to provide such support given the number of students they teach, their educational training, and the size of secondary schools (Eccles et al., 1993). Although elementary teachers seem sensitive to both internalized and externalized distress in children (Roeser & Midgley, 1997), secondary-school teachers may fail to notice children who are experiencing internalized distress and having difficulty adjusting to the transition to middle or high school. This seems especially true of children who struggle emotionally but continue to perform at an acceptable academic level (Juvonen et al., 2004; Lord, Eccles, & McCarthy, 1994). Consequently, because secondary teachers have so many students, they may not be able to be sensitive to mental health issues until these problems severely undermine academic performance or disrupt classroom activities. This creates a hole in the "safety net" available to children at a time when they are in particularly acute need of adult support and guidance (Simmons & Blyth, 1987).

Grade-level differences have also been identified for teachers' endorsement of mastery versus ability goals and related pedagogical practices. For example, Midgley and her colleagues (Midgley, 2002; Midgley, Anderman, & Hicks, 1995; Roeser et al., 1998a; Roeser, Midgley, & Maehr, 1994) found that, as children progress from elementary to middle school, both teachers (in reflecting on their own work environments and the learning environments for students in the school) and students (in reflecting on their school environments) report that their school environment is more focused on competition, relative ability, and social comparison than on learning, task mastery, and individual improvement. These changes occur during a time when adolescents are particularly vulnerable to social comparisons with peers. They are beginning to differentiate ability from effort and also are starting to view ability more as a "fixed capacity" than an incremental skill. Not measuring up to one's peers in terms of academic ability in school settings that increasingly emphasize ability differences is very likely to undermine academic motivation and well-being among students generally and vulnerable students in particular (Roeser & Eccles, 2000; Roeser et al., 1998b).

Finally, from the students' perspective, experiences of ethnic discrimination increase with grade level as well. Greene, Way, and Pahl (2006) found that African-American and Asian-American adolescents report increasing levels of discrimination from adults as they move through high school. African-American students also report an increasing amount of discrimination from peers during this same time period, suggesting that for African-American students, experiences of discrimination in general increase as they progress through high school. Interestingly, the Latino and Puerto Rican students in the same study did not show these same patterns; if anything these groups reported less ethnic discrimination as they moved through high school (Burchinal et al., 2008).

In summary, teachers' beliefs about themselves as a teacher and about the teaching role, about the students they teach, and about the goals and purposes of learning are all important factors that constitute a "psychological environment" that accompanies the pedagogical practices and forms of interaction related to these teacher beliefs. As such, these beliefs represent one important factor that can shape student outcomes in school indirectly through effects on teacher behavior as students move through the school system. In addition, many teacher beliefs "change" from the perspective of the developing child in ways that may be contraindicated with respect to the kinds of supports and learning environments young people need during adolescence. Next, we turn to the qualifications and quality of instruction that teachers deliver as a related set of factors that are consequential for child development at the teacher/classroom level of analysis.

Teacher Qualifications and Quality of Instruction

Teacher qualifications, in terms of their educational preparation and training, as well as teachers' ability to deliver high-quality classroom instruction, are the next school context factors we discuss that are important for child and adolescent development in schools.

Teacher qualifications. Research on teacher qualifications and student achievement outcomes has revealed that the qualifications of the teachers that children encounter, especially in the early years of school when foundational literacy and numeracy skills are the focus of the curriculum, have substantial effects on students' academic growth and subsequent educational trajectories through high school (Hill, Rowan, & Ball, 2005; Rowan, Correnti & Miller, 2002). In a review of evidence from three different national data sources, Darling-Hammond (1999) concluded that teacher preparation and certification are by far the strongest correlates of student achievement in reading and mathematics, even after taking account of students' socioeconomic and sociolinguistic background. The importance of teacher qualifications for student achievement has now been demonstrated in 46 countries that participated in the Trends in International Mathematics and Science Study (TIMMS) in 2003: Greater teacher qualifications were associated with increased mathematical achievement across nations (Akiba, LeTendre, & Scribner, 2007). In addition, evidence shows that teachers with greater qualifications also are more likely to use reform-oriented teaching practices in middle-school math classrooms (Smith, Desimone, & Ueno, 2005). Thus, it appears that teacher preparation and qualifications can improve instructional quality, which in turn can affect student achievement.

Darling-Hammond (1999) reviewed evidence showing that knowledge of the subject matter to be taught is essential to good teaching, but also that the returns of subject matter expertise in terms of improvements in student learning diminish as that expertise grows well beyond the curriculum to be taught. That is, beyond some basic mastery of the curricular content to be taught, other teacher qualifications such as the complexity of a teachers' pedagogical content knowledge (e.g., knowing how to teach a particular subject), developmental knowledge (e.g., knowing how to teach a particular subject to students of a particular age), and skill in bringing these to bear collectively on instruction matter more for student outcomes. For instance, research on effective teaching has shown that the most effective teachers are those who are flexible and able to adapt their teaching approaches to fit the needs of different students and the demands of different instructional goals or content (Doyle, 1985).

In addition, Darling-Hammond (1999) noted the troubling tendency of poor and ethnic-minority children to be over-exposed to "out-of-field" teachers teaching their subject matter classes. For instance, in Grades 5 through 8, it is estimated that 70% of poor and ethnic-minority adolescents have "math" teachers who do not possess even a college minor in math or a math-related field; the percentage is 50% during the high-school years (Peske & Haycock, 2006). Research among high-school students has demonstrated the negative achievement-related impact of having an out-of-field teacher on mathematics in particular (Goldhaber & Brewer, 2000). Research shows that not only are large proportions of the teaching staff in poor schools made up of non-credentialed or unqualified teachers, but substitutes also regularly fill the places of full-time teachers in these schools, there is little support for English-language learners (ELLs), and staff turnover is high (Darling-Hammond, 1997, 2000).

ELLs for whom English is a second language (ESL students) are also disproportionately exposed to unqualified teachers in US schools. Approximately 75% of ELLs in US schools speak Spanish (Fashola, Slavin, Calderon & Duran, 2001). Integrated language and subject matter courses that emphasize both receptive skills in listening and reading and production skills in speaking and writing are needed to assist ESL students in mastering both English and the subject matter (August & Hakuta, 1998; Valdes, 2001). Resistance to native language programs nationally and a shortage of teachers who are proficient in English and Spanish and who know how to prepare content instruction for ELL students hamper these efforts nationwide (Fashola et al., 2001).

In summary, teacher qualifications are an important source of educational inequality in US schools generally and the educational lifepaths and so-called "achievement gaps" involving poor and ethnic-minority children from particular racial/ethnic groups (African-, Latin-, and Native-American youth in particular). Although the NCLB Act of 2002 included a provision to redress inequality in teacher qualifications in high-concentration poor and ethnic-minority schools, such provisions did little to remedy the inequities. The lack of effect NCLB had on redressing real inequalities in teacher qualifications has been attributed in part to the relatively low standards for what constituted a highly qualified teacher in NCLB, and in part to the relatively low resources that were dedicated to teacher training by the law (Darling-Hammond, 2007; Peske & Haycock, 2006).

Instructional quality. As noted above, closely related to teacher qualifications is the quality of instruction that teachers deliver in the classroom. Research on instructional quality in both developed and developing nations has shown that it matters for students' learning and achievement (Heyneman & Loxly, 1983; Pianta & Hamre, 2009). Given the research reviewed above linking teacher qualifications and student outcomes, this research also suggests that instructional quality and teaching practices are important mediators between teacher qualifications and student achievement (e.g., Smith et al., 2005).

Although valid assessments of instructional quality remain a complex challenge in this area of research, recent research has shown that instructional quality is often mediocre in US public schools, especially if the students are poor (Pianta, Belsky, Houts & Morrison, 2007; Quint, 2006). Mashburn et al. (2008), for instance, in a study of over 2000 children enrolled in public pre-school programs, found that the quality of teachers' instruction predicted gains in academic and language skills. These authors also found that teacher quality was lower in classrooms with more than 60% low-income children, when teachers lacked a degree in early childhood education, and when they held less child-centered and more adult control-oriented beliefs concerning child development (Pianta et al., 2005).

Similarly, a study of elementary schools showed that teachers in high-poverty and high-minority schools are more likely to use certain kinds of pedagogical practices more than others, including the exercise of strong control over students and the limiting of their use of constructivist teaching practices, because, in part, they believe that poor children lack the inner control necessary to play a responsible role in their own learning (Solomon, Battistich, & Hom, 1996). Furthermore, because a substantial minority of low-income students are perceived as arriving to school with social–emotional and behavioral problems that compromise their readiness to learn (Adelman & Taylor, 1998), their teachers are more likely to experience feelings of burden in relation to their level of emotional needs (Roeser & Midgley, 1997); feel a need to distance themselves from their students emotionally (Solomon et al., 1996); and feel less efficacious as a teacher (Bandura, 2006). The use of heavy extrinsic inducements and controlling, teacher-centered forms of instruction in these environments may be a function of teachers' feeling overwhelmed and inefficacious in such settings and also the relative inexperience and high turnover of teachers in high-poverty, high-minority schools (Darling-Hammond, 1997, 2007). As these selected research studies indicate, at both elementary- and secondary-school levels, improvements in instructional quality remain a critical challenge for reform efforts (e.g., Pianta & Hamre, 2009; Quint, 2006). However, improvements in instructional quality often require other kinds of contingent reforms to be maximally effective (see Quint, 2006). For instance, Greenwald, Hedges, and Laine (1996) found that teachers' education, ability, and experience, in conjunction with being in small schools and lower teacher–student ratios, were the constellation of factors that mattered most for aggregate achievement at the school and district levels.

Changes in teacher qualifications and instructional quality.   Very little research has looked at how the nature of teacher qualifications or instructional quality changes over time from the perspectives of students as they progress through the school system. This represents one fruitful area for future research on human development in the contexts of schools.

Teacher–Student Relationships, Climate and Management

The nature of the classroom climate, referring to the general social-relational atmosphere of the classroom and its basis in teacher–student relationships, as well as how the classroom is organized and managed, is an important context feature at this level of analysis that can affect child and adolescent development.

Classroom climate and teacher–student relationships.   Research suggests that the quality of teacher–student relationships in terms of instrumental and social support, trust, and caring, and the fostering of a sense that all students are valued members of a learning community who belong in the classroom, is essential for the development of students' academic motivation, engagement, learning, and social–emotional well-being in school (Burchinal et al., 2008; Deci & Ryan, 2002; Eccles et al., 1998; Goodenow, 1993; NRC/IOM, 2004; Pianta, 1999; Roeser et al., 1996; Wentzel, 2002). Perceptions of teacher social support and sense of belonging and membership in a learning community are especially important precursors to individuals' motivation to learn (Osterman, 2000). Sense of belonging is perhaps especially critical for young people who must traverse significant ethnic and racial, socio-economic, and sociolinguistic borders to feel fully part of a school in which middle-class, majority cultural norms often predominate (Davidson & Phelan, 1999; Garcia-Reid, Reid, & Peterson, 2005; Lucas, Henze, & Donato, 1990). Correlational studies with adolescents show that students' perceptions of caring teachers enhance their feelings of self-esteem, school belonging, and positive affect in school (NRC/IOM, 2004; Roeser & Eccles, 1998; Roeser et al., 1996). In a naturalistic longitudinal study, Pianta et al. (2008) found that emotional supportive interactions in pre-school predicted trajectories of reading and math development across elementary school, though the associations were small. In sum, emotionally supportive teachers are a critical foundation for motivation to learn. The importance of relationships for reinvigorating education and reengaging disenfranchised students is at the heart of many of the most innovative approaches to school reform over the past couple of decades (Brown, 1997; Connell, 2003; Quint, 2006; Schaps, 2003).

Several researchers are studying how classroom climate is related to students' emotions in the classroom, and in turn their motivation and learning (Frenzel, Goetz, Ludtke, Pekrun, & Sutton, 2009; Frenzel, Pekrun, & Goetz, 2007; Goetz, Frenzel, Hall, & Pekrun, 2007; Goetz, Frenzel, Pekrun, Hall, & Ludtke, 2007; Goetz, Pekrun, Hall, & Haag, 2006; Pekrun, Goetz, Titz, & Perry, 2002). These researchers argue that emotional reactions to experiences in the classroom have a large impact on student engagement and learning; and have separated individual emotional reactions to classroom experiences from shared emotional reactions. Findings have revealed that shared emotional reactions across students within the same classroom are influenced by shared perceptions of teachers' enthusiasm and enjoyment (Frenzel et al., 2007). Furthermore, these shared positive and negative emotions were linked to the general level of achievement in the classroom: As a group, students in high-achieving classrooms reported more positive emotions (pride and enjoyment) and less extreme negative emotions (anxiety, shame, and hopelessness). Interestingly, at the individual level, there was a negative association between the average achievement level of the class and the individual student's positive emotional reactions during the class: Individual students reported more positive emotions if they were in a lower-achieving than a higher-achieving classroom, in part because they felt less pressure and a greater sense of control over their own achievements in the lower-achieving classroom (Pekrun, Goetz, & Frenzel, 2007).

Developmental changes in classroom climate and teacher–student relationships. Declines in perception of emotional support from their teachers and in a sense of belonging in the classrooms are quite common as students move from elementary into secondary schools (Burchinal et al., 2008; NRC/IOM, 2004; Roeser et al., 1994; Wigfield, Byrnes, & Eccles, 2006). This shift is particularly troublesome in our highly mobile society in which teachers represent one of the last stable sources of non-parental role models for adolescents. In addition to teaching, teachers in mobile societies such as the United States can provide guidance and assistance when socioemotional or academic problems arise. This role is especially important for promoting developmental competence when conditions in the family and neighborhood cannot or do not provide such supports (Eccles, Lord, & Roeser, 1996; NRC/IOM, 2004; Simmons & Blyth, 1987). Research on the importance of adult mentors in adolescents' lives, particularly in high-risk and very mobile communities, supports this point of view (DuBois, Holloway, Valentine, & Cooper, 2002). Although the positive effects are quite weak, adult mentors do provide stability for their mentees, and their mentees fare better in terms of school achievement, staying out of trouble, and maintaining positive mental health.

Classroom management. Work related to classroom management has focused on two general issues: orderliness/predictability and control/autonomy. With regard to orderliness and predictability, the evidence is quite clear: Student achievement and conduct are enhanced when teachers establish smoothly running and efficient procedures for monitoring student progress, providing feedback, enforcing accountability for work completion, and organizing group activities (e.g., Darling-Hammond & Bransford, 2005; Lee, 2000; Pintrich & Schunk, 2003). Unfortunately, such conditions are often absent, particularly in highly stressed and underfunded schools with inexperienced teachers (Darling-Hammond, 1997; Darling-Hammond & Bransford, 2005; NRC/IOM, 2004).

Research on autonomy versus control is equally compelling. Many researchers believe that classroom practices that support student autonomy are critical for fostering intrinsic motivation to learn and for supporting socioemotional development during childhood and adolescence (Deci & Ryan, 2002; Grolnick, Gurland, Jacob, & Decourcey, 2002; Ruthig et al., 2008). Support for this hypothesis has been found in both laboratory and field-based studies (Deci & Ryan, 2002; Grolnick & Ryan, 1987; NRC/IOM, 2004; Patall, Cooper, & Robinson, 2008; Roeser et al., 1998a). Pekrun and his colleagues have argued that students' perceptions of being in control of their academic outcomes lead to positive emotions, which, in turn, lead to increased engagement (e.g., Pekrun, 2006).

Other researchers have shown how student autonomy support needs to co-occur with other classroom management and instructional features such as adequate structure, orderliness, and relevant curriculum for its benefits on student motivation, engagement, and learning to be fruitful (Assor et al., 2002; Skinner & Belmont, 1993). The issue appears to be one of finding a proper balance between autonomy and structure (Deci & Ryan, 2002). This need for teachers to balance autonomy support and scaffolding and structure during learning activities is further complicated by the fact that the right balance between adult-guided structure and opportunities for student autonomy changes as the students mature: Older students desire more opportunities for autonomy and less adult-controlled structure, but teachers often are less trustful of older students and therefore look to control them more (Eccles et al., 1993). To the extent that students do not experience developmentally appropriate changes in the balance between structure and opportunities for autonomy as they pass through the K-12 school years, their school motivation should decline as they get older (Eccles et al., 1993).

Developmental changes in classroom management. Contrary to what one might expect to happen given the increasing developmental maturity of the children, secondary-school teachers, compared to elementary-school teachers, use more control-oriented strategies, enforce stricter discipline, and provide fewer opportunities for student autonomy and decision-making in the classroom (Midgley, 2002; Midgley & Feldlaufer, 1987; Midgley, Feldlaufer, & Eccles, 1988). Apparently, as children move from elementary to junior high-school environments, their teachers believe that they are less trustworthy and need to be controlled more. To explain this pattern, Willower and Lawrence (1979) suggested that, as children grow older, bigger, and more mature, and as peer subcultures become stronger during adolescence, teachers are increasingly likely to see students as a threat to their authority and thus respond with more control and discipline. Stereotypes about adolescents as unruly and out of control are likely to reinforce such beliefs and strategies. High-profile school violence cases likely increase teachers' concerns about their own safety as well as the safety of other school personnel and students, leading to even tighter controls over high-school students' behaviors (Elliott, Hamburg, & Williams, 1998; Lee & Smith, 2001). Finally, the demands of secondary-school environments, in which teachers have to deal with many students, may predispose them to use more controlling strategies as a way of coping with so many students.

Practices that provide less support for autonomy are likely to be especially problematic at early adolescence when children express an increased desire for opportunities to make choices and have their voices expressed in the classroom (Assor et al., 2009; Eccles et al., 1993). This may be particularly true for students who, because they are poor or have a history of academic or behavioral problems, are placed in low-ability tracks and classrooms where controlling strategies are particularly prevalent (Oakes, 2005). We discuss this further later. In summary, the set of research studies presented provides an example, collectively, of how complex causal chains across different levels of the school system, in this case involving organizational factors (large student loads), teacher beliefs (e.g., adolescents need to be controlled), and related teacher practices (less student autonomy in the classroom), can impact students' motivation, learning and achievement.

Motivational person–environment fit. The work on understanding group differences in achievement and achievement choices as a function of person (students)–environment (school context) configurations is another example of an attempt to identify a broad set of classroom characteristics that can affect child and adolescent motivation and development over time. Many investigators have suggested that students are maximally motivated to learn in situations that fit well with their interests, current skill levels, and psychological needs (e.g., Csikszent-mihalyi, Rathunde, & Whalen, 1993; Eccles et al., 1993; Krapp, Hidi, & Renninger, 1992; NRC/IOM, 2004). Research on female participation and achievement in mathematics in the classroom is one example of this approach. There are sex differences in adolescents' preference for different types of learning contexts that likely interact with subject area to produce sex differences in interest in different subject areas (Eccles, 1994, 2009; Hoffmann, 2002; Wigfield et al., 2006). Females appear to respond more positively to math and science instruction if taught in a cooperative or individualized manner rather than a competitive manner, if taught from an applied or person-centered perspective rather than a theoretical or abstract perspective, if taught using a hands-on approach rather than a book-learning approach, and if the teacher avoids sexism in its many subtle forms. The reason given for these effects is the student–classroom fit between the teaching style, the instructional focus, and females' own values, goals, motivational orientations, and learning styles. The few relevant studies support this hypothesis (Eccles & Harold, 1993; Hoffmann, 2002). If such classroom practices are more prevalent in one subject area (e.g., physical science or math) than another (e.g., biological or social science), one would expect sex differences in motivation to learn and subsequent pursuit of courses in these subject areas. The good news is that math and physical science do not have to be taught in these ways; more girl-friendly instructional approaches can be used. When they are, girls, as well as boys, are more likely to continue taking courses in these fields and to consider working in these fields when they become adults (Eccles, 1994, 2009).

Variations on this theme of **person–environment** fit being important in understanding classroom effects on students include research studies on aptitude by treatment interactions in the determination of student achievement (e.g., Roeser et al., 2002b) and theories stressing cultural match or mismatch as one explanation for group differences in school achievement and activity choices (e.g., Fordham & Ogbu, 1986; Suarez-Orozco & Suarez-Orozco, 2001). For example, Valencia (1991) concluded that a mismatch of the values of the school and the materials being taught contributed to the poor performance and high dropout rates among the Latino youth in the high school he and his colleagues studied. Dehyle and LeCompte (1999) made a similar argument in their discussion of the poor performance of Native-American youth in traditional middle-school contexts (see also Burchinal et al., 2008). The misfit between the needs of young adolescents and the nature of junior high-school environments is another example of these person–environment fit dynamics (Eccles et al., 1993; Konings, Brand-Gruwel, van Merrienboer, & Broers, 2008).

Summary of Teacher and Classroom Level of Analysis

In this section, we summarized studies of classroom- and teacher-related factors that suggest that development is optimized when students are provided with challenging tasks in a mastery-oriented environment that provides good emotional and cognitive support, meaning-ful material to learn and master, and sufficient support for their own autonomy and initiative. Furthermore, there is some evidence that quality instruction is related to teacher preparation and qualifications. Connell and Wellborn (1991) and Deci and Ryan (2002), in their **Self-Determination Theory**, suggested that humans have three basic needs: to feel competent, to feel socially attached, and to have autonomous control in one's life. Further, both sets of authors hypothesized that individuals develop best in contexts that provide opportunities for each of these needs to be met under the guidance of more-expert, qualified, and caring individuals. The types of classroom characteristics that emerge as important for both socioemotional and intellectual development characteristically seem to provide opportunities for students to meet these three basic needs and thereby to flourish more in their development. In addition, in their **Expectancy Value Theory** of achievement choices, Eccles and her colleagues argue that teacher and classroom characteristics like those discussed in this section influence the students' motivation to engage in learning through their impact on the students' expectations for success and the subjective value they attach to engaging in the learning activities provided by the teacher. We will see examples of such influences throughout this chapter.

LEVEL 4: ACADEMIC TRACKS AND CURRICULAR DIFFERENTIATION

The next level of influences is that of academic tracks or "curriculum differentiation policies." These terms refer to the regularities in the ways in which schools structure sets of learning experiences for different types of student (Oakes, 2005). The process of providing different educational experiences for students of different ability levels is a widespread yet very contro-versial practice in American schools.

Tracking takes different forms at different grade levels. It includes within-class ability grouping for different subject matters or between-class ability grouping in which different types of children are assigned to different teachers. Within-classroom ability grouping for reading and mathematics is quite common in elementary school. In the middle- and high-school years, between-class tracking becomes both more widespread and more broadly linked to the sequencing of specific courses for students bound for different post-secondary-school trajectories (college prep, general, vocational). Differentiated curricular experiences for stu-dents of different ability levels structure experience and behavior in three major ways: First, tracking determines the quality and kinds of opportunities to learn the child receives (Oakes, 2005); second, it determines exposure to different peers and thus, to a certain degree, the nature of social relationships that youths form in school (Fuligni, Eccles, & Barber, 1995); and, finally, it determines the social comparison group students use in assessing their own abilities and developing their academic identities (Marsh, Trautwein, Ludtke, Baumert, & Koller, 2007; Marsh, Trautwein, Ludtke, & Brettschneider, 2008).

Despite years of research on the impact of tracking practices, few strong and definitive answers have emerged (Fuligni et al., 1995). The results of these studies vary depending on the outcome assessed, the group studied, the length of the study, the control groups used for comparison, and the specific nature of the context in which these practices are mani-fest. The research situation is complicated by the fact that conflicting hypotheses about the likely direction and the magnitude of the effects of tracking emerge depending on the theoretical lens one uses to evaluate the practice. The strongest justification for tracking practices derives from a person–environment fit perspective. Children will be more moti-vated to learn if their educational materials and experiences can be adapted to their current competence level. There is some evidence consistent with this perspective for children placed in high-ability classrooms, high within-class ability groups, and college tracks (Fuligni et al., 1995; Gamoran & Mare, 1989; Kulik & Kulik, 1987; Pallas, Entwisle, Alexander, & Stluka, 1994).

The results for children placed in low-ability and non-college tracks do not confirm this hypothesis. By and large, when long-term effects are found for this group of children, they are usually negative primarily because these children are typically provided with inferior educational experience and support (e.g., Jackson & Davis, 2000; Lee & Smith, 2001; Pallas et al., 1994; Vanfossen, Jones, & Spade, 1987). Low track placements have been related to poor attitudes towards school, feelings of incompetence, and problem behaviors both within school (non-attendance, crime, misconduct) and in the broader community (drug use, arrests) as well as to educational attainments (Oakes, 2005). But whether academic tracks promote such outcomes or reflect preexisting differences remains a matter of considerable debate. It is also important to note that these negative effects result from the stereotypically biased implementation of ability-grouping programs. A different result might emerge for the low-competence students if the teachers implemented the ability tracking program more in keeping with the goals inherent in the person–environment fit perspective—that is, by providing *high*-quality instruction and motivational practices tailored to the current competence level of the students.

Social comparison theory leads to a different prediction regarding the effect of ability grouping and tracking on one aspect of development: ability self-concepts. People often compare their own performance with the performances of others to determine how well they are doing (Marsh, Chessor, Craven, & Roche, 1995; Marsh et al., 2007; Reuman, 1989). They typically conclude they are doing well, and that they have high ability, if they are doing better those around them. In turn, this conclusion should bolster their confidence in their ability to master the material being taught.

Ability grouping should narrow the range of possible social comparisons in such a way as to lead to declines in the ability self-perceptions of higher-ability individuals and to increases in the ability self-perceptions of lower-ability individuals. Marsh and his colleagues refer to this effect as the big fish in a small pond effect (BFSPE). Evidence supports this prediction. For example, Reuman (1989) found that being placed in a low-ability mathematics class in the seventh grade led to an increase in self-concept of mathematics ability and a decrease in test anxiety; and conversely, being placed in a high-ability mathematics class led to a decrease in self-concept of mathematics ability. Similarly, Marsh et al. (1995) found that being placed in a gifted and talented program led to a decline over time in the students' academic self-concepts. Additionally, Marsh and his colleagues have shown consistent evidence that attending a more academically elite high school leads to reductions in students' academic ability self-concepts that persist over time (Marsh et al., 2007). These results have led Marsh and his colleagues to conclude that academic tracking comes at a cost to confidence in one's academic abilities for academically able students. Similarly, Frenzel, Pekrun, and their colleagues have found that individual students experience slightly more negative emotions (anxiety, hopelessness, and shame) and slightly fewer positive emotions (enjoyment and pride) when they are in higher achieving classrooms (Pekrun et al., 2007).

Whether such reductions in students' academic self-confidence and increases in negative emotions actually undermine these students' academic achievement remains to be tested. The main educational argument for having such elite tracks and schools is that such educational environments provide more challenging and engaging educational experiences for academically able and gifted students—experiences that should lead to increased learning, performance, and motivational engagement. Consistent with this perspective, classic achievement motivation theorists predict, and have found supporting evidence, that individuals with a high need for achievement are most motivated to do their best work when the odds of success are at about .5 (Atkinson, 1957). If this is true then lowering the academic self-concepts of high-achieving students should actually increase their motivation to do their very best. The impact of these changes on other aspects of development likely depends on a variety of individual and contextual factors. If the net result of the BFSPE is to bring both low and high performers closer to the .5 probability level, then ability grouping should have a positive impact on all of the students in both ability groups who are highly motivated and a negative impact on all of the individuals in both ability groups who have low motivation to succeed. Theories focused on the importance of challenging material in a supportive environment suggest an increase in motivation for everyone provided that the quality of instruction leads to equally challenging material for all ability levels. Conversely, if the social comparison context also increases the salience of an entity view rather than an incremental view of ability (earlier discussion of teacher's views about intellectual ability; Dweck, 2002), then the decline in ability self-concepts of the high-ability individuals might lead them to engage in more failure-avoidant and ego-protective strategies.

Yet another way to think about the impact of ability grouping on development is in terms of its impact on peer groups: Between-classroom ability grouping and curricular differentiation promotes continuity of contact among children and adolescents with similar levels of achievement and engagement with school. For those doing poorly in school, such practices can structure and promote friendships among students who are similarly alienated from school and are more likely to engage in risky or delinquent behaviors (Dryfoos, 1990). The "collecting" of children with poor achievement or adjustment histories also places additional burdens on teachers who teach these classes (Oakes, 2005).

Tracking and ability grouping can also lead to the concentration of children with similar behavioral vulnerabilities. For instance, Kellam, Rebok, Wilson, and Mayer (1994) found that proportions of moderately to severely aggressive children ranged from 7–8% to 63% among two first-grade classrooms in the same elementary school. They found that these differing rates were a direct result of between-class ability grouping policy. As a result of this policy, children in these two classrooms were exposed to very different environments: one in which aggression was deviant (only 7–8% of students were aggressive) and one in which it was pretty much the norm (63% aggressive students). It seems likely that aggressive behavior would not necessarily lead to peer rejection in the classroom with high rates of aggression. On the contrary, in such an environment, aggression might confer status and social rewards among peers and thus be reinforced. By placing children with similar vulnerabilities in the same environment, both the reinforcement of negative behavior and promotion of friendships among similarly troubled children are more likely. This phenomenon has been well documented by Dishon and colleagues (Dishon, Poulin, & Burraston, 2001) in their intervention work with aggressive children and adolescents. They have found that aggressive and delinquent behavior often increases rather than decreases when aggressive youth are put together in an intervention group designed to decrease problem behavior.

In summary, between-class ability grouping and curriculum differentiation provide examples of how school policy, teacher beliefs and instruction, and student characteristics can all conspire to create maladaptive transactions that perpetuate poor achievement and behavior among low-ability children. Such a hypothetical sequence is depicted in Figure 8.2. The placement of many low-ability children in lower academic track classrooms may cause some teachers to feel overwhelmed and inefficacious. This might translate into poor instructional quality, a lowering of expectations for student success, and use of controlling strategies on the part of such teachers. These factors, in turn, could promote student disengagement (e.g., Kagan, 1990), which then feeds back into the teachers' beliefs and practices. Eventually, academic failure of certain low-ability children can result from these reciprocal processes. The BFSPE studied by Marsh and his colleagues demonstrates that there can also be disadvantages of tracking for high-ability students.

Another important and controversial aspect of curriculum differentiation involves how

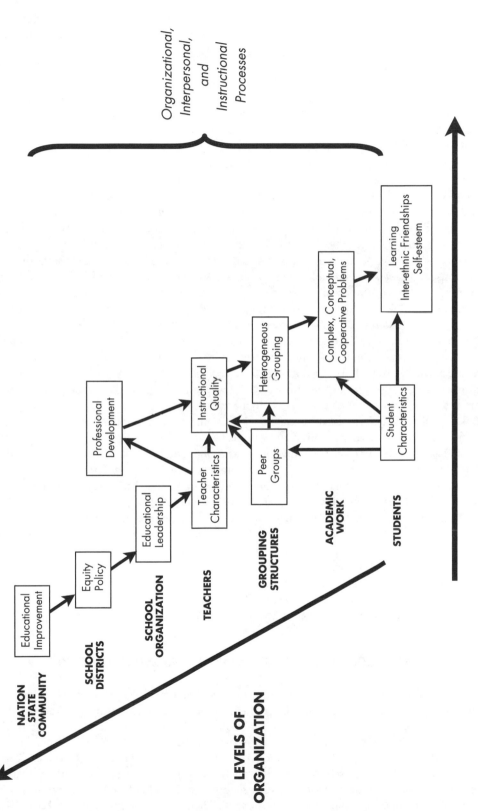

FIGURE 8.2 Causal chains of influence on child/adolescent development within a school system: The hypothesized case of using heterogeneous grouping and complex instruction as a means of increasing educational equity.

students get placed in different classes and how difficult it is for students to move between class levels as their academic needs and competencies change once initial placements have been made. These issues are important both early in a child's school career (e.g., Entwisle & Alexander, 1993) and later in adolescence when course placement is linked directly to the kinds of educational options that are available to the student after high school. Dornbusch (1994) described the impact of tracking on a large, ethnically diverse sample of high-school students in northern California. Analyzing the data course by course, Dornbusch found that 85% of his sample stayed in the same track during high school—there was little mobility. Furthermore, Dornbusch found that many average students were incorrectly assigned to lower track courses. This mistake had long-term consequences for these students, in effect putting them on the wrong path toward meeting the requirements for getting into California's higher educational system. Of particular concern was the fact that these youth and their parents, who were more likely to be of lower socioeconomic background and African- or Latin-American, were not informed of the potential consequences of course decisions made by school personnel during the child's early high-school career. In this case curricular differentiation practices and the absence of school–home communication exerted a profound influence on the lifepaths of these average students who, though able, were placed in lower-ability classrooms in high school.

Similar concerns have been raised about the marginalization and segregation of ESL students on middle- and high-school campuses (Valdes, 2001). There is also some evidence that students with limited English proficiency who are otherwise capable are placed in lower track classes (see Kao & Thompson, 2003). ESL programs are often housed on the periphery of regular school campuses and often fail to provide real opportunities for interaction with native English speakers. Furthermore, similar to the misassignment of African-American and Latino students to, and lack of mobility out of, low academic tracks (e.g., Dornbusch, 1994), there is some evidence that ESL students often get reassigned (downwardly) to ESL programs following school transition events even though they may have graduated from such programs into mainstream classes in their previous schools (Valdes, 2001).

A different perspective on tracking and educational equity comes from national studies using multilevel modeling analyses to examine how between-school differences in the extent of tracking and other reforms relate to student motivation and achievement. For instance, in a study of middle schools, Lee and Smith (1993) found that the extent to which middle schools had engaged in restructuring practices (less departmentalization, more team teaching, more heterogeneous grouping, etc.), students were more engaged in learning and learned more, and there was a more equitable social distribution of these outcomes. Studies of religious schools and high schools have shown similar results—the more that all students in a school are expected to learn a core curriculum, the less inequality there is in student achievement by social background factors (Bryk, Lee, & Holland, 1993; Lee & Bryk, 1989; Lee, Croninger, & Smith, 1997a; Lee & Smith, 1993, 1995; Lee, Smith, & Croninger, 1997b).

LEVEL 5: SCHOOLS AS ORGANIZATIONS WITH CULTURES

Schools also function as formal organizations that are characterized by various "cultures"—including a management/work culture for teachers and a learning culture for students. The effective schools research unequivocally established that features of the internal life of the school culture matter for student outcomes above and beyond students' initial social background characteristics (Good & Weinstein, 1986; Rutter & Maughan, 2002). As Lee (2000) summarized it: "Effective schools have strong leadership focused on academic outcomes. They closely monitor student work. In such schools, teachers hold high expectations for all students. Their social environments are purposeful. Their climates are orderly" (p. 126). These aspects of the school culture impact children's intellectual, socioemotional, and behavioral development. Below we review works on school organizational factors including fiscal resources and student characteristics (Lee, Bryk, & Smith, 1993; Lee & Smith, 2001); school size (Wyse, Keesler, & Schneider, 2008); the social, moral, and academic culture of the school as a whole (e.g, Roeser et al., 2009); unsupervised spaces in a school (Astor, Benbenishty, Zeira, and Vinokur, 2002; Bryk et al., 1993; Goodenow, 1993; Lee & Smith, 2001; Roeser et al., 2009); and school-wide practices such as school start and end times (Carskadon, 1990, 1997) and the yearly school calendar (Alexander, Entwisle, & Olson, 2007).

School Resources

School resources have been studied in various ways with respect to school, including in terms of per-pupil expenditures, the qualifications of the workforce (reviewed above), and the characteristics of the student body itself in terms of social capital. All of these forms of resources can affect developmental outcomes in schools (Greenwald et al., 1996). For instance, the schools attended by African- and Latin-American students generally, as well those attended by rural students in at least a dozen states, are schools with particularly high concentrations of impoverished students (Adelman & Taylor, 1998; Johnson & Strange, 2005). In terms of financial resources, these schools receive fewer state and local resources in terms of per-pupil expenditures than schools in more wealthy communities (Darling-Hammond, 2000; Johnson & Strange, 2005). This is due to the fact that K-12 education is largely funded at the state and local levels. Thus, the resources of a school or district are inextricably linked to where people live and the property wealth of their neighbors. Those in poor communities tend to go to schools with fewer resources, and those in affluent communities tend to go to well-resourced schools (Sawhill, 2006). Although the direct effect of per-pupil expenditures on achievement remains unclear, what is becoming clearer is how the lack of resources for hiring and retaining qualified teachers is a major way that under-resourced schools affect child and adolescent development through the qualifications of the teachers they hire (e.g., Loeb, Darling-Hammond, & Luczak, 2005).

In addition to the resource–teacher qualifications link, other studies have examined how the "mix" of socially disadvantaged students or those with significant emotional–behavioral difficulties has been associated with the educational outcomes of all students in a given school (Rutter & Maughan, 2002). In general, as the ratio of students who are socially disadvantaged goes up in a school, its aggregate achievement goes down. The aggregate behavioral histories of a school's student body also matter. LeBlanc, Swisher, Vitaro, and Tremblay (2007) found that between-school variation in the proportion of students with histories of disruptive problems predicted subsequent rates of classroom behavior problems among high-school students. A variety of mechanisms, including those of peer influences on motivation understood in the context of tracking, and social environments in which maladaptive norms develop, have been proposed to account for these influences (e.g., Rutter & Maughan, 2002).

School resources in terms of adequate materials, a safe environment, and qualifications of the teaching staff are important for students' learning and well being. School district level variations in such school resources are a major contributor to the continuing inequity in educational outcomes for several minority groups in the United States. Thirty-seven percent of African-American youth and 32% of Latin-American youth, compared to 5% of European-American and 22% of Asian-American youth, are enrolled in the 47 largest city school districts in this country; in addition, African-American and Hispanic youth attend some of the poorest school districts in the United States. Twenty-eight percent of the youth enrolled in city schools live in poverty, and 55% are eligible for free or reduced cost lunch, suggesting that class may be as important as (or more important than) ethnicity in the differences in achievement that emerge. Teachers in these schools report feeling less safe than teachers in other school districts, dropout rates are highest, and achievement levels at all grades are the lowest (Council of the Great City Schools, 1992; Lee & Smith, 2001). Finally, schools that serve these populations are less likely than schools serving more advantaged populations to offer either high-quality remedial services or advanced courses and courses that facilitate the acquisition of higher-order thinking skills and active learning strategies. Even adolescents who are extremely motivated may find it difficult to perform well under these educational circumstances.

School Size

Early studies of schools focused primarily on objective characteristics of schools such as school size, teacher–student ratios, number of books in the library, and per-pupil expenditures (Barker & Gump, 1964). School size emerges as one of the most important of these structural characteristics. Barker and Gump (1964) proposed that smaller secondary schools afford young people various opportunities not available in larger schools, opportunities that foster engagement and achievement. Such opportunities included (a) closer relationships between teachers and students, (b) greater adult monitoring of and responsibility for student progress; and (c) a particularly favorable roles-to-people ratio with respect to school extracurricular activities and the need for many students in the school to participate to fulfill those roles. By affecting these mediating processes, school size was hypothesized to affect student outcomes. Subsequent research has consistently verified these hypotheses.

For instance, in a national probability study of high-school students, Crosnoe, Johnson, and Elder (2004) found that students' attachment to school in general and to their teachers in particular was significantly negatively correlated with school size. Lee and Loeb (2000), in an urban Chicago sample of 264 (K-8) schools, found that in smaller schools (<400 students), teachers took greater responsibility for fostering students' learning and students showed greater 1-year gains in mathematics achievement.

Positive relationships, opportunities to participate in the life of the school, and closer monitoring by teachers are key mechanisms in translating school size into greater student bonding with school, motivation to learn and engagement (e.g., Hawkins, 1997; Hawkins, Kosterman, Catalano, Hill & Abbott, 2008). In a national study of high schools, Lee and Smith (1995) found that the greater the school size, the less positive were students' attitudes towards classes, investment of effort in school, and feelings of challenge. In summarizing the work on school size, Lee and Smith (1997) proposed that the most effective K-8 elementary schools with respect to student achievement gains are those that enroll 400 students or less, whereas the ideal 9–12 secondary school in this regard enrolls between 600 and 900 students. Students in elementary/middle schools that are larger than 400, and those in high schools smaller than 600 or larger than 1200, learn less in reading and mathematics. Findings regarding optimal size were consistent regardless of the social class and racial composition of the school. This work and studies by others suggest that the impact of school size on achievement depends on quality of instruction provided. If the schools focus primarily on social climate and devote limited focus to academic press, the students feel quite good about attending the school but their academic achievement is no higher than that of students attending much larger schools (Wyse et al., 2008). Again, this work provides a nice illustration of how complex configurations of factors in school systems, not single factors in isolation, account for "school effects" *per se* on students.

Others have studied issues of school size in the context of the schools-within-schools or small learning community approaches (Maroulis & Gomez, 2008; Ready & Lee, 2008). The schools-within-schools approach grew out of two concerns: reducing the size of each student's learning community without having to build new schools, and providing students with greater choice over their high-school curriculum. Educators decided that they could create several smaller learning communities within the existing large high-school buildings. Furthermore, they decided that they could increase student choice and sense of autonomy by focusing these smaller learning communities on specific subject matter or career topics such as math/science, the arts, health, and vocational education. Unfortunately, unless school administrators are very careful, these smaller learning communities often end up creating the same problems that we discussed under academic tracking; namely, tracking highly linked to the students' social class, which can then exacerbate problems of inequity in educational experiences (Ready & Lee, 2008). The students like these smaller learning communities and report feeling that their educational options fit better with their own career and educational goals, even though they acknowledge the status hierarchies associated with the different communities that can be created along social class lines in certain schools-within-schools programs.

Connell (2003; Connell & Klem, 2000) has created a major school reform model, *First Things First*, which uses small learning communities as a key component. He also requires that the schools create these communities in ways that do not segregate students based on current ability levels and social class. Finally, he provides the schools with major academic learning supports to keep the focus on learning rather than social climate. The results of his reform efforts in risk schools are quite promising. Not only has the reform succeeded in raising the academic performance of the schools, it has also reduced the differentials in performance across social class groups and increased both attendance and high-school graduation rates.

School Culture

The concept of the culture of the school as a whole, and the fact that different schools, like different communities, vary in their interpersonal, moral and academic cultures, expectations and goals for students, has made an important contribution to our understanding of school effects (e.g., Bandura, 2006; Bryk et al., 1993; Comer, 1980; Lee & Smith, 2001; NRC/IOM, 2004; Rutter, Maughan, Mortimore, & Ouston, 1979; Sarason, 1990). For example, in their analysis of why students achieve more in Catholic public schools, Bryk et al. (1993) discuss how both the academic and social cultures of Catholic schools fundamentally differ from those within most public schools in ways that positively affect the motivation of students, parents, and teachers. These cultures or general school climate are characterized by high value placed on learning, high expectations that all children can learn and master a core curriculum, and affirm the belief that though the business of school is learning, each person has inherent value and dignity and each person is a valued member of a social community (see also Lee & Smith, 2001). As a second example of general school culture factors that are consequential for student achievement, Bandura and his colleagues documented between-school differences in the aggregate level of teachers' efficacy beliefs (Bandura, 1994), a concept called collective efficacy. School-level differences in the collective efficacy of elementary-school teachers have been related to differences in students' aggregate reading and mathematics achievement (e.g., Goddard, Hoy, & Woolfolk Hoy, 2000).

Research and intervention work has also been done on how to create positive moral cultures in schools. This work, done by the Child Development Project (CDP) in Oakland, California, takes a school-level approach to fostering students' social and ethical development as well as their cognitive and academic development. Critically important to this approach are practices that directly engage students in cooperative and community-building activities at school. These include the use of cooperative learning techniques in classrooms, classroom management strategies that rely on student participation in norm setting and decision-making, teaching of conflict resolution skills, and curricula that focus students on themes of care. Research and intervention studies have shown that such practices foster a "community of care" that positively influences students' self-understanding, motivational beliefs and feelings of belonging, and in-school behavior (Battistich et al., 1999; Schaps, 2003).

Work in the area of school violence has also focused on the social and moral cultures of the school as a whole. Astor and his colleagues (Astor Meyer, & Behre, 1999; Astor et al., 2002; Benbenishty & Astor, 2007; Benbenishty, Astor, Zeira, & Vinokus, 2002) have shown that both the levels of school violence and students' concerns about their safety at school decrease as the social climate in the schools increases. It is likely that these two aspects of schools are reciprocally related: as climate decreases, violence increases, and as violence and bullying increase, the general social climate in the school further deteriorates.

In addition to the social and moral dimensions of the school culture, Maehr and Midgley (1996) argued that schools can be characterized by *academic* cultures as well. Just as teachers' instructional strategies are associated with and give rise to certain achievement goals in students, so too, these authors argue, do schools as a whole through their particular policies and practices (see also Midgely, 2002). The argument is that schools, through practices such as how they recognize students, create school-level emphasis on different achievement goals that then affect students' own goals and beliefs in their engagement and behavior (Midgley, 2002; Roeser et al., 1996; Urdan & Roeser, 1993). For example, schools' use of public honor rolls and assemblies for the highest achieving students, class rankings on report cards, differential curricular offerings for students of various ability levels, and so on are all practices that emphasize relative ability, competition, and social comparison in the school ("school ability orientation"). In contrast, through the recognition of academic effort and improvement, rewards for different competencies that extend to all students, and through practices that emphasize learning and task mastery (block scheduling, interdisciplinary curricular teams, cooperative learning), schools can promote a focus on discovery, effort and improvement, and academic mastery ("school task orientation"). Maehr and Midgley (1996) spent 3 years working with one middle school to test these ideas. Although it was quite difficult to actually change the school's practices, student motivation did increase as the school became more task-focused and less ability-focused (see also NRC/IOM, 2004).

Anderman, Maehr, and Midgley (1999) presented evidence that Maehr and Midgley's attempts to alter the school-level goal structure in their school improvement work influenced the goal structures students perceived in their classrooms. Anderman and his colleagues (1999) found that when students moved from elementary schools into the treatment middle school (where efforts were underway to create a mastery goal structure), they reported a slight decrease in personal performance goals whereas students entering the control middle school reported an increase in performance goals. In addition, students moving to the treatment school reported no change in their perceptions of a performance goal structure in their classrooms whereas those moving into the comparison middle school reported increased emphasis on performance goals.

The academic goal focus of a school has important implications for students' mental health as well. In a series of studies, Roeser and Eccles found that middle-school adolescents' belief that their school was ability-focused was associated with declines in their educational values, achievement, and self-esteem, and increases in their anger, depressive symptoms, and school truancy from seventh to eighth grade. These effects were found after controlling for prior levels of each adjustment outcome, adolescents' prior academic ability, and their demographic background (ethnicity, gender, family income; Roeser & Eccles, 1998; Roeser, Eccles, & Sameroff, 1998a). These results support the idea that schools that emphasize ability are likely to alienate a significant number of students who cannot perform at the highest levels, leading to anxiety, anger, disenchantment, and self-selection out of the school environment (Eccles & Midgley, 1989; Finn, 1989; Maehr & Midgley, 1996; Midgley, 2002). In contrast, schools that emphasize effort, improvement, task mastery, and the expectation that all students can learn appear to enfranchise more children in the learning process, promote adaptive attributions (e.g., achievement is based on effort and is therefore malleable), reduce depression, and decrease the frustration and anxiety that can be generated in achievement settings.

An extension of this work on academic climates with high-school students comes from a study by Fiqueira-McDonough (1986). She studied two high schools that were similar in intake characteristics and achievement outcomes, but differed in their academic orientation and rates of delinquent behavior. The high school characterized by a greater emphasis on competition and high grades (ability orientation) had higher delinquency rates, particularly among low-achieving students, than the school that was "more diverse in its goals and [took] a greater interest in students' non-academic needs," where school attachment (valuing of school, liking teachers) was greater on average. Furthermore, individual differences in school attachment were a primary predictor of delinquent activity: Students with lower school attachment were more involved in delinquency than students with higher school attachment. Fiqueira-McDonough (1986) concluded that the broader concern of this school with motivation and diverse needs of students enhanced adolescents' attachment to school, which, in turn, discouraged involvement in delinquency.

Research using students' perceptions of the school culture has documented that perception of the school academic culture is correlated with perception of the teacher–student relationships. For instance, adolescents who perceive a task orientation in their school also report that their teachers are friendly, caring, and respectful. These factors, in turn, predict an increased sense of belonging in school among adolescents (Roeser et al., 1996). In contrast, perceptions of a school ability orientation are negatively correlated with adolescents' perceptions of caring teachers (Roeser et al., 1996). From the adolescents' perspective, a de-emphasis on comparison and competition and an emphasis on effort and improvement are intertwined with their view of caring teachers. Other research has documented that adolescents' perceptions of a school performance goal structure are positively correlated with perceptions of racial discrimination in school among African- and Latin-American youth (Roeser & Peck, 2003; Roeser, 2004). It may be that by adolescence, certain ethnic-minority students become more aware of the differential reward structures and opportunities in the school, who the primary benefactors of these structures and opportunities are, and how such disparities in opportunities and outcomes mirror what youth see between racial/ethnic groups in the wider society. Focusing on task-oriented motivational strategies in schools may thereby reduce the salience and potentially debilitating effects of racial/ethnic stereotypes and relative ability-oriented rewards structures on the achievement of particular groups of students.

Research on school cultures has revealed that school-wide policies and practices can influence not only students' motivation and achievement, but also teachers' professional identities, work motivation, and pedagogy. As studies of "effective schools" have shown, competent leadership and a sense of mutual support among school staff are two important ingredients in effective schools (Good & Weinstein, 1986). However, not all schools have work environments in which there is equitable treatment of teachers, democratic decision-making processes, a spirit of innovation, and opportunities for the professional development of all teachers. From a goal theory perspective, it is hypothetically possible to describe the work environment of a school as emphasizing competition, social comparison, and differential treatment of teachers (e.g., a performance goal structure); cooperation, equity, and a spirit of innovation (e.g., a mastery goal structure); or to some degree, both. Roeser, Marachi, and Gehlbach (2000) found that when teachers perceived differential treatment of teachers by their administrators, and a sense of competitiveness among the teaching staff in the school, they were more likely to endorse classroom practices that highlighted ability differences and competition between students. On the other hand, when teachers in elementary and middle schools perceived support for innovation, experimentation, and even acceptance of "failure" when innovating from school leaders and their colleagues, they were more likely to emphasize these values and goals through their own classroom pedagogy. Together, these findings underscore the possibility that real change in students' motivation and learning through reform efforts may turn on whether or not a supportive work culture for teachers in which cooperation, innovation, and experimentation are valued exists in a school (Good & Weinstein, 1986; Maehr, 1991; Maehr & Midgley, 1996; Sarason, 1990). Again, this set of findings underscores interdependencies across levels of the school system when one is trying to understand the influence of schooling on child and adolescent development. As Sarason (1990, pp. xiii–xiv) put it:

> Schools have been intractable to change and the attainment of goals by reformers . . . the unreflective acceptance of the belief that schools exist only or primarily for children is one of the root causes of this intractability. Schools should exist equally for the development of both faculty and students . . . teachers cannot create and sustain the conditions for the productive development of children if those conditions do not exist for the teachers.

Unsupervised School Spaces

Another important physical dimension of school buildings is the non-instructional spaces that adolescents move in and through before school, after school, and between classes. These spaces include the parking lots and the school grounds, the hallways and the bathrooms, the sports fields (if any), and the cafeteria(s). One example of the importance of such spaces in the study of schooling and development comes from the work of Astor and his colleagues (1999) on school violence. These authors have found that even though students may respond affirmatively to a series of questions about how safe they feel in school in general, they still can show strong fears in particular areas of the school or school grounds at particular times of the day where violence is most likely to occur. For example, in a study of students in five high-school settings in southeastern Michigan, Astor and his colleagues (1999) found that most violent events reported by students occurred in what the authors called the "undefined public spaces" of the school—parking lots, bathrooms, particular hallways, and so on where no adults assumed supervisory jurisdiction. These spaces were undefined in terms of adult monitoring of behavior in them, and thus were the frequent sites for fights, unwanted sexual attention, and other negative behaviors.

School violence and bullying can have a negative impact on the target victims' and observing students' motivation and well-being (Nishina & Juvonen, 2005). In terms of the perpetrators, Fagan and Wilkinson (1998) reviewed theory and evidence that suggest several different functional goals that violence can serve for youth. These included the securing of high status among peers, acquisition of material goods, dominance of others and retribution for insults to the self, defiance of authority, and a form of "rough justice" in situations in which there is little legitimate adult authority. Thus, understanding the origins of school violence requires that we look at how school organizational factors and the psychological processes of the perpetrators co-contribute to school violence and its impacts on victims. In addition, understanding how undefined school spaces may offer disenfranchised students a venue to express themselves in antisocial ways at school may lead to new insights into how to reduce antisocial behavior by providing additional monitoring in unsupervised areas, as well as providing young people with more constructive opportunities for autonomy, belonging, status, competence, and well-being in the context of school and the way classrooms and the school as a whole are run.

School Hours and Schedules

Scholars have looked at two aspects of school schedules in terms of their impact on human development: school start and ending times, and the nature of the annual school calendar.

School start and end times.   School start time is yet another example of how regulatory processes associated with schools can interact with individual regulatory processes, here biological ones, to influence development. Research conducted by Carskadon (1990, 1997) has shown that as children progress through puberty they actually need more, not less, sleep. During this same period, as children move through elementary to middle and high school, schools typically begin earlier and earlier in the morning, necessitating earlier rise times for adolescents (Carskadon, 1997). In concert with other changes, such as the later hours at which adolescents go to bed, the earlier school start times of the middle and high school create a "developmental mismatch" that can both promote daytime sleepiness and undermine adolescents' ability to make it to school on time, alert, and ready to learn.

The "developmental mismatch" of increased need for sleep and earlier school start time can promote daytime sleepiness in adolescents.

The time at which school ends also has implications for child and adolescent adjustment. In communities where few structured opportunities for after-school activities exist, especially impoverished communities, children are more likely to be involved in high-risk behaviors such as substance use, crime, violence, and sexual activity during the period between 2 and 8 p.m. Providing structured activities either at school or within community organizations after school, when many children have no adults at home to supervise them, is an important consideration in preventing children and adolescents from engaging in high-risk behaviors (Carnegie Council on Adolescent Development, 1989; Eccles & Templeton, 2002) and for keeping educationally vulnerable students on track academically (Mahoney, Lord, & Carryl, 2005b; Peck, Roeser, Zarrett, & Eccles, 2008).

School calendar.   American schools typically are in session from September into June. This calendar reflects the historical need for students to be available to work on family farms during the summer. Such need is no longer typical for the vast majority of America's students. What is the consequence of this calendar for learning? This question has become highly salient in educational policy discussions due to increasing evidence that social class differences in school achievement result in large part because of social class differences in the "summer learning gap." Most recently, work by Alexander, Entwisle, and their colleagues showed that much of the social class differential in school achievement reflects differences that already exist when the students enter kindergarten and differences that accumulate over the elementary-school years in learning over the summer vacations. On average, children living in poor families learn less and forget more over the summer vacation than children living in middle-class and upper-class families, in part because these families are able to provide their children with a variety of structured learning experiences over the summer (Alexander et al., 2007). When they compared the actual rate of learning over the course of the school year across social class lines in the Baltimore school district, Alexander and his colleagues found little if any social class difference; in contrast, they found a substantial difference over the summer time. Work on summer schools has shown that well-designed summer school programs can help ameliorate this social-class differential (Alexander et al., 2007).

LEVEL 6: SCHOOL–HOME–COMMUNITY CONNECTIONS

Home–School Connections

Parent involvement in their child's schooling has consistently emerged as an important factor in promoting both academic achievement and socioemotional well-being (Comer, 1980; Eccles & Harold, 1993). Parent involvement in the form of monitoring academic activities and homework, providing assistance with homework, engaging children in educational enrichment activities outside of school, and active participation in classroom activities and in school organizations (e.g., governance, parent–teacher associations) (Epstein, 1992) communicates positive educational expectations, interest, and support to the child. Parent involvement also helps to establish a "safety net" of concerned adults (parents and teachers) that can support children's academic and socioemotional development and assist children if adjustment problems should arise (Jackson & Davis 2000; NRC/IOM, 2004).

Evidence also suggests that home–school connections are relatively infrequent during the elementary years and become almost non-existent during the middle- and high-school years (e.g., Carnegie Council on Adolescent Development, 1989; Eccles & Harold, 1993; Epstein, 1992; Stevenson & Stigler, 1992). This lack of involvement has been attributed to few efforts on the part of schools to involve parents, especially as children transition out of neighborhood-based elementary schools into the larger, more impersonal middle- and high-school environments (Eccles & Harold, 1993). The cultural belief that teachers are in charge of children's learning also contributes to the low levels of parent involvement in schools in the United States (Stevenson & Stigler, 1992). Other characteristics and experiences of parents that reduce involvement include a lack of time, energy, and/or economic resources, lack of knowledge, feelings of incompetence, failure to understand the role parents can play in education, or a long history of negative interactions of parents with the schools (Eccles & Harold, 1993; NRC/IOM, 2004).

School–Community Connections

Comer (1980) stressed the importance of school–community connections and partnerships. He argued that schools are a part of the larger community and that they will be successful only to the extent that they are well integrated into that community at all levels. For example, schools need to be well connected to the communities' social services so that schools can play a cooperative role in furthering children's and their families' well-being. Conversely, communities need to be invested in their schools in ways that stimulate active engagement across these two societal units. For example, when the business community is well connected to the school, there are likely to be increased opportunities for students to develop both the skills and knowledge necessary to make a smooth transition from school into the world of work. Such opportunities can range from frequent field trips to various employment settings to apprenticeships to direct involvement of employees in the instructional program of the school.

Concern about a stronger link between communities and schools has led to a recent increase in opportunities for students to be involved in community service-learning opportunities. In 1989, the Turning Points report (Carnegie Council on Adolescent Development, 1989) recommended that every middle school include supervised youth service in the community or school as part of the core academic curriculum. Today 25% of elementary schools, 38% of middle schools, and 46% of all high schools have students participating in either mandatory or voluntary service-learning activities (NCES, 2004).

Evidence for a positive impact of service-learning on various indicators of child and adolescent development is accumulating (NRC/IOM, 2004). For example, participants in well-designed service-learning programs do better than comparison groups on measures of problem-solving ability, reading and mathematics achievement, and course failure (Eyler, Root, & Giles, 1998; Fisher, 2001; Melchior & Bailis, 2002; Moore & Allen, 1996). Participation in service-learning programs is also linked to positive social assets, civic engagement, community involvement, and increased social and personal responsibility (e.g., Kahne, Chi, & Middaugh, 2002; Scales, Blyth, Berkas, & Kielsmeier, 2000), empathetic understanding (Scales et al., 2000), improved attitudes toward diverse groups in society (Yates & Youniss, 1996), altruistic motivation (Scales et al., 2000), closer communication with one's parents (Scales et al., 2000), more positive or mastery-oriented motivation for school work (Scales et al., 2000), greater commitment to academic learning (Scales et al., 2000), increased feelings of personal efficacy and self-esteem (Kahne et al., 2002; Yates & Youniss, 1996), and a better sense of oneself (Hamilton & Fenzel, 1988; Hart, Yates, Fegley, & Wilson, 1995). Finally, service-learning has also been related to reductions in problem behaviors. In a review of programs aimed at reducing adolescent pregnancy and unprotected sex, Kirby (2002) concluded that service-learning is an effective approach. Service-learning has also been linked to decreases in problem behavior in terms of lower course failure, school suspension, and school dropout (Allen, Philliber, Herrling, & Kuperminc, 1997), fewer discipline problems (Calabrese & Schumer, 1986), and reduced absenteeism (Melchior & Bailis, 2002).

Part-time employment is another example of school–community linkage that relates to the quality of adolescents' adjustment. Although part-time work outside of school hours can promote developmental competence by providing structured, safe opportunities in which adolescents can acquire skills, learn to follow structured routines, work cooperatively with others, and serve others (Mortimer, Shanahan, & Ryu, 1994), some have suggested that too much employment can undermine school success and promote engagement in problem behaviors. For instance, Steinberg, Fegley, and Dornbusch (1993) found that adolescents who work 20 hours or more per week show poor grades, lower school commitment, and less engagement in class activities than their non-working peers. One possible reason for these relations is that adolescents who work long hours are getting insufficient sleep. Steinberg et al. (1993) found that about one-third of the adolescents in their study who worked 20 hours a week or more also reported they were frequently too tired to do their homework and often chose easier classes to accommodate their heavy employment schedules. Although it is true that academically disengaged adolescents are more likely to seek out other settings such as part-time work to get their needs met, it is also true that increased work hours predict academic disengagement (Steinberg et al., 1993).

Mortimer and her colleagues found a much more positive association between working during the high-school years and successful adolescent development. In their multiyear longitudinal study of 1000 adolescents, they found that working an average of 20 hours a week or less bolsters self-confidence, time management skills, career exploration, and responsibility. It also was associated with increased likelihood of attending and completing college (Mortimer et al., 1994; Staff, Mortimer, & Uggen, 2004). Two issues are critical in explaining the differences in these two major studies: amount of time worked and prior academic and psychological functioning. Adolescents who take near full-time jobs while they are in high school, in part because they are already alienated from school, are likely to become further disengaged from schooling as they find a more rewarding niche at work. In contrast, working 10–20 hours per week is a positive growth experience for those adolescents who are doing adequately in other aspects of their development (Zimmer-Gembeck & Mortimer, 2006).

Closer ties between schools and communities may be especially important in high-risk neighborhoods. Both researchers and policy makers have become concerned with the lack of structured opportunities for youth after school (e.g., Carnegie Corporation of New York, 1992; Eccles & Gootman, 2002; Eccles & Templeton, 2002). In most communities, adolescents finish their school day by 2 or 3 in the afternoon. Also in most communities there are few structured activities available for these youths other than work. And typically, their parents are working until early evening—leaving the adolescents largely unsupervised. Such a situation is worrisome for two reasons: First, communities are missing an opportunity to foster positive development through meaningful activities and, second, adolescents are most likely to engage in problem behaviors during this unsupervised period. A closer collaboration between communities and schools could help solve this dilemma. At the most basic level, school buildings could be used as activity centers. At a more cooperative level, school and community personnel could work together to design a variety of programs to meet the multiple needs of their youth. We discuss this issue more extensively later in the chapter.

In this section, we summarized the multiple ways through which schools as complex organizations can influence child development. We stressed the fact that the various levels of organization interact in ways that shape the day-to-day experiences of children, adolescents, and teachers. We also stressed that there are systematic differences in these organizational features and that these differences help to explain differences in both teachers' behaviors and children's development within the school context. In the next sections, we provide three more specific examples of how these processes interact with each other and with the developmental level of the child to influence human development. The first focuses on transition into elementary school; the second and third focus on the transition from elementary school to either middle or junior high school and then on to high school. Both of these examples illustrate how children are exposed to systematic age-related changes in their out-of-family contexts of development and how these changes can impact their development.

SCHOOL TRANSITIONS AS WINDOWS ON THE INFLUENCE OF SCHOOL CONTEXT EFFECTS

Because they involve simultaneous changes in the school context and child developmental outcomes, school transitions provide a unique opportunity to assess school context effects on human development. All school districts must decide both when they allow children to begin school and how they will group the grade levels within the various school buildings. One common arrangement is to group children in kindergarten through sixth grade in elementary schools, children in Grades 7 through 9 in junior high schools, and children in Grades 10 through 12 in senior high schools. The other most common arrangement places the transitions after Grades 5 and 8—creating elementary schools, middle schools, and senior high schools. In both of these arrangements, children typically begin public schooling at age 5 with the entry into kindergarten. In addition, children typically move to a new and often larger building at each of the major school transition points (e.g., the move to middle or junior high school). These school transitions typically also involve increased bussing and exposure to a much more diverse student body. Despite sound theoretical reasons to expect that such transitions should influence children's development (Eccles, Midgley, & Adler, 1984), until recently there has been little empirical work on school transition effects. Because most of the empirical work has focused on the junior high-/middle-school transition, we emphasize this transition after briefly reviewing the work on the entry to elementary school.

Transition into Elementary School

Entrance into elementary school and then the transition from kindergarten to first grade introduces several systematic changes in children's social worlds (Perry & Weinstein, 1998). First, classes are age stratified, making age-independent ability social comparison much easier. Second, formal evaluations of competence by "experts" begin. Third, formal ability grouping begins usually with reading group assignment. Fourth, peers have the opportunity to play a much more constant and salient role in children's lives. Each of these changes should affect children's development. We know that first grade children modify both their expectations and their behavior more to failure feedback than children in preschool and kindergarten (Parsons & Ruble, 1977; Stipek & Hoffman, 1980). Changes such as those described above could certainly contribute to these changes in children's response to failure. We also know that parents' expectations for, and perceptions of, their children's academic competence are influenced by report card marks and standardized test scores given out during the early elementary-school years, particularly for mathematics (Alexander & Entwisle, 1988; Arbreton & Eccles, 1994).

Morrison and his colleagues have exploited the fact that schools have cut-off ages for eligibility to start school to examine the effects of age versus schooling on student development. As a result of these cut-offs, there is a group of children whose ages fall very near to the cut-off point (e.g., needing to be 5 years of age by September 1 of the school year). Those who make this cut-off get to start school; those who don't have to wait another year to begin formal schooling. By comparing the performance of these children on a variety of indicators, Morrison and his colleagues are able to estimate the effects of schooling versus maturing on various aspects of cognitive development (e.g., Christian, Morrison, Frazier, & Massetti, 2000). In general, they have found that the impacts of schooling are quite specific: Those children who attended kindergarten and first grade did better than children near in age who did not start school on tests of reading and letter recognition, mathematical skills, general information, and phonemic segmentation. In contrast, they did not do better on tests of receptive vocabulary and subsyllabic segmentation.

Evidence is emerging of significant long-term consequences of children's experiences in the first grade (Schulting, Malone, & Dodge, 2005). This is particularly true for experiences associated with ability grouping and within-class differential teacher treatment. Studies have shown that teachers use a variety of information in assigning first-grade students to reading groups, including temperamental characteristics (such as interest and persistence), ethnicity, gender, and social class (e.g., Alexander, Entwisle, & Dauber, 1994; Rist, 1970). Alexander et al. (1994) demonstrated that differences in first-grade reading group placement and teacher–student interactions have a significant and substantial effect (even after controlling for beginning differences in competence) on motivation, achievement, and behavior many years later. Furthermore, Pallas et al. (1994) demonstrated that these effects are mediated in part by differential instruction and in part by the exaggerating impact of ability group placement on parents' and teachers' views of the children's abilities, talents, and motivation.

The Middle Grades School Transition

There is substantial evidence of declines in academic motivation, interest in school, and achievement across the early adolescence years; particularly as these adolescents make the transition to middle or junior high school (approximately ages 11–14; see Anderman & Maehr, 1994; Anderman et al., 1999; Eccles et al., 1993; Juvonen et al., 2004; Rumberger, 1995; Wigfield, Eccles, & Pintrich, 1996). There are also increases in test anxiety (Wigfield & Eccles, 1989), focus on self-evaluation rather than task mastery (Nicholls, 1990), and both truancy and school dropout (NRC/IOM, 2004; Rosenbaum, 1976, 1991). Although these changes are not extreme for most adolescents, there is sufficient evidence of declines in various indicators of academic motivation, behavior, and self-perceptions and values over the early adolescent years to make one wonder what is happening. And although few studies have gathered information on ethnic or social class differences in these declines, academic failure and dropout are especially problematic among some ethnic groups and among youth from low-SES communities and families. It is probable then that these groups are particularly likely to show these declines in academic motivation and self-perceptions as they move into and through the secondary-school years (e.g., Roeser & Eccles, 1998; Roeser et al., 1999; Roeser & Peck, 2003).

Several explanations have been offered for these "negative" changes in academic motivation: Some point to the intraspsychic upheaval associated with early adolescent development (Blos, 1965). Others point to the simultaneous occurrence of several life changes. For example, Simmons and Blyth (1987) attributed these declines, particularly among females, to the coincidence of the junior high-school transition with pubertal development. Still others point to the nature of the junior high-school environment itself rather than the transition *per se*. Extending person–environment fit theory (Hunt, 1975) into a developmental perspective (stage–environment fit theory), Eccles and Midgley (1989) proposed that these negative developmental changes result from the fact that traditional junior high schools do not provide developmentally appropriate educational environments for early adolescents. They suggested that different types of educational environment are needed for different age groups to meet individual developmental needs and foster continued developmental growth. Exposure to the developmentally appropriate environment would facilitate both motivation and continued growth; in contrast, exposure to developmentally inappropriate environments, especially developmentally regressive environments, should create a particularly poor person–environment fit, which should lead to declines in motivation as well as detachment from the goals of the institution.

This analysis suggests several important developmental questions. First, what are the developmental needs of the early adolescent? Second, what kinds of educational environments are developmentally appropriate for meeting these needs and stimulating further development? Third, what are the most common school environmental changes before and after the transition to middle or junior high school? Fourth, and most importantly, are these changes compatible with the physiological, cognitive, and psychological changes early adolescents are experiencing? Or is there a developmental mismatch between maturing early adolescents and the classroom environments they experience before and after the transition to middle or junior high school that leads to a deterioration in academic and socioemotional development and performance for some children?

Stage–environment fit and the transition to junior high or middle school.   Until quite recently, few empirical studies focused on differences in the classroom or school environment across grades or school levels (Juvonen et al., 2004). Most descriptions focused on school-level characteristics such as school size, degree of departmentalization, and extent of bureaucratization. For example, Simmons and Blyth (1987) pointed out that most junior high schools are substantially larger than elementary schools and instruction is more likely to be organized departmentally. As a result, junior high-school teachers typically teach several different groups of students, making it very difficult for students to form a close relationship with any school-affiliated adult precisely at the point in development when there is a great need for guidance and support from non-familial adults. Such changes in student–teacher relationships are also likely to undermine the sense of community and trust between students and teachers, leading to a lowered sense of efficacy among the teachers, an increased reliance on authoritarian control practices by the teachers, and an increased sense of alienation among the students. Finally, such changes are likely to decrease the probability that any particular student's difficulties will be noticed early enough to get the student necessary help, thus increasing the likelihood that students on the edge will be allowed to slip onto negative motivational and performance trajectories leading to increased school failure and dropout. In the next sections, we discuss these issues in more detail.

Teacher control. First, despite the increasing maturity of students, junior high-school classrooms, compared to elementary-school classrooms, are characterized by a greater emphasis on teacher control and discipline, and fewer opportunities for student decision-making, choice, and self-management (e.g., Jackson & Davis, 2000; Juvonen et al., 2004; Midgley, 2002; Midgley & Feldlaufer, 1987). As outlined earlier, stage–environment fit theory suggests that the mismatch between young adolescents' desires for autonomy and control and their perceptions of the opportunities in their learning environments should result in a decline in the adolescents' intrinsic motivation and interest in school. Mac Iver and Reuman (1988) provided some support for this prediction: They compared the changes in intrinsic interest in mathematics for adolescents reporting different patterns of change in their opportunities for participation in classroom decision-making questions across the junior high-school transition. Those adolescents who perceived their seventh-grade mathematics classrooms as providing fewer opportunities for decision-making than had been available in their sixth-grade mathematics classrooms reported the largest declines in their intrinsic interest in mathematics as they moved from the sixth grade into the seventh grade.

Teacher–student relationships. As noted earlier, junior high-school classrooms are characterized by a less personal and positive teacher–student relationship than elementary-school classrooms. Given the association of classroom climate and student motivation reviewed earlier, it should not surprising that moving into a less supportive classroom leads to a decline in these early adolescents' interest in the subject matter being taught in that classroom, particularly among the low-achieving students (Dotterer, McHale, & Crouter, 2009; Juvonen et al., 2004; Midgley et al., 1988).

Teacher efficacy. Junior high-school teachers also feel less effective as teachers than elementary-school teachers, especially for low-ability students (Juvonen et al., 2004; Midgley et al., 1988). Given the association of teacher efficacy and students' beliefs, attitudes, motivation, and achievement (Ashton, 1985; NRC/IOM, 2004), it is again not surprising that these differences in teachers' sense of efficacy before and after the transition to junior high school contributed to the decline in early adolescents', particularly low-achieving adolescents', confidence in their academic abilities and potential (Midgley, Feldlaufer, & Eccles, 1989).

Groups and activity structures. The shift to junior high school is also associated with an increase in practices such as whole-class task organization and between-classroom ability grouping (Jackson & Davis, 2000; Juvonen et al., 2004; Oakes, Gamoran, & Page, 1992). As noted earlier, such changes should increase social comparison, concerns about evaluation, and competitiveness (Eccles et al., 1984; Rosenholtz & Simpson, 1984). They are also likely to increase teachers' use of normative grading criteria and more public forms of evaluation, both of which have been shown to have a negative effect on early adolescents' self-perceptions and motivation.

Grading practices.   There is no stronger predictor of students' self-confidence and efficacy than the grades they receive. If academic marks decline with the junior high-school transition, then adolescents' self-perceptions and academic motivation should also decline. In fact, junior high-school teachers use stricter and more social comparison-based standards than elementary-school teachers to assess student competency and to evaluate student performance, leading to a drop in grades for many early adolescents as they make the junior high-school transition (Eccles & Midgley, 1989; Roderick, 1993; Simmons & Blyth, 1987). This decline in grades is not matched by a decline in the adolescents' scores on standardized achievement tests, suggesting that the decline reflects a change in grading practices rather than a change in the rate of the students' learning (Kavrell & Petersen, 1984). Imagine what such decline in grades might do to early adolescents' self-confidence and motivation. Although Simmons and Blyth (1987) did not look at this specific question, they did document the impact of this grade drop on subsequent school performance and dropout. Even controlling for a youth's performance prior to the school transition, the magnitude of the grade drop following the transition into either junior high school or middle school was a major predictor of early school leaving (see also Roderick, 1993).

Pedagogical goals.   Several of the changes noted above are linked together in goal theory. Classroom practices related to grading practices, support for autonomy, and instructional organization affect the relative salience of mastery versus performance goals that students adopt as they engage in learning tasks at school. The types of change associated with the middle grades school transition should precipitate greater focus on performance goals. As noted earlier, Midgley and her colleagues found support for this prediction (Midgley, 2002; Midgley et al., 1995). In this study, both teachers and students indicated that performance-focused goals were more prevalent and task-focused goals were less prevalent in the middle-school classrooms than in the elementary-school classrooms. In addition, the elementary-school teachers reported using task-focused instructional strategies more frequently than did the middle-school teachers. Finally, at both grade levels the extent to which teachers were task-focused predicted the students' and the teachers' sense of personal efficacy. Not surprisingly, personal efficacy was lower among the middle-school participants than among the elementary-school participants.

Anderman et al. (1999) extended this work by comparing two groups of young adolescents: a group who moved into a middle school that emphasized task-focused instructional practices and a group who moved into a middle school that emphasized more traditional performance/ability focused instructional practices. Although these two groups of students did not differ in their motivational goals prior to the school transition, they did after the transition. As predicted, the adolescents who moved into the first type of middle school were less likely to show an increase in their extrinsic motivational and performance-oriented motivational goals.

School reform efforts.   Jackson and Davis (2000) summarized many middle-school reform efforts. They concluded that the following middle-school characteristics support both learning and positive youth development:

1. a curriculum grounded in rigorous academic standards and current knowledge about how students learn best, which is relevant to the concerns of adolescents
2. instructional methods designed to prepare all students to achieve at the highest standards
3. organizational structures that support a climate of intellectual development and a caring community with shared educational goals
4. staff who are trained experts at teaching young adolescents
5. ongoing professional development opportunities for the staff
6. democratic governance that involves both the adults and the adolescents
7. extensive involvement of parents and the community
8. high levels of safety and practices that support good health.

Similar conclusions were reached by Juvonen and her colleagues (2004).

Summary.   Changes such as those just reviewed are likely to have a negative effect on many children's motivational orientation toward school at any grade level. But Eccles and Midgley (1989) have argued that these types of school environmental changes are particularly harmful at early adolescence given what is known about psychological development during this stage of life. Evidence from a variety of sources suggests that early adolescent development is characterized by increases in desire for autonomy, peer orientation, self-focus and self-consciousness, salience of identity issues, concern over heterosexual relationships, and capacity for abstract cognitive activity (Brown, 2004; Eccles & Midgley, 1989; Keating, 1990; Simmons & Blyth, 1987; Wigfield et al., 1996). Simmons and Blyth (1987) argued that adolescents need safe, intellectually challenging environments to adapt to these shifts. In light of these needs, the environmental changes often associated with transition to junior high school seem especially harmful in that they emphasize competition, social comparison, and ability self-assessment at a time of heightened self-focus; they decrease decision-making and choice at a time when the desire for control is growing; they emphasize lower-level cognitive strategies at a time when the ability to use higher level strategies is increasing; and they disrupt social networks at a time when adolescents are especially concerned with peer relationships and may be in special need of close adult relationships outside of the home. The nature of these environmental changes, coupled with the normal course of individual development, is likely to result in a developmental mismatch so that the "fit" between the early adolescent and the classroom environment is particularly poor, increasing the risk of negative motivational outcomes, especially for adolescents who are having difficulty succeeding in school academically.

The High-School Transition

Although there is less work on the transition to high school, the existing work suggests quite similar problems (Coleman & Hoffer, 1987; Jackson & Davis, 2000; Lee & Smith, 2001; NRC/ IOM, 2004; Wehlage, Rutter, Smith, Lesko, & Fernandez, 1989). For example, high schools are typically even larger and more bureaucratic than junior high schools and middle schools. Lee and Smith (2001) provide numerous examples of how the sense of community among teachers and students is undermined by the size and bureaucratic structure of most high schools. There is little opportunity for students and teachers to get to know each other and, likely as a consequence, there is distrust between them and little attachment to a common set of goals and values. There is also little opportunity for the students to form mentor-like relationships with a non-familial adult and little effort is made to make instruction relevant to the students. Such environments are likely to further undermine the motivation and involvement of many students, especially those not doing particularly well academically, those not enrolled in the favored classes, and those who are alienated from the values of the adults in the high school. These hypotheses need to be tested.

Most large public high schools also organize instruction around curricular tracks that sort students into different groups. As a result, there is even greater diversity in the educational experiences of high-school students than in those of middle grades students; unfortunately, this diversity is often associated more with the students' social class and ethnic group than with differences in their talents and interests (Bryk et al., 1993; Lee et al., 1993; Lee & Smith, 2001). As a result, curricular tracking has served to reinforce social stratification rather than foster optimal education for all students, particularly in large schools (Dornbusch, 1994; Bryk et al., 1993; Lee et al., 1993; Lee & Smith, 2001). Bryk et al. (1993) documented that average school achievement levels do not benefit from this curricular tracking. Quite the contrary—evidence comparing Catholic high schools with public high schools suggests that average school achievement levels are increased when all students are required to take the same challenging curriculum. This conclusion is true even after one has controlled for student selectivity factors. A more thorough examination of how the organization and structure of our high schools influences cognitive, motivational, and achievement outcomes is needed.

Summary of School Transitions Research

In this section, we summarized the evidence related to the impact of school transitions on development. As one would expect, given what we now know about the ecological nature of the junior high-school transition, many early adolescents, particularly the low achievers and the highly anxious, experience great difficulty with this transition. In many ways, this transition can be characterized as a developmentally regressive shift in one's school context. Consistent with our stage–environment fit perspective, such a shift has negative consequences for many youths' school engagement and performance. Also consistent with our stage–environment fit perspective, there is an increasing number of intervention studies showing that the junior high-school transition does not have to yield negative consequences for vulnerable youth. Middle grades educational institutions can be designed in a developmentally progressive manner, and when they are, the majority of early adolescents gain from this school transition.

We have now completed our discussion of school influences on development. In this section, we outlined the many ways in which schools affect the socioemotional development and achievement of children and adolescents. We stressed the need to take both a systems level and a developmental perspective on the school. We now turn to a similar discussion of neighborhood influences. Like schools, neighborhoods are complex places in which children and adolescents spend a great deal of time. Unlike schools, much of this time is unstructured and unorganized. In addition, neighborhoods are far less well integrated contexts than schools. They include a wide array of people, contexts, and both opportunities and risks. Consequently, both the theoretical and the empirical research on neighborhood effects is much more diverse and scattered. It is also more recent, and therefore less voluminous. The major themes in this work are summarized in the next section.

NEIGHBORHOOD AND COMMUNITY INFLUENCES

Recent interest in the potential impact of neighborhoods and communities on human development has grown out of two major lines of work: Bronfenbrenner's articulation of an ecological view of development and renewed concerns with the impact of poverty on children and adolescents.

The publication of Wilson's book *The Truly Disadvantaged* in 1987 was probably the biggest single impetus to the study of poverty in the past 50 years. He outlined the problems of inner-city neighborhoods with unusually high concentrations of poverty, arguing that such neighborhoods pose major threats for socializing the next generation. According to Wilson, inner-city poverty of the 1980s and 1990s is quite different from inner-city poverty in previous generations because employment opportunities have moved out of these neighborhoods, leaving behind a situation in which the adults cannot find employment within their neighborhoods and communities. This in turn leads to high rates of unemployment, demoralization, and drug use, along with the deterioration of both the two-parent family and community well-being. Together these characteristics create a situation in which children have few successful role models and little obvious incentive to do well in school. Instead, they have many models of hopelessness and illegal behaviors. They also live in run-down housing with abundant health risks. Parents who do not have the economic means to leave these neighborhoods must cope with these conditions as they try to rear their children to become hopeful, healthy, and fully functioning members of the larger society. Wilson stressed just how difficult this task is if one lives in these truly disadvantaged neighborhoods.

Research related to Wilson's hypotheses, as well as to work by Bronfenbrenner and his colleagues (Bronfenbrenner & Morris, 1998) and the growing interest in the effects of poverty on human development (e.g., McLoyd, 1990; Sharkey, 2009), is accumulating. First and foremost, all researchers acknowledge the importance of studying both direct and indirect effects of neighborhood characteristics (Brooks-Gunn, Duncan, & Aber, 1997a, 1997b; Elder & Conger, 2000; Furstenberg et al., 1999; Runyan et al., 2009; Sampson, Raudenbush, & Earls, 1997). Most attention has been focused on the indirect effects of neighborhood characteristics mediated through the family, school, and peer networks. For example, the stresses on parents of living in poor, under-resourced neighborhoods are assumed to undermine effective parenting, especially for vulnerable parents (e.g., those who are unemployed or who have other major problems). In addition, the realities of the neighborhood are assumed to influence parents' goals and interactions with neighborhood institutions and residents (e.g., parents are likely to keep their children in the house or apartment as much as possible if the streets and parks in their community are dangerous). Similarly, because schools are funded to a great extent from neighborhood resources, the quality of the schools children attend is directly related to the incomes of the families living in their neighborhood. Finally, the kinds of peers children are likely to associate with are directly influenced by the types of children and families who live in their neighborhood. As noted below, work assessing these types of indirect influence is just beginning. Thus far, results support their importance (Brooks-Gunn et al., 1997a, 1997b).

Second, the nature and range of neighborhood influences on development differ by age. Infants and preschoolers are affected most by the indirect effects of neighborhood characteristics on their parents' behaviors and by the direct effects of varying health hazards associated with living in different types of communities. As children get older, they are affected more directly by the other institutions in the neighborhood, such as the schools and community recreational facilites, and by the peers and adults who reside in their neighborhood. These out-of-home neighborhood influences are especially influential during adolescence and young adulthood (Brooks-Gunn et al., 1997a, 1997b).

Third, we are just beginning to study the influences of neighborhood culture on development. Most work has focused on the establishing that there are neighborhood effects; that is, that children's development is affected by the characteristics of the neighborhoods in which they grow up independent of the characteristics of their families. This is not an easy thing to demonstrate because families living in different neighborhoods are also quite different from each other (Firkowska et al., 1978). The best example of this problem is family income. Poor families live in poor neighborhoods; rich families live in rich neighborhoods. How, then, does a researcher know if the relation of neighborhood poverty to children's school grades is due to "neighborhood effects" or to their parents' income? Researchers are still working out exactly how to answer this question.

An attempt to separate out these influences is the work by Rosenbaum and his associates (e.g., Rosenbaum, 1980, 1991; Rosenbaum, Kulieke, & Rubinowitz, 1988). In 1976, the courts in Chicago ordered the Chicago Housing Authority to redress ethnic discrimination in housing placement by offering poor families the opportunity to move to better housing. Families who accepted this offer were randomly assigned to housing either in a better inner-city neighborhood or in a middle-class suburban community outside of Chicago. Rosenbaum and his colleagues studied the long-term differences in developmental outcomes for the children in these two types of families. Youths reared in the suburbs were much more likely to graduate from high school, to complete a college track high-school academic program, and to attend college than youths reared in the alternative inner-city neighborhood. Given the experimental design of this study, it provides the strongest empirical support available that the neighborhood in which a child grows up has an impact on that child's developmental outcomes. The source of this effect, however, was not identifiable in this study. Researchers are now shifting their focus to understanding the processes that might account for such a neighborhood effect.

The US government enacted a major social policy experiment by providing a randomly selected group of very poor families in several large cities with the opportunity to move to middle-class neighborhoods in nearby suburbs (The Move to Opportunity Program—MTO). Researchers from several different disciplines are studying the consequences of this experiment for children's development. So far the evidence looks quite good for elementary-school-aged children and for mothers: The children are doing better in school and in general social functioning that the control group children, and the mothers are doing better on both schooling and employment outcomes than the control group mothers (Leventhal & Brooks-Gunn, 2004). The MTO adolescents are also less involved in criminal behavior than the control group adolescents.

These studies support the hypothesis that neighborhood characteristics should influence the course of human development for residents. But how do neighborhood characteristics influence development? Jencks and Mayer (1990) suggested three likely sources of influence that are of particular importance to this chapter: contagion, collective socialization, and resource exposure. By *contagion*, Jencks and Mayer (1990) were referring to the impact primarily of peer groups and young adults on children's behaviors, goals, and values. They argued that both good and bad behaviors are easily modeled and picked up by younger children as they watch the older children, adolescents, and young adults in their neighborhood. If most of the adolescents in a neighborhood drop out of school and use drugs and alcohol, then younger children are likely to adopt similar behavior patterns and values as they grow up. In addition, the older individuals in the neighborhood often actively recruit younger children and adolescents into the most typical activity settings (e.g., either gangs or more positive settings linked to faith-based or prosocial activity-based organizations such as Girl Scouts), further increasing the likelihood of children adopting the behavior patterns and values of the older residents in their communities. By and large, evidence supports this hypothesis (Brooks-Gunn et al., 1997a, 1997b; Furstenberg et al., 1999).

By *collective socialization*, Jencks and Mayer (1990) meant the collaborative efforts in the community to socialize the next generation. Somewhat like the recruitment component of the contagion effect discussed above, adults in a community sometimes have common goals for their children. If they are able to implement these goals with common strategies and socialization practices, they should be able to increase the likelihood of the children becoming the types of individuals they want them to become. Having abundant and consistent role models of the desired kinds of adult outcomes in the neighborhood should also increase this likelihood. Although work assessing this hypothesis is just beginning, initial findings provide promising support (Brooks-Gunn et al., 1997a, 1997b).

Closely related to this perspective is the work by Sampson et al. (1997) on collective efficacy. These researchers defined *collective efficacy* in terms of two components: social cohesion (shared values and goals) and confidence in shared social control mechanisms. After controlling for family-level characteristics such as income, education, and employment, and neighborhood-demographic characteristics such as the percentage of families living below the poverty line, the percentage of immigrant and African-American families, and the instability of the resident structure, Sampson et al. found that neighborhoods with a high sense of collective efficacy among the residents had lower rates of crime and delinquency. These investigators are also gathering extensive developmental data on the children in these neighborhoods. In the future, we will learn whether living in a neighborhood with a high sense of collective efficacy also serves as a protective factor in children's development.

By *resource exposure*, Jencks and Mayer (1990) meant the availability of opportunities versus dangers and risks. Communities vary in the presence and quality of such good things as schools, faith-based institutions, and other types of activity-base organization, recreational facilities, health facilities, access to affordable stores and markets, and police monitoring, as well as such risky things as the presence of liquor stores and drug outlets, the proportion of run-down versus quality housing, and both gang and police harassment. Jencks and Mayer argued that exposure to these types of risks and opportunities should influence the behaviors of all members of the community. The little available evidence is supportive of these predictions, but the effects of these general neighborhood characteristics are quite weak and, by and large, appear to be mediated through their impact of families and peer groups (Brooks-Gunn et al., 1997a, 1997b). In the next section we discuss the evidence for more positive effects of participating in organized activities, which are, typically, differentially available across various types of neighborhoods.

Furstenberg and his colleagues (1999) have suggested another mechanism of influence: *family management*. They suggested that the impact of neighborhoods on development would be moderated by the quality of parenting to which the children were exposed. Effective parents should adjust both their childrearing practices and the nature of their children's exposure to opportunities and risks outside the home depending on the type of community in which they live. In turn, these practices should either buffer the children from exposure to potential risks or facilitate their growth through exposure to positive opportunities. They referred to this set of practices as family management. The little available evidence suggests that many well-functioning parents do vary their practices depending on their community and that successfully implementing locally effective strategies does buffer against the negative impact of neighborhood risks on development, particularly in early and middle childhood periods (Brooks-Gunn et al., 1997a, 1997b; Duncan & Brooks-Gunn, 1997; Furstenberg, et al, 1999).

Summary of Neighborhood and Community Influences

There has been an increase in the amount and quality of work being done on neighborhood and community effects on human development. Although still in its infancy, this work has documented the influence of community characteristics on community members. As Bronfenbrenner (1979) predicted, communities influence the development of children primarily through their influence on the microsystem (i.e., through their influence on parenting practices, teacher behavior, school resources, and peer group behaviors). Because of the importance of the microsystem, the magnitude of neighborhood effects is quite small. Effective parents are able to buffer their children's development from the risks and dangers in many neighborhoods. Nonetheless, the impact of the neighborhood on development increases as children get older (Elliott et al., in preparation), partly because parental control and influences decrease as children move into adolescence and young adulthood. During these periods of life, individuals have much more control over their own behaviors and, consequently, their interactions with larger social units outside the home. This increasing independence can put them at greater risk to out-of-family influences on their development.

COMMUNITY- AND SCHOOL-BASED FREE-TIME ACTIVITIES

Communities and schools may also affect human development through their influence on the availability of structured leisure time activities. The release of *A Matter of Time* by the Carnegie Corporation of New York (1992) put the spotlight on the role of productive use of time in successful development. It illustrated how much discretionary time children and adolescents have and how much of this time is spent on unstructured activities such as "hanging out" with one's friends, watching television, and listening to music. The report stressed that constructive, organized activities are a good use of children's and adolescents' time because (1) doing good things with one's time takes time away from opportunities to get involved in risky activities; (2) one can learn good things (such as specific competencies, prosocial values and attitudes) while engaged in constructive activities; and (3) involvement in organized activity settings increases the possibility of establishing positive social supports and networks. To date, there has been relatively little longitudinal, developmentally oriented research focused on either the benefits or the costs of how children and adolescents spend their discretionary time. Most of the relevant research has been done in sociology and leisure studies, and most of the work has focused on adolescents.

Most of the sociological and psychological research on activity involvement has focused on extracurricular school activities. This research has documented a link between adolescents' extracurricular activities and adult educational attainment, occupation, and income, after controlling for social class and ability (Eccles & Templeton, 2002). This work also documented the protective value of extracurricular activity participation in reducing involvement in delinquent and other risky behaviors (e.g., Eccles, Barber, Stone, & Hunt, 2003; Mahoney, Larson, & Eccles, 2005a).

Research within leisure studies has taken a slightly different path, focusing on the differences between relaxed leisure and constructive, organized activities: Relaxed leisure is characterized as enjoyable, but not demanding (watching TV). In contrast, constructive, organized leisure activities (such as team sports, performing arts, and organized volunteer activities) require effort and commitment and provide a forum in which to express one's identity or passion (e.g., Larson, Hansen, & Moneta, 2006; Larson & Kleiber, 1993). These activities are assumed to have more developmentally beneficial outcomes than relaxed, unstructured leisure because they provide the opportunity (1) to acquire and practice specific social, physical, and intellectual skills that may be useful in a wide variety of settings; (2) to contribute to the well-being of one's community and develop a sense of agency as a member of one's community; (3) to belong to a socially recognized and valued group; (4) to establish supportive social networks of both peers and adults that can help one in both the present and the future; and (5) to experience and deal with challenges.

Recent research supports these assumptions about the positive effects of participation in organized activities (Larson & Hansen, 2005; Mahoney et al., 2005a, 2005b). For example,

Mahoney and Cairns (1997) and McNeal (1995) found that participation in extracurricular activities is related to lower rates of school dropout, particularly for high-risk youth. Mahoney (1997) also showed a connection to reduced rates of criminal offending. In addition, adolescents involved in a broad range of adult-endorsed activities report lower rates of substance use than their non-involved peers (Youniss, Yates, & Su, 1997b). Sport, in particular, has been linked to lower likelihood of school dropout and higher rates of college attendance (Eccles et al., 2003; McNeal, 1995), especially among low-achieving and blue-collar male athletes (Holland & Andre, 1987).

Participation in school-based extracurricular activities has also been linked to increases on such positive developmental outcomes as high-school grade point average, strong school engagement, and high educational aspirations (Barber, Eccles & Stone, 2001; Eccles & Barber, 1999; Lamborn, Brown, Mounts, & Steinberg 1992). Similarly, participation in high-school extracurricular activities and out-of-school volunteer activities predicts high levels of adult participation in the political process and other types of volunteer activities, continued sport engagement, and better physical and mental health (Barber et al., 2001; Glancy, Willits, & Farrell, 1986; Youniss, McLellan, & Yates, 1997a; Youniss et al., 1997b).

In contrast to these positive associations, sport has also been linked to increased rates of school deviance and drug and alcohol use (e.g., Eccles & Barber, 1999; Lamborn et al., 1992). These results suggest that participation in organized activities can have both positive and negative effects. Why? Several explanations for the positive results associated with participation have been offered: Rehberg (1969) suggested the importance of association with academically oriented peers, exposure to academic values, enhanced self-esteem, generalization of a high sense of personal efficacy, and superior career guidance and encouragement. Coleman (1961) stressed the values and norms associated with the different peer clusters engaged in various types of extracurricular activities. Otto and Alwin (1977) added skill and attitude acquisition (both interpersonal and personal) and increased membership in important social networks. Other investigators have focused on links among peer group formation, identity formation, and activity involvement (Eccles & Barber, 1999; Eccles & Templeton, 2002; Eckert, 1989; Mahoney et al., 2005a). For example, Fine (1992) stressed how participation in something like Little League shapes both the child's definition of himself as a "jock" and the child's most salient peer group. In turn, these characteristics (one's identity and one's peer group) influence subsequent activity choices, creating a synergistic system that marks out a clear pathway into a particular kind of adolescence.

Involvement in sports links an adolescent to a set of similar peers, provides shared experiences and goals, and can reinforce friendships.

This strong link between activity participation and peer group membership also provides an explanation for the negative influences of sports participation on drug and alcohol use. Knowing what an adolescent is doing often tells us a lot about whom the adolescent is with: It is very likely that participation in organized activity settings directly affects adolescents' peer group precisely because such participation structures a substantial amount of peer group interaction. One's co-participants become one's peer crowd. And such peer crowds often develop an activity-based "culture," providing adolescents with the opportunity to identify with a group having a shared sense of "style." Involvement in a school organization or sport links an adolescent to a set of similar peers, provides shared experiences and goals, and can reinforce friendships between peers (Larson, 1994; Mahoney et al., 2005a).

Participation in religious institutions, often called "congregations," and their affiliated youth groups is another important context of development that has been under-researched in the developmental sciences (King & Roeser, 2009; Roehlkepartain & Patel, 2006). A national study on religion showed that approximately half of all American adolescents attend religious services at a congregation weekly, with another quarter of youth attending services less than weekly but more frequently than just on the major religious holidays of their tradition (Smith & Denton, 2005). Furthermore, about half of all US adolescents (ages 13–17 years) indicate a strong, positive orientation to matters of religion, faith, and religious experience in their lives (Smith & Denton, 2005). With regard to this half of the youth population, a growing body of evidence shows links between religious participation/development and better health and well-being, as well as between religious participation and reduced rates of emotional distress and antisocial behavior (see King & Roeser, 2009; Oser, Scarlett, & Bucher, 2006).

Smith (2003) theorizes that religious institutions exert constructive influences on youth development, for instance by providing youth with three types of capital, including: (1) *spiritual capital* in the form of religious mentors and role models, moral and religious worldviews, and contexts for reflection and spiritual contemplation; (2) *cultural capital* in the form of opportunities for skill development (i.e., leadership skills) and for learning core cultural knowledge (e.g., Biblical events); and (3) *social capital* in the form of social ties across differently aged peers, non-parental adults, and members of wider communities and society. Such forms of capital, in turn, inform identity, activity choices, and the nature of one's social networks in positive and prosocial ways (King & Roeser, 2009). For instance, participation in religious congregational contexts has been linked to faith development (Roehlkepartain & Patel, 2006), defined as the degree to which a young person comes to internalize the priorities, commitments, and perspectives of their religious tradition (Benson, Donahue, & Erickson, 1989), and less contact with deviant peers and more contact with parents, non-parental adults, and non-deviant peers (King & Furrow, 2004; Larson et al., 2006; Martin, White, & Perlman, 2001).

PEER CULTURE AS A PRIMARY MEDIATOR OF SCHOOL, COMMUNITY, AND FREE-TIME ACTIVITY EFFECTS

Throughout our discussion of school, community, and organized activity effects on development, we have suggested ways in which particular characteristics might influence peer interactions. In this section, we discuss these connections in more detail. As discussed earlier, schools, activity settings, and communities provide the places in which a great deal of peer interaction takes place. Peer groups are often formed from among the residents in communities and the participants in organized activities. This geographical clustering of peer networks can have either positive or negative effects on development, depending on the nature of the individuals involved and the shared values and norms of the groups that emerge.

Researchers are just beginning to explore the full range of such influences. In this section, we explore this issue. We focus on those aspects of peer relations closely linked with the school, activity setting, and community contexts. Specifically, we focus on peers as co-learners, on the reinforcing and socializing mechanism within peer groups, and on the individual children's attempts to coordinate multiple goals.

Peers as Co-Learners

The extensive work on the advantages of cooperative learning provides one lens on the link between peers and schooling. This work has stressed several roles of peers as co-learners. Most directly, doing learning activities in a social context is usually more fun and, thus, intrinsically interesting (Slavin, 1990). Peers can also help each other understand and learn the material through group discussion, sharing of resources, modeling academic skills, and interpreting and clarifying the tasks for each other (NRC/IOM, 2004; Schunk, 1987). Each of these characteristics should influence achievement through its impact of the children's expectations for success, their valuing of the activity, and their focus on learning rather than performance goals. One way in which positive social interactions have been facilitated in classrooms is through cooperative learning (Slavin, 1990). Finally, cooperative learning is also linked to the mechanism discussed earlier: When cooperative learning is used in classrooms, children are more accepting of one another, and fewer children are socially isolated. Thus, greater use of such techniques can mitigate the effects of peer rejection and lack of belonging on students' academic motivation.

Closely related to the work on cooperative learning is the work on peer tutoring. Children learn a great deal from teaching other children (Eccles & Templeton, 2002; Jackson & Davis, 2000; McLaughlin, 2000; Sieber, 1979). Such an arrangement benefits both the tutor and the tutee. An interesting variant on peer tutoring is described in *Turning Points* (Carnegie Council on Adolescent Development, 1989): cross-age tutoring. A special group of eighth graders was trained and then allowed to tutor first graders in reading. What made the eighth graders special was the fact that all of them were doing quite poorly in school and were reading substantially below grade level. Nonetheless, they did read better than the first graders. It was hoped that the intervention would help both the eighth and first graders; and it did! Both the school engagement and performance of the group of eighth graders increased dramatically— so much so that they stayed in school and were reading at grade level when they graduated from high school. In addition, their tutees continued to read at grade level as long as they interacted with their older student tutor. This intervention demonstrates the power of cross-age tutoring as a way to provide older students with a meaningful and fulfilling task as well as younger children with the extra help they need to avoid falling behind.

Similar cross-age dynamics operate in communities. As noted earlier, older children and adolescents sometimes recruit younger children in the dominant peer group activity settings in particular neighborhoods; these can be either positive settings such as faith-based institutions or recreational centers or more negative settings such as gangs. Some of the most successful youth development programs discussed in *A Matter of Time* (Carnegie Corporation, 1992) involve cross-age mentoring programs like the one described earlier (see also McLaughlin, 2000).

Peer Group Influences

Much of the classic work on peer influences on development focused on the negative effects of peer groups on adolescents' commitment to doing well in school. Investigators have now turned their attention to understanding the specific mechanisms by which peer groups can either support or undermine positive development through their impact on both school engagement and involvement in other positive activities. This research has documented that children tend to cluster together in peer groups that share the same motivational orientations and activity preferences and that such clustering serves to reinforce their existing motivational orientation and activity preferences, leading to a strengthening of these individual differences over time (e.g., Berndt & Keefe, 1995; Berndt, Laychak, & Park, 1990; Epstein, 1983; Kindermann, McCollam, & Gibson, 1996; Youniss, 1980). But whether such effects are positive or negative depends on the nature of the peer groups' motivational values and behavioral orientations (Eccles et al., 2003). For example, high-achieving children who seek out other high achievers as friends should end up with more positive academic motivation as a result of their interactions with like motivated children. In contrast, low achievers who become involved with a group of friends who are also low achievers should become even less motivated to do school work and more interested in other activity settings (Fuligni et al., 1995; Kindermann, 1993; Kindermann et al., 1996).

The role of peer group influences is likely to vary across different ages. For example, peers may play an especially important role during adolescence. There are two major differences between children and adolescents in peer-group processes. Adolescents are more aware of, and concerned about, peer-group acceptance, and adolescents spend much more unsupervised time with peer groups in social, sports, and other extracurricular activities (Eccles & Templeton, 2002). For example, early adolescents rate social activities as very important to them, and like them better than most of the other activities they do, particularly academic activities (Brown, 2004; Wigfield, Eccles, Mac Iver, Reuman, & Midgley, 1991). Furthermore, Harter (1990) found that early adolescents' physical appearance and social acceptance are the most important predictors of their general self-esteem, much more important than their perceptions of their own cognitive competence. These results suggest that the potential role of peer groups should be greater during adolescence and that the nature of the effect should depend on the values of the peer group and the specific domains being considered. Hanging out with a group of friends highly motivated for school achievement should facilitate academic motivation and achievement, perhaps to the detriment of motivational commitment in other domains. Similarly, although hanging out with a low academic motivation group should undermine academic motivation, it may facilitate motivation and involvement in some other arena depending on the values of the peer group.

The work by Stattin and Magnusson (1990) provides an example of this process. They reported that some young women (early maturers) are particularly likely to be channeled into early heterosocial peer groups and activities. Because these females look sexually mature, they are more likely to become involved with older peers, particularly with older male peers who interact with them in a gender-role stereotypic manner. As these young women get caught up in this peer social system, they shift their attention away from academic activities and into heterosocial activities and roles. As a result, they lower their educational aspirations, shift the value they attach to academic pursuits and, in fact, end up obtaining less education than one would have predicted based on their prepubertal academic performance and motivation. Instead, they often marry and become parents earlier than their female classmates.

Work by Stattin, Kerr, Mahoney, Persson, and Magnusson (2005) elaborates on these early findings. They follow a sample of adolescents as they move through adolescence and into adulthood. Just like the girls in the Stattin and Magnusson study, these early maturing girls were likely to drop out of school earlier and then to both marry and have children earlier than their later maturing peers. But this was true for only a subset of the early maturing girls: those who attended community recreation centers, where they met and then began dating older males. Thus, Stattin et al. (2005) were able to document the pathway by which these early maturing girls moved into a risky older peer group. The recreation centers in their communities provided the setting in which these peer influences were able to be manifest.

Peers' Role in the Coordination of Multiple Goals

The work by Stattin et al. is also illustrative of the importance of coordinating multiple goals. Just as schools and communities are complex organizations with multiple purposes and goals, so individuals have multiple goals. Learning to coordinate and manage one's goals is a key developmental task. Peers can play a central role in this process by making various goals and activities more or less salient and more or less desirable. Adolescence is an ideal time in which to observe the dynamics of this process. Similar processes have been suggested for various ethnic groups. Several investigators have suggested that some groups are likely to receive less peer support for academic achievement than affluent European-American youth (e.g., Fordham & Ogbu, 1986; Willis, 1977). Steinberg, Dornbusch, and Brown (1992) concluded that both the lower performance of African-Americans and Latin-Americans and the higher performance of European-Americans and Asian-Americans are due more to ethnic differences in peer support for academic achievement than ethnic differences in either the value parents attach to education or the youths' beliefs regarding the likely occupational payoff for academic success. Even though the adolescents in each of these groups reported strong support for school achievement from their parents, the Latin-American and African-American students reported less support for school achievement among their peers than either the European-American or Asian-American students. Consequently there was less congruence between parents and peers in the valuing of school achievement. Some of the African-Americans indicated that they had great difficulty finding a peer group that would encourage them to comply with their parents' valuing of educational success. As a result, they reported that they had to be very careful in selecting which of their African-American peers to have as close friends. European-American and Asian-American students are much less likely to report this kind of peer dilemma.

Summary of Peer Effects

Peer influences are an integral part of both school and neighborhood effects. Spending time with one's peers is a major activity in both of these extra-familial contexts: In fact, the opportunity to spend so much time with one's peers is one of their major distinguishing characteristics. In this section, we have stressed that the impact of peers in these settings depends on the nature of the individuals and the inherent activities. Characteristics of both schools and neighborhoods influence the types of peers to whom, and the types of peer-group activities to which, children and adolescents will be exposed. If these peers have positive, prosocial values and behaviors, these associations are likely to facilitate positive developmental outcomes; if these peers have more problematic values and behaviors, these associations are likely to put the children's development at risk. Schools and neighborhoods also structure the kinds of activities individuals have the opportunity to engage in during their free time.

CONCLUSIONS

In this chapter, we have summarized the many ways in which schools, activity settings, and communities can influence child and adolescent development. We began by pointing out how the multiple levels of school organization interact to shape the day-to-day experiences of children and teachers. We stressed how one must think of schools as complex organizations to understand how decisions and regulatory processes at each level impact on schools as a context for development. We also stressed the interface of schools, as complex changing institutions, with the developmental trajectories of individuals. To understand how schools influence development, one needs to understand change at both the individual and the institutional level. The stage–environment fit theory provides an excellent example of the linking of these two developmental trajectories. Imagine two trajectories: one at the school level and one at the individual level. Schools change in many ways over the grade levels. The nature of these changes can be developmentally appropriate or inappropriate in terms of the extent to which they foster continued development toward the transition into adulthood and maturity. (The changes can also be developmentally irrelevant, but we did not discuss these types of changes.) Children move through this changing context as they move from grade to grade and from school to school. Similarly, children develop and change as they get older. They also have assumptions about their increasing maturity and the privileges it ought to afford them. We believe optimal development occurs when these two trajectories of change are in synchrony with each other; that is, when the changes in the context mesh well with, and perhaps even slightly precede, the patterns of change occurring at the individual level. Furthermore, we summarized evidence that the risk of negative developmental outcomes is increased when these two trajectories are out of synchrony—particularly when the context changes in a developmental regressive pattern.

We also discussed the relation of school characteristics to other contexts of development, particularly the community and the peer group. We then discussed how neighborhood characteristics can influence development independent of its association with schools. We summarized how both school and neighborhood influences are mediated by their impact on peer interactions and activity involvement. Throughout we stressed the need to look at interactions among these various contextual influences. Researchers seldom consider interactions across contexts of development. Instead, they tend to specialize in one context—for example, the family or the peer group. But people live in multiple contexts. Making sense of, and coordinating the demands of, these multiple contexts are among the more challenging developmental tasks. We know very little about how individuals manage these tasks and about how the ability to manage these tasks develops over time. We know relatively little about how characteristics of one context influence the characteristics of other contexts. We summarized some of the ways in which school, peer, leisure activity setting, and neighborhood characteristics influence the nature of children's peer groups and peer interactions. Much more such work and theorizing are needed.

Another way to think about multiple contexts is in terms of their relative ability to meet human needs. As we noted earlier, Connell and Wellborn (1991) suggested that individuals develop best in contexts that provide opportunities to feel competent, to feel socially connected and valued, and to exercise control over their own destiny. If this is true, then individuals ought to be drawn toward those contexts that provide these opportunities in developmentally appropriate doses. Variations across contexts on these characteristics could explain why individuals come to prefer one context over another—for example, adolescents who are not doing well in school or who are having difficulty getting along with their parents might turn to their peer group to find a sense of competence and positive self-esteem. Essentially, we are arguing that when individuals have some choice over where to spend their time, they will choose to spend the most time in those social contexts that best fulfill their needs for a sense of competence, for high-quality social relationship, for respect from others for their autonomy and individuality, and for a sense of being valued by one's social partners. If they can fulfill these needs within social contexts that reinforce normative behavior, they are likely to do well in school and other culturally valued institutions. If they cannot fulfill their needs in these types of social contexts, they are likely to seek out other social contexts, which, in turn, may reinforce more norm-breaking and problematic behaviors. Thus, if we want to support positive, normative developmental pathways for our children and adolescents, it is critical that we provide them with ample opportunities to fulfill their basic human needs in social contexts that reinforce positive normative developmental pathways.

ACKNOWLEDGMENTS

We would like to thank our colleagues and students for helping us think through the issues raised in this chapter and for helping us in preparing the manuscript. We would also like to thank the editors of this book for their comments and editorial suggestions.

REFERENCES AND SUGGESTED READINGS (📖)

Adelman, H. S., & Taylor, L. (1998). Reframing mental health in schools and expanding school reform. *Educational Psychologist, 33,* 135–152.

Akiba, M., LeTendre, G. K., & Scribner, J. P. (2007). Teacher quality, opportunity gap, and national achievement in 46 countries. *Educational Researcher, 36,* 369–387.

Alexander, K. L., & Entwisle, D. (1988). Achievement in the first two years of school: Patterns and processes. *Monographs of the Society for Research in Child Development,* 53 (2, Serial No. 218).

Alexander, K. L., Entwisle, D. R., & Dauber, S. L. (1994). *On the success of failure: A reassessment of the effects of retention in primary grades.* Cambridge, UK: Cambridge University Press.

Alexander, K. L., Entwisle, D. R., & Olson, L. S. (2007). Lasting consequences of the summer learning gap. *Sociology of Education, 72,* 167–180.

Allen, J. P., Philliber, S., Herrling, S., & Kuperminc, G. P. (1997). Preventing teen pregnancy and academic failure: Experimental evaluation of a developmentally-based approach. *Child Development, 64,* 729–742.

Ambady, N., Shih, M., Kim, A., & Pittinsky, T. L. (2001). Stereotype susceptibility in children: Effects of identity activation on quantitative performance. *Psychological Science, 12*(5), 385–390.

Ames, C. (1992). Classrooms: Goals, structures, and student motivation. *Journal of Educational Psychology, 84,* 261–271.

Anderman, E. M., & Maehr, M. L. (1994). Motivation and schooling in the middle grades. *Review of Educational Research, 64,* 287–309.

Anderman, E. M., Maehr, M. L., & Midgley, C. (1999). Declining motivation after the transition to middle school: Schools can make a difference. *Journal of Research and Development in Education, 32,* 131–147.

Arbreton, A. J. A., & Eccles, J. S. (1994, April). *Mothers' perceptions of their children during the transition from kindergarten to formal schooling: The effect of teacher evaluations on parents' expectations for their early elementary school children.* Paper presented at the American Educational Research Association Conference, New Orleans, LA.

📖 Aronson, J., & Steele, C. M. (2005). Stereotypes and the fragility of academic competence, motivation, and self-concept. In A. J. Elliot & C. S. Dweck (Eds.), *Handbook of competence and motivation.* New York: Guilford.

Ashton, P. (1985). Motivation and the teacher's sense of efficacy. In C. Ames & R. Ames (Eds.), *Research on motivation in education, Vol. 2: The classroom milieu* (pp. 141–171). Orlando, FL: Academic Press.

Assor, A., Kaplan, H., & Roth, G. (2002). Choice is good but relevance is excellent: Autonomy-enhancing and suppressing teacher behaviors predicting students' engagement in schoolwork. *British Journal of Educational Psychology, 72,* 261–278.

Assor, A., Vansteenkiste, M., & Kaplan, A. (2009). Identified versus introjected approach and introjected avoidance motivation in school and in sports: The limited benefits of self-worth striving. *Journal of Educational Psychology, 101*(2), 482–487.

Astor, R. A., Meyer, H. A., Behre, W. J. (1999). Unowned places and times: Maps and interviews about violence in high schools. *American Educational Research Journal, 36,* 3–42.

Astor, R. A., Benbenishty, R., Zeira, A., & Vinokur, A. (2002). School climate, observed risky behaviors, and victimization as predictors of high school students' fear and judgments of school violence as a problem. *Health Education & Behavior, 29,* 716–730.

Atkinson, J. W. (1957). Motivational determinants of risk taking behavior. *Psychological Review*, *64*, 359–372.

August, D., & Hakuta, K. (Eds.). (1998). *Educating language minority children*. Washington, DC: National Academy Press.

Ball, A. F. (2002). Three decades of research on classroom life: Illuminating the classroom communicative lives of America's at-risk students. In W. G. Secada (Ed.), *Review of research in education* (Vol. 26, pp. 71–112). Washington, DC: American Educational Research Association Press.

Bandura, A. (1994). *Self-efficacy: The exercise of control*. New York: W. H. Freeman.

Bandura, A. (2006). Toward a psychology of human agency. *Psychological Science*, *1*, 164–180.

Barber, B. L., Eccles, J. S., & Stone, M. R. (2001). Whatever happened to the Jock, the Brain, and the Princess?: Young adult pathways linked to adolescent activity involvement and social identity. *Journal of Adolescent Research*, *16*, 429–455.

Barker, R., & Gump, P. (1964). *Big school, small school: High school size and student behavior*. Stanford, CA: Stanford University Press.

Baumrind, D. (1971). Current patterns of parental authority. *Developmental Psychology Monograph*, *4*(1).

Battistich, V., Watson, M., Solomon, D., Lewis, C., & Schaps, E. (1999). Beyond the three R's: A broader agenda for school reform. *Elementary School Journal*, *99*, 415–432.

Benbenishty, R., & Astor, R. A. (2007). Monitoring indicators of children's victimization in school: Linking national-, regional-, and site-level indicators. *Social Indicators Research*, *84*, 333–348.

Benbenishty, R., Astor, R. A., Zeira, A., & Vinokus, A. D. (2002). Perceptions of violence and fear of school attendance among junior high school students in Israel. *Social Work Research*, *2*, 71–87.

Benson, P. L., Donahue, M. J., & Erickson, J. A. (1989). Adolescence and religion: A review of the literature from 1970 to 1986. *Research in the Social Scientific Study of Religion*, *1*, 153–181.

Berliner, D. (2003, May). *Heisenberg, high-stakes testing, and the honor of teachers*. Lecture at Stanford University School of Education, Stanford, CA.

Berndt, T. J., & Keefe, K. (1995). Friends' influence on adolescents' adjustment to school. *Child Development*, *66*, 1312–1329.

Berndt, T. J., Laychak, A. E., & Park, K. (1990). Friends' influence on adolescents' academic achievement motivation: An experimental study. *Journal of Educational Psychology*, *82*(4), 664–670.

Blos, P. (1965). The initial stage of male adolescence. *Psychoanalytic Study of the Child*, *20*, 145–164.

Blumenfeld, P. C. (1992). Classroom learning and motivation: Clarifying and expanding goal theory. *Journal of Educational Psychology*, *84*, 272–281.

Blumenfeld, P. C., Mergendoller, J., & Swartout, D. (1987). Task as a heuristic for understanding student learning and motivation. *Journal of Curriculum Studies*, *19*, 135–148.

Boyce, W. T., Frank, E., Jensen, P. S., Kessler, R. C., Nelson, C. A., Steinberg, L., et al. (1998). Social context in developmental psychopathology: Recommendations for future research from the MacArthur Network on Psychopathology and Development. *Development and Psychopathology*, *10*, 143–164.

Brody, G. H., Chen, Y.-F., Murry, V. M., Simons, R. L., Ge, X., Gibbons, F. X., et al. (2006). Perceived discrimination and the adjustment of African American youths: A five-year longitudinal analysis with contextual moderation effects. *Child Development*, *77*(5), 1170–1189.

Bronfenbrenner, U. (1979). *The ecology of human development: Experiments by nature and design*. Cambridge, MA: Harvard University Press.

Bronfenbrenner, U., & Morris, P. A. (1998). The ecology of environmental processes. In W. Damon (Series Ed.) & R. M. Lerner (Vol. Ed.), *Handbook of child psychology* (5th ed., Vol. 1, pp. 993–1028). New York: Wiley.

Brooks-Gunn, J., Duncan, G. J., & Aber, J. L. (Eds.) (1997a). *Neighborhood poverty* (Vol. 1). New York: Russell Sage Foundation.

Brooks-Gunn, J., Duncan, G. J., & Aber, J. L. (Eds.) (1997b). *Neighborhood Poverty* (Vol. 2). New York: Russell Sage Foundation.

Brophy, J. (1988). Research linking teacher behavior to student achievement: Potential implications for instruction of Chapter 1 students. *Educational Psychologist*, *23*, 235–286.

Brophy, J. E. (2004). *Motivating students to learn* (2nd ed.). Mahwah, NJ: Lawrence Erlbaum Associates.

Brown, A. L. (1997). Transforming schools into communities of thinking and learning about serious matters. *American Psychologist*, *52*, 399–413.

Brown, B. B. (2004). Adolescents' relationships. New York: Holt, Rinehart & Winston.

Bryk, A. S., Lee, V. E., & Holland P. B. (1993). *Catholic schools and the common good*. Cambridge, MA: Harvard University Press.

Burchinal, M. R., Roberts, J. E., Zeisel, S. A., & Rowley, S. J. (2008). Social risk and protective factors for African American children academic achievement and adjustment during the transition to middle school. *Developmental Psychology*, *44*(1), 286–292.

Calabrese, R., & Schumer, H. (1986). The effects of service activities on adolescent alienation. *Adolescence*, *21*(83), 675–687.

Calderhead, J. (1996). Teachers, beliefs, and knowledge. In D. C. Berliner & R. C. Calfee (Eds.), *Handbook of educational psychology* (pp. 709–725). New York: Simon & Schuster Macmillan.

Camarota, S. A., & McArdle, N. (2003). *Where immigrants live: An examination of state residency of the foreign born by country of origin in 1990 and 2000.* Washington, DC: Center for Immigration Studies.

Carnegie Corporation of New York (1992). *A matter of time: Risk and opportunity in the non school hours.* New York: Carnegie Corporation.

Carnegie Council on Adolescent Development (1989). *Turning points: Preparing American youth for the 21st century.* New York: Carnegie Corporation.

Carskadon, M. A. (1990). Patterns of sleep and sleepiness in adolescents. *Pediatrician, 17,* 5–12.

Carskadon, M. A. (1997, April). *Adolescent sleep: Can we reconcile biological needs with societal demands?* Lecture given at Stanford University, Stanford, CA.

Caspi, A., & Roberts, B. W. (2001). Personality development across the life course: The argument for continuity and change. *Psychological Inquiry, 12,* 49–66.

Cauce, A. M., Comer, J. P., & Schwartz, D. (1987). Long term effects of a systems oriented school prevention program. *American Journal of Orthopsychiatric Association, 57,* 127–131.

Chavous, T. M., Bernat, D. H., Schmeelk-Cone, K., Caldwell, C. H. Kohn-Wood, L., & Zimmerman, M. A. (2003). Racial identity and academic attainment among African American adolescents. *Child Development, 74*(4), 1076–1090.

Chavous, T. M., Rivas-Drake, D., Smalls, C., Griffin, T., & Cogburn, C. (2008). Gender matters, too: The influences of school racial discrimination and racial identity on academic engagement outcomes among African American adolescents. *Developmental Psychology, 44,* 637–654.

Christian, M. K., Morrison, F. J., Frazier, J. A., & Massetti, F. (2000). Specificity in the nature and timing of cognitive change. *Journal of Cognition and Development, 1*(4), 429–448.

Cohen, E. G., & Lotan, R. A. (Eds.). (1997). *Working for equity in heterogeneous classrooms: Sociological theory in practice.* New York: Teachers College Press.

Cole, M. (1996). *Cultural psychology: A once and future discipline.* Cambridge, MA: Harvard University Press.

Coleman, J S. (1961). *The adolescent society.* New York: Free Press.

Coleman, J. S., & Hoffer, T. (1987). *Public and private high schools. The impact of communities.* New York: Basic Books.

Collaborative for Academic, Social, and Emotional Learning (CASEL). (2003). *Safe and sound: An educational leader's guide to evidence-based social and emotional learning programs.* Chicago: CASEL. Retrieved October 1, 2003, from www.casel.org

Comer, J. (1980). *School power.* New York: Free Press.

Connell, J. P. (2003). *Getting off the dime: First steps toward implementing First Things First.* Report prepared for the US Department of Education. Philadelphia: Institute for Research and Reform in Education.

Connell, J. P., & Klem, A. M. (2000), You can get there from here: Using a theory of change approach to plan urban education reform. *Journal of Educational and Psychological Consultation, 11,* 93–120.

Connell, J. P., & Wellborn, J. G. (1991). Competence, autonomy, and relatedness: A motivational analysis of self-system processes. In R. Gunnar & L. A. Sroufe (Eds.), *Minnesota symposia on child psychology* (Vol. 23, pp. 43–77). Hillsdale, NJ: Lawrence Erlbaum Associates.

Council of the Great City Schools (1992). *National urban education goals: Baseline indicators, 1990–91.* Washington, DC: Council of the Great City Schools.

Covington, M. V. (1992). *Making the grade: A self-worth perspective on motivation and school reform.* New York: Cambridge University Press.

Covington, M. V. (2000). Goal theory, motivation, and school achievement: An integrative review. *Annual Review of Psychology, 51,* 171–200.

Crosnoe, R., Johnson, M. K., & Elder, G. H. (2004). School size and the interpersonal side of education: An examination of race/ethnicity and organizational context. *Social Science Quarterly, 85*(5), 1259–1274.

Csikszentmihalyi, M., Rathunde, K., & Whalen, S. (1993). *Talented teenagers: The roots of success and failure.* New York: Cambridge University Press.

Daniels, L. M., Haynes, T. L., Stupnisky, R. H., Perry, R. P., Newall, N. E., & Pekrun, R. (2007). *Contemporary Educational Psychology, 33,* 584–608.

Darling-Hammond, L. (1997). *The right to learn: A blueprint for creating schools that work.* San Francisco: Jossey-Bass.

Darling-Hammond, L. (1999). *Teacher quality and student achievement: A review of state policy evidence* (Document R-99-1). University of Washington: Center for the Study of Teaching and Policy.

Darling-Hammond, L. (2000). New standards and old inequalities: School reform and the education of African American students. *Journal of Negro Education, 69,* 263–287.

Darling-Hammond, L. (2007). Evaluating "No Child Left Behind". *The Nation,* May 21.

Darling-Hammond, L., & Bransford, J. (Eds.). (2005). *Preparing teachers for a changing world: What teachers should learn and be able to do.* San Francisco: Jossey-Bass.

Davidson, A. L., & Phelan, P. (1999). Students' multiple worlds: An anthropological approach to understanding students' engagement with school. In Urdan, T. C. (Ed.), *Advances in motivation: The role of context, Volume 11* (pp. 233–273). Stamford, CT: JAI Press.

Deci, E. L., & Ryan, R. M. (2002). Self-determination research: Reflections and future directions. In E. L. Deci & R. M. Ryan (Eds.), *Handbook of self-determination theory research* (pp. 431–441). Rochester, NY: University of Rochester Press.

Dehyle, D., & LeCompte, M. (1999). Cultural differences in child development: Navaho adolescents in middle schools. In R. H. Sheets & E. R. Hollins (Eds.), *Racial and ethnic identity in school practices: Aspects of human development* (pp. 123–140). Mahwah, NJ: Lawrence Erlbaum Associates.

Dewey, J. (1902/1990). *The child and the curriculum*. Chicago: University of Chicago Press.

Dishon, T. J, Poulin, F., & Burraston, B. (2001). Peer group dynamics associated with iatrogenic effect in group interventions with high-risk young adolescents. *New Directions for Child and Adolescent Development*, *91*, 79–82.

Dornbusch, S. M. (1994). *Off the track*. Presidential address at the biennial meeting of the Society for Research on Adolescence, San Diego, CA.

Dotterer, A. M., McHale, S. M., & Crouter, A. C. (2009). The development and correlates of academic interests from childhood through adolescence. *Journal of Educational Psychology*, *101*(2), 509–519.

Doyle, W. (1983). Academic work. *Review of Educational Research*, *53*, 159–200.

Doyle, W. (1985). Recent research on classroom management: Implications for teacher preparation. *Journal of Teacher Education*, *36*, 31–35.

Dryfoos, J. G. (1990). *Adolescents at risk: Prevalence and prevention*. Oxford, UK: Oxford University Press.

DuBois, D. L., Holloway, B. E., Valentine, J. C., & Cooper, H. (2002). Effectiveness of mentoring programs for youth: A meta-analytic review. *American Journal of Community Psychology*, *30*(2), 157–198.

Duncan, G. J., & Brooks-Gunn, J. (Eds.). (1997). *Consequences of growing up poor*. New York: Russell Sage Foundation.

Durlak, J. A., & Wells, A. M. (1997). Primary prevention mental health programs for children and adolescents: A meta-analytic review. *American Journal of Community Psychology*, *25*, 115–152.

Durlak, J. A., Weissberg, R. P., Taylor, R. D., & Dymnicki, A. B. (in press). The effects of school-based social and emotional learning: A meta-analytic review. *Child Development*.

Dweck, C. S. (2002). The development of ability conceptions. In A. Wigfield & J. S. Eccles (Eds.), *Development of achievement motivation* (pp. 57–88). San Diego, CA: Academic Press.

Dweck, C. S. (1992). The study of goals in psychology. *Psychological Science*, *3*, 165–166.

Eccles, J.S. (1983). Expectancies, values, and academic behavior. In J. Spence (Ed.), *Achievement and achievement motivation*. San Francisco: W.H. Freeman.

Eccles, J. S. (1984). Sex differences in achievement patterns. In T. Sonderegger (Ed.), *Nebraska symposium on motivation* (Vol. 32, pp. 97–132). Lincoln, NE: University of Nebraska Press.

Eccles, J. S. (1994). Understanding women's educational and occupational choices: Applying the Eccles et al. model of achievement-related choices. *Psychology of Women Quarterly*, *18*, 585–609.

Eccles, J. S. (2009). Who am I and what am I going to do with my life? Personal and collective identities as motivators of action. *Educational Psychologist*, *44*(2), 78–89.

Eccles, J. S., & Barber, B. L. (1999). Student council, volunteering, basketball, or marching band: What kind of extracurricular involvement matters? *Journal of Adolescent Research*, *14*, 10–43.

Eccles, J. S., Barber, B. L., Stone, M., & Hunt, J. (2003). Extracurricular activities and adolescent development. *Journal of Social Issues*, *59*, 865–889.

Eccles, J. S., & Gootman, J. A. (Eds.). (2002). *Community programs to promote youth development*. Washington, DC: National Academy Press.

Eccles, J. S., & Harold, R. D. (1993). Parent–school involvement during the early adolescent years. *Teachers' College Record*, *94*, 568–587.

Eccles, J., Lord, S., & Roeser, R. (1996). Round holes, square pegs, rocky roads, and sore feet: The impact of stage/environment fit on young adolescents' experiences in schools and families. In D. Cicchetti & S. L. Toth (Eds.), *Rochester symposium on developmental psychopathology, Volume VIII: Adolescence: opportunities and challenges* (pp. 47–93). Rochester, NY: University of Rochester Press.

Eccles, J. S., & Midgley, C. (1989). Stage/environment fit: Developmentally appropriate classrooms for early adolescents. In R. Ames & C. Ames (Eds.), *Research on motivation in education* (Vol. 3, pp. 139–181). New York: Academic Press.

Eccles, J., Midgley, C., & Adler, T. (1984). Grade-related changes in the school environment: Effects on achievement motivation. In J. G. Nicholls (Ed.), *The development of achievement motivation* (pp. 283–331). Greenwich, CT: JAI Press.

Eccles, J. S., Midgley, C., Wigfield, A., Buchanan, C. M., Reuman, D., Flanagan, C., & MacIver, D. (1993). Development during adolescence: The impact of stage–environment fit on adolescents' experiences in schools and families. *American Psychologist*, 48, 90–101.

Eccles, J. S., & Roeser, R. (2009). Schools, academic motivation and stage–environment fit. In R. M. Lerner & L. Steinberg (Eds.), *Handbook of adolescent psychology* (3rd ed., pp. 404–434). Hoboken, NJ: Wiley.

Eccles, J. S., & Templeton, J. (2002). Extracurricular and other after-school activities for youth. In W. S. Secada (Ed.), *Review of Educational Research* (Vol. 26, pp. 113–180). Washington DC: American Educational Research Association Press.

Eccles, J., & Wigfield, A. (1985). Teacher expectations and student motivation. In J. B. Dusek (Ed.), *Teacher expectations* (pp. 185–217). Hillsdale, NJ: Lawrence Erlbaum Associates.

Eccles, J. S., Wigfield, A., & Schiefele, U. (1998). Motivation. In N. Eisenberg (Ed.), *Handbook of child psychology* (5th ed., Vol. 3, pp. 1017–1095). New York: Wiley.

Eckert, P. (1989). *Jocks and burnouts: Social categories and identity in the high school.* New York: Teacher College Press.

Elder, G. H., & Conger, R. D. (2000). *Children of the land.* Chicago: University of Chicago Press.

Elias, M. J., Zins, J. E., Weissberg, R. P., Frey, K. S., Greenberg, M. T., Haynes, N. M., et al. (1997). *Promoting social and emotional learning: Guidelines for educators.* Alexandria, VA: Association for Supervision and Curriculum Development.

Elliott, D. S., Hamburg, B. A., & Williams, K. R. (1998). *Violence in American schools.* Cambridge, UK: Cambridge University Press.

Elliott, D. S., Menard, S., Rankin, B., Elliott, A., Wilson, W. J., & Huizinga, D. (in preparation). *Overcoming disadvantage: Successful youth development in high risk neighborhoods.*

Entwisle, D. R., & Alexander, K. L. (1993). Entry into school: The beginning school transition and educational stratification in the United States. *Annual Review of Sociology, 19,* 401–423.

Entwisle, D. R., Alexander, K. L. & Olson, L. S. (1997). *Children, schools and inequality.* Boulder, CO: Westview.

Epstein, J. L. (1983). The influence of friends on achievement and affective outcomes. In J. L. Epstein & N.L. Karweit (Eds.), *Friends in school* (pp. 177–200). New York: McGraw-Hill.

Epstein, J. L. (1992). School and family partnerships. In M. Alkin (Ed.), *Encyclopedia of educational research* (pp. 1139–1151). New York: Macmillan.

Eyler, J., Root, S., and Giles, D. E., Jr. (1998). Service-learning and the development of expert citizens: Service-learning and cognitive science. In R. Bingle and D. Duffey (Eds.), *With service in mind.* Washington, DC: American Association of Higher Education.

Fagan, J., & Wilkinson, D. L. (1998). Guns, youth violence and social identity. In M. Tonry & M. H. Moore (Eds.), *Youth violence* (pp. 373–456). Chicago: University of Chicago Press.

Fashola, O. S., Slavin, R. E., Calderon, M., & Duran, R. (2001). Effective programs for Latino students in elementary and middle schools. In R. E. Slavin & M. Calderon (Eds.), *Effective programs for Latino students* (pp. 1–66). Mahwah, NJ: Lawrence Erlbaum Associates.

Feldlaufer, H., Midgley, C., & Eccles, J. S. (1988). Student, teacher, and observer perceptions of the classroom environment before and after the transition to junior high school. *Journal of Early Adolescence, 8,* 133–156.

Fine, G. A. (1992). *With the boys: Little League baseball and preadolescent culture.* Chicago: University of Chicago Press.

Fine, M. (1991). *Framing dropouts: Notes on the politics of an urban public high school.* Albany, NY: State University of New York Press.

Finn, J. D. (1989). Withdrawing from school. *Review of Educational Research, 59,* 117–142.

Finn, J. D., (2006). *The adult lives of at-risk students: The roles of attainment and engagement in high school.* Report NCES 2006–328 to National Center of Educational Statistics. Washington, DC: US Department of Education.

Fiqueira-McDonough, J. (1986). School context, gender, and delinquency. *Journal of Youth and Adolescence, 15,* 79–98.

Firkowska, A., Ostrowska, A., Sokolowksa, M., Stein, Z., Susser, M., & Wald, I. (1978). Cognitive development and social policy. *Science, 200*(23), 1357–1362.

Fisher, D. (2001). "We're moving on up": Creating a schoolwide literacy effort in an urban high school. *Journal of Adolescent & Adult Literacy, 45*(2), 92–101.

Folkman, S., & Lazarus, R. S. (1984). If it changes it must be a process: A study of emotion and coping during three stages of a college examination. *Journal of Personality and Social Psychology, 48,* 150–170.

Ford, D. H., & Lerner, R. M. (1992). *Developmental systems theory: An integrative approach.* Newbury Park, CA: Sage.

Fordham, S., & Ogbu, J. U. (1986). Black students' school success: Coping with "the burden of 'acting white' ". *Urban Review, 18,* 176–206.

Fredricks, J. A., Blumenfeld, P. C., & Paris, A. H. (2004). School engagement: Potential of the concept, state of the evidence. *Review of Educational Research, 74,* 59–109.

Frenzel, A. C., Goetz, T., Ludtke, O., Pekrun, R., & Sutton, R. E. (2009). Emotional transmission in the classroom: Exploring the relationship between teacher and student enjoyment. *Journal of Educational Psychology, 101,* 705–716.

Frenzel, A. C., Pekrun, R., & Goetz, T. (2007). Perceived learning environments and students' emotional experiences: A multilevel analysis of mathematics classrooms. *Learning and Instruction*, *17*(5), 478–493.

Fuligni, A. J., Eccles, J. S., & Barber, B. L. (1995). The long-term effects of seventh-grade ability grouping in mathematics. *Journal of Early Adolescence*, *15*(1), 58–89.

Furstenberg, F. F., Cook, T., Eccles, J. S., Elder, G., & Sameroff, A. (1999). *Managing to succeed*. Chicago: University of Chicago Press.

Gamoran, A., & Mare, R. D. (1989). Secondary school tracking and educational inequality: Compensation, reinforcement, or neutrality? *American Journal of Sociology*, *94*, 1146–1183.

Garcia, E. E., Jensen, B., & Cuellar, D. (2006). Early academic achievement of Hispanics in the United States: Implications for teacher preparation. *New Educator*, *2*, 123–147.

Garcia Coll, C. T., Crnic, K., Hamerty, G., Wasik, B. H., Jenkins, R., Vazquez Garcia, H., & McAdoo, H. P. (1996). An integrative model for the study of developmental competencies in minority children. *Child Development*, *20*, 1891–1914.

Garcia-Reid, P., Reid, R. J., & Peterson, N. A. (2005). School engagement among Latino youth in an urban middle school context: Valuing the role of social support. *Education and Urban Society*, *37*(3), 257–275.

Glancy, M., Willits, F. K., & Farrell, P. (1986). Adolescent activities and adult success and happiness: Twenty-four years later. *Sociology and Social Research*, *70*, 242–250.

Goddard, R. D., Hoy, W. K., & Woolfolk Hoy, A. (2000). Collective teacher efficacy: Its meaning, measure and impact on student achievement. *American Educational Research Journal*, *37*, 479–507.

Goetz, T., Frenzel, A. C., Hall, N. C., & Pekrun, R. (2007). Antecedents of academic emotions: Testing the internal/external frame of reference model for academic enjoyment. *Contemporary Educational Psychology*, *33*, 9–33.

Goetz, T., Frenzel, A. C., Pekrun, R., Hall, N. C., & Ludtke, O. (2007). Between- and within-domain relations of students' academic emotions. *Journal of Educational Psychology*, *99*, 715–733.

Goetz, T., Pekrun, R., Hall, N., & Haag, L. (2006). Academic emotions from a social-cognitive perspective: Antecedents and domain specificity of students' affect in the context of Latin instruction. *British Journal of Educational Psychology*, *76*, 289–308.

Goldenberg, C. (1992). The limits of expectations: A case for case knowledge about teacher expectancy effects. *American Educational Research Journal*, *29*, 517–544.

Goldhaber, D. D. & Brewer, D. J. (2000). Does teacher certification matter? High school teacher certification status and student achievement. *Educational Evaluation and Policy Analysis*, *22*, 129–145.

Good, T., & Weinstein, R. (1986). Teacher expectations: A framework for exploring classrooms. In K. Zumwalt (Ed.), *Improving teaching* (pp. 63–85). Alexandria, VA: Association for Supervision and Curriculum Development.

Goodenow, C. (1993). Classroom belonging among early adolescent students: Relationships to motivation and achievement. *Journal of Early Adolescence*, *13*(1), 21–43.

Gottfredson, D. C., & Wilson, D. B. (2003). Characteristics of effective school-based substance abuse prevention. *Prevention Science*, *4*, 27–38.

Graham, S. (1991). A review of attribution theory in achievement contexts. *Educational Psychology Review*, *3*, 5–39.

Graham, S., & Barker, G. (1990). The downside of help: An attributional–developmental analysis of helping behavior as a low ability cue. *Journal of Educational Psychology*, *82*, 7–14.

Graham, S., & Taylor, A. Z. (2002). Ethnicity, gender, and the development of achievement values. In A. Wigfield & J. S. Eccles (Eds.), *Development of achievement motivation* (pp. 123–146). San Diego: Academic Press.

Greenberg, M. T., Weissberg, R. P., Utne O'Brien, M., Zins, J. E., Fredericks, L., Resnik, H., et al. (2003). Enhancing school-based prevention and youth development through coordinated social, emotional, and academic learning. *American Psychologist*, *58*, 466–474.

Greene, M. L., Way, N., & Pahl, K. (2006). Trajectories of perceived adult and peer discrimination among Black, Latino, and Asian American adolescents: Patterns and psychological correlates. *Developmental Psychology*, *42*, 218–238.

Greenwald, R., Hedges, L. V., & Laine, R. D. (1996). The effect of school resources on student achievement. *Review of Educational Research*, *66*, 361–396.

Grolnick, W. S., & Ryan, R. M. (1987). Autonomy in children's learning: An experimental and individual difference investigation. *Journal of Personality & Social Psychology*, *52*, 890–898.

Grolnick, W. S., Gurland, S. T., Jacob, K. F., & Decourcey, W. (2002). The development of self-determination in middle childhood and adolescence. In A. Wigfield & J. S. Eccles (Eds.), *Development of achievement motivation* (pp. 147–171). San Diego, CA: Academic Press.

Hamilton S. F., & Fenzel, L. M. (1988). The impact of volunteer experience on adolescent social development: Evidence of program effects. *Journal of Adolescent Research*, *3*(1), 65–80.

Harris-Britt, A., Valrie, C.R., Kurtz-Costes, B., & Rowley, S. J. (2007). Perceived racial discrimination and self-esteem in African American youth: Racial socialization as a protective factor. *Journal of Research on Adolescence*, *17*(4), 669–682.

Hart, D., Yates, M., Fegley, S., & Wilson, G. (1995). Moral commitment in inner-city adolescents. In M. Killen & D. Hart (Eds.), *Morality in everyday life: Developmental perspectives*. New York: Cambridge University Press.

Harter, S. (1990). Causes, correlates and the functional role of global self-worth: A life-span perspective. In J. Kolligian & R. Sternberg (Eds.), *Perceptions of competence and incompetence across the life-span* (pp. 67–98). New Haven, CT: Yale University Press.

Hawkins, J. D. (1997). Academic performance and school success: Sources and consequences. In R. P. Weissberg et al. (Eds.), *Enhancing children's wellness, Volume 8: Issues in children's and family's lives* (pp. 278–305). Thousand Oaks, CA: Sage.

Hawkins, J. D., Kosterman, R., Catalano, R. F., Hill, K. G., & Abbott, R. D. (2008). Effects of social development intervention in childhood 15 years later. *Archives of Pediatrics and Adolescent Medicine, 162,* 1133–1141.

Heyneman, S. P., & Loxley, W. A. (1983). The effect of primary-school quality on academic achievement across twenty-nine high- and low-income countries. *American Journal of Sociology, 88,* 1162–1194.

Hill, H. C., Rowan, B., & Ball, D. L. (2005). Effects of teachers' mathematical knowledge for teaching on student achievement. *American Educational Research Journal, 42,* 371–406.

Hoffmann, L. (2002). Promoting girls' interest and achievement in physics classes for beginners. *Learning and Instruction, 12,* 447–465.

Holland, A., & Andre, T. (1987). Participation in extracurricular activities in secondary school: What is known, what needs to be known? *Review of Educational Research, 57,* 437–466.

Hunt, D. E. (1975). Person–environment interaction: A challenge found wanting before it was tried. *Review of Educational Research, 57,* 437–466.

Jackson, A. W., & Davis, G. A. (2000). *Turning points 2000: Educating adolescents in the 21st century.* New York: Teachers College Press.

Jencks, C., & Mayer, S. E. (1990). The social consequences of growing up in a poor neighborhood. In L. E. Lynn, Jr. and M. G. H. McGeary (Eds.), *Inner-city poverty in the United States.* Washington, DC: National Academy Press.

Jennings, P. A., & Greenberg, M. (2009). The prosocial classroom: Teacher social and emotional competence in relation to child and classroom outcomes. *Review of Educational Research, 79,* 491–525.

Johnson, J., & Strange, M. (2005). *Why rural matters 2005: The facts about rural education in the 50 states.* Randolph, VT: The Rural School and Community Trust.

Jussim, L., Eccles, J. S., & Madon, S. (1996). Social perception, social stereotypes, and teacher expectations: Accuracy and the quest for the powerful self-fulfilling prophecy. In L. Berkowitz (Ed.), *Advances in experimental social psychology* (pp. 281–388). New York: Academic Press.

Jussim, L., Palumbo, P., Chatman, C., Madon, S., & Smith, A. (2000). Stigma and self-fulfilling prophecies. In T. F. Heatherton et al. (Eds.), *The social psychology of stigma* (pp. 374–418). New York: Guilford Press.

Juvonen, J. (2007). Reforming middle schools: Focus on continuity, social connectedness, and engagement. *Educational Psychologist, 42*(4), 197–208.

Juvonen, J., Le, V. N., Kaganoff, T., Augustine, C., & Constant, L. (2004). *Focus on the wonder years: Challenges facing the American middle school.* Santa Monica, CA: Rand.

Juvonen, J., Nishina, A., & Graham, S. (2006). Ethnic diversity and perceptions of safety in urban middle schools. *Psychological Science, 17*(5), 393–400.

Kagan, D. M. (1990). How schools alienate students at risk: A model for examining proximal classroom variables. *Educational Psychologist, 25,* 105–125.

Kahne, J., Chi, B., and Middaugh, E. (2002), *Cityworks evaluation summary, Surdna Foundation and Mills College.* Oakland, CA: CERG.

Kao, G., & Thompson, J. S. (2003). Racial and ethnic stratification in educational achievement and attainment. *Annual Review of Sociology, 29,* 417–442.

Karweit, N., & Hansell, S. (1983). School organization and friendship selection. In J. L. Epstein & N. Karweit (Eds.), *Friends in school: Patterns of selection and influence in secondary schools* (pp. 29–38). New York: Academic Press.

Kavrell, S. M., & Petersen, A. C. (1984). Patterns of achievement in early adolescence. In M. L. Maehr (Ed.), *Advances in motivation and achievement* (pp. 1–35). Greenwich, CT: JAI Press.

Keating, D. P. (1990). Adolescent thinking. In S. S. Feldman & G. R. Elliott (Eds.), *At the threshold: The developing adolescent* (pp. 54–89). Cambridge, MA: Harvard University Press.

Kellam, S. G., Rebok, G. W., Wilson, R., & Mayer, L. S. (1994). The social field of the classroom: Context for the developmental epidemiological study of aggressive behavior. In R. K. Silbereisen & E. Todt (Eds.), *Adolescence in context: The interplay of family, school, peers, and work in adjustment* (pp. 390–408). New York: Springer-Verlag.

Kindermann, T. A. (1993). Natural peer groups as contexts for individual development: The case of children's motivation in school. *Developmental Psychology, 29*(6), 970–977.

Kindermann, T. A., McCollam, T. L., & Gibson, E., Jr. (1996). Peer networks and students' classroom engagement during childhood and adolescence. In K. Wentzel & J. Juvonen (Eds.), *Social motivation: Understanding children's school adjustment.* (pp. 279–312). Boston: Cambridge University Press.

King, P. D., & Roeser, R. W. (2009). Religion and spirituality in adolescent development. In R. M. Lerner & L. Steinberg (Eds.), *Handbook of adolescent psychology* (3rd ed.). Hoboken, NJ: Wiley.

King, P. E., & Furrow, J. L. (2004). Religion as a resource for positive youth development: Religion, social capital, and moral outcomes. *Developmental Psychology, 40*(5), 703–713.

Kirby, D. B. (2002). Effective approaches to reducing adolescent unprotected sex, pregnancy, and childbearing. *Journal of Sex Research, 39*, 51–57.

Konings, K. D., Brand-Gruwel, S., van Merrienboer, J. J. G., & Broers, N. J. (2008). Does a new learning environment come up to students' expectations? A longitudinal study. *Journal of Educational Psychology, 100*(3), 535–548.

Krapp, A., Hidi, S. & Renninger, K. A. (1992). Interest, learning and development. In K. A. Renninger, S. Hidi, & A. Krapp (Eds.), *The role of interest in learning and development* (pp. 3–25). Hillsdale, NJ: Lawrence Erlbaum Associates.

Kulik, J. A., & Kulik, C. L. (1987). Effects of ability grouping on student achievement. *Equity & Excellence, 23*, 22–30.

Lamborn, S. D., Brown, B. B., Mounts, N. S., & Steinberg, L. (1992). Putting school in perspective: The influence of family, peers, extracurricular participation, and part-time work on academic engagement (pp. 153–181). In F. M. Newmann (Ed.), *Student engagement and achievement in American secondary schools*. New York: Teachers College Press.

Larson, R. (1994). Youth organizations, hobbies, and sports as developmental contexts. In R. K. Silberiesen & E. Todt (Eds.), *Adolescence in context*. New York: Springer-Verlag.

Larson, R. W. (2000). Toward a psychology of positive youth development. *American Psychologist, 55*, 170–183.

Larson, R., & Hansen, D. (2005). The development of strategic thinking: Learning to impact human systems in a youth activism program. *Human Development, 48*, 237–349.

Larson, R., Hansen, D., & Moneta, G. (2006). Differing profiles of developmental experiences across types of organized youth activities. *Developmental Psychology, 42*, 849–863.

Larson, R., & Kleiber, D. (1993). Free time activities as factors in adolescent adjustment. In P. Tolan & B. Cohler (Eds.), *Handbook of clinical research and practice with adolescents* (pp. 125–145). New York: Wiley.

Larson, R., & Richards, M. (Eds.). (1989). Introduction: The changing life space of early adolescence. *Journal of Youth and Adolescence, 18*, 501–509.

Lazarus, R. S. & Folkman, S. (1984). *Stress, appraisal and coping*. New York: Springer.

LeBlanc, L., Swisher, R., Vitaro, F., & Tremblay, R. E. (2007). School social climate and teachers' perceptions of classroom behavior problems: A ten-year longitudinal and multilevel study. *Social Psychology in Education, 10*, 429–442.

Lee, V. E. (2000). Using hierarchical linear modeling to study social contexts: The case of school effects. *Educational Psychologist, 35*, 125–142.

Lee, V. E. & Bryk, A. S. (1989). A multilevel model of the social distribution of high school achievement. *Sociology of Education, 62*, 172–192.

Lee, V. E., Bryk, A. S., & Smith, J. B. (1993). The organization of effective secondary schools. In L. Darling-Hammond (Ed.), *Review of research in education* (Vol. 19, pp. 171–267). Washington, DC: American Educational Research Association.

Lee, V. E., Croninger, R. G., & Smith, J. B. (1997a). Course taking, equity, and mathematics learning: Testing the constrained curriculum hypothesis in U.S. secondary schools. *Educational Evaluation and Policy Analysis, 19*, 99–121.

Lee, V. E., & Loeb, S. (2000). School size in Chicago Elementary Schools: Effects on teacher attitudes and student achievement. *American Educational Research Journal, 37*, 3–31.

Lee, V. E., & Smith, J. B. (1993). Effects of restructuring on the achievement and engagement of midde-grade students. *Sociology of Education, 66*, 164–187.

Lee, V. E., & Smith, J. B. (1995). Effects of high school restructuring and size on early gains in achievement and engagement. *Sociology of Education, 68*, 241–270.

Lee, V. E., & Smith, J. B. (1997). High school size: Which works best for whom? *Educational Evaluation and Policy Analysis, 19*, 205–227.

Lee, V. E., & Smith, J. (2001). *Restructuring high schools for equity and excellence: What works*. New York: Teachers College Press.

Lee, V. E., Smith, J. B., & Croninger, R. G. (1997b). How high school organization influences the equitable distribution of learning in mathematics and science. *Sociology of Education, 70*, 128–150.

Leventhal, T., & Brooks-Gunn, J. (2004). Diversity in developmental trajectories across adolescence: Neighborhood influences. In R. L. Lerner & L Steinberg, *Handbook of adolescent psychology* (2nd ed., pp. 451–486). Hoboken, NJ: Wiley.

Loeb, S., Darling-Hammond, L., & Luczak, J. (2005). How teaching conditions predict teacher turnover in California schools. *Peabody Journal of Education, 80*, 44–70.

Lord, S., Eccles, J. S., & McCarthy, K. (1994). Risk and protective factors in the transition to junior high school. *Journal of Early Adolescence, 14*, 162–199.

Lucas, T., Henze, R., & Donato, R. (1990). Promoting the success of Latino language-minority students: An exploratory study of six high schools. *Harvard Educational Review, 60,* 315–340.

Mac Iver, D. J., Reuman, D. A., & Main, S. R. (1995). Social structuring of school: Studying what is, illuminating what could be. In M. R. Rosenzweig & L. W. Porter (Eds.), *Annual review of psychology* (Vol. 46). Palo Alto, CA: Annual Reviews.

Mac Iver, D., & Reuman, D. A. (1988, April). *Decision-making in the classroom and early adolescents' valuing of mathematics.* Paper presented at the annual meeting of the American Educational Research Association, New Orleans, LA.

Madon, S., Smith, A., Jussim, L., Russell, D. W., Eccles, J. Palumbo, P., et al. (2001). Am I as you see me or do you see me as I am? Self-fulfilling prophecies and self-verification. *Personality and Social Psychological Bulletin, 27,* 1214–1224.

Maehr, M. L. (1991). The "psychological environment" of the school: A focus for school leadership. In P. Thurstone & P. Zodhiates (Eds.), *Advances in educational administration* (Vol. 2, pp. 51–81). Greenwich, CT: JAI Press.

Maehr, M. L., & Midgley, C. (1996). *Transforming school cultures to enhance student motivation and learning.* Boulder, CO: Westview Press.

Mahoney, J. L. (1997, April). *From companions to convictions: Peer groups, school engagement, and the development of criminality.* Paper presented at the Biennial Meeting of the Society for Research on Child Development, Washington, DC.

Mahoney, J. L., & Cairns, R. B. (1997). Do extracurricular activities protect against early school dropout? *Developmental Psychology, 33,* 241–253.

Mahoney, J. L., Larson, R., & Eccles, J. (Eds.). (2005a). *Organized activities as contexts of development: Extracurricular activities, after-school and community programs.* Hillsdale, NJ: Lawrence Erlbaum Associates.

Mahoney, J. L., Lord, H., & Carryl, E. (2005b). An ecological analysis of after-school program participation and the development of academic performance and motivational attributes for disadvantaged children. *Child Development, 76,* 811–825.

Maroulis, S., & Gomez, L. M. (2008). Does "connectedness" matter? Evidence from a social network analysis within a small-school reform. *Teachers College Record, 110,* 1901–1929.

Marsh, H. W., Chessor, D., Craven, R., & Roche, L. (1995). The effects of gifts and talented programs on academic self-concept: The big fish strikes again. *American Educational Research Journal, 32,* 285–319.

Marsh, H. W., Trautwein, U., Ludtke, O., Baumert, J., & Koller, O. (2007). The big-fish–little-pond effect: Persistent negative effects of selective high schools on self-concept after graduation. *American Educational Research Journal, 44,* 631–669.

Marsh, H. W., Trautwein, U., Ludtke, O., & Brettschneider, W. (2008). Social comparison and big-fish–little-pond effects on self-concept and other self-belief constructs: Role of generalized and specific others. *Journal of Educational Psychology, 100,* 510–524.

Martin, T. F., White, J. M., & Perlman, D. (2001). Religious socialization: A test of the channeling hypothesis of parental influence on adolescent faith maturity. *Journal of Adolescent Research, 18*(2), 169–187.

Mashburn, A. J., Pianta, R. C., Hamre, B. K., Downer, J. T., Barbarin, O. A., Bryant, D., et al. (2008). Measures of classroom quality in prekindergarten and children's development of academic, language, and social skills. *Child Development, 79*(3), 732–749.

McLaughlin, M. W. (2000). *Community counts: How youth organizations matter for youth development.* Washington, DC: Public Education Network.

McLoyd, V. C. (1990). The impact of economic hardship on Black families and development. *Child Development, 61,* 311–346.

McNeal, R. B. (1995). Extracurricular activities and high school dropouts. *Sociology of Education, 68,* 62–81.

McPartland, J. M. (1990). Staffing decisions in the middle grades. *Phi Delta Kappan, 71*(6), 465–469.

Meece, J. (1991). The classroom context and students' motivational goals. In M. Maehr & P. Pintrich (Eds.), *Advances in motivation and achievement* (Vol. 7, pp. 261–286). Greenwich, CT: JAI.

Meece, J. L., Glienke, B. B., & Burg, S. (2006). Gender and motivation. *Journal of Social Psychology, 44,* 351–373.

Meier, J. (2008). Introduction to the special section on European perspectives on the role of education in increasingly diverse European societies. *Child Development Perspectives, 2,* 92.

Melchior, A. & Bailis, L. N. (2002). Impact of service-learning on civic attitudes and behaviors of middle and high school youth: Findings from three national evaluations. In A. Furco & S. H. Billig (Eds.), *Service-learning: The essence of the pedagogy* (pp. 201–222). Greenwich, CT: Information Age.

Midgley, C. (2002). *Goals, goal structures, and patterns of adaptive learning.* Mahwah, NJ: Lawrence Erlbaum Associates.

Midgley, C., Anderman, E., & Hicks, L. (1995). Differences between elementary and middle school teachers and students: A goal theory approach. *Journal of Early Adolescence, 15,* 90–113.

Midgley, C., & Feldlaufer, H. (1987). Students' and teachers' decision-making fit before and after the transition to junior high school. *Journal of Early Adolescence, 7,* 225–241.

Midgley, C., Feldlaufer, H., &, Eccles, J. S. (1988). The transition to junior high school: Beliefs of pre- and post-transition teachers. *Journal of Youth and Adolescence, 17*, 543–562.

Midgley, C. M., Feldlaufer, H., & Eccles, J. S. (1989a). Changes in teacher efficacy and student self- and task-related beliefs during the transition to junior high school. *Journal of Educational Psychology, 81*, 247–258.

Midgley, C., Feldlaufer, H., & Eccles, J. S. (1989b). Student/teacher relations and attitudes toward mathematics before and after the transition to junior high school. *Child Development, 60*, 981–992.

Mind and Life Educational Research Network (submitted for publication). *Contemplative practices and mental training: Prospects for American education*.

Moore, C., & Allen, J. P. (1996). The effects of volunteering on the young volunteer. *Journal of Primary Prevention, 17*, 231–258.

Moos, R. H. (1979). *Evaluating educational environments*. San Francisco: Jossey-Bass.

Mortimer, J. T., Shanahan, M., & Ryu, S. (1994). The effects of adolescent employment on school-related orientation and behavior. In R. K. Silbereisen & E. Todt (Eds.), *Adolescence in context: The interplay of family, school, peers, and work in adjustment* (pp. 304–326). New York: Springer-Verlag.

Murayama, K., & Elliot, A. J. (2009). The joint influence of personal achievement goals and classroom goal structures on achievement-relevant outcomes. *Journal of Educational Psychology, 101*, 432–447.

National Center for Education Statistics (2004). *Service-learning and community service in K-12 public schools*. Washington, DC: US Department of Education.

National Center for Education Statistics (2005). *The condition of education 2005* (NCES 2005–094). Washington, DC: US Department of Education.

National Center for Education Statistics (2006). *The condition of education 2006* (NCES 2006–071). Washington, DC: US Department of Education.

National Center for Education Statistics (2007). *Status and trends in the education of racial and ethnic minorities* (NCES 2007–039). Washington, DC: US Department of Education.

National Research Council (1997). *The new Americans: Economic, demographic, and fiscal effects of immigrations*. Washington, DC: National Academy Press.

National Research Council and Institute of Medicine (2004). *Engaging schools*. Washington, DC: National Academies Press.

Newmann, F. M., Wehlage, G. G., & Lamborn, S. D. (1992). The significance and sources of student engagement. In F. M. Newmann (Ed.), *Student engagement and achievement* in *American secondary schools* (pp. 11–39). New York: Teachers College Press.

Nicholls, J. G. (1990). What is ability and why are we mindful of it? A developmental perspective. In R. J. Sternberg & J. Kolligian (Eds.), *Competence considered*. New Haven, CT: Yale University Press.

Nichols, S. L., & Berliner, D. C. (2007). *Collateral damage: How high stakes testing corrupts America's school*. Boston: Harvard Education Press.

Nichols, S. L., & Berliner, D. C. (2008). Testing the joy out of learning. *Educational Leadership, 65*, 14–18.

Nisbett, R. E. (2008). *Intelligence and how to get it*. New York: W. W. Norton.

Nishina, A., & Juvonen, J. (2005). Daily reports of witnessing and experiencing peer harassment in middle school. *Child Development, 76*(2), 435–450.

Noddings, N. (2005a). *The challenge to care in schools: An alternative approach to education*. New York: Teachers College Press.

Noddings, N. (Ed.) (2005b). *Educating citizens for global awareness*. New York: Teachers College Press.

Oakes, J. (2005). *Keeping track: How schools structure inequality* (2nd ed.). New Haven: CT: Yale University Press.

Oakes, J., Gamoran, A., & Page, R. N. (1992). Curriculum differentiation: Opportunities, outcomes, and meanings. In P. Jackson (Ed.), *Handbook of research on curriculum* (pp. 570–608). New York: Macmillan.

Orfield, G. (1999). *Resegregation in American schools*. Cambridge, MA: Harvard University Press.

Oser, F. K., Scarlett, W. G., & Bucher, A. (2006). Religious and spiritual development throughout the lifespan. In W. Damon & R. M. Lerner (Series Eds.) & R. M. Lerner (Volume Ed.), *Handbook of child psychology, Vol. 1: Theoretical models of human development* (6th ed., pp. 942–998). New York: Wiley.

Osterman, K. F. (2000). Students' need for belonging in the school community. *Review of Educational Research, 70*(3), 323–367.

Otto, L. B., & Alwin, D. (1977). Athletics, aspirations and attainments. *Sociology of Education, 50*, 102–113.

Pallas, A. M., Entwisle, D. R., Alexander, K. L., & Stluka, M. F. (1994). Ability-group effects: Instructional, social, or institutional? *Sociology of Education, 67*, 27–46.

Parsons, J. E., & Ruble, D. N. (1977). The development of achievement–related expectancies. *Child Development, 48*, 1075–1079.

Parsons, J. S., Kaczala, C. M., & Meece, J. L. (1982). Socialization of achievement attitudes and beliefs: Classroom influences. *Child Development, 53*, 322–339.

Partnership for 21st Century Skills (2008). See www.21stcenturyskills.org

Patall, E. A., Cooper, H., & Robinson, J. C. (2008). The effects of choice on intrinsic motivation and related outcomes: A meta–analysis of research findings. *Psychological Bulletin, 134,* 270–300.

Pearce, N. J., & Larson, R. W. (2006). How teens become engaged in youth development programs: The process of motivational change in a civic activism organization. *Applied Developmental Science, 10,* 121–131.

Peck, S., Roeser, R. W., Zarrett, N. R. & Eccles, J. S. (2008). Exploring the role of extracurricular activity involvement in the educational resilience of vulnerable adolescents: Pattern- and variable-centered approaches. *Journal of Social Issues, 64,* 135–156.

Pekrun, R. (2006). The control-value theory of achievement emotions: Assumptions, corollaries, and implications for educational research and practice. *Educational Psychology Review, 18,* 315–341.

Pekrun, R., Goetz, T., & Frenzel, A.C. (2007, April). *Achievement and individual emotion: A multi-level analyses.* Symposium paper presented at American Educational Research Association, San Diego, CA.

Pekrun, R., Goetz, T., Titz, W., & Perry, R. P. (2002). Academic emotions in students' self-regulated learning and achievement: A program of qualitative and quantitative research. *Educational Psychologist, 37,* 91–105.

Perry, K. E., & Weinstein, R. S. (1998). The social context of early schooling and children's school adjustment. *Educational Psychologist, 33,* 177–194.

Peske, H. G., & Haycock, K. (2006). *Teaching inequality: How poor and minority students are shortchanged on teacher quality.* Washington, DC: Education Trust.

Pianta, R. C. (1999). *Enhancing relationships between children and teachers.* Washington, DC: American Psychological Association.

Pianta, R. C., Belsky, J., Houts, R., & Morrison, F. (2007). Opportunities to learn in 'America's elementary classrooms. *Science, 5820,* 1795–1796.

Pianta, R., Belsky, J., Vandergrift, N., Houts, R., & Morrison, F. J. (2008). Classroom effects on children's achievement trajectories in elementary school. *American Educational Research Journal, 45,* 365–398.

Pianta, R. C., & Hamre, B. K. (2009). Conceptualization, measurement and improvement of classroom processes: Standardized observation can leverage capacity. *Educational Researcher, 38,* 109–119.

Pianta, R., Howes, C., Burchinal, M., Bryant, D., Clifford, R., Early, D., et al. (2005). Features of pre-kindergarten programs, classrooms, and teachers: Do they predict observed classroom quality and child–teacher interactions? *Journal of Applied Developmental Science, 3,* 144–159.

Pianta, R. C., & Shuhlman, M. W. (2004). Teacher–child relationships and children's success in the first years of school. *School Psychology Review, 33,* 444–458.

Pintrich, P. R., & Schunk, D. H. (2003). *Motivation in education: Theory, research, and application* (2nd ed.). Englewood Cliffs, NJ: Merrill-Prentice Hall.

Portes, A., & Rumbaut, R. G. (2001). *Legacies: The story of the immigrant second generation.* Berkeley, CA: University of California Press.

Quint, J. (2006). *Meeting five critical challenges of high school reform: Lessons from research on three reform models.* New York: Manpower Demonstration Research Corporation. Retrieved November 11, 2009, from www.mdrc.org/publications/428/execsum.pdf

Ready, D. D., & Lee, V. E. (2008). Choice, equity, and schools-within-schools reform. *Teachers College Record, 110*(9), 1930–1958.

Rehberg, R. A. (1969). Behavioral and attitudinal consequences of high school interscholastic sports: A speculative consideration. *Adolescence, 4,* 69–88.

Renninger, K. A. (2000). Individual interest and its implications for understanding intrinsic motivation. In C. Sansone & J. M. Harackiewicz (Eds.), *Intrinsic and extrinsic motivation* (pp. 373–404). San Diego, CA: Academic Press.

Reuman, D. A. (1989). How social comparison mediates the relation between ability-grouping practices and students' achievement expectancies in mathematics. *Journal of Educational Psychology, 81,* 178–189.

Rist, R. C. (1970). Student social class and teacher expectations: The self-fulfilling prophecy in ghetto education. *Harvard Educational Review, 40,* 411–451.

Roderick, M. (1993). *The path to dropping out.* Westport, CT: Auburn House.

Roehlkepartain, E. C., & Patel, E. (2006). Congregations: Unexamined crucibles for spiritual development. In E. C. Roehlkepartain et al. (Eds.), *The handbook of spiritual development in childhood and adolescence* (pp. 324–336). Thousand Oaks, CA: Sage.

Roeser, R. W. (2004). Competing schools of thought in achievement goal theory? In M. L. Maehr & P. R. Pintrich (Eds.), *Advances in motivation and achievement, Volume 13: Motivating students, improving schools* (pp. 265–299). New York: Elsevier.

Roeser, R. W., & Eccles, J. S. (1998). Adolescents' perceptions of middle school: Relation to longitudinal changes in academic and psychological adjustment. *Journal of Research on Adolescence, 88,* 123–158.

Roeser, R. W., & Eccles, J. S. (2000). Schooling and mental health. In A. J. Sameroff, M. Lewis, & S. M. Miller (Eds.), *Handbook of developmental psychopathology* (2nd ed., pp. 135–156). New York: Plenum.

Roeser, R. W., Eccles, J. S., & Freedman-Doan, C. (1999). Academic and emotional functioning in middle adolescence: Patterns, progressions, and routes from childhood. *Journal of Adolescent Research, 14,* 135–174.

Roeser, R. W., Eccles, J. S., & Sameroff, J. (1998a). Academic and emotional functioning in early adolescence. Longitudinal relations, patterns, and prediction by experience in middle school. *Development and Psychopathology, 10*, 321–352.

Roeser, R. W., Eccles, J. S., & Strobel, K. (1998b). Linking the study of schooling and mental health: Selected issues and empirical illustrations at the level of the individual. *Educational Psychologist, 33*, 153–176.

Roeser, R. W., & Galloway, M. G. (2002). Studying motivation to learn in early adolescence: A holistic perspective. In T. Urdan & F. Pajares (Eds.), *Academic motivation of adolescents: Adolescence and education* (Vol. 2, pp. 331–372). Greenwich, CT: Information Age Publishing.

Roeser, R. W., Marachi, R., & Gehlbach, H. (2002a). A goal theory perspective on teachers' professional identities and the contexts of teaching. In C. Midgley (Ed.), *Goals, goal structure, and patterns of adaptive learning* (pp. 204–239). Mahwah, NJ: Lawrence Erlbaum Associates.

Roeser, R. W., & Midgley, C. M. (1997). Teachers' views of aspects of student mental health. *Elementary School Journal, 98*(2), 115–133.

Roeser, R. W., Midgley, C. M., & Maehr, M. L. (1994, February). *Unfolding and enfolding youth: A development study of school culture and student well-being.* Paper presented at the Society for Research on Adolescence, San Diego, CA.

Roeser, R. W., Midgley, C., & Urdan, T. C. (1996). Perceptions of the school psychological environment and early adolescents' psychological and behavioral functioning in school: The mediating role of goals and belonging. *Journal of Educational Psychology, 88*, 408–422.

Roeser, R. W., & Peck, S. C. (2003). Patterns and pathways of educational achievement across adolescence: A holistic–developmental perspective. *New Directions for Child and Adolescent Development, 101*, 39–62.

Roeser, R. W., & Peck, S. C. (2009). An education in awareness: Self, motivation, and self-regulated learning in contemplative perspective. *Educational Psychologist, 44*, 119–136.

Roeser, R. W., Shavelson, R. J., Kupermintz, H., Lau, S., Ayala, C., Haydel, A., et al. (2002b). The concept of aptitude and multidimensional validity revisited. *Educational Assessment, 8*, 191–205.

Roeser, R. W., Stephens, J. C., & Urdan, T. (2009). School as a context of motivation and development. In K. Wentzel & A. Wigfield (Eds.), *Handbook of motivation.* Mahwah, NJ: Lawrence Erlbaum Associates.

Roeser, R. W., Strobel, K. R., & Quihuis, G. (2002c). Studying early academic motivation, social–emotional functioning, and engagement in learning: Variable- and person-centered approaches. *Anxiety, Stress, and Coping, 15*(4), 345–368.

Roeser, R. W., Urdan, T. C., & Stephens, J. M. (2009). School as a context of motivation and development. In K. R. Wentzel & A. Wigfield (Eds.), *Handbook of motivation at school* (pp. 381–410). New York: Routledge.

Romo, H. D., & Falbo, T. (1996). *Latino high school graduation.* Austin, TX: University of Texas Press.

Rosenbaum, J. E. (1976). *Making inequality: The hidden curriculum of high school tracking.* New York: Wiley.

Rosenbaum, J. E. (1980). Social implications of educational grouping. *Review of Research in Education, 7*, 361–401.

Rosenbaum, J. E. (1991). Black pioneers: Do their moves to the suburbs increase economic opportunity for mothers and children? *Housing Policy Debate, 2*(4), 1179–1213.

Rosenbaum, J. E., Kulieke, M. J., & Rubinowitz, L. S. (1988). White suburban schools' responses to low-income Black children: Sources of successes and problems. *Urban Review, 20*, 28–41.

Rosenbloom, S. R., & Way, N. (2004) Experiences of discrimination among African American, Asian American, and Latino adolescents in an urban high school. *Youth and Society, 35*, 420–451.

Rosenholtz, S. J., & Simpson, C. (1984). The formation of ability conceptions: Developmental trend or social construction? *Review of Educational Research, 54*, 301–325.

Rosenthal, R. (1969). Interpersonal expectations effects of the experimenter's hypothesis. In R. Rosenthal & R. L. Rosnow (Eds.), *Artifacts in behavioral research* (pp. 182–279). New York: Academic Press.

Rosenthal, R. (1974). *On the social psychology of the self-fulfilling prophecy: Further evidence for Pygmalion effects and their mediating mechanisms.* New York: MSS Modular Publications.

Roseth, C. J., Johnson, D. W., & Johnson, R. T. (2008). Promoting early adolescents' achievement and peer relationships: The effects of cooperative, competitive and individualistic goal structures. *Psychological Bulletin, 134*, 223–246.

Ross, L., & Nisbett, R. E. (1991). *The person and the situation: Perspectives of social psychology.* New York: McGraw-Hill.

Rowan, B., Correnti, R., & Miller, R. J. (2002). What large-scale survey research tells us about teacher effects on student achievement: Insights from the Prospects Study of Elementary Schools. *Teachers College Record, 104*, 1525–1567.

Rowley, S. J., Burchinal, M. R., Roberts, J. E., & Zeisel, S. A., (2008). Racial identity, social context, and race-related social cognition in African Americans during middle childhood. *Developmental Psychology, 44*, 1537–1546.

Ruggiero, K. M., & Taylor, D. M. (1995). Coping with discrimination: How disadvantaged group members perceive the discrimination that confronts them. *Journal of Personality and Social Psychology, 68*, 826–838.

Rumberger, R. W. (1995). Dropping out of middle school: A multilevel analysis of students and schools. *American Educational Research Journal, 32*, 583–625.

Runyan, D. K., Hunter, W. M., Socolar, R. R. S., Amaya-Jackson, L., English, D., Landswerk, J., et al. (2009). Children who prosper in unfavorable environments: The relationship to social capital. *Pediatrics, 101*(1), 12–18.

Ruthig, J. C., Perry, R. P., Hladkyj, S., Hall, N. C., Pekrun, R., & Chipperfield, J. G. (2008). Perceived control and emotions: Interactive effects on performance in achievement settings. *Social Psychology Education, 11*, 161–180.

Rutter, M. (1983). School effects on pupil progress: Research findings and policy implications. *Child Development, 54*, 1–29.

Rutter, M., & Maughan, B. (2002). School effectiveness findings 1979–2002. *Journal of School Psychology, 40*, 451–475.

Rutter, M., Maughan, B., Mortimore, P., & Ouston, J. (1979). *Fifteen thousand hours: Secondary schools and their effects on children.* Cambridge, MA: Harvard University Press.

Sable, J., and Garofano, A. (2007). *Public elementary and secondary school student enrollment, high school completions, and staff from the common core of data: School year 2005–06* (NCES 2007–352). Washington, DC: National Center for Education Statistics. Retrieved June 18, 2007, from http://nces.ed.gov/pubsearch/pubsinfo.asp?pubid=2007352

Sameroff, A. (1983). Developmental systems: Contexts and evolution. In W. Kessen (Ed.) and P. H. Mussen (Series Ed.), *Handbook of child psychology: Volume 1. History, theory, and methods* (pp. 237–294). New York: Wiley.

Sampson, R. J., Raudenbush, S. W., & Earls, F. (1997). Neighborhoods and violent crime: A multilevel study of collective efficacy. *Science, 277*, 918–924.

Sarason, S. B. (1990). *The predictable failure of school reform.* San Francisco: Jossey-Bass.

Sawhill, I. V. (2006). Opportunity in America: The role of education. *Future of Children Policy Brief*, Fall, 1–7.

Scales, P. C., Blyth, D. A., Berkas, T. H., & Kielsmeier, J. C. (2000). The effects of service-learning on middle school students' social responsibility and academic success. *Journal of Early Adolescence, 20*(3), 332–358.

Schaps, E. (2003). The heart of a caring school. *Educational Leadership, 60*, 31–33.

Schulting, A. B., Malone, P. S., & Dodge, K. A. (2005). The effect of school-based kindergarten transition policies and practices on child academic outcomes. *Developmental Psychology, 41*(6), 860–871.

Schunk, D. H. (1987). Peer models and children's behavioral change. *Review of Educational Research, 57*, 149–174.

Sellers, R. M., Caldwell, C. H., Schmeelk-Cone, K. H., & Zimmerman, M. A. (2003). Racial identity, racial discrimination, perceived stress, and psychological distress among African American young adults. *Journal of Health and Social Behavior, 44*(3), 302–317.

Sharkey, P. (2009). *Neighborhoods and the Black–White mobility gap.* Report to Economic Mobility Project of the Pew Charitable Trusts, Washington, DC. See www.economicmobility.org

Shih, M., Pittinsky, T. L., & Ambady, N. (1999). Stereotype susceptibility: Identity salience and shifts in quantitative performance. *Psychological Science, 10*(1), 80–83.

Shulman, L. S. (2005). Signature pedagogies in the professions. *Daedalus, 134*, 52–59.

Sieber, R. T. (1979). Classmates as workmates: In formal peer activity in the elementary school. *Anthropology and Education Quarterly, 10*, 207–235.

Simmons, R. G., & Blyth, D. A. (1987). *Moving into adolescence: The impact of pubertal change and school context.* Hawthorn, NY: Aldine de Gruyter.

Skinner, E. A., & Belmont, M. J. (1993). Motivation in the classroom: Reciprocal effects of teacher behavior and student engagement across the school year. *Journal of Educational Psychology, 85*, 571–581.

Slavin, R. E. (1990). Achievement effects of ability grouping in secondary schools: A best-evidence synthesis. *Review of Educational Research, 60*, 471–499.

Slavin, R. E. & Calderon, M. (2001). *Effective programs for Latino students.* Mahwah, NJ: Lawrence Erlbaum Associates.

Sleeper, M. E. & Strom, M. S. (2006). Facing history and ourselves. In M. J. Elias & H. Arnold (Eds.), *The educators' guide to emotional intelligence and academic achievement: Social–emotional learning in the classroom* (pp. 240–246). Thousand Oaks, CA: Corwin Press.

Smith, A. E., Jussim, L., & Eccles, J. S. (1999). Do self-fulfilling prophecies accumulate, dissipate, or remain stable over time? *Journal of Personality and Social Psychology, 77*, 548–565.

Smith, C. (2003). Theorizing religious effects among American adolescents. *Journal for the Scientific Study of Religion, 42*, 17–30.

Smith, C., & Denton, M. L. (2005). *Soul searching: The religious and spiritual lives of American teenagers.* Oxford, UK: Oxford University Press.

Smith, T. M., Desimone, L. M. & Ueno, K. (2005). "Highly qualified" to do what? The relationship of NCLB teacher quality mandates and the use of reform-oriented instruction in middle school mathematics. *Educational Evaluation and Policy Analysis, 27*, 75–109.

Solomon, D., Battistich, V., & Hom, A. (1996). Teacher beliefs and practices in schools serving communities that differ in socioeconomic level. *Journal of Experimental Education, 64*, 327–347.

Staff, J., Mortimer, J. T., & Uggen, C. (2004). Work and leisure in adolescence. In R. L. Lerner & L. Steinberg (2004). *Handbook of adolescent psychology* (2nd ed., pp. 429–450). Hoboken, NJ: Wiley.

Stattin, H., Kerr, M., Mahoney, J., Persson, A., & Magnusson, D. (2005). Explaining why a leisure context is bad for some girls and not for others. In J. L Mahoney, R. W. Larson, & J. S. Eccles. (Eds.). *Organized activities as contexts of development: Extracurricular activities, after-school and community programs* (pp. 211–234). Hillsdale, NJ: Lawrence Erlbaum Associates.

Stattin, H., & Magnusson, D. (1990). *Pubertal maturation in female development*. Hillsdale, NJ: Lawrence Erlbaum Associates.

Steinberg, L., Dornbusch, S., & Brown, B. (1992). Ethnic differences in adolescents' achievements: An ecological perspective. *American Psychologist, 47*, 723–729.

Steinberg, L., Fegley, S., & Dornbusch, S. M. (1993). Negative impact of part-time work on adolescent adjustment: Evidence from a longitudinal study. *Developmental Psychology, 29*, 171–180.

Stevens, R. J., & Slavin, R. E. (1995). The cooperative elementary school: Effects on students' achievement, attitudes, and social relations. *American Educational Research Journal, 32*, 321–351.

Stevenson, H. W., & Stigler, J. W. (1992). *The learning gap: Why our schools are failing and what we can learn from Japanese and Chinese education*. New York: Summit Books.

Stipek, D. J., & Hoffman, J. M. (1980). Children's achievement-related expectancies as a function of academic performance histories and sex. *Journal of Educational Psychology, 72*, 861–865.

Strobel, K., & Roeser, R. W. (1998, April). *Patterns of motivation and mental health in middle school: Relation to academic and emotional regulation strategies*. Paper presented at the Annual Meeting of the American Educational Research Association, San Diego.

Suarez-Orozco, C., & Suarez-Orozco, M. (2001). *Children of immigration*. Cambridge, MA: Harvard University Press.

Szalacha, L. A., Erkut, S., Garcia Coll, C., Alarcon, O., Fields, J. P., & Ceder, I. (2003). Discrimination and Puerto Rican children's and adolescents' mental health. *Cultural Diversity and Ethnic Minority Psychology, 9*, 141–155.

Tschannen-Moran, M., Woolfolk Hoy, A., & Hoy, W. K. (1998). Teacher efficacy: Its meaning and measure. *Review of Educational Research, 68*, 202–248.

Turner, J. C., Midgley, C., Meyer, D. K., Ghenn, M., Anderman, E. M., Kang, Y., et al. (2002). The classroom environment and students' reports of avoidance strategies in mathematics: A multimethod study. *Journal of Educational Psychology, 94*, 88–106.

Urdan, T., Midgley, C., & Anderman, E. (1998). The role of classroom goal structure in students' use of self-handicapping strategies. *American Educational Research Journal, 35*, 101–122.

Urdan, T. C., & Roeser, R. W. (1993, April). *The relations among adolescents' social cognitions, affect, and academic self-schemas*. Paper presented at the annual meeting of the American Educational Research Association, Atlanta, GA.

Valdes, G. (2001). *Learning and not learning English: Latino students in American schools*. New York: Teachers College Press.

Valencia, R. R. (Ed.) (1991). *Chicano school failure and success: Research and policy agendas for the 1990s*. London: Falmer Press.

Vanfossen, B. E., Jones, J. D., & Spade, J. Z. (1987). Curriculum tracking and status maintenance. *Sociology of Education, 60*, 104–122.

Vernez, G., Abrahamse, A., & Quigley, D. D. (1996). *How immigrants fare in U.S. education*. Santa Monica, CA: Rand Corporation.

Wehlage, G., Rutter, R., Smith, G., Lesko, N., & Fernandez, R. (1989). *Reducing the risk: Schools as communities of support*. Philadelphia: Falmer Press.

Weiner, B. (1991). On perceiving the other as responsible. In R. A. Dienstbier (Ed.), *Perspectives on motivation: Nebraska symposium on motivation, 1990* (pp. 165–236). Lincoln, NE: University of Nebraska Press.

Weinstein, R. (1989). Perceptions of classroom processes and student motivation: Children's views of self-fulfilling prophecies. In C. Ames & R. Ames (Eds.), *Research on motivation in education: Vol. 3: Goals and cognitions* (pp. 13–44). New York: Academic Press.

Wentzel, K. (2002). Are effective teachers like good parents? Teaching styles and student adjustment in early adolescence. *Child Development, 73*, 287–301.

Whitbeck, L. B., Simons, R. L., Conger, R. D., Wickrama, K. A. S., Ackley, K. A. & Elder, G. H. (1997). The effects of parents' working conditions and family economic hardship on parenting behaviors and children's self-efficacy. *Social Psychology Quarterly, 60*, 291–303.

Wigfield, A., Byrnes, J. B., & Eccles, J. S. (2006). Adolescent development. In P. A. Alexander & P. Winne (Eds.), *Handbook of educational psychology* (2nd ed.). Mahwah, NJ: Lawrence Erlbaum Associates.

Wigfield, A., & Eccles, J. S. (1989). Test anxiety in elementary and secondary school students. *Educational Psychologist, 24*, 159–183.

Wigfield, A., Eccles, J. S., & Pintrich, P. R. (1996). Development between the ages of eleven and twenty-five. In D. C. Berliner and R. C. Calfee (Eds.), *The handbook of educational psychology* (pp. 148–185). New York: Macmillan.

Wigfield, A., Eccles, J. S., Schiefele, U., Roeser, R., Davis-Kean, P. (2006). Motivation. In N. Eisenberg (Ed.), *Handbook of child psychology* (6th ed., Vol. 3, pp. 933–1002). New York: Wiley.

Wigfield, A., Eccles, J., Mac Iver, D., Reuman, D., & Midgley, C. (1991). Transitions at early adolescence: Changes in children's domain-specific self-perceptions and general self-esteem across the transition to junior high school. *Developmental Psychology*, *27*, 552–565.

Willis, P. L. (1977). *Learning to labor: How working class kids get working class jobs*. Driffield, UK: Nafferton.

Willower, D. J., & Lawrence, J. D. (1979). Teachers' perceptions of student threat to teacher status and teacher pupil control ideology. *Psychology in the Schools*, *16*, 586–590.

Wilson, D. B., Gottfredson, D. C., & Najaka, S. S. (2001). School-based prevention of problem behaviors: A meta-analysis. *Journal of Quantitative Criminology*, *17*, 247–272.

Wilson, W. J. (1987). *The truly disadvantaged: The inner city, the underclass and public policy*. Chicago: University of Chicago Press.

Wong, C. A., Eccles, J. S., & Sameroff, A. J. (2003). The influence of ethnic discrimination and ethnic identification on African-Americans adolescents' school and socioemotional adjustment. *Journal of Personality*, *71*, 1197–1232.

Wyse, A. E., Keesler, V., & Schneider, B. (2008). Assessing the effects of small school size on mathematics achievement: A propensity score-matching approach. *Teachers College Record*, *110*(9), 1879–1900.

Yates, M., & Youniss, M. (1996). A developmental perspective on community service in adolescence. *Social Development*, *5*(1), 85–111.

Youniss, J. (1980). *Parents and peers in social development*. Chicago: University of Chicago.

Youniss, J., McLellan, J. A., & Yates, M., (1997a). What we know about engendering civic identity. *American Behavioral Scientist*, *40*, 619–630.

Youniss, J., Yates, M., & Su, Y. (1997b). Social integration: Community service and marijuana use in high school seniors. *Journal of Adolescent Research*, *12*, 245–262.

Zalantino, S. D., & Sleeman, P. J. (1975). *A systems approach to learning environments*. Pleasantville, NY: Redgrave.

Zimmer-Gembeck, M. J., & Mortimer, J. T. (2006). Adolescent work, vocational development, and education. *Review of Educational Research*, *76*, 537–566.

Zins, J. E., Weissberg, R. P., Wang, M. C., & Walberg, H. J. (2004). *Building academic success on social and emotional learning*. New York: Teachers College Press.

CHILDREN AND THE LAW: EXAMPLES OF APPLIED DEVELOPMENTAL PSYCHOLOGY IN ACTION

Lindsay C. Malloy, Michael E. Lamb, and Carmit Katz
University of Cambridge

INTRODUCTION

Each year, increasing numbers of children come into contact with the legal, social service, and child welfare systems around the world, often as a result of child maltreatment, parental separation/divorce, and delinquent behavior. As a result, children represent "a large and growing legal constituency, one that possesses a special set of constraints involving basic developmental competencies, including cognitive, social, and emotional, that may constrain their effective participation" (Bruck, Ceci, & Principe, 2006, p. 777). In response to these trends, the amount of research concerning children and the law has grown rapidly and continues to grow, making it one of the fastest-growing areas in all of developmental psychology (Bruck et al., 2006). Lawyers, judges, social workers, jurors, parents, and others must make important (often life-transforming) decisions about children's lives in different contexts every day. Psychological research can and should guide these crucial decisions. But does it?

Although legal and social service intervention is often justified by reference to children's best interests, the interventions themselves are seldom informed by reference to developmental theory or the results of scientific research. Instead, political, ideological, and cultural values may guide the development of policies such as those that allow the prosecution of juvenile offenders in adult courts or emphasize family preservation rather than the termination of parental rights when children have been severely and persistently abused by their parents. It is unfortunate that policy makers sometimes fail to take advantage of a burgeoning and increasingly sophisticated understanding of child development in this way because superior public policy and law would surely emerge if policies and practices were better informed.

Psychological research can be and has been used to guide the treatment of children in legal contexts, however, and we use these instances to demonstrate in this chapter how applied and basic psychological research can complement one another, with researchers helping guide practitioners and the latter in turn offering insights and asking questions that foster a more complete understanding of developmental processes. Our discussion focuses on the role and relevance of psychological research in relation to child maltreatment, divorce, and juvenile justice.

When developmental psychology emerged as a distinct discipline about a century ago, it focused very heavily on applied issues, with psychologists regularly providing advice to parents, teachers, and paediatricians (Clarke-Stewart, 1998; Sears, 1975). By the middle of the twentieth century, however, psychologists shifted their focus to basic research questions, apparently fearing that a concern with applied issues made developmental psychology less credible as a science. Today, we see a new appreciation for applied research simultaneously enhancing children's welfare while yielding insights into normative developmental processes that could not be obtained by basic research alone.

As far back as 1843, British psychologists used the "insanity defence" in a case involving a man who attempted to assassinate the Prime Minister of the United Kingdom (Brigham, 1999). Psychology and the legal system thus share a long (and often tumultuous) history. The first legal brief to cite social science evidence was filed in 1908 (*Muller v. Oregon*) and perhaps the best known legal brief informed by psychologists was submitted to the US Supreme Court in 1954 to demonstrate the effects of racial segregation on children's education (*Brown v. Board of Education*, 1954).

More than a century ago, Munsterberg (1908) argued that "The time for such applied psychology is surely near . . . all are ready to see that certain chapters of Applied Psychology are sources of help and strength for them. The lawyer alone is obdurate [pp. 9–10]. . . . It is surprising and seems unjustifiable that lawyers and laymen alike should not have given any attention, so far, to the . . . many . . . methods of the psychological laboratory—methods in the study of memory and attention, feeling and will, perception and judgment, suggestion and emotion. In every one of these fields, the psychological experiment could be made helpful to the purposes of court and law" (p. 76). Munsterberg's claims were met with skepticism and hostility from some legal professionals (e.g., Wigmore, 1909), and even some social scientists (e.g., Cairns, 1935), who reflected opinions and sentiments that prevail to this day, despite considerable evidence that applied psychologists have made substantial contributions with respect to policy concerning children's eyewitness testimony, divorce, and juvenile justice, as shown in the next section.

We begin by defining applied and basic psychology, and then discuss the ways in which both types of research have informed policy and practice regarding these three topics, while also highlighting challenges that were overcome, lessons learned along the way, and issues of continued concern.

APPLIED VERSUS BASIC RESEARCH

What better place to start than with the common misconceptions about applied and basic research? Applied psychological research is often (mis)characterized as atheoretical and methodologically inferior to basic research, while basic research is often (mis)characterized as "that which sits on shelves for other academics to read." Although this may be true in some cases, neither of these characterizations is fair. Furthermore, although applied and basic research may be differently motivated, the distinction need not be framed in an "either/or" format (e.g., Should my research attempt to understand natural phenomena, *or* solve a social problem? Should I make a contribution to theory *or* improve lives?). Both types of research can and often do improve the quality of individuals' lives significantly but, according to Groark and McCall (2005, p. 558), the issue is "how soon, how directly, and what other information is needed before such knowledge guides practice and action."

Applied research has been defined as "research conducted to solve a problem or in order to provide information that can be put to some specific use," whereas basic research is defined as "research motivated by the desire to expand knowledge" (Zigler & Finn-Stevenson, 1999, p. 555). Often basic research is thought of as "knowledge for the sake of knowledge" with unknown but potentially broader implications than applied research aimed at solving a particular problem, usually in a specific setting or context (Campbell, 1978; Cialdini, 1980; Lewin, 1946). Because applied psychology's goal is to provide knowledge relevant to particular circumstances in real-world contexts, it is often conceptualized as "action scholarship" (Groark & McCall, 2005). As such, applied psychology defines and addresses, and aims to solve real-world problems as well as related research questions.

Differences between applied and basic research are also evident in the associated research and dissemination processes including such features as timing, speed, criterion, control, and methodology (Groark & McCall, 2005). For example, applied research faces more stringent deadlines: It must be completed fast enough that the information gleaned is still relevant to the real-world problem at hand. Applied psychologists may take advantage of methods that appear applicable rather than those that might be considered "scientifically ideal" under other circumstances (McCall & Green, 2004). Psychologists conducting applied research also look beyond traditional avenues, such as academic journals, for dissemination, engaging in dialogues with practitioners, policy makers, and other end-users. Because they must simultaneously ensure that they are conducting rigorous empirical research while being aware of concerns and practices in the field, psychologists conducting applied research may find themselves making difficult decisions and choosing among contradictory options more often than psychologists conducting basic research.

As mentioned earlier, applied research and basic psychological research are not mutually exclusive. Not only is there considerable overlap, but they need and complement one another in unique and important ways. For instance, applied psychology typically involves assessing the generalizability of basic theories or findings (Groark & McCall, 2005). In addition, field findings can be understood by putting them in the context of basic research. For example, we show later how applied research has promoted children's welfare, but also how the close study of children's experiences and performance in real-world settings has enhanced our understanding of developmental processes. This point deserves emphasis because psychologists often view applied research as intellectually and methodologically inferior, unlikely to enhance our broader understanding.

While basic research has the "presumed advantage of being guided by and contributing to theory" (Groark & McCall, 2005, p. 558), research concerning children and the law is solidly grounded in developmental theory while still addressing applied issues. There is much to gain, methodologically and substantively, from studying children in both experimental analog and real-world contexts. Grappling with real-world problems and contexts, applied psychology has also "produced innovative developmental paradigms, theories, and frameworks" that augment and enhance the tools available for future research (Bruck et al., 2006, p. 776). Through various outlets, the answers to these questions are then conveyed to the field and public at large. In the following pages, we illustrate these processes in relation to three topics: children's eyewitness testimony, parental separation and divorce, and juvenile justice issues. For each topic, we review (a) the impetus for this line of work, (b) successful applications of applied and basic research, including problems encountered and solutions devised along the way, and (c) areas that reflect further challenges.

CHILD MALTREATMENT AND CHILDREN'S EYEWITNESS TESTIMONY

Although we try, as a society, to protect children, the prevalence of child maltreatment (physical, sexual, and psychological abuse, as well as neglect) makes clear that too many children do not live in safe and secure circumstances. For example, in the United States, about 3.5 million investigations or assessments are carried out annually following reports of suspected child maltreatment. Following these investigations, nearly 800,000 children were classified as victims of maltreatment in 2007 (US Department of Health and Human Services, Administration on Children, Youth, and Families, 2009). The situation is alarming elsewhere as well. In 2003, approximately 235,000 child maltreatment investigations were conducted in Canada, and almost half of these cases were substantiated by child protection workers (Trocmé et al., 2001). Between 2001–02 and 2005–06, the number of child protection notifications in Australia almost doubled from 138,000 to 267,000, with increases in the number of substantiated cases as well (Australian Institute of Health and Welfare, 2007). In England, 570,000 cases were referred in 2002–2003, and over 30,000 of these cases were registered or substantiated (Creighton, 2004).

Although many factors affect children's adjustment, maltreatment can profoundly affect children's cognitive, socioemotional, and even physical development (Celano, Hazzard, Campbell, & Lang, 2002; Cicchetti, in press; Dodge, Pettit, Bates, & Valente, 1995; Egeland, Yates, Appleyard, & van Dulmen, 2002; Feiring, Taska, & Lewis, 1998; Lyon & Saywitz, 1999; National Research Council, 1993; Shonk & Cicchetti, 2001; Sternberg, Baradaran, Abbott, Lamb, & Guterman, 2006a; Valle & Silovsky, 2002). Importantly, these effects can be long-lasting: Child maltreatment is a major risk factor for short- and long-term adjustment problems, including adult psychopathology (see reviews by Alexander, 1992; Beitchman, Zucker, Hood, DaCosta, Akman, & Cassavia, 1992; Briere & Runtz, 1993; Cicchetti, in press; Finkelhor, 1990; Finkelhor & Browne, 1988; Green, 1993; Sternberg, Lamb, Guterman, & Abbott, 2006b). Early identification of maltreatment is critical for ending victimization, protecting children, and providing children, families, and potentially perpetrators with appropriate services and treatment.

Early identification is easier said than done, however, because child maltreatment is a crime that is extremely difficult to investigate. For one thing, the crimes often occur behind closed doors and are shrouded in secrecy. Especially in the case of sexual abuse, furthermore, corroborative evidence rarely exists either because the nature of the abuse does not lend itself to physical evidence (e.g., fondling), or physical evidence has disappeared due to delayed reporting, which is quite common (Goodman-Brown, Edelstein, Goodman, Jones, & Gordon, 2003; London, Bruck, Ceci, & Shuman, 2005; Pipe, Lamb, Orbach, & Cederborg, 2007). Even in the rare cases where physical evidence exists, it may not identify the perpetrator. As a result, children's eyewitness testimony is often critical. Without it, justice will not be served, children will not be protected, and victims will not be treated. Thus, it is imperative that children's reports are clear, consistent, detailed, and accurate. When children's accounts are vague, inconsistent, and/or incomplete, their reports tend to be met with skepticism (e.g., Leippe, Manion, & Romanczyk, 1992; see Myers, 1992), whereas "aside from a smoking pistol, nothing carries as much weight with a jury as the testimony of an actual witness" (Loftus & Ketcham, 1991, p. 16).

Children most often testify about maltreatment, but they can also be called upon to provide statements as victims or witnesses to other crimes (domestic violence, murder, etc.) or in civil proceedings (e.g., custodial disputes, removals of children or adults from their homes) (Bruck et al., 2006; Lamb, 2003; Lamb, Hershkowitz, Orbach, & Esplin, 2008). As a result, research on children's eyewitness testimony has mushroomed.

Impetus for This Line of Research

Coinciding with and in response to the growing awareness of child maltreatment and a desire to see it dealt with aggressively (Bruck et al., 2006; Lamb, 2003), several barriers to children's participation in the legal system were removed in the 1980s. For example, in the United States, Canada, and the UK, most jurisdictions ceased requiring corroborative evidence when children alleged that they had been sexually abused. These changes made it possible for children to participate in the legal system, which they had rarely done before (Ceci & Bruck, 1995), in part because they were thought to be incompetent witnesses. Unfortunately, several well-publicized but controversial child sexual abuse cases have certainly contributed to the persistence of this reputation (e.g., *California v. Raymond Buckey et al., Commonwealth of Massachusetts v. Cheryl Amirault LeFave; New Jersey v. Michaels, Lillie and Reed v. Newcastle City Council & Ors, North Carolina v. Robert Fulton Kelly Jr., State v. Fijnje*).

In the McMartin Preschool Abuse case in California, for example, dozens of children alleged that Raymond Buckey and colleagues working in the preschool subjected children to months of ritual sexual abuse (*California v. Raymond Buckey et al.*). Alleged victims claimed bizarre experiences (e.g., they were taken into tunnels underneath the school; they saw witches fly; they went on hot air balloon rides; and they witnessed human and animal sacrifice) but no physical evidence confirming the allegations ever emerged. The charges were eventually dropped after years of investigation and criminal trials. Defendants in other cases were not so lucky, often serving time in jail before their convictions were overturned (Ceci & Bruck, 1995; Nathan & Snedeker, 1995).

In these cases, which rested almost entirely on children's allegations, it was the jury's task to determine whether the children could be believed. Juries had to make such decisions in the face of contradictory claims by prosecutors that children never lie about sexual abuse, and by defence attorneys that children were easily led to provide false reports following repeated suggestive interviews by zealous therapists. At the time, there was virtually no relevant scientific evidence (Bruck et al., 2006) so research on children's eyewitness testimony was nudged into existence. It has continued to flourish in response to a continuing stream of high-profile cases. Of note, some of these cases (as described above) highlight children's vulnerabilities and susceptibility to suggestion (i.e., **suggestibility**) while others demonstrate the ability of even young children to provide accurate and detailed testimony. In one widely publicized case, for example, 5-year-old Sarah Ahn described both the driver who had abducted her friend, Samantha Runnion, while they were playing at their apartment complex, and his vehicle. The girl's description was critical in the arrest of the perpetrator and subsequent trial, which ended in the perpetrator being sentenced to death for the abduction, sexual assault, and murder of Samantha Runnion (Lewin, 2002; Luna, 2005).

How Did Psychologists Respond to the Need for Research on Children's Eyewitness Testimony?

Certainly, research relevant to some of the issues raised by these cases already existed, but there was uncertainty about the extent to which psychologists could use the basic developmental literature to understand children's eyewitness testimony, how the results could be translated into practical guidelines and conclusions, and how unanswered questions might best be framed and addressed.

Basic research on some topics, the development of memory and language in particular, clearly informed our understanding of children's eyewitness testimony. For example, psychologists had long been aware of age-related improvements in children's memory capacity and ability to structure narrative accounts of remembered events (Bauer, 2006; Fivush & Haden, 2003; Nelson & Fivush, 2004; Schneider & Bjorklund, 1998), but researchers now faced real-world problems that could not be addressed using the results of studies largely focused on children's memories for number lists and other non-stressful events. Researchers thus began the arduous task of developing innovative methods and paradigms balancing the need for **ecological validity** with ethical concerns.

To increase ecological validity (i.e., relevance to memories of abuse), researchers began studying children's ability to remember stressful medical procedures, inoculations, and medical examinations (e.g., Baker-Ward, Gordon, Ornstein, Larus, & Clubb, 1993; Goodman, Hirschman, Hepps, & Rudy, 1991b; Goodman, Quas, Batterman-Faunce, Riddlesberger, & Kuhn, 1997; Howe, Courage, & Peterson, 1996; Ornstein, Baker-Ward, Gordon, & Merritt, 1997; Pipe et al., 1997; Quas et al., 1999; Saywitz, Goodman, Nicholas, & Moan, 1991). Such events included some abuse-relevant elements (e.g., stress, bodily touch, salience) and thus increased ecological validity without exposing children to unnecessary distressing events. Furthermore, unlike most instances of abuse, the events in these studies were objectively verifiable, allowing researchers to investigate children's accuracy in response to different types of question.

In a further effort to increase ecological validity, some researchers began testing some of the relevant issues specifically among maltreated children (e.g., Eisen, Qin, Goodman, & Davis, 2002; Howe, Cicchetti, Toth, & Cerrito, 2004; Lyon, Malloy, Quas, & Ahern, in press; Lyon, Malloy, Quas, & Talwar, 2008; Lyon & Saywitz, 1999) whereas most research on child witnesses has involved children who have not been maltreated (e.g., Bruck et al., 2006; see Lyon, 2007). By creatively making research more applicable and ecologically valid, psychologists have obtained an increasingly clear picture of children's capacities and limitations.

Even if some elements are similar, however, medical examinations and procedures are not the same as maltreatment, so some researchers began to conduct field studies to determine systematically (a) how children were actually interviewed in investigative settings, and (b) how children responded to different types of questions when asked by investigators about possible experiences of abuse. This research represented a shift from simply labeling children as competent or incompetent as well as recognition of the importance of field research for true progress in this area. Instead, researchers sought to identify the most effective ways of interviewing children in order to capitalize on their capabilities and competencies while also recognizing their limitations. In other words, given what had been learned about children's abilities, capacities, limitations and the factors that influence them, how might they be interviewed to best effect? This research on investigative interviewing illustrates the contributions of both applied and basic psychologists to the development of knowledge and its dissemination, resulting in improved investigative techniques around the world.

The Investigative Interview

For the reasons described above (e.g., lack of corroborative evidence), suspected victims (and other witnesses) of maltreatment are typically interviewed about their experiences, and these **investigative interviews** typically set into motion criminal proceedings and a variety of interventions for children and families, making the encounters between children and investigative interviewers critically important.

Despite variations in legal traditions and social welfare policies, there is substantial international consensus about the types of forensic interviews that elicit the most accurate and complete information, a consensus fuelled by mounting evidence regarding children's linguistic, communicative, social, and memorial capacities (e.g., American Professional Society on the Abuse of Children, 1990, 1997; Home Office, 1992, 2007; Lamb et al., 2008; Poole & Lamb, 1998). First, there is an agreement among researchers that interviewers should first establish a supportive relationship ("rapport") with children, and encourage them to correct the interviewers and/or seek clarification when necessary before questioning them about the alleged criminal incidents. Second, many experts recommend that interviewers should allow children to practice providing narrative descriptions of events and should introduce them to the interviewing style before starting to explore possible abuse. Most professionals also agree that investigative interviews should be conducted using **open-ended questions** (e.g., "Tell me about everything that happened to you") with focused but not suggestive (e.g., "When did it happen?") questions used as seldom and as late in the interview as possible. Such recommendations are supported by experimental evidence suggesting that open-ended questions are preferable because they access free recall memory which is more likely to be accurate, whereas focused questions tend to engage both memory processes that are more prone to error *and* narrow information retrieval.

Reaching the End-Users of Results

This research has been used to craft best-practice guidelines (e.g., Achieving Best Evidence, Home Office, 2007; Memorandum of Good Practice, 1992; NICHD Investigative Interview Protocol, 2000—see below) in the hope that these guidelines would reform interview practice, although consensus about the manner in which interviews should be conducted does not mean that interviews are typically conducted in accordance with these recommendations. As is common in other fields (see Grol & Grimshaw, 2003 for a review of implementing best-practice guidelines in the medical field), practitioners often fail to abide by best-practice guidelines and recommendations (Aldridge & Cameron, 1999; Memon, Wark, Holley, Bull, & Köhnken, 1996; Warren, Woodall, Hunt, & Perry, 1996).

For example, Sternberg, Lamb, Davies, & Westcott (2001a) evaluated the effect of the Memorandum of Good Practice on the investigative interview conducted by police officers in the UK interviewing children about alleged abuse. Despite the Memorandum's call for open questions, forensic interviewers relied heavily on **closed questions** (47%) (e.g., "Where did he touch you?"), option-posing utterances (29%) (e.g., "Did he touch you over or under your clothes?"), and suggestive prompts (5%) (e.g., "He hurt you, right?"). Open-ended questions (e.g., "Tell me what happened when you were with X") were infrequently (6%) employed to elicit information from children. As a result, the information obtained was of uncertain quality: 40% of the information that children provided was obtained using option-posing and suggestive questions, which yield less reliable information than open-ended questions do (Dent, 1982, 1986; Goodman, Bottoms, Schwartz-Kenney, & Rudy, 1991a; Hutcheson, Baxter, Telfer, & Warden, 1995; Lamb et al., 1996).

Studies conducted in Israel, the US, and Sweden similarly revealed that many interviewers did not adhere to best-practice guidelines. The widespread similarities in interview practices across countries and cultures was noteworthy and alarming primarily because the extant practices were at considerable odds with practices recommended by researchers and professional advisory groups around the world (e.g., American Professional Society on the Abuse of Children, 1990; Home Office, 1992, 2007). In other words, despite consistent research documenting the superiority of certain ways of obtaining information, interviewers around the world continued to employ inferior and potentially dangerous practices when they interviewed alleged victims. Such findings raised questions about the effectiveness of guidelines that are not rigorously evaluated in the field and underscored the need for greater investment in ongoing training and supervision to bring about major changes in the quality of investigative interviewing (Lamb, Orbach, Hershkowitz, Esplin, & Horowitz, 2007). This was a difficult but useful lesson to learn, one that has been painstakingly learned by psychologists and professionals in other fields as well (e.g., Grol & Grimshaw, 2003; Hohmann & Shear, 2002).

Why don't forensic interviewers adhere to recommended interview practices? There are many potential reasons. A good investigative interview demands a great deal of interviewers. Among other things, it requires accommodating children's limited language abilities and vocabulary, asking appropriate questions, obtaining detailed evidence about sensitive topics, and maintaining children's often limited attention. Furthermore, the daily routines of investigative interviewers typically leave no time to access the latest findings. In addition, some interviewers sincerely believe that they are following best-practice guidelines (e.g., Aldridge & Cameron, 1999; Powell & Wright, 2008; Warren et al., 1999) despite evidence to the contrary.

In response to interviewer needs, researchers developed detailed guidelines to make it easier for interviewers to achieve best practice (e.g., Cognitive Interview, Fisher, Brennan, & McCauley, 2002; Finding Words technique or the RATAC (Rapport, Anatomy Identification, Touch Inquiry, Abuse, and Closure) protocol, Walters, Holmes, Bauer, & Vieth, 2003; NICHD Investigative Interview Protocol, Lamb et al., 2008). Only the NICHD Protocol has been extensively and internationally validated in the field, however, so we discuss it in detail, describing how it was developed, implemented, evaluated, revised, and maintained.

NICHD Investigative Interview Protocol

The NICHD Protocol was designed to translate professional recommendations into operational guidelines (Lamb et al., 2008; Orbach, Hershkowitz, Lamb, Esplin, & Horowitz, 2000) and guide interviewers to use prompts and techniques that maximize the amount of information elicited from free-recall memory. It covers all phases of the investigative interview.

Pre-substantive phase. In the *introductory phase*, the interviewer introduces himself/herself, clarifies the child's task (the need to describe events in detail and to tell the truth), and explains the ground rules and expectations (i.e., that the child can and should say "I don't remember," "I don't know," "I don't understand," or correct the interviewer when appropriate). This phase was developed with sensitivity to the fact that children are usually unused to being the sole source of information and often fail to ask for clarification when they do not understand (e.g., Lamb, Sternberg, Orbach, Hershkowitz, & Esplin, 1999; Saywitz, Snyder, & Nathanson, 1999; Sternberg et al., 1997; Waterman, Blades, & Spencer, 2000, 2004). This phase also reflects the legal system's demands that interviewers include questions designed to establish that children understand the difference between true and false statements. In the NICHD Protocol, this is done in a developmentally appropriate manner that takes account of young children's difficulty defining abstract concepts (e.g., truth, lies) (Lyon, 2000; Lyon et al., 2008; Lyon & Saywitz, 1999).

The *rapport-building phase* was designed to create a relaxed, supportive environment for children and to establish rapport between children and interviewers in light of evidence that children are more likely to be cooperative when interviewers are friendly (e.g., Bottoms, Quas, & Davis, 2007; Quas, Wallin, Papini, Lench, & Scullin, 2005; Roberts, Lamb, & Sternberg, 2004). Also, children are prompted to describe a recently experienced neutral event in detail. This "training" is designed to familiarize children with the open-ended investigative strategies and techniques used in the substantive phase while demonstrating the specific level of detail expected of them.

In a *transitional part* between the pre-substantive and the substantive phases of the interview, a series of prompts are used to identify the target event/s under investigation nonsuggestively and with prompts that are as open as possible. The interviewer only moves on to some carefully worded and increasingly focused prompts (in sequence) if the child fails to identify the target event/s.

Substantive phase. If the child makes an allegation, the *free-recall phase* begins with an invitation ("Tell me everything . . ."), followed by other free-recall prompts or invitations (see Table 9.1). As soon as the first narrative is completed, the interviewer asks whether the incident occurred "one time or more than one time" and then proceeds to secure incident-specific information using follow-up ("Then what happened?") and cued (e.g., "Earlier you mentioned a [person/object/action]. Tell me everything about that") invitations, making reference to details mentioned by the child to elicit uncontaminated free-recall accounts of the alleged incident/s.

Only after exhaustive free-recall prompting do interviewers proceed to directive questions (focused recall questions that address details previously mentioned by the child and request information within specific categories [e.g., time, appearance] such as "When did it happen?" or "What color was that [mentioned] car?" If crucial details are still missing, interviewers then ask limited option-posing questions (mostly yes/no or forced-choice questions referencing new issues that the child failed to address previously). Suggestive utterances, which communicate to the child what response is expected, are strongly discouraged.

Implementation. Although the Protocol took advantage of mounting psychological evidence about children's abilities, researchers next had to determine whether it would "work" in the field. Israel was the first country to ask this question (Orbach et al., 2000), and the implementation was difficult. As is common in other fields, practitioners in the field were reluctant to admit that their methods were not useful and found it difficult to make changes to rely on the new guidelines. Through intensive efforts to create and maintain a constructive relationship based on mutual respect and good faith, however, the Protocol was evaluated. In

TABLE 9.1
Interviewer Prompt Types and Examples

Prompt Type	Examples
Invitation	Tell me everything that happened as well as you can remember.
	Then what happened?
	Tell me more about that.
Cued invitation	Think back to that [day/night] and tell me everything that happened from [some action mentioned by the child] until [a later action described by the child].
	Tell me more about [person/object/activity mentioned by the child].
	You mentioned [person/object/activity mentioned by the child]; tell me everything about that.
Direct/Focused	You mentioned [person/object/activity], When/what/where [completion of the direct question]?
	You mentioned you were at the shops. Where exactly were you? [pause for response] Tell me about that shop.
	Earlier you mentioned that your mother "hit you with this long thing." What is that thing? [pause for response] Tell me about that thing.
Questions to AVOID	Yes/No questions (e.g., Did he touch you?)
	Option posing questions (e.g., Was that over or under your clothes?)
	Questions that encourage children to imagine events (e.g., Tell me what might have happened.)
	Suggestive questions (e.g., He hurt you, didn't he?)

These and other examples can be found in Lamb et al. (2008).

light of the successes outlined below, the Israeli Department of Youth Investigation made the Protocol mandatory. Since 1998, every investigative interview of young alleged victims, witnesses, or suspects has been conducted using the Protocol.

Evaluation. Findings obtained in independent field studies in four countries (Cyr & Lamb, 2009; Lamb et al., 2008; Orbach et al., 2000; Sternberg, Lamb, Orbach, Esplin, & Mitchell, 2001b) showed dramatic improvements in the quality of their interviews once they began using the Protocol. Simply publishing best-practice guidelines may not work, but interviewers can be trained to conduct better interviews, regardless of their jurisdiction or profession (e.g., social workers, police officers; Sternberg et al., 1997; Sternberg, Lamb, Esplin, & Baradaran, 1999).

When using the Protocol, interviewers use at least three times more open-ended and approximately half as many option-posing and suggestive prompts as they do when exploring comparable incidents, involving children of the same age, without the Protocol. Interviewers using the Protocol also introduce option-posing and suggestive questions later in the interview process than do peers not using the Protocol. Because option-posing and suggestive questions by definition involve the introduction of information by investigators, they may contaminate later phases of the children's reports, especially when younger children are involved (Bjorklund, Bjorklund, Brown, & Cassel, 1998; Ceci & Bruck, 1995; Memon et al., 1996), and thus their delayed utilization is forensically important. When priority was given to open-ended strategies and techniques in Protocol interviews, there were also significant increases in the number of facilitators and other supportive comments addressed to child witnesses (Hershkowitz, Orbach, Lamb, Sternberg, & Horowitz, 2006); this further enhanced the recall and reporting of information by encouraging children to be more cooperative.

When forensic investigators follow the structured NICHD Protocol, they thus obtain better information from alleged victims. In each study, about half of the informative and forensically relevant details and more than 80% of the initial disclosures of sexual abuse were provided in response to free-recall prompts. This is important because, as noted earlier, details elicited using free recall or open-ended prompts are more likely to be accurate than details elicited using more focused prompts in both field and laboratory analog contexts (Dale, Loftus, & Rathbun, 1978; Dent, 1986; Dent & Stephenson, 1979; Goodman et al., 1991a; Hutcheson et al., 1995; Lamb & Fauchier, 2001; Lamb et al., 2007; Orbach & Lamb, 2001).

Interestingly, all of the above findings were replicated in the US, the UK, Israel, and Canada, without differences in the proportions of prompts that were open-ended, differences in the proportions of details elicited using open-ended prompts, age differences, or differences in the proportion of the interviews completed before the first use of option-posing questions. The lack of age differences raised doubts about the interpretation and generalization of the results obtained in experimental laboratory analog settings, illustrating how applied research can lead basic researchers to re-evaluate their findings and interpretations.

Of course, it is important to consider multiple perspectives and goals when conducting applied research, and researchers must decide carefully how to determine whether an intervention was successful (Westmaas, Gil-Rivas, & Silver, 2007). As described above, the Protocol was evaluated in terms of how it changed interviewer practice and questioning and also how it improved children's reports. Subsequent research asked whether introduction of the Protocol made a difference to the ways in which cases were evaluated and adjudicated. As predicted by the developers of the Protocol, Pipe, Orbach, & Lamb (2008) found that, following introduction of the Protocol, proportionally more cases were referred for prosecution and more were resolved by conviction.

The Importance of Long-Term Evaluation and Training

As mentioned above, professional consensus alone did not yield changes in interviewers' behavior even when they knew what they should do and believed that they were following those recommendations (Aldridge & Cameron, 1999; Warren et al., 1999). Studies on the effective interviewing of children have also demonstrated how difficult it is to alter the ways in which interviewers typically perform. Practitioner training and even education of the public often yields improvement in trainees' knowledge but no meaningful changes in the ways in which they actually behave (see Grol & Grimshaw, 2003; Westmaas et al., 2007 for public health examples).

Recognizing this, training in use of the Protocol has always been accompanied by efforts to provide continued support, guidance, and feedback after interviewers start using the Protocol; these strategies are supported by the results of experimental research in other contexts (Adams, Field, & Verhave, 1999; Clark, 1971; Frayer & Klausmeier, 1971; Gully, 1998; Sweet, 1966). In the case of the NICHD Protocol, improvements occurred only after interviewers started reviewing and receiving critical feedback from expert consultants and fellow interviewers (Lamb et al., 2002c). Unfortunately, improvements derived from this close monitoring and feedback rapidly diminished when the interviewers stopped attending regular feedback sessions. Within 6 months after the training/supervision ended, police officers in the US were conducting interviews that resembled their original interviews more than when they were getting the expert feedback (i.e., fewer open-ended prompts, earlier introduction of more focused prompts) (Lamb et al., 2002b).

The adverse effects of termination of supervision and feedback have important, although somewhat sobering, implications for those attempting to apply information gleaned from research in the real world. Clearly, it is possible to employ professionals' accumulated knowledge of memory and communicative development to improve the quality of information elicited from alleged victims of child abuse, but these benefits are obtained only when extensive efforts are made not only to train interviewers to adopt recommended practices, but to ensure the maintenance of these practices as well. Regardless of their skillfulness, interviewers continue to maintain or improve their skills only when they regularly review their own and others' interviews closely, discussing their strategies, successes, and mistakes with other interviewers. In Israel, for example, all interviewers are required to continue attending regular peer-review sessions of this sort and this seems to have ensured that the investigative interviews conducted there are of high quality (87% of all substantive questions were open according to a recent study by Katz & Hershkowitz, in press), suggesting that good interviewers can continue to get better in the right circumstances.

In all, the NICHD Protocol and its training model illustrate an effective collaboration between academia and the field, with researchers and practitioners working together to generate solutions to real-world problems (Lamb et al., 2008). This model, which has been applied with success in Israel, Canada, the US, and parts of the UK, has led to improvements in the quality of interviews with children who are alleged victims of sexual or physical abuse. It is an influential example of collaboration between researchers and practitioners. Continued evaluation of the Protocol, its components, and its implementations highlight the importance of a continuous feedback loop between applied researchers, basic researchers, and the field.

How Does the Protocol Continue to Influence Research and Practice?

The continued collaboration between practitioners and academia not only has allowed for the evaluation and validation of the Protocol but also has cast light on further research questions and problems for research psychologists to address. For example, a more recent version of the

Protocol can be used when interviewing witnesses who are not victims (Lamb, Sternberg, Orbach, Hershkowitz, & Horowitz, 2003b), and another version has been developed and used to interview youthful suspects (Hershkowitz, Horowitz, Lamb, Orbach, & Sternberg, 2004); this is discussed further below. Currently, Lamb and his colleagues are field-testing a revision designed to provide additional reassurance for children who are unusually reluctant to talk about their experiences (Hershkowitz, Horowitz, & Lamb, 2005; Hershkowitz et al., 2006; Hershkowitz, Lamb, & Horowitz, 2007; Pipe et al., 2007), and are trying to determine whether the Protocol can be used effectively to interview children with learning or mental difficulties— an important question because such individuals are disproportionally likely to be abused (Crosse, Kaye, & Ratnofsky, 1993; Hershkowitz et al., 2007; Sullivan & Knutson, 2000).

Furthermore, those who study linguistic, communicative, and memory development among young children have long believed that preschoolers were incapable of providing narrative responses to invitations (Bourg et al., 1999; Hewitt, 1999; Kuehnle, 1996). However, applied research demonstrated that, when invitations were carefully formulated and children appropriately prepared for their roles as informants, even children as young as four years of age were capable of providing detailed responses (Lamb et al., 2003a). The fact that the Protocol is effective with preschoolers is not of interest only to interviewers who often have difficulty interviewing very young children but also to those who conduct basic developmental research. Of course, such findings also prompt questions about the most effective techniques to use with even younger children.

Through a combination of applied and basic research, it has been possible to enhance our understanding of normative developmental processes *and* improve the quality of investigative interviewing of children. This careful research has made it possible to enhance the value of children's testimony in ways that should enable law enforcement, child protection, and judicial agencies to protect children better from maltreatment.

Summary

In the past few decades, literally hundreds of studies conducted by an internationally and disciplinarily diverse group of researchers have shed light on children's abilities, capacities, and limitations while elucidating the factors that influence children's eyewitness testimony. By identifying children's strengths, weaknesses, and characteristics, researchers have fostered improvements in the quality of forensic interviewing and the evaluation of the information elicited from children. Clearly, it is possible to obtain valuable information from children, but doing so requires careful investigative procedures, a realistic awareness of children's capacities and limitations, and an appreciation of the restrictions imposed on interviews by real-world characteristics. Ongoing feedback and training is critical to ensure that interviewers continue to adhere to the Protocol and do not drift back.

THE EFFECTS OF PARENTAL SEPARATION AND DIVORCE

Forensic interviewing is not the only real-world problem to have been illuminated by applied developmental science, of course. Many social scientists have documented the extent to which children's development can be affected by their parents' separation, and applied developmental psychologists have, in turn, shown how psychological research not only helps explain these effects, but also informs the development of social policies and practices that can help ameliorate the more negative effects.

Divorce and parental separation clearly affect more children than child maltreatment; about half the children in the US spend at least part of their childhood living with a single parent, and similar experiences affect considerable (though slightly smaller) numbers of children in most other industrialized countries. Researchers have clearly demonstrated that, on average, children benefit from being raised in two-[biological or adoptive]parent families rather than separated, divorced, or never-married single-parent households (Amato, 2000; Aquilino, 1996; Carlson, 2006; Clarke-Stewart & Brentano, 2006; Clarke-Stewart, Vandell, McCartney, Owen, & Booth, 2000; Hetherington, 1999; Hetherington & Kelly, 2002; McLanahan, 1999; McLanahan & Teitler, 1999; Simons, Lin, Gordon, Conger, & Lorenz, 1999), although there is considerable variability within groups, and the differences between groups are relatively small. Indeed, although children growing up in fatherless families are, on average, disadvantaged relative to peers growing up in two-parent families with respect to psychosocial adjustment, behavior and achievement at school, educational attainment, employment trajectories, income generation, involvement in antisocial and even criminal behavior, and the ability to establish and maintain intimate relationships, the majority of children with divorced parents enjoy average or better-than-average social and emotional adjustment as young adults (Booth & Amato, 2001; Clarke-Stewart & Brentano, 2006; Hetherington & Kelly, 2002; Kelly & Emery, 2003). Approximately 25% of children in post-separation and divorced families give evidence of adjustment problems, compared to 12–15% in married families. Thus, the majority of children from separated families evince no psychopathology or behavioral symptoms, although they are likely to experience psychic pain for at least some period of time (Emery, 1998; Hetherington & Kelly, 2002; Laumann-Billings & Emery, 2000; Schwartz & Finley, in press).

Such individual differences in outcomes force us to identify more precisely both the ways in which divorce/single parenthood may affect children's lives and the factors that might account for individual differences in children's adjustment following their parents' separation. Several interrelated factors appear to be especially significant.

Economic Stresses

Typically, single parenthood is associated with a variety of social and financial stresses with which custodial parents must cope, largely on their own. Single-parent families are more economically stressed than two-parent families, and economic stresses or poverty appear to account (statistically speaking) for many effects of single parenthood (Hetherington & Kelly, 2002; McLanahan, 1999).

Reductions in the Quality of Relationships with Children

Because single mothers need to work more extensively outside the home than married or partnered mothers do, parents spend less time with children in single-parent families and the levels of supervision and guidance are lower and less reliable than in two-parent families (Hetherington & Kelly, 2002; McLanahan, 1999). Reductions in the level and quality of parental stimulation and attention may affect achievement, compliance, and social skills while diminished supervision makes antisocial behavior and misbehavior more likely (Hetherington & Kelly, 2002).

Conflict between Parents

Conflict between the parents commonly precedes, emerges during, or increases during the separation and divorce processes, and often continues for some time beyond them. Interparental conflict is an important correlate of children's psychosocial adjustment just as marital harmony, its conceptual inverse, appears to be a reliable correlate of positive adjustment

(Cummings Goeke-Morey, M. C., & Raymond, 2004; Cummings, Merrilees, & George 2010; Johnston, 1994; Kelly, 2000). The negative impacts of high levels of marital conflict on the quality of parenting of both mothers and fathers have been well documented. In general, parental conflict is associated with more rejecting, less warm and nurturing parenting by mothers, and with fathers' withdrawal from parenting and engagement in more intrusive interactions with their children (Cummings & Davies, 1994; Grych, 2005). Anger-based marital conflict is associated with filial aggression and externalizing behavior problems, perhaps because such parents and children have similar difficulty regulating negative affect (Katz & Gottman, 1993). These and other data support the observation that some of the "effects of divorce" are better viewed as the effects of marital or parental conflict and violence (Kelly, 2000).

The adversarial legal system tends to promote conflict between already vulnerable parents because of its win–lose orientation and the way it fosters hostile behaviors and demands. Although the adversarial process purports to focus on children's "best interests," parents' psychologically driven legal strategies more often represent their own needs and perceived entitlements, and the effect is to diminish the possibility of future civility, productive communication, and cooperation (Kelly, 2003).

Quality and Type of Parenting

The quality and type of parenting have emerged as important influences on the post-separation/divorce adjustment of school-aged children and adolescents. Deterioration in the quality of parenting after separation has long been recognized (Belsky, Youngblade, Rovine, & Volling, 1991; Clarke-Stewart & Brentano, 2006; Hetherington, 1999; Sturge-Apple, Davies, & Commings, 2006; Wallerstein & Kelly, 1980). Many parents are preoccupied, stressed, emotionally labile, angry, and depressed following separation, and their "diminished parenting" includes less positive involvement and affection expressed with their children, and more coercive and harsh forms of discipline. External factors such as absorption in dating, new partners, cohabitation, remarriage, and poverty and financial instability are also associated with reductions in the quality of parenting (Amato, 2000; Hetherington, 1999; Kelly, 2000; Pruett, Williams, Insabella, & Little, 2003; Simons et al., 1999; Wallerstein & Kelly, 1980).

By the same token, specific aspects of parenting can moderate the impact of separation and divorce on children's social, emotional, and academic adjustment, and potentially protect children against the harmful impacts of high conflict. Such effective parenting is characterized by warmth and engagement, authoritative discipline (setting limits, non-coercive discipline and control, enforcement of rules, appropriate expectations), academic skill encouragement, and monitoring of the children's activities (Amato & Fowler, 2002; Amato & Gilbreth, 1999; Finley & Schwartz, 2007; Hetherington, 1999; Martinez & Forgatch, 2002; Simons et al., 1999).

Disruptions in Relationships with Fathers

Divorce commonly disrupts one of the child's most important and enduring relationships, that with his or her father. As Amato (1993; Amato & Gilbreth, 1999) has shown with particular clarity, however, the bivariate associations between father absence and children's adjustment are much weaker than one might expect. Indeed, Amato and Gilbreth's (1999) meta-analysis revealed no significant association between the frequency of father–child contact and child outcomes, largely because of the great diversity in the types of "father-present" relationships. We might predict that contacts with abusive, incompetent, or disinterested fathers are likely to have much different effects than relationships with devoted, committed, and sensitive fathers. As expected, Amato and Gilbreth (1999) found that children's well-being was significantly enhanced when their relationships with nonresident fathers were positive, when the nonresident fathers engaged in active parenting, and when contact was frequent. Clarke-Stewart and Hayward (1996), Dunn, Cheng, O'Connor, and Bridges (2004), Finley and Schwartz (2007), Hetherington, Bridges, and Insabella (1998), and Simons and Associates (1996) likewise reported that children benefited when their nonresident fathers were actively involved in routine everyday activities, and the conclusion was clearly supported in recent analyses by Carlson (2006) of data from the National Longitudinal Study of Youth. Carlson showed that father involvement was associated with better adolescent adjustment and that paternal involvement partially mediated the effects of family structure (notably divorce or single parenthood) on adolescents' behavioral outcomes. Similarly, higher levels of paternal involvement in their children's schools were associated with better grades, better adjustment, fewer suspensions, and lower dropout rates than were lower levels of involvement (Nord, Brimhall, & West, 1997). Active engagement in a variety of specific activities and ongoing school-related discussions between fathers and their adolescents significantly lowered the probability of school failure when compared to adolescents with less actively engaged fathers.

Another meta-analysis indicated that, on multiple measures of emotional and behavioral adjustment and academic achievement by mothers, fathers, teachers, and clinicians, children in joint physical **custody** were better adjusted than children in sole custody arrangements. In fact, children in shared custody were as well adjusted as children whose parents remained married (Bauserman, 2002). Although joint physical custody parents reported less past and current conflict than did sole physical custody parents, conflict did not explain the superiority of the children in joint custody arrangements. Again, the clear implication is that active paternal involvement, not simply the number or length of meetings between fathers and children, predicts child adjustment. This suggests that post-divorce arrangements should specifically seek to maximize positive and meaningful paternal involvement rather than simply allow minimal levels of visitation. As in non-divorced families, in other words, the quality of continued relationships with the parents—both parents—is crucial (Kelly & Lamb, 2000; Lamb & Kelly, 2009). Stated differently and succinctly, the better (richer, deeper, and more secure) the parent–child relationships, the better the children's adjustment, whether or not the parents live together (Lamb, 2002a, 2002b; Lamb & Kelly, 2009).

Unfortunately, those conducting custody and visitation awards do not always appear to understand what sort of interaction is needed to consolidate and maintain parent–child relationships. As a result, their decisions seldom ensure either sufficient amounts of time or adequate distributions of that time for children and parents. Decision makers have typically failed to recognize and take advantage of the knowledge of children's psychological needs and the developmental trajectories that have been compiled over the past few decades of intensive research. This research is invaluable both because an understanding of normative developmental phases helps us understand how parental separation and divorce may affect children's development and adjustment, and because it can be useful when designing post-divorce living arrangements most likely to benefit children (Kelly & Lamb, 2000; Lamb & Kelly, 2009). Basic research on early social development and descriptive research on the multifaceted correlates of divorce combine to yield a clearer understanding of the ways in which divorce affects children and of how the welfare of many children could be enhanced by changes in common practices. Furthermore, research on the impacts of divorce enhances our understanding of developmental processes by providing a new context in which to examine children's social development.

In the next paragraphs, we briefly review attachment research. Then we demonstrate how it has been applied successfully by the legal and child welfare systems before identifying areas of continued concern and challenge.

Attachment

Attachment is one of the most frequently researched aspects of child development, and researchers have documented long-lasting effects of attachment styles (Cassidy & Shaver, 2008; Thompson, 1999, 2006). According to attachment theorists, infants form attachments to those who have been available regularly and have responded to the infants' signals and needs (Lamb, Thompson, Gardner, & Charnov, 1985; Thompson, 2006; see also Lamb & Lewis, Chapter 6, this volume). As described by Bowlby (1969), and largely confirmed by subsequent research (for detailed review, see Thompson, 2006), infant–parent attachments pass through four broad developmental phases, during the first three of which infants learn to discriminate among adult carers and gradually develop emotional attachments to them.

Responses to separation become increasingly intense as attachments to parents and other important carers strengthen between 6 and 24 months of age (Yarrow; 1963; Yarrow & Goodwin, 1973). Most infants initially prefer the parent who provides most of their care and are more likely to seek out their preferred parents for comfort when distressed (Lamb, 2002a). Non-preferred parents remain emotionally important, however, and are sought out for other social and emotional needs, and, when primary carers are not available, for comfort. Although infants and toddlers may resist transitions between parents in the second year, just as they sometimes protest (even more strongly) daily transitions to out-of-home care providers, they generally comfort quite quickly once the transition is accomplished. This is particularly likely when both parents have the opportunity to engage in normal parenting activities (feeding, playing, soothing, putting to bed, etc.) while attachments are being established and consolidated.

Infants and toddlers need regular interaction with their "attachment figures" in order to foster, maintain, and strengthen their relationships (Lamb, Bornstein, & Teti, 2002a; Thompson, 2006). This means that young children need to interact with both parents in a variety of contexts (feeding, playing, diapering, soothing, reading, putting to bed, etc.) to ensure that the relationships are consolidated and strengthened. In the absence of such opportunities for regular interaction across a broad range of contexts, infant–parent relationships may weaken rather than grow stronger. Relationships with parents continue to play a crucial role in shaping children's social, emotional, personal, and cognitive development into middle childhood and adolescence (Lamb & Lewis, Chapter 6, this volume).

Attachment and Implications for Parental Separation and Divorce

When parents divorce, do judges and legal practitioners incorporate and apply this information about attachment and early relationships when making decisions? The answer is complex and perhaps best given as "sometimes" or "increasingly."

Attachment research tells us that the ideal post-divorce situation is one in which children with separated parents have opportunities to interact with both parents frequently in a variety of functional contexts (feeding, play, discipline, basic care, limit-setting, putting to bed, etc.) (Kelly & Lamb, 2000; Lamb, 2002b; Lamb & Kelly, 2001, 2009). However, even though children's best interests are usually served by keeping both parents actively involved in their children's lives, many custody and access arrangements do not foster the maintenance of relationships between children and their nonresident parents. Unfortunately, policy makers, judges, and lawyers in many jurisdictions have not been very attentive to the importance of promoting children's relationships with both of their parents. Arbitrary and one-size-fits-all restrictions on the amounts of time children spend with their fathers have been the norm regardless of the quality of the father–child relationships. Traditional "visiting guidelines" in many jurisdictions assign every other weekend to the nonresident parent (with perhaps a brief midweek visit), and mental health professionals often rely on unsubstantiated beliefs that every other weekend is best for children because it ensures that children continue to have only one "real home."

These plans have left much to be desired for many families, and have caused great dissatisfaction and sense of loss to the majority of children in post-divorce arrangements (Fabricius, Braver, Diaz, & Schenck, 2010). Research on children's and young adults' retrospective views of their post-divorce living arrangements indicates that the majority express strong wishes and longing for more time with their fathers, a desire for more closeness, and favorable views of shared physical custody arrangements (Fabricius et al., 2010; Fabricius & Hall, 2000; Laumann-Billings & Emery, 2000; Smith & Gallop, 2001).

What Recommendations Follow from the Attachment Research?

In order to ensure that both parents become or remain attached to their children, post-divorce **parenting plans** need to encourage participation by both parents in as broad as possible an array of social contexts on a regular basis. That is, brief dinners and occasional weekend visits do not provide a broad enough or extensive enough basis for such relationships to be fostered, whereas weekday and weekend daytime and nighttime activities are important for children of all ages. Even young children should spend overnight periods with both parents when both have been involved in their care prior to separation, even though neo-analysts have long counseled against this (Kelly & Lamb, 2000; Lamb & Kelly, 2009). When both parents have established significant attachments and both have been actively involved in the child's care, overnight "visits" will consolidate attachments and child adjustment, not work against them. Consistent with this reasoning, the results of research by Pruett, Insabella, and Gustafson (2005) show that regular overnight visits were associated with better adjustment on the part of toddlers and young children. Parents who have been actively involved before divorce but are then denied overnight access to their children are thereby excluded from an important array of activities, and the strength or depth of their relationships suffers as a result. In the absence of sufficiently broad and extensive interactions, many fathers drift out of their children's lives, and children see their fathers as increasingly peripheral, placing these children at risk psychologically and materially (Fabricius et al., 2010).

Furthermore, to minimize the deleterious impact of extended separations from either parent when children are young, and still consolidating their attachments, attachment theory tells us that there should be more frequent transitions than would perhaps be desirable with older children (Lamb & Kelly, 2009). To be responsive to young children's psychological needs, in other words, the parenting schedules adopted for children under age two or three should actually involve more transitions, rather than fewer, to ensure the continuity of both relationships and to promote the children's security and comfort. Although no empirical research exists testing specific parenting plans following separation, it is likely, for example, that infants and toddlers who are attached to committed and competent fathers would remain most comfortable and secure with a schedule that allowed them to see their fathers at least three times a week, including at least one extended overnight stay, so that there is no separation of greater than 2–3 days. From the third year of life, the ability to tolerate longer separations begins to increase, so that most toddlers can manage two consecutive overnights with each parent without stress.

Best Practices in the Case of Parental Separation and Divorce

There are a number of empirically based practices that mental health professionals can provide to help separating parents reduce the risks that children face. Firstly, they can prepare parents to talk to their children about those aspects of the separation and divorce that directly affect them. Remarkably, most children are not informed about the details and meaning of the parental separation for them, are not invited to ask questions nor allowed an opportunity to give suggestions regarding their new living arrangements, and are not consulted regarding schedule changes (Dunn, Davies, O'Connor, & Sturgess, 2001; Smart, 2002; Smart & Neale, 2000), which leaves children to cope with these major changes in their lives without either emotional support or cognitive clarity.

Many jurisdictions have introduced education programs that explain to separating parents the effects of divorce on children, the impact of parent conflict, the particular risk when parents use their children to express their anger and disagreement, the need to separate children's needs from adult needs, and parenting skills, and often provide skill-based training to minimize conflict and promote more effective communication. At least in the short term, these courses appear to be effective (e.g., Arbuthnot & Gordon, 1996; Bacon & McKenzie, 2004; Ellis & Anderson, 2003; Pedro-Carroll, Nakhnikian, & Montes, 2001), particularly when the content is empirically based and includes skill-based training and role-play exercises. More extensive research-based parent education programs appear to bring about meaningful behavioral changes in both mothers and fathers (for reviews, see Braver, Griffin, Cookston, Sandler, & Williams, 2005; Haine, Sandler, Wolchik, Tein, & Dawson-McClure, 2003).

Secondly, because transitions between households provide opportunities for discussion and argument, it is important to ensure that these exchanges take place in neutral settings and at times that limit contact between the parents when there is a history of conflict. For example, one parent might drop the children off at school or day care, with the other parent picking them up at the end of the day. Parenting coordinators report that many children benefit from the elimination of face-to-face parent confrontations at the family residence or other meeting places, and conflict becomes a much less frequent experience. Similarly, visitation exchange centers allow children to be brought by one parent without making it necessary for the parents to encounter one another directly. Such arrangements may be especially helpful when either the parents or children are fearful, and have been shown to increase the frequency of contact between nonresident parents and their children while reducing levels of conflict between the parents (Flory, Dunn, Berg-Weger, & Milstead, 2001).

Other practices have also been developed to address conflict between separating parents. Of these, custody and divorce mediation has been best evaluated and validated (Emery, 1994; Emery, Laumann-Billings, Waldron, Sbarra, & Dillon, 2001; Kelly, 2002, 2004). The potential benefits are substantial in both the short term (e.g., earlier settlement of parenting disputes, reduced parental conflict, improved parental support) and the longer term (e.g., more sustained contact between nonresident fathers and children 12 years later), relative to parents using the traditional adversarial system (Emery et al., 2001; Kelly, 2004).

Parenting coordinators are also increasingly used in the United States, representing an effort to address the needs of children where there is very high conflict between the parents. Parenting coordination is a child-focused dispute resolution process designed to help parents settle disputes regarding their children in a timely manner, while facilitating compliance with parenting plans and related court orders. A non-adversarial intervention, the parenting coordination role combines case and conflict management, relevant parent education, mediation, and sometimes arbitration of certain child-related disputes that the parents cannot settle on their own. Parenting coordination is generally viewed as a post-decree process for parents who have demonstrated a continuing inability to settle child-specific disputes through other means, including private negotiations, mediation, specialized parent education groups, settlement conferences, or following trial. Most parenting coordinators serve by stipulation of the parents and court order, or by private consent agreements. In general, the judiciary has been supportive and enthusiastic; other professionals involved with these families have also indicated in surveys that parent coordinators can be very effective, especially in reducing the frequency and intensity of disputes (Coates, Deutsch, Starnes, Sullivan, & Sydlik, 2004). The Guidelines for Parenting Coordination (2006) were developed by an AFCC task force, and their value, as well as the need for extensive training, has been discussed at length by Kelly (in press). Although there has been no systematic research on long-term effectiveness, dramatic decreases in the rates of litigation (court appearances) in the first year after parenting coordinators were appointed were reported in one unpublished dissertation (Johnston, 1994). Several articles on the most problematic post-divorce families make clear that parenting coordinators are among the most important interventions available to smooth the post-separation and divorce transitions (Coates et al., 2004; *Family Courts Review*, 2001).

Thirdly, professionals can become familiar with and promote awareness of various models for parenting plans that have been informed by applied research. Instead of one standard visiting pattern, a menu of different time-sharing options for children of different ages would encourage parents, professionals, and courts to consider children's ages and developmental needs and achievements; the quality of parent–child relationships; parents' interest and capacity to be involved in their children's lives; and children's voices and input when appropriate. Model parenting plans typically include multiple options for various living arrangements that range from traditional visiting, expanded access involving more midweek and weekend time, and various shared physical custody arrangements. Many model plans available include highly detailed templates to guide parental choices with respect to legal decision-making and parental responsibilities. It is important that agreements and court orders are sufficiently detailed so that both parents know when, where, and how their children will make the transitions between households, eliminating the ambiguity that angry parents exploit and which often cause one or both parents to argue in front of their children. Orders that make vague references to "liberal visitation" invite sustained argument, and, when mothers remain angry, do not sufficiently protect children's relationships with their fathers. Even in legal cultures that emphasize "private ordering," lawyers, therapists, and custody evaluators should help parents develop specific schedules for children's time with each parent, and courts should routinely expect such language and detail.

Fourth, custody evaluators should become familiar and stay current with the empirical literature regarding attachment, child development, parent–child relationships, parental separation, and children's adjustment. If they are to make recommendations to the court—a subject currently generating some controversy (Tippins & Wittmann, 2005)—these recommendations should be grounded in and supported by the current research literature, rather than theory or subjective bias (Kelly & Johnston, 2005; Lamb & Kelly, 2009; Warshak, 2000).

Overall, decisions following divorce/separation, especially those involving custody and parenting plans, should be attentive to individual circumstances and sensitive to the parents' and children's strengths, schedules, and needs (Kelly, 2005, 2007; Smyth & Chisholm, 2006). And, of course, practitioners should make use of the wealth of psychological research relevant to attachment and parental separation/divorce.

Why Aren't These Best Practices Followed More Often?

As in the case of investigative interviewing, practitioners making decisions about children's lives in the context of parental separation may sincerely believe that they are doing the "right" thing. However, many of their beliefs are unfounded, and unsupported by empirical research.

For example, the prohibition of overnight "visitation" has been justified by prejudices and beliefs rather than by any empirical evidence (Warshak, 2000), which has demonstrated benefits of overnight visitation for many children. Such beliefs are often rooted in stereotypes about the traditional role of fathers in children's lives. For example, the lingering resistance to overnights among professionals working with divorcing families appears to reflect the view that fathers are not important attachment figures. Thus, even psychologists who have long recognized the need to minimize the length of separations from attachment figures when devising parenting plans have typically focused only on separations from mothers, thereby revealing the presumption that young children are not meaningfully attached to their fathers.

The adversarial legal system in the United States may also be partly responsible for the plans devised and decisions made following parental separation, encouraging rather than reducing conflict in the process. Although the adversarial process purports to focus on children's "best interests," parents' psychologically driven legal strategies more often represent their own needs and perceived entitlements, and the effect is to diminish the possibility of future civility, productive communication, and cooperation (Kelly, 2003). Our focus should remain on the children's best interests, not "fairness" to the parents.

Summary

Both applied research on divorce and basic research on attachment point to the central importance of maintaining meaningful relationships with both parents. Many innovative practices and programs have been developed over the past few decades as increasing numbers of professionals have come to recognize the importance of promoting continued relationships between children and both of their separating parents. There is a still long way to go, however. Unfortunately, reasoned discussion about the potential benefits of greater involvement by nonresident parents has often been drowned out by poisonous rhetoric from groups and individuals mired in gendered concerns about fairness for parents rather than children's best interests. Also, long-held beliefs and stereotypes about parents, particularly fathers, have influenced the uptake of psychological research in this arena.

Interestingly, although decisions about the disposition and living arrangements of children in the case of divorce appear to downplay the importance of the parents' involvement, family preservation programs in the case of child maltreatment tend to overstate the importance of family involvement. In fact, the legal system tends to privilege family relationships in some situations where it is deleterious (Gelles, 1996) while failing to strengthen and promote parent–child relationships when parents separate in divorce, despite being committed and competent parents. Because so many children are affected by their parents' separation or by social service interventions, it is critical to determine which decisions are in the best interests of children and how best to apply what we know about the importance of children's relationships.

JUVENILE JUSTICE

Psychological research has also made significant contributions to juvenile justice, particularly with respect to **culpability** and **competence to stand trial**. In this section, we discuss the seminal role that developmental research played in the US Supreme Court decision to abolish the death penalty for adolescents (*Roper v. Simmons*, 2005), and then turn to an issue that has not yet been much affected by psychological research—interrogating juvenile suspects. As discussed above, basic and applied psychological research played a significant role in informing and changing the ways that young victims and witnesses are interviewed, but despite similarities in the developmental principles, research on capacities and limitations has not been taken into account where young suspects are concerned.

A Brief History

When the juvenile justice system in the United States was designed, there was clear recognition of developmental differences between adults and juveniles. With these differences (e.g., maturity of judgment, malleability) in mind, the system emphasized **rehabilitation** rather than punishment. Following a dramatic shift in policy and public concern about juvenile crime in the 1980s, however, a very different system is evident today (see Fagan, 2008; Scott & Steinberg, 2008; Steinberg, 2009; Steinberg & Scott, 2003 for reviews). Adolescents are increasingly adjudicated in adult court where they face more severe punishments including, up to a few years ago, the death penalty. Harsher and more punitive sanctions are being levied on adolescents who are found guilty of committing crimes, leading some to refer to the "criminalization" of the juvenile justice system (Feld, 1993). Indeed, Fagan writes (2008, p. 82), "As adolescents came increasingly to be feared as perpetrators of the most serious and violent crimes, the principles of rehabilitation that were essential to the juvenile court were largely abandoned."

Role of Developmental Research in the Juvenile Justice System

The juvenile justice system is characterized by difficult and distinct decisions and judgments (e.g., status or age-defined offenses; judgments concerning adolescents' competency to stand trial, risk for future harm, and potential response to treatment) made by individuals who would surely benefit from an understanding of child and adolescent development. For example, judges might thus weigh information about immaturity of judgment and behavior regulation when sentencing; defence attorneys could learn how better to communicate with and represent clients who are faced with important decisions (e.g., whether to accept a plea bargain); and prosecutors could consider developmental issues when deciding whether to charge young suspects as juveniles or adults (Steinberg, 2009). Although, as Steinberg notes, the consideration of developmental psychology in decisions concerning juvenile justice is not a "panacea," decision-making can and should be informed by the lessons learned by developmental psychologists. The US Supreme Court's decision to abolish the death penalty for adolescents is illustrative.

Abolition of the Death Penalty for Adolescents

In *Roper v. Simmons* (2005), the United States Supreme Court ruled that the execution of offenders for crimes committed at the age of 16 or 17 constituted cruel and unusual punishment in violation of the Eighth Amendment to the Constitution. In prior decisions, the death penalty had already been deemed unsuitable for those under 15 in *Thompson v. Oklahoma* (1988), but left standing for 16- and 17-year-olds in *Stanford v. Kentucky* (1989). The court's decision in *Roper v. Simmons* was based on evidence mitigating adolescents' culpability as a result of their developmental status summarized in an amicus curiae brief (American Medical Association et al., 2004) submitted by a coalition of academic professional bodies (i.e., the American Medical Association, the American Psychiatric Association, the American Society for Adolescent Psychiatry, the American Academy of Child & Adolescent Psychiatry, the American Academy of Psychiatry and the Law, the National Association of Social Workers, the Missouri Chapter of the National Association of Social Workers, and the National Mental Health Association). The brief outlined decades of research on adolescent development and adolescent offending conducted by those who study cognitive, social, and moral development; criminology; and even neuroscience. Much of the research was basic in nature, while some was conducted specifically to test certain aspects of adolescent offending, as is typically done when applied psychologists address a specific problem. The overarching claim was that "Older adolescents behave differently than adults because their minds operate differently, their emotions are more volatile, and their brains are anatomically immature" (p. 4), as explained in the following paragraphs.

Basic Research Relevant to Juvenile Justice

In terms of cognitive and psychosocial development, laboratory research using several paradigms (e.g., gambling tasks, computerized driving games; Cauffman et al., in press; Steinberg et al., 2008) finds that adolescents are more impulsive and less future-oriented than adults, even young adults (e.g., Steinberg et al., 2009). Adolescents live for the moment. If they consider the future consequences of their actions at all, they tend to focus on potential short- rather than long-term consequences, perhaps because their greater sensitivity to rewards than to risks makes their judgements immature (Cauffman & Steinberg, 2000; Steinberg & Cauffman, 1996; Steinberg et al., 2008, 2009). In the amicus brief, researchers claimed that "Adolescents are inherently more prone to risk-taking behavior and less capable of resisting impulses because of cognitive and other deficiencies" (p. 5). One of these "other" deficiencies is related to their **emotional regulation**. Adolescents often let their emotions "get the better of them" and tend to be more emotionally volatile even in comparison to young adults who are just a few years older. For example, Steinberg notes (2009, pp. 480–481), "Although basic cognitive competence matures by the time individuals reach age 16, many of the social and emotional capacities that influence adolescents' judgment and decision making, especially outside the psychologist's laboratory, continue to mature into late adolescence and beyond."

Socially, adolescents are more affected by peer pressure or peer influence—especially when they are in groups. For example, adolescents take more chances and make more risky decisions when in groups (e.g., Gardner & Steinberg, 2005). When their choices involve clothing or music, the increased susceptibility to peer influence may have limited long-term consequences for themselves or others, but when choices involve whether to commit an illegal act or engage in other risky behavior, the susceptibility to peer influence becomes more problematic.

In recent years, impressive technological advances have allowed researchers to explore the biological basis of these changes (see Johnson, 2010). Anatomical differences between the brains of adolescents and adults demonstrate that adolescents are not fully mature until after the age of 18 (see Scott & Steinberg, 2008; Steinberg, 2007, 2008, for reviews). Important differences are evident in the frontal lobes, for example—areas of the brain known to play critical roles in executive function, planning, and decision making. The frontal lobes are underdeveloped in terms of myelination and pruning, both of which affect how the brain functions. As noted in the amicus brief (p. 12), "Research shows that adolescent brains are more active in regions related to aggression, anger, and fear, and less active in regions related to impulse control, risk assessment, and moral reasoning than adult brains." This basic neuroscience research thus confirms what research psychologists have learned about adolescent behavior.

Applied Research Concerning Juvenile Justice

Applied research also helped the authors of the amicus brief to reach an important conclusion, "Executing adolescents does not serve the recognized purposes of the death penalty"

(p. 21). One such purpose is to deter future crime. However, research on the increasingly punitive orientation of the juvenile justice system shows that these policies (e.g., transfer to adult criminal court) fail to deter future crime and may actually increase recidivism (Bishop & Frazier, 2000; Singer & McDowall, 1988; see Fagan, 2008 for review). Reporting on the consistent failure of harsher sanctions to deter juvenile offending, Fagan (2008, pp. 100–101) writes, "Rarely do social scientists or policy analysts report such consistency and agreement under such widely varying sampling, measurement, and analytic conditions . . . Few modern criminologists or correctional administrators maintain the illusion that incarceration has either broad therapeutic benefits or a strong deterrent effect." Not only does more severe treatment fail to achieve its intended purpose (e.g., increasing public safety), but it is also extensively costly to taxpayers (Greenwood, 2006), and it jeopardizes the safety, mental health, and future prospects of many juveniles (e.g., Bishop & Frazier, 2000; Cesaroni & Peterson-Badali, 2005; Forst, Fagan, & Vivona, 1989; see Fagan, 2008). This is critical because mental illness and mental health symptoms are very common among juvenile offenders, especially female offenders, upon entering the juvenile justice system (e.g., Cauffman, 2004; Cauffman, Lexcen, Goldweber, Shulman, & Grisso, 2007; Teplin, Abram, McClelland, Dulcan, & Mericle, 2002; Wasserman, McReynolds, Lucas, Fisher, & Santos, 2002).

Applied research in this field has also helped to document the **age–crime curve** and has led to the delineation of two primary groups of offenders—adolescent limited and life-course persistent (Moffitt, 1993). Decades of research conducted around the world demonstrates that most juvenile offenders cease offending after adolescence, whether or not they come into contact with the legal system; a very small proportion of adolescent offenders continue committing crimes later in life (e.g., Moffitt & Caspi, 2001; Moffitt, Caspi, Harrington, & Milne, 2002; Odgers et al., 2008). Complementing the basic research on adolescence discussed above, this real-world research has (or should have) critical implications for the treatment and punishment of juvenile offenders.

The Death Penalty Decision

In 2002 (*Atkins v. Virginia*), the US Supreme Court abolished the death penalty for individuals with intellectual disabilities, in part because of their "disabilities in areas of reasoning, judgment, and control of their impulses." Of course, adolescents share these characteristics, and this influenced the Supreme Court's later decision to abolish the death penalty for adolescents as well.

Writing for the majority, Justice Kennedy referred to important characteristics of adolescence that had been described in the amicus brief, including adolescents' diminished decision-making capacity and their related tendency to engage in risky and irresponsible behavior; their increased susceptibility to external pressure, especially from peers; and the changing nature of their identity. In reference to the developing adolescent character, Justice Kennedy wrote that it was "less supportable to conclude that even a heinous crime committed by a juvenile is evidence of irretrievably depraved character." In fact, because of considerable and rapid changes in adolescent character, researchers have referred to adolescents as "moving targets" (Grisso, 1998). When trying to conduct psychological assessments and predictions about future behavior, it is quite difficult to "hit" such moving targets, but, the court opined, adolescents would most likely "outgrow" their criminal behavior as they matured.

What Else Have We Learned from Research Concerning Juvenile Justice?

Certainly, basic and applied developmental researchers have made significant contributions in the field of juvenile justice: The abolition of the death penalty for juvenile offenders is literally a matter of life and death for some young people. Importantly, research pertaining to adolescent development and juvenile justice has done more than merely inform legal practices; it has informed our understanding of normative developmental processes as well, again demonstrating the reciprocal relationship between basic and applied research.

Developmental psychologists clearly recognize adolescence as a formative period during which rapid change is apparent while adolescents "make substantial progress in acquiring and coordinating skills that are essential to filling the conventional roles of adulthood" (Steinberg, 2009, p. 480). Certain developmental "tasks" (e.g., education, vocational training, dating and intimate relationships, goal setting, cooperation in groups) help adolescents to both develop psychologically and transition successfully into young adulthood and the new roles that may await them (e.g., parent, member of the work force). Steinberg (2009, p. 480) notes that:

> This process of development toward psychosocial maturity is one of reciprocal interaction between the individual and her social context. Several environmental conditions are particularly important, such as the presence of an authoritative parent or guardian, association with prosocial peers, and participation in educational, extracurricular, or employment activities that facilitate the development of autonomous decision making and critical thinking.

It is clear that juveniles in the justice system, particularly those who are incarcerated, are accomplishing (or not accomplishing) these developmental tasks in a very different environment than other youths. Their environment primarily includes peers, with less opportunity for education and vocational training than would be available "on the outside." They also lack the influence of caring adult role models, including parents/guardians and older siblings. Such differences likely influence their developmental trajectories at least in comparison with those spending their formative years in more normative contexts such as schools, neighbourhoods, and families.

Researchers have studied these youth to learn about basic psychological processes in different developmental contexts. For example, this research has allowed us to understand better peer influence and the potential iatrogenic effects of incarceration and other interventions for problematic behavior. Several studies have found that surrounding delinquent teenagers with other delinquent teenagers actually escalates their bad behavior, especially among those considered "high risk" or most in need of intervention (e.g., Dishion, Spracklen, Andrews, & Patterson, 1996; Patterson, Dishion, & Yoerger, 2000; Poulin, Dishion, & Burraston, 2001; see Cécile & Born, 2009; Dishion, McCord, & Poulin, 1999, for reviews). In intervention settings, incarceration in particular, adolescents may literally learn how to be better offenders—a phenomenon that Dishion et al. (1999, p. 756) term "deviancy training." This work has implications not only for the legal system but also for mental health professionals who may conduct or recommend group therapy.

Interrogation of Juvenile Suspects

In the section on investigative interviewing, we discussed decades of research on children's eyewitness testimony and the many steps that have been taken to help ensure that they provide accurate testimony. There is much at stake when juvenile suspects are questioned as well. Oddly, while the legal and child protection systems have responded to developmental research with policies and protocols for interviewing young people who are victims or witnesses to crime, research has not similarly affected practice where juveniles are suspected of committing crimes. Noting the neglect of relevant research in this area, Owen-Kostelnik, Reppucci, and Meyer (2006, p. 286) wrote: "Our assumption is that 'kids are kids' no matter the context in which they find themselves; being suspected of committing a crime does not make a child an adult."

False Confessions

In what is commonly known as "the Central Park jogger case," five teenage boys confessed to the brutal assault and rape of a woman in New York City (Kassin, 2002). Twelve years into their prison sentence, DNA and confession evidence confirmed the identity of the actual rapist—Matias Reyes (*People of the State of New York v. Kharey Wise et al.*, 2002). The boys, who were now young men, were exonerated and released from prison. Although this case is extremely well known, it is unfortunately not an isolated incident. False confessions are more common than people realize.

Left: Kharey Wise as he looked in court when he was arraigned in the Central Park jogger rape case. (Photo by John Pedin/NY Daily News Archive via Getty Images). Right: Kharey Wise testifies against the death penalty at a hearing before the New York State Assembly at Pace University. Wise, who was wrongfully convicted of beating and raping a woman jogger in Central Park in 1989, spent 15 years in prison. He was released when the real assailant confessed to the crime. (Photo by Debbie Egan-Chin/NY Daily News Archive via Getty Images.)

Over the past 20 years, advances in DNA testing have exonerated over 200 individuals in the United States, some of whom were on death row at the time. Although it is difficult to determine precisely, a surprising 15% to 25% of all DNA exonerations included a false confession or admission which contributed, at least in part, to the wrongful conviction (Garrett, 2008; Scheck, Neufeld, & Dwyer, 2000; Innocence Project, www.innocenceproject.org, last accessed September 1, 2009). Unfortunately, false confessions do not result from a particular legal system or set of procedures—proven false confessions have been documented in England, Australia, New Zealand, China, Japan, Norway, Finland, Germany, Iceland, the Netherlands, and Canada (Kassin et al., 2010). Researchers have identified dispositional and situational factors associated with the risk that individuals will make a false confession (see Kassin & Gudjonsson, 2004; Kassin et al., 2010 for reviews). Although false confessions, whether in the real world or in the laboratory, occur at all ages, young people appear disproportionately likely to confess falsely.

Youth as a Dispositional Risk Factor for False Confession

Field research. In the Central Park Jogger case, each of the five boys recanted his confession immediately, claiming that he had confessed in order to be allowed home. This exemplifies some of the principles of adolescent development discussed above, including immaturity of judgment, focus on short-term consequences, and impulsivity.

In a study of individuals whose innocence had been verified using DNA evidence, Gross, Jacoby, Matheson, Montgomery, and Patel (2005) found that whereas only 13% of the adults had confessed falsely, 42% of the juveniles had done so, with the youngest exonerees (12 to 15 years old) confessing to murder or rape at an alarming rate (69%). In a study of "proven false confession cases," mostly involving serious crimes, Drizin and Leo (2004) found that 33% involved false confessions from juveniles, and 55% of these were from juveniles who were 15 and under—even though juveniles typically represent only 8% and 16% of all arrests for murder and rape, respectively (Snyder, 2006).

Self-report data also speak to the frequency with which juveniles confess falsely (of those interrogated, 6% in Viljoen, Klaver, & Roesch, 2005; 7.3% in Gudjonsson, Sigurdsson, Asgeirsdottir, & Sigfusdottir, 2006; 8.8% in Gudjonsson, Sigurdsson, Sigfusdottir, & Asgeirsdottir, 2008). Furthermore, more frequent interrogation is associated with greater risk (Gudjonsson et al., 2006). In a large international study, youth from various parts of Europe (i.e., Iceland, Norway, Finland, Latvia, Lithuania, Russia, and Bulgaria) were asked about their experience of interrogation and false confession. Of the 11.5% (2,726) interrogated by the police, 14% claimed to have falsely confessed (Gudjonsson, Sigurdsson, Asgeirsdottir, & Sigfusdottir, in press).

Responses to hypothetical vignettes have also been studied. For example, when presented with hypothetical interrogation situations, 25% of male juvenile offenders indicated that they would choose to confess falsely in at least one of the scenarios (Goldstein, Condie, Kalbeitzer, Osman, & Geier, 2003). Grisso et al. (2003) presented community and justice-system-involved juveniles and young adults with vignettes describing police interrogation situations and asked participants to indicate the "best choice" for the suspect—confess, remain silent, or deny the offense. Younger individuals were more likely to choose the "confess" option: over half of 11- to 13-year-olds and approximately one-fifth of adults did so. Although the vignettes did not indicate that suspects were innocent and that confessions were necessarily false, this research is consistent with youths' propensity to confess. For instance, Viljoen et al. (2005) found that 55% of juvenile defendants confessed when questioned as suspects by the police, with confessors significantly younger than those who remained silent.

In addition to false confessions, field research indicates that juveniles also make other decisions in the interrogation room that put them at risk. For example, younger suspects are more likely to misunderstand or to waive their Miranda rights and/or right to counsel and rarely ask for attorneys to be present (Grisso, 1980; Viljoen et al., 2005; see Grisso, 1981, 1997 for reviews).

Laboratory research.   As in the case of children's eyewitness testimony, researchers have struggled to develop ecologically valid *and* ethical research paradigms to mimic interrogation situations. For example, Kassin and Kiechel (1996) introduced a creative solution—the "Alt key" methodology. In this paradigm, participants complete a reaction time task after being warned that data will be lost and the computer will crash if they press the "Alt" key. Inevitably, the computer crashes and participants are accused of pressing the forbidden key. They are asked to sign a statement indicating that their actions caused the computer to crash.

To increase the ecological validity of this paradigm, Redlich and Goodman (2003) added heftier consequences to the equation—participants would have to complete 10 hours of data entry after the experiment finished if they admitted pressing the forbidden key, and the study revealed clear linear developmental differences in the risk of making false confessions. Young adults were the least likely to take responsibility for crashing the computer (59%). Twelve and 13-year-olds were the most likely (78%) to sign the statement; 15- and 16-year-olds did so 72%

of the time. Similar developmental differences were found in the participants' willingness to question authority—the majority (65%) of 12- and 13-year-olds were willing to sign the statement taking responsibility for crashing the computer without asking a single question, but this tendency decreased with age (46% of the 15- and 16-year-olds and 33% of the young adults).

Hypothetical vignette studies have also been conducted with normative populations. These studies show similar improvements in legal decision making and legal reasoning with age (e.g., Grisso et al., 2003; Peterson-Badali & Abramovitch, 1993; Redlich, Silverman, & Steiner, 2003). This research confirms the importance of developmental status in legal decision making, regardless of whether youth are involved in the justice system.

Developmental Influences in the Interrogation Room

Several of the basic psychological principles that influence young people's ability to provide eyewitness testimony (discussed in the "Child Maltreatment and Children's Eyewitness Testimony" section above) and make them ineligible for the death penalty also increase their vulnerability in the interrogation room. Several of these characteristics also pertain to individuals with intellectual disabilities (Gudjonsson, 2003; Gudjonsson & MacKeith, 1994). Specifically, adolescents are characterized by immature decision making, and impulsivity; they also are less future-oriented, are more suggestible, are more compliant with authority, tend to emphasize short- over long-term consequences, and are more susceptible to pressure from peers and other external influences (e.g., lawyers, parents) (e.g., Cauffman & Steinberg, 2000; Gardner & Steinberg, 2005; Gudjonsson & Singh, 1984; Richardson, Gudjonsson, & Kelly, 1995; Richardson & Kelly, 2004; Singh & Gudjonsson, 1992; Steinberg et al., 2008, 2009). Perhaps not surprisingly, then, exactly half (19) of the proven multiple false confession cases examined by Drizin and Leo (2004) involved false confessions from multiple juvenile suspects to the same crime. As discussed above, youth involved in the justice system are disproportionately affected by mental impairments, including mental health issues and impairments in intellectual ability (e.g., Cauffman, 2004; Closson & Rogers, 2007; Quinn, Rutherford, Leone, Osher, & Poirier, 2005). Given that individuals with mental impairments are also at increased risk for false confession (e.g., Gudjonsson, 1990; Redlich, Summers, & Hoover, 2010), juveniles may be in "double jeopardy" (Redlich, 2007, p. 610) when questioned as suspects. Redlich adds (p. 610), "The fact that all juveniles have one false confession risk factor (young age) and that most have two risk factors (young age and mental impairment) underscores the need for immediate reforms in the interrogation of minors." Youths' developmental capacities and limitations are of importance in the interrogation room, although they have been largely ignored and even exploited to date.

In the Interrogation Room

The "Reid Technique" (Inbau, Reid, Buckley, & Jayne, 2001), now in its fourth edition, is taught and used by interrogators around the world. The website claims to have trained over 500,000 investigators in the United States, Canada, Europe, Asia, and the Middle East (Reid & Associates, 2009). Also, self-report studies of investigators in the US and Canada indicate the high prevalence of Reid-like techniques (e.g., Kassin et al., 2007; Leo, 1996; Meyer & Reppucci, 2007). This technique involves creating a confrontational environment in which the ultimate goal is to obtain a confession because detectives have already concluded that the suspect is guilty; the "interview" has thus become an "interrogation." The technique includes such tactics as lying to suspects, presenting false evidence, minimizing and justifying the crime and its consequences, interrupting and disallowing denials, asking suspects to report hypothetical details of the crime, and other tactics known to increase false reports among children and adults in other contexts (e.g., Garven, Wood, Malpass, & Shaw, 1998; Libby, 2003; Wade, Garry, Read, & Lindsay, 2002; see Loftus, 1997, 2003 for reviews).

Despite the developmental differences discussed earlier in this chapter, proponents of Reid-like techniques (the most prevalent method in the United States; Kassin et al., 2010) pay little or no attention to the age of the suspect being interviewed. In fact, when interrogating adolescents, the Reid training manual recommends, "the same general rules prevail as for adults" (Inbau et al., 2001, p. 99). This is evident in the use of Reid-like techniques with juveniles in self-report and observational studies (Feld, 2006; Meyer & Reppucci, 2007), even at the same rates that they claim to use the techniques with adult suspects (Meyer & Reppucci, 2007).

Regarding young suspects, the Reid technique actually recommends outright exploitation of their developmental characteristics. For example, Inbau et al. (2001) recommended exploiting juveniles' "restless energy, boredom, low resistance to temptation, and lack of supervision" (Kassin et al., 2010, p. 20). They also suggest that police "play one [suspect] against the other." Given what we know about adolescents and peer pressure, they are right in concluding that this tactic may work especially well with young, first-time offenders (Inbau et al., 2001, pp. 292–293).

Recognizing that juveniles (and others with intellectual vulnerabilities) are at increased risk for false confession, recent versions of the training manual (Inbau et al., 2001) do recommend taking some precautions concerning juvenile suspects, however. In discussing the presentation of fictitious evidence, for example, they note, "This technique should be avoided when interrogating a youthful suspect with low social maturity" (p. 429) and with those with diminished mental capacity (e.g., mental retardation), but it is not clear that police interrogators are capable of making judgments about adolescents' social maturity.

Of course, even if they are not recommended, these methods remain perfectly legal, regardless of the suspect's age! And, in several high-profile cases, these tactics have been extremely effective in obtaining confessions from juvenile suspects (see Drizin & Colgan, 2004; Firstman & Salpeter, 2008; Kassin et al., 2010; and Lambert, 2008 for more details of these cases). Michael Crowe, a 14-year-old boy who confessed falsely to murdering his sister, was told several lies by police before confessing, including that his hair was found in her hands, his blood found in her room, and that he had failed a lie detector test. Marty Tankleff, a 17-year-old boy who discovered his stabbed parents, confessed after several hours of denial. He was presented with false evidence against him; most persuasive of all was when the police told him that his father had awoken from his coma and accused his son of the crime. It took almost two decades before Marty was released from prison.

Where to Go From Here?

Kassin et al. (2010, p. 30) state, "There is a strong consensus among psychologists, legal scholars, and practitioners that juveniles and individuals with cognitive impairments or psychological disorders are particularly susceptible to false confession under pressure. Yet little action has been taken to modulate the methods by which these vulnerable groups are questioned when placed into custody as crime suspects." The authors thus recommend that, for one thing, individuals who conduct interviews and interrogations with juveniles should receive special training, concerning the risks associated with youthful age (as well as the risks associated with other vulnerabilities such as mental retardation and mental illness). Ideally, this training would cover relevant principles of developmental psychology and interview strategies and structure.

Recent attempts at revising the NICHD Investigative Interview Protocol for use with suspects are promising in this regard. Hershkowitz et al. (2004) used a modified version of the protocol to interview alleged perpetrators of sexual abuse between the ages of 9 and 14. Surprisingly, suspects who fully or partially admitted their involvement were very responsive to open-ended prompts. In fact, the total number of details provided by the suspects did not vary depending on whether they fully or partially admitted the allegations. Kassin et al.'s (2010) call for more systematic research on such alternatives to typical interrogations should be heeded.

Summary

Although suspects are considered "innocent until proven guilty," juveniles cannot be considered "vulnerable until suspected of a crime." If children and adolescents need certain protections or techniques when interviewed as victims or witnesses, they should not be treated like adults when suspected of criminal behavior. The legal system cannot have it both ways.

As we have seen, adolescents have several characteristics that reduce their culpability but increase their risk when they come into contact with the law. These "moving targets" are difficult to study, yet basic and applied psychological researchers have produced mounting evidence of key differences between adolescents and adults that should affect how they are treated in the legal system. When writing about these "fundamental differences," Steinberg (2009, p. 481) concludes, "Taken together, the lessons of developmental science offer strong support for the maintenance of a separate juvenile justice system in which adolescents are judged, tried, and sanctioned in developmentally appropriate ways."

Crucial reforms, most notably the US Supreme Court abolition of the death penalty for adolescents, have used developmental knowledge successfully. Other areas, however, are still in need of reform. The interrogation of juveniles is one arena in which we could make better use of current knowledge and also heed calls for more research on alternative interviewing strategies. As Kassin et al. (2010, p. 30) point out, in light of existing research, "It is uniformly clear to all parties that vulnerable suspect populations—namely, juveniles and people who are cognitively impaired or psychologically disordered—need to be protected in the interrogation room."

CONCLUSIONS

By using examples regarding children and the law, this chapter illustrates the richness and multifaceted value of applied developmental science. In the areas of children's eyewitness testimony, parental separation/divorce, and juvenile offending, basic and applied psychological research have combined to offer creative and empirically based solutions to real-world problems. Furthermore, applied research has not only promoted children's welfare in these various contexts, but also advanced our understanding of developmental processes and theories more generally, helped test the validity and generalizability of findings obtained previously through experimental research, and led to the creation of new and creative research methodologies.

The road has not been easily travelled, and much work remains to be done. Due to the "large and growing legal constituency" of youth (Bruck et al., 2006, p. 777), we chose to focus on examples from children and the law to illustrate both successes and challenges. Unfortunately, many decision-makers in the legal community fail to take advantage of a burgeoning and increasingly sophisticated understanding of child development when making crucial decisions about children's lives. However, as we have shown in this chapter, psychological research has been used to guide the treatment of children in some legal contexts. We have used these examples to demonstrate how applied and basic psychological research can inform and complement one another, with researchers helping guide practitioners and the latter in turn offering insights and asking questions that foster a more complete understanding of developmental processes.

In the field of children's eyewitness testimony, basic research on children's cognitive and social development has allowed researchers to devise and implement forensic interview practices that have enhanced the quality of forensic interviewing around the world. Through a combination of applied and basic research, it has been possible to improve the value of children's testimony in ways that should allow society to protect children better from maltreatment *and* further our understanding of normative developmental processes. Also, this research has illustrated an important lesson: Simply publishing best-practice guidelines may not be enough to change practice in the field, at least in the long term, highlighting the importance of ongoing training and continued evaluation. The NICHD Protocol and its training model illustrate an effective and influential example of collaboration between academia and the field to generate and disseminate solutions to real-world problems.

In the field of divorce, basic research on attachment and applied research on the impact of parental divorce/separation on children have informed the development of social policies and practices that can help ameliorate the more negative effects of divorce while providing a new context in which to examine children's social development. Unfortunately, decisions about custody and visitation (e.g., amount and distributions of parent–child time) often reflect a lack of knowledge or long-held biases about parent–child relationships, especially concerning father–child relationships. Although several innovative practices have been developed over the past few decades, there is still a long way to go in devising ways to promote children's best interests and their continued relationships with both of their separating parents.

In the field of juvenile justice, basic and applied psychological researchers have clarified how adolescents should be evaluated and treated in the legal system. This research not only has influenced the US Supreme Court's decision to abolish the death penalty for adolescents, but has informed our understanding of normative developmental processes as well (e.g., peer influence), again demonstrating the reciprocal relationship between basic and applied research. Although the death penalty is now off the table for juveniles, they are increasingly being transferred to adult criminal court where they face a more punitive environment. Discussing this trend, Fagan (2008, p. 93) writes, "While the law has moved toward waiving increasingly younger teens to adult criminal court, social and biological evidence suggests moving in the other direction. Perhaps it's time for the law to change course and follow the science."

The interrogation of juveniles is another area in which we could make better use of current knowledge. Several of the basic psychological principles that influence youths' ability to provide eyewitness testimony and make them ineligible for the death penalty also increase their vulnerability in the interrogation room. However, these vulnerabilities are largely ignored or even exploited when juveniles are interrogated about suspected crimes. Additional research and reforms are needed.

The Importance of Influencing Legal Practice with Science (and Vice Versa)

Why should we, as social scientists, care whether our work has implications for the legal system? Ogloff provides an answer (2000, p. 459): "The law is among the most pervasive forces in society. For psychology to have an impact on society, it is crucial for psychology to have an impact on the law."

This is easier said than done, of course. Psychology and the legal system share a long (and often tumultuous) history. Conflict between two disciplines is quite common (e.g., behavioral science and public health; Muehrer et al., 2002), and professionals in academia and the field alike must make efforts toward mutual respect and collaboration. We must strive to inform practice with science (and vice versa) so that the best information can be obtained and disseminated. This may mean greater awareness of and sensitivity to differences in training, motivations, goals, and professional "cultures." Scholars have observed that those in the psychology and legal professions come from two different "cultures" (Brigham, 1999), which may be, in part, responsible for the doubt and even suspicion on both sides. Certainly, the chance of successful collaboration is enhanced by overcoming barriers, including differences in training and communication.

This should be "a two-way street." Psychologists must work to understand the law and the legal system if they wish to make an impact—they cannot expect the field to operate exactly as it does in the laboratory. Those who fail to consider the applied context in which they are working risk making inappropriate conclusions or recommendations. Because legal professionals must operate within the context and confines of *their* own field, guidelines that ignore real-world conditions and are impractical will be disregarded and may also discourage future relationships and research uptake. In response to Munsterberg's (1908) claims that psychologists could help address difficult legal questions, Wigmore (1940, p. 367) responded, "Whenever the Psychologist is ready for the Courts, the Courts are ready for him."

Importantly, psychologists cannot expect to be the "ones with all the answers," dispensing information and advice to those in the legal community. They must be prepared for the feedback loop and the reciprocal relationships which can enhance their research, right down to the identification of new and timely research questions (Ogloff, 2000).

Dissemination

For applied psychological research to have an impact, the findings need to reach the field. Most academics conduct research in the laboratory, present it to other academics at conferences, and publish it in academic journals, which are inaccessible literally or figuratively to most non-psychologists. Most psychological studies will *remain* inaccessible unless psychologists attempt to reach other audiences. Even some of the books that have addressed issues discussed in this chapter accessibly (e.g., Ceci & Bruck, 1995; Scheck et al., 2000; Warshak, 2001) have had limited success bringing those in academia and the field together to debate relevant issues. Conferences aimed at practitioners and academics have perhaps had more success in facilitating the exchange of ideas and knowledge and encouraging debate (e.g., American Psychology Law Society, International Investigative Interviewing Research Group).

Applied psychologists must engage in dialogues with practitioners, policy makers, and other end-users. To this end, Sommer (2006) calls for "dual dissemination," which involves psychologists writing their own articles for publication to more general audiences in parallel to their publications for more specialized academic audiences. In so doing, psychologists must retrain themselves to write for or speak to other audiences. When writing for judges and other legal practitioners, for example, it is important to keep publications focused and practical. Jargon should be eliminated completely, and simple rather than technical language should be used whenever possible. When research findings are disseminated to new and different audiences, they may reach individuals who can apply and test the findings in new contexts, potentially leading to novel research questions.

The amount of research concerning children and the law has grown rapidly and continues to grow. While promoting children's welfare and legal reform, this research has contributed to developmental knowledge, theory, and methodology more generally. Applied developmental psychology has a long and rich history and continues to influence the legal system and other realms. This is critical because "How are we as psychologists to regard a discipline that succeeds primarily in speaking to itself?" (Gergen, 1995).

REFERENCES AND SUGGESTED READINGS (📖)

Adams, B. J., Field, L., & Verhave, T. (1999). Effects of unreinforced conditional selection training, multiple negative comparison training, and feedback on equivalence class formation. *Psychological Record*, *49*, 685–702.

Aldridge, J., & Cameron, S. (1999). Interviewing child witnesses: Questioning techniques and the role of training. *Applied Developmental Science*, *3*, 136–147.

Alexander, P. C. (1992). Application of attachment theory to the study of sexual abuse. *Journal of Consulting and Clinical Psychology*, *60*, 185–195.

Amato, P. R. (1993). Children's adjustment to divorce: Theories, hypotheses, and empirical support. *Journal of Marriage and the Family*, *55*, 23–38.

Amato, P. R. (2000). The consequences of divorce for adults and children. *Journal of Marriage and the Family*, *62*, 1269–1287.

Amato, P. R., & Dorius, C. (2010). Fathers, children, and divorce. In M. E. Lamb (Ed.), *The role of the father in child development* (5th ed.). Hoboken, NJ: Wiley.

Amato, P. R., & Fowler, F. (2002). Parenting practices, child adjustment, and family diversity. *Journal of Marriage and Family*, *64*, 703–716.

Amato, P. R., & Gilbreth, J. G. (1999). Non-resident fathers and children's well-being: A meta-analysis. *Journal of Marriage and the Family*, *61*, 557–573.

American Medical Association, American Psychiatric Association, American Society for Adolescent Psychiatry, American Academy of Child & Adolescent Psychiatry, American Academy of Psychiatry and the Law, National Association of Social Workers, Missouri Chapter of the National Association of Social Workers, & National Mental Health Association. (2004, July). *Amici curiae brief submitted to Roper v. Simmons, 543 U.S. 551 (2005)*.

American Professional Society on the Abuse of Children (1990). *Guidelines for psychosocial evaluation of suspected sexual abuse in young children*. Chicago, IL: APSAC.

American Professional Society on the Abuse of Children (1997). *Guidelines for psychosocial evaluation of suspected sexual abuse in young children* (revised). Chicago, IL: APSAC.

Aquilino, W. S. (1996). The life course of children born to unmarried mothers: Childhood living arrangements and young adult outcomes. *Journal of Marriage and the Family*, *58*, 293–310.

Arbuthnot, J., & Gordon, D. A. (1996). Does mandatory divorce education for parents work? A six-month outcome evaluation. *Family & Conciliation Courts Review*, *34*, 60–81.

Atkins v. Virginia, 536, U.S. 304. (2002).

Australian Institute of Health and Welfare (2007). *Child protection Australia 2005–06*. Child welfare series no. 40, Cat. no. CWS 28. Canberra, Australia: AIHW.

Bacon, B. L., & McKenzie, B. (2004). Parent education after separation/divorce: Impact of the level of parental conflict on outcomes. *Family Court Review*, *42*, 85–98.

Baker-Ward, L., Gordon, B. N., Ornstein, P. A., Larus, D. M., & Clubb, P. A. (1993). Young children's long-term retention of a pediatric examination. *Child Development*, *64*, 1519–1533.

Bauer, P. J. (2006). Event memory. In D. Kuhn & R. Siegler (Volume Eds.), W. Damon & R. M. Lerner (Eds. in Chief), *Handbook of child psychology, Volume 2: Cognition, perception, and language* (6th ed., pp. 373–425). Hoboken, NJ: Wiley.

Bauserman, R. (2002). Child adjustment in joint-custody versus sole-custody arrangements: A meta-analytic review. *Journal of Family Psychology*, *16*, 91–102.

Beitchman, J. H., Zucker, K. J., Hood, J. E., DaCosta, G. A., Akman, D., & Cassavia, E. (1992). A review of the long term effects of child sexual abuse. *Child Abuse & Neglect*, *16*, 101–118.

Belsky, J., Youngblade, L., Rovine, M., & Volling, B. (1991). Patterns of marital change and parent–child interaction. *Journal of Marriage and the Family*, *53*, 487–498.

Bishop, D., & Frazier, C. (2000). Consequences of transfer. In J. Fagan & F. Zimring (Eds.), *The changing borders of juvenile justice* (pp. 227–277). Chicago: University of Chicago Press.

Bjorklund, D., Bjorklund, B., Brown, R., & Cassel, W. (1998). Children's susceptibility to repeated questions: How misinformation changes children's answers and their minds. *Applied Developmental Science*, *2*, 99–111.

Booth, A., & Amato, P. R. (2001). Parental predivorce relations and offspring postdivorce well-being. *Journal of Marriage and the Family, 63*, 197–212.

Bottoms, B. L., Quas, J. A., & Davis, S. L. (2007). The influence of the interviewer-provided social support on children's memory, suggestibility, and disclosures. In M. E. Pipe et al. (Eds.), *Child sexual abuse: Disclosure, delay, and denial* (pp. 135–157). Mahwah, NJ: Lawrence Erlbaum Associates.

Bourg, W., Broderick, R., Flagor, R., Kelly, D. M., Ervin, D. L., & Butler, J. (1999). *A child interviewer's guidebook.* Thousand Oaks, CA: Sage.

Bowlby, J. (1969). *Attachment and loss: Vol. 1. Attachment.* New York: Basic Books.

Braver, S. L., Griffin, W. A., Cookston, J. T., Sandler, I. N., & Williams, J. (2005). Promoting better fathering among divorced nonresident fathers. In W. M. Pinsof & J. Lebow (Eds.), *Family psychology: The art of the science* (pp. 295–325). New York: Oxford University Press.

Briere, J., & Runtz, M. (1993). Childhood sexual abuse: Long-term sequelae and implications for psychological assessment. *Journal of Interpersonal Violence, 8*, 312–330.

Brigham, J. (1999). What is forensic psychology anyway? *Law and Human Behavior, 23*, 273–298.

Brown v. Board of Education, 375 U.S. 483. (1954).

Bruck, M., Ceci, S. J., & Principe, G. F. (2006). The child and the law. In K. A. Renninger, I. E. Sigel, W. Damon, & R. M. Lerner (Eds.), *Handbook of child psychology* (6th ed., Vol. 4, pp. 776–816). Hoboken, NJ: Wiley.

Cairns, H. (1935). *Law and the social sciences.* London: Kegan Paul, Trench Trubner and Co.

California v. Raymond Buckey et al., Los Angeles County Sup. Ct. #A750900.

Campbell, D. T. (1978). Qualitative knowing in action research. In M. Brenner, P. March, & M. Brenner (Eds.), *The social contexts of method* (pp. 184–209). London: Croom Helm.

Carlson, M. J. (2006). Family structure, father involvement, and adolescent behavioural outcomes. *Journal of Marriage and the Family, 68*, 137–154.

Cassidy, J., & Shaver, P. R. (Eds.) (2008). *Handbook of attachment: Theory, research, and clinical applications* (2nd ed.). New York: Guilford Press.

Cauffman, E. (2004). A statewide screening of mental health symptoms among juvenile offenders in detention. *Journal of the American Academy of Child and Adolescent Psychiatry, 43*, 430–439.

Cauffman, E., Lexcen, F. J., Goldweber, A., Shulman, E. P., & Grisso, T. (2007) Gender differences in mental health symptoms among delinquent and community youth. *Youth Violence and Juvenile Justice, 5*, 288–307.

Cauffman, E., Shulman, E. P., Steinberg, L., Claus, E., Banich, M., Graham, S., et al. (in press). Age differences in affective decision making as indexed by performance on the Iowa Gambling Task. *Developmental Psychology.*

Cauffman, E., & Steinberg, L. (2000). (Im)maturity of judgment in adolescence: Why adolescents may be less culpable than adults. *Behavioral Sciences and the Law, 18*, 741–760.

Ceci, S. J., & Bruck, M. (1995). *Jeopardy in the courtroom: A scientific analysis of children's testimony.* Washington, DC: APA Books.

Cécile, M., & Born, M. (2009). Intervention in juvenile delinquency: Danger of iatrogenic effects? *Children and Youth Services Review, 31*, 1217–1221.

Celano, M., Hazzard, A., Campbell, S. K., & Lang, C. B. (2002). Attribution retraining with sexually abused children: Review of techniques. *Child Maltreatment, 7*, 65–76.

Cesaroni, C., & Peterson-Badali, M. (2005). Young offenders in custody: Risk and assessment. *Criminal Justice and Behavior, 32*, 251–277.

Cialdini, R. B. (1980). Full cycle social psychology. In L. Bickman (Ed.), *Applied social psychology annual.* Newbury Park, CA: Sage.

Cicchetti, D. (in press) Developmental psychopathology. In R. M. Lerner (Gen. Ed.), M. E. Lamb & A. Freund (Vol. Eds.), *Handbook of lifespan development, Volume 2: Social and personality development.* Hoboken, NJ: Wiley.

Clark, D. C. (1971). Teaching concepts in the classroom: A set of prescriptions derived from experimental research. *Journal of Educational Psychology Monograph, 62*, 253–278.

Clarke-Stewart, K. A. (1998). Historical shifts and underlying themes in ideas about rearing young children in the United States: Where have we been? Where are we going? *Early Development & Parenting, 7*, 101–117.

Clarke-Stewart, A. & Brentano, C. (2006). *Divorce: Causes and consequences.* New Haven, CT: Yale University Press.

Clarke-Stewart, K. A., & Hayward, C. (1996). Advantages of father custody and contact for the psychological well-being of school-age children. *Journal of Applied Developmental Psychology, 17*, 239–270.

Clarke-Stewart, K. A., Vandell, D. L., McCartney, K., Owen, M. T., & Booth, C. (2000). Effects of parental separation and divorce on very young children. *Journal of Family Psychology, 13*, 304–326.

Closson, M., & Rogers, K. M. (2007). Educational needs of youth in the juvenile justice system. In C. L. Kessler & L. J. Kraus (Eds.), *The mental health needs of young offenders: Forging paths toward reintegration and rehabilitation* (pp. 229–240). New York: Cambridge University Press.

Coates, C. A., Deutsch, R., Starnes, H., Sullivan, M. J., & Sydlik, B. (2004). Parenting coordination for high-conflict families. *Family Court Review, 42*, 246–262.

Commonwealth of Massachusetts v. Cheryl Amirault LeFave, 1999.

Creighton, S. J. (2004). Prevalence and incidence of child abuse: International comparisons. *National Society for the Prevention of Cruelty to Children*. Retrieved September 5, 2009, from www.nspcc.org.uk/Inform/research/Briefings/prevalenceandincidenceofchildabuse_wda48217.html

Crosse, S. B., Kaye, E., & Ratnofsky, A. C. (1993). *A report on the maltreatment of children with disabilities*. Washington, DC: National Center of Child Abuse and Neglect.

Cummings, E. M., & Davies, P. T. (1994). Maternal depression and child development. *Journal of Child Psychology and Psychiatry and Allied Disciplines*, *35*, 73–112.

Cummings, E. M., Goeke-Morey, M. C., & Raymond, J. (2004). Fathers in family context: Effects of marital quality and marital conflict. In M. E. Lamb (Ed.), *The role of the father in child development* (4th ed., pp. 196–221). Hoboken, NJ: Wiley.

Cummings, E. M., Merrilees, C. E., & George, M. R. W. (2010). Fathers, marriages, and families: Revisiting and updating the framework for fathering in the family context. In M. E. Lamb (Ed.), *The role of the father in child development* (5th ed.). Hoboken, NJ: Wiley.

Cyr, M., & Lamb, M. E. (2009). Assessing the effectiveness of the NICHD investigative interview protocol when interviewing French-speaking alleged victims of child sexual abuse in Quebec. *Child Abuse & Neglect*, *33*, 257–268.

Dale, P. S., Loftus, E. F., & Rathbun, L. (1978). The influence of the form of the question of the eyewitness testimony of preschool children. *Journal of Psycholinguistic Research*, *74*, 269–277.

Dent, H. R. (1982). The effects of interviewing strategies on the results of interviews with child witnesses. In A. Trankell (Ed.), *Reconstructing the past: The role of psychologists in criminal trials* (pp. 279–297). Stockholm: Norstedt.

Dent, H. R. (1986). Experimental study of the effectiveness of different techniques of questioning child witnesses. *British Journal of Social and Clinical Psychology*, *18*, 41–51.

Dent, H. R., & Stephenson, G. M. (1979). An experimental study of the effectiveness of different techniques of questioning child witnesses. *British Journal of Social and Clinical Psychology*, *18*, 41–51.

Dishion, T. J., McCord, J., & Poulin, F. (1999). When interventions harm: Peer groups and problem behavior. *American Psychologist*, *54*, 755–764.

Dishion, T. J., Spracklen, K. M., Andrews, D. W., & Patterson, G. R. (1996). Deviancy training in male adolescent friendships. *Behavior Therapy*, *27*, 373–390.

Dodge, K. A., Pettit, G. S., Bates, J. E., & Valente, E. (1995). Social information-processing patterns partially mediate the effect of early physical abuse on later conduct problems. *Journal of Abnormal Psychology*, *104*, 632–643.

Drizin, S. A., & Colgan, B. (2004). Tales from the juvenile confession front: A guide to how standard police interrogation tactics can produce coerced and false confessions from juvenile suspects. In G. D. Lassiter (Ed.), *Interrogations, confessions, and entrapment* (pp. 127–162). New York: Kluwer Academic/Plenum.

Drizin, S. A., & Leo, R. A. (2004). The problem of false confessions in the post-DNA world. *North Carolina Law Review*, *82*, 891–1007.

Dunn, J., Cheng, H., O'Connor, T. G. & Bridges, L. (2004). Children's perspectives on their relationships with their nonresident fathers: Influences, outcomes and implications. *Journal of Child Psychology and Psychiatry*, *45*, 553–566.

Dunn, J., Davies, L., O'Connor, T., & Sturgess, W. (2001). Family lives and friendships: The perspectives of children in step-, single-parent, and two-parent families. *Journal of Family Psychology*, *15*, 272–287.

Egeland, B., Yates, T., Appleyard, K., & van Dulmen, M. (2002). The long-term consequences of maltreatment in the early years: A developmental pathway model to antisocial behavior. *Children's Services: Social Policy, Research, & Practice*, *5*, 249–260.

Eisen, M. L., Goodman, G. S., Qin, J., Davis, S., & Crayton, J. (2007). Maltreated children's memory: Accuracy, suggestibility, and psychopathology. *Developmental Psychology*, *43*, 1275–1294.

Eisen, M. L., Qin, J., Goodman, G. S., & Davis, S. L. (2002). Memory and suggestibility in maltreated children: Age, stress arousal, dissociation, and psychopathology. *Journal of Experimental Child Psychology*, *83*, 167–212.

Ellis, D., & Anderson, D. Y. (2003). The impact of participation in a parent education program for divorcing parents on the use of court resources: An evaluation study. *Conflict Resolution Quarterly*, 169–187.

Emery, R. E. (1994). *Renegotiating family relationships: Divorce, child custody, and mediation*. New York: Guilford Press.

Emery, R. E. (1998). *Marriage, divorce, and children's adjustment* (2nd ed.). Thousand Oaks, CA: Sage.

Emery, R. E., Laumann-Billings, L., Waldron, M. C., Sbarra, D. A., Dillon, P. (2001). Child custody mediation and litigation: Custody, contact, and coparenting 12 years after initial dispute resolution. *Journal of Consulting and Clinical Psychology*, *69*, 323–332.

📖 Fabricius, W. V., Braver, S. L., Diaz, P., & Schenck, C. (2010). Custody and parenting time: Links to family relationships and well-being after divorce. In M. E. Lamb (Ed.), *The role of the father in child development* (5th ed.). Hoboken, NJ: Wiley.

Fabricius, W. V., & Hall, J. (2000). Young adults' perspectives on divorce: Living arrangements. *Family & Conciliation Courts Review, 38*, 446–461.

Fagan, J. (2008). Juvenile crime and criminal justice: Resolving border disputes. *Future of Children, 18*, 81–118.

Family Courts Review (2001). Special issue, *39*(3).

Feiring, C., Taska, L., & Lewis, M. (1998). The role of shame and attributional style in children's and adolescents' adaptation to sexual abuse. *Child Maltreatment, 3*, 129–142.

Feld, B. C. (1993). Criminalizing the American juvenile court. *Crime & Justice, 17*, 197–280.

Feld, B. (2006). Police interrogations of juveniles: An empirical study of policy and practice. *Journal of Criminal Law and Criminology, 97*, 219–316.

Finkelhor, D. (1990). Early and long-term effects of child sexual abuse: An update. *Professional Psychology: Research and Practice, 21*, 325–330.

Finkelhor, D., & Browne, A. (1988). Assessing the long-term impact of child sexual abuse: A review and conceptualization. In G. T. Hotaling et al. (Eds.), *Family abuse and its consequences: New directions in research* (pp. 270–284). Thousand Oaks, CA: Sage.

Finley, G. E., & Schwartz, S. J. (2007). Father involvement and young adult outcomes: The differential contributions of divorce and gender. *Family Court Review, 45*, 573–587.

Firstman, R., & Salpeter, J. (2008). *A criminal injustice: A true crime, a false confession, and the fight to free Marty Tankleff.* New York: Ballantine Books.

Fisher, R. P., Brennan, K. H., & McCauley, M. R. (2002). The cognitive interview method to enhance eyewitness recall. In M. Eisen, G. Goodman, & J. Quas (Eds.), *Memory and suggestibility in the forensic interview* (pp. 265–286). Mahwah, NJ: Lawrence Erlbaum Associates.

Fivush, R., & Haden, C. A. (Eds.). (2003). *Autobiographical memory and the construction of a narrative self: Developmental and cultural perspectives.* Mahwah, NJ: Lawrence Erlbaum Associates.

Flory, B. E., Dunn, J., Berg-Weger, M., & Milstead, M. (2001). An exploratory study of supervised access and custody exchange services. *Family Court Review, 39*, 469–482.

Forst, M. A., Fagan, J., & Vivona, T. S. (1989). Some paradoxical effects of the treatment—custody dichotomy for adolescents in adult prisons. *Juvenile and Family Court Journal, 40*, 1–15.

Frayer, D. A., & Klausmeier, H. J. (1971). *Variables on concept learning: Task variables.* Theoretical paper No. 28. Madison, WI: Wisconsin Research and Development Center for Cognitive Learning.

Gardner, M., & Steinberg, L. (2005). Peer influence on risk-taking, risk preference, and risky decision-making in adolescence and adulthood: An experimental study. *Developmental Psychology, 41*, 625–635.

Garrett, B. (2008). Judging innocence. *Columbia Law Review, 108*, 55–142.

Garven, S., Wood, J. M., Malpass, R. S., & Shaw, J. S., III. (1998). More than suggestion: The effect of interviewing techniques from the McMartin Preschool case. *Journal of Applied Psychology, 83*, 347–359.

Gelles, R. J. (1996). *The book of David: How preserving families can cost children's lives.* New York: Basic Books.

Gergen, K. J. (1995). Postmodern psychology: Resonance and reflection. *American Psychologist, 50*, 394.

Goldstein, N., Condie, L., Kalbeitzer, R., Osman, D., & Geier, J. (2003). Juvenile offenders' Miranda rights comprehension and self-reported likelihood of false confessions. *Assessment, 10*, 359–369.

Goodman, G. S., Bottoms, B. L., Schwartz-Kenney, B. M., & Rudy, L. (1991a). Children's testimony about a stressful event: Improving children's reports. *Journal of Narrative and Life History, 1*, 69–99.

Goodman, G. S., Hirschman, J. E., Hepps, D., & Rudy, L. (1991b). Children's memory for stressful events. *Merrill-Palmer Quarterly, 37*, 109–157.

Goodman, G. S., Quas, J. A., Batterman-Faunce, J. M., Riddlesberger, M. M., & Kuhn, J. (1997). Children's reactions to and memory for a stressful event: Influences of age, anatomical dolls, knowledge, and parental attachment. *Applied Developmental Science, 1*, 54–75.

Goodman-Brown, T. B., Edelstein, R. S., Goodman, G. S., Jones, D. P. H., & Gordon, D. S. (2003). Why children tell: A model of children's disclosure of sexual abuse. *Child Abuse & Neglect, 27*, 525–540.

Green, A. H. (1993). Child sexual abuse: Immediate and long-term effects and intervention. *Journal of the American Academy of Child & Adolescent Psychiatry, 32*, 890–902.

Greenwood, P. (2006). *Changing lives: Delinquency prevention as crime control policy.* Chicago: University of Chicago Press.

Grisso, T. (1980). Juveniles' capacities to waive Miranda rights: An empirical analysis. *California Law Review, 68*, 1134–1166.

Grisso, T. (1981). *Juveniles' waiver of rights: Legal and psychological competence.* New York: Plenum.

Grisso, T. (1997). The competence of adolescents as trial defendants. *Psychology, Public Policy, and Law, 3*, 3–32.

Grisso, T. (1998). *Forensic evaluation of juveniles.* Sarasota, FL: Professional Resource Press.

Grisso, T., Steinberg, L., Woolard, J., Cauffman, E., Scott, E., Graham, S., et al. (2003). Juveniles' competence to stand trial: A comparison of adolescents' and adults' capacities as trial defendants. *Law and Human Behavior, 27*, 333–363.

Groark, C. J., & McCall, R. B. (2005). Integrating developmental scholarship into practice and policy. In

M. H. Bornstein & M. E. Lamb (Eds.), *Developmental science: An advanced textbook* (5th ed., pp. 557–601). Mahwah, NJ: Lawrence Erlbaum Associates.

Grol, R., & Grimshaw, J. (2003). From best evidence to best practice: Effective implementation of change in patients' care. *Lancet, 362*, 1225–1230.

Gross, S. R., Jacoby, K., Matheson, D. J., Montgomery, N., & Patel, S. (2005). Exonerations in the United States, 1989 through 2003. *Journal of Criminal Law & Criminology, 95*, 523–553.

Grych, J. H. (2005). Interparental conflict as a risk factor for child maladjustment: Implications for the development of prevention programs. *Family Court Review, 43*, 97–108.

Gudjonsson, G. H. (1990). One hundred alleged false confession cases: Some normative data. *British Journal of Clinical Psychology, 29*, 249–250.

Gudjonsson, G. H. (2003). *The psychology of interrogations and confessions: A handbook*. Chichester, UK: Wiley.

Gudjonsson, G. H., & MacKeith, J. A. C. (1994). Learning disability and the Police and Criminal Evidence Act of 1984. Protection during investigative interviewing: A video-recorded false confession to double murder. *Journal of Forensic Psychiatry, 5*, 35–49.

Gudjonsson, G. H., Sigurdsson, J. F., Asgeirsdottir, B. B., & Sigfusdottir, I. D. (2006). Custodial interrogation, false confession, and individual differences: A national study among Icelandic youth. *Personality and Individual Differences, 41*, 49–59.

Gudjonsson, G. H., Sigurdsson, J. F., Sigfusdottir, I. D., & Asgeirsdottir, B. B. (2008). False confessions and individual differences: The importance of victimization among youth. *Personality and Individual Differences, 45*, 801–805.

Gudjonsson, G. H., Sigurdsson, J. F., Asgeirsdottir, B. B., & Sigfusdottir, I. D. (in press). Interrogation and false confession among adolescents in seven European countries: What background and psychological variables best discriminate between false confessors and non-false confessors? *Psychology, Crime, and Law*.

Gudjonsson, G. H., & Singh, K. K. (1984). Interrogative suggestibility and delinquent boys: An empirical validation study. *Personality & Individual Differences, 5*, 425–430.

Guidelines for Parenting Coordination (2006). AFCC Task Force on Parenting Coordination. *Family Court Review, 44*, 164–181.

Gully, S. M. (1998). The influences of self-regulation processes on learning and performance in a team training context. *Dissertation Abstracts International: Section B: the Sciences & Engineering, 58* (9-B), 5175.

Haine, R. A., Sandler, I. N., Wolchik, S. A., Tein, J.-U., & Dawson-McClure, S. R. (2003). Changing the legacy of divorce: Evidence from prevention programs and future directions. *Family Relations, 52*, 397–405.

Hershkowitz, I., Horowitz, D., & Lamb, M. E. (2005). Trends in children's disclosure of abuse in Israel: A national study. *Child Abuse and Neglect, 29*, 1203–1214.

Hershkowitz, I., Horowitz, D., Lamb, M. E., Orbach, Y., & Sternberg, K. J. (2004). Interviewing youthful suspects in alleged sex crimes: A descriptive analysis. *Child Abuse and Neglect, 28*, 423–438.

Hershkowitz, I., Lamb, M. E., & Horowitz, D. (2007). Victimization of children with disabilities. *American Journal of Orthopsychiatry, 77*, 629–635.

Hershkowitz, I., Orbach, Y., Lamb, M. E., Sternberg, K. J., & Horowitz, D. (2006). Dynamics of forensic interviews with suspected abuse victims who do not disclose abuse. *Child Abuse and Neglect, 30*, 753–769.

Hetherington, E. M. (Ed.). (1999). Should we stay together for the sake of the children? In E. M. Hetherington (Ed.), *Coping with divorce, single parenting, and remarriage* (pp. 93–116). Mahwah, NJ: Lawrence Erlbaum Associates.

Hetherington, E. M., Bridges, M., & Insabella, G. M. (1998). What matters? What does not? Five perspectives on the association between marital transitions and children's adjustment. *American Psychologist, 53*, 167–184.

Hetherington, E. M., & Kelly, J. (2002). *For better or for worse: Divorce reconsidered*. New York: Norton.

Hewitt, S. D. (1999). *Assessing allegations of sexual abuse in preschool children*. Thousand Oaks, CA: Sage.

Hohmann, A. A., & Shear, M. K. (2002). Community-based intervention research: Coping with the "noise" of real life in study design. *American Journal of Psychiatry, 159*, 201–207.

Home Office. (1992). *Memorandum of good practice on video recorded interviews with child witnesses for criminal proceedings*. London: Home Office with Department of Health.

Home Office. (2007). *Achieving best evidence in criminal proceedings: Guidance on interviewing victims and witnesses, and using special measures*. London: Home Office.

Howe, M. L., Cicchetti, D., Toth, S. L., & Cerrito, B. M. (2004). True and false memories in maltreated children. *Child Development, 75*, 1402–1417.

Howe, M. L., Courage, M. L., & Peterson, C. (1996). "How can I remember when I wasn't there?": Long term retention of traumatic experiences and emergence of the cognitive self. In K. Pezdek & W. P. Banks (Eds.), *The recovered memory/false memory debate* (pp. 121–149). San Diego, CA: Academic Press.

Hutcheson, G. D., Baxter, J. S., Telfer, K., & Warden, D. (1995). Child witness statement quality: Question type and errors of omission. *Law and Human Behavior, 19*, 631–648.

Inbau, F. E., Reid, J. E., Buckley, J. P., & Jayne, B. C. (2001). *Criminal interrogation and confessions* (4th ed.). Gaithersberg, MD: Aspen.

Innocence Project. (2009). Understand the causes: False confessions. Retrieved September 4, 2009, from www.innocenceproject.org/understand/False-Confessions.php

Johnson, M. H. (2010). Developmental neuroscience, psychophysiology, and genetics. In M. H. Bornstein & M. E. Lamb (Eds.), *Developmental science: An advanced textbook* (6th ed., pp. 201–240). Hove, UK: Psychology Press.

Johnston, T. (1994). *Analysis of Santa Clara County, CA case files*. Unpublished dissertation.

Kassin, S. M. (2002, November 1). False confessions and the jogger case. *New York Times*, p. A31.

Kassin, S. M., Drizin, S. A., Grisso, T., Gudjonsson, G. H., Leo, R. A., & Redlich, A. D. (2010). Police-induced confessions: Risk factors and recommendations. *Law and Human Behavior, 34*, 3–38.

Kassin, S. M., & Gudjonsson, G. H. (2004). The psychology of confessions: A review of the literature and issues. *Psychological Science in the Public Interest, 5*, 35–69.

Kassin, S. M., & Kiechel, K. L. (1996). The social psychology of false confessions: Compliance, internalization, and confabulation. *Psychological Science, 7*, 125–128.

Kassin, S. M., Leo, R. A., Meissner, C. A., Richman, K. D., Colwell, L. H., Leach, A.-M., et al. (2007). Police interviewing and interrogation: A self-report survey of police practices and beliefs. *Law and Human Behavior, 31*, 381–400.

Katz, L. F., & Gottman, J. M. (1993). Patterns of marital conflict predict children's internalizing and externalizing behaviors. *Developmental Psychology, 29*, 940–950.

Katz, C., & Hershkowitz, I. (in press). The effect of drawing on the richness of accounts provided by alleged victims of child sexual abuse. *Child Maltreatment*.

Kelly, J. B. (2000). Children's adjustment in conflicted marriage and divorce: A decade review of research. *Journal of the American Academy of Child Psychiatry, 39*, 963–973.

Kelly, J. (2002). Psychological and legal interventions for parents and children in custody and access disputes: Current research and practice. *Virginia Journal of Social Policy and Law, 10*, 129–163.

Kelly, J. (2003). Parents with enduring child disputes: Multiple pathways to enduring disputes. *Journal of Family Studies, 9*, 37–50.

Kelly, J. B. (2004). Family mediation research: Is there support for the field? *Conflict Resolution Quarterly, 22*, 3–35.

Kelly, J. B. (2005). Developing beneficial parenting plan models for children following separation and divorce. *Journal of American Academy of Matrimonial Lawyers, 19*, 237–254.

Kelly, J. B. (2007). Children's living arrangements following separation and divorce: Insights from empirical and clinical research. *Family Process, 46*, 35–52.

Kelly, J. B. (in press). Training for the parenting coordinator role. *Journal of Child Custody*.

Kelly, J. B., & Emery, R. E. (2003). Children's adjustment following divorce: Risk and resilience perspectives. *Family Relations, 52*, 352–362.

Kelly, J. B. & Johnston, J. R. (2005). Commentary on Tippins and Whitmann's "Empirical and ethical problems with custody recommendations: A call for clinical humility and judicial vigilance". *Family Court Review, 4*, 233–241.

Kelly, J. B., & Lamb, M. E. (2000). Using child development research to make appropriate custody and access decisions for young children. *Family and Conciliation Courts Review, 38*, 297–311.

Kelly, J. B., & Lamb, M. E. (2003). Developmental issues in relocation cases involving young children: When, whether, and how? *Journal of Family Psychology, 17*, 193–205.

Kuehnle, K. (1996). *Assessing allegations of child sexual abuse*. Sarasota, FL: Professional Resource Press/ Professional Resource Exchange.

Lamb, M. E. (2002a). Infant–father attachments and their impact on child development. In C. S. Tamis-LeMonda & N. Cabrera (Eds.), *Handbook of father involvement: Multidisciplinary perspectives* (pp. 93–117). Mahwah, NJ: Lawrence Erlbaum Associates.

Lamb, M. E. (2002b). Placing children's interests first: Developmentally appropriate parenting plans. *Virginia Journal of Social Policy and the Law, 10*, 98–119.

Lamb, M. E. (2003). Child development and the law. In R. M. Lerner, M. A. Easterbrooks, & J. Mistry (Eds.), *Handbook of psychology, Volume 6: Developmental psychology* (pp. 559–577). Hoboken, NJ: Wiley.

Lamb, M. E., Bornstein, M. H., & Teti, D. M. (2002a). *Development in infancy* (4th ed.). Mahwah, NJ: Lawrence Erlbaum Associates.

Lamb, M. E., & Fauchier, A. (2001). The effects of question type on self-contradictions by children in the course of forensic interviews. *Applied Cognitive Psychology, 15*, 483–491.

Lamb, M. E., Hershkowitz, I., Orbach, Y., & Esplin, P. W. (2008). *Tell me what happened: Structured investigative interviews of child victims and witnesses*. Hoboken, NJ: Wiley.

Lamb, M. E., Hershkowitz, I., Sternberg, K. J., Esplin, P. W., Hovav, M., Manor, T., et al. (1996). Effects of investigative utterance types on Israeli children's responses. *International Journal of Behavioural Development, 19*, 627–637.

Lamb, M. E., & Kelly, J. B. (2001). Using the empirical literature to guide the development of parenting plans for young children: A rejoinder to Solomon and Biringen. *Family Court Review, 39*, 365–371.

Lamb, M. E., & Kelly, J. B. (2009). Improving the quality of parent–child contact in separating families with infants and young children: Empirical research foundations. In R. M. Gatalzer Levy, L. Kraus, & J. Galatzer-Levy (Eds.), *The scientific basis of child custody decisions* (2nd ed., pp. 187–214). Hoboken, NJ: Wiley.

Lamb, M. E., & Lewis, C. (2010). The development and significance of father–child relationships in two parent families. In M. E. Lamb (Ed.), *The role of the father in child development* (5th ed.). Hoboken, NJ: Wiley.

Lamb, M. E., Orbach, Y., Hershkowitz, I., Esplin, P. W., & Horowitz, D. (2007). A structured forensic interview protocol improves the quality and informativeness of investigative interviews with children: A review of the research using the NICHD Investigative Interview Protocol. *Child Abuse & Neglect, 31,* 1201–1231.

Lamb, M. E., Sternberg, K. J., & Esplin, P. W. (1998). Conducting investigative interviews of alleged sexual abuse victims. *Child Abuse and Neglect, 22,* 813–823.

Lamb, M. E., Sternberg, K. J., Orbach, Y., Esplin, P. W., & Mitchell, S. (2002b). Is ongoing feedback necessary to maintain the quality of investigative interviews with allegedly abused children? *Applied Developmental Science, 6,* 35–41.

Lamb, M. E., Sternberg, K. J., Orbach, Y., Esplin, P. W., Stewart, H., & Mitchell, S. (2003a). Age differences in young children's responses to open-ended invitations in the course of forensic interviews. *Journal of Consulting and Clinical Psychology, 71,* 926–934.

Lamb, M. E., Sternberg, K. J., Orbach, Y., Hershkowitz, I., & Esplin, P. W. (1999). Forensic interviews of children. In R. Bull & A. Memon (Eds.), *The psychology of interviewing: A handbook* (pp. 253–278). New York: Wiley.

Lamb, M. E., Sternberg, K. J., Orbach, Y., Hershkowitz, I., & Horowitz, D. (2003b). Differences between accounts provided by witnesses and alleged victims of child sexual abuse. *Child Abuse and Neglect, 27,* 1019–1031.

Lamb, M. E., Sternberg, K. J., Orbach, Y., Hershkowitz, I., Horowitz, D., & Esplin, P. W. (2002c). The effects of intensive training and ongoing supervision on the quality of investigative with alleged sex abuse victims. *Applied Developmental Science, 6,* 114–125.

Lamb, M. E., Thompson, R. A., Gardner, W. P., & Charnov, E. L. (1985). *Infant–mother attachment.* Hillsdale, NJ: Lawrence Erlbaum Associates.

Lambert, B. (2008, July 1). Freed after 17 years in prison, L.I. man will not face new trial. *New York Times,* p. A1.

Laumann-Billings, L., & Emery, R. E. (2000). Distress among young adults in divorced families. *Journal of Family Psychology, 14,* 671–687.

Leippe, M. R., Manion, A. P., & Romanczyk, A. (1992). Eyewitness persuasion: How and how well do fact finders judge the accuracy of adults' and children's memory reports? *Journal of Personality and Social Psychology, 63,* 181–197.

Leo, R. A. (1996). Inside the interrogation room. *Journal of Criminal Law and Criminology, 86,* 266–303.

Lewin, K. (1946). Action research and minority problems. *Journal of Social Issues, 2,* 34–35.

Lewin, T. (2002, July 22). Ideas & trends; above expectation: A child as witness. *New York Times,* section 4, p. 3.

Libby, L. K. (2003). Imagery perspective and source monitoring in imagination inflation. *Memory and Cognition, 7,* 1072–1081.

Lillie and Reed v. Newcastle City Council & Ors [2002] EWHC 1600 (QB).

Loftus, E. F. (1997). Creating false memories. *Scientific American, 277,* 70–75.

Loftus, E. F. (2003). Make-believe memories. *American Psychologist, 58,* 864–873.

Loftus, E. F., & Ketcham, K. (1991). *Witness for the defense: The accused, the eyewitness, and the expert who puts memory on trial.* New York: St Martin's Press.

London, K. L., Bruck, M., Ceci, S. J., & Shuman, D. W. (2005). Disclosure of child sexual abuse: What does the research tell us about the ways that children tell? *Psychology, Public Policy, and Law, 11,* 194–226.

Luna, C. (2005, July 23). Girl's killer gets death. *Los Angeles Times,* p. B1.

Lyon, T. D. (2000). Child witnesses and the oath: Empirical evidence. *Southern California Law Review, 73,* 1017–1074.

Lyon, T. D. (2007). False denials: Overcoming methodological biases in abuse disclosure research. In M. E. Pipe et al. (Eds.), *Disclosing abuse: Delays, denials, retractions and incomplete accounts.* Mahwah, NJ: Lawrence Erlbaum Associates.

Lyon, T. D., Malloy, L. C., Quas, J. A., & Ahern, E.C. (in press). Children's reasoning about adult transgression secrecy: Effects of adult identity, child age, and maltreatment. *Child Development.*

Lyon, T. D., Malloy, L. C., Quas, J. A., & Talwar, V. (2008). Coaching, truth induction, and young maltreated children's false allegations and false denials. *Child Development, 79,* 914–929.

Lyon, T. D., & Saywitz, K. J. (1999). Young maltreated children's competence to take the oath. *Applied Developmental Science, 3,* 16–27.

Martinez, C. R., & Forgatch, M. S. (2002). Adjusting to change: Linking family structure transitions with parenting and boys' adjustment. *Journal of Family Psychology, 16,* 107–117.

McCall, R. B. & Green, B. L. (2004). Beyond the methodological gold standards of behavioral research: Considerations for practice and policy. *Society for Research in Child Development Social Policy Reports, 18,* 1–19.

McCall, R. B., Green, B. L., Strauss, M. S., & Groark, C. J. (1997). Issues in community-based research and program evaluation. In I. E. Sigel & K. A. Renninger (Eds.), *Handbook of child psychology* (Vol. 4, 5th ed., pp. 955–997). New York: Wiley.

McLanahan, S. S. (1999). Father absence and the welfare of children. In E. M. Hetherington (Ed.), *Coping with divorce, single parenting, and remarriage* (pp. 117–146). Mahwah, NJ: Lawrence Erlbaum Associates.

McLanahan, S. S., & Sandefur, G. (1994). *Growing up with a single parent: What hurts, what helps.* Cambridge, MA: Harvard University Press.

McLanahan, S. S., & Teitler, J. (1999). The consequences of father absence. In M. E. Lamb (Ed.), *Parenting and child development in "nontraditional" families* (pp. 83–102). Mahwah, NJ: Lawrence Erlbaum Associates.

Memon, A., Wark, L., Holley, A., Bull, R., & Köhnken, G. (1996). Reducing suggestibility in child witness interviews. *Applied Cognitive Psychology, 10,* 503–518.

Memorandum of Good Practice (1992). London: Her Majesty's Stationery Office.

Meyer, J. R., & Reppucci, N. D. (2007). Police practices and perceptions regarding juvenile interrogations and interrogative suggestibility. *Behavioral Sciences and the Law, 25,* 757–780.

Moffitt, T. (1993). Adolescence-limited and life-course persistent antisocial behavior: A developmental taxonomy. *Psychological Review, 100,* 674–701.

Moffitt, T. E., & Caspi, A. (2001). Childhood predictors differentiate life-course persistent and adolescence-limited antisocial pathways among males and females. *Development & Psychopathology, 13,* 355–375.

Moffitt, T. E., Caspi, A., Harrington, H., & Milne, B. J. (2002). Males on the life-course-persistent and adolescence-limited antisocial pathways: Follow-up at age 26 years. *Development & Psychopathology, 14,* 179–207.

Muehrer, P. R., Salovey, P., Abdelmonem, A. A., Coyne, J. C., Kring, A. M., Merson, M. H., et al. (2002). Overcoming barriers to collaboration between basic behavioral scientists and public health scientists in research on mental disorders. *Journal of Clinical Psychology in Medical Settings, 9,* 253–265.

Muller v. Oregon, 208 U.S. 412 (1908).

Munsterberg, H. (1908). *On the witness stand.* Garden City, NY: Doubleday.

Myers, J. E. B. (1992). *Legal issues in child abuse and neglect.* Newbury Park, CA: Sage.

Nathan, D., & Snedeker, M. (1995). *Satan's silence: Ritual abuse and the making of a modern American witch hunt.* New York: Basic Books.

National Research Council (1993). *Understanding child abuse and neglect.* Washington, DC: National Academy Press.

Nelson, K., & Fivush, R. (2004). The emergence of autobiographical memory: A social cultural developmental theory. *Psychological Review, 111,* 486–511.

Nord, C., Brimhall, D., & West, J. (1997). *Fathers' involvement in their children's schools.* Washington, DC: National Center for Education Statistics.

New Jersey v. Michaels, 625 A.2d 579 aff'd 642 A.2d 1372 (1994).

North Carolina v. Robert Fulton Kelly Jr., 456 S.E.2d 861 (1995).

Odgers, C. L., Moffitt, T. E., Broadbent, J. M., Dickson, N., Hancox, R. J., Harrington, H., et al. (2008). Female and male antisocial trajectories: From childhood origins to adult outcomes. *Development and Psychopathology, 20,* 673–716.

Ogloff, J. R. P. (2000). Two steps forward and one step backward: The law and psychology movement(s) in the 20th century. *Law and Human Behavior, 24,* 457–483.

Orbach, Y., Hershkowitz, I., Lamb, M. E., Esplin, P. W., & Horowitz, D. (2000). Assessing the value of structured protocols for forensic interviews of alleged child abuse victims. *Child Abuse and Neglect, 24,* 733–752.

Orbach, Y., & Lamb, M. E. (2001). The relationship between within-interview contradictions and eliciting interviewer utterances. *Child Abuse and Neglect, 25,* 323–333.

Ornstein, P. A., Baker-Ward, L., Gordon, B. N., & Merritt, K. A. (1997). Children's memory for medical experiences: Implications for testimony. *Applied Cognitive Psychology, 11,* S87–S104.

Ornstein, P. A., Gordon, B. N., & Larus, D. M. (1992). Children's memory for a personally experienced event: Implications for testimony. *Applied Cognitive Psychology, 6,* 49–60.

Owen-Kostelnik, J., Reppucci, N. D., & Meyer, J. D. (2006). Testimony and interrogation of minors: Assumptions about maturity and morality. *American Psychologist, 61,* 286–304.

Patterson, G. R., Dishion, T. J., & Yoerger, K. (2000). Adolescent growth in new forms of problem behavior: Macro- and micro-peer dynamics. *Prevention Science, 1,* 3–13.

Pedro-Carroll, J., Nakhnikian, E., & Montes, G. (2001). Assisting children through transition: Helping parents protect their children from the toxic effects of ongoing conflict in the aftermath of divorce. *Family Court Review, 39,* 377–392.

People of the State of New York v. Kharey Wise, Kevin Richardson, Antron McCray, Yusef Salaam, & Raymond Santana: Affirmation in Response to Motion to Vacate Judgment of Conviction (2002). Indictment No. 4762/89, December 5, 2002.

Peterson-Badali, M., & Abramovitch, R. (1993). Grade related changes in young people's reasoning about plea decisions. *Law & Human Behavior, 17,* 537–552.

Pipe, M. E., Goodman, G. S., Quas, J., Bidrose, S., Ablin, D., & Craw, S. (1997). Remembering early experiences during childhood: Are traumatic events special? In J. D. Read & D. S. Lindsay (Eds.), *Recollections of trauma: Scientific evidence and clinical practice* (pp. 417–423). New York: Plenum Press.

☐ Pipe, M. E., Lamb, M. E., Orbach, Y., & Cederborg, A.-C. (2007). *Child sexual abuse: Disclosure, delay and denial.* Mahwah, NJ: Lawrence Erlbaum Associates.

Pipe, M. E., Orbach, Y., & Lamb, M. E. (2008, March). The effect of the NICHD Interview Protocol on the outcomes of child sexual abuse investigations. In M. E. Lamb, *How does the quality of interviews with alleged victims of child abuse affect investigation and intervention?* Symposium presented at the annual meeting of the American Psychology Law Society, Jacksonville, FL.

Poole, D. A., & Lamb, M. E. (1998). *Investigative interviews of children: A guide for helping professionals.* Washington, DC: American Psychological Association.

Poulin, F., Dishion, T. J., & Burraston, B. (2001). 3-Year iatrogenic effects associated with aggregating high-risk adolescents in cognitive–behavioral preventive interventions. *Applied Developmental Science, 5,* 214–224.

Powell, M. B., & Wright, R. (2008). Investigative interviewers' perceptions of the value of different training tasks on their adherence to open-ended questions with children. *Psychiatry, Psychology and Law, 15,* 272–283.

Prohaska, T. R., & Rozensky, R. H. (2002). Overcoming barriers to collaboration between basic behavioral scientists and public health scientists in research on mental disorders. *Journal of Clinical Psychology in Medical Settings, 9,* 253–265.

Pruett, M. K., Insabella, G. M., & Gustafson, K. (2005). The Collaborative Divorce Project: A court-based intervention for separating parents with young children. *Family Courts Review, 43,* 38–51.

Pruett, M. K., Williams, T. Y., Insabella, G., & Little, T. D. (2003). Family and legal indicators of child adjustment to divorce among families with young children. *Journal of Family Psychology, 17,* 169–180.

Quas, J. A., Goodman, G. S., Bidrose, S., Pipe, M. E., Craw, S. & Ablin, D. S. (1999). Emotion and memory: Children's long-term remembering, forgetting, and suggestibility. *Journal of Experimental Child Psychology, 72,* 235–270.

Quas, J. A., Wallin, A. R., Papini, S., Lench, H., & Scullin, M. H. (2005). Suggestibility, social support, and memory for a novel experience in young children. *Journal of Experimental Child Psychology, 91,* 315–341.

Quinn, M. M., Rutherford, R. B., Leone, P. E., Osher, D. M., & Poirier, J. M. (2005). Youth with disabilities in juvenile corrections: A national survey. *Exceptional Children, 71,* 339–345.

☐ Redlich, A. D. (2007). Double jeopardy in the interrogation room: Young age and mental illness. *American Psychologist, 62,* 609–611.

Redlich, A. D., & Goodman, G. S. (2003). Taking responsibility for an act not committed: Influence of age and suggestibility. *Law and Human Behavior, 27,* 141–156.

Redlich, A. D., Silverman, M., & Steiner, H. (2003). Pre-adjudicative and adjudicative competence in juveniles and young adults. *Behavioral Sciences and the Law, 21,* 393–410.

Redlich, A. D., Summers, A., & Hoover, S. (2010). Self-reported false confessions and false guilty pleas among offenders with mental illness. *Law & Human Behavior, 34,* 79–90.

Reid & Associates (2009). Interviewing and interrogation. Retrieved September 1, 2009, from www.reid.com/ training_programs/interview_overview.html

Richardson, G., Gudjonsson, G. H., & Kelly, T. P. (1995). Interrogative suggestibility in an adolescent forensic population. *Journal of Adolescence, 18,* 211–216.

Richardson, G., & Kelly, T. P. (2004). A study in the relationship between interrogative suggestibility, compliance and social desirability in institutionalised adolescents. *Personality and Individual differences, 36,* 485–494.

Roberts, K. P., Lamb, M. E., & Sternberg, K. J. (2004). The effects of rapport building style on children's reports of a staged event. *Applied Cognitive Psychology, 18,* 189–202.

Roper v. Simmons, 543 U.S. 551 (2005).

Saywitz, K. J., Goodman, G. S., Nicholas, E., & Moan, S. F. (1991). Children's memories of a physical examination involving genital touch: Implications for reports of child sexual abuse. *Journal of Consulting and Clinical Psychology, 59,* 682–691.

Saywitz, K. J., Snyder, L., & Nathanson, R. (1999). Faciliating the communicative competence of the child witness. *Applied Developmental Science, 3,* 58–68.

Scheck, B., Neufeld, P., & Dwyer, J. (2000). *Actual innocence.* Garden City, NY: Doubleday.

Schneider, W., & Bjorklund, D. F. (1998). Memory. In W. Damon (Series Ed.) and D. Kuhn & R. S. Siegler (Vol. Eds.), *Handbook of child psychology: Volume 2. Cognition, perception, and language* (pp. 467–521). New York: Wiley.

Schwartz, S. J., & Finley, G. E. (in press). Mothering, fathering, and divorce: The influence of divorce on reports of and desires for maternal and paternal involvement. *Family Court Review.*

☐ Scott, E., & Steinberg, L. (2008). *Rethinking juvenile justice.* Cambridge, MA: Harvard University Press.

Sears, R. R. (1975). Your ancients revisited: A history of child development. In E. M. Hetherington (Ed.), *Review of child development research.* Oxford, UK: University of Chicago Press.

Shonk, S. M., & Cicchetti, D. (2001). Maltreatment, competency deficits, and risk for academic and behavioral maladjustment. *Developmental Psychology, 37,* 3–17.

Sigurdsson, J. F., & Gudjonsson, G. H. (2004). Forensic psychology in Iceland: A survey of members of the Icelandic Psychological Society. *Scandinavian Journal of Psychology*, *45*, 325–329.

Simons, R. L. and Associates (Eds.). (1996). *Understanding differences between divorced and intact families*. Thousand Oaks, CA: Sage Publications.

Simons, R. L., Lin, K. H., Gordon, L. C., Conger, R. D., & Lorenz, F. O. (1999). Explaining the higher incidence of adjustment problems among children of divorce compared with those in two parent families. *Journal of Marriage and the Family*, *61*, 1020–1033.

Singer, S. I., & McDowall, D. (1988). Criminalizing delinquency: The deterrent effects of the New York Juvenile Offender Law. *Law and Society Review*, *22*, 521–536.

Singh, K., & Gudjonsson, G. H. (1992). Interrogative suggestibility among adolescent boys and its relationship to intelligence, memory, and cognitive set. *Journal of Adolescence*, *15*, 155–161.

Smart, C. (2002). From children's shoes to children's voices. *Family Court Review*, *40*, 307–319.

Smart, C. & Neale, B. (2000). "It's my life too"—Children's perspectives on post-divorce parenting. *Family Law*, March, 163–169.

Smith, A. B., & Gallop, M. M. (2001). What children think separating parents should know. *New Zealand Journal of Psychology*, *30*, 23–31.

Smyth, B. M., & Chisholm, R. (2006). Exploring options for parental care of children following separation: A primer for family law specialists. *Australian Journal of Family Law*, *20*, 193–218.

Snyder, H. (2006). *Juvenile arrests 2004*. Washington, DC: Office of Juvenile Justice and Delinquency Prevention, Office of Justice Programs.

Sommer, R. (2006). Dual dissemination: Writing for colleagues and the public. *American Psychologist*, *61*, 955–958.

Sroufe, L. A. (1979). The coherence of individual development: Early care, attachment, and subsequent developmental issues. *American Psychologist*, *34*, 834–841.

Stanford v. Kentucky, 492 U.S. 361 (1989).

State v. Fijnje, 11th Judicial Circuit Court, Dade Country, Florida, #84–19728 (1995).

State of New Jersey v. Michaels, 136 N.J. 299, 642 A.2d 1372 (1994).

State of Washington v. Manuel Hidalgo Rodriguez, Washington Court of Appeals No. 17600–2-III (Sept. 22, 1999).

State of Washington v. Carol M.D. and Mark A.D., 983 P.2d 1165 (Wash. Ct. App. 1999).

Steinberg, L. (2007). Risk-taking in adolescence: New perspectives from brain and behavioral science. *Current Directions in Psychological Science*, *16*, 55–59.

Steinberg, L. (2008). A social neuroscience perspective on adolescent risk-taking. *Developmental Review*, *28*, 78–106.

Steinberg, L. (2009). Adolescent development and juvenile justice. *Annual Review of Clinical Psychology*, *5*, 459–485.

Steinberg, L., Albert, D., Cauffman, E., Banich, M., Graham, S., & Woolard, J. (2008). Age differences in sensation seeking and impulsivity as indexed by behavior and self-report: Evidence for a dual systems model. *Developmental Psychology*, *44*, 1764–1778.

Steinberg, L., & Cauffman, E. (1996). Maturity of judgment in adolescence: Psychosocial factors in adolescent decision making. *Law and Human Behavior*, *20*, 249–272.

Steinberg, L., Graham, S., O'Brien, L., Woolard, J., Cauffman, E., & Banich, M. (2009). Age differences in future orientation and delay discounting. *Child Development*, *80*, 28–44.

Steinberg, L., & Scott, E. (2003). Less guilty by reason of adolescence: Developmental immaturity, diminished responsibility, and the juvenile death penalty. *American Psychologist*, *58*, 1009–1018.

Sternberg, K. J., Baradaran, L. P., Abbott, C. B., Lamb, M. E., & Guterman, E. (2006a). Type of violence, age, and gender differences in the effects of family violence on children's behavior problems: A mega-analysis. *Developmental Review*, *26*, 89–112.

Sternberg, K. J., Lamb, M. E., Davies, G. M., & Westcott, H. L. (2001a). The Memorandum of Good Practice: Theory versus application. *Child Abuse & Neglect*, *25*, 669–681.

Sternberg, K. J., Lamb, M. E., Esplin, P. W., & Baradaran, L. P. (1999). Using a scripted protocol in investigative interviews: A pilot study. *Applied Developmental Science*, *3*, 70–76.

Sternberg, K. J., Lamb, M. E., Guterman, E., & Abbott, C. B. (2006b). Effects of early and later family violence on children's behavior problems and depression: A longitudinal, multi-informant perspective. *Child Abuse & Neglect*, *30*, 283–306.

Sternberg, K. J., Lamb, M. E., Hershkowitz, I., Yudilevitch, L., Orbach, Y., Esplin, P. W., et al. (1997). Effects of introductory style on children's abilities to describe experience of sexual abuse. *Child Abuse and Neglect*, *21*, 1133–1146.

Sternberg, K. J., Lamb, M. E., Orbach, Y., Esplin, P. W., & Mitchell, S. (2001b). Use of a structured investigative protocol enhances young children's responses to free-recall prompts in the course of forensic interviews. *Journal of Applied Psychology*, *86*, 997–1005.

Sturge-Apple, M. L., Davies, P. T., & Cummings, E. M. (2006). Hostility and withdrawal in marital conflict: Effects on parental emotional unavailability and inconsistent discipline. *Journal of Family Psychology*, *20*, 227–238.

Sullivan, P. M., & Knutson, J. F. (2000). Maltreatment and disabilities: A population-based epidemiological study. *Child Abuse and Neglect, 24*, 1257–1273.

Sweet, R. C. (1966). *Educational attainment and attitude toward school as a function of feedback in the form of teachers' written comments.* Technical Report No. 15. Madison, WI: Wisconsin Research and Development Center for Cognitive Learning.

Teplin, L., Abram, K., McClelland, G., Dulcan, M., & Mericle, A. (2002). Psychiatric disorders in youth in juvenile detention. *Archives of General Psychiatry, 59*, 1133–1143.

Thompson v. Oklahoma, 487 U.S. 815 (1988).

Thompson, R. A. (1999). Early attachment and later development. In J. Cassidy & P. R. Shaver, *Handbook of attachment: Theory, research, and clinical applications* (pp. 265–286). New York: Guilford Press.

Thompson, R. A. (2006). Early sociopersonality development. In W. Damon, R. A. Lerner, & N. Eisenberg (Eds.), *Handbook of child development, Volume 3: Social, emotional, and personality development* (6th ed.). Hoboken, NJ: Wiley.

Tippins, T. M. & Wittmann, J. P. (2005). Empirical and ethical problems with custody recommendations: A call for clinical humility and judicial vigilance. *Family Court Review, 43*, 193–222.

Trinder, L. & Lamb, M. E. (2005). Measuring up? The relationship between correlates of children's adjustment and both family law and policy in England. *Louisiana Law Review, 65*, 1509–1537.

Trocmé, N., MacLaurin, B., Fallon, B., Daciuk, J., Billingsley, D., Tourigny, M., et al. (2001). *Canadian Incidence Study of Reported Child Abuse and Neglect: Final Report.* Ottawa, Canada: Minister of Public Works and Government Services.

US Department of Health and Human Services, Administration on Children, Youth, and Families (2009). *Child maltreatment 2007.* Washington, DC: US Government Printing Office.

Valle, L. A., & Silovsky, J. F. (2002). Attributions and adjustment following child sexual and physical abuse. *Child Maltreatment, 7*, 9–25.

Viljoen, J., Klaver, J., & Roesch, R. (2005). Legal decisions of preadolescent and adolescent defendants: Predictors of confessions, pleas, communication with attorneys, and appeals. *Law and Human Behavior, 29*, 253–278.

Wade, K. A., Garry, M., Read, J. D., & Lindsay, D. S. (2002). A picture is worth a thousand lies: Using false photographs. *Psychonomic Bulletin and Review, 9*, 597–603.

Wallerstein, J. & Kelly, J. (1980). *Surviving the breakup: How children and parents cope with divorce.* New York: Basic Books.

Walters, S., Holmes, L., Bauer, G., & Vieth, V. (2003). *Finding words: Half a nation by 2010: Interviewing children and preparing for court.* Alexandria, VA: National Center for Prosecution of Child Abuse.

Warren, A. R., Woodall, C. E., Hunt, J. S., & Perry, N. W. (1996). "It sounds good in theory, but …": Do investigative interviewers follow guidelines based on memory research? *Child Maltreatment, 1*, 231–245.

Warren, A. R., Woodall, C. E., Thomas, M., Nunno, M., Keeney, J. M., Larson, S. M., et al. (1999). Assessing the effectiveness of a training program for interviewing child witnesses. *Applied Developmental Science, 3*, 128–135.

Warshak, R. A. (2000). Blanket restrictions: Overnight contact between parents and young children. *Family and Conciliation Courts Review, 38*, 422–445.

Warshak, R. A. (2001). *Divorce poison.* New York: Regan Books.

Wasserman, G. A., McReynolds, L., Lucas, C., Fisher, P. W., & Santos, L. (2002). The Voice DISC–IV with incarcerated male youth: Prevalence of disorder. *Journal of the American Academy of Child and Adolescent Psychiatry, 41*, 314–321.

Waterman, A. H., Blades, M., & Spencer, C. P. (2000). Do children try to answer nonsensical questions? *British Journal of Developmental Psychology, 18*, 211–226.

Waterman, A. H., Blades, M., & Spencer, C. P. (2004). Indicating when you do not know the answer: The effect of question format and interviewer knowledge on children's "don't know" responses. *British Journal of Developmental Psychology, 22*, 335–348.

Westmaas, J. L., Gil-Rivas, V., & Silver, R. C. (2007). Designing and implementing interventions to promote health and prevent illness. In H. S. Friedman & R. C. Silver (Eds.), *Foundations of health psychology* (pp. 52–70). New York: Oxford University Press.

Wigmore, J. H. (1909). Professor Munsterberg and the psychology of testimony. *Illinois Law Review, 3*, 399–434.

Wigmore, J. H. (1940). *Evidence in trials at common law* (3rd ed.). Boston: Little, Brown.

Yarrow, L. J. (1963). Research in dimensions of early maternal care. *Merrill-Palmer Quarterly, 9*, 101–114.

Yarrow, L. J., & Goodwin, M. (1973). The immediate impact of separation: Reactions of infants to a change in mother figures. In L. J. Stone, H. T. Smith, & L. B. Murphy (Eds.), *The competent infant* (pp. 1032–1040). New York: Basic Books.

Zigler, E. F., & Finn-Stevenson, M. (1999). Applied developmental psychology. In M. H. Bornstein & M. E. Lamb (Eds.), *Developmental science: An advanced textbook* (4th ed.) (pp. 555–598). Mahwah, NJ: Lawrence Erlbaum Associates.

GLOSSARY

Achievement: The attainment of specific academic and educational goals.

Achievement goal theory: A social–cognitive understanding of motivated behavior in achievement settings that posits that students' responses to success and failure depend on the achievement goals they have. Students who have performance goals are most concerned with how well they do compared to others and are likely to select tasks on which they are certain they can succeed. In contrast, students with mastery goals are most concerned about learning and so are likely to select tasks from which they can learn the most even if they have difficulty succeeding.

Action theory: A conceptualization of human development as an intentional, dynamic, and reciprocal process of "action feedback–self-organization–further action" in which individuals create behavioral regulators that moderate exchanges occurring between them and the context.

Age–crime curve: The robust empirical finding that the onset of criminal offending is between ages 8–14, peaks in prevalence between ages 15–19, and declines towards adult levels between ages 20–29.

Agency: Individuals' intrinsic curiosity, competence, motivation, and exploratory behaviors that promote their capacity to act in the world and contribute to their own development in school.

Agentic: A characteristic of a person who feels that they can influence their world and the behaviors of those around them and then acts accordingly.

Aggression: High levels of relational aggression (e.g., threatening friendship withdrawal) *within* the friendship, and high levels of exclusivity, jealousy, and intimacy, characterize the friendships of relationally aggressive children. In contrast, overtly aggressive children direct their overt aggression *outside* their friendship dyads, and report low levels of intimacy (Grotpeter & Crick, 1996).

Analysis of variance (ANOVA): Statistical technique based on the general linear model used to assess differences among group means that can accommodate a wide variety of experimental designs, including between-subject effects, within-subject effects, or within- and between-subject (or mixed) effects.

Artifact: Species-specific features of shared and inherited material culture that mediate and coordinate human beings with the physical world and with each other.

Attachment: Biologically and culturally influenced system of interrelated social behaviors between caregiver and child that provide emotional security and encourage environmental exploration.

Attachment theory: Conceptual framework for describing and explaining normative and individual differences in caregiver–child interactions first developed by Bowlby, stressing the foundational influence of the social and emotional qualities of this dyadic relationship (typically mother–infant) in the healthy development of later interpersonal relationships.

Authoritarian parenting: Parenting style, described by Baumrind, characterized by valuing obedience and the forceful imposition of the parents' will; this parenting style has been found more commonly among fathers than mothers, when the child under discussion was a son, and within some cultural contexts to be associated with increased levels of behavior problems.

Authoritative parenting: Parenting style, described by Baumrind, characterized by the encouragement of independence and the influencing of children's behavior using rational explanation that is sensitive to, and facilitates, children's changing sense of self; this parenting style is associated with social competence and conformity to cultural and societal norms.

Autobiographical memory: Emerging after the third birthday, personal memories of past events of one's life that rely upon a sense of self that is central to the narrative account, organizing and giving meaning to the events that are remembered.

Behavior genetics: The quantitative study of the degree to which genotypic variability is associated with phenotypic variability in a population; historically behavior genetic studies have focused on estimating the heritability of an observed behavioral trait (e.g., intelligence, personality, psychopathology) by comparing samples of monozygotic (identical) and dizygotic (fraternal) twins.

Behavioral inhibition: A moderately stable self-regulatory response that causes some children to withdraw from unfamiliar people and situations.

Behaviorism: The name coined early in the 20th century by James B. Watson and his colleagues to distinguish their emphasis on the study of observable behavior from the study of introspection of unobservable psychological processes.

Bioecological theory: Bronfenbrenner's conceptualization of human development within the context of four interrelated and nested ecological levels (i.e., *microsystem, mesosystem, exosystem,* and *macrosystem*) which influence individual developmental outcomes in relation to the chronosystem.

Bio-social-behavioral shifts: Qualitative rearrangements in the emergence and organization of behavior resulting from the synthesis of biological and social factors interacting over time within cultural contexts.

Bio-social-cultural change: A generalized cultural (or cultural-mediational) alternative to classical theories in which human development is seen as an emergent process of biological and social changes that interact within and are mediated by culture, the accumulated knowledge, experience, and learning of prior generations.

Categorical data analysis: Class of statistical procedures used to determine whether observed proportions or frequencies differ significantly or are correlated with one another. Examples include chi-square analysis, logistic regression, and log-linear analysis.

Classroom climate: The general social-relational atmosphere of the classroom resulting from the organization and management of the learning environment as well as the character of teacher–student relationships.

Closed questions: Queries for information posed to interviewees that specify a response or set of particular responses (e.g., "Did he touch you over or under your clothes?", "Who did you tell?"). These types of questions are typically regarded as less preferable to open-ended questions in investigative interviews in part because they restrict the memory search to certain aspects of the event.

Competence to stand trial: The judgment that a person has the capacity to assist counsel in preparing his or her legal defense and to understand the nature of the proceeding sufficiently to participate in and make decisions about rights afforded to defendants; one of the areas of juvenile justice developmental science has contributed significantly to informing legal statutes and practice.

Conceptual splits: Instances in which questions about the nature of human development are framed in terms of opposing explanations such as nature versus nurture, continuity versus discontinuity, and stability versus instability.

Conduct disorder: Repetitive and persistent pattern of behaviors in which social norms or the basic rights of others are violated. These can include aggressive conduct towards other people or animals, behavior that causes property loss or damage, deceitfulness, theft, and serious violations of rules.

Confidence interval: Estimated range of values that surround the point-estimate of a population parameter and indicates the precision, or likely accuracy, of the point estimate.

Conflict: Interpersonal interactions characterized by quarreling, active hostility (assaults and threats) and reactive hostility (refusals and resistance) among individuals.

Conscience: Relationally influenced cognitive and affective processes which govern how young children construct and act consistently with generalizable, internal standards of conduct.

Construct validity: Degree to which a variable, as operationally defined, represents an intended theoretical construct; threats to construct validity occur when variables either underrepresent the intended construct or include extraneous factors.

Continuity: Consistency in group-based, normative perceptual abilities between time points.

Continuity–discontinuity issue: A conceptual split that stresses qualitative or quantitative similarity (continuity) or dissimilarity (discontinuity) of the description or explanation of behaviors at different points in the life span.

Co-regulation: "A form of coordinated action between participants that involves a continuous mutual adjustment of actions and intentions" (Fogel & Garvey, 2007) in which participants (e.g., child and adult) are best described as a single system rather than as two separate individuals.

Co-rumination: Intimate self-disclosure characterized by dwelling on emotionally charged and intimate everyday occurrences and feelings in negative ways.

Cross-cultural psychology: Research that explores the causes and consequences of cultural differences in which culture is treated as an antecedent or independent variable that acts on psychological processes.

Culpability: The judgment that a person is sufficiently responsible for a criminal act or negligence to be at fault and liable for the conduct; one of the areas of juvenile justice developmental science that has contributed significantly to informing legal statutes and practice.

Cultural evolution: Nineteenth-century anthropologists' belief that cultures could be classified according to their level of development—characterized by the sophistication of their technology and the complexity of their social organization—which represented progressively advanced stages of the development of humankind.

Cultural influence: The impact of cultural norms and values in defining the "meanings" of social behaviors that affect group and individual beliefs, attitudes, and value systems.

Cultural practices: Recurrent ways of accomplishing valued social activities in concert with some group of one's proximally circumscribed social unit.

Cultural psychology: An approach in which culture is treated as the species-specific medium of human life within which people acquire and share symbolic meanings and practices that contribute to the development of psychological processes within a given cultural group.

Culture: The residue in the present of past human activity in which human beings have variously transformed nature to suit their own ends and passed the cumulated artifacts down to succeeding generations in the form of tools, rituals, beliefs, and ways of conceiving of the world. Psychological and material aspects of culture are inextricably interconnected in a medium of conceptual systems, social institutions.

Custody (child): A legal finding in which the care, control, and maintenance of a child is awarded to one or both parents following a divorce or separation proceeding.

Design: The structure or plan of investigations that defines the extent and means by which investigators exercise control over their independent, and all other variables, that may be operating in an investigative context. Design variations guard against different threats to the validity of the investigation and determine the conclusions that can be appropriately drawn from the research.

Developmental contextualism: Lerner's conceptualization of human development that emphasizes bidirectional, changing relations among multiple levels of organization involved in human life (e.g., biology, psychology, social groups, culture, history).

Developmental niche: An individual's "life world" in which the complex set of socio-cultural-ecological relations form the proximal environment of development. Developmental niches consist of (1) the physical and social settings in which a child lives, (2) the culturally regulated childrearing and socialization practices of a child's society, and (3) the psychological characteristics of a child's parents, including parental theories about the process of child development and their affective orientation to the tasks of childrearing.

Developmental regulation: The processes of dynamic person-context relations that are a shared feature of systems theories of human development.

Developmental systems theories: a family of related theories of human development that share four components: (1) change and relative plasticity; (2) relationism and the integration of levels of organization; (3) historical embeddedness and temporality; and (4) an emphasis on the limits of generalizability, diversity, and individual differences.

Differential susceptibility hypothesis: The view that some temperamental or genetic characteristics render children more susceptible to positive as well as negative environmental influences.

Discrimination: The impugning of an individual's intellectual ability based on ethnicity, race, or gender that may undermine the benefits of education by increasing mental health concerns and decreasing academic motivation and by anticipation of future discrimination in the labor market.

Display rules: Social rules governing the appropriate expression of emotion in social situations.

Dynamic systems theory: A conceptualization of human development combining biological and psychological systems approaches with those of complex and nonlinear systems in physics and mathematics in which systematic changes over time can be explained across different species, age levels, or domains of development.

Ecological validity: The degree to which empirical findings obtained under experimentally controlled conditions are generalizable to real-world situations and settings.

Effect size: An estimate of the magnitude of a population difference or association often obtained by a standardized mean difference statistic or correlation coefficient and used to convey the importance or strength of a statistical result.

Efficacy: Generally, individual beliefs regarding the personal capability to causally effect a desired outcome. Teachers' efficacy beliefs regarding their ability to perform the core tasks of teaching have been shown to be associated with their teaching behaviors in the classroom, professional achievement, and psychological well-being. Students' confidence in their ability to succeed at a task predicts their engagement in that task.

Effortful control: A temperamental quality that concerns the ability to focus and/or shift attention, thinking, or behavior to accomplish one's goals.

Emotion(al) regulation: The management of emotions to accomplish one's goals.

Ethics: Principles of right and wrong behavior that govern the conduct of research. Ethical standards are established to maximize benefits and minimize harms; and to ensure the rights, protection, and fair treatment of all who conduct, participate in, and use the results of, research.

Expectancy Value Theory: A theory of human motivation in which individuals' choice, persistence, and performance are explained by their expectations for success, and the extent to which they value the activity.

Exploratory data analysis: Informal data analysis techniques for understanding the characteristics and meaning of data. Examples include constructing graphs, charts, and plots, and calculating simple descriptive statistics.

External validity: The extent to which the study results are applicable (or generalizable) to individuals, settings, treatments, and times different from those characterizing the original study.

Externalizing problems: Behavioral difficulties in adolescence such as delinquency, conduct disorder, attentional difficulties, and substance abuse associated with peer rejection in childhood.

Fisherian analysis: Class of statistical procedures addressing research questions involving longitudinal changes or cross-sectional differences in average performance. Examples include *t*-tests and various types of analysis of variance (ANOVA).

Friendships: Close, mutual, and voluntary dyadic relationships characterized by reciprocity and a feeling of perceived equality between individuals that provide children with support, security, intimacy, affection, and both instrumental and informational assistance. Outcomes of friendships include consensual validation of interests, hopes, and fears, the creation of prototypes for later romantic, marital, and parental relationships, and growth in interpersonal sensitivity.

Functionalist approach: Explains emotion in terms of goal attainment in everyday experience: "(e)motion is thus the person's attempt or readiness to establish, maintain, or change the relation between the person and his or her changing circumstances, on matters of significance to that person" (Saarni, et al., 2006, p. 227).

Garden metaphor of culture: A variant of the culture-as-medium view in which the heuristic value of conceiving of culture as the holistic and internally organized artificial environment-for-growing-living things based on that incorporates knowledge, beliefs, and material tools.

Generalized linear model: Broad class of analytic techniques that apply to both quantitative and categorical data and extend the basic concepts of regression and ANOVA to settings where the response variables are discrete and are not assumed to have a normal distribution.

Holistic person–context interaction theory: Magnusson's conceptualization of human development emphasizing the individual as an active, intentional part of a complex and continuous dynamic person–environment system of interdependent mental, behavioral, and biological components of the individual (person) and of social, cultural, and physical components of the environment (context).

Interactionism: The name given to a perspective on development emphasizing the combined role of both biogenetic factors and experience in shaping human development. Most contemporary psychologists embrace this resolution of the age-old nature–nurture debate.

Internal validity: Correct inferences about the causal connectedness between independent variable and dependent variable in a particular investigation; factors that threaten internal validity are commonly referred to as *confounds*.

Internal working models: Mental representations of the self, other people, and relationships that young children construct from their interactions with attachment figures.

Internalizing problems: Behavioral and emotional problems across the lifespan such as low self-esteem, anxiety problems, loneliness, and depressive symptoms that are associated with peer rejection in childhood.

Investigative interviews: Interviews conducted with witnesses or suspected victims of maltreatment concerning their experiences, the outcomes of which typically set into motion criminal proceedings and a variety of interventions for children and families. Empirical research on the impact of various features of investigative interviews has been used to craft best-practice guidelines for professionals overseeing and conducting investigative interviews.

Joint attention: A child's shared attention with another via eye contact, often established through referential pointing and shared emotional expression.

Learning theorists: Emphasize the role of observable patterns of stimuli and responses which affect the likelihood that specific behaviors will be more or less likely to be repeated depending on whether the responses are punishing or rewarding.

Life-course theory: A conceptualization of human development emphasizing the integrated and dynamic view of the entire course of human life that encompasses growth and decline and integrates individual ontogenies with their changing historical and social contexts.

Life-span developmental theory: Baltes' conceptualization of human development emphasizing lifelong adaptive processes from conception through old age.

Longitudinal design: Developmental design in which individuals are studied over time in order to study normative changes and individual differences in development.

Maturationist: Maturationism is a perspective emphasizing the extent to which development unfolds along a biogenetically determined pathway, little influenced by varying experiences. Arnold Gesell was a key proponent of maturationism in the first half of the 20th century.

Measurement: The research operations that are used to obtain relevant and high quality—standardized, reliable, and valid—scores for analysis. Measurement is sometimes called *scaling*.

Measurement validity: The degree to which an observed variable accurately measures a theorized construct; examples of measurement validity include face, content, factorial, predictive, concurrent, and construct.

Molecular genetics: The study of the structure and function of specific gene polymorphisms and their behavioral correlates.

Multiple determination: Multi-determinism is the realization that most aspects of development are affected by a variety of factors that mutually reinforce one another. As a result, development can often appear unaffected when one or more of the important causal factors are missing.

Multivariate analysis: Type of statistical procedure used to analyze multiple scores obtained from the same individual (or other unit of sampling).

Nativist: Philosophical assertion that some kinds of knowledge do not rely on experience and thus that human beings enter the world with a sensory apparatus equipped (at the very least) to order and organize their percepts.

Nature and nurture: The nature–nurture debate is the label given to the long-standing philosophical debate about the relative importance of biogenetic factors (such as heredity) and experience in shaping individual differences in development. Most psychologists now agree that both nature and nurture are critically important, and have embraced interactionism as a way of explaining how they work together.

Neurotransmitters: Biochemical substance which is released by the presynaptic neuron at synapses that transmits information to another neuron.

Nonexperimental designs: Research designs that employ neither randomization nor adequate control conditions and produce results from which causal inferences cannot be made.

Null hypothesis testing: Multistep procedure for judging the statistical significance of data relative to a research question.

Observational learning: Socialization processes that do not involve the intentional and direct action of parents but occur through children's observations of the parents' social behaviors.

Ontogenesis: The developmental history of an individual, typically the object of psychological theory and research.

Open-ended questions: Queries for information posed to interviewees that do not specify a response or set of particular responses (e.g., "Tell me what happened"). These types of questions are typically regarded as preferable to closed questions in investigative interviews in part because they allow for an extensive memory search.

Parental sensitivity: Individual differences in mothers' or fathers' perception of, and responsiveness to, the affective needs of children that can influence attachment security.

Parenting: The dynamic construct of how parents relate to their children across the lifespan that includes similarities and differences in parenting styles of both mothers and fathers within the context of larger family, social, and cultural contexts.

Parenting plans: Legal provision in the case of parental separation or divorce created to ensure that both parents become or remain attached to their children by encouraging parental participation by both parents in as broad as possible an array of social contexts on a regular basis.

Pearsonian analysis: Class of correlation-based statistical procedures addressing research questions involving the correlates of individual differences or the consistency of individual differences across time, settings, or behaviors. Examples include correlation, regression, factor analysis, and structural equation modeling.

Peer acceptance: The experience of being liked and accepted by peers.

Peer rejection: The experience of being disliked and not accepted by peers.

Peers: Similar-age individuals with whom children socialize.

Perceived popularity: The degree to which children are regarded as are "popular," cool, central, or highly visible by their peers.

Perceived social competence: An awareness of one's own peer acceptance or social skillfulness; children with higher perceived social competence tend to be more popular with peers.

Person–environment fit: A theory of human motivation that suggests students are maximally motivated to learn in situations that fit well with their own interests, current skill levels, and psychological needs.

Phylogenesis: The developmental history of life on earth or, more specifically, a species that constitutes the biological history of the newborn individual.

Plasticity: The potential for relative systematic change in human development across the life span and the multiple levels of organization comprising the ecology of human development (see Ch. 2). In the context of neurological development, the state of not yet having achieved specialization at some level that is an inherent property of brain growth and development, rather than simply the recovery of function after early brain damage.

Power: The probability of correctly rejecting a false null hypothesis that depends on various factors including the size of the effect, Type I error rate, and sample size.

Predictive validity: The degree to which experiences in early childhood are associated with aspects of social and emotional development later in the lifespan.

Privileged domain: A core area of development believed to be largely innate that provide the basis for domain-specific knowledge and behavior.

Psychoanalytical: Psychoanalytical theory was developed by Sigmund Freud and his colleagues early in the 20th century to explain the dynamic, often unconscious processes explaining individual behavior and development. This approach has been discredited in scientific psychology, but has left a popular legacy and is still employed by some clinicians.

Qualitative research methods: Approaches aimed at capturing, describing, and interpreting developmental phenomena through language or other non-quantifiable modalities rather than through statistical analyses. Qualitative approaches are grounded in epistemologies other than positivism.

Quantitative data analysis: Class of statistical procedures used to analyze continuous, multipoint, and ordered data that include ratio, interval, and near-interval scores. Examples include correlation, regression, and various ANOVA techniques.

Quasi-experiments: Research designs in which control procedures are applied but assignment to conditions is not random, limiting the degree to which causal inferences can be made of results.

Reciprocity: Behaviors in which partners take turns acting and reacting to another's behavior.

Regression analysis: General approach, based on the general linear model, to analyzing quantitative data that can be used to answer research questions regarding group trends and those involving individual differences.

Rehabilitation: A central feature of juvenile justice that focuses on preparing youthful offenders for a productive life upon release from detention that is based upon both historical assumptions about adolescents (e.g., maturity of judgment, malleability) as well as more recent empirical research on risk-taking, impulse control, and emotional regulation.

Rejection sensitivity: The tendency to defensively expect, readily perceive, and overreact to peer rejection.

Reliability: The dependability, consistency, or generalizability of a measured variable or score based upon its stability over time, across situations, among observers, or across items comprising a scale.

Repeated-measures analysis: Type of statistical procedure used to analyze a score repeatedly assessed over time or setting.

School transitions: Changes in one's school building that typically occur at elementary (ages 5–10), middle (ages 10–14), and high school (ages 14–18) that may result in either progressive or regressive developmental shifts.

Schooling: Based on a nineteenth-century European model of education, a widely practiced and organized form of socialization typified by teaching-learning activities that are removed from contexts of practical activity, involve a distinct social structure, value system, and mediational means (writing).

Schooling effects: Research findings in which children with schooling experience exhibit behavior and levels of performance different than that of children without schooling experience.

Security of attachment: According to attachment theory, the degree to which infants use attachment figures as secure bases from which to explore the novel environment.

Self-Determination Theory: A theory of human motivation and personality emphasizing individuals' inherent growth tendencies and their innate psychological needs as well as the motivation behind their choices apart from external influences.

Sex-role models: Students of gendered behavior believe that both adults and children often strive to imitate the behavior of others and thus that same-sex modeling is one of the ways that boys and girls come to behave in conventionally masculine and feminine ways.

Skeletal principles: Biological constraints that serve to bias developing children's attention to relevant features of a behavioral domain yet also require infusion of cultural input to develop past a rudimentary starting point.

Social cognition: Reasoning about the mental states and processes of others—including goals, intentions, and beliefs—based on their verbal and non-verbal behaviors.

Social information-processing: Rubin and Rose-Krasnor's model of interpersonal problem-solving in which children sequentially select a social goal, examine the task environment, access and implement a chosen strategy, and then evaluate the outcome relative to the initial social goal.

Social learning theorists: e.g., Albert Bandura emphasize the importance of learning how to behave not only through imitating the behavior of others but also by responding to the rewarding or punishing cues they give and by making conscious efforts to achieve certain goals or states.

Social participation: Parten's description of six developmentally sequential categories of social interactions, including unoccupied behavior, solitary play, onlooker behavior, parallel play, associative play, and cooperative play.

Social skills: Behaviors and abilities that promote successful initiation and maintenance of social interactions.

Socialization: The developmental process of acquiring interpersonal skills, abilities, and understanding that influence social behavior and interactions across the lifespan.

Social-emotional learning: Inter- and intrapersonal "non-content" domains—including self-awareness, social awareness, responsible decision making, self-management, and relationship management—that relate to content learning. Research findings suggest that social and emotional learning programs delivered in classrooms are positively associated with a wide range of educational and developmental outcomes.

Sociometric popularity: Method of categorizing children into status groups based on the number of positive ("like") and negative ("dislike") nominations received from peers.

Stability–instability issue: A conceptual split that distinguishes similarities and differences that arise between people within groups as a consequence of within-person change: a person's position relative to his or her reference group may remain the same (stability) or change (instability) with development.

Standardization: Measurement procedures intended to ensure that the assessed scores for all participants are procedurally comparable.

Statistical conclusion validity: The validity of the outcome of a statistical test resulting in a correct or incorrect decision; the latter result can be represented as a threat to validity when a researcher mistakenly rejects a true null hypothesis or fails to reject a false null hypothesis (Type II error).

Stereotype: Commonly held beliefs about groups of people that may or may not be accurate, e.g., the belief that males are better at sports than females.

Suggestibility: The degree to which a person is susceptible or vulnerable to suggestive influences based upon individual traits or situational demands.

Temperament: The biological basis of the affective arousal, expression, and regulatory components of personality that contribute to a wide range of developmental outcomes, including individual personality characteristics.

Theory of mind: A type of social cognition in which individuals construe others in terms of their mental states and traits, often investigated through the use of "false-belief" tasks.

Tracking: The educational practice of grouping students by ability level within or between classroom settings which determines their educational opportunities, social relationships with peers, and self-evaluation of academic abilities.

True experiments: Research designs that include manipulation of the independent variable by the investigator and control of extraneous variables by random assignment of participants to conditions.

Univariate analysis: Type of statistical procedure used to analyze a single score from each sampling unit (e.g., individual).

Vulnerability: A term used to describe the extent to which some behaviors of some people may be more prone to influence than others. Some people appear more susceptible than others, who are sometimes described as resilient.

AUTHOR INDEX

SUBJECT INDEX

ABOUT THE AUTHORS

Craig B. Abbott is a Senior Research Assistant and Statistician in the Comparative Behavioral Genetics Section at the Eunice Kennedy Shriver National Institute of Child Health and Human Development. He received his B.S. from Brigham Young University and his M.S. and Ph.D. from the University of Utah. His research interests are in the effects of family violence on the social and emotional development of children and adolescents; the development and assessment of techniques for interviewing child witnesses and victims of alleged sexual abuse; and parent–adolescent relationships.

Marc H. Bornstein is Senior Investigator and Head of Child and Family Research in the Program in Developmental Neuroscience at the Eunice Kennedy Shriver National Institute of Child Health and Human Development. He holds a B.A. from Columbia College, M.S. and Ph.D. degrees from Yale University, and an honorary doctorate from the University of Padua. Bornstein was a Guggenheim Foundation Fellow and has received awards from the Human Relations Area Files, National Institutes of Health, American Psychological Association, the Theodor Hellbrügge Foundation, the American Mensa Education and Research Foundation, the Japan Society for Promotion of Science, and the Society for Research in Child Development. Bornstein has held faculty positions at Princeton University and New York University as well as visiting academic appointments in Bamenda, London, Munich, New York, Paris, Santiago, Seoul, Tokyo, and Trento. He sits on the Governing Council of the SRCD and the Executive Committee of ISIS. Bornstein is coauthor of *Development in Infancy* (5 editions), *Development: Infancy through Adolescence*, and *Lifespan Development* and general editor of the *Crosscurrents in Contemporary Psychology Series* (10 volumes) and the *Monographs in Parenting* (8 volumes). He has also edited the *Handbook of Parenting* (Vols. I–V, 2 editions) and the *Handbook of Cultural Developmental Science*, and he coedited *Developmental Psychology: An Advanced Textbook* (6 editions) as well as numerous other volumes. He is author of several children's books, videos, and puzzles in *The Child's World* and *Baby Explorer* series. Bornstein is Editor Emeritus of *Child Development* and Founding Editor of *Parenting: Science and Practice*. He has contributed scientific papers in the areas of human experimental, methodological, comparative, developmental, crosscultural, neuroscientific, pediatric, and aesthetic psychology.

Julie Bowker is an Assistant Professor of Psychology in the Department of Human Development at the University at Buffalo, the State University of New York. She received her B.S. in Human Development and Family Studies at Cornell University and her Ph.D. in Human Development from the University of Maryland, College Park. Her research program focuses on the roles that peer relationships, particularly friendships, play in social and emotional development during late childhood and early adolescence.

Xinyin Chen is Professor of Psychology at the University of Western Ontario. Chen received his B.A. at East China Normal University and M.A. and Ph.D. at the University of Waterloo.

He was a William T. Grant Scholar. Chen's research interests include children's and adolescents' socioemotional functioning (e.g., shyness-inhibition, aggression, and social competence), peer relationships including groups and networks, and family influences, with a focus on crosscultural issues.

Michael Cole is Professor of Communication and Psychology at the University of California—San Diego, where he is director of the Laboratory of Comparative Human Cognition. He received his B.A. at UCLA and his Ph.D. at Indiana University. After spending a postdoctoral year in Moscow where he worked with Alexander Luria and Eugene Sokolov, he became involved in crosscultural research focused on cognitive development and the consequences of engaging in cultural practices associated with literacy and schooling. This work is published in *The Cultural Context of Learning and Thinking* and *The Psychology of Literacy*. He is a Fellow of the American Academy of Arts and Sciences, the Society of Experimental Psychologists, and the Academies of Education of the United States and Russia. He has engaged in research creating model cultural systems and studying the consequences of participation for children of varying ages and backgrounds. His books include *Cultural Psychology: A Once and Future Discipline* and *The Development of Children*.

Robert Coplan is a Professor of Psychology at Carleton University (Ottawa, Canada) and Editor of the journal *Social Development*. He received his B.Sc. at McGill University and his M.A. and Ph.D. at the University of Waterloo. Coplan conducts research and publishes in the area of children's peer relationships and social development, with a specific focus on the development of anxiety and internalizing problems in childhood. He is coauthor of *The Development of Shyness and Social Withdrawal* and *Social Development in Childhood and Adolescence: A Contemporary Reader* and author of *What Teachers Needs to Know about Shy Children at School*.

Jacquelynne S. Eccles is McKeachie/Pintrich Distinguished University Professor of Psychology and Education at the University of Michigan. Eccles received her Ph.D. from UCLA and has served on the faculty at Smith College, the University of Colorado, and the University of Michigan. At the University of Michigan, she served as Chair of the Combined Program in Education and Psychology as well as acting chair of the Psychology Department. She is also a Research Scientist at the Institute for Social Research at the University of Michigan and a visiting World Scholar at the Institute of Education, University of London, UK. She chaired the MacArthur Foundation Network on Successful Pathways through Middle Childhood and was a member of the MacArthur Research Network on Successful Pathways through Adolescence. She is past-president of the Society for Research on Adolescence and Division 35 of APA. Her awards include a Spencer Foundation Fellowship, the Sarah Goddard Power Award, the APS Cattell Fellows Award, SPSSI's Kurt Lewin Award, Distinguished Life Time Career awards from APA Division 15 and from the Society for the Study of Human Development, and the University of Michigan Faculty Recognition Award for Outstanding Scholarship. She is a Fellow in the American Psychological Association, American Psychological Society, American Educational Research Association, and Society for the Psychological Study of Social Issues. She has conducted research on gender-role socialization, identity formation and action, classroom influences on motivation, social development in the family, school, peer, and wider cultural contexts. Her recent work focuses on the ways in which ethnicity and gender become part of the self and influence experiences with others and the relation of self-beliefs and identity to the transition from mid to late adolescence and then into adulthood. She is coeditor of books focused mostly on topics linked to motivation and to gender, and is Editor of the *Journal of Research on Adolescence* and incoming Editor of *Developmental Psychology*.

Rebecca Goodvin is an Assistant Professor of Psychology at Western Washington University. She received her B.A. from Gonzaga University and her M.A. and Ph.D. from the University of Nebraska—Lincoln. Her research focuses on children's emotional and social-cognitive development in the context of parent–child relationships, and in particular on the development of self-concept in early childhood. She has focused on attachment theory and parent–child communication as frameworks for understanding this development, and seeks to integrate the concept of internal working models in attachment theory with a growing understanding of young children's social cognition. In addition, she has a strong interest in the social and institutional contexts surrounding and supporting child development, and worked for the University of Nebraska's Center on Children, Youth, Families, and Schools, and for the University of Nebraska's Center on Children, Families, and the Law on projects including an Early Head Start evaluation, the Midwest Child Care Consortium, and an NIH funded study addressing the context of child neglect in Nebraska.

Donald P. Hartmann is Emeritus Professor of Psychology in the Department of Psychology at the University of Utah. He received his Ph.D. from Stanford University. He is a fellow of three APA divisions: Developmental, Clinical, and Applied Behavior Analysis. He previously served as Editor or Associate Editor of *Behavioral Assessment*, *Behavior Therapy*, and *Journal of Applied Behavior Analysis*. His writings include *Child Behavior Analysis and Therapy* and *Using Observers to Study Behavior*. His research interests have been in children's friendship loss and MAD (measurement, analysis, and design).

Carmit Katz is a Research Associate within the Department of Social and Developmental Psychology at Cambridge University, UK. She received her Ph.D. from the School of Social Work at Haifa University in Israel. Katz has conducted several studies with the Unit of Investigative Interviewers in Israel; she has also conducted individual and group training sessions with investigative interviewers. Katz's main professional interest is in promoting the well-being of children who are involved in the legal system. In the course of conducting field studies, Katz is intensively involved in writing and disseminating practical guidelines for investigative interviewers (e.g., the integration of drawings into interviews, interviewing reluctant children about alleged abuse). Katz is coeditor of *Children's Testimony: A Handbook of Psychological Research and Forensic Practice*.

Michael E. Lamb is Professor and Head of the Department of Social and Developmental Psychology at the University of Cambridge, UK. He received his Ph.D. from Yale University, honorary doctorates from the University of Goteborg, Sweden, and the University of East Anglia, UK, and the Association for Psychological Science's James McKeen Cattell Award for Lifetime Contributions to Applied Psychological Research. Lamb is coauthor of *Development in Infancy*, *Socialization and Personality Development*, *Infant–Mother Attachment*, *Child Psychology Today*, *Investigative Interviews of Children*, and *Tell Me What Happened: Structured Investigative Interviews of Child Victims and Witnesses*. He has edited books on fathers and father–child relationships, including *The Role of the Father in Child Development*, founded and coedited *Advances in Developmental Psychology*, as well as *Developmental Science: An Advanced Textbook*, and has edited other books on child abuse, children's testimony, day care, infant social cognition, social and personality development, sibling relationships, social policy, and parent–child relationships in diverse social and cultural circumstances.

Richard M. Lerner is the Bergstrom Chair in Applied Developmental Science and the Director of the Institute for Applied Research in Youth Development at Tufts University. He went from kindergarten through Ph.D. within the New York City public schools, completing his doctorate at the City University of New York. Lerner was the founding editor of *Journal of Research on Adolescence* and of *Applied Developmental Science*, which he continues to edit. He was a fellow at the Center for Advanced Study in the Behavioral Sciences and is a fellow of the American Association for the Advancement of Science, the American Psychological Association, and the Association for Psychological Science. Prior to joining Tufts University, he was on the faculty and held administrative posts at The Pennsylvania State University, Michigan State University, and Boston College, where he was the Anita L. Brennan Professor of Education and the Director of the Center for Child, Family, and Community Partnerships. Lerner serves on the Advisory Board of the John Templeton Foundation, and held the Tyner Eminent Scholar Chair in the Human Sciences at Florida State University. He is known for his theory of relations between lifespan human development and social change and for his research about relations between adolescents and their peers, families, schools, and communities. As illustrated by his *Liberty: Thriving and Civic Engagement among America's Youth* and *The Good Teen: Rescuing Adolescence from the Myth of the Storm and Stress Years*, his work integrates the study of public policies and community-based programs with the promotion of positive youth development and youth contributions to civil society.

Selva Lewin-Bizan is a Post-Doctoral Fellow at the Institute for Applied Research in Youth Development at Tufts University, working in the 4-H Study. She received a B.A. from Tel-Aviv University, an M.A. from University of Chicago, and a Ph.D. from Boston College. Lewin-Bizan has clinical experience with children, adolescents, and parents in the United States and abroad, in both civilian and military settings. Her research explores how family dynamics and monetary resources affect the lives of children and parents, with special emphasis on fatherhood. This research has a threefold purpose: first, to understand how fathers parent and why; second, to understand how fathering affects fathers themselves; and third, to understand the role of fathers in children's and adolescents' development. Lewin-Bizan's research focuses on policy implications, particularly for economically disadvantaged families.

Charlie Lewis is Professor of Family and Developmental Psychology at Lancaster University. He trained as a clinical psychologist and gained a Ph.D. from Nottingham University. He is the author or coauthor of *Becoming a Father*, *Fathers, Work and Family Life*, *Family Understandings*, and *How Children Develop Social Understanding*. He has edited *Reassessing Fatherhood*, *Children's Early Understanding of Mind*, and a six-volume series on *Developmental Psychology*. His research is focused on children's social-cognitive development, particularly in constructing accounts of social understanding in infants and preschoolers that contrast with the "theory of mind" hypothesis; fathering; the influences of advertising and product placement on children; children's testimony, particularly in those in special education; social and language development of children with autism; and theory in cognitive developmental psychology.

Lindsay C. Malloy is a Postdoctoral Research Associate in the Department of Social and Developmental Psychology at the University of Cambridge, UK. She received her Ph.D. from the University of California, Irvine. Malloy has published in *Developmental Psychology*, *Child Development*, and *Journal of the American Academy of Child and Adolescent Psychiatry*. She received a dissertation award from the American Psychology Law Society and a Regional Research Award from Psi Chi. She is coeditor of *Children's Testimony: A Handbook of Psychological Research and Forensic Practice*. Her research is concerned with developmental and sociocontextual factors on children's memory and suggestibility, including the effects of cognitive, social, and emotional factors on their reports, and children's and adolescents' disclosure of traumatic or negative experiences.

Kristina L. McDonald is a Postdoctoral Research Associate in the Department of Human Development, University of Maryland, College Park. She received her B.A. from Illinois Wesleyan University and her M.S. and Ph.D. from Duke University. Her research interests include the social relationships of children, adolescents, and emerging adults, with a particular focus on how individuals handle conflict with relationship partners, cultural and contextual influences on social interaction, and the socioemotional experiences (e.g., loneliness) associated with characteristics of social relationships.

Martin Packer is Associate Professor of Psychology at Duquesne University and at the University of the Andes, in Bogotá, Colombia. He received his B.A. at Cambridge University, UK and his Ph.D. at the University of California, Berkeley. His research has explored interactions between neonates and their mothers, early childhood peer relationships, conflict among adolescents, and the way schools change the kind of person a child becomes. He has taught at the University of California, Berkeley and the University of Michigan. He is coeditor of *Entering the Circle: Hermeneutic Investigation in Psychology* and *Cultural and Critical Perspectives on Human Development* and is author of *The Structure of Moral Action, Changing Classes: School Reform and the New Economy*, and *The Science of Qualitative Research: Towards a Historical Ontology*. He is one of the founding coeditors of the journal *Qualitative Research in Psychology*.

Kelly E. Pelzel is a licensed psychologist at the University of Iowa Hospitals and Clinics Center for Disabilities and Development, which is affiliated with the University of Iowa Children's Hospital. She received her B.A. from the University of Northern Iowa and her Ph.D. from the University of Utah. She is a member of the Society for Research in Child Development and the World Association for Infant Mental Health. Her professional interests include social perspective-taking, early childhood mental health, and autism spectrum disorders.

Robert W. Roeser is an Associate Professor in the Department of Psychology and Senior Program Coordinator for the Mind and Life Institute at Portland State University. He received his B.A. from Cornell University, an M.A. from Holy Names College, and M.A. and Ph.D. from the University of Michigan. Roeser has been a William T. Grant Faculty Scholar and a William J. Fulbright Scholar in India. His research focuses on school as a central cultural context of human development, with a special emphasis on how educational program and environments shape outcomes such as motivation to learn, well-being, identity, and self-regulatory capacity.

Kenneth H. Rubin is Director and Professor, Center for Children, Relationships, and Culture in the Department of Human Development, University of Maryland. He received his B.A. from McGill University and his M.S. and Ph.D. from the Pennsylvania State University. Rubin is a fellow of the Canadian and American Psychological Associations and the Association of Psychological Science; he has been a recipient of the International Society for the Study of Behavioral Development Award for Distinguished Contributions to the International Advancement of Research and Theory in Behavioral Development and the American Psychological Association Mentor Award in Developmental Psychology. He twice served as an Associate Editor of *Child Development* and is past-president of the International

Society for the Study of Behavioral Development. Rubin's research interests include the study of children's peer and family relationships and their social and emotional development. He is the senior author of three chapters that have appeared in *The Handbook of Child Psychology—Play* and *Peer Interactions, Relationships, and Groups.*

Ross A. Thompson is Professor of Psychology at the University of California, Davis. He received his A.B. from Occidental College and his A.M. and Ph.D. from the University of Michigan. Thompson was previously the Carl Happold Distinguished Professor of Psychology at the University of Nebraska. He has been a Visiting Scientist at the Max Planck Institute for Human Development and Education in Berlin, Germany, a Senior NIMH Fellow in Law and Psychology at Stanford University, and a Harris Visiting Professor at the University of Chicago. He received the Ann L. Brown Award for Excellence in Developmental Research, the Outstanding Research and Creative Activity Award from the University of Nebraska system, and the Boyd McCandless Young Scientist Award for Early Distinguished Achievement from the American Psychological Association, as well as many teaching awards. Thompson is a founding member of the National Scientific Council on the Developing Child, and was a member of the Committee on Integrating the Science of Early Childhood Development of the National Academy of Sciences that wrote *From Neurons to Neighborhoods: The Science of Early Childhood Development.* He has twice been Associate Editor of *Child Development.* His books include *Preventing Child Maltreatment through Social Support: A Critical Analysis, The Postdivorce Family: Children, Families, and Society,* and *Toward a Child-Centered, Neighborhood-Based Child Protection System.* He also edited *Socioemotional Development* and is coauthor of *Infant–Mother Attachment.* His research interests are in early parent–child relationships, the development of emotional understanding and emotion regulation, conscience development, and the growth of self-understanding as well as the applications of developmental research to public policy concerns, including school readiness and its development, early childhood investments, and early mental health.

Amy Eva Alberts Warren is a Post-Doctoral Fellow at the Institute for Applied Research in Youth Development and Project Director of the John Templeton Foundation funded study, The Role of Spiritual Development in Growth of Purpose, Generosity, and Psychological Health in Adolescence. She received a B.A. Clark University and M.A. and Ph.D. from Tufts University. Warren is interested in how people come to be compassionate, socially just, and peaceful. She is particularly interested in the role that parents and educators play in nurturing such development and in how social policies and popular beliefs shape these roles.

Abby C. Winer is a doctoral student at the University of California, Davis and a research assistant at the Social and Emotional Development Lab. She received her A.B. from Georgetown University. While at Georgetown, she assisted with the Early Care and Education Lab assessing the quality of early child care environments and experiences as part of a longitudinal investigation of child care and children's temperaments over time. She was also involved with the Parent–Child Health Project at the George Washington University, examining familial influences on early infant and toddler mental health and temperament. Her current work examines relational influences of attachment, parent–child conversations, and social representations on preschoolers' prosocial and conscience development. Her research interests include the study of the relational contexts and ecologies of children's social and emotional development, both constructive and deconstructive behaviors, as well as the implications and applications of this research to public policy and intervention programs.